PETE MOULTON
with the assistance of Jason Moulton

Telecommunications Survival Guide

PH
PTR

Prentice Hall PTR, Upper Saddle River, NJ 07458
www.phptr.com

Library of Congress Cataloging-in-Publication Data

CIP data available.

Editorial/Production Supervision: *Kathleen M. Caren*
Acquisitions Editor: *Mary Franz*
Editorial Assistant: *Noreen Regina*
Marketing Manager: *Dan DePasquale*
Development Editor: *Jim Markham*
Manufacturing Manager: *Alexis R. Heydt*
Cover Design Direction: *Jerry Votta*
Cover Design: *Talar Agasyan*
Cover Illustration: *Tom Post*
Series Design: *Gail Cocker-Bogusz*

 © 2001 Prentice Hall PTR
Prentice-Hall, Inc.
Upper Saddle River, NJ 07458

Prentice Hall books are widely used by corporations and government agencies for training, marketing, and resale.

The publisher offers discounts on this book when ordered in bulk quantities. For more information, contact Corporate Sales Department, Phone: 800-382-3419; fax: 201-236-714; email: corpsales@prenhall.com or write Corporate Sales Department, Prentice Hall PTR, One Lake Street, Upper Saddle River, NJ 07458.

Printed in the United States of America

10 9 8 7 6 5 4 3 2 1

ISBN 0-13-028136-0

Prentice-Hall International (UK) Limited, *London*
Prentice-Hall of Australia Pty. Limited, *Sydney*
Prentice-Hall Canada Inc., *Toronto*
Prentice-Hall Hispanoamericana, S.A., *Mexico*
Prentice-Hall of India Private Limited, *New Delhi*
Prentice-Hall of Japan, Inc., *Tokyo*
Simon & Schuster Asia Pte. Ltd., *Singapore*
Editora Prentice-Hall do Brasil, Ltda., *Rio de Janeiro*

This book is dedicated to the people at the Moulton Company and my immediate family. Jason Moulton, Phil Lowry, Phil Crouse, Melissa Clawson, Ellen (Jona) Mayes, and Colby (John) Smith, Herb Brooks, and Matt Baker have all traveled extensively to permit me to sit and write. Susan, Joe, and Jenna Witkowski have put me up in my travels. Jeremy Moulton contributed to some of the best stories. Better him putting a telephone wire in his mouth than I. Jacob and Jared may one day become his assistants in this world of evolving technology. Josh Moulton for ordering and sending back all the gear we needed to get this book done. Finally, Cate Dolan the woman who always knows the correct answer ("Yes" or "C.") for every question.

CONTENTS

CHAPTER 4

Telephony Today   97

CHAPTER 5

Data Communications and WAN Fundamental Concepts 175

CHAPTER 6

Local Area Networks   255

CHAPTER 7

Saving Telecommunications Costs 373

CHAPTER 8

RF, Satellite, and Cellular Communications 465

CHAPTER 9

Telecommunications Technologies
Providing New Business Opportunities 537

CHAPTER 10

Looking Down the Road . . .   621

Appendix   *633*
Index   *659*

INTRODUCTION

The overall objectives of this book are to help business professionals understand new telecommunications technologies, and to share information about how these technologies can be deployed to save costs and develop new business. Business professionals include management, sales, development, administrative, and maintenance staff at all levels of an organization.

The book identifies new computer and telecommunications technologies that will impact business operations over the next several years. Plain language and simple explanations of technologies and technical terms are used because people tend to make technology more complex and difficult than it really is. How telecommunications impacts business is illustrated by example and practical experience. Readers are helped to clearly understand these technologies and how they may be applied to save costs and develop new business. The book describes and explains classic, fundamental telecommunications technologies, products, and services, including:

- Voice communications or telephony networks designed to carry voice.
- Data communications or Wide Area Networks (WANs) designed originally to carry text and numbers.
- Local Area Networks (LANs) designed originally to carry data in a small geographic area such as a building or a floor in a building.
- Wireless networking.
- The Internet.

Today, voice, data, image, and video communications are delivered to desktop computer systems around the planet by a combination of data communications, such as Wide Area Networks (WANs), voice communications, and LAN technologies. The classic voice, data (WAN), and LAN technologies are converging so that voice, data, image and video communications travel across the same network using the same protocols (rules of communications). All communications have largely become digital. The Internet is becoming the sole planet-wide communications network as existing voice telephone networks slowly disappear. LANs deliver the Internet to the desktop 24 hours a day, seven days a week.

Networking technologies and products are converging to provide new business opportunities and services to consumers and to other businesses. Business-to-Business (B2B) commerce Web companies and their Web sites are an example of the way in which telecommunications is rapidly changing business activity and saving substantial costs over traditional distribution mechanisms. Residential users are beginning to be provided with increasingly useful information and services from the Internet like the emerging bill paying services, specialty shopping services with related information services, and investment services.

Implementing such new businesses and the technologies required to support them is not without problems and glitches. This book provides practical insight into what to expect and how to manage deployment of new telecommunications services and implementation of new telecommunications products.

Broadly stated, the goals of this book are to present in a simple and entertaining fashion descriptions of telecommunications technologies that are and will continue to change not only the way business is conducted, but what will happen in our day-to-day personal lives.

For example, telecommunications technologies are rapidly changing how we listen to music. New sound compression technologies implemented in MP3 compression algorithms (an algorithm is just a mathematical procedure or formula and MP3s use some cool math to compress music while preserving the original sound quality) permit storing and transmitting CD-quality sound across the Internet. This is, as I write, altering the way we listen to music and the music industry. Today, the most searched for word on the Internet is no longer "sex," but rather "MP3."

Telecommunications includes voice (telephony), data (WAN), LAN, wireless, Personal Computer (PC), and other technologies. These are blended together today to form the Internet, which is a very large WAN, and intranets, which are our LANs that deliver voice, data, and multimedia information to both corporate and residential computer appliances and PCs. This blending is labeled convergence in the telecommunications Industry. This is the reason why people are so excited today, because everything is converging together into one big happy network with everyone connected 24 hours a day from everywhere around the world.

Telecommunications networking fundamentals describe the application of computer and telecommunications technologies in global and enterprise networks.

Who this Book is For

The target audience of this book is entry-level and experienced professionals that manage businesses, as well as those that sell, design, administer, and maintain telecommunications networks. Readers should understand some PC basics (the difference between bits and bytes) and some fundamental electrical concepts (for example, what is voltage). Don't worry too much about terminology; we explain all the terms used in this book.

This book includes practical explanations of basic telephony, data communications, LANs, and wireless communications as they relate to telecommunications technologies and products sold today. These concepts are directly related to the topic being covered (e.g., multiplexing is combining multiple streams of information into a single river of information and being able to split the river back into the individual streams) as it relates to cellular telephony and how that in turn relates to TDMA and CDMA. (TDMA and CDMA are means that cell phones use to communicate to cell towers). It is not a general book on fundamental PC and electronics concepts.

If you become bogged down or burdened by some details, stop and step up to the higher conceptual level. It is not necessary to understand the details in this book. Actually, many technical people would say this book is not detailed. However, it is their job to design and build telecommunications components and networks. To do that requires a good knowledge of the exact details on how to build, manufacture, and implement telecommunications components. That is why there is specialized training on Cisco, Microsoft, and other technical products. This book presents only those details required to understand the basic technologies. After reading this book, you should understand telecommunications components and understand what questions you need to ask so you can more fully understand the telecommunications world around you. Increased knowledge in any one area is left to books that specialize in that area.

Some people plan to retire before telecommunications technology impacts their job. Regardless, there is no escape. "Resistance is futile" as the Star Trek Borg would say. Even in retirement, changing telecommunications technologies and services will impact our lives. For example, the Dial-Pad.com free telephone service saves long distance charges when calling family and friends, and the free Web services from Netzero.com and Freeweb.com save Internet access charges. Thus, using these telecommunications technologies and free services in retirement to communicate with family and friends when income is limited saves money. No one can escape the impact of telecommunications technology and services on their professional and personal life, even if they retire. There is no turning back from the telecommunications technologies insidiously invading all aspects of our lives.

In the new information millennium, those that master the application of telecommunications and information technologies will be the "haves" of the planet. Those that do not will become the "have nots." Bill Gates best exemplifies this. He was the right person at the right place at the right time with the motivation to put it all together. There will be other Bill Gates' in the future, just as there was an Andrew Carnegie and a J. D. Rockefeller. None of us are likely to be so lucky as any of these people. However, in our own small way, we can become much more effective than people that ignore telecommunications technologies and the impending changes that they will impose on our lives. If you want to survive telecommunications and master telecommunications technologies in a way that will enchance your life, this book is for you!

How the Book is Organized

The structure of this book is to present an historic perspective of the evolution of telecommunications technologies. The historic perspective helps us better understand both the limitations imposed upon the implementation of new technologies and the development of new products and services based upon these technologies. The evolution description begins with original telephony (Chapters 1-4), then progresses on to data communications (Chapters 5 and 6), and finally concludes with wireless technologies (Chapters 7-10). Blended throughout the book are the impacts of PC and microelectronic technologies because these are the driving forces behind telecommunications convergence.

Conventions Used

Pictures with supporting text are used to explain the concepts. This is my own personal bias. I am not much of a reader—I guess it was the classic comics I read for book reports in high school—but more of a picture person. Maybe it is better to think "A picture is worth a thousand words." Regardless, pictures make it easy for me to explain and for the reader to grasp the concepts presented.

Review questions and answers are included at the end of each chapter for your enjoyment. It is always fun to test your knowledge so that you avoid "technical harassment."

Technical harassment is a "Pete" term describing the all-too-common situation where one is sitting across the table from the resident geek and they are saying we must absolutely implement ATM because everyone else is implementing ATM. This implies that you know what ATM is besides some terminals (machines) that spit out money. It also is designed to intimidate you into signing off on the $1,000,000 project. That is "technical harassment."

Finally, "Brain Teaser" sidebars are provided throughout the book to induce practical thinking. Here's an example:.

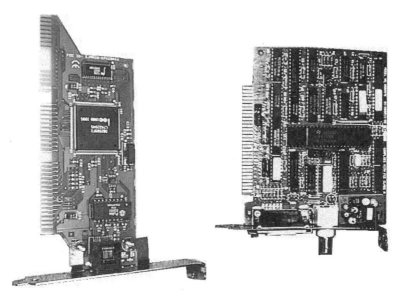

Figure A   *Ethernet boards.*

Brain Teaser

Your Technical Common Sense

Regardless of how non-technical we feel, we still possess common sense that can help us understand technology. Old and new Ethernet LAN boards are shown in Figure A. What makes the new Ethernet board distinguishable from the old board? How can one tell a new PC card from an old one?

In the case of our Ethernet cards, the key distinguishing factor is:

1. The number of chips.
2. The bus connector at the bottom of the board.
3. The Ethernet cable connectors on the metal "L"-shaped connector.

All answers distinguish one board from the other, but the best answer is the number of chips. New PC boards use fewer chips. In our case, only one or two chips are required.

OK, now for a tougher question, what chip on the old Ethernet board does the most work? The common sense answer is as plain as the nose on your face. It is the BIG chip!

Our goal here is to illustrate that even the most non-technical person can understand technology using their own common sense thinking. Enjoy the book!

Telecommunications Evolution and Future

This chapter describes the evolution of telephony (voice communications), data communications, and LAN systems. It highlights how new microelectronic (small semiconductor chip), computer, and PC technologies are pushing the convergence of telephony, data communications, and LAN technologies. The future of telecommunications is postulated.

Telephony vs. Telecommunications

Telecommunications is the science of communicating over a long distance using telephone or radio technology. This involves using microelectronic (small semiconductor chip), computer, and PC technologies to transmit, receive, and switch voice, data, and video communications over different transmission media, including copper, fiber, and electromagnetic transmissions.

This definition implies that we are doing more than just voice communications. Further, it does not imply using analog transmission exclusively. Many forms of analog and digital transmission are employed in telecommunications today. Analog communication is like a dimmer switch for light because it has an almost unlimited number of brightness settings. In contrast, digital communication works like a simple light switch that has only on or off.

When people use the word "telecommunications," most think of the classical analog telephone. That is *telephony*. Telephony is focused on voice communications. Telecommunications has evolved into much more.

The telephone network was originally designed to carry human voice and not digital information such as data, music, or video. It supported telephony (voice communications), but not telecommunications (data, image, and video). Realizing this helps us to understand some of the problems occurring as telephony (voice communications), WAN, LAN, wireless communications, and PC technologies merge to become telecommunications in the next millennium.

The scary thought is that any person born today will not know a world without portable PCs to serve them. They will have no concept of products that last and last for years. Gone are the days of the old telephone that was designed to work for 40 years.

Telephony

Telephony is traditional voice communications. It is communications facilitated by the telephones we have all come to know and love. We dial the number of another phone and talk into the headset microphone while listening to the headset speaker. Our voice is sent from one phone to the other, regardless of the distance. The drawback is that a wire, or more accurately, a channel (a communications path similar to a trough of water) must connect the phones for the duration of the call. This channel is switched into place by the telephone network for the duration of the call. All telephones and telephone subscribers share the facilities of the telephone network. This means that we cannot all talk at the same time because the telephone network is not designed to handle such a large load of telephone calls.

One reason people were told not to call each other just as the next millennium began was that everyone calling would overload the telephone network. The result would be everyone hearing the fast busy signal. Then they would think that the phone network was down because of some strange Y2K bug, when it was really brought down by an overload of unnecessary calls.

Today we occasionally have peak periods when the telephone network is overloaded, particularly during disasters when huge chunks of the telephone network infrastructure is incapacitated. Sometimes on Mother's Day the network also becomes overloaded.

The definition of telephony has been expanded by the telephone industry to embrace other types of transmission. They define telephony as the science of transmitting voice, data, video, or images over a distance that is greater than one can shout. Regardless of this expanded definition, telephony retains its largely voice communications flavor.

Telephony is used by the telephone industry to describe their business. Because they were voice network providers, this definition fit. As the use of communications networks changed, the telephone industry incorporated more than just voice communications; they began carrying data, and video. Further, they moved away from the traditional wired approach to delivering services to some new wireless delivery systems.

To better fit the new business model, the telephone industry used telecommunications to describe their business. Today, the telephone industry uses telecommunications to describe the transmission of voice, video, image, and data across today's telephone infrastructure.

Telecommunications and Convergence

Telecommunications is the merging of voice, data (WAN), LAN, video, image, and wireless communications technologies with PC and microelectronic technologies to facilitate communications between people or to deliver entertainment, information, and other services to people. Microelectronics is the technology of constructing electronic circuits and devices in very small packages such as computer chips. Telecommunications represents a convergence of these technologies into networks and systems that serve people planet-wide.

Traditional data communications, or WAN communications, were the transmission of data (at that time text and numbers) between sites. They encompassed all the necessary computer hardware, electronics, optical equipment, and signaling techniques required to send encoded information.

LANs distributed information around a single facility or a campus of facilities. Television required delivery of video information to distribution points (TV stations). Images were sent by facsimile (fax) transmission because the images could not be easily encoded as data. Wireless transmission evolved from early two-way radio systems (walkie-talkies) that permitted instant intercom-like communications between people, regardless of their physical location.

All these forms of communication have been hugely influenced by the rapid and incessant changes in microelectronic technologies since these changes helped to shrink all these devices. These technological advances are rapidly making the old Dick Tracy wrist TV a practical reality. They are the fuel for convergence and the rapid evolution of new products and communications services. The Internet provides a focal point of standardization (TCP/IP and HTML), and a platform for developing and delivering new services to consumers. The master of these technologies and the Internet will dominate the planet. This is a scary thought, but true.

Convergence Implications

Convergence occurs because data, voice, video, and other information is encoded as a stream of 1's and 0's, making them digital communications. Since everything is sent digitally, these types of transmissions can be combined and sent over the same high-speed transmission channels or pipes. That has been done for years in the telephone network. What is changing today is that the delivery of these diverse types of data is via one composite (or combined) digital stream on a single physical network to the business or residential site instead of delivering voice, video, and data communications via different digital streams on different physical networks. This will soon reach the telecommunications device that is attached to the "nut behind the keyboard"—me. We are beginning to implement composite stream Internet Protocol (IP) communications to business and residential sites. IP is used in the Internet to route data from source to destination points. IP uses physical network facilities more effectively than traditional analog and digital communications. Tomorrow it may be implemented in a wearable computer-communications appliance on my belt.

For example, DialPad.com provides a new, popular voice communications service. DialPad provides long-distance telephony from desktop PCs to phones anywhere in the continental U.S. This is the delivery of voice telephony by an IP network to a residential user. Voice over IP (VoIP) is simply putting voice communications over a digital packet network like the Internet instead of the traditional analog voice telephone network.

Another example is Cisco's VoIP router/gateways. These VoIP router/gateways are installed on a customer site and plugged into the Private Branch Exchange (PBX), or phone system, and data/LAN network connections. They also attach via a high-speed channel to an IP network. This IP network can be a private IP network or the Internet.

Cable modems (similar to analog telephone line modems) are used by cable companies to send digital data to residential users. They are a good example of how a coaxial copper cable carrying your television channels can also provide data connectivity into the Internet. Cable networks can carry simultaneous voice communications as well. Expect the cable companies to offer voice services as competition increases.

The total can be more than the sum of the parts because consumers will require all different communications services. Voice, video, and Internet access are the most visible today. This means that the business that synergistically provides these services as a single package is likely to dominate communications in this millennium. For example, companies like AT&T have allied themselves with TCI and @Home (Media One) to offer a variety of options to consumers, making them not only a "phone company," but also an overall communications company. They provide high-speed channels and connectivity into different target services—voice telephony, television and movies, and the Internet. They are becoming a single communications provider that does it all, a Broadband Integrated Communications Provider (BICP).

Table 1-1 shows the basic progression of computer technology over the last five years. The table compares CPU (Central Processing Unit) speeds, amount of RAM (Random Access Memory), disk drive size, and communication speeds.

Table 1.1 *Microelectronic and Communications Evolution*

Year	1995	1996	1997	1998	1999	2000
CPU Speed	60MHz	100MHz	200MHz	400MHz	600MHz	1GHz
PC RAM Size	8MB	16MB	32MB	64MB	128MB	256MB
PC Disk Drive Capacity	500MB	1.2GB	3.2GB	6.4GB	37GB	70GB
WAN Transmission Speed	28.8-Kbps Modem	33.6-Kbps Modem	56-Kbps Modem	56-Kbps Modem	400-Kbps to 800-Kbps Cable Modem	Mbps xDSL and Cable Modem

The CPU does all the work in the PC. Better-known CPU manufacturers are Intel and AMD. RAM is like chalkboard space for your PC. When you work on your PC, data is copied from the fixed disk drives into RAM, where it is manipulated by the CPU chip. The more chalkboard space or RAM you have, the more data you can manipulate at one time. Fixed disk drives are the physical location where data files are stored. Fixed disk drives are basically large file cabinets.

These are common values found in a computer system purchased during the designated year. Recently, IBM made another storage technology breakthrough that has the potential of increasing disk storage capacities 100-fold over what we have available today. This will be just in time, as we need more storage to contain the multimedia video information that is fast becoming part of our everyday lives.

In Table 1-1, the 1995 PC cost was about $2000 to $3000. Its main function was to perform word processing and spreadsheet analysis (number crunching), and to help you improve your Solitaire skills. In 2000, PCs still cost about $2000 to $3000. However, the tasks the PC performs have changed to focus on multimedia (data, sound, and video) tasks as well as continuing to improve your Solitaire skills. A computer is not usually purchased for faster word processing, but rather to support increased productivity by enabling voice dictation and videoconferencing. These are applications that would have choked and killed a 1995 PC.

So today, how much is that 1995 PC worth? It can still do word processing. However, the best you could probably get for the entire PC, monitor included, is about $150. Basically, old PCs are throw-away devices just like old telephones. How much will the 2000 PC be worth in two or three years? As PCs become cheaper and more disposable, the planet and our personal and business activities will be inextricably intertwined with computers.

Telecommunications convergence is tele-computing that combines voice, data, and LAN communications with PC technologies. Major communications companies such as AT&T, PSI Net, MCI, and Comcast are positioning themselves to be your one-stop communications provider of all communications, shopping, and entertainment services. These services require high-speed (millions of bits per second speeds) communications facilities that deliver data, image, voice, and video information to our office and home desktop (or kitchen countertop) computers. The communications network will attach to your office or in-home network, but a single connection may use wireless (microwave-like radio broadcast transmission) or a wired (coaxial cable or telephone wire) connection. Wireless connection means simply no wires, and a wired connection using wires is sometimes referred to as a wireline connection. Desktop, mobile, hand-held, and wearable PCs are the universal communications appliance that these service providers will plug their networks into to supply all your communication, shopping, and entertainment needs and more. Using one device, one network, and one provider is where telecommunications is headed. This book intends to help you understand exactly where we're going and how these technologies are merging as we move forward in this new millennium.

Brain Teaser

Describing a Communications Network Today and Tomorrow

How would you in the simplest terms describe a telecommunications network? Is it composed of fire, earth, water (a smoke signal network), copper, and other elements? What do you think?

It is important to understand and develop a simple approach to networking that gives us the practical perspective and reference points we need to cope with the dizzying changes in communications technologies. It needs to become your own simple conceptual framework for networking. You guessed it. I am stretching this out to give you time to ponder the question.

The simple view is that all networks are composed of hardware, channels, and software. Hardware is the tools and materials that we use to build our network. Today it is very reliable and, in many cases, redundant. Channels are the pipes interconnecting the network hardware components. Bits ("0's" and "1's") are stuffed in one end and spit out the other. Pipes come in various sizes and materials. Some are the quarter-inch copper pipes connected to the faucet in our kitchen sink; others are the 3-inch Poly Vinyl Chloride (PVC) drain pipes; and still others are the cement water mains delivering water to our neighborhoods. Finally, there is software. Software is the glue that holds all this stuff together. It is a complex glue, consisting of millions of programs written by millions of people. Actually, so many people are involved that it is a wonder it works at all. Fortunately, good, long-tested software code forms the building blocks or the foundation for new software. It is always easier to reuse electronic information than to create it from scratch.

Communications networks are all composed of hardware, channels, and software. Troubleshooting a communications network is identifying which component is malfunctioning or misconfigured. Building a communications network is selecting and purchasing the hardware and its associated software and the channels needed to interconnect all components. Then these are installed (connected together) and configured to make the network operate.

1. Which network component is the pipe?
2. Which network component functions as glue?
3. Which component is left?

The goal here is to provide a simple conceptual framework for understanding the complex telecommunications networks with which we live today.

Telecommunications Evolution

To understand the impact that computer and telecommunications technologies are having on your company, we need to understand the love/hate relationship between computer and telecommunications technologies. These two technologies are now combining to form balanced tele-computing (Tele-computing is Pete's word for the convergence of voice, data, and LAN communications with PC technologies. In an enterprise, it signifies the total integration of telecommunications and computing functions into a single organization-wide network) networks upon which most organizations are vitally dependent.

Telephony Evolution

Many telecommunications managers got their start by monitoring telephone bills from AT&T. In the mid-1970s to mid-1980s, telecommunications described the technologies for communicating voice. At that time, telecommunications management controlled communications expenses and telephone abuse within an organization. Soon, telecommunications began to incorporate image and messaging technologies. Telecommunications competition expanded when Judge Harold Greene completed divestiture in 1984. Soon, enterprise-wide communications networks began to integrate more non-AT&T services, and more importantly, a wider range of telecommunications technologies. Today we have entered in earnest the era of digital networking, that is, having widespread digital communications supporting voice, imaging, and data communications to the desktop (see Figure 1-1).

Why is a book on telecommunications focusing on the PC as the root cause of new telecommunications and computing technologies in the future? It is simply because the primary tool for most workers in any industry is a microprocessor-based PC. Such PCs range from desktop PCs to laptop PCs to special hand-held devices performing specific work functions (such as the PCs used by Federal Express and UPS to track shipments). These PCs are attached to telecommunications channels and services to perform their work activity support functions.

Today we are in the process of implementing a balanced tele-computing work environment. Balanced tele-computing is the label for matching both computing and telecommunications tools to an employee's work functions and job activities. It is the balance between the capabilities of the desktop or hand-held PC, the capabilities of the communications channels, and the pro-

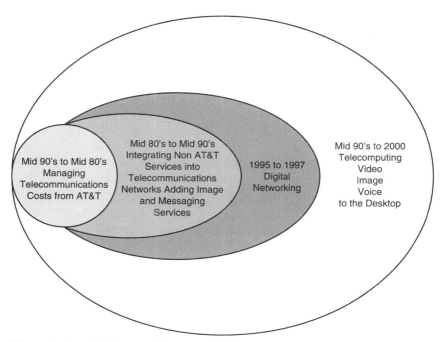

Figure 1–1 *Telephony evolution.*

cessing and database support provided by network servers. It is like technologically-oriented industrial engineering—giving an employee the computer and communications technologies that make them most productive in their job.

Not all concepts are wisely implemented. For example, thinking balanced tele-computing—matching computer tools to work functions—I purchased a pen-based laptop PC. The purpose was to have people that visited our booth at computer conferences complete a seminar interest form on the pen-based laptop PC, entering the data directly into an electronic database, and thus eliminating paper index cards. This would save trees, have the data electronically available more quickly, and more. Unfortunately, I lost perspective of the practicality of the pen-based laptop PC. After all, don't they do things like this in the movies? I discovered that by the time the first person completed the electronic form *correctly* using the pen-based laptop PC, a three-day conference would be over. It would have been easier and quicker for them to enter the data using the PC's keyboard than by using the electronic pen for input. Truly, at some point in time, this dream will become reality, but not today.

It is important today to understand voice, data, and LAN technologies because all are fast becoming part of telecommunications in the era of convergence. Convergence merges voice, video, image, and data over one network connection.

Data Communications Evolution

Any organization can be viewed as a large beast that performs useful functions for its customers as long as it is fed dollars of sales. Today, organizations also must be fed technology to live long and prosper. New technologies must be incorporated into business operations at a dizzying rate to assure an organization's competitive edge. The real difficulty here is that a technological edge like weaponry superiority is fleeting. Consequently, organizations must continually seek new technologies to maintain their competitive standing in their market.

One single piece of technology is driving this revolution in computing and telecommunications technologies—the microprocessor, or the computer on a chip. Its implementation into small desktop personal computers has caused a major restructuring of the computer industry. Companies that led the computer industry for years have suddenly found their major market strength is no longer a strength but rather a boat anchor. New companies created solely from PC-related products dominate American business today.

Old networks were based upon providing access to mainframe computers from terminals or later PCs spread throughout an organization. IBM's System Network Architecture (SNA) and Digital Equipment Corporation's DECnet were the dominant networking architectures. These are now labeled "legacy networks." Today's networks focus on PC LANs as the building blocks for enterprise-wide communications. In less than twenty years' time, the tinker toy PCs have broken apart the traditional role of computers in organizations. Also, these PCs reshaped the telephone and entertainment industries.

In the battle between computers and telecommunications, the computer people controlled centralized mainframe computers that provided information services—accounting, inventory management, and sales monitoring—to management. The computer people were powerful because the organization believed that they understood computers and that computers were complex machines. IBM promoted this image in its vain attempt to maintain its monopoly in the computer industry. In 1987, IBM made a marketing mistake. They introduced a proprietary PC following their traditional strategy for monopolizing the computer industry. It failed. In 1995, IBM announced the demise of its micro-channel architecture PC. IBM is now the fourth-ranked PC manufacturer worldwide today.

The future of computers and telecommunications was shaped by a war between PC software rivals. It began with Microsoft and Novell. Each had technical and market strengths in different areas. Microsoft dominated PC operating environments, while Novell dominated PC LAN software. Each saw the impending battle over PC market share focused around PC communications. The war started in earnest in 1995 with the release of Windows NT servers and Windows 95 clients. The Transmission Control Protocol/Internet Protocol (TCP/IP) communications software built into these Microsoft products takes PC communications to new levels. Today, the Microsoft vs. Novell war is over before it really began, and Microsoft won.

But, a new war is developing between Linux and the legions of Linux followers and implementers, and Microsoft and Windows. Further, Microsoft is fighting on another front to dominate PC access to the Internet. The justice department monopoly litigation against Microsoft was started by Microsoft's competitive practices against Netscape, a rival Web browser manufacturer. The winners here will play a significant role in shaping how we use communications and computers in the office and at home. Every company in the computer and communications industry understands that any company dominating the Internet and the devices that deliver the Internet to our homes and offices can become the monopoly IBM was in the computer industry of the 1960s through 1980s.

Turf wars in the telecommunications industry are continuous. The goal for every organization is to become the company that delivers one device, one network, and the information and entertainment services everyone uses. PCs today are migrating toward one universal communications application, the Web browser! Microsoft has integrated into the Windows Internet Explorer the ability to view desktop publishing files produced by Microsoft Word. The Internet Explorer also permits users to listen to music. With Windows, active desktop news and other information is delivered to the desktop in video form as well. However, regardless of how integrated Microsoft's products are, Microsoft dominance of the PC is not assured. So, computer-communications turf battles continue (see Figure 1-2).

LAN Evolution

Local Area Networks have played a significant role in effectively integrating PCs and communications into the workplace. The need to easily and quickly share files and printers was obvious in the early days of PCs (the early 1980s). The first LANs emerged in 1983.

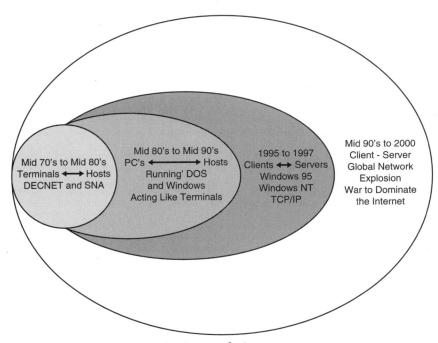

Figure 1–2 *Data communications evolution.*

Most businesses began connecting their PCs together with a network to facilitate sharing of financial and administrative data and collaboration on special projects. These LANs soon provided backbone communications for businesses. Today virtually every PC is connected to a LAN or some other form of communications to permit file and printer sharing and to provide email service and more sophisticated group collaboration on business projects.

Soon LANs will play a significant role in the home. Households with an old and a new PC are networking them together. As PC prices fall lower still and the number of PCs in a household increases, more households will have a LAN. Specialized PCs will be added to perform specific functions; for example, the entertainment center-controlling PC that plays MP3 music, records video for later viewing, and gathers the news like a newspaper for us to read at our desired down time. A LAN interconnects regular workstation PCs with specialized PCs and the Internet. This makes 24/7 functions possible.

For example, when backing up critical household data, most PCs today use PBB (Prayer-Based Backup—praying that nothing fails). However, off-

Figure 1–3 *Backup service advertised by SGII.com.*

site backup using connections over the Internet are now being offered. The SGII.com site is one of the first to offer this service (see Figure 1-3).

What makes these services and technologies possible is the LAN connectivity between PCs in a single facility or campus area. Connecting these business and household LANs to the Internet with high-speed transmission links opens the door to diverse information services and capabilities.

There are four key areas competing to provide high-speed LAN access to the Internet. They are:

- Cable modems—The first services out of the chute and being championed by AT&T and all cable television companies.

- Digital Subscriber Lines (DSLs)—A service promoted by the telephone companies. This looks to be the big, early competitor of cable modems.

- Radio Frequency (RF) broadband distribution—These services are easy to deploy via satellite or terrestrial links. We should see them in the next several years.

- Electrical power network links—These are the last dark horse competitor. Since there is good copper wire into every house, why let it go to waste?

These approaches are the key technical areas explored in this book. There is more on each of these areas in subsequent chapters.

The Influence of PC Technologies

PC CPU, RAM, and disk technologies are quickly advancing. The PC itself is rapidly becoming our home communications and entertainment appliance. For example, PCs are quickly becoming the music systems in our homes. Attach amplified speakers to a PC playing an MP3 and it rivals the music produced by the best home entertainment systems today. Soon they will exceed their capabilities. IBM's technical break-through in disk storage technology announced in March 2000 can increase disk storage capacity 100 times from current capabilities. This can have a profound impact in the amount of information retained by PCs at home and at work. It can also mean that every work of art, every movie, and every book ever written can be available on-line across the Internet.

Microcomputer technology pushes convergence because as computer speeds, storage capacities, and communications speeds to the Internet improve, they are not only used for word processing, Web surfing, and email, but also for increased voice and video communications. The common applications that we run in the future will be video/voice conferencing, voice recognition, and graphic editing. Microcomputers are simply the one-stop communications appliance of the present and the future.

At MIT, they are working on the Oxygen project, a $40 million research project. The goal is to make everyone a node on a network, reachable anytime, anyplace. Oxygen is based around four key components:

- The "Handy21," a portable unit appearing to be a cellular phone. It has a high-contrast screen, a digital camera, a Global Positioning System (GPS) module for locating it, an infrared transmitter-receiver in addition to the RF transmitter-receiver, and a powerful microprocessor. Handy21 can be a phone, a two-way radio, a television, a pager, a hand-held computer, a pointing device, and more, depending on the software dynamically loaded into it. This device reconfigures its hardware based upon the programs being run in it to perform the task desired by the person using it. The software is retained on servers attached to the network.
- The "Enviro21," a larger non-hand-held computer in an office, car trunk, or home closet. The "Enviro21" does everything hand-held "Handy21" does and more. An Enviro21 can control physical devices such as a furnace or door locks.
- The "N21" network, a new World Wide Web using steroids, linking all Handy21s and Enviro21s to servers. The N21 network connects everyone to everyone and everything.

- The last important component is the ability to communicate through voice commands and speech, as though you were talking to a person rather than a silicon-based device.

There are similar concepts that like Oxygen are designed through powerful microelectronic technology to provide the ability for a network to know where you are and what you need to use at any time. Out jogging with just an earphone and microphone? The hand-held device and network adjust to the way you can communicate. At home watching a movie? In that case, the network can determine whether to interrupt you or not.

Convergence and advanced microelectronic technologies will make these concepts reality within ten years.

Brain Teaser

Cellular Phones

Go to the Internet and shop for cellular phones. What are the key features you find today?
Is physical size a feature with the smaller the better? What is the smallest phone you have found?
Is battery life important? What descriptive terms are found for battery life? Standby and talk time are the common features.
Are there additional features? Do some act as pagers and display text paging? Are others able to surf the Web?
Our goal is to see what wireless phones are provided today and contrast their features with the features of the next-generation mobile communications information systems of the near future.

Telecommunications Future

Tele-computing has several implications. The first is that it should be tailored to the person at work or at home. The goal is to serve employees and residential users. This means it is end-user-driven. Technology must not be cumbersome. It must be very easy to use. Further, it must be reliable. Once people count on these PC-based devices for all their information needs, the devices and supporting networks cannot ever fail.

Our PCs will become video telephones, using flat panel displays that can be hung on any wall. PCs will also become more portable and wearable. They must, however, have a more reliable operating environment than Windows 95/98/ME and even Windows NT/2000. We will have special-use systems aimed at a primary function or two. They will be small but have big displays and make loud sounds. The most important PCs will be wearable and part of our garments, just as many cell phones are worn on the hip today.

Telecommunications and Telephony

All telephony will migrate to IP networks (for instance, the Internet). The voice telephone network as we know it is history. It is being transformed into a high-speed IP delivery system between distribution networks. Distribution networks will cover the last mile to the home or office using telephone wire, coaxial cable, radio frequency channels, or power wiring. Each of these will compete vigorously for the around $200 per month each household will spend on communications. New services will cater to consumer and business needs. Those that master these technologies, have the dollars of investment behind them, and meet present and future needs will become the Microsoft-like companies of tomorrow. Those that do not master these technologies will be absorbed like Digital Equipment Corporation.

Residential Telecommunications

Residential services will depend on high-speed Internet access. High-speed today is 100 Kbps to 900 Kbps. This will increase in the future to 1 Mbps to 10 Mbps for each household. This will be driven by the entertainment industry selling video over the Internet. At first, downloading a movie over several hours will be acceptable. But soon, only a few seconds will be tolerated. Several residential communications technologies, including cable modems, telephone company DSLs, radio frequency channels, and electric power distribution channels, will compete for consumer communications spending. Prices will drop because these services can be delivered effectively with few employees. The services must be highly reliable. Those that provide high reliability, high-speed, and low cost will dominate the market in the geographical areas they serve.

This means that people will no longer be bound to cities for high-paying jobs, provided high-speed communications are universally available in rural and other areas. This should radically change the way we work and manage workers.

Telecommunications and Business

Video telephony is anywhere and everywhere. We already wear cell phones. Some have push to talk (intercom-like) features and the ability to surf the

Web. GPS tracking/locating and more is on the way. The net result is that businesses will need to reinvent themselves on two fronts, how they deal with employees and how they deal with customers.

In dealing with employees, working hours and locations will become more fluid and less definable. Access to key data and public information must be provided securely to any working location. Network and PC operation can have no glitches. The cost of a single outage may not be the cost of lost time, but rather the loss of that million-dollar sale.

In dealing with customers, there are new opportunities to track and identify customers. These abilities must weighted against the invasion of customer privacy they produce or bring about. There are also opportunities to provide new products and services that are highly cost-effective. These services will rely heavily on electronic delivery, but will not be able to split themselves from other physical advertising and delivery mechanisms. Mouse clicks and mortar will beat mouse clicks every time. This means that the company that has the facilities and electronic presence (mouse clicks and mortar) will beat the electronic company (mouse clicks) every time.

Brain Teaser

Communications Service Availability

Check your local cable company and telephone company to see if they are offering cable modems or DSLs.
Is service available for your home?
What transmission speeds are advertised?
Is it possible to get 1.544-Mbps service from either cable modem or DSL service?
The goal here is to see what high-speed Internet access is available in your geographic area.

Balanced Tele-computing

Enterprise networks support a combination of telecommunications, data communications (WANs), and LANs. Enterprise networks are large networks that allow everyone in a business or government organization to communicate with one another from every facility on the planet 24 hours a day. Enterprise networks are not new. In the 1970s, enterprise networks provided communications between terminals and mainframe computers. In the mid 1970s enterprise networks were largely based upon IBM's System Network Architecture (SNA, software and hardware products from IBM, conforming to IBM-developed communications procedures) and Digital's DECnet (software and hardware products from Digital Equipment Corporation (DEC), conforming to a set of DEC-developed communications procedures products. TCP/IP (software products conforming to standard international communications procedures that run the Internet) networks transformed enterprise networks with a worldwide addressing mechanism. Today's PC LAN-based enterprise networks also conform to international standard addressing specified by the International Organization for Standardization (ISO).

The big change in the 1990s was that any PC could get to any data on any server (provided the user was authorized) through an addressing scheme that was structured like an organization chart (NetWare Directory Services—NDS—Novell) or telephone directory (Domain Name Services—DNS—UNIX). The Domain Name Service (DNS) approach is used in the Internet and will become the dominant approach for connecting users with the information they seek in all networks. This is evidenced by Microsoft Windows 2000 moving to DNS addressing for enterprise networks. Enterprise networks using different addressing schemes are connected via Internet gateways. The implication here is that everyone on the planet connected to the Internet at any location can access any information on any computer planetwide (provided they are authorized).

Tele-computing is the convergence of voice, data, and LAN communications with PC technologies. This convergence delivers to the office or home PC data, image, voice, and video information. Tele-computing makes desktop, mobile, hand-held and wearable PCs universal communication appliances.

Balanced tele-computing extends this concept by simply matching computer-communications tools to job functions (see Figure 1-4). Balanced tele-computing becomes even more difficult as we move into the future because our tele-computing choices are forever growing. What is a good combination of computer and communications technologies today may not be the most effective combination tomorrow. So, balancing technology to meet information and communications needs becomes a interesting problem. When you think of balancing technologies to meet user needs, effective (not necessarily cheap) solutions seem more obvious. In the home, balanced tele-computing is matching the PC tools and communications services to the information and entertainment needs of the household. The focus is on providing the computer-communications tools and services that help people in their work and improve their personal lives.

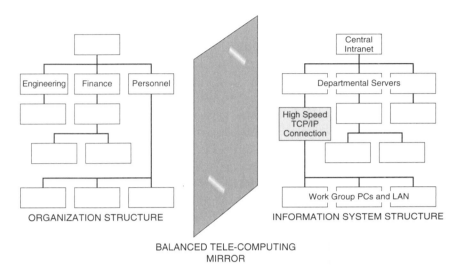

Figure 1–4 *The balanced tele-computing concept.*

How networks are built and how they work are much less important here than what they do for us. The driving force behind networks is how they make everyone more productive. This is what I call balanced tele-computing—matching the computer and communications capabilities to the work functions performed by an employee. The goal is to increase the employee's productivity. This goal is accomplished by balancing the computing done at the desktop (or in the wearable computer) with the available communications/transmission capacities and computing done in the supporting servers.

For example, the paperless office was a concept promoted in the 1980s and 1990s. Now I ask, are our offices any less paperless today? I think not! So what have all these PCs and networks done for us? They make the amount of information we digest daily increase by a factor of 50,000 or more (provided a picture is worth 1,000 words, what is a video worth? A 1,000,000 words?). Further, the information we see is filtered down to that information which is really important to us individually. So, our productivity and effectiveness is much greater than before. The information provided depends upon the PC, communications links, and servers gathering and filtering the information presented.

In the following sections, let's explore some examples of other ways balanced tele-computing can impact work.

Vending Machine Example

In the vending machine industry, what is the greatest cost? Our seminar students guess the cost of the machines, cost of servicing the machines, or the cost of space in which to place the machines. While these are all significant costs, the biggest cost is having the person standing in front of the machine with their dollar out ready to spend and having nothing in the machine to buy. Now the vending machine has lost the revenue and margin that pays all the other costs. Hold this thought for a second while we approach from another direction.

College students, especially the ones who work late at night in their computer labs (yes, I am a nerd who wore a bamboo slide rule in college), need sustenance. Food is no problem because there are usually several pieces of cold pizza or some Doritos left from the early evening meal. However, a beverage is needed, meaning the student has to leave the safe confines of their computer lab to go to the closest soda machine to acquire the needed thirst-quenching, caffeine-saturated beverage only to find often that the soda machine is empty.

Because they do not like risking leaving the safe confines of the lab and returning empty-handed, and because they are inventive, the students develop and implement electronic boards that track the sodas in the soda machine. Further, they connect these boards and the machines up to the Internet. This permits them to query the soda machine and determine the availability of soda right from the safe confines of the laboratory. In some cases, they can even set up an electronic account so that they can purchase the required soda without using coins. They debit their account and then issue the eject soda command to the soda machine. Then, a minute or two later, the machine spits out the selected soda.

Now back to our vending machines. We cannot put every vending machine on the Internet today. There are not enough IP addresses to go around—not at least until Internet II with 64-bit addressing comes along. However, it is possible to give every vending machine its own cell phone. Then the vending machine, like ET (the Extra Terrestrial), can phone home. The vending machines could report in late at night or, in the event of emergency (they ran out of products to sell), during the day as needed.

If a person winning the Darwin Award (an award given by nerds posthumously to people killing themselves in an incredibly stupid fashion and thus increasing the overall intelligence level of the planet) attempted to break into the vending machine, it could phone the police. One Darwin Award winner rocked a soda machine back and forth so it fell on them and caused their death. Soda machines weigh around 1,000 pounds. That soda machine could have phoned 911 and said "Help, someone is breaking into me, oops too late."

This vending machine example combines communications technologies with microelectronic and PC technologies to make servicing vending machines much more productive and effective. It should reduce the number of cases when someone had the dollar ready to spend and was faced with an empty machine. It balances remote computing capabilities with cost-effective communications and central computing support.

Laptop Example

Laptop PCs are a second example. Today, most traveling businesspeople have a laptop PC that accompanies them everywhere they go. My job involves heavy travel as well. I teach seminars on telecommunications mostly throughout the U.S., but sometimes elsewhere on the planet as well. I also write. That means that wherever I go, I need to take all my work as well as the ability to write, occasionally using speech-to-text software. This means that my PC is industrial-strength, as compared to those carried by most travelers, which only need to send and receive email or enter orders into an automated order system.

Again, balanced tele-computing, matching computer and communications tools to job functions, is applied. I am balancing my remote computing needs with the available communications facilities and central site services.

PC in the Kitchen

Finally, why have PCs not invaded the kitchen? They could be productively employed for tracking household inventories, counting calories, preparing grocery lists, purchasing essentials, presenting recipes, and entertaining the cook and bottle washers. My guess is the large monitor. There is no counter space for it to sit upon. However, flat panel monitors are becoming increasingly cheaper and of better quality.

So soon, PCs connected with special kitchen-oriented software will appear there. They will be of course be connected to the refrigerator so that when anything is removed or added, they update their food inventory list. The inventory will be based upon special detectable tags and not bar codes. So when the door closes, the kitchen PC will hold roll call to see who has been added and who is missing and presumably eaten. It could then connect on-line to the grocery store and update our shopping list from the weekly specials or stores with the lowest prices. Also, the "Shame on us" message for eating too many calories would appear with the appropriate sonic alarm.

New Internet Services

New Internet services are aimed specifically at consumers. Can you find some on the Web? List three that you would use in the following spaces.

1.

2.

3.

The goal here is for you to see how balanced tele-computing is pushing new telecommunications technologies and services into our everyday lives. I personally like the lottery-like Web site iWon.com, the electronics shopping and most other shopping sites, and my email. These are my choices, not necessarily yours.

■ Summary

This chapter has presented the difference between telephony and telecommunications, introduced the concept of balanced tele-computing, and described in summary fashion how telecommunications evolved into what it is today as well as projected where it is heading in the future. Telecommunications is the convergence of voice, data (WAN), LAN, video, image, and wireless communications technologies with PC and microelectronic technologies to facilitate communications between people or to deliver entertainment, information, and other services to people. Balanced tele-computing focuses on matching computer-communications tools to job functions. The implication is that we balance what a PC or hand-held device does with what the supporting network and servers do. Finally, the future of constant and instant unobtrusive communications was described. This is a future moving toward one device, one network, one provider, and one application.

▲ CHAPTER REVIEW QUESTIONS

1. *What ways will not provide high-speed access to the Internet to the home?*
   A. Cable modems
   B. Water pipe
   C. Cellular radio

    D. Telco DSL connections

    E. Satellite communications

    F. Power lines

2. *DSL stands for*

    A. Digital Subscription Line

    B. Data Subscription Line

    C. Digital Subscriber Line

    D. Data Subscriber Line

3. *What units of measure are used to represent transmission speeds to the home?*

    A. Bps

    B. Kbps

    C. Mbps

    D. Gbps

4. *Cable modems operate at what speeds?*

    A. Bps

    B. Kbps

    C. Mbps

    D. Gbps

5. *Analog modems operate at what speeds?*

    A. Bps

    B. Kbps

    C. Mbps

    D. Gbps

6. *What technologies are converging?*

    A. Voice, WAN, LAN, video, image, and wireless with microelectronic technologies

    B. Voice, WAN, LAN, video, and wireless with microelectronic technologies

    C. Voice, data, LAN, video, and wireless with microelectronic technologies

    D. Voice, data, LAN, image, and wireless with microelectronic technologies

7. *What kind of company is promoting DSL?*
   A. Electric power company
   B. Retailer
   C. Wholesaler
   D. Cable television company
   E. Satellite company
   F. Telephone company

8. *Which provides the highest speed?*
   A. Cable modems
   B. DSL lines
   C. RF links
   D. Satellite communications
   E. Power lines

Telecommunications Standards

This chapter identifies some standards bodies and points out just what is essential to understand about standards. The Open System Interconnection (OSI) seven-layer networking model is described and how it works is illustrated. This seven-layer model (hereinafter referred to as the OSI model) is the key to understanding the technologies involved with telecommunications because every product and service fits somewhere into this model. The implementation and functions of the layers in the OSI model are discussed, along with its importance to us in understanding telecommunications.

Standards Overview

Standards for building telephony voice communications, data communications, LAN, and wireless communications hardware and software products are developed by several national and international standards groups (see Table 2-1). Some key international standards organizations include:

- The International Telecommunications Union (ITU) is a Geneva, Switzerland-based agency of the United Nations.
- The Consultative Committee of International Telegraph & Telephone (CCITT) was formed in 1956. The CCITT studies telegraphy and telephony technical, operating, and tariff questions. The CCITT is now part of the International Telecommunications Union (ITU).
- The International Organization for Standardization (ISO), founded in 1947, is a specialized international agency that develops and promotes worldwide standards. It is a voluntary, non-treaty group with members from over 80 countries.
- European Telecommunications Standards Institute (ETSI), formed in 1988, writes technical standards. It is composed of representatives from Post, Telephone, and Telegraph (PTTs) ministries, computer and telecommunication vendors, manufacturers, users, and research bodies.

There are several key American standards bodies as well, including:

- The American National Standards Institute (ANSI), which has developed data communications and other standards like the American national Standard Code for Information Interchange (ASCII code).
- The Electronic Industries Association, which plays a role in developing communications hardware standards, including the venerable EIA-232D (formerly Recommended Specification-232, or RS-232) specification.
- The Institute for Electrical and Electronic Engineers (IEEE), which has taken the lead in developing LAN (the 802.x standards) and other high-speed networking standards.

The standards developed by lead groups are reviewed and incorporated into worldwide standards by the ITU and other organizations.

Standards are developed over a period of time by meetings between interested individuals and organizations having a vested interest in the specific standards. There are several steps and votes required before a particular standard is approved and issued for the industry to follow. The main problem is that products and technologies are evolving so quickly and so profusely, it is difficult for the standards organizations to keep pace.

It is best for us to view standards as the starting point or foundation on which our telecommunications networks rest. Planet-wide, there are general overlying telecommunications standards, but in general, North American telecommunications standards are slightly different. For example, in the U.S., T-1 service is sold (T-1 is just a digital pipe that connects to a telephone network or data network at speeds of 1.544 Mbs), but in Europe, E-1 service is sold. An E-1 channel is the European equivalent to a T-1 channel, but it operates at 2,048 Mbps. Standards are reviewed and expanded regularly, accommodating the construction of larger, faster networks using newer technologies that rest on those standards. The networks themselves incorporate some proprietary, non-standard equipment that solves special problems for the network. Hopefully, if wisely selected, the proprietary equipment can be easily replaced with industry-standard equipment as it becomes available.

Recognizing and understanding the role that standards play in telecommunications networks is key to effectively designing and implementing them. So, let us look further.

In my short stint as a lobbyist for General Electric Information Services Company (GEISCO), I attended a CCITT standardization meeting hosted by the State Department at one of their buildings in Washington, D.C. It was like fifty men in blue and gray suits (and one man in a sport coat with a pocket protector in the pocket) sitting around a big table. Each participant had stacks of paper in front of him. They were passionate about their work, and all that came through to me was boring. Actually, it was very, very boring. I was fortunate that my stint as a lobbyist did not last. Now that is not to say that standardization work is unimportant. Quite the contrary, it is a very important first step in achieving what we really need – hardware, software, and channels that all work together to form a network.

Standards need to be developed in one years' time, tops. This should be possible if the process uses electronic proposal posting, review, commenting, and voting. When this is not the case, standards run the risk of being obsolete before they are approved.

The Importance of Standards

Standards are especially important for telecommunications because they are the first step to assuring inter-operability of products and services from many telecommunications vendors. When products are manufactured to a standard, they do not necessarily work together. For example, when ten tax accountants are given the same exact income tax information on an indi-

Table 2.1 *Standards Bodies*

Abbreviation	Full Name, Address, Telephone Number, and Web Site
ANSI	American National Standards Institute 1430 Broadway New York, New York 10018 Telephone: (212) 642-4900 www.ansi.org
EIA	Electronic Industries Alliance Corporate Engineering Department 2500 Wilson Boulevard Arlington, Virginia 22201 Telephone: (703) 907-7500 www.eia.org
ETSI	European Telecommunications Standards Institute 650, route des Lucioles 06921 Sophia Antipolis, France Telephone:+33 49 294.42. 00 www.etsi.org
ITU (CCITT)	General Secretariat International Telecommunications Union Place des Nations Ch-1211 Geneva 20, Switzerland Telephone: +41-22-730.51.11 www.itu.int
ECMA	European Computer Manufacturers Association 114 Rue Du Rhone Ch-1204 Geneva, Switzerland Telephone: +41-22-849.60.00 www.ecma.ch
ISO	International Organization for Standardization Central Secretariat 1 Rue De Varembe Ch-1211 Geneva, Switzerland Telephone: 41-22-749.01.11 www.iso.ch
IEEE	The Institute of Electrical and Electronic Engineers 802 Committee Secretary, IEEE Standards Board 345 East 47th Street New York, New York 10017 USA Telephone: (212) 419-7900 www.ieee.org

vidual and fill out the same standard income tax return, we get ten different implementations of that standard income tax return. In theory, all tax accountants should have produced the exact same return. But life does not work that way. Ten manufacturers building communications equipment to the same standard oftentimes produce ten different variations of communications equipment that does not work together. However, these different pieces of equipment are closer to working together than if they had not been built to the same standard.

Telephony standards vary from data communications and LAN standards because they are more often established through international standards bodies and less through market share recognition. AT&T created all early American telephony standards. International telephony standards were not created by AT&T and vary in many ways from American telephony standards.

De Jure Standards

Standards created by a single organization for the industry or standards bodies are called de jure standards. Most telephony standards are de jure standards. They are developed by the international standards bodies and finalized so the product developers can construct compatible hardware and software products. The drawback here is that they take time to be developed and adopted. So much so that unless the standard covers some very consistent or constantly used technology, it may not be so useful. Standards bodies have decreased the time it takes them to create a standard because they understand that the standard may be obsolete if they take too long to create it. In contrast, they must create standards, otherwise proprietary products would dominate the telecommunications market. An example of a de jure standard is the V. 90 modem specification standardized by the ITU.

De Facto Standards

Some standards have been established de facto because specific PC and LAN products dominated the market by out-selling their competition. This is basically the idea of whoever sells the most wins. The original de facto PC industry standard was the IBM PC. Most PC consulting gurus at the time would advise, "Buy your software first, then get your hardware." They were very wrong. In the early 1980s, if software did not run on an IBM PC, it did not run. At that time, it was best to buy the hardware first (an IBM PC). I learned this painfully when I tried running some special accounting software on a Columbia Data Products PC. It did not run and I had to eat $6,000 of expenses.

However, the IBM PC de facto standard lost out around 1990 when IBM introduced the PS-2. (Pretty Stupid Computer –2… Oops! Sorry, my opinions are showing.) Although innovative, it failed to motivate the market to mimic it, and as a result, IBM's PC market share dropped to about 10% from a high of around 85% share. With that decline, the IBM PC ceased to be the PC industry de facto standard. However, in the 1990s, Microsoft Windows became the de facto industry standard for PCs.

The Microsoft Windows operating environment continues to be the de facto driving standard for the PC industry. No one is holding a gun to our head, forcing us to buy Microsoft products, but Microsoft does twist our arm a little bit. Windows is a software de facto standard around which other PC applications software is built. Periodically, Microsoft publishes a PC hardware design document for PC manufacturers that directs them how to design PC hardware that will work with future Windows releases. So, Windows today is the de facto standard, driving both PC hardware and software. This is good as long as Microsoft publishes complete information needed by other hardware and software developers so that they can develop competitive and reliable products.

Microsoft knows that Windows is only a de facto standard and that Windows could be replaced at any time by another de facto standard. This could be the Macintosh operating system or even the dread Linux operating system. For us, the most important standards are those that relate to telephony, data communications, LANs, wireless communications, etc. The focal point for these standards is the OSI model. The OSI model is the key to understanding how all telecommunications and PC technology fits together. We will discuss this shortly.

Inter-operability

Standards are especially important for telecommunications because they assure product compatibility. However, more important is inter-operability of products and services from different telecommunications vendors. Inter-operability means that the products can be plugged together to form a network that carries voice, data, image, and video.

It is nice to have products meet standards. Conforming to a common standard is an important step in having products inter-operate. However, what we must have is inter-operable products to construct working networks. Inter-operable products come more from de facto standards than from de jure standards. If you are building a network or just connecting to the Internet from your home, you must select inter-operable products to have that connection work. Fortunately, there are many inter-operable products from which to choose for consumers. In business, network design and implementation commonly involve a pilot test to assure that all involved vendors solve inter-operability problems before product purchase commitments are made. Contracts also include clauses obligating communications hardware, software, and service vendors to fix any inter-operability problems that occur through the life of the network.

Brain Teaser

Modem Standards

Go to a computer store that sells PC modems. Alternatively, shop for modems using the Internet. Select several modems from different manufacturers that support data, fax, and video communications. What standards do they support and advertise?
1. Can you find some ITU standards listed?
2. Are there any American standards identified?
3. Will these modems inter-operate?
Compare what you found to the specifications for the Supra modem listed in Figure 2-1.

The objective here is to illustrate that any telecommunications equipment meets a variety of specifications, and it is important to identify those specifications to assure that the telecommunications equipment can inter-operate with other telecommunications equipment and software. In this case, because the PC modem market is mature and most all modems are made using Rockwell International-designed chips, all PC modems inter-operate with most other PC modems.

OSI Model

To understand what telecommunications products do in a network, we need to first understand the OSI model for networking. This model provides a yardstick, or common measuring system, for explaining the functions of telephony, data communications, LAN, and wireless hardware—software—services. Once the layers of the OSI model in which a product works are

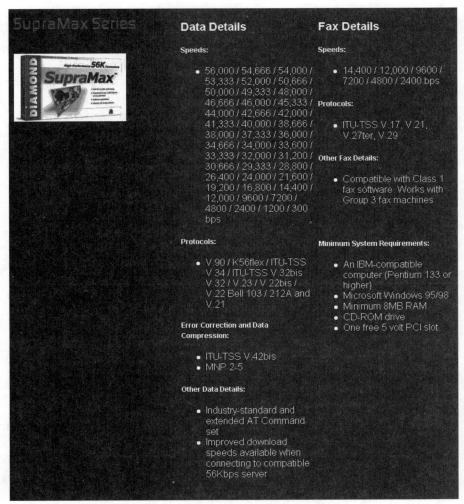

SupraMax Series

Data Details

Speeds:

- 56,000 / 54,666 / 54,000 /
  53,333 / 52,000 / 50,666 /
  50,000 / 49,333 / 48,000 /
  46,666 / 46,000 / 45,333 /
  44,000 / 42,666 / 42,000 /
  41,333 / 40,000 / 38,666 /
  38,000 / 37,333 / 36,000 /
  34,666 / 34,000 / 33,600 /
  33,333 / 32,000 / 31,200 /
  30,666 / 29,333 / 28,800 /
  26,400 / 24,000 / 21,600 /
  19,200 / 16,800 / 14,400 /
  12,000 / 9600 / 7200 /
  4800 / 2400 / 1200 / 300
  bps

Protocols:

- V.90 / K56flex / ITU-TSS
  V.34 / ITU-TSS V.32bis
  V.32 / V.23 / V.22bis /
  V.22 Bell 103 / 212A and
  V.21

Error Correction and Data
Compression:

- ITU-TSS V.42bis
- MNP 2-5

Other Data Details:

- Industry-standard and
  extended AT Command
  set
- Improved download
  speeds available when
  connecting to compatible
  56Kbps server

Fax Details

Speeds:

- 14,400 / 12,000 / 9600 /
  7200 / 4800 / 2400 bps

Protocols:

- ITU-TSS V.17, V.21,
  V.27ter, V.29

Other Fax Details:

- Compatible with Class 1
  fax software. Works with
  Group 3 fax machines

Minimum System Requirements:

- An IBM-compatible
  computer (Pentium 133 or
  higher)
- Microsoft Windows 95/98
- Minimum 8MB RAM
- CD-ROM drive
- One free 5 volt PCI slot

Figure 2–1 *Supra modem specifications from the Internet.*

identified, then the functionality and contribution to that network are identified in a consistent manner.

The OSI model is academic. It was constructed conceptually from networking descriptions like that provided by IBM for its System Networking Architecture (SNA), which started with three layers and ended up having seven, matching up with the OSI model layers. The networking products in existence at the time this model was developed were largely proprietary, with IBM's being a de facto standard of the time. These real networking products performed the functions assigned by the OSI model to the seven layers, but

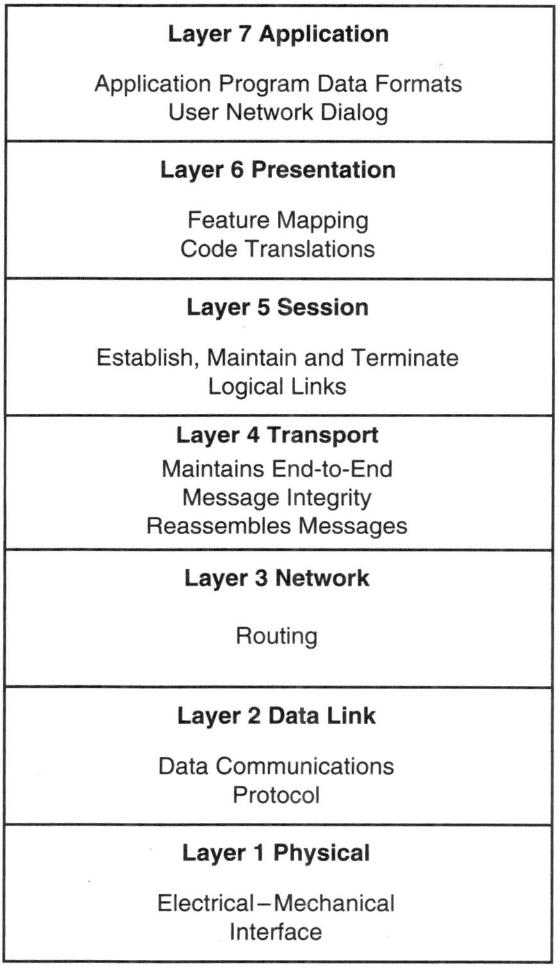

Layer 7 Application Application Program Data Formats User Network Dialog
Layer 6 Presentation Feature Mapping Code Translations
Layer 5 Session Establish, Maintain and Terminate Logical Links
Layer 4 Transport Maintains End-to-End Message Integrity Reassembles Messages
Layer 3 Network Routing
Layer 2 Data Link Data Communications Protocol
Layer 1 Physical Electrical–Mechanical Interface

Figure 2–2 *OSI model.*

their design structure and implementation did not follow formal boundaries. My analogy is that the hardware and software boundaries in these products was more like the Mexican-American border than like the Berlin Wall. Some functions were placed upon one side or the other of the border, depending upon the whim of the designer. Networks did not really use mix-and-match components. Most connections were mirrored with manufacturers' components on each end. Networks worked, but they were not cheap and flexible. Product shortages slowed network expansion.

The OSI model (see Figure 2-2) was a key step in changing the products and methods of networking. OSI began the process that led to the opening up of networking to products from many different manufacturers. The quest for market dominance and market share is not necessarily good business sense. An open market with cheap products promotes more revenue than a closed, proprietary market dominated by a single company. For example, the long-distance telephone market is now open to many competitors. In spite of rates for calls declining more than 80%, the overall dollar volume of long distance calls has increased steadily since the market was opened to competition in 1984. With increases in productivity, this long-distance market remains a cash cow to several large companies, including AT&T, the original U.S. long-distance monopoly. Voice over Internet Protocol (VoIP) technology is now increasing revenue margins in that marketplace, which over the next several years will spur additional long-distance rate reductions.

The OSI model is important for us because it promotes competition between telecommunications product and service vendors, and because it provides a consistent measure of a product's functionality in the network. It is a means of understanding how this complex jigsaw puzzle on networking hardware, software, and channels fits and functions together.

To understand the OSI reference model, we first need to understand compatibility. Compatibility is required to establish communications between a PC and a server. This permits communications between the PC and the server.

This explanation of the OSI model does take certain liberties for the sake of most people understanding the model. OSI purists could easily criticize the details here. The details are much less important to our understanding than the overall picture. Telecommunications product designers and standards developers need to get the details exactly correct. We do not need to be so precise.

Compatibility

As an aid to understanding the functions in the OSI model and how they evolved into the seven layers, we must examine how to make a terminal compatible with a host computer. Both the terminal and the host computer must meet specific criteria to permit them to communicate with each other. The criteria are divided into data format compatibility and networking compatibility (see Figure 2-3).

DATA FORMAT COMPATIBILITY

Data format compatibility is getting usable data from the server. I think of it as data usability ("usability" is my word invention). Data format compatibil-

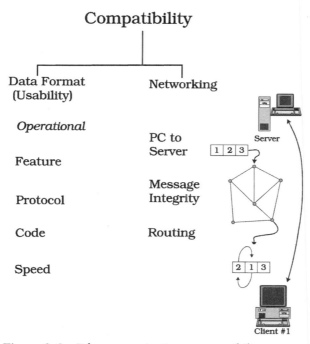

Figure 2–3 *Telecommunications compatibility.*

ity criteria begin with simple data transmission *speed* compatibility, or matching transmission speeds. Both the PC and the host must communicate at the same speed, or bits per second transmission rate. If they do not exactly match speed, then no communication is possible. This is the same for humans, because most of us like to communicate at somewhere between 100 to 150 words per minute, depending on where you grew up. For grins, try talking too slow or too fast to another human being. Try 30 words per minute, which is about one word every two seconds. That speed is slow enough to drive just about anyone crazy. Next try 400 words per minute. Only Jason and I can talk that fast, and when we do, not much is really understood. Data communications work in the exact same way. They need to have speed compatibility because if you go too fast, or too slow, network components, like people, will not communicate. Think of how difficult it might be for a native of New Orleans to communicate with a native of New York City. They both tend to communicate at different speeds. Speed compatibility is determined by the modems and LAN boards (Network Interface Cards) used.

What speeds are modems capable of today? The fastest operate in theory at 56 Kbps down from the network and at 33.6 Kbps up to the network. In fact, they are somewhat slower than that depending upon circuit quality and other limiting factors. What LAN speeds are there today? Ethernet runs at 10 Mbps, 100 Mbps, and is moving to 1 Gbps. If a LAN board were to attempt to talk with a modem card, nothing would happen because they operate at different transmission speeds (and they have different electrical interfaces due to the differences in transmission media and speeds).

A code is the mechanism used by the computer to translate the "0's" and '1's" manipulated by the computer into displayed and printed alphanumeric text we humans understand. A code is defined more formally as a system of symbols, letters, or signals used to represent a message. *Code* compatibility is simple to solve because most all computers today use either ASCII (American national Standard Code for Information Interchange) code or EBCDIC (Extended Binary Coded Decimal Interchange Code) code. (If you can survive that last sentence, this is as difficult as this book gets, so you should survive the rest.) IBM mainframe computers use primarily EBCDIC code, while most all other remaining computers on the planet use ASCII code. Generally, if it is a computer of any sort, it is using ASCII code. Internationally, the equivalent is called International Alphabet #5. What is the maximum number of characters or bit combinations that must be handled with code compatibility? There are 256 possible combinations of eight bits. If we were to have a computer translate from one code to another, e.g., map 256 things of one code to 256 things in another code, how difficult would that be? For a computer, it would be a no-brainer. So converting from ASCII code to EBCDIC is nothing today.

Our next criterion is protocol compatibility. What is a protocol? This question I ask seminar students just to get them thinking of the descriptions of a protocol that they have heard about. Some say it is handshaking. Others say rules of the road. These are somewhat true and descriptive of how a protocol accomplishes its goal. But the definition of a protocol should really focus on the goal of the protocol more than on how it works.

For you to understand protocols, you need to repeat the little protocol description mantra, "The goal of a protocol is to get information from Point A to Point B error-free." The real goal of a protocol is to get whatever we send into one end of a pipe to the other end of the pipe error-free. Protocols accomplish this by acting like a language with handshakes to coordinate transmitting and receiving devices. A more formal definition of a protocol is rules for communications that get information from Point A to Point B error-free.

Protocol compatibility is more difficult than code compatibility because we must account for every protocol handshaking scenario. Protocols use specific handshakes, or etiquette messages, to coordinate information exchange between sending and receiving devices, similar to a language. Visualize if you can the English language handshake messages for a local phone call. When you call someone, the first thing the person must say if they're following proper protocol is "Hello." If you hear nothing but static on-line, then you will respond "Is anyone there?" As a human, you're trying to use the proper protocols to begin communication, and if no one answers, you hang up because you cannot communicate. Once communication has been established, to signify the communication is over, one person must say "Goodbye!" The other person will then verify that the phone call is over by also saying "Goodbye." Then the proper phone protocols have been followed and information has been transferred between Point A and Point B error-free. Typical protocol handshake messages are:

> *Caller – Hello*
> *Answerer – This is Pete. Can I help you?*
> *Caller – Is Jason there?*
> *Answerer – No, he is teaching today.*
> *Caller – OK, I will call again tomorrow.*
> *Answerer – Goodbye*
> *Caller – Goodbye.*

Just for fun, try breaking the basic telephone protocol humans use by breathing heavily into the phone when someone calls and see what protocol handshakes they use in response. This can be quite funny.

Each phone call scenario must be covered to achieve protocol compatibility.

Feature compatibility is the next level. Features are hardware characteristics that we can usually touch, feel, or see such as keyboards, keypads, or monitors of different sizes and resolutions. This requires matching the keyboard keys and display size to what the communicating software expects. How many readers have worked with a PC such as a Digital Equipment Corporation VTnnn terminal on a VAX (Virtual Architecture eXtended), or used a PC as a 3270 terminal on an IBM host? For those readers having done this, how well did you like the keyboard mapping and display layout? What happened when it came time to display 132 characters on the PC's 80-character wide-screen? Did you get the display to wrap everything after 80 characters to the line below so that unreadable sentences resulted, or did the display show an 80-character window that moved to the right for those lines having more than 80 characters? Either approach is a pain to work with.

Another example is the telephone keypad. Telephone keypads do not have keys corresponding to all the letters in the alphabet. How are we able to enter an alphabetic name into cell phone memory without keys corresponding to the alphabetic letters "A" through "Z"? There is a correspondence between the numeric keypad keys on a telephone and the letters of the alphabet. The "2" key also represents the letters "A," "B," and "C." When a "C" is required in an entry, we can push the "2" key three times to produce the "C". This is a further example of feature compatibility.

Operational compatibility is determined by the data formats used by the application program. Lotus spreadsheets use WKS or WK1 files, while Excel spreadsheets use XLS files. Can you identify some different image file formats? We have BMP—Bit-Mapped Picture, TIF—Tagged Interface File, PCX, TGA, JPG, GIF, WPG—WordPerfect Graphic, RLE, and many more. What happens when you are using a graphics program that does not recognize a WPG format and you try to load a WPG image? You got it, nothing. The early Web browsers used to display only JPG and GIF formats. Today they display a much wider variety of image formats. They have wider operational compatibility.

Terminal emulation required speed-code protocol and feature compatibility. These criteria permitted dumb terminals to work with software in host computer systems. PCs running stand-alone software required us to be cognizant of operational compatibility. Data could not be effectively exchanged between PCs unless the programs in each PC had a common operational data format.

NETWORKING

Networking compatibility is concerned with sending data across complex networks. A complex network is comprised of nodes and links. In Figure 2-3, the nodes are the little circles and the links are the lines connecting them. A node is usually a facility with its own internal LAN. Links are high-speed communications channels, terminating in routers at each node. Complex networks are commonly arranged in a mesh or web-like arrangement. The goal with a complex network is to have data stuffed in at the source node and then have it pop out at the destination node. The network must perform three functions to transfer the data from source to destination across a complex network.

The first function is that the data must be *routed* between source and destination. Which way does it travel through a network? Does it go down the right-hand pathway, the left-hand pathway, or the straight through pathway?

Routing requires all end nodes to have unique and compatible addresses. A network with unique and compatible addresses is the postal network. Everyone who wants to receive mail must have a mailing address which is unique to the network. If it is not unique, then someone else could receive their mail. Postal addresses also must be compatible, or presented in the exact same format. When we want to send a letter, we must write down the full mailing address, including a person's full name, street address, city, state, and Zip code. We can't just write down on an envelope a person's first name and stick the envelope into a mailbox. This address is incomplete and consequently incompatible. The first name-only address is also not unique. All networks must have some form of unique and compatible addresses.

Next, data must be sent through the network in small chunks rather than as a single block. The opportunity for having an error in a large block of data is very high. When an error occurs, the entire block must be re-transmitted. With smaller chunks, the chance of error is much less and only the small chunk must be re-transmitted. However, smaller chunks introduce the problem of *message integrity*, that is, reconstructing the original message from the smaller chunks. If we chop up a message into Chunk 1, 2, and 3, when it is received, it must be reassembled as 1, 2, and 3. We have to be sure that Chunk 2 belongs to us and not someone else. It would be very embarrassing to get a rude phrase sent by someone else in a message sent to our mother.

Finally, a one-to-one or end-to-end connection, or logical link, must be established and maintained between the source of data (client) and the destination for the data (server). This *logical link* must be maintained for the duration of the communications activity. In LANs, this end-to-end connection is sometimes visible on the PC client as extra disk drives.

A logical link operates similar to a telephone call. When someone answers a phone, a fixed point-to-point connection between them and the caller is established for the duration of the call. This is like the logical link between sending and receiving devices on a network. The network logical link is established for the duration of the communication. When communications are concluded, the network resources assigned to the logical link are relinquished to serve other users.

Understanding how to make a terminal compatible with a host computer lays the foundation for understanding the OSI layers. Now that we have finished discussing terminal-host compatibility, we can relate compatibility to the OSI seven-layer networking model.

Brain Teaser

Protocol Handshakes

When we call on the phone, we use a language-based protocol to communicate error-free between Person A and Person B. What are the key handshakes of this protocol?
1. Does the called party answer first?
2. What handshake is used to answer the phone?
3. What is the response from the calling party?
4. When an error happens, what handshakes identify it as an error?
5. How is the error corrected? What happens when there are constant errors?
6. Who signals the end of the call?
7. How is the call terminated?
This exercise helps us document the simple handshakes we use in an everyday phone call into more formal handshake messages. Some dial-up protocols follow similar handshake message patterns, but use more cryptic commands to get data from Point A to Point B error-free.

OSI Functions and Implementation

The OSI model formally assigns communications functions into layers.

It is easiest to split the OSI model into two major sections, hardware and software. Layers 1 and 2 are hardware, and hardware is things we can touch, feel, shoot with a gun, set on fire, or throw out windows. Layers 1 and 2 look like a wire or a box with flashing lights. They are always something physical. A good example of Layers 1 and 2 would be an Ethernet card and wire.

Layers 3, 4, 5, 6, and 7 are software. This layer is again subdivided. Layers 3, 4, and 5 cover communications software. We never see communications software working, but it is always there. A good example is TCP/IP software. Communications software is overworked and under-appreciated.

Layers 6 and 7 are also software. This software (Layers 6 and 7) gets all the glory because it is the software that we interface with as the PC user. Layer-6 and Layer-7 software include windows and screens and application programs.

The important thing to remember here besides there being seven layers is that Layer 1 is the bottom layer. The top layer must then be Layer__? Seven is correct. So far, you have done well.

Layer 7 is the most intelligent OSI layer, but also the slowest. In contrast, Layer 1 is the fastest layer, but least intelligent. As you move from top to bottom, the intelligence decreases and the speed increases. Each layer knows how to directly communicate with the layers above and below it through interfaces. Finally, Layer 1 is the only layer that can directly communicate to itself. Now we have the basic understanding of what the seven-layer model is all about, because everything in telecommunications can be explained using this model. Using the OSI seven-layer model, you can understand the telecommunications products and services used in your network.

Next we need to understand how a layered model works. It is based upon protocols and interfaces. Protocols are used to communicate horizontally between the layers, and interfaces are used to move information vertically up and down the stack of layers.

PROTOCOLS AND INTERFACES

If you and I were communicating using the OSI layers, then Layer 4 in me would communicate to Layer 4 in you using a protocol. My Layer 4 cannot communicate to your Layer 5 or Layer 6; it can only communicate with your Layer 4.

For my Layer 4 to communicate with your Layer 4, it needs to pass data to my Layer 3. My Layer 3 then passes the data down to my Layer 2, and finally, my Layer 2 passes it on to my Layer 1. This is necessary because the only physical connection between us is at Layer 1.

To pass data from my Layer 4 to my Layer 3, the data must pass through an interface between Layer 4 and Layer 3. The interface between software layers is mainly a contractual agreement on how to behave, like how you are contracted to make your house or rent payment once a month by check. It is sent to a certain address and is a specific amount. Similarly, data is delivered to a specific range of memory addresses and is a certain size and structure. Physical interfaces are similar, but physically implemented, like how we stop our cars for red lights or go through them for green lights. Interfaces are sometimes called Application Program Interfaces (APIs). This has nothing to do with the top layer of the seven-layer OSI model. APIs loosely describe software interfaces between adjacent layers.

Protocols and interfaces remind me of an old Smothers Brothers song: "Crabs walk sideways and lobsters walk straight, so… a crab cannot have a lobster for a date." Yes, Virginia, there is such a song!

PROTOCOLS

The crabs in our case are protocols carrying data between equivalent layers in different devices. They communicate with the same layer in the other device using header information added to the block of data sent to the other device. Only the equivalent layer in the receiving device can decipher the header information and determine what to do with the information received.

INTERFACES

The lobsters are the interfaces between adjacent layers in the same device, carrying data up and down the OSI seven-layer stack. There are software and hardware interfaces. Both operate similarly. They transfer rigidly structured data between adjacent layers. They signal the adjacent layer that data is available. They respond to a specific set of commands, like "get" and "put" commands. Interfaces are called APIs, regardless of the level at which they operate. Driver programs implement software to hardware interfaces for the exact hardware device installed.

Two well-known interfaces are the WinSock32 API and the Telephone Server Application Program Interface (TSAPI), implemented in Windows software. The WinSock32 API interfaces higher layer software to the TCP/IP software of Windows, and the TSAPI is a similar interface for Windows software applications aimed at telephony.

The OSI Model

The ISO was the focal point for the development of the OSI networking model. (Yes, you might think of this as the ISO-OSI networking model. Confused? Keep in mind that the "S" is always in the center spot.)

This seven-layer networking model divides up communications in an arbitrary (but logical) fashion among the layers. In the real world of making communications hardware and software products that work reliably, communications products perform the functions. These products do not necessarily follow precisely the hierarchical structure defined by the OSI model. Let's match compatibility to the seven layers. First, the seven layers are:

Application	Layer 7
Presentation	Layer 6
Session	Layer 5
Transport	Layer 4
Network	Layer 3

| Data Link | Layer 2 |
| Physical | Layer 1 |

Most telephony, data, image, LAN, and wireless communications products today are described and discussed in the context of the OSI model. This model provides the frame of reference for understanding how communications products should be constructed so that they can communicate with each other (be interconnected).

OSI Layers vs. Compatibility vs. Components

Matching the compatibility types up with the OSI layers further explains the communications functions performed in each layer. OSI layer purists are likely to say our function assignments are not precisely correct. For us to use the model, they do not need to be exactly correct, because we are using the OSI model to generally understand the operation of many different communications hardware and software components. The design of these components does not precisely follow the OSI model either. However, because communications hardware and software generally follows the OSI model, we can answer the question: "Which layer does speed compatibility fall into?" The layers vs. compatibility are:

- **Layer 1** covers speed compatibility. The *physical layer* wiring and electrical transmission can be summarized into two simple data communications parameters: speed and distance. The greater the transmission speed, the shorter the distance the electrical signal carries. Layer 1 is communications hardware like cabling. Hardware interfaces to Layer 2.
- **Layer 2**—The *data link layer* handles data link protocol compatibility. The function of a data link protocol is to get information from Point A to Point B error-free. It uses message handshakes to perform its function. Layer 2 is also communications hardware such as an Ethernet card with flashing lights. Layer 2 interfaces to Layers 1 and 3.
- **Layer 3**—The *network layer* performs routing compatibility, sending data from source to destination. Layer 3 is communications software. Internet Packet (IP) protocol software used to address and to route Internet messages is an example of Layer 3. Layer 3 interfaces to Layers 2 and 4.
- **Layer 4**—The *transport layer* provides end-to-end message integrity compatibility. It assures that entire messages are moved through a network from source to destination. It is communications software. Transmission Control Protocol (TCP) software assuring message

ISO (International Standards Organization)
or
OSI (Open Systems Interconnection Model)
Seven Layers

ISO Layer	Compatibility	PC Component
7 – Application	Operational	Application
6 – Presentation	Feature/Code	Windows
5 – Session	PC to Server	TCP
4 – Transport	Message Integrity	TCP
3 – Network	Routing	IP
2 – Data Link	Protocol	LAN Board
1 – Physical	Speed	LAN Board

Figure 2–4 *Compatibility vs. OSI layers vs. PC components.*

integrity for information sent across the Internet is an example of Layer 4. Layer 4 interfaces to Layers 3 and 5.

- **Layer 5**—The *session layer* provides the logical one-to-one or end-to-end connection. *Layer 5* is the software entry point to the network. Layer 5 is communications software. Again, TCP, a software used to make point-to-point connections across the Internet, is an example of Layer 5. Layer 5 interfaces to Layers 4 and 6.

- **Layer 6**—The *presentation layer* provides feature compatibility. This is performed by the PC's operating environment. Layer 6 is software that we sometimes see. An example of Layer-6 software would be the Windows Graphical User Interface program (GUI.EXE). Layer-6 interfaces to Layers 5 and 7.

- **Layer 7**—The *application layer* covers operational compatibility. It is largely the function of the application program to solve operational compatibility. Today, many programs accept data files in different operational formats. Netscape Navigator is an example of Layer-7 software. Layer-7 software interfaces with Layer-6 software.

See Figure 2-4 for an overview of which compatibility criteria are assigned to which OSI layers and which PC components implement those layers.

We need to now fit all the pieces of the OSI puzzle together using a PC example. This example can be extended to all communications. For example, in the days of Alexander Graham Bell, the seven layers existed for all phone calls. One layer was implemented in the phones and the remaining six layers were implemented in the people talking on the phones. They just did not know that they were implementing six layers.

OSI Model Flow Example

To better understand the model, let's see how the OSI model applies to communications products. In Figure 2-5, we transmit data from a PC on the left (Point A) through a modem eliminator cable (null modem cable) to the PC on the right (Point B). When I type "A" at the terminal on the left, the "A" appears on the screen of the PC on the right. When "A" is typed at the PC on the left, we are at the user or applications layer, Layer 7. The keyboard scans the keys to determine that it should create the ASCII code (1000001) for "A". This is performed at the presentation layer, Layer 6. This layer's function is performed by the PC hardware.

Layer 5 is the session layer, maintaining a one-to-one connection between transmitting and receiving PCs. There is not much to do here because the physical connection only permits a single termination. Layer 5 specifies that the transmission is destined for Point B. Layer 4 is the transport layer responsible for end-to-end message integrity. It states one block; this is it! Layer 3 is the routing layer, routing the block from Point A to Point B.

The data is passed to the communications software that implements Layer 2, the data link layer. The data link layer adds a parity error check and a transmission envelope of start and stop bits.

The data is passed to the serial interface implementing the physical layer. The RS-232 physical interface transmits positive and negative voltages corresponding to the bits in the "A". Equivalent layers reverse the process in the receiving PC. The serial interface converts the voltages back to bits used by the PC software. The software strips the start and stop bits forming the transmission envelope, checks the parity bit, and hands the data to the character generator hardware of the PC display. The character generator transforms the bits of ASCII "A" into the dots on the display screen that in turn we at the user level see on the screen. The character "A" begins its journey at the top left of Figure 2-5, then travels down to the bottom of Figure 2-5. At the physical layer, the bottom of Figure 2-5, the "A" travels horizontally across to the destination computer, and finally travels back up to the top on the right-hand side of Figure 2-5. This is the basics of the seven layer model.

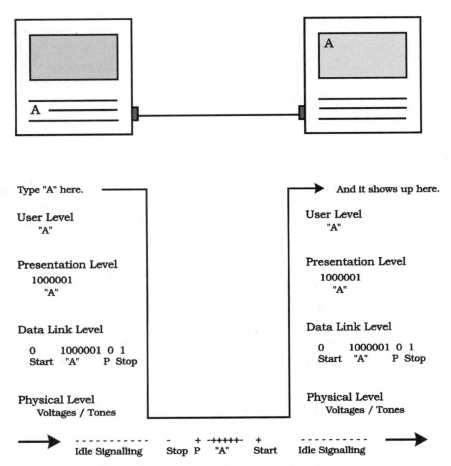

Figure 2–5 *OSI layers in action.*

Telecommunications Components

The OSI model, while important, must relate to what is purchased and used to implement real networks. This is the hardware and software interconnected by communications channels. To communicate, we must have all three components present and they must inter-operate. Hardware is our PC or our telephone, channels are the wire and telephone switching equipment used in the telephone network, and software is Windows or UNIX and applications software programs that makes the system function as a cohesive whole. Network components are illustrated in Figure 2-6.

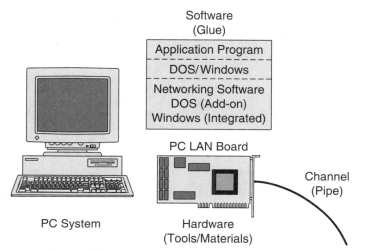

Figure 2–6   *Telecommunications hardware, channels, and software.*

COMPONENTS VS. LAYERS

In our PC example in Figure 2-6, the PC communications card implements Layers 1 and 2. The electronics on the board determine the type of media and the electrical (or optical) signaling that travels across the media. This in turn results in a maximum bits per second speed and a maximum distance between communicating devices that can be traveled before the signal must be boosted to travel further. An Ethernet card that implements Layers 1 and 2 is shown in Figure 2-7.

The dotted line represents the driver program needed to communicate between Windows and the hardware. This is sometimes labeled a Mini-Port Driver or .MPD file. Hardware generally covers Layers 1 and 2. Layers 3 and up are implemented in software. TCP/IP is implemented in software at Layers 3, 4, and 5. All you need for TCP/IP is the software built into Windows 95/98/ME and Windows NT/2000. The IP part covers Layer 3 and the routing function. VoIP software interfaces directly to this Layer-3 software. TCP is focused on data transmission and implemented in Layers 4 and 5. Finally, Layer 6 is implemented in Windows. The Graphics Device Interface (GDI.EXE) and the user interface (USER.EXE) are the software components that perform many of these functions. Finally, the Windows application program implements Layer 7. So, a Web browser on the dial pad site would at Layer 7 perform some VoIP telephony for us as the person using the PC.

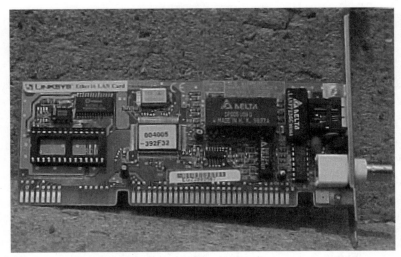

Figure 2–7 *Ethernet hardware.*

This is a highly simplified example of how the OSI model is implemented. I have again taken liberties with the precise implementation of the layers to breathe some reality into a generally uninteresting but important concept. One last shot before we finish. What exactly is Asynchronous Transfer Mode (ATM) when it comes to PCs?

ATM

Asynchronous Transfer Mode (ATM) is a PC card that implements (like Ethernet cards implement) OSI Layers 1 and 2. To bring ATM directly to any PC would require installing an ATM card in that PC. An ATM card is shown in Figure 2-8.

The ATM in all new telecommunications transmission technologies boils down to hardware and some supporting software. It is nothing special or awesome, but rather, just the latest telecommunications technology implemented in hardware and software.

Applying the OSI Model

We will use the OSI model throughout this book as a frame of reference for describing and explaining the functionality of telecommunications products and services.

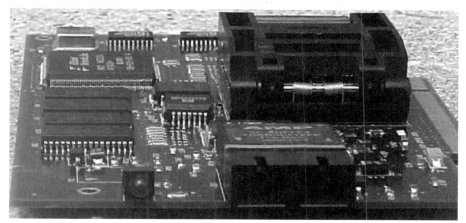

Figure 2–8 *Asynchronous Transfer Mode (ATM) hardware.*

The OSI model is the keystone for understanding telecommunications hardware and software components. Once you understand the OSI seven-layer model, you can use it to figure out what functions any telecommunications product or service provides or performs.

The OSI model provides a roadmap for understanding how the hardware, communications channel, and software pieces fit together to form today's telecommunications networks. It is a vital tool for facilitating the development of inter-operable telecommunications products and services, as well as an important tool to facilitate our understanding of telecommunications networks. You have been warned! Remember the OSI model.

<hr>

Brain Teaser

Identifying Windows ATM Software

Open the Windows 98 **Control Panel** (select **Start** → **Settings** → **Control Panel**). Then, select **Network** → **Add Adapter**.
1. Are any ATM adapters listed?
2. Can you find an efficient networks adapter?
3. Next, select **Protocol**. Are there any special ATM protocols built into Windows 98?
The purpose of this exercise is to illustrate that new PCs support ATM telecommunications technology for voice, data, image, and video communications. Later in the book, we will illustrate why this support is compelling and important for future telecommunications networks.

■ Summary

This chapter has presented an overview of telecommunications standards and a practical perspective of their implementation and use in networking. The OSI model for networking was introduced. OSI layer functions and implementation were examined and discussed. The importance of the OSI model to us as a tool for understanding the functionality of telecommunications products was presented at the conclusion of the chapter.

▲ Chapter Review Questions

1. *What does OSI stand for?*

   A. Open System Internetworking

   B. Open System Interconnection

   C. Open System Internet-architecture

   D. Open Service Interconnection

2. *What does TCP/IP stand for?*

   A. Transmission Control Protocol/Internet Packet protocol

   B. Transaction Control Protocol/Internet Protocol

   C. Transmission Control Protocol/Intranet Protocol

   D. Transmission Control Protocol/Internet Protocol

3. *How many layers are in the OSI model?*

   A. Three

   B. Five

   C. Seven

   D. Nine

4. *An Ethernet card covers which OSI layers?*

   A. Layers 1 and 3

   B. Layers 2 and 3

   C. Layer 2 only

   D. Layers 1 and 2

5. *What is the function performed by OSI Layer 3?*

    A. Message integrity

    B. Electrical signaling

    C. Error-free transmission

    D. Routing

6. *What layer(s) implement the IP?*

    A. Layer 1

    B. Layer 3

    C. Layer 2

    D. Layers 3, 4, and 5

7. *What layer(s) is responsible for message integrity?*

    A. Layer 4

    B. Layer 3

    C. Layer 2

    D. Layers 4 and 5

8. *ATM is*

    A. A PC card

    B. Layers 1 and 2

    C. Asynchronous Transfer Mode

    D. All of the above

    E. None of the above

9. *Telecommunications networks are built using what?*

    A. The OSI layers

    B. Hardware, software, and channels

    C. PC boards

    D. Layers 1, 2, 3, 4, and 5

10. *Network cabling is in which layer(s) of the OSI model?*

    A. Layer 4

    B. Layer 3

    C. Layer 2

    D. Layers 1 and 2

    E. None of the above

Voice Basics

This chapter presents the basics of telephony and voice communications networks. This lays the foundation for examining how telephone networks have technologically evolved into telecommunications networks. It covers basic analog and digital telephone operation.

Voice Communications

The voice communications network was originally designed to carry only human voice. Telephony is derived from two Greek words: tele, meaning far and phone, meaning sound. Combined into telephony, they imply sound at a distance.

Voice communications have very specific operating characteristics. These characteristics are similar to those of video transmission. Voice communications are a continuous stream of information with few interruptions. Voice communications require a reliable, continuously operating network; there must be no transmission delays. The information representing a voice signal must arrive in the same order as it was transmitted. A fixed transmission speed is required, and few transmission errors are permitted. Let's examine these characteristics some more.

The voice network must be very reliable. We have come to expect that telephones will always work. Since telephones always work, we depend upon them. If they failed to work or were significantly less reliable, we would become upset today. This reliance on any technical tool causes us to depend upon them always being available to serve us. When they fail, we become very stressed.

Voice was originally transmitted as analog signals that were a simple conversion of analog sounds into analog electrical signals. Analog voice transmission was basically just a bunch of waves. Today, analog voice sounds are converted to analog electrical signals and then into a continuous digital stream of pulses we think of as "0's" and "1's". The time between the digital "0's" and "1's" must be constant, or fixed. Any delays or hesitations would cause the voice to sound warbled and distorted. Further, the "0's" and "1's" representing voice must arrive in the same sequence in which they were transmitted. Having one phrase arrive before another would render speech unintelligible. Good voice or speech quality requires sending a constant 64,000-bits-per-second stream from source to destination. Quality of speech improves as the output more closely resembles the analog signal input. To represent music (a very demanding digital representation of sound), CDs over-sample the analog signal to produce digital encoding in the 160,000-bits-per-second or greater bit stream.

Data communications have quite different characteristics. We will examine these at the beginning of Chapter 5.

Telephone networks are evolving rapidly into so much more than just mechanisms for voice communications. However, their ability to transport and deliver to consumers other types of information is influenced by the original intent and design of the network to carry voice. Understanding basic telephony will help us understand the constraints imposed upon this evolution into a 21st century telecommunications network.

Basic Voice Network Components and Their Functions

Voice networks are comprised of inter-operable components that permit the establishment of calls between end-users. A call may be point-to-point between two users or a multi-point conference connection between several users.

The voice network has an architecture that provides:

- Terminals—A telephone is used to make and receive voice calls and to process call control information. Terminals are usually thought of as analog phones, but today, they are fast becoming computers with multimedia output.
- Access—Access to wide area connection components is provided by local loops that connect terminals to local telephone company offices. The access can take several forms, from the common analog transmission loop to leased lines, T-1 digital lines, and cellular links.
- Connectivity—This feature permits users at telephone terminals to make and receive calls. Telephone company switching equipment usually accomplishes connectivity.
- Features—These are provided to the caller by the telephone company. Some features are call forwarding, instant re-dial, caller ID, etc.
- Services—These are additional network functions that go beyond basic calling features. Voice mail, protocol conversion, and the like are services.

Our current telephone network is composed of several visible and many invisible components. Next we will examine the basic technology behind voice communications and the components implementing this technology.

Voice Communications Frequencies

To understand voice communications technology, we need to look quickly at how we communicate by voice. Our spoken voice is an analog signal that has frequency and amplitude characteristics. This analog voice signal can be represented by an electrical analog (or duplicate) of the human voice signal.

Electrical signals can be analog or digital. The phone system was built originally for analog voice communications in a narrow range of frequencies

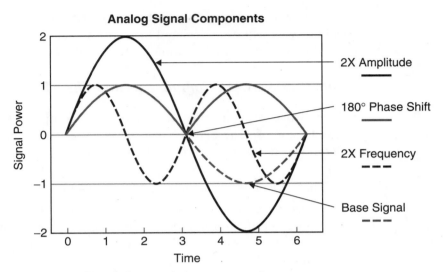

Figure 3–1 *Signal characteristics, or properties.*

to mimic our voices. Analog electrical signals have the following as primary electrical characteristics:

- Amplitude (volume or power).
- Frequency (pitch).
- Phase.

Voice communications, or sounds, are analog signal communications. When anyone says analog, you should think of an ocean wave or a lazy S (see Figure 3-1).

This wave is defined one way by height. The wave's height is its amplitude. Amplitude is the power, or strength, of the wave. When we talk, we transmit analog waves. The louder we talk, the more power in the wave and the higher the wave's amplitude. When we talk softly, the power is low and the amplitude or wave height is small.

When one lazy S is complete, the wave has completed a single cycle. When waves complete several cycles in a second, we refer to that as the frequency of the wave. If a wave completes two cycles in a second, for instance, it would have a frequency of two Cycles Per Second (CPS).

Frequency is measured in CPS or Hertz (Hz). The range of frequencies used by a communications device determines the communication channel and communicating device's bandwidth, or information carrying capacity. Humans hear in the range of 10Hz to 16,000Hz, or a bandwidth of 16,000-10 = 15,990Hz. When you hear the whine from a PC color monitor, you hear

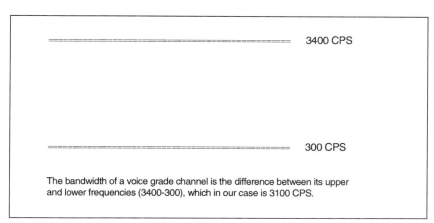

Figure 3–2 *Telephone line bandwidth.*

15,790Hz. Specifications on tape cassette player headphones usually state that they can produce sound from 20Hz to 20,000Hz. Twenty Hertz is earthquake frequency. At that frequency with loud amplitude, buildings shake. Our ability to hear high frequencies diminishes with age. I think babies are capable of hearing 18,000Hz frequencies at 18 months. However, it does not do them much good then. My ability to distinguish frequencies tops out around 12,000Hz.

In the telephone system, the frequencies it passes are restricted to between 300Hz to 3400Hz. No matter what frequencies enter, only those between 300Hz and 3400Hz are produced at the other end. In this case, the telephone network bandwidth is 3400Hz – 300Hz, or about 3100Hz (see Figure 3-2).

Could the telephone network be built to deliver frequencies from 0Hz to 20,000Hz? Sure it could, but at what cost? The voice telephone network is a compromise between high-quality sound signals (0Hz to 20,000Hz) and the cost of delivering those signals to all subscribers. It was a good compromise, because when we talk on the phone, we get all the content we need. We can recognize the voice of the other person, we can tell their mood (happy, angry, or sad), whether they are ill, and more.

Electronic communications are moving to higher and higher frequencies because higher frequencies can carry more information. This is like an angry person speaking in an increasingly higher tone voice. Frequencies (mostly electronic frequencies) are measured or expressed as:

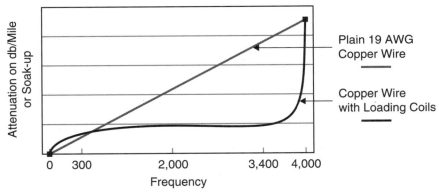

Signal Soak-up (Attenuation) on Telephone Wire

Plain 19 AWG
Copper Wire

Copper Wire
with Loading Coils

Attenuation on db/Mile
or Soak-up

0   300   2,000   3,400 4,000
Frequency

Figure 3–3 *Telephone wire signal absorption (soak-up).*

Kilohertz = 1KHz = 1,000Hz

Megahertz = 1MHz = 1,000,000Hz

Gigahertz = 1GHz = 1,000,000,000Hz

Amplitude is the power, or volume, that a particular signal has in a given frequency. Analog signals are comprised of frequency, amplitude, and phase components (see Figure 3-3). Although the phone has a bandwidth of 3100Hz, each frequency does not have equal amplitude. A human ear works somewhat similarly—it hears 2KHz sounds much better than 14KHz sounds.

Humans primarily use amplitude and frequency in voice communications. Humans may hear phase changes, but they cannot distinguish changes in phase. Try listening to a modem on a telephone line calling another modem if you would like to hear what changes in phase sound like. Analog electrical signals can be modulated. Modulation is changing, or regulating, waves so that meaningful information is represented by the waves. As you drive to work, you may listen to FM or AM radio. FM stands for Frequency Modulation because FM radio changes the frequency, or timing, of the wave to carry information. AM stands for Amplitude Modulation because it changes the height, or amplitude, of the wave to carry information.

A voice signal can be represented electronically by the equation $A \sin (\phi + \lambda t)$, where "A" represents the amplitude of the signal, "ϕ" represents the phase, "λ" represents the frequency, and "t" represents the time interval. This equation can produce a simple sinusoidal curve similar to those we all learned in trigonometry. This equation can be modulated electronically to carry meaningful information.

Bandwidth defines the amount of information one can transmit in a signal. Signals are like pipes. Since very small pipes like the water faucet in your kitchen deliver quarts of water, they have a small bandwidth. A water main connected to a fire hydrant can deliver swimming pools of water, so it has a much larger bandwidth. In the analog world, bandwidth is described as a difference in frequencies or Hz. To derive an analog signal's bandwidth, you take the highest frequency and subtract from it the lowest frequency. The difference is the signal bandwidth. A signal with a high frequency of 4000 CPS and a low frequency of 0 cycles per second has a bandwidth of 4000 CPS, or 4KHz. Telephone voice channels use frequencies from 4000 CPS Hz to 0Hz, and they have a 4KHz analog signal bandwidth.

Voice Channel Pass Window

Loading coils and other filtering equipment limit the frequencies transmitted across a voice-grade analog channel. This was caused by early telephony working across copper wire. Copper wire soaks up an electrical signal sent down it. This works similar to us shouting down a pipe. Someone a short distance down the pipe would hear us shouting easily because the pipe contains and focuses the energy of our voice. However, if someone were a long distance away down the pipe, they would not hear our voice because it would be all soaked up.

It is even worse with copper wire because high frequencies are soaked up more than low frequencies as shown in Figure 3-4. So if say Lurch from the Addams Family were to talk on the phone, his very low voice would get through with no problem. Tiny Tim's high falsetto voice, on the other hand, would be largely absorbed and we would hear little over the phone. Installing loading coils in telephone lines solves this problem. A loading coil is a coil of wire that alters the electrical characteristics of copper telephone wire. It flattens out the signal loss between 300 and 3400 CPS at the expense of having the signal soaked up at an even higher rate above 3400 CPS. Figure 3-4 also shows this. With loading coils installed, both Lurch and Tiny Tim can use the phone with equal confidence that they will be heard at the receiving end.

The impact of loading coils can be illustrated another way by drawing a graph of the typical telephone channel and making the vertical axis signal power (the more power, the louder the signal) and the horizontal axis signal frequency (see Figure 3-5). A voice-grade channel with loading coils installed permits signal power between the frequencies of 300 and 3400 CPS. Below 300 and above 3400 CPS, all signal power is soaked up or absorbed by the telephone network. (The total frequency range used by the telephone company is 0 to 4000 CPS. Guard bands limit the effective voice range from 300

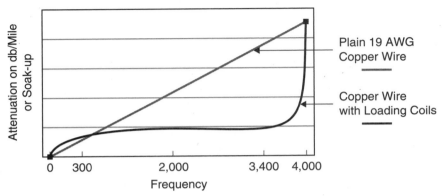

Figure 3–4 *Telephone wire signal absorption (soak-up).*

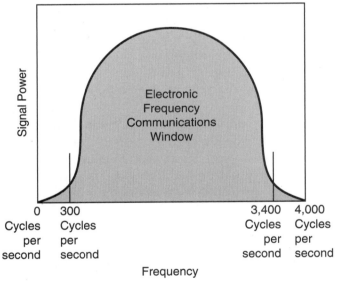

Figure 3–5 *Telephone pass window.*

to 3400 CPS.) This graph is referred to as the pass window for voice-grade telephone lines. It is, the window through which specific frequencies, those above 0 and below 4000 CPS, pass, or are transmitted (carried), end-to-end by the telephone network.

Telephone Operation

Most home telephones are analog devices using a current loop driven to carry voice from the telephone's microphone to the telephone company central office and from the telephone company central office to the telephone's speaker.

ANALOG PHONES

Analog telephone current signaling permits analog signals to travel long distances (miles) over copper telephone wire. What voltage is used in telephones? Is it 12 volts like in our automobiles or 120 volts like in the wall outlet? It is neither, but rather 48-volts Direct Current (DC). This is relatively low voltage, but you can get a shock from the telephone line. Anyone can wire up a phone. There are two to six wires in a phone jack. The wire color codes for the primary phone line are red and green. Green is for tip (the tip of the phone jack plug in the old manual switchboards) and red is for ring. The second line uses yellow and black wires. Sometimes there are blue and white wires. These carried power for the light on the Princess™ telephones. A small word of caution when wiring phones: if you have two hands but need three, do not use your mouth for a hand. The 48-volt DC power in the phone line will give you a memorable jolt. It is not like testing a 9-volt battery with your tongue. Further, if the phone were to ring, the telephone company would send 90-volt Alternating Current (AC) power down the line once per second to cause the phone to ring. This would give you a very memorable jolt.

The way an analog telephone works is that it is normally on-hook or resting in its cradle (see Figure 3-6). In this case, the DC circuit is broken between the telephone company and the phone. DC current flows in one direction only. It cannot flow across any breaks in the circuit. When the phone rings, the telephone company sends a 90-volt AC signal (like the current in any power outlet). AC current moves out the back or in both directions. It cannot cross the switch in the phone, but it can pass through a capacitor (two metal plates very close to one another) because it first charges and then discharges the plates on each side of the capacitor. This permits the AC current to ring the bell in the phone.

When we answer, the DC begins to flow and the equipment in the telephone company senses this and instantly (well, to humans instantly) stops the AC signal from traveling down the line. Then, as we hear the person at the other end speak, the telephone company increases and decreases the current flow to mimic the analog voice at the other end of the circuit. The phone

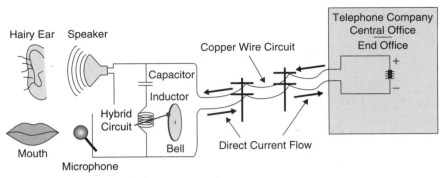

Figure 3–6 *Analog telephone circuit diagram.*

creates sound in its speaker using this variation in current flow. The sound created is heard in our Figure 3-6 by the ear. The DC current flow exits the speaker and runs through a hybrid circuit that returns it to a constant flowing current—no variations in flow. It is then run into the microphone in the telephone.

The microphone consists of two metal plates separated by carbon granules. The current flows from one plate through the carbon granules to the other plate. The granules are a resistor that varies depending upon how close the metal plates are to one another. The voice entering the microphone vibrates the plates, changing the resistance and thus creating a varying current flow mimicking the voice analog signal. This travels down the copper telephone wire into the telephone central office where it is further processed and transmitted to its destination.

The telephone current loop provides our familiar telephone interface—dial tone, keypad DTMF (Dual Tone Multi-Frequency) tones, busy signals, and more. Ringing signals use 90-volt AC to ring the telephone's bell. Most phones in homes are analog telephones operating basically in this fashion.

DIGITAL TRANSMISSION AND HIGH FREQUENCIES

Digital (square wave) transmission carries information as "0's" (no signal) or "1's" (signal). Square waves are either present or absent, not like analog signals which can be 10%, 20%, ... , 90%, or 100% there. A square wave signal is shown in Figure 3-7.

Square waves present some problems for the telephone network as it was originally designed and constructed. High frequencies are required to create square wave (digital) signals. Let me illustrate. If we were to send a

Figure 3–7 *Square wave signal.*

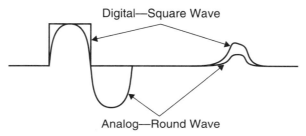

Figure 3–8 *Round waves (analog) vs. square waves (digital).*

round wave down a telephone copper wire, it would be soaked up more than a digital square wave.

In Figure 3-8, we see a 1000-CPS signal. This could be used to send digital information, but it is soaked up more than the square wave with its nice sharp corners. So, we need to use true square waves to send digital signals.

But, square waves require high frequencies to produce the nice sharp square corners that are their hallmark. Figure 3-9 illustrates how high frequencies, or harmonics, are needed to produce square waves.

In the top of Figure 3-9, we show a 1000-CPS signal and its 11th harmonic (an 11,000-CPS signal). In the time it takes the 1000-CPS signal to go up and down once (one full cycle), the 11th harmonic signal completes 11 full up and down cycles. In the bottom of Figure 3-9, a square wave is constructed by tracing the upward path of the 11,000-CPS signal's first cycle, then the level is held high until the downward path of the 6th cycle. The 6th cycle's downward path is used to form a square wave. The resulting square wave looks almost like an ideal square wave.

The purpose here is to illustrate two basic points key to understanding telephony and telecommunications. The points are:

- Digital transmission can cross wires that are capable of supporting high frequencies. Otherwise, they are all soaked up and do not get through.

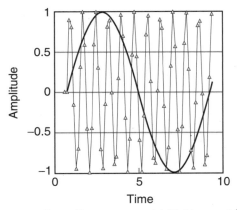

Base Frequency and 11th Harmonic

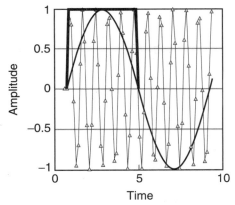

Square Wave Based Upon 11th Harmonic

Figure 3–9   *Digital signals require high frequencies.*

- Higher frequencies can support higher bits per second transmission speeds than lower frequencies. So, a GHz signal can carry more bits per second than a MHz signal.

These points play an important role in understanding the impediments and technical tradeoffs made to implement digital transmission over existing telephone facilities and the capabilities of different wireless communications systems.

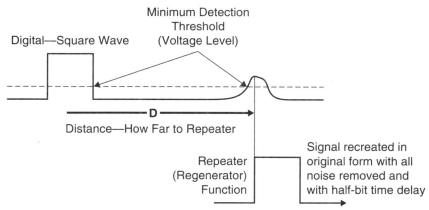

Figure 3–10 *Digital repeater function.*

DIGITAL PHONES

Integrated Services Digital Network (ISDN) phones use digital (square wave) transmission to carry all information to and from the telephone company. So, the digital phone has a computer in it and there is no longer an analog current flowing between it and the telephone company central office. Transmission is digital using high-frequency square waves that are levels of voltage. For example, a zero could be − 5 volts and a one could be + 5 volts. These square waves travel over existing telephone wire with one modification. What is the modification? Think, the loading coils! They limit high frequencies to less than 4000 CPS. What frequency did we need to send our square waves? 11,000 CPS. With loading coils in the telephone circuit, this frequency would be all soaked up.

When a telephone company constructs an ISDN circuit, they set it up for high-frequency square wave transmission by removing the loading coils and then test to assure that the digital signals are received at a sufficient level at each end of the circuit (see Figure 3-10). When the digital signals fall below the minimum detectable threshold, no transmission is received.

Digital phones convert our voice analog signal into digital transmission in the phone. Analog phones rely on equipment in the telephone network to perform the conversion. We will discuss the conversion process soon. ISDN phones implement a 2B + D connection between the phone and the telephone company central office. This 2B + D is called a Basic Rate Interface, or BRI. The B is a Bearer channel running at 64,000 bits per second. It can carry (or bear) voice, data, image, or video traffic depending upon the equipment

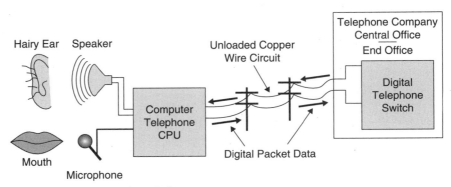

Figure 3–11 *ISDN digital phone.*

attached to each end of the B channel. An ISDN BRI has two B channels for a total of 128,000 bits per second information carrying capacity. It can carry two telephone voice connections simultaneously and thus support mini-conference calls between three parties. The D channel is a Data channel that carries the telephone signaling information.

Signaling is a key telephony term which calls the handshake signals used primarily by telephones to establish a call and break down a call so other callers can use the circuit. Signaling is the dial tone, numbers dialed, the busy or ringing signal, call waiting signals, caller ID signals, the hang-up signal, and more. These signals are carried by the D channel in an ISDN line.

To make an ISDN call, we pick up the phone and hear a dial tone created by the computer in the ISDN phone for our benefit, then we type the number we are calling into a keypad. The computer in the ISDN phone converts the number into ASCII code characters and places them in a chunk of data that it sends to the digital telephone switch in the central office. The digital telephone switch completes the call and sends back chunks of data, indicating that the target phone is ringing or engaged. The computer in the ISDN phone creates the appropriate sounds for us to hear. If the call is answered, a B channel is used to carry a continuous stream of digital information representing our voice between our phone and the target phone. When the call is terminated, the phones and the telephone switches exchange more signaling chunks of data to release the communications channels used by the call (see Figure 3-11).

COMMON CHANNEL VS. IN-BAND SIGNALING

There are two different ways to perform signaling. Our analog telephones provide in-band signaling, while ISDN phones use common channel signaling.

In-band signaling was the first type of signaling deployed in the telephone network. In-band signaling is defined as voice and signaling information sharing the same communications path. Think of this: When you are talking on your analog home phone and your fingers hit keys on the telephone's numeric keypad, what do you hear? You hear the DTMF beeps in the middle of your conversation. That is because analog telephones use in-band signaling. The signaling information (beeps) is carried in the main and only communications channel.

In common channel signaling, voice information and signaling information travel on separate paths. If you were dialing an ISDN phone that had common channel signaling, you could press the keypad keys and talk to someone at the same time without them hearing the keypad tones. The signaling information and voice information travel separate paths and do not interfere with each other. Sometimes this may be referred to as out-of-band signaling. Compare the channel capacity your voice requires to the channel capacity required to send telephone numbers (signaling information). Voice transmission requires much more capacity than call setup information (the telephone number dialed). Further, signaling information (the call setup information) is data transmission that comes at the beginning of the call and the end of the call with much wasted time between the signaling data packets. So why waste communications capacity to set up a phone call? A separate signaling network can easily accommodate signaling. This network is a data communications network that carries signaling information efficiently from many callers simultaneously because data chunks (packets or frames) can be interleaved on a single channel. This describes the technique used by Signaling System 7 (SS-7) that is discussed later in this chapter.

With ISDN phones, common channel (D channel) signaling is used. The signaling travels as chunks of digital data on the separate D channel. In-band signaling is used today only for signaling between our analog home phones and the telephone company. The telephone backbone (supporting) network employs common channel signaling, or out-of-band signaling, over separate D channels to manage all calls passing through it.

2-Wire vs. 4-Wire Channels

There are 2-wire and 4-wire channels in the telephone network. Service to our analog home phone is 2-wire service. Only two wires are required to communicate. As we saw earlier, one wire carries the analog signal from the telephone company to the phone while the other wire carries our analog voice signal to the telephone company. This is a full duplex connection—we can speak and listen at the same time. Common analog telephones use just two wires (although four are typically present in telephone cable) to transfer voice between the phone and the telephone company central office. This represents a single path carrying information in both directions.

Analog connections between telephone switching equipment such as trunk lines from telephone company end offices to telephone company toll offices use four wires to provide two separate message pathways. Each pathway has a full pass window. Thus, a 4-wire circuit has two separate pass windows and a greater bandwidth than a 2-wire circuit. Class 5 end offices support 2-wire switching, while toll offices switch 4-wire circuits.

4-wire circuits are much less important today with the backbone support network being largely high-speed digital transmission channels.

Quality of Service

In telecommunications networks, Quality of Service (QoS) is guaranteeing a measurable minimum level of transmission delay, data loss, and transmission errors. The goal is to maintain the equivalent voice communications quality to that of the analog telephone network as telephony is moved from an analog circuit-switched network to a digital packet (or cell) delivery network.

A circuit-switched network defines a point-to-point guaranteed bandwidth that no one else can use. Imagine a room of people. To set up a connection from one side of the room to the other, each person in the room must hold another person's hand. These people are forming a point-to-point circuit, or channel. Once they hold someone else's hand, they cannot hold another hand. No one else in the room can add their hand to the point-to-point circuit. This guarantees a fixed, constant bandwidth and a defined path.

In contrast, a packet-switched network is a network that does not have a defined circuit path. In this case, imagine the group of people tossing small white, blue, and pink coffee sweetener packets to each other. They start at one side of the room and are tossed from person to person until all the white, blue, and pink coffee sweetener packets make it to the other side of the room. The problem with tossing packets is now that they can travel the same pathways (reducing bandwidth), they can get out of sequence, there can be delays, and there is the risk of packet losses (transmission errors). QoS is a measure of how well a digital network (tossing sweetener packets) matches up with a circuit-switched network (holding hands).

The goal is to have the new digital packet networks perform as well as the older circuit-switched analog/digital networks.

Central to the QoS concept is the fact that transmission speeds, error rates, and other characteristics can be measured and guaranteed in advance. Continuous transmission of high-bandwidth video and multimedia information requires a high QoS. Transmitting this kind of content dependably is difficult in public networks using data communications protocols and products.

The Internet is a packet network that does not guarantee on-time or complete delivery of all packets passing through it. To carry voice communications across the Internet, there must be QoS guarantees that provide performance equivalent to that of the circuit-switched voice network. The Internet's Resource Reservation Protocol (RSVP) provides this QoS. With RSVP protocol data passing through the Internet, communications components can be expedited based on QoS policy and reservation criteria arranged in advance. This permits the Internet to effectively carry voice communications traffic. Similarly, Asynchronous Transfer Mode (ATM) also lets a company or user pre-select a level of quality for ATM service. In ATM, technical transmission details like the average delay at a gateway, the variation in delay in a group of cells (cells are 53-character (byte) transmission units), cell losses, and the transmission error rate can be measured and guaranteed to achieve a specific QoS level.

Brain Teaser

Types of Analog Signals

Pick up any phone and call an AOL access number. Wait until the modem answers, then hang up. What did you hear during this phone call?

1. When you dialed the AOL access port telephone number, did you hear the in-band DTMF tones while dialing?

2. Did you hear the ringing signal from the AOL number called? What created this ringing signal? Was it the telephone company switch, the Private Branch Exchange (PBX) switch in your office, or the digital telephone you were calling from? Try a phone at home to see if the ringing signal sounds different.

3. What did the modem sound like when it answered the phone? Did it at some time change frequencies? Did the answering modem change signal amplitude (get softer or louder)? What was the final sound it made? Was it that awful background static-type noise (sometimes referred to as white noise)? That was a phase encoded analog signal. Yup, humans cannot hear phase changes, but modems can.

The goal here is to illustrate the different types of signaling that are used in making a dial-up connection to the Internet.

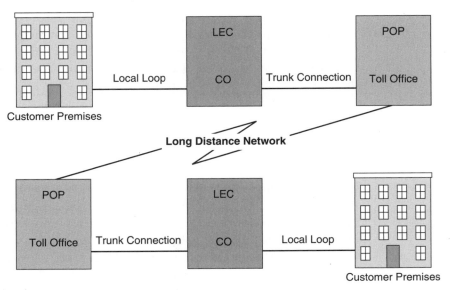

Figure 3–12   *Voice network components.*

Voice Network Components

The telephony network was originally designed to carry only human voice. Voice was carried over analog circuit-switched connections that amplified the signal so that it was audible at the other end of the circuit-switched connection.

Today our telephone networks are evolving rapidly into so much more. The original analog voice is digitally encoded into 64-Kbps data streams (64 Kbps is a very good number to remember). This has turned the backbone telephony network into a high-speed digital transport system that has the ability to transport data, digital video, and much more. The components in the voice network are still largely influenced by the original intent and design of the telephone network to carry voice.

The basic voice communications network connects from a telephone inside a customer premise to a telephone network Central Office (CO) facility through a local loop of copper wire (see Figure 3-12). This local loop is a single line for the voice telephone network subscriber. A telephone company CO connects to and serves up to 100,000 subscribers. In it resides a branch exchange switch. This is a high-end switch that connects the subscriber lines to one another or to the trunk lines that run to other voice network COs.

A trunk line is simply a line that connects two telephone switches together. Trunk lines are implemented using a variety of communications technologies, ranging from 4-wire analog channels to high-speed digital fiber optic SONET channels. Anyone having a phone system like Jason and I have trunk lines connecting them to the telephone company CO.

Some voice network COs connect directly to other subscribers, while others act as relay points to other voice communications networks. Trunk circuits run between COs. These are most often high-speed digital links composed of fiber. Sometimes these were 4-wire analog circuits. They were also called tie lines. Long-distance or Inter-Exchange Carriers (IXCs or IECs) connect to our local telephone network via a Point-Of-Presence (POP).

The POP is a room full of telephone switching gear. It is commonly built by the Local Exchange Carrier (LEC). IXCs/IECs rent space to co-locate their switching equipment with that of the LEC. Then, circuits connect the IXC/IEC to the LEC's switching equipment. The long-distance network is similarly configured. It consists of many COs connected by high-speed fiber optic trunk circuits. More detail of the voice network is provided in Figure 3-13. When we look at this diagram, we start at the customer premise. The telephone company equipment (any telephone company equipment) installed on a customer premise is Customer Premise Equipment (CPE). CPE can be leased from the telephone company or purchased from some system vendor.

Customer Premise Equipment

In Figure 3-13, the CPE is a telephone. It runs through in-house wiring maintained by the telephone subscriber to a demarcation point. This is commonly a terminating block that connects the customer premise wiring to the telephone company local loop running to the CO. A demark refers to the demarcation point, which is the "line in the sand" that delineates customer maintenance responsibility from telephone company responsibility. In other words, the demark is the point where responsibility for the wiring shifts from the telephone company to the subscriber. If a telephone has problems and the telephone service person comes into the customer premise to test the customer premise (or in-house) wiring to locate the problem, their time is billable to the customer.

Whenever there are telephone problems, check to see that the telephone network is working properly beyond the demarcation point. A simple test for an analog phone line is to plug in an analog phone and listen for a dial tone. If there is no dial tone, call the phone company to fix the problem. When there is a dial tone, check your phones and wiring before calling the telephone company.

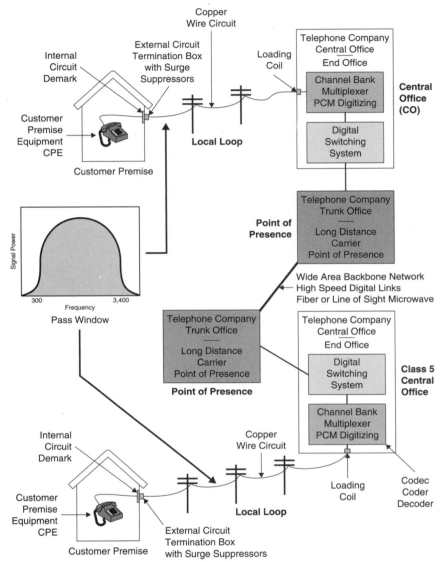

Figure 3–13   *Voice network component details.*

The demarcation point for most homes is outside the house at that little box where the telephone company plugs in its wires. For businesses, the demark point could be outside or inside the facility, depending on how telephone service was installed. Sometimes telephone company personnel refer to the cross-connect point. This is where an internal telephone network connects physically to the telephone company network. In businesses, this is commonly between two punch-down blocks. Punch-down block cross connections make it easier and more convenient to implement changes when tying the telephone network to customer premise network equipment.

Oftentimes, surge suppressors in the telephone line cause problems. These surge suppressors are located in the telephone box on the outside of the customer premise. They are the responsibility of the telephone company. Telephone service personnel will test them and replace them as needed because that is part of the telephone service they provide.

Whenever businesses have problems with their telephone network, they must test and verify that their internal network is working up to the demarcation point. They can then call the telephone company and tell them everything is working fine up to the demarcation point, but something malfunctioning beyond that point is causing a problem. Even if the telephone company is told that you have tested and found that the problem lies on their side of the demark point, the telephone company may still say everything on their side is working properly. Later they may call you back and say they found a problem in their network and they made a mistake. The problem was their fault. To resolve telephone network problems often requires a battle with the telephone company over where the problem lies. To win the battles, you need to know exactly on which side of the demark the source of the problem lies.

Local Loops

A local loop is the wire that runs from your facility to the closest telephone CO. It is generally within 2 to 25 miles of 19 AWG (American Wiring Gauge) unshielded twisted pair wire. Today local loops are terminated at one point in a customer premise facility. It is then the responsibility of the facility owner to route the local loop wires to their final destination within the customer premise. Some local loops are trunk lines that carry more than a single call. Other local loops provide high-speed digital voice access to the telephone company CO. They typically run over glass fiber links rather than the more common copper wire.

The problem with local loops is that everyone has a local loop. This local loop was designed to carry analog voice and not high-speed digital communications. Local loops are the one component of the telephone network that needs upgrading the most. However, local loops will be the last telephone network component upgraded because there are just so many of them and everyone does not need high-speed digital communications yet.

Loading coils are devices placed in analog local loops to assure constant, predictable signal loss across the 300-cycle to 3400-cycle frequency range. This range of frequencies carries our voice on the telephone network. As we discussed earlier in this chapter, loading coils cannot be used on digital transmission links because they absorb the digital pulses, effectively absorbing all digital pulses. Remember this by thinking that loading coils hate digital signals. To provide high-speed digital communications to access the Internet, the telephone company must remove those digital transmission-hating loading coils.

Local loops terminate in surge suppression frames in the CO. The CO closest to the subscriber is called a Class 5 end office. The Class 5 designation came from the AT&T switching hierarchy office class designations. The local loop has surge suppression equipment in each end to prevent lightning strikes from damaging CPE and telephone equipment.

Sometimes CO facilities are extended using Remote Terminals (RTs). These are the little green boxes in neighborhoods often referred to as pedestals. The RT is essentially a channel bank located remotely and connected by digital transmission facilities to the Class 5 end office. A Subscriber Line Carrier (SLC-96) is a similar CO extension that serves up to 96 subscriber lines with four active (or two compressed) and one spare T-1 digital line. Think of T-1 at this moment in time as simply a high-capacity digital pipe that allows 24 simultaneous voice conversations at one time. More details on T-1 vs. DS-1 connections follow in this chapter. The remote connections provide a one-for-one subscriber line channel to a telephone company CO. The latest SLC device from Lucent Technologies is an SLC-2000 that connects up to 2,048 subscriber lines to a CO.

Channel Bank Multiplexers

Channel banks are multiplexing/de-multiplexing analog-to-digital and digital-to-analog conversion devices. A multiplexer is a device that funnels several different streams of communications into a single common stream over a single channel. A multiplexer also de-multiplexes, which is simply separating the multiple streams from the common stream and sending them over several individual lines. A channel bank multiplexer combines individual analog channels into one common digital line.

It is not important to memorize the Digital Signal (DS) level, T-1, and T-3 definitions used in the next few paragraphs just yet. The definitions are discussed in more detail later in the book. They are used here to familiarize you with how they are commonly used.

Each channel bank terminates 24 subscriber lines. A channel bank converts the analog signal from a phone into a Digital Signal Level Zero (DS-0) 64-Kbps digital signal. This digital DS-0 signal is then time division multiplexed (combined) with the DS-0 64-Kbps signals of the other subscriber line phone signals and passed as a Digital Signal Level One (DS-1) to the CO branch exchange switch. The branch exchange switch then circuit switches individual lines into trunk circuits, depending upon the number they are calling. The trunk circuits use T-1 electrical signaling to send digital information long distances between COs. DS-1 and T-1 circuit connections are shown in Figure 3-14.

DS-1 circuits are internal to the CO. They support 24 voice channels at 64 Kbps with framing overhead. This results in an aggregate speed of 1.544-Mbps transmission on the DS-1 channel. T-1 channels are equivalent to DS-1 channels except that they run between COs and thus use different physical layer (Layer 1 – Yup, it is those pesky OSI layers) electrical signaling. Finally, the T-1 channels feed into higher capacity T-3 digital channels. A T-3 channel is a larger digital pipe than a T-1 channel.

The channel banks must send some data to the CO switch, so they rob bits from the voice channels to send this data. The data is essential to send error, operating status, and other data between the channel bank and branch exchange switch. This means that our voice channels are bit-robbed.

Can we hear several bits being robbed from 64 Kbps? Nope, we do not notice the bits being robbed. It is like the time I bought a set of Bruce Springsteen CDs for $45. It was his live album. At any rate, when I put the CD into the CD player, I noticed that it was smudged. So I tried cleaning it with Windex™ and a soft tissue. That was ineffective, so I thought what would remove almost anything from anything?—and up popped acetone. So I got some nail polish remover, put it on a new tissue, and started to blot the smudge. As I moved to blot the smudge, I thought, "You know, Pete, acetone might just eat through that plastic on the CD." Oops! It was too late. So I had a big smudge. But being a digital media, I hoped that old Bruce might make it through the smudge. When I played the CD, Bruce sang fine for 30 seconds, then nothing. Because CDs are written in spirals with a synchronization signal, the big smudge obliterated the synchronization signal, causing the CD to become useless. I killed a lot of bits, not just one or two. So I took the CD back to the store and told them that it was smudged.

The voice channels between the channel bank multiplexer and the branch exchange switch are bit-robbed. ISDN channels have extra overhead, so they are not bit-robbed.

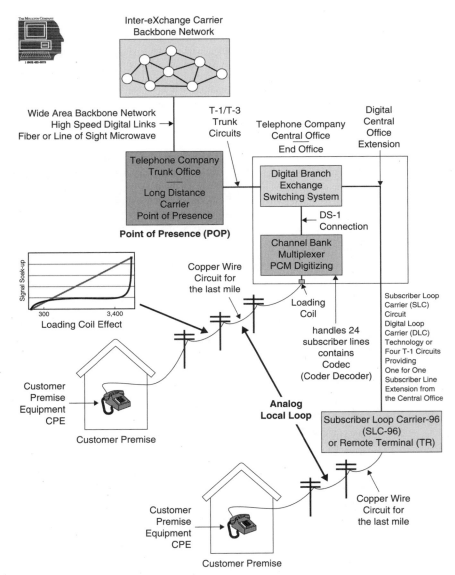

Figure 3–14 *DS-1/T-1 and Central Office Extensions.*

Coders/Decoders and Pulse Code Modulation

Typically, digital encoding of a voice analog signal is done using Pulse Code Modulation (PCM). The process goes through several steps that we will sim-

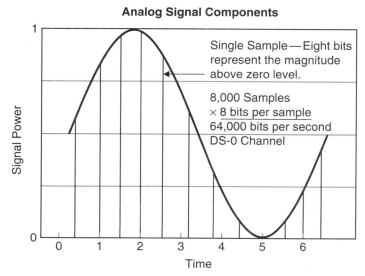

Figure 3–15 *Analog signal sampling.*

plify here. The end result of this process is the magical 64,000 bits per second voice channel carrying a single analog voice telephone call. The analog-to-digital conversion process involves looking at the analog signal and representing it as 8-bit bytes (characters). Our voice-grade channel frequencies fit into an overall range of 4,000 cycles. It is possible for a frequency to change in one-half a cycle. Consequently, the digital encoding must sample (look at) the analog signal 8,000 times a second (4,000 X 2).

This "8,000" is a constant number in the telephone network. The worldwide telephone network does things 8,000 times every second. In some cases, 8 bits are created to produce our 64-Kbps DS-0 channel (8 X 8,000 = 64,000) and in others, 24 DS-0 channels are combined into (8-bit X 24 + a frame bit = 193 bits) 193-bit frames that are transmitted 8,000 a second to produce a DS-1 channel (see Figure 3-15).

PCM that converts our analog voice into a 64,000 bits per second DS-0 channel is performed by Coders/Decoders (CODECs) in the channel bank multiplexer. The voice channel is then combined with 23 other subscriber line voice channels to form a 24-line multiplexed DS-1 channel that goes across the CO into a branch exchange switching system.

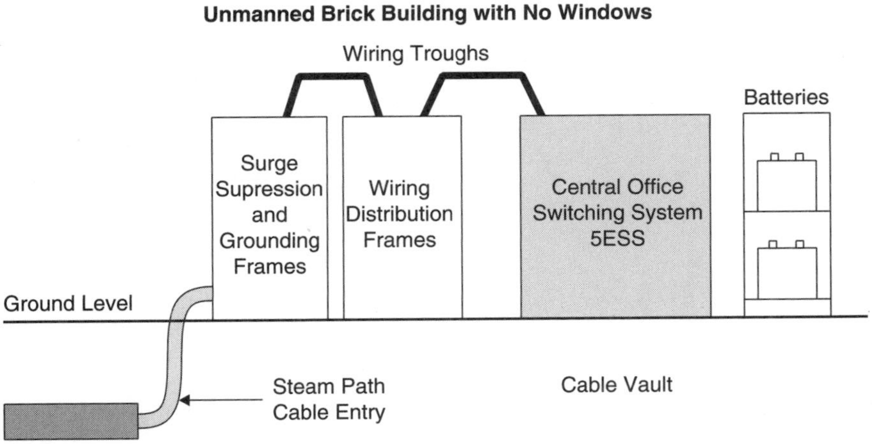

Unmanned Brick Building with No Windows

Figure 3–16 *Class 5 CO configuration.*

Central Offices

A telephone company CO is often an all-brick building with no windows. It has no markings on the outside. There is a single entry door colored an olive drab color with a numeric keypad next to it. A nicely manicured lawn and shrubs surround the CO. It can withstand the onslaught of a Category-5 tornado. It is the proverbial brick house. Inside resides a branch exchange switch and racks of batteries, providing power in the event of power failure. There are surge suppression frames designed to stop lightning surges from reaching the telephone branch exchange and other sensitive electronic components. There are also distribution frames used to route individual subscriber lines around the CO and terminate them in the channel bank multiplexers attached to the switch. Figure 3-16 shows a typical Class 5 CO configuration.

Central Office Switches

Operators manually making the connections between subscriber phones performed the first telephone switching. Electromechanical switches soon replaced manual switching. Early electromechanical telephone switches were called stepper switches because they had fingers that would rotate to make contacts. Several of these rotary mechanisms were stacked together, forming a vertical ladder of rotary switches that the rotating contacts would step up or down. Stepper switches were invented in 1891.

5XB—AT&T Electromechanical Cross Bar Switch

1AESS—ATT& End Office Electronic Switch
  Computer Controlled Cross Bar Switching

4AESS—AT&T Trunk Office Electronic Switch
  Time Space Time (TST) Switching
  100,000 Trunk Capacity
  50,000+ Active Connections

5ESS—AT&T End Office Electronic Switch
  Modular Growth
  Time Space Time (TST) Switching
  Message Switching for Network Communication
  Fiber Links
  CENTREX Support
  100,000 Line Capacity

Figure 3–17 *CO Branch exchange evolution.*

An undertaker invented stepper switches. In the very early telephone days in La Porte, Indiana, there were two undertakers. The wife of one undertaker was also the telephone operator for the town (there were no telephone switches at that time). Whenever anyone asked the operator to connect them to an undertaker, she would plug them into her husband's phone. His business prospered and the other undertaker's, Mr. Almon B. Strowger's, business waned. Upon discovering the cause for the lost business, Strowger invented the first stepper telephone switch to assure impartial switching of telephone calls. At least this is the story.

The next electromechanical switch was the crossbar switch. This is an analog device supporting switching functions only (see Figure 3-17). Crossbar switches used multiple vertical and horizontal paths with basically electromagnetic relay switches to interconnect any one of the vertical paths with any of the horizontal paths. These crossbar switches were referred to as Telephone Exchange Crossbar (TXC) switches. Crossbar switches were first used in the late 1930s. A common telephone company end office switch was the Number 5 Crossbar (5XB) switch. Crossbar switches performed space-type switching, with each circuit being connected through its own separate physical path.

The next type of switch was an electronic switch. These switches were computer-controlled electromechanical or electronic switching devices. They switched largely analog signals. The control of these switches changed from processing each digit as it was dialed to storing the number in a register and then making the dialed connection. These switches were called common control switches. They soon advanced to stored program control. The first stored program control switch used in 1965 was the Number 1–Electronic Switching System (1ESS). It was a computer-controlled crossbar switch. Such switches were sometimes referred to as Telephone Exchange Digital (TXD) switches because they performed switching using computers.

The ESS switches had to use an identical or "generic," program in each class of switch. The differences between offices were determined by parameters used by the "generic" program. Parameters included the number and location of active lines and trunks, tone or rotary dialing, etc. The CPU of the ESS was upgraded in the mid 1970s to provide better call processing. This upgraded ESS was the 1AESS. Both the 1ESS and 1AESS were basically computer-controlled crossbar switches.

The first computer-controlled digital switch was the 4ESS, which was aimed at toll switching. It used the 1AESS CPU coupled with a Time Multiplexed Switch (TMS) capable of handling over 50,000 simultaneous connections. Time multiplexing switched connections by giving each connection its own unique time slot on a shared bus. The toll switch dealt mainly with digital signals. However, local offices had to interface with the analog local loops over which voice traveled and they had to ring the phone with a nearly 90-volt AC. Semiconductors were not good at those tasks. The 5ESS solved these problems. Now no longer were analog signals switched at the local office, but rather they were converted to digital form and switched by a stored program in a computer.

The 5ESS from Lucent is a Time Space Time (TST) digital switch capable of handling up to 100,000 lines. A TST switch combines switching with different physical circuit paths (space-type switching) and time multiplexed switching. The current switches are identified as Telephone Exchange Electronic (TXE) because they employ electronic switching as opposed to electromechanical means like crossbar or stepper switches.

Northern Telecom is another manufacturer of digital telephone switches designated as DMS-100, DMS-200, and DMS-250. Each is tailored to specific switching functions.

Cellular switch vendors market PBXs or CO switches reconfigured with software to support mobile subscribers. Three of the major U.S. cellular switch equipment suppliers, AT&T, Ericsson, and Northern Telecom, are also leading suppliers of CO switches.

Branch exchange CO switches work on contention. They switch subscriber lines on to trunk lines. There are far fewer trunk lines than subscriber lines. So when all trunk lines are occupied, we get a fast busy signal. The number of trunk lines and switching capacity of the branch exchange switch are predicated upon the average phone call being four minutes' duration. The average call duration was at one time three minutes, then we all had long-distance calls charge for the first three minutes and then minute by minute after that three-minute interval. When calls are much longer—like calls for surfing the Web (twenty minutes duration)—then the contention design of the telephone company network is thrown off and we can have all trunks occupied.

During disasters and on Mother's Day, the call volume into specific areas exceeds the trunk capacity into those areas and calls are blocked. The trunk capacity needed to support a specific number of subscriber lines with a specific call duration is determined using an Erlang B statistical distribution function. There are tables based upon call duration and number of lines that for one call in 100 blocked tell the number of trunks required to provide that level of service.

DS-1 vs. T-1

The DS-0 and T-1 transmission speed is the same, 1.544 Mbps. DS-1 specifies the circuits that connect telephony components in a CO. T-1 specifies the circuits interconnecting different COs. T-1 circuits are inter-office circuits and DS-1 connections are intra-office connections. Both T-1 and DS-1 channels are broken down into 24 DS-0 time division multiplexed channels, with each individual channel assigned its own unique time slot on the T-1 or DS-1 channel (refer back to Figure 3-14).

Point-Of-Presence

T-1 trunk circuits run from a Class 5 CO to toll offices and on to the POP of the IXC/IEC. The POP is a room owned by a local telephone company. The function of the POP is to interconnect networks. Actually, any site where networks interconnect is quite often referred to as a POP. The equipment and T-1 connecting circuits for the local telephone company and different long-distance carriers terminate at the POP. In the POP, interconnections between the networks are made using DS-1 or other types of circuits. Long-distance calls carried by AT&T are routed to the closest POP interconnecting AT&T's

network into the local telephone company network. Similarly, calls carried by MCI *Worldcom* are routed to POPs that interconnect MCI *Worldcom's* network to the local telephone company network. The POP for both AT&T and MCI *Worldcom* could be the same physical facility because a single POP site could interconnect the local telephone company to several IXCs/IECs. The long-distance carrier that originally had the most POPs was AT&T.

Inter-Exchange Carriers, or Long-Distance Carriers

IXCs/IECs, or long-distance carriers, have their own network of high-speed digital circuits that run nationwide and connect to other worldwide networks. These networks were at one time arranged in a hierarchical fashion to facilitate switching long-distance calls. When trunks between lower level switching offices were blocked, calls were routed to a higher level switching office. Each IXC/IEC constructs its own backbone network facilities or leases facilities from other IXCs/IECs or local telephone companies to build its nationwide long-distance network. Most facilities built today run across fiber. Some run down railroad rights of way. That is where SPRINT originally began. SPRINT originally stood for Southern Pacific Railroad Internal Network Telecommunications. GTE changed the acronym to Switched Private Network Telecommunications (as in GTE Sprint). Southern Pacific Rail gave birth to Sprint as a U.S. long-distance carrier in the 1970s. Qwest Communications was formed originally in 1988 from Southern Pacific Rail as the Southern Pacific Telecommunications Company (SPT). SPT began by laying fiber optic cable along Southern Pacific's railroad rights-of-way to provide long-distance carriers with increased network capacity. Qwest continues to build its network in a similar fashion.

These IXC/IEC long-distance networks use automated switching equipment to complete long-distance calls through their facilities. Very little human involvement is required to run a long-distance network today. That and fierce competition is why long-distance rates continue to decline. There is now a shaking up and a consolidation of telephone companies. The original competing long-distance carriers, AT&T and MCI, are acquiring companies that permit them to enter the local telephone market, while the local telephone companies are planning to get into handling long-distance calls. Other high-speed backbone networks are aimed at carrying Internet traffic. All these networks are similar in that they employ largely high-speed fiber channels to interconnect their switching and POP access sites.

Central Office Hierarchy

In the 1980s, AT&T had a CO hierarchy that ranged from Class 5 COs to Class 1 sectional offices. The office designations from top to bottom were:

- Class 1—Regional center.
- Class 2—Sectional center.
- Class 3—Primary center.
- Class 4—Toll center.
- Class 5—End office.

Subscriber lines were connected to Class 5 end offices. The Class 5 end offices connected via trunk lines to Class 4 toll centers and other Class 5 end offices. Similarly, Class 4 toll centers connected to Class 3 primary centers and other Class 4 toll centers. The hierarchy continued in a similar manner such that a call that could not be routed directly between Class 5 end offices was pushed up to higher level offices until the connection was completed. That meant it was possible during peak calling times to have a local New York State call routed to its destination via a Class 1 regional center in California. While possible, this would be a really rare, once-in-a-lifetime event—kind of like talking on a hand-held Iridium satellite phone (you bet, I did that once in my lifetime).

Today the telephone network routes calls using more sophisticated mesh routing algorithms and not the simpler hierarchical routing algorithms. The mesh routing algorithms are much more effective in utilizing today's more complex telephone network facilities and are needed to provide FCC-mandated capabilities such as number portability (the ability to keep a phone number regardless of which telephone company provides your local service).

Brain Teaser

Voice Network Circuits

Get a voltmeter and set it to measure DC volts. Use it to measure the voltage on a telephone line. You may be able to do this by probing the RJ-11 (Recommended Jack-11) wall outlet, but you should take the faceplate off the outlet to get better access to the wire leads.

1. What voltage did you read? Was it about 48 Volts or something different?
2. When you examined the wires connecting to the wall outlet, what colors were they? Were they red, green, yellow, and black?
3. How many wires were connected using the RJ-11 connector, two or four?
4. Examine the RJ-11 cable going from the phone wall outlet to the phone. How many wires does it

connect? Two or four? What are the colors of the wires? Use the underside of the RJ-11 jack to view the colors.

5. Tour your neighborhood. What telephone termination boxes do you see? Are they simple wire terminations (small cylindrical canisters) or something larger (cabinet-size SLC-96 units)?

The goal here is to physically see analog telephone connections that are in customer premises and to identify telephone network components used to connect customer premises to the telephone company Class 5 COs.

Signaling System Seven (SS-7)

Signaling System Seven (or SS-7) is a packet-switched data network that carries telephone signaling data between switching components in the voice network.

SS-7 is the magic behind the telephone network. The telephone companies love SS-7 because their networks can provide more services and carry more calls using fewer lines. Plain and simple, they can make more money with existing infrastructure. You use it when you pick up a phone and dial. Usually by the time you put the phone to your ear, it is ringing. This is because SS-7 has already set up the phone call. Before we had SS-7, we had SS-6. Before we used common channeling signaling, we used in-band signaling throughout the telephone network and call setup time could be as long as 20 seconds; today it's usually less than five seconds.

Signaling data includes the number dialed, the calling number, busy signals, ringing signals, off-hook notification, on-hook notification, and more. This information is encoded in cryptic commands and sent as data packets over the SS-7 connections between voice network switches (see Figure 3-18).

Packet-switched data travels from one routing node to another through a Packet-Switched Network (PSN). Packet-switched data is routed consistently (always the same) for the duration of a call because the same routing algorithms are used to route the data for the duration of the connection. If network components fail or loading increases, the packets may be re-routed across a different set of links to compensate for the outage or data overload and to maintain the connection. In Figure 3-18 our data traffic could, if needed, be re-routed over several different paths between the telephone switches.

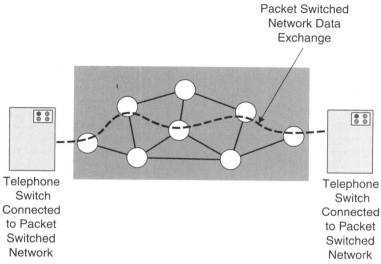

Figure 3–18   *Packet-switched connection.*

Packet-Switched Network using HDLC

The packets for SS-7 are formed using High-Level Data Link Control (HDLC) protocol, a Link Access Protocol Data (LAPD) variation. HDLC/LAPD is a hardware protocol, or Layer 2 protocol. This version of HDLC is specifically aimed at telephony data exchange. Because none of us at this time is going to design switching software, it is not necessary to know the details of HDLC/LAPD. That falls under the category of TMI—Too Much Information. The HDLC frame format shown in Figure 3-19 conforms to ISDN D Channel LAPD ITU-T Recommendation I.441 (Q.921).

Please do not quit reading right here, because it is not important for you to remember the details from Figure 3-19. What is important for you to remember is that the signaling data controlling the telephone network is sent from telephone switch to telephone switch on a separate packet-switched data network. This means that SS-7 implements common channel signaling and not in-band signaling. All telephone calls are controlled by this packet-switched data network. SS-7 is also the mechanism that implements advanced telephony services such as caller ID, just in time *69, number portability, and more.

An SS-7 network and some general handshake exchanges are shown in Figure 3-20.

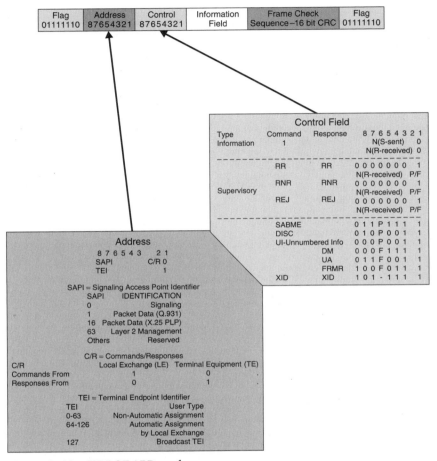

Figure 3–19 *HDLC/LAPD packet.*

There are several types of SS-7 components. These components are in SS-7 networks run by the local telephone company (the LEC) and in networks run by the IXC/IEC as shown in Figure 3-20.

SS-7 Nodes

SS-7 networks have several different node types. These types of nodes are arranged by function. To provide reliable service, there is redundancy in the nodes of each SS-7 network. The node types are:

- Service Switching Point (SSP)—An SSP can be any system switching calls and functioning as an SS-7 node. This begins the process.

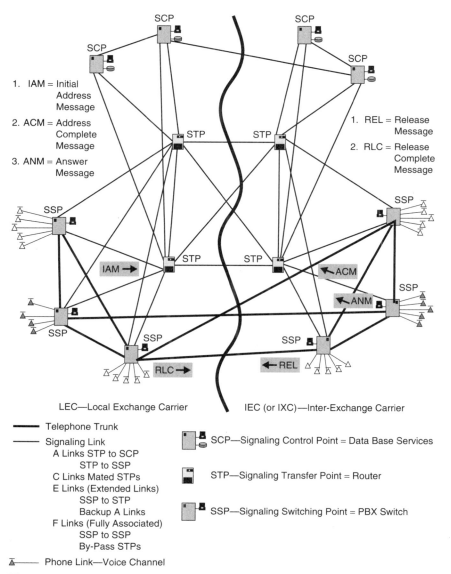

1. IAM = Initial
   Address
   Message

2. ACM = Address
   Complete
   Message

3. ANM = Answer
   Message

1. REL = Release
   Message

2. RLC = Release
   Complete
   Message

LEC—Local Exchange Carrier   IEC (or IXC)—Inter-Exchange Carrier

━━━ Telephone Trunk

─── Signaling Link
   A Links STP to SCP
      STP to SSP
   C Links Mated STPs
   E Links (Extended Links)
      SSP to STP
      Backup A Links
   F Links (Fully Associated)
      SSP to SSP
      By-Pass STPs

△── Phone Link—Voice Channel

SCP—Signaling Control Point = Data Base Services

STP—Signaling Transfer Point = Router

SSP—Signaling Switching Point = PBX Switch

Figure 3–20 *SS-7 components.*

- Signaling Transfer Point (STP)—An STP is a router for SS-7 signaling packets. This just routes the signaling information.

- Service Control Point (SCP)—An SCP provides the intelligence to the signaling network. It determines the route for the call, implements other advanced telephone network calling services, and holds information on calling cards, 800 numbers, and cellular roaming data. SCP is redundant to provide constant service in the event of the failure of one SCP.

SS-7 packet-switched trunk circuits are 64-Kbps or higher speed circuits that carry HDLC/LAPD packets between SSPs, STPs, and SCPs. These links are separate from the voice communications channels, but they may run across the same physical facilities. With redundancy of SS-7 nodes and multiplicity of packet routes, SS-7 is very reliable. Each carrier has its own SS-7 network to control the routing of voice calls within its network. These SS-7 networks are interconnected and constantly exchange signaling packets. Figure 3-21 shows how a LEC SS-7 network can connect to a Competitive Local Exchange Carrier (CLEC) SS-7 network that has only one switching facility. The CLEC SS-7 switching facility would contain the software needed to perform signal switching, signal transfer, and signal control functions. The single site would have redundant hardware to provide the required voice network reliability.

So think of every LEC, every CLEC, and every IXC/IEC having its own SS-7 network that is connected to every other SS-7 network. When a voice telephone call is placed, these networks exchange lots of packets to route the call, make the connection, break down the call, and provide special extra-charge signaling services.

SS-7 Operation

When we go to make a voice network call, we pick up the phone and dial the destination or target phone's area code and number. The SS-7 switching point to which our telephone is attached sends an Initial Address Message (IAM) to the SS-7 network. This message travels across the SS-7 network through other SSPs and STPs as needed to arrive at an SCP. If an SSP knows how to route a call because that call has been made frequently, the IAM may be routed to the destination telephone's SSP. This would happen for many local (non-toll) calls in extended metropolitan areas.

The target SSP responds with an Address Complete Message (ACM) and rings the target (destination) telephone. When the phone is answered, the destination, target or called telephone's SSP sends an Answer Message (ANM). SSPs then complete the circuit using the voice network facilities and the call proceeds between the two telephones. The voice network facilities are circuit-switched, 64-Kbps digital channels that originate and terminate in analog local loop subscriber lines.

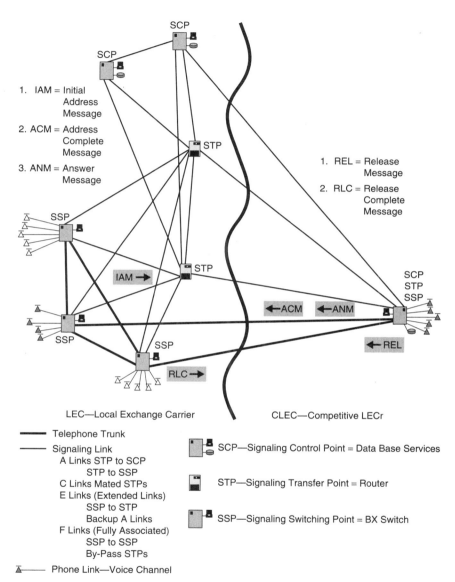

1. IAM = Initial Address Message

2. ACM = Address Complete Message

3. ANM = Answer Message

1. REL = Release Message

2. RLC = Release Complete Message

LEC—Local Exchange Carrier   CLEC—Competitive LECr

━━━ Telephone Trunk

─── Signaling Link
   A Links STP to SCP
      STP to SSP
   C Links Mated STPs
   E Links (Extended Links)
      SSP to STP
      Backup A Links
   F Links (Fully Associated)
      SSP to SSP
      By-Pass STPs

△─── Phone Link—Voice Channel

SCP—Signaling Control Point = Data Base Services

STP—Signaling Transfer Point = Router

SSP—Signaling Switching Point = BX Switch

Figure 3–21   *SS-7 LEC/CLEC connections.*

Once our conversation is complete, we place our telephones on-hook, making them ready to complete another call. At that time, SS-7 springs into action again. A Release (REL) message is sent to the other SSP, thus completing the call. This message signals that the circuit facilities can now be broken down and returned to the available inventory of circuits, ready to be used to complete other calls. When the corresponding SSP releases its circuits, it sends a Release Complete (RLC) message back to the other SSP.

SS-7 and ISDN

Both ISDN and SS-7 employ common channel signaling. But they are not the same thing. ISDN is the technology for delivering digital telephone services to telephone subscribers. It provides a mechanism for CPE to interact and more directly control telephone network facilities. Many companies use ISDN Primary Rate Interfaces (PRIs) to interface their PBX switches to the telephone network because the D signaling and control channel can now get SS-7 packets from the telephone company SSPs and use them to perform advanced call routing features with their internal telephones. Further, an ISDN-attached switch can place and receive video teleconferencing (H channel) calls. A video teleconference call requires the equivalent of six Bearer (B) channels to deliver full-motion standard TV video between the video teleconferencing equipment at two sites.

SS-7 is the telephone technology that makes ISDN services possible. However, it also makes it possible to deliver those advanced services to any analog phone as well. As a result, ISDN for the home voice telephone consumer does nothing more than what they already have available on their analog telephone with the exception of high-speed (128 Kbps) digital transmission to their PC, hence the It Still Does Nothing (ISDN) label for the Integrated Services Digital Network.

The PRI D channel provides more effective interaction with the telephone network switching components provided that the PBX switch has ISDN functionality and related features installed.

The final point to realize about SS-7 is that SS-7 nodes may not be separate from voice telephone network switching equipment. That is to say, SS-7 switching and routing functionality may reside in telephone network switching equipment as added installed software. SS-7 SCPs are likely to be separate computers dedicated to the control function alone in larger LEC and IXC/IEC voice switching networks. Figure 3-22 illustrates the commonality of SSP and STP functions in LEC and IXC/IEC telephone switching components.

The CPE PBX is connected to a telephone company Class 5 end office branch exchange switch via an ISDN PRI. Signaling data travels between the CPE PBX and CO switch over the Data (D) channel as HDLC/LAPD packets. The signaling information next jumps on top of the SS-7 network of the LEC telephone company. It then runs into the IXC/IEC SS-7 network to finally

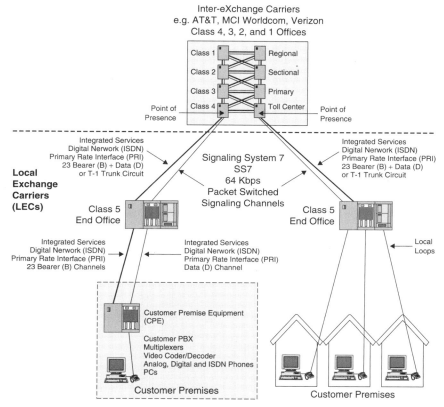

Figure 3–22   *SS-7 integrated in branch exchange switches.*

arrive at the branch exchange switch in the Class 5 CO attached to the telephone subscriber being called.

SS-7 Common Channel Signaling

Both SS-7 and ISDN use common channel signaling. This means that the signaling data that establishes and breaks down a voice telephone call travels across an exclusive signaling channel. In the case of an ISDN connection, the signaling channel is the D channel. In-band signaling was used before common channel signaling was implemented. This required the voice telephone network to open a full voice channel between telephone switches to pass the signaling information before the call was completed. If the distant end was occupied and a busy signal was returned, the voice channel remained open until the calling party placed the telephone back on-hook. This meant that voice channels that could carry voice conversations were occupied with signaling traffic. Common channel signaling eliminated this unneeded use of voice channels and permitted them to be dedicated to handling voice traffic alone. As a result, when the long-distance network was converted to SS-7 in the late 1970s and early 1980s, it could handle more simultaneous voice telephone calls. Using SS-7 common channel signaling increased the voice telephone network capacity by about one-third and saved AT&T from building some added voice network facilities for several years.

SS-7 is the backbone packet-switched data network that carries voice network signaling data exclusively. So, a ringing or busy signal from a called phone is no longer the analog sound we hear coming out of our telephone handset, but rather packets of data sent to our local switch on the separate SS-7 packet-switched data network. Our local switch converts those packets into the in-band signaling that we hear coming from the telephone handset. The only in-band signaling today is performed between an analog telephone and the CO switch.

For caller ID to analog telephones, the SS-7 calling number information in the HDLC/LAPD is converted to in-band signals sent to the special caller ID box attached to the analog telephone. These in-band caller ID signals are sent before the ringing signal is sent as a 90-volt AC in-band signal to the analog telephone.

The SS-7 backbone network uses common channel signaling. Analog telephone subscriber lines use common channel signaling once they leave the CO switch. In-band signaling is used by residential phones. SS-7 is what really controls phone calls and telephone features. However, SS-7 operates behind the scenes for residential phones.

Brain Teaser

SS-7 Packet Sizes

How large is an SS-7 packet? Is it like 1,000 characters (bytes) of data or more like 100 characters (bytes) of data? Write down your gut guess now before proceeding further. Our goal here is to give you a feel for the practical thinking you should use when dealing with seemingly complex topics.

1. Refer back to Figure 3-19 and now write down your guess as to the SS-7 packet size. Did you change your mind from your first guess?

2. Now think of how big our telephone numbers are today. Are they 4, 7, 10, or more digits? To complete a call, we use the called number and the calling number. How many digits is that total? Now, how big in characters do the commands between switches need to be? 10 characters or 100

characters? Remember, switches do not need to read English. Reading books and sentences is for humans. Write down your guess as to how big SS-7 packet sizes are now? Did you change your mind again?

The goal was to make you think of very technical telephony concepts from the practical perspective we already know. To cope with rapidly and relentlessly advancing technology, we must continually use this practical perspective as a means to understand the reality of how high-technology systems, e.g., SS-7 switching, operate. Generally, the maximum number of digits in any phone number is around 10, but certainly less than 20. Two phone numbers means a maximum of 40 characters, and with 10 characters for cryptic SS-7 commands, my guess is that SS-7 frames are under 100 characters in size.

■ Summary

This chapter has presented the basics of voice communications, or telephony. It first described basic telephone, or voice communications technology, and voice network components. Voice-grade channel operation, local loops, and telephone CO equipment were examined. Then, SS-7 was presented. SS-7, implemented in the early 1980s, had profound impact on the operation and future capabilities of the switched telephone network.

▲ CHAPTER REVIEW QUESTIONS

1. *What is a difference between analog and digital signals?*

   A. Analog signals are soaked up (attenuated) by wire and digital signals are not.

   B. Analog signals are tones and frequencies and digital signals are pulses.

   C. Analog signals are electrical signals and digital signals are not.

   D. Analog signals travel slower than the speed of light and digital signals do not.

2. *What are the operating frequencies in a voice-grade channel?*

   A. 0Hz to 3400Hz

   B. 300Hz to 4000Hz

   C. 300GHz to 3400GHz

   D. 300Hz to 3400Hz

3. *What device is placed in a telephone line to provide constant signal loss across the voice-grade channel frequencies?*

     A. Repeater

     B. Amplifier

     C. Loading coil

     D. Coder/Decoder

4. *What is the line running from the customer premise to the local Telephone Company Central Office called?*

     A. Copper Wire

     B. Subscriber Loop

     C. Local Loop

     D. 4-wire analog circuit

5. *What type of transmission requires the ability to transmit and receive high frequencies?*

     A. Digital Transmission

     B. Analog Transmission

     C. Voice Transmission

     D. Data Transmission

6. *What device terminates subscriber lines in a local Telephone Company Central Office?*

     A. Branch Exchange Switch

     B. Channel Bank Multiplexer

     C. Wiring Distribution Frames

     D. A Coder/Decoder

7. *What speed is DS-0?*

     A. 1.544 Mbps

     B. 3,400 Hz

     C. 10 Mbps

     D. 64 Kbps

     E. 53 Kbps

8. *What channel operates at the same speed as a T-1 channel?*
   A. DS-0
   B. H0
   C. PRI
   D. DS-3

Telephony Today

This chapter continues examining voice communications. Because politics and telephony are inseparable companions, regulation for both local and long-distance telephony communications is also examined along with the current competitive environment for telephone services. Finally, the chapter examines telephone switches and PBXs contrasting them with CENTREX service.

North American Numbering Plan

AT&T originally designed the North American Numbering Plan (NANP) back in 1947. It conforms to the ITU Recommendation E.164, the international standard for numbering plans. NANP is the system for assigning area codes, telephone numbers, and other important network codes throughout the U.S. and 17 other countries. The system covers World Zone 1 for the Public Switched Telephone Network (PSTN) in the U.S. and its territories (e.g., Guam), Canada, Bermuda, and many Caribbean nations, including Anguilla, Antigua & Barbuda, Bahamas, Barbados, British Virgin Islands, Cayman Islands, Dominica, Dominican Republic, Grenada, Jamaica, Montserrat, St. Kitts and Nevis, St. Lucia, St. Vincent and the Grenadines, Trinidad and Tobago, and Turks & Caicos.

Bell Communications Research, or Bellcore, was created during the divestiture of the Bell System in 1984 to serve the Bell operating companies by providing a center for technological expertise and innovation. Bellcore has become Telcordia Technologies today. After divestiture in 1984, Bellcore administered the NANP, and not so surprisingly, controversy over a conflict of interest began. The argument was that Bellcore, owned by the Regional Bell Operating Companies (RBOCs), favored both the RBOCs and AT&T with special numbering assignments. This controversy heightened with the exhaustion of area codes. All area codes were designated as having a 0 or 1 as their middle number (see below). Today, many metropolitan areas must use additional area codes.

As a result, the Federal Communications Commission (FCC) intervened in October 1992. The involvement of the FCC caused Bellcore to withdraw as administrator of the NANP in August 1993. Bellcore agreed to remain on as plan administrator for 12 to 18 months, permitting the FCC to select a new administrator. Lockheed-Martin began to administer the NANP, and today, NeuStar, Inc performs the task.

Current NANP Numbering

NANP geographic area codes were three-digit numbers formatted X any digit 2 through 9, then either 0 or 1, and X any digit 0 through 9. A seven-digit subscriber number followed the area code. The subscriber number, previously an NNX-XXXX format, is now an NXX-XXXX, allowing the use of 0 or 1 as the second digit. The N (0 or 1) X format has a maximum of $8 \times 2 \times 10$, or 160 combinations, while the NXX has a maximum of $8 \times 10 \times 10$, or 800 combinations.

As the demand for area codes in North America grew, Bellcore proposed an integrated numbering plan for World Zone 1, essentially North America and the Caribbean. The new plan went into effect in January 1995 and changed the numbering system from an N (0 or 1) X NXX-XXXX format to an NXX-NXX-XXXX format. This change increased the quantity of available ten-digit phone numbers from about one billion to six billion. The most current area code information is available at the NANPA (North American Numbering Plan Administration) Web site sponsored by NeuStar, Inc, the current NANP administrator. The NANPA link is:

http://www.NANPA.com

The above Web site reference is to the new NANP codes. An old NANP map is shown in Figure 4-1.

Area Code Exhaustion

The phenomenal growth of telecommunications over the last 20 years is the reason for the current area code shortage. High-growth areas include:

- Cellular phones.
- Fax machines.
- Portable beepers.
- Multiple number services.
- Direct-Inward Dialing (DID) numbers.
- Pay-per-view applications.
- Special ringing features.

These and many other applications consume large blocks of seven-digit numbers. Consequently, there are not enough seven-digit numbers to keep up with demand.

However, the way phone numbers are assigned is changing. Originally, when a telephone company needed a new phone number to provide service to a single residential customer and there were no telephone numbers assigned to that geographic area, the telephone company would allocate a block of 10,000 numbers. Those 10,000 numbers were set aside to support a single residential customer. The unused 9,999 numbers would sit idle. With number pooling, telephone companies have to return to a pool of numbers not being used. Further, telephone numbers are allocated in blocks of 1,000 numbers and not the wasteful blocks of 10,000 numbers.

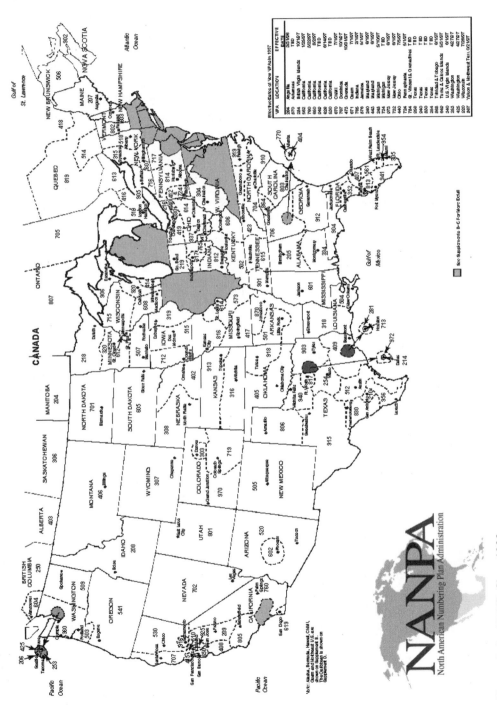

Figure 4-1 *NANP, Circa 1999.*

AREA CODE SUBDIVISIONS

Initially, area codes were subdivided geographically. I am in Maryland. When the Maryland 301 area code was nearly exhausted, it was split geographically into two area codes, the old 301 area code and a new 410 area code. With the geographic split, I was forced to get new numbers because all my phones but one were in the new 410 area code geographic area. The one foreign exchange line that ran into Laurel, Maryland kept the same phone number because it was in the 301 area code geographic coverage area.

AREA CODE OVERLAYS

The initial area code split in Maryland lasted several years. But the explosive growth in phone number usage caught up and two new area codes were assigned using the NXX NXX-XXXX numbering scheme. The original geographic assignments looked somewhat like familiar area codes because they had 0's and 1's as the middle number (e.g., N0X or N1X – 301 and 410 in my case). The new area codes were area code overlays. This meant that the 301 and 410 number assignments did not change and any new subscribers were assigned the new overlay area codes 240 and 443.

The 240 area code almost resembles an N0/1X area code, so it has movie star quality. My geographic area did not get that assignment. It must be that all the Bell Atlantic executives lived in the 301 geographic area, which was assigned the 240 overlay code. In my case, we were assigned the Joan Rivers area code, 443. Who would think of 443 as anything but a yucky area code? So I got as many 410 numbers as I could before the 443 area code was assigned to new telephone numbers.

With area code overlays, my next-door neighbor can have a 443 area code while I have a 410 area code. With area code overlays comes 10-digit dialing. To make local calls, 10 digits must be dialed. Someday, everybody will have to dial 10 digits. However, none of my 410 numbers had to change with the area code overlay unless they changed with the area code geographic subdivision.

NUMBER PORTABILITY

With the advent of local telephone competition, telephone subscribers do not have to change their telephone number when they move from one local telephone company to another. This feature or requirement is mandated by the FCC and is called local number portability. It is dependent upon SS-7 SCPs having a database of telephone numbers for the geographic areas they service. With disk storage technology today, it would not be a problem to store routing data for all telephone numbers on a pair (redundancy for reliability) of SCPs. It would require 6 billion numbers with say 100 characters of data for each number, or about 600GB of disk storage space—a small amount of storage by today's standards.

LOCAL ACCESS AND TRANSPORT AREAS

Local Access and Transport Areas (LATAs) were established after divestiture to permit telephone companies to charge subscribers for access to local or regional exchanges and to the inter-exchange toll telephone network for sending and receiving intra-LATA and interstate calls. LATAs are geographic areas generally smaller than a state, but bigger than a county. A LATA is also smaller than an area code and bigger than a local exchange. LATAs follow telephone boundaries (not state boundaries).

There are intra-LATA toll charges and inter-LATA toll charges. Maryland has four LATAs and four area codes. The area codes are not assigned to individual LATAs. Intra-LATA calls do not leave the LATA. LECs bill you for intra-LATA calls. Intra-LATA calls often look like local calls, but they are really local toll calls. Such local toll calls can have charges that are greater than long-distance charges. Today, the LEC is not the only telephone company that can carry local toll calls. Long-distance providers can also carry local toll calls. Inter-LATA phone calls go from one LATA to another LATA. These are considered long-distance calls. In most cases, whenever a call leaves a LATA, it physically connects to a long-distance provider who completes the call. This stops LECs from competing with long-distance carriers. The LATA and area code assignments for Maryland are shown in Figure 4-2.

I think of this crossed LATA assignment as the cross your heart assignment, or the "you are blessed" assignment. To me, it seems more logical to assign the LATA numbers for Maryland in a clockwise fashion rather than crossing them as they are assigned. LATAs are artificial structures for the purpose of telephone billing. Cellular phone calls do not charge for inter-LATA and intra-LATA calls, or in some cases for interstate calls. For example, my NEXTEL and my old Cellular One phones can call from Virginia to Pennsylvania without incurring intra-LATA or inter-LATA toll charges. As we move towards tariffs becoming less distance-dependent, the need for LATAs will disappear. At some point in time, we will pay for network access only, regardless of where we call.

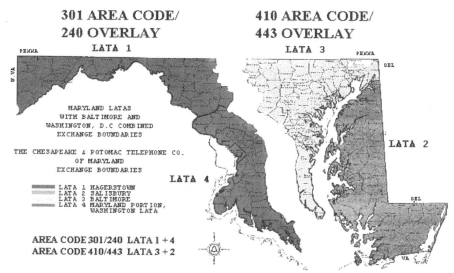

Figure 4–2 *Maryland LATAs and area codes.*

Carrier Identification Codes

Carrier Identification Codes (CICs) are numeric codes that, as originally devised, enabled LECs, as providers of inter-Exchange (IXC) access services, to identify access customers in order to bill and route traffic to such customers. The NANP administrator assigns these codes using guidelines developed by the Industry Carriers Compatibility Forum (ICCF), under the auspices of the Carrier Liaison Committee (CLC) that is sponsored by the Alliance for Telecommunications Solutions (ATIS), an industry forum. CICs are used for purposes beyond those for which they were originally designed. CICs facilitate competition by enabling callers to use the services of any number of telecommunications service providers.

For example, they enable callers to reach any carrier (pre-subscribed or otherwise) from any telephone by dialing a Carrier Access Code (CAC) that includes a CIC (e.g., 10-10-220 for MCI *WorldCom).* For Feature Group (FG) B, the CAC is in the format 950-XXXX, where XXXX is the FG B CIC. The more familiar CAC is for FG D. The FG D CAC is dialed using the a 7-digit format (101XXXX), where X = 0 through 9. Thus, the MCI network is accessed by dialing 10-10-220 or 101-0220. The Lucky Dog Network (AT&T) is accessed by dialing 10-10-345 or 101-0345. FG B differs somewhat from

FG D in that an IXC's/IEC's customer must first dial 101 and then the CIC to place a call.

Firms seeking and obtaining CICs provide useful information on the entry of new firms into the long-distance market. Prior to 1986, interstate access services were made available on a non-discriminatory basis to end-users as well as to IXCs/IECs. CIC information is current because firms acquiring CICs for the first time are reported within 30 days.

An IXC/IEC or other access customer must have a CIC to purchase FG D or FG B interconnection access from a local telephone company. FG D allows a customer of an IXC/IEC to place calls on a "1-plus" basis, the "equal access" capability deployed by the Bell telephone companies following their divestiture from AT&T.

Firms not assigned a CIC may also offer long-distance telecommunications services for sale. Typically, these firms resell services provided by others. Other firms engaged in long-distance telecommunications use special access or engage in selling transmission capacity to carriers and therefore do not need a CIC number. As competition has developed, CICs, which initially were two digits in length, have been expanded to three and four digits to assure there are enough CICs to meet the demand for them.

Some FG B CICs used to route and bill calls in the PSTN and the companies to which they are assigned are:

CIC	Designation	Company
2	TET	*WorldCom* Inc.
4	ATZ	ATX Telecommunications Services
5	MYC	Macy's of California
15	HWT	Hawaiian Telephone Company
16	TSD	TMC Long Distance *dba* Cherry Communications Inc.
19	TSD	TMC Long Distance *dba* Cherry Communications Inc.
25	ICL	Inter Continental Telephone
35	CWK	Qwest Communications
60	ECY	Economy Telephone, Inc.
62	KTC	Kentucky Telephone Corp.
65	ISA	ISACOMM, Inc. [Sprint]
80	ALS	*WorldCom* Inc.
86	MAD	Global Crossing Telecommunications, Inc.
189	GSR	State of Texas - GSC

CIC	Designation	Company
211	RTC	Frontier Communications International Inc.
220	TDD	Telecom*USA [MCI]
223	TDX	Cable & Wireless Communications, Inc. (TDX)
272	PJC	Bell Atlantic Communications, Inc.
356	EKN	Eastman Kodak Company
375	WUT	AT&T EasyLink Services
652	NNC	Bell Atlantic Communications, Inc.
872	UTC	Sprint
888	MCG	MCI *WorldCom*
5008	UOM	WinStar
5010	SUS	Qwest Communications
5011	AUD	Qwest Communications
5036	MLW	Merchant-Link, Inc.
5037	MLW	Merchant-Link, Inc.
5047	NYC	Bell Atlantic Communications
5048	NYC	Bell Atlantic Communications
5050	AAX	Ameritech Services
5051	AKB	Arkansas Blue Cross Blue Shield
5052	AKB	Arkansas Blue Cross Blue Shield
5061	BSO	BellSouth Business Systems
5062	BSO	BellSouth Business Systems
5063	BSL	BellSouth Long Distance
5979	REG	Reliant Energy Communications, Inc.
5999	DLX	Deluxe Data Systems

This FG B list is not comprehensive. It represents a small sampling of the FG B carriers.

The FG D list is similar in size and content to the FG B list. Some entries from it are:

CIC	Designation	Company
1	MAL	*WorldCom* Inc.
2	TET	*WorldCom* Inc.

CIC	Designation	Company
3	RTC	Frontier Communications International, Inc.
4	ATZ	ATX Telecommunications Services
7	TAM	TeleMarketing Communications Inc.
9	EQN	EqualNet Corporation
10	VTD	Valley Telephone Long Distance
12	JJJ	Qwest Communications
15	HWT	Hawaiian Telephone Company (GTE)
16	TSD	TMC Long Distance *dba* Cherry Communications Inc.
18	SNK	Sprint Local Telecommunications Division
19	TSD	TMC Long Distance *dba* Cherry Communications Inc.
22	MCI	MCI *WorldCom*
23	IDS	IDS Long Distance, Inc
30	VWF	U.S. Long Distance, Inc.
44	ALN	Global Crossing Telecommunications, Inc.
57	VDC	Nationwide Long Distance
60	ECY	Economy Telephone, Inc.
62	KTC	Kentucky Telephone Corp.
93	MBU	Melbourne International Comm. Ltd.
113	AKD	Ameritech Long Distance Services
125	AQT	Atlantic Telephone Company, Inc.
126	SNU	Ameritech Communications, Inc.
220	TDD	Telecom*USA {MCI *WorldCom*}
221	CPL	Capital Telecommunications, Inc.
222	MCI	MCI *WorldCom*
223	TDX	Cable & Wireless Communications, Inc.
224	AMU	Telecom*USA [MCI *WorldCom*]
226	ONE	One Call Communications
236	LTL	Qwest Communications
239	AZU	Brooks Fiber Communications [*WorldCom*]
241	ALG	American Long Lines
245	TDT	Frontier Communications International, Inc.

CIC	Designation	Company
272	PJC	Bell Atlantic Communications, Inc.
273	EDS	EDS
288	ATX	AT&T Communications
291	CSF	Call Savers Inc.
297	LWH	Long Distance Wholesale Club (Excel Communications)
314	MWZ	AT&T Wireless Services, Inc.
333	UTC	Sprint
335	THA	Touch America, Inc.
345	ATX	Lucky Dog Phone Company (AT&T)
5000	---	Reserved for Testing Purposes Only
5003	NNN	Northern Communications, Inc.
5008	UOM	WinStar
5010	PPY	PRE-PAY U.S.A. Inc.
5011	JCV	Jones Communications, Inc
6123	AAX	Ameritech
6124	VLO	Valor Telecommunications Southwest, LLC
6125	WNL	Wantel, Inc
6970	AXG	AP&T Long Distance
6971	DMV	Gulf Pines Communications, LLC
6979	SSW	Tri-Star Communications
6981	WVL	Warwick Valley Telephone Co.
6982	LAE	Local Access Network, LLC
6984	NRI	Northwest Telephone Inc.
6988	PMM	Premiere TeleMedia, Inc.
6990	THI	Telehop Communications Inc.
6996	ORL	Orlando Telephone Company Inc.
6998	YWL	Yukon-Waltz Telephone Co.
6999	ICG	ICG Telecom Group, Inc.

An applicant obtains a CIC by purchasing access from an access provider. The access provider in turn applies to NANPA for the assignment on behalf of the access purchaser. Reflecting their origin, CICs may be classified as FG B or FG D, depending on the type of access purchased. The following procedure is used to request a CIC assignment:

1. Complete the CIC application form. One application form is required per CIC request. The CIC applicant completes all required entries on the CIC application form to the best of his/her knowledge and signs the form.

2. Contact an access provider, i.e., the LEC, and request the assignment of a CIC. The CIC application form is presented to the access provider when requesting access service.

3. Place a valid order for FG B or FG D trunk access service, or FG B translation access service. This depends on the type of CIC being requested and the service availability. The access provider indicates the three CIC choices in order of preference.

4. Provide the access provider a list of all CICs currently held, indicating the name of the CIC holders if other than the entity applying for the CIC.

CICs are assigned according to the guidelines developed by the ATIS-sponsored Industry Numbering Committee. The guidelines and an application form can be found at:

ftp://ftp.atis.org/pub/clc/inc/95012706.doc

The FCC, with input from the North American Numbering Council, is reviewing fundamental issues concerning entitlement to and use of CICs.

A 1997 summary of CIC assignments showed that 37 CICs were assigned for intra-LATA calls, 15 were assigned to Canadian carriers, 6 were assigned to offshore and Caribbean carriers, 54 were assigned to AT&T, 48 assigned to MCI (now MCI *WorldCom*), 234 were assigned to other long-distance companies (some of which have been since acquired by *WorldCom*), 8 codes (211, 311, 411, etc.) were not usable, and 000-199 were not used because of 900-number service.

International Numbers

Calling overseas with U.S.-based long-distance services can be reasonably straightforward. For example, international calls with a specific carrier use a CAC then 01, a country code, a city code, and a local telephone number.

Calls to USA from Overseas
Carrier Access Code + Area Code + Local Telephone Number

Calls from USA to Overseas

Carrier Access Code + 01 + Country Code + City Code + Local Telephone Number

Some selected country codes for calls originating in the U.S. and terminating in the designated country are shown in Table 4-1.

Table 4.1 *International Calling Prefixes*

Country	Calling Prefix	
Australia	61	
Austria	43	Ach 7727, Bludenz 5552, Graz 316, Innsbruck 512, Kitzbuhel 5356, Klagenfurt 463, Krems An Der Donau 2732, Linz 70, Linz Donau 70, Neunkirchen Niederosterreich 2635, Salzburg 662, Vienna 1, Villach 4242, Wels 7242, Wiener Neustadt 2622
United Kingdom ATT	44	Belfast 1232, Birmingham 121, Bournemouth 1202, Cardiff 1222, Durham 191, Edinburgh 131, Glasgow 141, Gloucester 1452, Ipswich 1473, Liverpool 151, London (inner) 171, London (outer) 181, Manchester 161, Nottingham 115, Prestwick 1292, Sheffield 1944, Southhampton 1703
United Kingdom BT	44	Belfast 1232, Birmingham 121, Bournemouth 1202, Cardiff 1222, Durham 191, Edinburgh 131, Glasgow 141, Gloucester 1452, Ipswich 1473, Liverpool 151, London (inner) 171, London (outer) 181, Manchester 161, Nottingham 115, Prestwick 1292, Sheffield 1944, Southhampton 1703
United Kingdom Mercury	44	Belfast 1232, Birmingham 121, Bournemouth 1202, Cardiff 1222, Durham 191, Edinburgh 131, Glasgow 141, Gloucester 1452, Ipswich 1473, Liverpool 151, London (inner) 171, London (outer) 181, Manchester 161, Nottingham 115, Prestwick 1292, Sheffield 1944, Southhampton 1703
USA	1	Current list of area codes
Uruguay	598	Canelones 33, Florida 352, Las Piedras 324, Maldonado 42, Mercedes 532, Minas 442, Montevideo 2, Paysandu 722, Punta Del Este 42, San Jose 342.
U.S. Virgin Islands	340	

A more complete listing of country codes and international networks using AT&T services is provided at:

http://www.att.com/traveler/

Some countries are reorganizing their calling prefixes to route calls to specific destinations and services. Some special prefix routing is:

Australian Calling Prefixes:

00 Emergency and International (001, 0010, etc.)

01 Satellite (mobile - 014, 015,018; paging 016, 019)

02 Geographic services

03 Geographic services

04 Mobile

05 Spare

06 Spare

07 Geographic services

08 Geographic services

09 Spare

10 Interim dial access (Optus long distance (1), followed by area or ID code)

11 Public, community mass calling services

17 Universal personal telecommunications services

18 Freephone, charge card, controlled and Virtual Private Network Services (VPNS)

19 Information, facsimile

New UK Calling Prefixes:

00 International numbers

01 Geographic numbers

02 New geographic numbers (e.g., London, Northern Ireland, and Cardiff)

07 Mobiles, pagers, and all "follow-me" services

08 Free, local, or national rate calls

09 Premium-rate calls

U.S. long-distance carriers make international calling relatively easy, although it is difficult for Americans to understand international telephone numbering plans.

The international standard that governs the length of telephone numbers has increased the maximum length of a telephone number, including country code, from 12 to 15 digits. Changes are not immediately planned for telephone numbers in World Zone 1, but other countries may take advantage of the new standard. However, a primary strength of the INPA code plan is retention of the current 10-digit telephone number format. This allows for expansion without requiring changes to currently assigned telephone numbers. Thus, the impact and cost of implementing the plan, while substantial for the telecommunications industry, is minimal for subscribers.

The Network Operations Forum has designed an NANP-wide test facility for interchangeable NPAs. Two separate test numbers are to provide INPA announcements and answer supervision for checking billing programs.

Brain Teaser

International Numbers

Find some international phone numbers using AOL's software. AOL has access in many countries worldwide. Such access can be used to verify the correctness of international telephone numbers. Select the access numbers option.

1. Now pick the United Kingdom as the country and view the AOL access numbers. What calling prefix do they have? Make a note of it.

2. Now pick Australia as the country and view the AOL access numbers. What calling prefix do they have? How do they match up with the Australian prefixes listed above?

3. Now try Ghana as the country and view the AOL access number. What calling prefix does it have? Does it match up with UK or Australian prefixes in any way?

The goal here is to understand international numbering plans and the confusion that surrounds them. It also presents a practical means of getting information about telephone numbers in different foreign countries.

Telephone Companies and Regulation

The U.S. telephone companies were largely formed from the breakup of AT&T. They are one class of vendor for communications services or channels. In 1984, to purchase communications services, you dealt with a Regional Bell Operating Company (RBOC), a Local Exchange Carrier (LEC) that was a wholly owned subsidiary of the Regional Bell Operating Company, and Inter Exchange Carrier (IXC/IEC) that provided long-distance circuits. The RBOCs, LECs and IXCs/IECs and their transformation into the current entities that are competing for both long-distance and local dial tone services, are described here.

The telephone market can be viewed as the long-distance calling market and the local subscriber access market (local dial tone). Within these markets, there are large customers (the cream) and small customers (the individual household subscribers). Changes that shaped the current telephone market began with the large long-distance customers, then moved to long distance for individual household subscribers. Now the focus is on providing dial tone service to large local business customers and to high-density, individual household subscriber areas. The next phase, which is almost upon us full throttle, is to provide every subscriber with high-speed or broadband Internet access. This is needed to deliver the new Internet information, shopping, consumer, and entertainment services, to businesses and households.

Pre-divestiture - "Universal Service"

Politics and telephones have been bedmates since the beginning of telephony in the U.S. Because telephones were viewed as being delivered by a monopoly (a single company that provided all the telephony services), political agendas were attached to the regulation of telephone services. Further, the telephone companies employed lots of people. In true political fashion, politicians running for public office would pander to this large segment of voters by promising, as they always do, that the government would take care of their employment concerns and personal lives. Of course, we truly know that all such political promises are either outright lies or come with so many strings attached that they are worthless.

The initial politics of telephony was "universal service." This meant that regardless of what it cost to deliver telephone service to a subscriber, every subscriber was charged about the same price for service. Because the most significant expense in the delivery of telephone service was the cost of connecting (wiring up a service area) subscribers to the telephone company CO, rural subscribers paid about the same as urban subscribers for telephones when it actually cost more to connect them up. This was good at the time because it meant that everyone nationwide got telephone service. It caused voice telephony to be universally available throughout the U.S. Universal service fees are levied on all phone calls to assure that low-income and rural telephone subscribers have access to affordable telephone service.

In the long term, this results in some subscribers subsidizing the service costs of other subscribers. Today, business subscribers pay a higher cost (because they presumably have more money) than residential subscribers. A business phone costs more than a residential phone, it has pay-by-the-minute rates for all calls (local and long distance), and the long-distance rates are higher during business hours than during evening hours.

Figure 4-3 illustrates how long-distance voice calls were delivered to household telephone subscribers. AT&T used a hierarchical switching structure connected to telephone subscriber lines. When you attempted to make a local call from one Class 5 CO to another, and the tie line trunk circuits between those switching systems were busy (occupied servicing other calls), your call would be bounced up to a Class 4 toll center. The Class 4 toll center would attempt to use its trunk circuits to another Class 4 toll center to com-

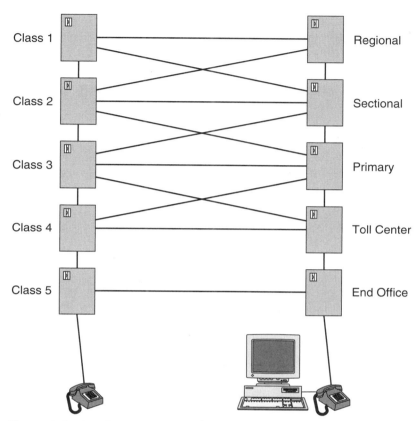

Figure 4–3   *Pre-divestiture network switching hierarchy.*

plete the call, but if they were occupied, it would then bump the call up to a Class 3 primary center and so on until the call could be completed.

With "universal service," AT&T, GTE, and United Telecommunications were the larger telephone companies delivering phone services in the U.S. At the same time, there were also over 1,500 smaller telephone companies and telephone cooperatives providing local service in smaller communities across the U.S.

Divestiture - Modified Final Judgment - "Equal Access"

Technology changed the telephone industry. The company that began the change process was Microwave Communications Incorporated (MCI), which became MCI Communications Corporation. They started by providing communications to trucking firms using line-of-sight microwave communications links. The resultant network could support long-distance telecommunications services as well. But MCI needed to connect to local subscriber telephones. New telecommunications and microelectronic technologies made it possible for MCI to cost-effectively build a long-distance voice telephone network that could compete with AT&T. MCI petitioned the FCC to get into the long-distance business, and well, the rest is history. The federal government won the court case. Judge Green in the Modified Final Judgment broke up AT&T into a long-distance company competing at the time largely with MCI and seven Regional Bell Operating Companies (RBOCs). The RBOCs were originally holding companies that owned LECs. The LECs were the local telephone companies that provided the IXC/IEC access to subscriber telephone lines. With the Modified Final Judgment, the era of "equal access" began.

The goal of divestiture and "equal access" was to promote long-distance competition. The politics of divestiture was "equal access." "Equal access" is successful because long-distance call costs have declined substantially. The cost of a long-distance call has declined more than 80% from what it was in 1984, and it continues to decline today as new technology is introduced into the voice telephone network and competitive long-distance market. The lowest long-distance costs are now around five cents per minute. Another interesting phenomenon is that the total dollars spent on long-distance calls has increased from the dollar volume of 1984. There is actually a bigger pie of revenue to split up among long-distance competitors today than there was in 1984. So lowering monopoly-set costs resulted in more revenue because calling volume increased. (It is interesting to note that MCI was at one time thought to be an acronym for Money Coming In because of the incredible revenues MCI made.)

The government is close to making a similar mistake with the Internet. If the Internet is taxed, business activity on it will diminish. Further, the economy will slow down and there will be a lower income tax base on which the government can earn revenues. We have a budget surplus right now because of lower taxes, not because taxes were increased. We are at such high tax rates that the volume of business activity will lower with increased taxation. The lower business activity, even with the higher tax, rate will produce less revenue for the government than would a lower tax rate and the resultant increased economic activity. Raising prices or taxes on technical economic activity is a mistake, as has been demonstrated by the lowering of long-distance rates through increased competition and the results produced by the "no tax" policy on Internet activities.

All along, new telecommunications and microelectronic technologies improved the quality of telephone calls. The backbone voice network of all telephone service vendors is excellent. Certainly, there were some early instances where the quality of long-distance voice calls over vendors other than AT&T was poor. Such low-quality connections today are rare.

Figure 4-4 shows the IXCs/IECs having equal access to subscriber phones at the Class 5 COs. With equal access, each long-distance carrier is free to provide long-distance service to any telephone subscriber.

The Inter-Exchange Carriers

Inter-Exchange Carriers (IXCs/IECs) are telephone companies that transport calls between telephone exchanges. They carry long-distance and toll charge calls. AT&T, MCI *WorldCom*, Qwest, Cable and Wireless, and others are IXCs/IECs. Since the breakup of AT&T in 1984, IXCs/IECs interface with local telephone companies at POPs. The POPs serve offices set up in each LEC. The POP is the point to which the local telephone company connects its customers for long-distance dial-up and leased-line communications between telephone exchanges.

As we discussed earlier, toll calls are made within and between LATAs in the telephone network. A LATA is smaller than a state and bigger than a county; smaller than an area code and bigger than a single exchange. It is an artificial entity created by telephone companies for the purpose of computing toll charges. There are intra-LATA (within) and inter-LATA (between) toll charges. The boundaries are drawn so as to maximize telephone company revenues.

Calls to locations outside a LATA require the LEC to pass the call to a designated IXC/IEC POP. The IXC/IEC transports the call to a LEC at the destination LATA. Basically, IXCs/IECs transport calls from LATA to LATA.

Regional Bell Operating Companies

The seven RBOCs, or baby Bells, created from AT&T in the 1984 divestiture include:

- NYNEX—Covers New York and New England.
- Bell Atlantic—Covers the Mid-Atlantic states.
- Bell South—Operates in the Southeastern states.
- Ameritech—Covers the Midwest.
- U.S. West —Covers the mountain states and Northwest.
- Pacific Telesis—Operates in California and Nevada.
- Southwestern Bell—Covers Texas and southern states west of the Mississippi.

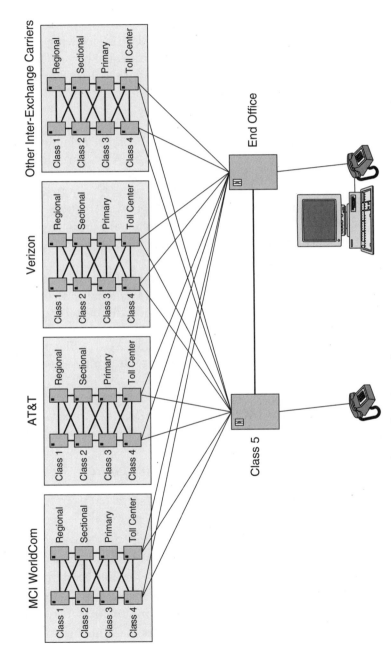

Figure 4–4 *Equal access network switching hierarchy.*

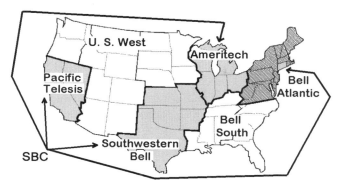

Figure 4–5 *RBOCs and mergers.*

These RBOCs were set up as part of the Modified Final Judgment implemented in January 1984. Recent legislation has significantly altered how these RBOCs can do business and what communications services they can provide. As a result, they are all pursuing mergers and new opportunities. Bell Atlantic and NYNEX have already merged to become a bigger Bell Atlantic. Then, Bell Atlantic merged with GTE to form Verizon. Ameritech, Pacific Telesis, Southwestern Bell, and SNET have merged to become SBC Communications. U.S. West and Qwest have merged as well.

RBOC	Targeted Percentage of Lines Using Digital Transmission (1998 Data)
NYNEX	97.4
Pacific Telesis	94.8
Bell Atlantic	93.3
Bell South	92.1
Ameritech	89.9
U.S. West	68.4
Southwestern Bell	66.6

The big long-distance telecommunications merger is the MCI World-Com merger, which included WorldCom, MCI, and Sprint. Figure 4-5 shows some of the RBOCS and mergers.

Local Exchange Carriers

The RBOCs were holding companies for their subsidiaries, the LECs. LECs provide local dial tone to residential subscribers. Thus, residential telephone subscribers are provided basic telephone network access by a physical connection from their customer premises to a local LEC CO. This connection is a dial-up connection, or a dedicated trunk connection, like a leased T1 (1.544-Mbps) channel.

For dial-up connections, after the phone is dialed, the subscriber accesses a variety of telephone services and call-handling features provided by the LEC. These telephone services and functions are for connections in the LEC's LATA.

For dedicated trunk lines, the local segment is set up and maintained by LECs at each end, while the inter-LATA portion of the circuit is established and maintained by an IXC/IEC.

LECs were set up as part of the 1984 divestiture decision. However, the separate company designations are gone today. For example, all Bell Atlantic and NYNEX LECs are now known as just Verizon. Figure 4-6 shows the 1984 LECs.

Other Common Carriers and Specialized Common Carriers

Other Common Carriers (OCCs) or Specialized Common Carriers (SCCs) offer unique communications services. They may be domestic and international record carriers supporting international telex communications, or domestic satellite carriers providing satellite communications services authorized by the FCC.

Telex is a low-speed message communications system that is available worldwide. Internet email and facsimile message services are replacing telex. However, telex message communications are still important, especially in the banking and shipping sectors, due to their legal validity and wide availability in all parts of the world.

They may provide backbone voice network support to other telephone companies, but their primary focus is on their unique specialized communications services.

Competitive Access Providers

Competitive Access Providers (CAPs) provide fiber optic and microwave communications links that connect to IXCs/IECs. These links compete with

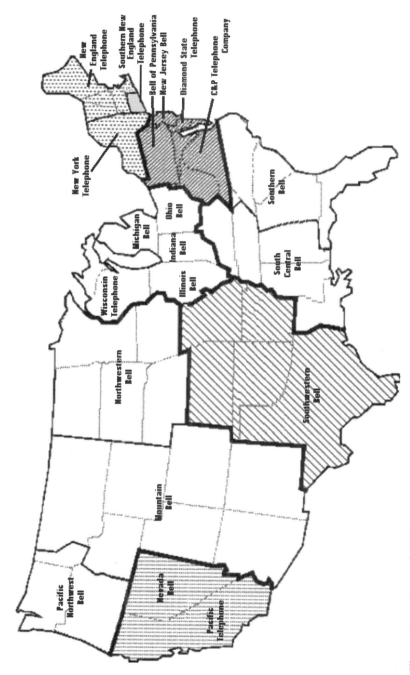

Figure 4–6 *Original LECs.*

LEC networks in the top 25 metropolitan areas nationwide, as well as in many smaller metropolitan areas. CAPs compete with CATV (Cable Television) service providers. FCC rulings helped CAPs quickly become viable competitors to LECs.

Metropolitan networks first appeared with the spread of cable television. Although these networks limited television signal distribution from satellite downlinks to residential communities, the early cable systems became the prototypes of Metropolitan Area Networks (MANs). In the early 1980s, satellite uplink operators built teleports and local access networks to offer direct private satellite transmission services to large organizations.

While the 1984 breakup of AT&T increased competition in the long-distance and communications markets, it left the local connectivity market monopoly essentially intact. However, entrepreneurs soon began to offer long-distance service using teleport satellite circuits combined with private local access networks to their customers' premises. CATV companies also deployed fiber for high-traffic routes and explored using fiber for connections to subscriber premises.

The spread of such metropolitan local access networks eroded the LEC monopoly over local loop connectivity to subscribers. Further, CAPs demanded access to LECs operations centers and COs. CAPs exerted extensive pressure on the FCC to achieve these goals. LECs strongly resisted this encroachment on their business base. Today, LECs are forced to allow CAPs to co-locate with their physical facilities. This is expanding to allow CAPs to directly connect with LEC central offices in some areas, providing alternative access to the LEC's local switch.

CAPs have many individual networks supporting users with heavy data traffic. These CAP networks offer customers up to 100-Mbps transmission speed and redundant routing for point-to-point transmission at lower prices. Further, CAPs generally use more fiber optic transmission facilities and deliver higher speed circuits at lower cost than do the LECs.

The Telecommunications Act of 1996

The Telecommunications Act of 1996 was enacted by the U.S. Congress on February 1, 1996, and signed into law by the President on February 8, 1996. This act made major changes in laws governing CATV, telecommunications (telephony), and the Internet. The law's main purpose was to stimulate competition in local telecommunication services. The law specified how local telephone carriers can compete, how and under what circumstances LECs can provide long-distance services, and the deregulation of CATV rates.

FCC 1996 Ruling and Current Rulings

The goal of the Telecommunications Act of 1996 was to promote local tele-communications competition. In August 1996, an FCC ruling enhanced the competitive position of Competitive Local Exchange Carriers (CLECs) in the local telecommunications marketplace by defining precisely and uniformly the terms and conditions under the Telecommunications Act of 1996, whereby CLECs may interconnect with Incumbent Local Exchange Carriers (ILECs) to originate and terminate calls. The ruling adopted broad guide-lines, but charged states with implementing the requirements of the order. Some key points of the ruling were:

- Points of interconnection—CLECs and ILECs must interconnect their networks to facilitate local and long-distance telephone calls. Such network interconnections may be at the ILEC local end office, toll (tandem) office, or other points of aggregation along ILEC loops. Interconnection at other mutually agreed-upon network points is encouraged to provide more flexibility for competitive providers to route and complete calls.

- Reciprocal compensation—ILEC telephone companies must be com-pensated for the traffic they handle. A pricing methodology for trans-port and termination of local telephone traffic should be a reciprocal compensation based on a Total Element Long Run Incremental Cost (TELRIC) study. Interim default rates are established for use by states that have not yet completed TELRIC cost studies. Bill-and-keep arrangements between companies are permitted if ordered by the state. Bill-and-keep arrangements reduce administrative barriers, allowing CLECs to more quickly offer local exchange services. Both the default rates for interconnection and the alternative bill-and-keep arrangements permitted by the FCC provide lower interconnection rates than negotiated rates.

- Unbundled network elements—CLEC costs are direct, unbundled costs. Competitive local providers access cost-based unbundled ILEC network elements based on a TELRIC methodology and permit CLECs to combine network elements without restriction. This gives CLECs access to cost-based unbundled loops, which greatly enhances their competitive position in offering integrated solutions to end-users. Unbundled switching elements priced based on cost can be assessed additive access charges. However, these additive charges do not apply to CLECs using their own switches and not the ILEC's switches.

- Resale—A resale rate equal to the ILEC retail rate less the costs avoided by the ILEC as a wholesale provider establishes an interim default discount range of 17 to 25 percent for states with no resale rules in place. The mandated range represents a balanced approach that does not impede the CLEC's ability to offer competitively priced facilities-based local exchange products and also offer competitively priced local exchange resale products.
- Wireless local loop—Wires do not need to run to a customer facility to provide service.
- Dialing parity—Extra digits, like an access code, do not need to be dialed if someone is using a provider that does not own the local exchange.
- Number portability—You have the right to take your phone numbers with you when changing providers.
- Co-location—Competitive telephone service providers have the right to place their equipment in the incumbent LEC's COs.
- Access charge reform—The FCC has committed to restructure access charges in the future. The FCC's intention to restructure access charges matches many CLECs' long-term business strategies, including providing wireless local loops.Within the framework of this ruling, CLECs can negotiate much more quickly and effectively the fair, competitive interconnection agreements with LECs that are essential to fostering full competition in local telecommunications markets. This act encourages just about anyone to become a telecommunications provider because the FCC wants to motivate competition.

INCUMBENT LOCAL EXCHANGE CARRIERS

ILECs are the original LECs that were spun off from AT&T in 1984 by the Modified Final Judgment. They own the facilities or network elements that originate and terminate calls from subscriber phone lines. My ILEC is now Verizon, which was formed by the merger of GTE and Bell Atlantic.

COMPETITIVE LOCAL EXCHANGE CARRIERS

CLECs are the competition entering the local telephone service market. They are initially servicing business customers with high-revenue volumes. The cost of servicing such business customers is less than the cost of serving residential customers because a large volume of telephone traffic for the business customer is from a single easy-to-reach facility. Residential subscribers in contrast require lots of facilities for servicing little traffic.

Because telephone tariffs can be more competitive now, this is presenting an interesting dilemma. Traditionally, businesses have subsidized residential phones. Business phone line charges are higher and daily rates for dial-up calls (during business hours) are higher. The facilities to deliver these services are the same facilities as those that deliver residential services. With CLECs capturing the lucrative business customers and leaving the less lucrative (subsidized) residential customers to be serviced by the ILECs, ILECs are considering raising residential rates to compensate for their loss of revenue. This means residential phone subsidies, e.g., "universal service," could disappear. When this happens, the CLECs will find that servicing residential customers is very profitable as well as servicing the business customers they captured from the ILEC.

New technologies and lower labor costs permit the CLECs to deliver telephone services to business and residential customers for lower prices than the ILECs. Figure 4-7 conceptualizes how CLECs and ILECs could provide telephone service to business and residential customers.

In the case of residential customers, the last mile of wire would most likely be owned by the ILEC. The CLEC would need to connect into the ILEC wiring at an ILEC Class 5 end office. In the case of business customers, the CLEC is likely to construct its own network access mechanism or install its own wire connecting the business directly to the CLEC Class 5 CO.

Brain Teaser

CLEC and ILEC Information on the Web

Using an Internet search engine, perform the following searches:
1. Search for CLEC and ILEC. Do these terms (CLEC and ILEC) lead to more telecommunications Web sites?
2. Search for the Telecommunications Act of 1996. Can you find a 14-point checklist? What do the points cover? Do they match up with the list in Figure 4-8?
The goal here is to understand the regulations that are shaping competition in the telecommunications industry.

Telephony Services

Common carriers are organizations providing regulated telephone, telegraph, telex, and data communications services. For the last few decades, the telephone network was optimized to carry voice telephone calls. Digital voice

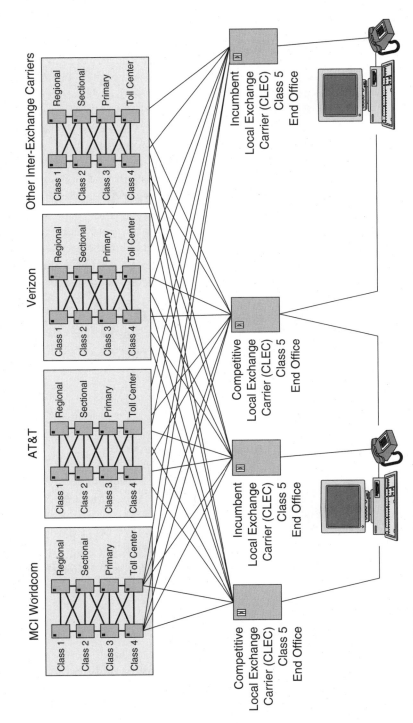

Figure 4–7 *CLEC network switching hierarchy.*

Telecommunications Act of 1996—14-Point Checklist Overview

1. Intercommunication.
2. Non-discriminatory access to network elements.
3. Non-discriminatory access to Bell-owned poles, ducts, and rights-of-way.
4. Unbundled local loop transmission from the central office to the customer premise.
5. Unbundled transport from the trunk side of the local switch.
6. Unbundled local switching (routing calls) separate from transmission services.
7. Non-discriminatory access to 911, E911, directory assistance, and operator call completion.
8. White pages directory listings for competitors' customers.
9. Non-discriminatory access to telephone numbers by competitors' customers until numbering administration has been given to organizations other than Bell companies.
10. Non-discriminatory access to databases and signaling required for call routing and completion.
11. Interim telephone number portability via remote call forwarding or direct-inward dialing until new arrangements are complete fro full number portability.
12. Non-discriminatory access to services that allow completive carriers to supply dialing parity, i.e., dial 1 to access customer's PIC for toll and non-toll calling.
13. Reciprocal compensation arrangements for Bell and competitive carriers to carry each others' calls.
14. Resale of telecommunications services as stated above, at cost, without provision of profit for the Bells.

Figure 4–8 *Telecommunications Act 14-point checklist.*

and data traffic have rapidly increased. Data communications traffic differs from digital voice traffic because digital voice traffic can lose transmission bits and still be acceptable to the customer, while data communications traffic cannot lose a single bit. This section focuses on voice communications services alone. Other types of services are covered in later sections.

Types of Channels

The types of communications channels we can purchase are measured use, leased channels, or packet-switched network channels. They can be a voice-grade analog channel or an ISDN channel. Other channels are high-speed digital channels that provide the capacity of many voice-grade lines (see Figure 4-9).

MEASURED USE OR DIAL-UP

A measured use or dial-up channel is a single dial-up telephone line. Cost for the channel is based upon usage. For local calls, you pay a flat fee for access to the local telephone network and then either a flat fee or a metered usage fee

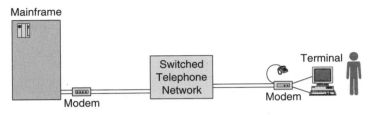

SWITCHED — MEASURED USE — DIAL-UP LINES

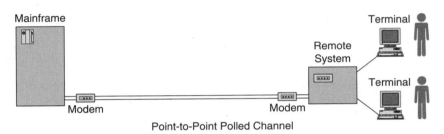

Point-to-Point Polled Channel

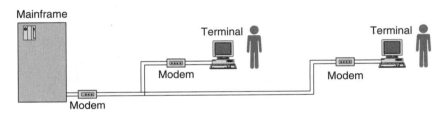

Multi-Point Polled Channel

LEASED — FULL PERIOD DIGITAL CHANNELS

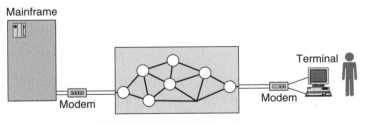

PACKET SWITCHED NETWORK

Figure 4–9 *Telecommunications channels.*

They contend for telephone trunks. Contention is first come, first served operation. The phone requesting trunk access first gets the trunk for the duration of its call, then releases the resource for other telephones to use. With dial-up services, if all phones were to request trunks at the same time (like when there is a natural disaster in some geographical area—a San Francisco earthquake, for instance), the local telephone facilities would be overloaded and only about 10% of the calls would be completed.

Measured use circuits can be voice-grade analog channels or ISDN channels.

VOICE-GRADE ANALOG CHANNELS • A voice-grade analog dial-up channel is the ubiquitous telephone line used for voice and modem communications. Voice-grade analog channels dial-up lines are 2-wire service because they use two wires. In contrast, voice-grade leased lines are commonly 4-wire service.

Voice-grade channels and circuits are designed to carry voice frequencies in the audio frequency speech transmission range of 300 to 3400Hz. The overall channel bandwidth of a voice channel is 0 to 4000Hz, or 4KHz. Voice-grade channels provide a usable bandwidth of about 3KHz. This effectively limits the amount of information they can carry.

Voice-grade channels were more than adequate for the voice and low-speed data communications telephony of the 1960s, 1970s, and most of the 1980s. The maximum transmission speeds attainable by today's dial-up modems are 53 Kbps (down)/33.6 Kbps (up). Today, requirements are changing rapidly. The Internet is a driving force in that change. Much higher speed access to the Internet is needed to access the new Internet-delivered multimedia services.

INTEGRATED SERVICES DIGITAL NETWORK CHANNELS • ISDN Basic Rate Interface (BRI) channels are equivalent to two dial-up voice-grade analog telephone lines. A BRI is composed of two B channels and one 16-Kbps D channel. The B channels are 64-Kbps digital transmission channels that can carry voice, image, or video traffic. The D channel is the signaling and control channel that carries caller ID, call waiting, number dialed, and other signaling data. An ISDN BRI is connected to an ISDN phone with a 4-wire connection, but services can be delivered to the customer premise over two wires.

ISDN channels use contention for local telephone trunk facilities when placing dial-up calls just like voice-grade analog channels. Actually, ISDN and voice-grade analog channels often compete for the same trunk circuits because both terminate in the same local telephone company branch exchange switch. Costs for ISDN BRI channels have a fixed monthly access fee component and very often a per minute usage fee for each separate B channel.

The main difference between an ISDN channel and a voice-grade analog channel is that the ISDN channel can deliver 128-Kbps digital access to the Internet, while a single voice-grade analog channel cannot. The primary motivation for using an ISDN channel is to access the Internet at higher speeds than analog voice channels provide. Otherwise, most of the popular ISDN services or features can be provided by analog voice-grade channels at lower cost. This means that there is little incentive to purchase ISDN unless it is for 128-Kbps access to the Internet.

In some cases, an ISDN PRI Channel is a measured use channel. A PRI consists of 23 B channels and a 64-Kbps D channel. The B and D channels perform the same functions as they perform in the BRI. In the case of the PRI, it is possible to switch several B channels together. This means that an ISDN H0 channel is composed of six B channels. The H0 channel delivers the 384 Kbps needed for video teleconferencing. An H0 channel can be a switched measured use channel subset of a PRI. This saves money for many organizations because it is cheaper to pay for PRI access to the telephone network from two video conference locations and the H0 channel measured use calls than it is to pay for a leased high-speed channel between the same two video conference facilities. Further, if there are three or more video conference facilities, then the savings can be even larger because the cost for each facility for ISDN PRI access to the telephone network is much less than the cost of dedicated leased facilities between all three video teleconferencing sites.

LEASED

Leased lines are sometimes referred to as private lines or dedicated lines. They are leased 24 hours a day, 7 days a week, or 24/7. Their full capacity is available to the telephone subscriber all the time. Unfortunately, most telephone subscribers only use a leased line during peak activity times and its capability is unused at other times. Leased lines are charged for on a flat rate, depending upon their source and destination. The telephone company constructs dedicated facilities to that leased line between its origination point and its termination point. Often, leased line charges incorporate a distance-sensitive component so the longer the distance a leased line travels, the more it costs. There is no contention for telephone company trunks with a leased line.

Leased line circuits are mostly digital channels today. A leased line channel is most often a point-to-point channel. A point-to-point channel connects two separate facilities directly to one another. Another type of leased channel is a multi-point or multi-drop channel connecting several different facilities to a single central facility.

POINT-TO-POINT • Point-to-point leased channels provide high-speed digital pipes between geographically separate facilities. They can be implemented as

T-1/T-3 channels, ISDN PRI channels, or much higher speed Optical Carrier (OC) channels. OC channels are delivered using Synchronous Optical Network, or Synchronous Optical Network Technologies (SONET).

Leased line point-to-point channels are often terminated into multiplexers and that connect to a LAN routers and telephone PBX telephone switches at each site. This enables the point-to-point circuit to carry both voice and data traffic between the sites. The ability to carry simultaneous voice and data traffic is not dynamic, but rather fixed with a specific proportion of the channel dedicated to voice traffic and another (lesser proportion) dedicated to data traffic.

Most companies today seek to reduce costs by making the use of point-to-point leased line facilities much more dynamic and able to quickly shift the entire channel from voice to data traffic as needed to meet communications needs. Because data traffic is less time-sensitive than voice traffic, dynamic bandwidth (capacity) allocation provides more effective use of dedicated leased point-to-point communications channels.

MULTI-POINT • Wide area network multi-point leased channels are data channels. The devices attached to those channels share the capacity of the channel using a polling protocol. The central facility polls each device attached to the multi-point channel for data. When the device has data to send, it transmits the data. Otherwise, a short response signals the central facility to poll (solicit data) from the next device on the multi-point channel. The entire channel is controlled by a single central facility. The central facility performs the polling of all devices in the multi-point facilities, receives data inputs from them, prepares responses to the data inputs, and transmits the responses to the appropriate remote multi-point device.

The classic multi-point channel system was the airline reservations system. Few multi-point airline reservations systems remain today because LAN PC-based systems have replaced them.

PACKET NETWORK SERVICES

Newer communications services are delivered as packet network services. In this case, a site leases high-speed access to a Packet-Switched Network (PSN) POP. The voice, data, image, or video traffic is received at the PSN POP and broken into packets that are then sent through the PSN to a destination POP attached by high-speed access to the destination site. The packets of voice, data, image, or video information are reassembled at the PSN POP and passed across the high-speed access line to the destination site.

Packet network charges are fixed monthly charges for the high-speed access line, and usage charges for the amount of data that is sent across the

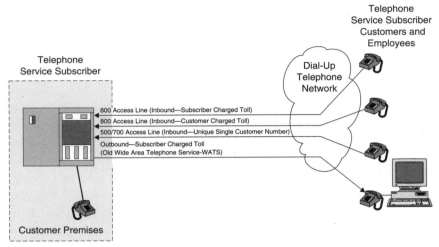

Figure 4–10 *Telephone network services.*

packet network. The Internet is a PSN. Networks using Internet technology are referred to as Internet Packet (Internet Packet protocol), or IP networks.

Dial-up Network Services

There are several services available generally to businesses (but are sometimes used by individual telephone subscribers) beyond basic dial-up services. The services described here, 500-, 555-, 700-, 800-, and 900-number services have been used differently by businesses, but are all somewhat similar to 800-number services. Their names are derived from the first three digits of the ten-digit phone numbers implementing these services. These services provide voice-grade communications channels, but bill for them at special rates (see Figure 4-10).

Whenever someone signs up for telephone service, they must designate a long-distance (IXC/IEC) carrier for each telephone line. This is sometimes called the pre-subscribed carrier.

500-NUMBER SERVICES

In 1993, a new set of codes for personal communications services was established. Area code 500 was designated for this purpose. One of the potential uses for 500 codes is for an individual or business to keep the same phone number (NXX-XXXX) if it moves from its CO code area (NXX), even to another state. Five hundred codes would thus allow non-geographic numbering.

More often, 500-number service is used as a single-number telephone service for individuals on the move. Some telephone service providers offer nationwide "follow-me" phone numbers for mobile customers. The service uses the "500 access code" designated under the NANP for nationwide telephone numbers. A 500-number service lets customers be reached at any location and on any equipment instead of different numbers for business, cellular, fax, and home phones. One 500-number can be called to reach a subscriber on any type of phone anywhere.

Companies offering "500-number service" receive office codes, each of which can be used for 10,000 telephone numbers. All 500 calls that are dialed as 1-500-550-XXXX are routed to MCI, regardless of the last four digits dialed. Similarly, calls that are dialed as 1-500-288-XXXX are routed to AT&T. Because each of 1,000 office codes can be associated with 10,000 line numbers, there are theoretically 10,000,000 potential 500 numbers. As a practical matter, however, fewer than 80% of these potential numbers are usable. Telephone numbers that begin with a 1 or 0, for example, are not used.

555-NUMBER SERVICES

The assignment of 555 line numbers differs from 500-number service codes. The 555 numbers represent a special office code and remain constant. The numbers assigned are special service line numbers. For example, one 555 number used for many years is 555-1212. It is used for nationwide directory assistance. This particular 555 number continues to be used for that purpose. Non-communications companies as well as communications companies can obtain line number assignments for 555 line numbers. Like the telephone number for directory assistance, these numbers are to be used for special informational purposes.

555 line numbers are being assigned on a national or regional basis. A national 555 number is assigned to an entity for use in most or all of the area codes in the U.S., whereas a regional 555 number is assigned to an entity for use in a specific geographic area (less than 30% of the area codes, states, or provinces). Thus, a regional 555 number may be assigned to more than one entity if it is to be used in different geographic regions. A national number cannot be assigned to more than one entity.

700-NUMBER SERVICES

The 700-number system handles calls automatically sent to the pre-sub-scribed long-distance (IXC/IEC) carrier. These 700 numbers support a variety of applications, including access to long-distance message applications such as weather, traffic, and database applications. The 700-number service can be used for closed user group services, such as limiting access to a group of telephone numbers, e.g., a virtual network. Long-distance carriers selling a select service exclusively to their customers use 700-number services as the means to offer value-added services to customers without making them available to the public.

800, 888, 877, AND 866 SERVICES

800-number, 888-number, 877-number, and 866-number services are toll-free services. In this case, the called party pays for the call. Prior to 1993, toll-free 800 calls were routed in a manner similar to that being used for 500-number, 700-number, and 900-number calls, with the NXX office code indicating the long-distance carrier handling the call. In 1993, procedures for routing 800-number calls were changed. The first three digits of 800-number calls no longer indicate the carrier handling the call.

The new system enables customers to change long-distance carriers while still retaining the same 800 number. This system of "portability" relies on an 800-number routing database originally maintained by Bellcore. During the two years since 800-number portability was implemented, the number of working 800 telephone numbers tripled. This growth caused the near exhaustion of 800 numbers. In 1996, the 888 code was added to support the increase in demand for toll-free numbers. The 888 code has nearly 8 million combinations. The 888 numbers were quickly exhausted as well because every business having a special 800 number, like our 800 4-DANERD, requested an equivalent 888 number. Consequently, 877 and 866 numbers are now being used to support toll-free services.

The 800-number services are among the most famous carrier services for business. AT&T introduced the 800-number service in the 1960s. The 800-number service provides switched, voice-grade channels for transmission of either voice or data. These channels are toll-free, inbound service for callers dialing an 800 number. The called 800 number subscriber pays for the call. Volume discounts are sometimes given to 800-number subscribers based on exceeding specific call volumes each month. An 800 number may be local, regional, national, or international in coverage, and it can be quickly assigned to any local access phone line. Our radio show has a toll-free 888 number assigned from 5:00 PM to 6:00 PM every Sunday night. Calls at other times are not completed to that number.

Providing toll-free, inbound telephone numbers for customers is a powerful business tool. At one time, AT&T sponsored a survey of telephone buying habits that found three out of four shoppers were more likely to do business with a company providing an 800 number.

There are many different 800-number service offerings. For example, some offerings provided by AT&T included the original 800-number service introduced in 1967, which gave inter-state and/or intra-state service for businesses receiving less than 500 hours of inbound calls per month. A single access line to the switched network is required for voice, data, or facsimile transmission. Also included was an advanced 800-number service with additional features. The advanced 800-number features were grouped into two packages:

- Feature Package I—800 Single Number Service, 800 Area Code Routing, 800 Time Manager, and 800 Day Manager.
- Feature Package II—Feature Package I plus 800 Exchange Routing and 800 Call Allocator services.

These features are used either independently or in combination to match inbound call-handling to specific subscriber operations. The following are call-handling operations these services provide:

- The primary 800-number Single Number Service uses the same 800 number for interstate, intrastate, and Canadian calls. This is the 500-hour or less inbound call service. A low-end 800-number starter service targeted at companies with less than three hours of 800-number calls per month is also offered. Calls are routed over existing dial-up lines. Subscribers terminate 800 calls from all 50 states, Puerto Rico, and the U.S. Virgin Islands. Postalized rates (no distance bands, i.e., same price from New York to New Jersey as New York to California) are used. This means that one rate is charged for full U.S. coverage.
- 800-number Area Code Routing uses one 800 number, but directs callers to different local numbers or departments based on a call's originating location.
- 800-number Exchange Routing routes calls using area code and exchange digits. Calls from different exchanges within an area code can be routed to specific locations. An exchange cannot be routed to more than one location, and this feature must be combined with 800 Area Code Routing and Automatic Number Identification (ANI) features for calls originating in LEC equal access areas.

- 800-number Time Manager and 800-number Day Manager routes calls to specific locations based on time of day, day of week, or both. The 800-number Time Manager can distribute calls to different locations throughout a 24-hour day based upon time of day. A schedule can be defined in 15-minute or five-minute increments. A maximum of 96 routes can be scheduled, provided all intervals total 24 hours. Once selected, an entire 24 hours is programmed. The schedule then repeats every 24 hours, observing Daylight Savings Time in spring and fall. The 800-number Day Manager distributes calls to destinations by days of the week. Each week starts on Sunday and ends the following Saturday. Each day begins at one second past midnight. Calls route differently by individual days or combinations of days. Routing must be specified for each weekday. A defined weekly schedule applies to every week in the year.
- 800-number Command Routing sets an alternate route when a specific event occurs. Up to 255 contingency routes are stored in a database, each defining one path for a single alternate route. Only one path is used at a time. The other routes are disabled. This feature is activated by using a terminal and dialing into a special user support system or by calling a special advanced features service center and giving them an assigned security identification code.
- 800-number Call Allocator is a load-balancing distribution function. Calls to an 800 number are routed to different centers or access line groups by specifying a percentage of calls distributed to each. Percentages are in whole numbers (0 through 100) and must add up to 100%. The percentages remain fixed and cannot be quickly changed by the user.
- 800-number Call Prompter provides menu or database routing. Call Prompter directs calls to specific destinations via voice menu prompts (recorded announcements) stored in the network. For menu routing, callers route their own calls by pressing digits on a touchtone telephone according to stored menu instructions. Database routing pre-screens calls using an account number, ID number, or other numeric code entered by a caller. Based on the number entered, calls are directed to a specific destination. Each routing can have as many as 1,023 codes, and each code can have a maximum of 15 digits.
- 800-number Courtesy Response presents a message to callers when a business is closed. It must be combined with another 800-number service such as the advanced features like 800 Day Manager, 800 Time Manager, or 800 Command Routing. Messages must conform to regulatory rules, always play from the beginning, and must not repeat.

- 800-number Call Attempt Profile records the volume of call attempts to an 800 number, providing a measured response and lost calls.
- 800-number Routing Control Services allow control over routing patterns without initiating a service order. A user support system is accessed via a dial-up connection to review or change routing plans.
- 800-number Routing Control Service 1 (RCS 1) permits changing the time-of-day and/or day-of-week and destination parameters used to route calls.
- 800-number Routing Control Service II (RCS II) permits adding, changing, or deleting any Feature Package II routing, announcement, or routing-on-demand features without initiating a service order.

Other 800-number services provided by AT&T include:

- 800 Information Forwarding (known as 800 INFO) is an order-taking process allowing businesses to sell products and services to a pre-determined customer base. CATV services use this to permit subscribers to place last-minute orders to watch feature films or other premium programs.
- The 800 READYLINE service has a single 800 number serving both interstate and intrastate calls at no extra charge. The 800 READYLINE service uses existing dial-up lines, permitting the line to make and receive local and long-distance calls, and to receive 800-number dialed calls. Two 800 READYLINE service options are: basic service supporting interstate and intrastate inward calling over the same lines from anyplace in the U.S., including Alaska and Hawaii, Puerto Rico, and the U.S. Virgin Islands; and custom service that allows subscribers to define specific areas from which they can receive calls.
- Other higher end 800-number services terminate interstate, intrastate, and Canadian 800 traffic on a single dedicated 800-number line with subscribers receiving a single bill instead of multiple bills, and increased discounts. Some high-end services are targeted at subscribers with ten or more lines and over 450 hours of monthly usage. They allow businesses to create toll-free calling areas by combining area codes from the U.S. mainland, Alaska, Hawaii, Puerto Rico, Canada, and the U.S. Virgin Islands. This type of high-end service is delivered directly from an AT&T serving office or POP using dedicated digital T1 facilities. Enhancements include Split Access Flexible Egress Routing (SAFER) and Alternate Destination Call Redirection (ADCR). An ISDN 800 INFO-2 feature provides ANI and a service monitor gives subscribers comprehensive daily, weekly, or monthly reports on call

activity, detailing call attempts, incompletes, busies, abandons, etc., as well as warning when call rates drop below specified levels.

- An 800 Speech Recognition Service prompts callers to speak a number from one to nine corresponding to menu options. Calls are routed based upon the menu item selected. The 800 Speech Recognition Service gives subscribers call routing flexibility using voice recognition technology.

- Other multimedia 800-number services transmit multimedia messages at 56 Kbps or 64 Kbps. The network determines if a toll-free call requires voice or multimedia service and routes it accordingly. Thus, subscribers continue single-number 800 service, but eliminate separate voice and data networks. A multimedia 800 call uses appropriate connections regardless of the local service provider or long-distance (IXC/IEC) carrier and works with equipment from several vendors. ISDN is used to deliver this multimedia 800-number service, but it is not a prerequisite. Callers with 56-Kbps lines or with an ISDN BRI and a compatible multimedia PC can use the service's simultaneous voice, data, and image functionality. This 800-number service provides remote access to LANs, video teleconferencing, and desktop collaboration. Customers might use multimedia applications to inspect inventory parts, to view a catalog while placing an order, or to watch a presentation containing detailed installation or maintenance instructions.

AT&T service examples were used because they present the full variety of 800-number services and features. With the advent of equal access long distance competition, it is easy for any subscriber business or resident to have simple 800-number service where the 800-number subscriber pays for the call. MCI was giving out private 800 numbers for all its long distance customers. While this depleted the 800-number pool, it was a good business strategy aimed at increasing MCI revenues.

900-NUMBER SERVICES

The 900-number services are services for which the calling party is charged for the call at rates different from those charged for ordinary long-distance calls. Sometimes this is referred to as Calling Party Pays (CPP).

The 900-number services started in 1980 as a mechanism to create profits for information providers. The first major 900-number service application was used during the Jimmy Carter and Ronald Reagan debates. More than one-half million callers used a 900-number over three nights to vote on the debate winner. The 900-number services permit callers to respond to prompts using touch-tone keypads.

900-number services more commonly provide information services such as sports scores, music industry updates, stock quotes, and weather forecasts. A common 900-number service is the personal advertisements in a newspaper. Some companies use 900 numbers for software support—with callers, in effect, paying a per-minute consulting fee.

Some 900-number service subscribers are the more colorful long-distance services such as those targeted at hapless contest winners (they win a larger telephone bill, but no prize), psychic friends (my psychic friend tells me that there is a lot of money in being a psychic friend), and the phone sex lines. Most people remain cautious about using 900 numbers because of these more colorful and sleazy services and the adverse publicity received by 900-number services when these services first began.

The 900-number services are outgrowing their association with novelty services (e.g., phone sex and psychic friends). Today they provide respectable business applications, including retailing and information distribution.

Today's 900-number service applications often turn cost centers into revenue centers. Subscriber callers receive written information through fax-back technology. Callers dial a 900 number and select information that is sent immediately to their fax. TV surveys are routinely performed via 900-number services. Technical support lines for PC products use 900-number services rather than toll-free or local exchange numbers combined with credit card accounts. Depending upon the cost for the user, 900-number services could be less expensive for callers than mail-based or fax-based responses. This greatly depends upon the amount of time and the convenience of using alternatives. Information retrieval over a 900-number service is more easily integrated into corporate databases than is paper-based information retrieval. In the future, any customer service now provided over 800-number services lines could conceivably be provided by a 900-number service.

Provisioning or configuring a 900-number service typically involves two parties: a carrier to handle the transmission and an entertainment or information provider. The information provider is not regulated by the FCC, but is regulated by the Federal Trade Commission with respect to advertising, billing 900-number services, and the message preamble. The carrier that transmits a 900-number call usually handles the billing and collections as well. Because billing and collections are non-regulated, charges for this activity are usually covered by contract. The carrier typically charges both a per-minute fee for the actual transmission of the message plus a share of the gross receipts for handling the billing and collections.

The assignment of 900-number codes is similar in many respects to the assignment and use of 500-number codes discussed above. Not all of the 900-number codes assigned are in use at any particular time. In some cases, a firm that has acquired a 900-number code may not yet have commenced operation. In other cases, firms may have merged or terminated operations and the numbers have not yet been re-assigned.

A current problem with 900-number services is that sometimes unscrupulous operators represent a 900 number as an 800 number. You are given an 800 number to call, and then when the phone is answered, a voice message says that if you stay on the line, you will be transferred to a 900 number, the CCP number. The voice message is required by law for 900 numbers. However, unless you immediately terminate the call, a 900-number charge appears on your bill.

Billing and Tariffs

With telephone services, we receive a bill. Bills represent our cost for those services. We are billed for telephone network access and usage. The bills may reflect metered use or 24/7 full-time use. The bills are computed from telephone tariffs, the regulated, registered, or advertised prices for telephone services.

Tariffs have been complex and confusing for years. This was a natural and intentional outgrowth to telephone industry regulation. When there is a monopoly from which a service can only be purchased, then the only way to price that service is to determine the cost of delivering the service and permit a fair return to investors on their money above the cost for delivering the service. That is great in theory, but stinks in fact. The result is ever-increasing service costs, and little technical innovation in services offered. In a monopoly situation, there is little incentive to behave differently. If I were placed in the same position as the telephone companies, I would do the same thing.

To get a tariff set by a Public Service Commission or Public Utility Commission (PSC or PUC), the telephone company would tell a lie. The bigger the lie, the higher they could set the rate. In most cases, it was impossible for anyone to truly understand how telephone infrastructure costs were allocated accurately among the myriad of telephone network services. For example, what part of my Class 5 CO branch exchange switch cost should be allocated to delivering my 800-number service vs. delivering my dial-up line service? My bet is that no telephone company financial analyst could accurately answer that question. So, any good, logical, plausible story presented by the telephone company that made sense would be used to set the telephone tariff for a specific service. Who could refute such a story if it was logical and plausible?

For example, if I were facing a tariff hearing, I would think up a plausible tariff explanation like my fishing story. Yeah, I went fishing in this pond one time and caught such a big fish that I had to use a tractor to pull it out. When I wanted to weigh the fish, it was so big that none of the scales would work, so I threw it on a semi-truck and drove it into town to weigh it on the truck scales. Unfortunately, it was too big to weigh there, so I just took a picture of the fish and weighed the picture. The picture weighed 50 pounds. Now, could I get a nice high tariff for that whopper?

My point here is that in a regulated industry, pricing is set based upon costs and testimony. There is little incentive to innovate and reduce costs (there is some incentive, but it is not highly compelling). As a result, over the last 30 years, telephone costs have increased to extraordinarily high levels, especially intrastate telephone tariffs. The painful mechanism for correcting these bloated telephone service tariffs is to promote competition, competition made possible by new telecommunications technologies, and competition that results in lower prices and increased business activity. The long-distance market illustrates this with prices dropping more then 70%, but overall revenues spent on long-distance calls increasing.

What this means today is that we are in a transition period between regulation and competition. Some telephone charges will make sense, while others will not. Saving money means examining all alternatives to obtain the most favorable rate for telephone services, even when it means doing something that seems totally illogical, because it seems there is no logic to regulated telephone tariffs.

PUBLIC SERVICE COMMISSIONS

Within states, PSCs or PUCs regulate the telephone companies. Generally, when telephone services traverse state boundaries, they fall under the FCC's jurisdiction. The FCC also sets nationwide policy for telecommunications that state PSCs and PUCs implement. This means that the telephone industry and politics are inseparable. Telephone companies influence the composition of the PSCs and PUCs so that they would get favorable rate treatment.

INTRASTATE VS. INTERSTATE

Consequently, intrastate telephone tariffs are generally higher than interstate telephone tariffs. For example, a telecommunications networking manager at Chemical Bank in New York City remarked to me that it cost more to run a

T-1 channel from lower Manhattan to mid-town Manhattan than it cost to run the same T-1 line from New York City to Chicago. Intrastate and inter-city rates were higher than FCC-mandated interstate rates.

Similarly, telephone channels run from northern California to southern California were often terminated in the knee bend of Nevada. The circuit would be terminated there and not really connected to any equipment. The reason was that the termination in Nevada made the circuit an interstate cir-cuit subject to the lower interstate tariffs, thus saving substantial costs.

Dial-up toll charges are higher for intrastate calls than for interstate calls. Sometimes, 800-number services are not configured for intrastate calls as well. This just epitomizes the differences between interstate and intrastate tariffs and leads back to my previous statement: "Saving money means exam-ining all alternatives to obtain the most favorable rate for telephone services, even when it means doing something that seems totally illogical."

METERED USE

Dial-up contention services are charged for metered use. That means that the LEC runs a stop-watch on our long-distance calling and reports the number of minutes (seconds) we called long distance for each hour (or minute) dur-ing the day. Then our long-distance carrier computes our long-distance charges by applying this usage pattern to our negotiated long-distance rates.

How metered charges are calculated can impact a telephone bill signifi-cantly. Metered charges can be calculated by the full minute, by 30-second intervals, 15-second intervals, 6-second intervals (0.1-minute intervals), or rounded to the nearest second. When a metered rate call is made, are the charges calculated second-by-second (the most desirable), do you pay for the first three minutes and then full minute-by-full minute thereafter (the origi-nal AT&T long-distance rate), or do you pay for 30 seconds and then tenth of a minute (6-second) intervals thereafter? Check your metered charge details, otherwise your metered call bill could be much larger than you expect.

Since the cost per minute has dropped and seems to be a consumer flashpoint, some long-distance carriers offer special calling plans with a fixed monthly fee and a low per minute rate. To account for distances, older dialed or switched services like outbound Wide Area Telephone Service (WATS) used pricing bands, with more distant bands being charged higher prices. Some newer dialed, measured use, and switched services favor a similar mile-age-based, time-of-day/day-of-week-based rate structure. Often discounts are offered for bulk usage and long-term commitments.

Another metered use approach is to charge for data circuits based upon the amount of packets transmitted. In the case of metered billing based upon

$$\text{Air Line Miles} = \sqrt{\frac{(H1\text{-}H2)^2 + (V1\text{-}V2)^2}{10}}$$

Figure 4–11 *Airline mile computation using V and H coordinates.*

packets, full packets cost less than empty packets. A small data load that used lots of packets could cost as much as a heavier load using fewer packets.

LEASED CIRCUIT

Leased line prices have no usage component. Thus, the user has full-time, full-capacity use of the leased channel for the fixed monthly price paid. Leased circuits are charged a fixed rate, often depending upon the distance the circuit spans. Distances used to be measured in airline miles from telephone exchange to telephone exchange. The old FCC published tariff #264 listed Vertical and Horizontal (V and H) coordinates for every telephone exchange in the U.S. V and H coordinates are still listed in a popular telecommunications dictionary under V & H. These coordinates could be plugged into the formula shown in Figure 4-11.

Today the FCC provides a searchable database of longitude and latitude references for U.S. communities. They are found at:

http://www.fcc.gov/mmb/asd/bickel/atlas2.html

These can be used to compute airline miles between two sites. Precise circuit costs are best obtained from the telephone company or service provider.

SLAMMING AND TARIFF SCAMS

Equal access produced some high-powered sales activities and the practice of slamming. Slamming is changing a subscriber's primary long-distance carrier without their knowledge or authorization. I have been slammed more than once.

SLAMMING • The last time I was slammed, I got a phone call from someone that sounded like they were the billing service for my LEC. They said that all my local and long-distance calling charges could come on a single bill from the LEC. All they needed to do this was to get my numbers straight. So they asked for the numbers that I have. I have about 10 phone lines (because I am a nerd). Once they had the numbers, I was then asked to verify this conversation with a supervisor. I responded OK, only to be switched to a supervisor that said all my long-distance calls would now be handled by a new carrier at

$0.25 per minute. My response was NO! Stop right there! Cancel everything! I am happy exactly where I am! So they stopped, or so it seemed.

About three months later, I got a long-distance phone bill for about $1,000. This was three times my normal long-distance bill. When I investigated, I found that the one line on which most of my long-distance calls were placed had been switched to a new long-distance carrier at $0.25 per minute. This was up from the $0.075 per minute that I was normally charged. Yup, illegally slammed. After some nasty words with the LEC, I found out that these people that called were not what they represented. They were not associated with the LEC, they were not associated with the LEC billing service, but they could get the LEC billing service to switch the billing on the one phone line on which all my long-distance calls were made over to them.

With all this said, this could have been easily avoided by requesting them to fax me a description of the deal in detail, on letterhead, with their signature. That should be an irrefutable policy for any and every telephone solicitation. Anyone that has a legitimate offer would surely be able to do that, and anyone who is a crook would not.

OTHER ILLICIT TELEPHONE SCAMS • There are other illicit telephone scams in addition to the more traditional slamming. Some of the more effective ones have a person representing themselves as the telephone company or a credit card company. They seek telephone number information, telephone switch trunk access, or credit card information.

At a large company, the front desk guards intercepted all the night-time telephone requests to place long-distance calls using the internal PBX and long-distance services paid for by the company. For about a week, the Executive Vice President of Marketing was requesting regularly every night to use an outgoing trunk line from the internal PBX to make long-distance calls because he was "negotiating an important multi-million dollar deal." This particular Vice President was someone using one of the AT&T blue calling card telephones in New York City. They dialed 800-numbers from the calling card phone (no change is required). When an 800 number was answered automatically by a telephone PBX, they then dialed the outside trunk access code for Lucent or Northern Telecomm switches. The front desk guards at the large company who intercepted this night-time call posed as the Executive Vice President of Marketing to get access to the long-distance trunk line. Once they got the trunk line, all their calls to relatives in South and Central America were made for free. The telephone bill for this million dollar deal was around $30,000. Paying close attention to telephone bills can save a lot of money.

Another scam is similar, but aimed at residential subscribers. An AT&T service technician calls to conduct a test on telephone lines. They state that to complete the test, you need to dial nine (9), zero (0), the pound sign (#), and then hang up. The 90# number on some telephone branch exchange switches may transfer the incoming caller to an outgoing trunk circuit, thus enabling them to make long-distance calls. This did not work with my LEC.

I checked this out on the Internet, searching for telephone scams. The FCC site had it listed as a telephone scam, but only for businesses. It appears that only users of certain types of telephone switching equipment (PBXs to be exact) are vulnerable to this scam. Furthermore, the PBX must be improperly configured to be vulnerable. The vast majority of telephones, including residential telephones, are not affected by this scam.

To avoid such scams, all that any employee needs to do is ask for a call-back number or for the name and number of the caller's supervisor. Then they should hang up.

TARIFF SUMMARY

Today, some pricing more reflects the demand for the service rather than pricing based upon old cost justification procedures. Demand-based pricing is pricing with a single rate ($.17 per minute, regardless of distance called) for anywhere in the U.S. These rates are sometimes referred to as postalized rates because they provide a flat rate for calls anywhere in the U.S. Similarly, for the price of a first-class stamp, you can send a letter anywhere in the U.S. (This is not true for packages where postal rates vary with distance.) The increased telephone service competition pushes telephone service vendors from "car sales" pricing (where you can never really know the true price you are paying) to the easier to understand demand-based pricing.

We have presented some general explanations of telephone service pricing here. However, whenever you are selecting communications services, you must determine the exact pricing for comparative services carrying your communications load. The old billing for channel mileage is fast disappearing in favor of flat network access charges and metered traffic charges.

Brain Teaser

Long-Distance Costs

Get calling plan information from some long-distance companies using their Web sites. I am going to compare two published plans. The plans are:

A 5¢ plan. This plan provides direct dialed state-to-state long-distance calls from home at just 5¢ a minute, all day, every day. You get this great long-distance rate for a monthly cost of $8.95 plus 5¢ a minute.

A 7¢ plan. This plan provides the same direct dialed state-to-state long-distance calls from home at just 7¢ a minute, all day, every day for a monthly fee of just $4.95.

1. How many minutes a month would you need to talk on the phone to make the 5¢ plan better than the 7¢ plan? My computation shows 200 minutes, or about 3.33 hours.

2. What is the cost of a telephone call if you only talk two hours on the 5¢ plan? I am calculating about 12.5¢ a minute.

3. What is the cost of a telephone call if you only talk two hours on the 7¢ plan? I am calculating about 11.12¢ a minute.

4. How much use would be required to get the calls down to 8¢ a minute? I am calculating 495 minutes (8.25 hours) at a total cost of $39.60 for the 7¢ plan. For the 5¢ plan, it appears that only 299 minutes and $23.90 are needed.

The goal here is to understand current long-distance pricing. These long-distance plans sound great until compared to an 8¢ plan with no fixed fees when you consider that to save money, you would need to talk from five to eight hours every month to just get the rate down to 8¢ a minute. Try comparing long-distance plans from other companies to see how they compare, but make sure you add in all possible fees, not just per minute charges.

Private Branch Exchanges and CENTREX

There are two approaches for providing telephones and telephone services in large facilities. The facility can purchase their own telephone switch or PBX, or they can purchase Central Office Exchange (CENTREX) services from a local telephone company.

In general, a PBX is a box with flashing lights that works behind the scenes to originate and terminate calls from telephones at the desk. Usually, the more flashing lights, the better. PBXs and CENTREX are the classic phone systems solutions for the office. When you buy a PBX, the drawback is usually that you bought a proprietary phone system that only works with components and software produced by that switch manufacturer. If a telephone breaks, a replacement is not found at the local electronics store. Replacement phones are purchased from the original manufacturer at a premium price. However, a PBX system is maintained internally and can be changed at any time.

In contrast, CENTREX is leasing or renting a phone system from a LEC or telephone service provider. The end-user does not see any major differences between a PBX and CENTREX. They still use a telephone to make calls, but they might need to dial some added digits.

The latest PBX and CENTREX competitor is the UNPBX. It's a PBX, but not a classic PBX. VoIP telephony and LAN server-based PBX systems can replace traditional PBX and CENTREX systems. Such UNPBX systems are based on less proprietary PC technology. They cost less than a classic PBX. However, UNPBXs may not be as reliable as traditional PBX and CENTREX systems. However, reliability of UNPBX systems can be made to rival the reliability of both PBX and CENTREX systems.

Traditional PBXs act as a telephone switch. They switch incoming calls from trunks to phone lines, route outgoing calls to the appropriate trunk lines, provide intercom and voice mail services, and more.

An offshoot of these PBXs is the Automatic Call Directors (ACDs). An ACD combines intelligence with call switching to route calls to specific phones based upon caller menu selection, caller area code, etc.

PBXs became more prevalent in the 1990s because of physical size and cost reductions. They are now multi-function systems that provide organizations with more than voice switching capabilities. With the integration of computers and digital technology, PBXs can now support voice communications, wireless/cordless communications, messaging, facsimile, video conferencing, and multimedia applications. PBXs are sometimes referred to as PABXs (Private Automatic Branch Exchanges) and EPABXs (Electronic Private Automatic Branch Exchanges). All PBXs have similar components. Knowledge of general PBX architecture can be helpful when it comes time to evaluate a particular PBX. Common components include the control system, trunk adapters, line adapters, user stations, and switching subsystems. At one time, PBXs were physically very large systems and very expensive systems.

Today's PBXs are small and efficient, often occupying only a small room or part of a room. Further, their cost has dropped substantially, so they are affordable by a small business. I saw one not so long ago in the checkout line at Staples while I was purchasing file folders. A display said pick up your own PBX today for $895. It worked with analog phones and was easy to install.

A typical PBX configuration is shown in Figure 4-12.

PBX Evolution

The PBX evolution followed that of CO switches. Early PBX systems were analog switching systems that switched voice lines. They evolved to computer-controlled switches, to analog phone to T-1 trunk, to digital phone to T-1 trunk, and finally to switches that could handle analog phones, T-1 trunks, digital phones, ISDN trunks, and ISDN phones. See Figure 4-13 for

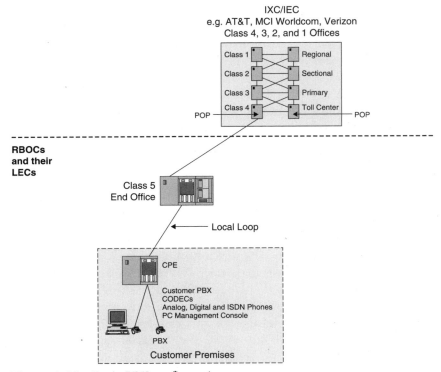

Figure 4–12 *Basic PBX configuration.*

Private Branch Exchange Evolution

Analog Phone to Analog Trunk - Cross Bar Switching
Analog Phone to Analog Trunk - Computer Controlled
Analog Phone to T-1 Trunk
Digital Phone to T-1 Trunk
Digital Phone to ISDN Trunk
ISDN Phone to ISDN Trunk

Figure 4–13 *PBX evolution.*

the more detailed steps. Originally, PBXs consisted of large crossbar switching complexes. Their size alone made them impractical for small offices.

Newer PBX systems are virtually all-digital systems. Digital switching using computer and semiconductor components have greatly reduced the physical size of PBXs. Our office has a digital hybrid key system (a small digital PBX). It connects about 13 user terminals (phones), two fax machines, the front doorbell, a Pentium PC, and 10 trunk lines through the digital

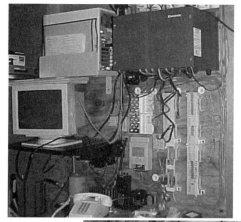

Figure 4–14 *Small PBX installation.*

switch. The unit is expandable to 250 user terminals. This hybrid PBX fits into about six cubic feet. Though physically small, it handles all phone traffic, and simultaneous voice and data communications, while providing us with voice mail. Figure 4-14 shows our PBX.

On the bottom right of the small PBX in Figure 4-14, we can see the PBX cards in the gray cabinet exposed. On the right is the CPU card with all the lights. Next to it is the memory card. This card contains the PBX software that is written into Read Only Memory (ROM) chips. Then there are a couple of Loop Start Cards (LSCs) terminating our analog voice-grade channel trunks into the telephone company CO. Next are Digital Line Cards (DLCs) that connect to the digital phones throughout the facility. The left-most component is the power supply powering the switch. In the top left part of the figure, you can see the PC next to the PBX that provides the voice mail service for our company.

Today, most PBXs perform digital switching. These digital PBXs are all computer-controlled. That means that all system control is provided by the equivalent of a PC.

A PC-like CPU card installed in the chassis provides system control of our PBX. The CPU, in addition to making all the internal PBX switching connections, is responsible for testing all PBX components, collecting data for analysis, allocating resources for calls, maintaining these allocations during the entire call, and releasing them upon call termination. As you can imagine, the CPU is the heart and brains of a PBX. Today, small PBX systems use the same RISC CPUs as the larger CO switching systems. PBX operation can be tailored to a specific organization's needs. Features implemented by new PBX software are easily added, like ARS (Automatic Route Selection) or the more sophisticated Least Cost Routing (LCR).

To provide uninterrupted service, protective measures must be used to keep your PBX running. For example, all PBXs need a UPS on the system. What happens to your ability to call for help during a power outage without a UPS attached to your PBX? Bad things, you can be sure.

TRADITIONAL PBX

Figure 4-15 shows a generalized structure of a computer-controlled PBX. There are adapter cards for trunks and lines. The trunk cards connect to the telephone company and the line cards connect to subscriber telephones. A central computer controls switching and performs advanced functions like ARS or the more sophisticated LCR. There are typically separate voice and control buses in the PBX.

COMMON VOICE FEATURES

Common voice call processing features are Direct-Inward Dialing (DID), automated attendant, and voice mail. Other features include voice mail messaging, voice response, voice recognition, and related applications. Interactive Voice Response (IVR), audio text, and voice mail are key features in new PBXs.

Normally when a PBX is called, an attendant answers and then routes the call to the requested individual's phone. Other PBXs send incoming calls to several phones, regardless of dialing information. This permits anyone to answer the incoming call. Our PBX is programmed to operate this way.

DIRECT-INWARD DIALING • DID routes callers to individual internal phone extensions attached to the PBX based upon the number they dial. In this manner, every phone looks as though it is a private phone and no phone sys-

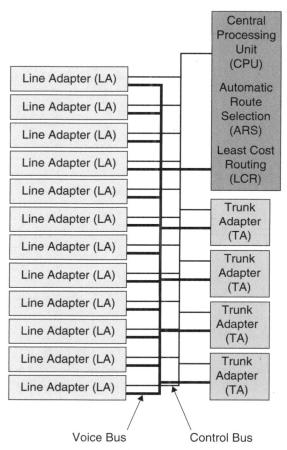

Figure 4–15 *General PBX architecture.*

tem attendants are required. When a call is unanswered, the calling party is routed to the voice mailbox of the user assigned that extension. Callers are also given an option to talk with an attendant in the event immediate attention is needed.

AUTOMATED ATTENDANT • In contrast to PBX systems that send calls to a PBX operator or attendant, an automated attendant has the caller select from a list of services or options through a voice menu. One option is to dial the extension of the party they are calling. Other options direct them to hunt for groups or special services like customer support, sales, etc.

When you're sick and tired of listening to an automated attendant, just mash the "0" key on the telephone keypad. Mashing the "0" key on many PBX systems sends you to a live human operator. However, I recently mashed the "0" key and the PBX struck back by requiring me to listen to the entire message over again, plus a reading of *War and Peace*. Whoever programmed that automated attendant feature was wise to our tricks.

VOICE MAIL • Voice mail systems provide voice mail for inbound calls as a basic personal telephone answering service. When an extension is called but not answered within a specified number of rings (like three or four rings), the caller is switched to a mailbox in the voice mail system. When they leave a message, the phone extension called enables a visible indicator that a new voicemail has been received.

Voice mail is a pain because today we have to check it, email, faxes, cell phone voice mail, and desk phone voice mail. Technology called unified messaging promises to solve this hassle and simplify our lives. With unified messaging, Microsoft Outlook or Lotus Scheduler can display all your email, faxes, cell phone voice mail, and desk phone voice mail. A PC can play back voice mail without using the phone.

VOICE MAIL MESSAGING • Voice mail messaging is the ability to distribute voice mail to other telephone subscribers. Major voice mail systems can provide a class-of-service mailbox feature that distributes incoming messages among several mailboxes, similar to an ACD.

In this case, personal voice mailboxes may back up Telephone Service Representative (TSR) personal extensions when the caller is directed to a specific, unavailable TSR.

Callback messaging provided by ACD systems delivers voice messages from callers as incoming call assignments automatically when call traffic is slow or on demand by a TSR.

PC-based voice mail uses both Microsoft's messaging standard, MAPI (Messaging API), and the computer telephony standard, TAPI (Telephony API), supported by Windows 95/98/ME and Windows NT/2000. The software requires an inexpensive voice card or a modem with voice capability to turn a standard server into a robust voice mail system that can connect directly to a PBX or voice telephone network. It runs on a general office LAN instead of a proprietary system. An open and scalable architecture allows for easy integration with other computer messaging technologies such as facsimile, email, and groupware systems such as Microsoft Exchange and Lotus Notes, as well as internet-based email.

Other PC-based voice mail features include enhanced message notification and priority delivery; increased storage capacities with decreasing hardware prices; support for Application Program Interfaces (APIs) for access among different vendors' products; desktop PC access to voice, electronic, and fax messages; TDD (Telecommunications Device for the Deaf) facilities for hearing-impaired telephone messaging; AMIS (Audio Messaging Interchange Specification) analog networking capability; combined voice messaging, interactive voice response, and fax platforms; voice recognition interfaces; LAN connectivity using multiple clients and application servers; and cellular phone voice messaging for missed call coverage and voice mail.

Our PC-based voice mail runs on Operating System 2 (OS 2, or what I call Operating Stupidity 2 because it never really sold). It is a simple system lacking the advanced features identified here.

INTERACTIVE VOICE RESPONSE • IVR accepts input from either a telephone keypad or the caller's voice and uses that input to send back synthesized voice or pre-recorded messages offering callers choices on how they can complete their call. This is often just information in response to a query or a menu service provided by PBX systems. An IVR PBX would answer a phone call and prompt the caller to respond to its menu selections by pushing buttons on a touch-tone phone. An example would be telephone banking. This is a key component to Computer Telephony Integration, or CTI.

HUNT GROUPS • A hunt group is a group of lines that share the same phone number. When a call comes in using the assigned phone number, the PBX hunts for an available line in the group. The first available line in the group is rung. When the call is answered, that line becomes busy and is not used to answer subsequent calls to the hunt group's phone number. Once the phone is hung up again, it is returned to the hunt group pool of lines to service subsequent calls. Hunt groups are used for special calls like technical support or service calls, sales department calls, or shipping status calls.

PICKUP GROUPS • A pickup group is similar to a hunt group. Several lines share the same phone number for both the pickup group and the hunt group. When a call comes in using the assigned phone number, the PBX rings all lines in the pickup group so any phone in the group can answer the phone. The first phone answering the call becomes busy and is not used to answer subsequent calls to the pickup group's phone number. Once the phone is hung up again, it is returned to the pickup group to service new calls. Like hunt groups, pickup groups are used for special calls like technical support or service calls, sales department calls, or shipping status calls.

A fun thing to do on April Fools Day, is to program your PBX to turn off its dial tone. Some phone systems support this. Without dial tone, people think that a phone is broken, but the phone still works. Time how long it takes them to figure out that the dial tone is turned off. This is an easy April Fools joke because humans expect dial tone when using the phone. However, the PBX doesn't need dial tone.

OTHER PBX FEATURES

Some other features offered with PBX systems include cordless telephone handsets, video conferencing support, and connections to pagers.

CORDLESS CONNECTIONS • Cordless or wireless PBXs (CPBXs) often implement wireless phones as add-ons to existing PBX products. Wireless handsets enable users to be mobile around a facility while having access to the PBX and the features of wired telephones.

One wireless PBX product is targeted at small businesses. It is a full-featured PBX supporting generally under 20 handsets. It allows every user to work from anywhere in the home or office, and yet remain completely accessible for important calls from outside or within. Unlike other cordless products, you can take a business call in your office while someone else takes another call just outside the office or while two other users talk from their desks between offices. The wireless small-office PBX supports all the tasks a small office or busy home demands from a desk station and mobile handsets. The handsets use their LCD screens to provide caller ID and caller ID on call waiting, speed dial/redial, call restrictions, handset paging, room monitoring, a remotely accessible digital answering machine that answers separately for each line, a smart fax/modem port, and more.

VIDEO CONFERENCING SUPPORT • Video conferencing allowing different locations to communicate using real-time audio and video is still at the leading edge of PBX applications. Its growth is being driven by the availability of inexpensive desktop PC video conferencing systems. These inexpensive systems use BRI ISDN links. Other larger PBXs support the switching of H0 channels over ISDN PRIs, facilitating full-motion video connections between video conferencing sites.

PAGER CONNECTIONS • PBXs can now route DID calls to pagers, cell phones, voice mail, or other destinations when a person is not at their phone. Most of these new routing capabilities use basic PBX switching functionality and externally attached systems perform the additional pager, cell phone, or voice mail functions.

FAX CONNECTIONS • Calls for specific printed information can be routed to facsimile servers for processing. Through IVR menu selection, callers can request to fax specific documents directly to a fax number specified by them. This feature is often used by technical support organizations to deliver documentation and other information to customers and service personnel.

PBX Architecture and Operation

Refer to Figure 4-16 while we discuss PBX architecture and operation. The operation of the PBX is controlled by the CPU, which is one laid-back, cool dude. Dissimilarly, the line adapters are really hyper individuals that just jump the gun at every event. So if we make an internal extension-to-extension intercom call, the PBX would process the call in this manner: We would pick up our telephone extension handset. This would send a packet of data into the line adapter signaling off-hook. Well, the line adapter is now beside itself and does not know what to do (the intelligence is in the CPU). It runs in circles, muttering, "What should I do now; what can I do now?" Soon it figures out that it should talk to the CPU about what happened. No, there is no psychic thinking here on the part of the line adapter, because the only PBX component it can talk to is the CPU. So it sends a message across the data bus to the CPU saying, "Someone took the handset off-hook; what do I do, what can I do, what should I do?" The CPU responds saying, "Just chill out! Did they dial a number? Look for numeric keypad input!" The line card replies, "OK," and proceeds to look for keypad input.

When the extension number is dialed, the line card gets a packet of data from the telephone. Again, the line adapter is exasperated and does not know what to do next, so it runs in circles muttering, "What should I do now; what can I do now?" Soon it thinks of asking the CPU what to do again, and passes the extension number across the control bus to the CPU in the message. "I got an extension number; now what do I do, what can I do, what should I do?" The CPU responds, "Chill out, dude! I will handle things from here, no sweat!" The line card replies, "OK."

Now the CPU sends a command across the control bus to the line card servicing the extension dialed. It says to the line card, "Another extension dialed your extension number." But before the CPU can say another word, the line card replies, "What do I do, what can I do, what should I do?" The CPU responds, "Just chill out! Ring the telephone extension. Now look to see if the phone is answered." The line card replies, "OK," and proceeds to ring the extension phone and look for the handset going off-hook.

After two rings, the phone is answered. Now the line card passes a message to the CPU across the control bus stating, "Someone answered the phone; now what do I do, what can I do, what should I do?" The CPU responds, "Chill out! I will now complete the call!" The line card replies, "OK." The CPU then proceeds to assign a 64-Kbps time slot on the voice bus to each line card, completing the circuit connection between the extensions

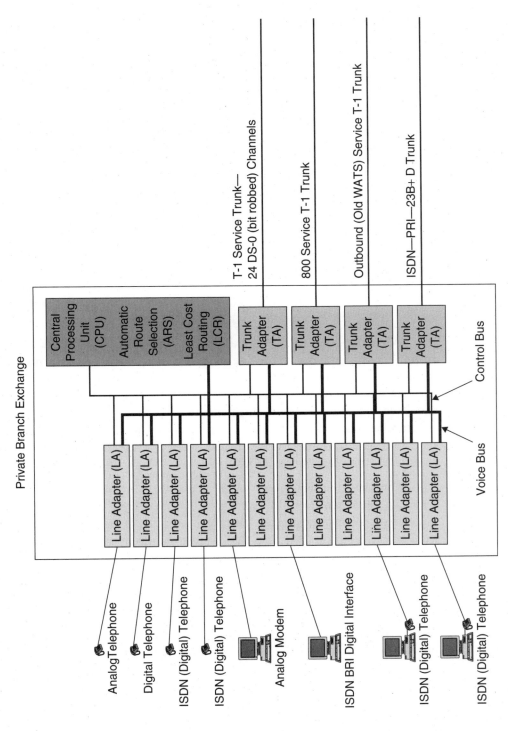

Figure 4–16 *Traditional PBX connectivity.*

and permitting voice to travel from the handset of one extension to the handset of the other extension.

A similar procedure is followed when the call is complete and the connection needs to be broken down so the voice bus time slot can be reused to service other calls.

The point of my little scenario here is to illustrate the interaction of the line cards, the trunk cards (they behave just like line cards – actually line cards and trunk cards are sometimes interchangeable), the control bus, the voice bus, and the CPU. Whenever a switch handles any outgoing or incoming call, it performs similar procedures and may use much more sophisticated stored program logic to route the call from a trunk card to a line card, or vice versa.

Often, the PBX software runs on a version of the UNIX operating system. The reason for this is that UNIX was developed by Bell Labs. That weird software running on your PBX is probably a version of UNIX. The software is a special application that performs telephone switching, voice mail, and other voice telephone operating and management functions.

LINE CARDS

There are several types of line cards. Analog line cards handle analog telephones and analog trunk lines. They may be ground-start or loop-start. Ground-start cards are the less sophisticated cards that route the telephone line voltages to earth ground. Loop-start cards loop the signal back to the other end of the connection. This provides better analog signaling (circuit control).

Digital line cards interface to digital phones. They may use RJ-11 jacks and CAT-5 twisted pair wiring (there is more information on CAT-5 wiring in Chapter 6.) Signaling and voice information travel as digital signals between the telephone extension and the switch. Some digital phones may conform to ISDN standards. In this instance, the line card would need to support ISDN B and ISDN D channel multiplexing and ISDN signaling handshakes.

Analog line cards can interface to fax machines, analog telephone trunks, special input devices (e.g., front door ringers), and more to provide enhanced PBX features. The device it is connected to and the software program in the PBX switch determine the ultimate function of an analog line card.

TRUNK CARDS

A wide range of digital communications trunks is available from local telephone companies. These high-speed trunks provide high-quality voice and data transfer to and from local telephone company CO switches. PBXs use different trunk cards to connect to these high-speed communications trunks. The physical trunk adapter may be the same for different trunk interfaces. The only difference between one card and another is the PBX software controlling the card.

T-1 TRUNK CARDS • T-1 trunks are the traditional bulk trunk interface between the PBX and the telephone company CO. T-1 trunks are just digital pipes. T-1 trunks are digital communications links composed of 24 multiplexed DS-0 64-Kbps channels. The aggregate digital rate of a T-1 trunk is 1.544 Mbps. T-1 trunks carry any signal or data that is converted into digital form. When a T-1 trunk is in a private point-to-point system, no special signaling or switching occurs because the PBXs at each end of the private system are typically from the same manufacturer. If the T-1 trunk is going through an IXC/IEC, control, switching, and diagnostic equipment can corrupt T-1 communication. The T-1 trunk must match carrier control, switching, and diagnostic signaling to prevent corruption.

A T-1 trunk carries command and control data, analog voice, and video conferencing information. Individual DS-0 channels are interchanged while transmitting T-1 traffic from one location to another. A private T-1 line can interconnect two PBX systems.

Individual T-1 channels can also be used to connect data terminals and LANs. With the appropriate multiplexers, T-1 trunks can be subdivided into individual DS-0 channels, which can be connected to the PBX and to data transmission equipment and LAN routers. The T-1 multiplexer can be separate from the PBX, or it may be incorporated into the PBX. The DS-0 channel data multiplexer is usually a separate network component. T-1 multiplexers that "front-end" a PBX are sometimes called bandwidth managers.

A T-1 trunk card may have a physical twisted pair or fiber optic interface. It can handle inbound, outbound, 800-number, or other calls. The software assigned to the card would be different for trunk cards handling 800-number inbound calls and trunk cards handling outbound calls.

ISDN PRI TRUNKS • ISDN trunks differ from T-1 trunks in that they provide a separate path, the 64-Kbps D channel, for signaling information. ISDN is still just a digital pipe, but it is more intelligent than a T-1 digital pipe. ISDN cards also have a different physical layer interface from that of T-1 cards.

ISDN offers simultaneous data, voice, and video connections as well as remote telemetry.

ISDN PRI lines are 23B+D. They provide 23 64-Kbps clear B channels and 1 64-Kbps D channel. ISDN uses common channel signaling facilities and packet mode data transmission to process call signaling information (e.g., call establishment and supervisory operations). PBXs supporting ISDN interfaces must understand D channel packet mode transmission, common channel signaling message formats, etc. When they do, they can more effectively interact with the SS-7 telephone company signaling network and as a result provide more sophisticated call processing features and functions.

At one time, WATS and 800-number services provided reduced call rates for large calling areas. Today, telephone tariffs are time-dependent and flat rate (postalized) for both outgoing and incoming 800-number service. PBX systems are programmed to use these lines depending upon time of day or depending upon the number dialed. Several simultaneous incoming calls can be rolled over to other trunks supporting multiple calls to a single number. Our 800 number can roll incoming calls over three trunks. The call rollover feature is provided by the telephone company but supported by our PBX. The key feature here is providing for outgoing calls in the ARS, or least-cost routing.

800-NUMBER TRUNKS • The 800-number service trunks are often assigned to special functions like sales, order processing, and customer service. The calls coming in on these trunks require special handling and routing to PBX hunt and pickup groups of extensions. They must support Direct Number Identification Service (DNIS) which routes calls to hunt groups depending upon the specific 800-number dialed, e.g., sales is 800 800-8001, order processing is 800 800-8002, and customer service is 800-800-8003. The software assigned to some T-1 and ISDN PRI trunks performs Automatic Number Identification (ANI). The calling number identified is used to route the call to an appropriate telephone service person (sales, order processing, or customer service) and to provide them with a screen of the account information for the person calling. The screen of information is produced by the switch sending a message containing the ANI telephone number to a computer that retrieves the account information and then directs it to the screen of the operator whose phone is ringing. This is the functionality of an ACD system. Generalized PBX systems have this capability, but heavy-volume order entry or customer support sites generally use a special industrial-strength ACD system.

ANALOG TRUNKS • Analog trunks are ordinary 2-wire, or they may be 4-wire circuits connecting to a telephone company CO switch. In this case, the telephone company CO switch is unaware that it is talking to a PBX. It treats every trunk line like an analog phone. The PBX can implement special functions for the analog lines like music on hold and ARS. The PBX can be programmed to provide hunt groups, fax on demand, fax machine support, pick groups (or pickup groups), and other call processing features for the analog trunk lines.

CPU

PBXs have ARS or LCR features for outgoing calls. Different programs installed on the PBX's CPU do this call handling.

AUTOMATIC ROUTE SELECTION • ARS routes using a lookup table that lists the attached trunks identified by their exchange numbers (e.g., 301-596, 410-988, 410-531). ARS is the least sophisticated routing technique provided by PBXs. Tables stored in the PBX CPU's memory based upon which telephone exchanges connect toll-free to which trunk lines provide the data used by the PBX to automatically select the trunk line over which to place an outgoing call. A limit to routing sophistication sometimes depends on the amount of RAM (Random Access Memory) or data storage available to the controlling CPU.

LEAST COST ROUTING • LCR uses the cost of making a call over a specific trunk to route calls. Cost is a simple ranking of available trunk lines, or a more sophisticated algorithm that incorporates IXC/IEC tariffs and time-of-day information. For example, the LCR algorithm determines that a call is a long-distance (toll) call and attempts to route it over the cheapest IXC/IEC trunk line to save money. A sophisticated LCR switch may use tariffs for several IXCs/IECs. When all trunk lines are busy, the LCR algorithm queues the call or routes it over alternate facilities. LCR algorithms often incorporate day of week and time of day in their route selection decisions.

COST CONTROL AND REPORTING • Cost control and reporting are primarily performed by call accounting and cost allocation tele-management functions. These are now basic features that can be provided with any PBX. PBXs provide the capability to manage these functions by linking with PCs and Structured Query Language (SQL) database systems. Data from the PBX is then analyzed using SQL applications to monitor and allocate telephony costs. These tele-management functions can be performed from any authorized PC on an enterprise network.

AUTOMATIC CALL DIRECTORS – AUTOMATIC CALL DISTRIBUTION • ACDs support call centers and other types of customer information services. A call center processes incoming telephone calls to support business activities and provide customers information. Call centers improve business operation by supporting and managing telephone contact with customers. Call centers increase staff productivity and thus lower service costs. A call center can operate as a simple hunt group or it may use the sophisticated call queuing and distribution capabilities of an ACD.

Key elements for all call centers are:

- A sophisticated ACD providing call statistics and management analysis.
- Calling party ID use.
- Up-to-date customer databases.
- Computer Telephony Integration (CTI).
- Voice processing technologies.

The most cost-effective means of streamlining call centers use ACDs and voice processing. ACDs fall into several categories: standalone, PBX integrated, CO-based, network-based, PC-based, and third-party. PC-based ACDs and service bureaus are very attractive for businesses with varied needs because they inexpensively support efficient customer service. As we briefly discussed earlier, ANI and DNIS are used to match callers with services in ACDs or PBXs.

DIALED NUMBER IDENTIFICATION SERVICE • DNIS passes the specific number called from a trunk of 800 numbers to the PBX or ACD. If 800 800-8001 were dialed from 410 988-9294, DNIS would pass the exact 800 number called, 800 800-8001, to the PBX or ADC. When 800 800-8002 is called, that number, 800 800-8002, is passed to the PBX or ADC. The switch uses the number called to route the call to specific hunt groups of telephone extensions. In this manner, 800 800-8001 would be the telephone extensions of the sales department, 800 800-8002 the order processing staff telephone extensions, and so forth as we described previously.

AUTOMATIC NUMBER IDENTIFICATION • ANI permits PBXs and ACDs to identify the specific number of the calling phone. When a person dials from 410 988-9294, AIN provides that phone number (410 988-9294) to the ACD or PBX. The PBX then uses that phone number to form a database query message to pull up the account information associated with that customer on a SQL or other database system. When the information is retrieved, it is routed to the terminal screen of the next customer service agent. The PBX sends the terminal ID of the agent whose phone is ringing to the database system so that the database system sends the customer account data retrieved to the appropriate terminal device. It is similar to caller ID, but ANI cannot be blocked. ANI was originally used for telephone company billing functions.

TELE-MANAGEMENT FEATURES • Call management, or tele-management, helps manage equipment inventory, the cable and wire plant, work orders, and network problems. PBX tele-management applications encompass many functions from call accounting to traffic engineering. Users are able to install tele-management software in mainframes, mid-range SQL servers, or PCs. Vendors can provide comprehensive systems using PC, PC-LAN, and client/server platforms. Some vendors offer more limited PC tele-management systems at lower costs. Requirements for real-time network management capabilities also drive this market. Traditional tele-management software fits the following categories:

- Call accounting.
- Cost allocation.
- Telephone asset inventory.
- Spares, supplies, and expendables inventory management.
- Cable and wire plant management.
- Traffic analysis, network design, and network optimization.
- Telephone directory management.
- Installation/Modification/Upgrade work order reporting.
- Problem reporting/resolution management.
- Telephone network security.

Tele-management systems must soon integrate voice, data, and video systems with network management capabilities.

COMPUTER TELEPHONY INTEGRATION

CTI covers automating a spectrum of call processing activities by combining external computer processing with the real-time call controls of PBXs. For example, Novell provides telephony services for NetWare.

One form of CTI is merging a computerized database with a phone system. CTI is a very cost-effective solution for call centers. Using this database, CTI customer calls that have to be answered by a live representative can be reduced. CTI can track live, up-to-date customer information to increase efficiency and to more effectively support customers.

Jason's favorite example using CTI is a local pizza chain. The first time Jason called for a pizza, the pizza person picked up the phone and said, "Is this the Moulton residence?" Jason said, "Why, yes it is." Next they asked, "Who am I speaking to?" Jason replied "Jason Moulton." Then they asked, "What would you like to order?" Jason replied, "One large pizza with vegetables and four liters of Mountain Dew. Please deliver the order." They replied, "Thank you." Jason quickly queried, "Could I pay for that with my credit card?" They replied, "Okay!" The pizza then showed up in twenty minutes.

The second time Jason called, they said, "Is this Jason Moulton?" Jason replied, "Yes." They then asked, "Would you like your regular order of one large pizza with vegetables and four liters of Mountain Dew delivered and charged to your credit card?" Jason said, "Yes." Then the pizza showed up again in twenty minutes. Amazing!

Jason knew something was going on. So he visited the pizza place and found that they had a caller ID box next to a computer. Each time someone called, they typed the telephone number into the computer and saw who it was. If they had ordered before, that information was stored in the computer and displayed. They were using an inexpensive version of CTI.

The third time Jason called the pizza place, as soon as they picked up the phone, he said, "Food," and hung up. They then called Jason back and he said, "Food," and hung up again. They called again and Jason said, "This is Jason Moulton and I want food." They said, "Okay." The pizza was delivered with 4 liters of Mountain Dew in twenty minutes.

Novell provides telephony services for NetWare consisting of a Telephony Server NetWare Loadable Module (NLM) linking a PBX, a NetWare server, and a set of client/server APIs. Developers are using the NLM and APIs to create applications that access and control PBXs from PCs attached to NetWare LANs. The Novell/AT&T Telephony Services API (TSAPI) is the standard language of communications used between the PBX and NetWare Server APIs.

In other cases, a CTI-enabled PC may act as a PBX. This requires adding telephone boards and special software to the PC. The prime benefit here is that you have a fully functional PBX based upon cheap PC technologies. It would be possible to replace my PBX today with a CTI-enabled PC at around one-half the cost of my PBX. The PC would perform voice mail, call routing, and other PBX functions (see Figure 4-17).

Other CTI configurations aimed at different functions are possible as well.

ELECTRONIC TELEPHONE DIRECTORY • In the case of the Novell CTI configuration above, it could be used to implement an electronic telephone directory. The simplest implementation would have an administrator continually enter the telephone extensions into a SQL database that was resident upon the NetWare server. The database could be updated daily or more frequently, depending upon changes in telephone extension assignments. All PCs in the facility could retrieve data from the telephone directory database. The tele-

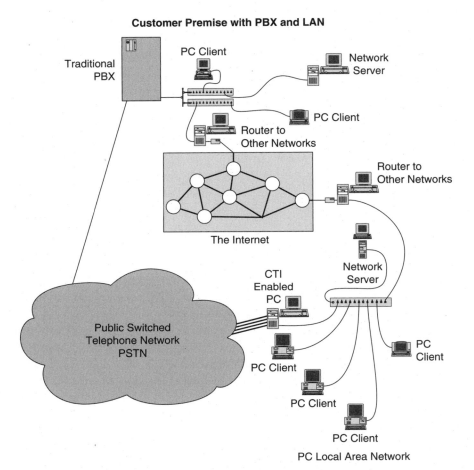

Figure 4–17 *CTI-enabled PC.*

phone switch would need a special software module that supported Novell's TSAPI. AT&T PBX switches have this software support. The PBX would also need to be connected to the facility LAN. The NetWare server would need to have NetWare's TELEPHONY.NLM installed. The TELEPHONY.NLM is a software program that runs on NetWare servers and provides the ability to communicate with TSAPI-enabled PBXs.

Now comes the fun part. When one person in the facility wanted to call another person at an extension in the facility, they could access the telephone directory database and search for the person's name, their title, picture, or whatever. Once the directory entry for that person was located, the caller could double-click on the entry. Now the server springs into action, and using the TELEPHONY.NLM and TSAPI, it sends commands to the PBX that cause both the calling telephone extension and the called telephone extension to ring simultaneously. Sophisticated CTI directory features could provide a screen for the called party, email messaging in the event of no answer, and more. The CTI configuration supporting an electronic telephone directory is shown in the top right of Figure 4-18.

SERVER-BASED PBX • A server-based PBX is a network server (a PC on steroids) that has special telephone interface boards and software installed. The telephony interface boards connect the server to analog telephone trunk and extension lines, to digital extension lines, or to T-1 trunk lines. The server-based PBX could then route telephone traffic to analog or digital telephone handsets next to each PC, or using the LAN directly, to the PC itself, making it the telephone.

The T-1 or analog PC cards would interface the server-based PBX into the Plain Old Telephone Service (POTS) analog network or into a T-1 connection directly to the local telephone company switch. Server-based PBX software is generally an integrated package providing call routing, call accounting, and integrated voice mail using the server's disk drives to store voice mail messages.

Sometimes server-based PBXs are popularly referred to as UnPBXs because they are not traditional, custom-designed, computer-controlled switches running a UNIX operating system. An UnPBX configuration is illustrated at the bottom of Figure 4-18. The reasons people are interested in server-based PBXs is because they can configure everything themselves, the costs are low, and functionality is growing. The drawback is the number of users that a server-based system can support. Generally these are 256 telephones or less. The number of supported phones is growing. We have seen server-based PBXs deployed in offices of 16 or 32 people. Offices of thousands usually require a classic PBX to service that many users.

VOICE OVER IP PBX • A specialized server-based PBX would be a VoIP PBX. VoIP is simply putting voice over your data network. In this case, a LAN attached to the PBX would carry both voice and data traffic to the PC of each PBX user. One LAN wire would be used for both voice and data traffic. This can substantially save wiring costs. Further, a VoIP server-based PBX can route voice and data traffic across any high-speed IP network or the Internet. This can save voice toll charges between facilities that have similar (or better yet, identical) VoIP server-based PBXs. VoIP technology is the future and offers significant voice and data cost savings for long distance and huge cost savings for international voice and data communications.

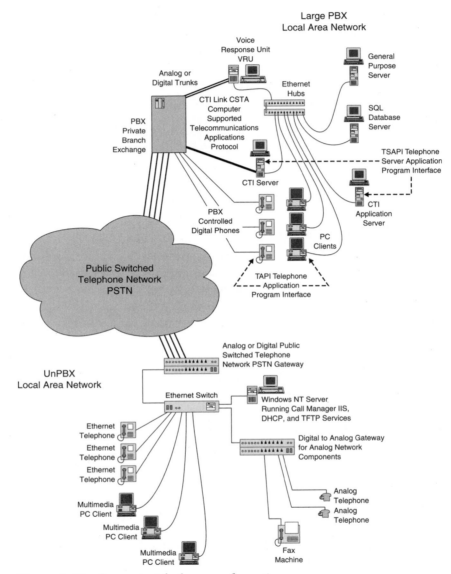

Figure 4–18 *Computer telephony configurations.*

PBX Selection

Some general considerations in selecting a PBX are:

1. Identify the number of subscriber lines (telephones)—This is a simple head or room count. When first purchasing a PBX, it is prudent to purchase 10% spares for the telephone handsets. Such spares will be used for repairs and system expansion. If they are purchased later, their price can be much higher than they cost when purchased with the PBX.
2. Determine the required trunks needed to support the subscriber lines—An Erlang-B calculation determines the number of trunks, depending upon the number of phones and the average call duration. The PBX vendor often provides the Erlang-B trunk line determination. If there are distinct usage groups, e.g., voice callers and Internet callers with one usage group having longer call durations (holding times) than the other usage group, then separate calculations should be performed for the lines assigned to each group.

These steps size the PBX. Then the PBX call processing features are determined from the following steps:

1. Next, document normal call processing. Do calls come to one attendant? Or do they directly ring the called party's line? Further, what new business functions need to be supported? Do you need a voice doorbell? What about paging? Or linking to cell phones? This determines what features the PBX needs to provide.
2. Examine how well the vendor PBX offerings match ISDN and other standards for future telecommunications.
3. Finally, examine other considerations such as:
   Does the system provide a smooth migration from low- to high-end systems?
   Do networked systems appear as a single system to users?
   Can ISDN and data capabilities be incorporated within existing installations?
   Can users have voice mail and management features in their PBX?
   Does the vendor provide comprehensive service and maintenance?
   Does the PBX support VoIP telephony or can it be easily upgraded to VoIP telephony? When are VoIP upgrades available for purchase?
   Does the PBX improve security and reduce risk of security breaches, theft, and assault on CPE?
4. Last but not least, get at least three different bids from different vendors. Pitting one vendor against another is the best way to get a competitive price.

When purchasing a PBX, keep in mind that during the initial purchase negotiations, the advantage lies with the PBX purchaser, not the seller. So negotiate everything into the purchase contract that you can. For example, ask to keep the contract pricing for replacement and upgrade components for five years. Ask for two or more years of on-site maintenance to be part of the purchase price. Ask for training and the ability to program (configure the software) in your switch. Ask for performance and reliability guarantees that the PBX vendor must meet over the life of the contract. Write the agreement in such a way that the vendor will meet the contract commitments or pay penalties if the contract terms are not met.

Once a contract is signed, the advantage now shifts to the PBX vendor because most PBX systems use proprietary hardware and software. They are not commodity items like PC hardware and software (unless it is a server-based PBX). Consequently, if you need a part or an upgrade component, the vendor can charge you a premium price for that component unless specified differently by the purchase contract.

Brain Teaser
_____

Telephones

Examine several telephones at your office and compare them to the phones at your home.
1. Do the phones at home have any special buttons or features? Write them down. Is there a hold feature? Do you have caller ID? How is call waiting activated, by a special button or on-hook/off-hook flash?
2. What buttons do you find on the phones at work? Do some phones have more features and buttons than others?
3. Do any phones have an LCD? Are the LCD sizes all the same? What functions can be programmed from the phone? Is there a manual that explains the extension programming functions that you can review?
4. Are any PCs used as phones? If they are, that is way cool!
The objective is to make you familiar with the features and functions of your telephone at work. These features and functions are dependent upon the PBX system to which the phone is attached.

CENTREX - Central Office Exchange

CENTREX (Central Exchange) is a generic name for telecommunications services, similar to those provided by CPE PBXs, offered through CO switches. While a PBX is located at a customer's site, a CENTREX system is located at a local telephone company's CO (see Figure 4-19). The CENTREX

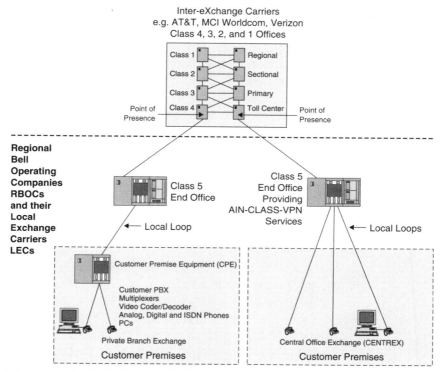

Figure 4–19   *CENTREX vs. PBX.*

customer leases a dedicated partition of the CO exchange, which is part of the public telephone network. Special switching functions, user features, as well as access to the public telephone network are provided from the CO switch. In this case, specific trunks and phone lines are defined to the CO switch software as reserved for a specific organization. This private designation is marketed as a CO feature called CENTREX.

Today's CENTREX provides enhanced features and functionality, including non-blocking service, voice mail, automated attendant features, voice messaging, Station Message Detail Recording (SMDR), and ACD, making it an able competitor to PBXs.

CENTREX VS. PBX

The advantage of CENTREX is freedom from dealing with on-site PBX equipment maintenance and upgrades. CENTREX is also good for applications intolerant of outages or downtime. CENTREX disadvantages include: less control over CENTREX services, recurring cost of lines, limited systems integration and customization, and restricted data communications capabilities.

To select CENTREX or PBX, an analysis life cycle cost analysis of owning a PBX vs. the recurring costs associated with the same communications functions provided by CENTREX service should be performed. CENTREX costs vary from LEC to LEC.

For example, we recently analyzed CENTREX service in a western city. The CENTREX costs turned out to be around $100 per month per subscriber line. Normal phone lines run from $20 to $35 per month for fixed rate (unlimited local calls) lines. So, the price of CENTREX service in this case was about $65 per line per month. This could be highly cost-effective for two to four lines. But small, cheap PBX systems (like the one at my office superstore checkout) make cost justification of CENTREX difficult. The $895 system shared four trunk lines with up to eight phones, and you could add a master console for $300. With purchased installation, the system might run $1,200 to $2,000. At $65 per line per month for four lines, it does not take long to pay for the small PBX.

Potential users need to carefully evaluate the advantages and disadvantages of both CENTREX and owning a CPE PBX. What functions exactly does the CENTREX provide over the PBX? One clear advantage is reliability. CPE PBXs require redundant and battery backed-up power to continue operation in the event of power failure. How long will they operate with the power out? In the case of my PBX, you can measure the time in minutes. CENTREX, in contrast, should be able to function for hours, and should have telephone company personnel and equipment rushing to the site for repairs in the event of a major disaster. No such luck with my PBX.

CENTREX's key selling point is the Advanced Intelligent Network (AIN) Virtual Private Network (VPN) function. COs offer advanced functions based upon intelligent switches. The CO 5ESS switch is capable of implementing PBX functions for directly attached subscriber lines using a portion of the CO switch and can integrate these functions with other 5ESS switches located in distant COs.

ADVANCED INTELLIGENT NETWORK

AIN is a popular term. The telecommunications industry is nothing but a bunch of acronyms that is easily described by the OSI seven-layer model. It seems whoever comes up with the best acronyms has the best technology. AIN is an awesome acronym. Think from the salesperson's perspective: If you want to sell a product, "advanced" is a great word to use. It's better than "normal" and "basic." "Intelligent" is another excellent term to use. It's better than "stupid" or "idiotic." "Network" is another great term because everything has to do with a network today. I would love it if someone tried to sell me a super-duper Advanced Amazing Unbelievably Intelligent Genius Network, or SAAUIGN, because that just sounds really too good to be true, and how can you turn that down? Even better, instead of calling it "AIN," maybe they should have called it "normal dumb network," but that would not have sold so well. What AIN does is bring intelligence and more features to the telephone network using SS-7.

Telecommunications carriers can use the SS-7 backbone to provide AIN service to customers that rely on the PSTN for their telecommunications networking. AIN services satisfy the following generic customer applications:

- Call management.
- Time-of-day/Date call forwarding.
- Directory number-to-fax translation.
- Multi-location extension dialing and portability.
- Automatic call distribution.
- Emergency hotlines.
- Private virtual networking.
- Routing to messaging services.
- Routing to calling line identification/Client host database match.

AIN is a catch-all term for future PBX equivalent services being provided through the LEC's network. One key AIN capability is VPN, which makes many geographically dispersed sites look like they are all part of a single, central telephone system.

VIRTUAL PRIVATE NETWORK

VPNs are CO software-based services that provide the features, functionality, and reliability equivalent to a private network. VPNs operate using public switched network telecommunications facilities. VPN benefits are shifting the technological risks from the customer to the telephone company; expanding and enhancing networks, adding new staff, and purchasing additional equipment; and providing the ability to easily integrate communications to accommodate business changes like a merger.

A VPN has the ability to make a few employees located in many facilities spread around a geographic area appear to be on a single telephone system at a single large facility. (In the data communications world, VPN permits remote users to connect securely to the central facility communications network across the Internet. This is a similar but different meaning for VPN.)

For example, The Moulton Company has employees that sometimes work from home. One employee is a two-day-a-week telecommuter and the other is an occasional telecommuter. They live in Bel Air, Maryland and around Bowie, Maryland, respectively. With AIN CENTREX service, we could have a phone line in each home for say $100 per month and some lines in our Columbia, Maryland headquarters (our world headquarters looks like the basement of my house) that would make us all look like we're in a single building on the same PBX. The Bel Air, Bowie, and Columbia phones would connect to different Class 5 CO switches. The AIN software in each CO switch would make all phones appear to be on the same switch at a single site. We could perform four-digit extension dialing, have music on hold, transfer calls, and more, all because of the AIN software running in the telephone company switches.

To provide equivalent service with my PBX would require a software (and likely a hardware) upgrade, and getting 4-wire analog leased (Foreign Exchange service – FX) lines from Bel Air and Bowie to Columbia. We already have a Berwyn Heights, Maryland leased FX line service that costs around $50 per month. Bel Air and Bowie are more distant from Columbia than Berwyn Heights, so the leased FX line service costs there would likely be significantly higher than $50 per month. In this case, VPN service is probably less costly and would provide equivalent or better features than leasing FX lines and connecting the remote sites through my PBX.

Banks with small branches spread around a metropolitan area find VPN services are an excellent way to make all branches look like they are part of a single bank telephone system.

The disadvantage of VPNs is possible loss of control over an organization's network's future direction and costs. Telecommunications costs can unexpectedly rise from increases in fees and charges. Such increased changes are not directly controlled by any subscriber organization. The goal of the LEC providing CENTREX service is to increase tariff rates because they still remain in a monopolistic business environment.

VPNs provide the operating benefits of centralized billing, increased reliability, and potential cost savings over operating a private network. In contrast, VPN providers often have their hands stuck out for setup fees, usage fees, features charges, and annual fees. VPN services implemented using 64-Kbps lines may not adequately service data traffic.

To decide if the benefits outweigh the costs, potential VPN users must consider the telecommunications traffic which remains inside the organization and the duration of the calls (e.g., how long individual lines remain in use), the networking features and functions they require and the costs for both CENTREX service and purchasing and operating a customer premise PBX.

CUSTOM LOCAL AREA SIGNALING SERVICES

Custom Local Area Signaling System (CLASS) services include:

- Selective call acceptance.
- Selective call forwarding.
- Selective call rejection.
- Distinctive ringing.

Each feature uses the Calling Line Identity (CLI) sent via an SS-7 network to provide end-users with increased call management capabilities, privacy, security, and convenience. The SS-7 network passes the calling number to the CLASS-enabled switch at the destination office for the call. The destination office's switch then screens the call to perform call forwarding, selective call rejection, important call alerts (like calls from the President), and more.

CENTREX LINE ASSIGNMENT SERVICE

The CENTREX Line Assignment Service (CLAS) permits CENTREX subscribers to change their class of service by using a PC to connect to the local telephone company's CENTREX switch control computer and changing operating parameters directly. In this manner, the subscriber is not dependent upon the local telephone company to perform day-to-day, routine CENTREX configuration functions. CLAS permits changing:

- CENTREX phone numbers.
- Turning on and off specific features.
- Adding numbers to speed dialing.
- Changing pickup groups.

The requested changes are implemented within 24 hours by the CENTREX switch, provided there are no conflicts or errors. A report of the change results is available to the CENTREX subscriber to verify that the requested changes were implemented. The principal benefit of CLAS is that it saves subscribers money because CLAS is a single monthly fee. In contrast, for each change requested to a CENTREX system, the subscriber is charged an administration fee.

Brain Teaser

CENTREX Features

Go to a local telephone company's Web site and search for CENTREX. I used the Bell Atlantic site here:

`http://www.bellatlantic.com/largebiz/cent_cp_cf.htm`

Check the CENTREX features offered.

1. Are any CLASS features offered? Bell Atlantic offered some CLASS features, including distinctive ring. Some other CLASS call handling features appeared to be offered as well.

2. Is the CLAS capability listed? It appears that for the high-end CENTREX service (CustoFLEX), an enhanced system management feature is offered.

3. Is pricing published? The prices we saw were found by searching for "CENTREX, costs." They were tariff publications with the CENTREX line costs buried at the end of the document. Costs for CENTREX service in Maryland were about $20 to $40 over the cost of the basic phone line as best we could ascertain from the tariffs.

4. Get a quick verbal quote from your local phone company for CENTREX service for a 10-telephone line office. How do the costs compare to the cost of service without CENTREX?

This analysis should help you better understand CENTREX service benefits and limitations. It should also provide some information for a cursory CENTREX vs. PBX comparison analysis.

■ Summary

In this chapter, we saw while examining the changing landscape of telephone companies and regulation that politics and telephony are inextricably tied together. In the long term, there will likely be about 5 to 10 global telecommunications companies. All the global companies will have a U.S. presence and compete vigorously in both local and long-distance U.S. markets. We looked at different voice telephony services and saw what capabilities they provided for business and other organizations. Finally, we examined PBX and CENTREX service offerings to see how they could effectively support voice communications in any organization. Our voice solution could be satisfied using a PBX, CENTREX, or even an UNPBX. They are all similar boxes with similar flashing lights that provide equivalent functions. The choice is up to you.

▲ Chapter Review Questions

1. *In 1985, how many RBOCs were there?*
   A. 7
   B. 6
   C. 5
   D. 4

2. *What connects the IXC/IEC networks to the LEC networks?*
   A. Branch exchange switch
   B. POP
   C. Router
   D. Class 4 toll office

3. *What led to the breakup of the AT&T telephone monopoly in 1984?*
   A. Judge Harold Green
   B. MCI
   C. Advancing technology
   D. The RBOCs wanting freedom from AT&T

4. *What has happened to long-distance rates since 1984?*
   A. They have risen
   B. They declined 50%
   C. No change
   D. They declined more than 70%

5. *Are there any true 5¢ per minute rates?*
   A. Yes
   B. No
   C. Yes, for businesses
   D. Maybe

6. *How are communications costs computed?*
   A. Based upon distance
   B. Based upon time
   C. Depends upon the service
   D. Based upon data volume
   E. All of the above
   F. None of the Above

7. *Automatic Route Selection software is more sophisticated than Least Cost Routing software.*

    A. True

    B. False

    C. They are the same

    D. Don't care

8. *A universal PBX features is?*

    A. Least cost routing

    B. Voice mail

    C. Hunt and pickup groups

    D. Cell phone and pager routing

9. *What feature permits the subscriber to control the CENTREX switch directly?*

    A. CLASS

    B. CLAS

    C. PBX

    D. PC software

10. *What makes CENTREX a cost-effective alternative to a PBX?*

    A. Nothing

    B. CLAS

    C. VPN

    D. Reliability

Data Communications and WAN Fundamental Concepts

Data communications networks and technologies initially supported data transmission at low speeds with high error rates. These early data communications networks were sometimes called Wide Area Networks (WANs) because they were national or global in coverage. They were designed to carry text and numeric data. Voice was not envisioned as something that would travel across data communications networks. WAN, or data communications technologies and products, provided a foundation for the evolution of all WAN and LANs to the high-speed, low-error-rate networks of today that carry voice, video, and data traffic.

Data traffic is different from voice traffic. They have different requirements that must be met. Classic data traffic requires no errors but can handle delays. Voice traffic requires continuous flow (no delays) and can tolerate occasional errors in communications. Voice communications does not try to correct errors because that would cause delays and hesitations in speech. Delays are worse than errors because humans expect instant response when talking. Delivering voice information requires encoding an analog signal into a digital signal, delivering it in a circuit-switched fashion to a destination, then converting it back to an analog signal. Data communications traffic starts as a digital signal. It is then converted to an analog signal, equivalent to a voice analog signal, and sent through the voice network to a destination. At the destination, the analog signal is converted back to the digital signal used by the computer. The data process takes place outside (in an environment surrounding) the voice network. WANs then rely on the underlying voice network to again encode the analog signal (now containing data and no voice) to a new and different digital signal, deliver it to its destination, and then convert it back to an analog signal. At this point, it is handed to the WAN equipment at the other end for final delivery (see Figure 5-1).

Data traffic may look the same as voice traffic, but it has different communications performance requirements than voice traffic. Voice traffic is a continuous stream of "0's" and "1's." To the voice network, encoded data appears the same as voice traffic. However, to the data equipment at the other end, the data traffic arrives as wads or chunks of useful information with gaps of time in between. Now you may be getting the idea why sending data through the voice network wastes network capacity. Many of the voice network "0's" and "1's" are just wasted, idle bits for the data equipment. If only they could be used for something else when not required for sending data, there would not be so much waste.

In the voice network, as we saw in Chapter 4, if some bits are lost, it's no big deal. The humans at each end of a voice line adapt to the lost bits marvelously. They only complain when lots and lots of bits are lost often (like with a cell phone). Data equipment is very persnickety. Data must, like the coffee, be good to the last bit. Any lost bits or incorrectly received bits cause the computers expecting those bits to search for them frantically. They will request transmission of the data in error incessantly until the transmission is received without error.

Table 5-1 summarizes the differences between voice and data transmission. Voice network traffic must not be interrupted. The network must be much more reliable than a data network. There can be no delays or irregular arrival times between bits. They cannot be bunched up or spread out, other-

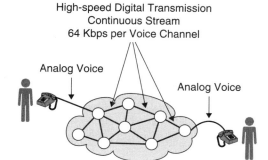

High-speed Digital Transmission
Continuous Stream
64 Kbps per Voice Channel

Analog Voice

Analog Voice

Voice Network
Analog Voice Encoded as Digital "0's" and "1's"
Delivered to Destination
"0's" and "1's" then Decoded to Analog Voice

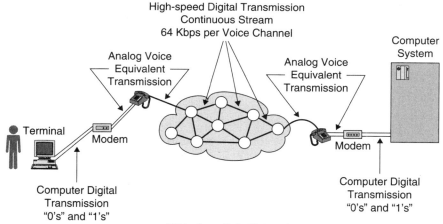

High-speed Digital Transmission
Continuous Stream
64 Kbps per Voice Channel

Computer
System

Analog Voice
Equivalent
Transmission

Analog Voice
Equivalent
Transmission

Terminal

Modem

Modem

Computer Digital
Transmission
"0's" and "1's"

Computer Digital
Transmission
"0's" and "1's"

Wide Area Data Network
Surrounds Voice Network
Digital "0's" and "1's" Modulated into Analog Voice Equivalent
Then Analog Voice Equivalent Encoded as Digital "0's" and "1's"
Delivered to Destination
"0's" and "1's" Then Decoded to Analog Voice Equivalent and
Analog Voice Equivalent is Demodulated into Digital "0's" and "1's"

Figure 5–1 *Data traversing the voice network.*

wise our voice would sound warbled. The bits sent in a 1-2-3-4 sequence must arrive in a 1-2-3-4 sequence. There can be no out-of-sequence bits, otherwise one phrase would arrive ahead of another, making our conversation unintelligible. A constant 64-Kbps (higher for video) stream of "0's" and

"1's" is needed to deliver the voice to its destination. A few dropped bits are okay, because humans ignore them. Video has the same characteristics as voice, but is transmitted at higher speeds (384 Kbps for full-motion standard television).

Table 5.1 *Data and Voice Characteristics*

Data	Voice/Video
Less reliable	More reliable
Delays	No delays
Not time-dependent	Time sequenced arrival
Variable bandwidth	Constant high bandwidth
No errors	Errors OK

Data transmission is a query followed by a response from the target computer. Surfing the Web is like this. We click on a hyper-link; a small chunk (or wad) of characters is sent through the Internet to a server holding a Web page. The server now returns a large chunk (or wad) of data, the Web page to which the hyper-link points, to us. If the PC fails (as it surely does quite often), we blame Bill Gates and Windows and start muttering four-letter phrases to ourselves. When the response takes several seconds to appear on our screen, we play Solitaire and blame Netscape or the Web site for being slow. The data can be sent out of sequence, provided our Windows PC knows how to reassemble it into the proper sequence for final display. Since we are sending chunks of data, sometimes we need all the bits and sometimes we do not need any bits. Our requirement for communications channel capacity (bandwidth) varies as we request and receive data from the network. The aggravating point about data is that it must be exactly correct. If we were visiting www.paytrust.com, we would be very upset if a transmission error moved our bank account balance decimal point a couple of digits to the left. Similarly, we might feel falsely secure if an error placed the decimal point several places to the right. In any event, data has to be exactly correct. Computers do not tolerate any errors.

As we proceed with the remainder of this book, we will see where blending voice and data in the same network to save costs proves interesting because of these distinctly different characteristics. Understanding how new high-speed networking technologies like Asynchronous Transfer Mode (ATM) are adapted to handle voice and data is important when using them in any network. Keep our data characteristics in mind as we now explore WANs, or data communications.

Data Communications Fundamentals

Several basic concepts must be covered to understand data networks. The concepts include serial vs. parallel transmission, data encoding, synchronous and asynchronous transmission, duplex and half-duplex, modem operation, baud vs. bits per second, and multiplexing. These concepts are also used in voice networks and LANs. The concepts are explained here in their simplest form to make it exactly clear how they work. The real world of networks employs concepts in combination in different products and services, so it is more difficult to understand how they operate. However, understanding the basic concepts permits us to say that multiplexing applies this way and duplex transmission applies here, thus enabling us to grasp more fully how a combination of concepts works as a whole.

For example, cellular telephone networks use different channels and different types of multiplexing to communicate between the cell phones and the cell phone switching equipment. Understanding which type of multiplexing goes with which type of cell phone helps to explain why some cell phones are better than others. Now, let's examine basic data communications, or WAN, transmission concepts. We begin with data codes.

Serial vs. Parallel

Serial vs. parallel transmission simply describes how bits travel from one component to another component across a network. In a computer, parallel transmission is used because distances are short and data must be manipulated quickly. Once outside the PC, serial transmission dominates. Serial transmission is single-file, Indian-style transmission, where one bit follows another down a single pathway as shown in Figure 5-2.

Serial transmission requires one, two, or four wires, depending upon the electrical properties of the signal. In contrast, parallel transmission requires a single wire or path for every bit. This could mean 8 wires, 16 wires, or more, depending upon the width of the pathway (number of bits, 8, 16, 32, or 64). 32-bit CPU chips use 64-bit or 128-bit data pathways internally in PCs. The next step is to 64-bit CPU chips and even wider data pathways.

Serial transmission runs across copper wire, optical fiber, and Radio Frequency (RF) channels in telecommunications networks. Virtually all WANs (data communications) and LANs are serial links. On a PC, the parallel port connecting to a printer is the remaining parallel transmission interface and this will soon disappear when Universal Serial Bus (USB) printers

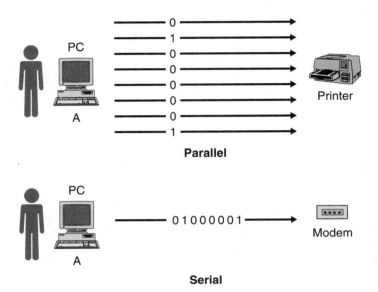

Figure 5–2 *Serial vs. parallel transmission.*

and peripherals take over in the next couple of years. The USB interface uses (as you have already guessed) bit serial transmission.

Data Codes

A code gives something else meaning. For example, Morse code gives dots and dashes meaning by turning them into letters and numbers. Fundamentally, computers just deal with voltage levels. We do not need to understand voltage level details, but we do need to understand that different voltage levels can represent "0's" and "1's." Still, most humans do not read "0's" and "1's" (binary information), so we need to convert them into another form such as the following ASCII code. The voltages represent binary numbers, a "0" or a "1." A one-bit message can have two possibilities—0 or 1. A two-bit message can have four possibilities:

$$2^1\ 2^0$$
$$0\ \ 0\ =0$$
$$0\ \ 1\ =1$$
$$1\ \ 0\ =2$$
$$1\ \ 1\ =3$$

A three-bit message has eight possibilities:

$$2^2 \ 2^1 \ 2^0$$

0	0	0	= 0
0	0	1	= 1
0	1	0	= 2
0	1	1	= 3
1	0	0	= 4
1	0	1	= 5
1	1	0	= 6
1	1	1	= 7

To compute the decimal value of a binary pattern, use $2^0=1$, $2^1=2$, and $2^2=4$.

Computers generally take binary numbers in combinations of eight at once (which nerds call a byte—a combination of four binary numbers is called a nibble) to form the equivalent of the decimal numbers 0 to 255. Computers store letters and other characters by assigning a number for each one. So, eight binary numbers is equal to one byte, which in turn is equal to one character.

A data code translates printed or displayed symbols into "0's" and "1's" that a computer can manipulate into the letters (or characters) humans use. Humans see the letter "A" and a computer sees a pattern of voltages, 0 volts representing a 0 and +5 volts representing a 1 (see Figure 5-3).

Computers use eight bits at a time to represent a single character. Different patterns of "0's" and "1's" are used for every displayed character. The patterns are specified by a code set. The two better-known code sets are the ASCII code set and the EBCDIC code set. ASCII is called a 7-level code because it uses seven of the eight bits. EBCDIC uses all eight bits to represent characters. Eight bits provide a maximum of 256 patterns of "0's" and "1's," and ASCII's seven bits provide 256 divided by 2, or 128 different patterns of "0's" and "1's" to represent printed characters.

How many printed characters are there? There are:

- 26 A through Z—Uppercase
- 26 a through z—Lowercase
- 10 0 through 9—Numeric
- 32 "'!@#$%^&*()-_+={}[]:;/?.>,<\|`~ —Special
- 94 Unique characters, minimum

Computers   **People**

+0 +5 +0 +0 +0 +0 +0 +5   A
Voltages   Letters

Data Representations			
Binary Bits 0 or 1	HEX 0 to F	Decimal 0 to 9	ASCII Letter
1111 1111	F F	2 2 5	(Blank)
0110 0001	6 1	9 7	a
0100 0001	4 1	6 5	A
0000 0000	0 0	0	(Null)

Figure 5–3   *Data representation.*

This depends upon the language used, but for U.S. English, there are 96 printed characters because we need a space character (we all occupy space) and a delete (remove the character directly above the cursor) character. Therefore, the ASCII 7-bit code has plenty of combinations that can represent the standard 96 printable characters we use everyday.

One of the early code sets used for sending data was Baudot code (named after a French mathematician, Emile Baudot). It was a five-bit (or level) code providing 32 different patterns. Because of the paucity of patterns, Baudot code had only uppercase characters and required reusing codes to represent numbers and punctuation symbols. The shift between letters and numbers was accomplished during transmission by sending a special shift sequence of characters. Baudot code was used on early Teletype machines.

AMERICAN STANDARD CODE FOR INFORMATION INTERCHANGE (ASCII)

ASCII (pronounced ass-key, which leads to some fun word games) code is the dominant code used in computers and communications systems worldwide. ASCII translates patterns of seven binary numbers ("0's" and "1's") into one of the standard 96 printable characters. Computers then combine a character number with a font representation to display or print the character. The numbers used in ASCII range from all "0's" (equal to 0) to all "1's" (equal to 255).

The American National Standards Institute (ANSI) in ANSI Standard X3.4 first defined ASCII in 1968. The ASCII code is an international standard known as IA5 (International Alphabet #5). The ASCII 7-bit code can represent a maximum of 128 characters. The eighth bit of every byte is used as a "parity check" bit. What does parity mean to you? How does it check for errors?

PARITY CHECKING • The best explanation of parity I have ever heard is that parity acts like a clothes dryer. Just think, every time you dry your clothes, you put in an even number of socks and the dryer produces an odd number of socks. (Socks are equivalent to ones.) Odd parity counts the ones in a character and adds an extra one to assure the ones (socks) are always odd. Similarly, even parity assures that every character has an even number of ones by adding a one as needed to characters with normally an odd number of ones. The thought here is that single-bit errors in data transmission within a character can be detected.

Let us just think here for a moment. If one bit changes during transmission in a character and the receiving device recomputes the parity for that character, would the parity match? It would most certainly not match. What if two bits were to change? Oh, it would match, and the character error would go undetected. So parity can only detect errors when 1, 3, 5, or 7 bits are changed, and it does not detect errors when 2, 4, 6, or 8 bits are changed. Using binomial probability theory, we might determine (and no, I did not do the calculation, but I do know what binomial probabilities are) that this is 95% effective in detecting errors. Pretty good odds until you think of the terabytes transmitted on networks every millisecond. This means there are many undetected data errors, which is not good.

Parity was and is sometimes used in PC memory to detect errors. Why? RAM (Random Access Memory) errors are usually only single-bit errors, while many data communications errors are more likely to be multiple-bit errors. So the parity bit in ASCII code is not used as an error-detecting bit. ASCII characters are sent as eight bits with no parity. Actually, today an extra ninth bit is often added to each eight bits in computer memory. The resulting extra four memory bits in every 36 bits of RAM are used to detect and correct single-bit errors in every 36 bits of RAM. The ninth bit from every character is processed using an Error Correcting Code (ECC) algorithm (that employs more sophisticated math than binomial probabilities) to detect every multiple-bit error and to detect and correct every single-bit error.

In data communications systems, even parity is used in asynchronous transmission and odd is used in synchronous transmission. We discuss asynchronous and synchronous transmission later in this chapter. Parity can be set as even, odd, no parity (preferred), mark (always a one), or space (always a zero). Parity setup problems can be a source of aggravation, but if in doubt, use eight bits and no parity for ASCII characters. Remember, these are just ways to check for and correct errors. Parity just checks for errors and can easily be fooled. ECC checks and corrects some errors and cannot be fooled.

DECIMAL REPRESENTATION • Each ASCII code can be translated into a decimal number using bit patterns. It is helpful to know the decimal representation of ASCII characters sometimes because PC software can be made to use a specific character when you input the decimal number equivalent. The way the binary to decimal translation works is that each bit position starting from the right represents a decimal number. The right-most bit is 1, then 2, 4, 8, 16, 32, and 64 for each of the seven remaining bits. You guessed it—these are 2^0, 2^1, 2^2, 2^3, 2^4, 2^5, and 2^6. Remember, the decimal value is derived from 2^0 =1, 2^1=2, 2^2=4, 2^3 =8, 2^4=16, 2^5=32, and 2^6=64.

So, for our capital "A" in Figure 5-3, we would multiply the binary number by the value, then add them together to get the decimal number equivalent to the binary pattern. This means that the decimal equivalent would be 64 X 1 plus 1 X 1, or 65. Now try the lowercase "a" to get 96.

THE ASCII CODE • The ASCII code set is shown in Figure 5-4. The code table has sixteen rows. Printable characters are in the six right-most columns. Six times 16 gives us the standard 96 printable characters. These characters as shown in the table include upper- and lowercase letters, numbers, and some punctuation symbols. The left-most columns contain device and communications control characters. The device control characters are in the shaded area on the bottom, while the communications control characters are in the shaded area on the top of columns one and two.

The communications control characters are:

- NUL (The null character)—It does nothing but occupy space.
- SOH (Start Of Header)—Precedes the address field in a block of data.
- STX (Start of Text)—Precedes the data (generally text) field in a block of data.
- ETX (End of Text)—Signals the end of the data (text) field.
- EOT (End Of Transmission)—The "That's All Folks" character, which resets a line to default status.

- ENQ (Enquiry)—Solicits data from a terminal, or polls the terminal.
- ACK (Acknowledgement)—Positive acknowledgement that all was received okay.
- BEL (Rings the terminal's bell)—This is a fun character. It causes PCs to beep.
- DLE (Data Link Escape – Used for special communications functions.
- DC1 or XOFF (Data Control 1)—Used to signal transmitter to stop sending data.
- DC2 and DC4 (Data Control 2 and Data Control 4)—Provide user-specific communications functions.
- DC3 or XON (Data Control 3)—Used to signal transmitter to start (resume) sending data.
- NAK (Negative Acknowledgement)—Negative acknowledgement that transmission went badly; no good data was received.
- SYN (Synchronous idle)—Used to frame blocks of data in synchronous transmission.
- ETB (End Transmission Block)—Terminates an intermediate block of data that is not the last block in the message. ETB is similar to ETX. EOT signals the end of a message.
- CAN (Cancel)—Terminates or cancels activity.

The device control characters are:

- BS (Backspace).
- HT (Horizontal Tab).
- VT (Vertical Tab).
- FF (Form Feed)—Ejects the page.
- CR (Carriage Return).
- SO (Shift Out).
- SI (Shift In).
- EM (End of Medium).
- SUB (Substitute character)—Marks the end of a DOS text file.
- ESC (Escape character)—Yes, it is a real character, unlike Ctrl and Alt, which do not produce characters.
- FS, GS, RS, and US (Form Separator, Group Separator, Record Separator, and Unit Separator).

Generally, the name of the device control character describes its function.

Let's use the table to create the codes for "A." On the left, the first four bits are given. These bits are the right-most bits of the binary pattern for "A." Locate the row for "A," move left to find "0 0 0 1," now move to the top of the

American Standard Code for Information Interchange (ASCII)

Row Number	Bits # 7 6 5 4 3 2 1	000	001	010	011	100	101	110	111
0	0 0 0 0	NUL	DLE	SP	0	@	P	`	p
1	0 0 0 1	SOH	DC1 (XON)	!	1	A	Q	a	q
2	0 0 1 0	STX	DC2	"	2	B	R	b	r
3	0 0 1 1	ETX	DC3 (XOFF)	#	3	C	S	c	s
4	0 1 0 0	EOT	DC4	$	4	D	T	d	t
5	0 1 0 1	ENQ	NAK	%	5	E	U	e	u
6	0 1 1 0	ACK	SYN	&	6	F	V	f	v
7	0 1 1 1	BEL	ETB	'	7	G	W	g	w
8	1 0 0 0	BS	CAN	(	8	H	X	h	x
9	1 0 0 1	HT	EM	)	9	I	Y	i	y
10 = A	1 0 1 0	LF	SUB	*	:	J	Z	j	z
11 = B	1 0 1 1	VT	ESC	+	;	K	[	k	{
12 = C	1 1 0 0	FF	FS	,	<	L	\	l		
13 = D	1 1 0 1	CR	GS	-	=	M	]	m	}
14 = E	1 1 1 0	SO	RS	.	>	N	^	n	~
15 = F	1 1 1 1	SI	US	/	?	O	_	o	DEL
Column Number ⟶		0	1	2	3	4	5	6	7

Column Correspondence — Use With Ctrl Key

Figure 5–4 *ASCII codes.*

⌐— ASCII File —⌐		⌐—EBCDIC File—⌐		Letter
0 1 0 0	1 0 0 0	1 1 0 0	1 0 0 0	H
0 1 1 0	1 0 0 1	1 0 0 0	1 0 0 1	i
0 0 0 0	1 1 0 1	0 0 0 0	1 1 0 1	CR
0 0 0 0	1 0 1 0	0 0 1 0	1 0 1 0	LF

Text File Contents Look to Us Like This:

Hi

Figure 5–5 *ASCII vs. EBCDIC file.*

column to add bits 7, 6, and 5. You should find "1 0 0." Combining should produce "1 0 0   0 0 0 1," or the seven bits for "A."

We can determine the decimal numeric value for "A" from the table as well. The decimal value of NUL is 0, and the decimal value of SI is 15. That means that the decimal value of DLE is 16, SP (Space) is 32, "0" is 48, and @ is 64. Since "A" is under @, its value is one more than 64, or 65.

The final way this table is useful is the key correspondence between the printable characters in column 6 and column 0 and the printable characters in column 7 and column 1. To create a Backspace (BS) character, I would hold down the Ctrl key on the keyboard and tap the "h," which is the column 6 key in the same row as BS. Similarly, FF is "Ctrl" plus "l," or "Ctrl l." Bell is "Ctrl g." Line Feed is "Ctrl j." What are XON and XOFF? They are "Ctrl q" and "Ctrl s," respectively. We will do one more trick in our study break exercise coming up soon.

Extended Binary Coded Decimal Interchange Code (EBCDIC) • IBM developed EBCDIC code. It was an enhancement to the Binary Coded Decimal (BCD) code used in early IBM computers. EBCDIC is an 8-bit code having 256 possible characters. It has the exact same 96 standard characters as does ASCII, but differs in the device and communication control characters supported as shown in Figure 5-5. EBCDIC supports all ASCII device and control characters, but there are some added characters like NL (New Line)—a combination of Carriage Return and Line Feed characters. The control characters in EBCDIC sometimes perform different functions on different IBM computer peripherals and components.

The most important thing to remember about EBCDIC code is where it is used and where it is not used. EBCDIC code is used in some large IBM (mainframe or server) computers and in some large computers made by other manufacturers. All other computers use ASCII code. So any computer you see is using ASCII code, especially if it talks to other computers. An ISDN phone uses ASCII code. My Timex Data-Link watch uses ASCII code (it is a computer). The caller ID box next to the analog phone uses ASCII code. Cell phones use ASCII code (all of them are computers). So, a few thousand computers on the planet still use EBCDIC code and the remaining millions of computers on the planet use ASCII code.

Code translation between ASCII and EBCDIC is not difficult. To all computers that need to translate code, it is a snap to match the 128 characters of ASCII into the 256 characters of EBCDIC. It is not overly difficult to match the 256 characters of EBCDIC into the 128 characters of ASCII because the odd control characters may often be discarded without consequence.

UNICODE TRANSLATION • To fully represent foreign alphabets and character formats, Unicode translation is used. Before Unicode, there were hundreds of different encoding systems for assigning numbers to letters. No single encoding (number to letter assignment) could contain enough characters. European countries alone required several different translations to cover all the European languages. Even for English, a single translation or encoding was not adequate to represent all the letters, punctuation, and technical symbols in common use. Character translation systems often conflicted with one another by using the same number for two different characters, or they used different numbers for the same character.

Servers and other computers need to support many different translations. Whenever data is passed between different translations (encoding systems) on different computers, data runs the risk of corruption. Unicode changed all that by providing a unique number for every character, no matter what the computer, no matter what the software, no matter what the language. Unicode is an international standard adopted by the computer industry. Many operating systems, Web browsers, and other computer products support it. With Unicode translation, 16 bits represent characters, providing over 65,000 numbers to translate into characters for all languages. While 65,000 characters are sufficient for encoding most of the many thousands of characters used in major languages of the world, the Unicode standard also provides an extension mechanism called UTF-16. The extension mechanism allows for translating (or encoding) as many as a million more characters. This is sufficient for all known character translation requirements, providing full coverage for all modern and historic scripts known on this planet.

Keep in mind that these are just codes that allow you to represent information in another form.

Brain Teaser

ASCII Code

> To test the decimal equivalent of any ASCII character, use any PC keyboard with a numeric keypad. Open a DOS window, then with the cursor in the DOS window, hold down the Alt key and while holding it down, tap the decimal number of the ASCII character you wish to create.
> 1. Use Alt plus 65. Do you get "A"?
> 2. Try Alt plus 97. Do you get "a"?
> 3. What is Alt 71? It is "G". This made a broken keyboard usable for me once. The "G" key would not work, so I used Alt 72 to make "G's."
> The goal here is to show how understanding a few things about ASCII code can be useful when working with any PC.

Data Transmission Concepts

Now we need to examine the fundamental concepts behind data transmission. These concepts are analog vs. digital transmission, synchronization, and the perplexing plexes: duplex, half-duplex, and simplex. Once we understand these data communications concepts, they will help us understand how new telecommunications products and services work.

ANALOG VS. DIGITAL TRANSMISSION

In Chapter 4, we discussed some analog and digital transmission concepts. Here we explore them further. While we examine them, refer to Figure 5-6.

Analog transmission uses an electrical analog of the original signal. Analog transmission (i.e., voice communications) uses frequency, amplitude, and sometimes phase changes to an analog wave (a sine wave, or sinusoidal wave) to communicate information between a sender and receiver. As humans, we can understand frequency and amplitude changes to our voice signal. Frequency changes are high and low pitch sounds. Amplitude changes are loud and soft sounds. However, we cannot detect changes in phase. A phase-encoded signal sounds like a hissing noise (sometimes called white noise).

Analog signals traveling down the wire are soaked up. It is like my voice. If I were to shout "Hello" in the middle of a field, people very close by might hear my "Hello." If they were some distance away, they most likely would

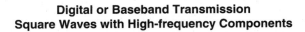

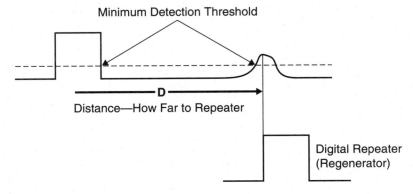

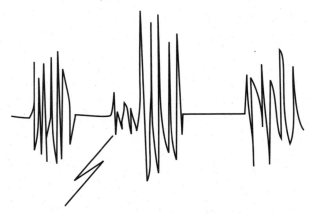

Figure 5–6 *Analog vs. digital transmission.*

think that they heard a sound, but would not pay much attention to it. If I were to shout down a pipe, my voice would travel further because the energy of my voice would be focused in the pipe. However, if the pipe were to run from NYC to LA, someone at the LA end would hear nothing if I were shouting at the NYC end. My voice would need to run through the multi-mega watt Public Address (PA) system with super sub-woofer speakers to permit it to travel any distance down the pipe toward LA. The multi-mega watt PA system with super sub-woofer speakers would amplify my analog voice signal so it would travel further down the pipe toward LA. Of course, if the sound started in NYC, they still might not hear it in LA.

What would they hear if water was dripping near the microphone input on the multi-mega watt PA system with super sub-woofer speakers? The dripping of the water and my "Hello" would be combined into a single amplified analog transmission to LA. They might hear something like "Hello – drip" or "drip – Hello." The point is that amplified analog signals amplify both the signal and unwanted noise as the analog signal travels through amplifiers (sometimes referred to in telephony as analog repeaters) from the signal source to the signal destination.

Analog transmission can be summarized by the following characteristics:

- Analog transmission is in tones (frequencies), amplitudes, and phases.
- Analog equipment amplifies both signals and noise.
- Modems (Modulators/Demodulators) are required to convert PC digital data to analog signals.
- Analog frequencies are susceptible to distortion, e.g., some frequencies travel faster than others frequencies across telephone lines.

Digital transmission is square waves or pulses. These pulses are composed of high-frequency analog signal components. However, digital signals are either present or absent, "0" or "1." The square waves are also soaked up by wire, so they may not exceed the minimal voltage level to be detected by the receiving device. In this case, they must be sent through a digital repeater or signal regenerator that samples the old signal mid-point and then creates an exact fresh duplicate of the original digital pulse and passes it on to the receiver. Well, it is almost an exact duplicate. It is identical in every respect to the original signal except that it is delayed one-half pulse width.

While this does not seem like much and often is not significant, if we were to run a digital signal coast-to-coast, it might require signal regenerators every 6,000 feet, or every mile, for about 3,000 miles. This produces 1,500 bits of delay, or about 150 characters. At 33,600 bits per second, it would be about 44.7-milliseconds delay.

To understand wiring rules for networks, we need to go way back to when we were children. Think of the summertime when life was simple. No school, hot sunny days, nothing to do, and you had a rope in your hand! So you whipped it up, then down, and you saw a pulse (digital transmission) travel down the rope. Cool! Now you tried a different rope and saw that the pulse didn't travel as far. Then you tried several other ropes and saw that some were really good while others were not so good at having the pulse travel down them. Next you tried whipping a rope really hard. The up and down hard whip made the pulse travel further down the rope as compared to the distance produced by a wimpy wrist flick. Next you went for high-speed transmission by rapidly whipping the rope up and down. This shortened the distances pulses could travel. Didn't you do this as a child? I sure did. It must have been early training for my present job.

Our simple rope analogy tells us all we need to know about digital transmission across wires. Some wire is better than other wire in carrying digital signals. Category-5 (CAT-5) wire is better than Category-3 (CAT-3) wire. We discuss CAT-5 and CAT-3 wires more in Chapter 6. The stronger the electrical signal, the further the pulse travels. Different transmission components at OSI Layer 1 have different electrical properties and hence transmit digital pulses longer or shorter distances. And finally, the higher the transmission speed, the shorter the distance the signal travels. So high-speed digital transmission can run over any wire for a short distance before the receiving device has difficulty detecting it.

Why are more and more functions put into the CPU chip? Because at CPU clock speeds in the MHz and GHz range, signals do not travel very far before they are all soaked up and require a repeater. Also, traveling any distance slows down the data from reaching its destination and also slows down the PC. So shorter signal run distances (like inside the chip alone) make faster PCs.

Digital transmission can be summarized by the following characteristics:

- Digital transmission is discrete pulses.
- Digital repeaters, or signal regenerators, remove transmission noise and retransmit pulses at their original strength.
- A Channel Service Unit/ Data Service Unit (CSU/DSU, sometimes also called an ISDN modem) is required to interface data communications equipment to digital transmission facilities.
- The CSU permits the telephone company to perform loopback and other channel tests to customer premises.
- Digital transmission, "0" or "1" signals and repeaters, eliminate the effects of noise on our transmitted information.

In summary, information can be transmitted either in analog or digital fashion. Analog is a continuous wave, which is harder to re-create. Digital is a pulse that only has two values, on and off, and is easier to re-create. We are moving more towards digital because we can cram more information down a digital pipe than can be sent down an analog pipe.

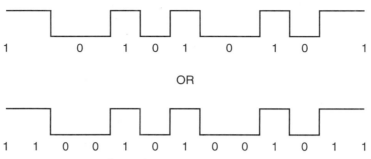

Figure 5–7   *Digital signal interpretations.*

ASYNCHRONOUS VS. SYNCHRONOUS VS. ISOCHRONOUS

Now we need to deal with the issue of synchronization, or timing. This requires synchronizing the transmitting and receiving devices. When I think of synchronization, I think of dancing, because if you and your partner are out of step, then disaster ensues. Fred Astaire and Ginger Rogers were dance partners that were always in step, or synchronized. Communications devices work the same way. There is bit, character (byte), and message (block frame packet) synchronization that must occur before data can be sent and received across a communications channel. Bit serial transmission places special demands upon sending and receiving equipment to perform bit, byte (character), and message synchronization. Figure 5-7 illustrates the problem of synchronization.

The problem illustrated in Figure 5-7 is to determine which is the correct interpretation of the incoming signal? Is the top case with alternating "1's" and "0's" correct, or is the bottom case with "0's" and "1's" sometimes repeated correct? From our perspective, we would most likely guess the bottom interpretation. Why? It seems that some pulses, or square waves, are longer than others.

Now let us put ourselves in the place of the receiving communications equipment. How does it know that some pulses are longer than others? It cannot view them like we can. Consequently, it must time them with a stopwatch (or clock). When timing is done and the correct bits are interpreted from the data stream, bit synchronization is being performed.

There are three techniques that are used for bit synchronization: asynchronous transmission, synchronous transmission, and isochronous transmission.

Bit synchronization—This is required for the receiving machine to determine when to sample (determine the voltage level) for a bit. The sampling rate is determined by a clock provided by the Data Communications Equipment (DCE, or modem) or the Data Terminal Equipment (DTE, or PC).

Character synchronization—This is required for receiving equipment (the DTE, or PC) to determine which bits are in a character. The DTE counts the bits to determine the character length. Agreement on character length is established and set into the PC and the server before communication begins. Asynchronous transmission uses 10 bits per character; synchronous and isochronous transmission use 8 bits per character.

Message synchronization—This is required for the receiving device (DTE, or PC) to determine the start and end of records or messages. The DTE, using handshakes and message formats established by the Level-2 data link protocol, performs message synchronization.

There are two ways to perform the timing for bit synchronization: with an internal clock, or wristwatch, in each device or with an external clock, or wall clock. Asynchronous transmission uses the wristwatch (internal clock) in every device. Synchronous transmission uses the wall clock (external clock). A wall clock works as the analogy here because most all wall clocks plug into an electrical outlet so they get their timing from the same source, the 60-cycle alternating electric current.

ASYNCHRONOUS TRANSMISSION • In asynchronous transmission, both the sending and receiving devices have wristwatches. The wristwatch is their internal timer. They use the wristwatch and specific agreements on transmission speed, character length, and line terminating characters between sending and receiving devices to perform bit, character, and message synchronization.

Asynchronous transmission is a transmission technique in which each character of information is individually synchronized by using a "start" bit (start bit = 0) at the beginning of the character and a "stop" bit (stop bit = 1) at the end of the character (refer to Figure 5-8). In asynchronous transmission, bit synchronization is performed using the "start" and "stop" bits and a wristwatch (crystal oscillator) in every terminal device. This allows characters to be sent at random or irregular time intervals (asynchronous intervals) after the preceding character has been transmitted.

In asynchronous transmission, when no data is being sent, the transmitting device sends idle signals down the channel. The idle signals are continuous ones—"1's." The start bit is always a zero. The receiving device, seeing a 1 to 0 change on the channel, senses that data is beginning to arrive. It then uses its wristwatch to time each individual bit received based upon the agreed transmission speed. The bit duration is dependent upon the

Clocked Units of Time

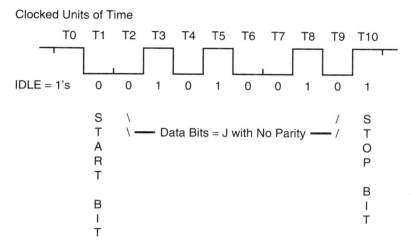

* Code Bits Plus One Start Bit and One Stop Bit
* 8-bit Code Equals 10 Transmission Bits

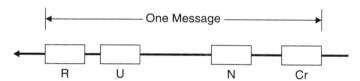

Figure 5–8   *Asynchronous transmission.*

transmission speed setting, with higher transmission speeds having shorter bit times (durations). Both sender and receiver must be set at the same speed. The stop bit is always 1. It returns the channel to the idle state. This prepares the receiving device for the next character.

The receiver counts 10 bits to then expect the end of a character. This is eight data bits and the start and stop bits. Message synchronization is performed by sensing the Carriage Return (CR) or Line Feed (LF) characters. They signal the end of a line of data. When CR or LF are detected, the host system processes the line of text information it has just received.

SYNCHRONOUS TRANSMISSION • Synchronous transmission is a data transmission technique in which a common central clock in the communications channel holds the sending and receiving stations in synchronization with each other. In this case, bit synchronization is accomplished using a master clock, or wall clock. This wall clock for each circuit is maintained either by high-accuracy clocks in the host computer system, the modem, or the communications channel, or by timing signals included in the transmitted data.

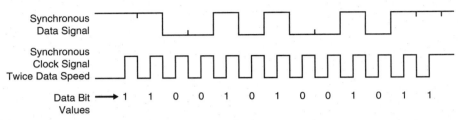

Figure 5–9 *Synchronous transmission clock.*

Example: BISYNC "Poll" Message

First Bit of Character   Last Bit of Character
/   \
0 Synch Bytes   Control Unit   Device   Poll   7
                              Address   Address   Character

← 11	00110010	00110010					00101101	11 ←
	SYN	SYN	C	C	D	D	ENQ	

* Synchronization Using SYN Characters
* No Breaks Between Characters in Messages
* 8-bit Code Equals Eight Transmission Bits
  (All Characters Are in EBCDIC Code)
* Clocking Provided by Modem or Master Circuit Clock
* Used for High-speed Transmission

Figure 5–10 *Synchronous transmission.*

The bit synchronization of both receiver and transmitter is performed using the central (wall clock) clock signal received as a separate signal from the communications channel. The synchronous clock signal is twice the data rate so that the pulse transitions used for bit synchronization are precisely in the middle of the data bit received (see Figure 5-9). In synchronous transmission, bits are sent at fixed times and messages are sent in blocks, frames, packets, or cells. The sending and receiving devices always know the exact bit values sent and received because of the common clock signal. They do not readily know the characters and messages represented by the bits until they find framing characters.

Character synchronization and message synchronization are performed using special communications control characters (framing characters) or octets, e.g., the Synchronous Data Link Control (SDLC) flag byte of zero, six ones, and a zero, or the Binary Synchronous Communications (BSC) protocol SYN (Synchronous Idle) character. The receiving device has no idea when a block of data is to arrive. It must continually search for framing characters. In Figure 5-10, a character is used for message framing.

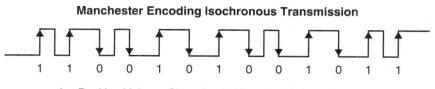

Manchester Encoding Isochronous Transmission

1 1 0 0 1 0 1 0 0 1 0 1 1

0 = Positive Voltage Changing to Negative Voltage
1 = Negative Voltage Changing to Positive Voltage
For Two 1's or Two 0's in a Row, the Voltage Must Be Reset

Figure 5–11 *Manchester encoding.*

Figure 5-10 depicts IBM's BSC protocol operation using EBCDIC character codes. When the receiving device detects one SYN (message framing) character, it clocks in eight more bits and checks for a second SYN character. Since a single character could easily occur by chance, two SYN characters or more precede each block of data. If the second character is a SYN character, then a block of data is truly being received and the receiving device clocks in the bits eight at a time, checking each set of eight bits for other communications control characters. Such characters would signal the end to the block being received. Poll messages are ended with the ENQ (Enquiry) character. In this manner, character synchronization and message synchronization are performed during synchronous transmission.

ISOCHRONOUS TRANSMISSION • Isochronous transmission has the clock and data combined into a single signal. It has properties of asynchronous transmission and synchronous transmission. Voice and video streams are sent with isochronous transmission because they require a continuous, in-sequence stream of precisely timed data that occasionally has single bits missing.

An easy way to understand a combined timing and data signal is to examine Manchester data encoding used in Ethernet LANs. Manchester encoding represents a zero by a positive voltage changing to a negative voltage and a one by a negative voltage changing to a positive voltage (refer to Figure 5-11).

In this fashion, when many "0's" or "1's" are repeated in a Manchester-encoded bit stream, there are more signal transitions than if there was a bit stream of alternating "0's" and "1's." The electronics on Ethernet LAN boards use the voltage transitions to perform bit synchronization. Character and message synchronization are performed in a fashion similar to synchronous transmission, with framing sequences signaling the beginning and ending of a message. The framing sequence is, in the case of Ethernet, a special, unique coding violation (it doesn't follow the Manchester-encoding convention) that signals the beginning or end of a frame of data.

We have described the simple timing techniques that permit communications devices to dance properly with other communications devices. We do this because we do not want devices stepping on each others' toes, or really, losing bits.

THE PERPLEXING PLEXES: SIMPLEX, HALF-DUPLEX, AND FULL DUPLEX

Communications channels may operate in simplex, half-duplex, or duplex (full duplex) transmission mode. This defines how devices can communicate. Simplex means that only you can talk. For example, Dilbert believes that managers seem to only talk while employees are forced to listen. They could not ever switch. Half-duplex means you can talk or you can listen, but you cannot do both at the same time. This is what most humans do in normal conversation. Duplex means you can talk and listen at the same time, which usually takes place in a Jerry Springer Show-type argument. These terms are perplexing because they describe the physical channel, character flows across the channel, and message flows on the channel. So, a channel may be at the same time full duplex and half-duplex. The physical channel, in this case, is full duplex and the message flows are half-duplex.

A channel/circuit/line is an electrical transmission path between two points. It is usually some type of copper wire, but may be optical fiber or an RF link as well. Channels may be classified as simplex, half-duplex, or duplex (full duplex). These terms are illustrated in Figure 5-12. A simplex channel transmits data in only one direction. This is like a presentation. One person speaks, the remainder listen. Printer transmission is simplex transmission.

A half-duplex channel permits two-way transmission, one way at a time. This is similar to a question-and-answer format. One person first asks a question, then the second person replies with an answer. Most terminal-to-host communication is half-duplex. Duplex, or full duplex, is two-way simultaneous transmission. This is like an argument. Both persons speak simultaneously. Host-to-host communications may be full duplex. A full duplex channel is composed of a simplex transmitting channel and a simplex receiving channel. So, two simplex channels are needed to make a full duplex channel. These definitions are simple enough. The confusion comes when they are applied.

Full duplex and half-duplex are used at any time to describe the physical channel, character flows across the channel, or message flows on the

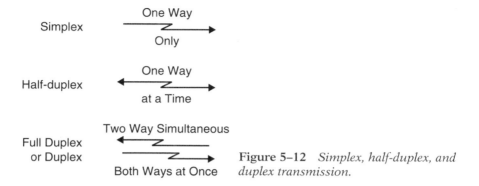

Figure 5–12 *Simplex, half-duplex, and duplex transmission.*

channel. Most channels are physically full duplex, while computer to terminal message flows are half-duplex (see Figure 5-13).

In Figure 5-13, a character typed on the keyboard is transmitted down the channel to the WAN server. The WAN server remembers the character received and then immediately transmits that character back to the thin dial-up client. The physical channel is full duplex along with the character flows. Message flows are half-duplex because an entire message must be received before the WAN server processes it and returns a response to the thin dial-up client; for example, logging a PC in on a dial-up connection to an Internet Service Provider (ISP). When we log in, the ISP's host computer sends out a request for a user name. We respond and type in our name. Our name appears on our display screen. The ISP's host computer echoes characters (full duplex character flows) to our PC. Once we press Enter (which creates CR and LF characters), the host looks up our user name and then sends a message requesting our password (half-duplex message flows). We enter the password, but nothing appears on our PC screen because the dial-up host suppresses the character echo back to our PC (half-duplex character flows). In all instances, the physical channel has two simplex pathways forming a physical full duplex channel. The major benefit of duplex operation is that we know the host computer received our data correctly. It provides us visual verification of the data received. This is how most dial-up connections work today.

When our PC is set to local echo, or half-duplex operation (highly unusual), the instant we type a character, the PC displays it and simultaneously sends it into the ISP's host computer system. Here we see the character immediately on typing it, but we lose verification that the WAN server received what we typed correctly.

Virtually all dial-up communications employ echoplex, or full duplex transmission. With echoplex, the host echoes any characters sent by the PC

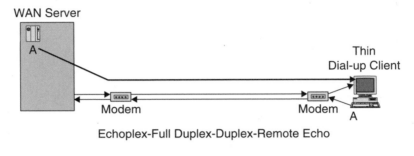

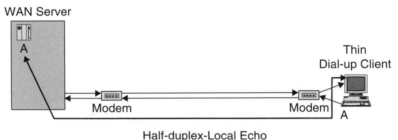

Figure 5–13 *Terminal duplex vs. half-duplex operation.*

or terminal. In this case, the PC or terminal must disable local echo, or double characters result. Terminals do not have a local echo on/off switch. Instead, the switch is often labeled HDX (Half-Duplex)/FDX (Full Duplex). HDX means local echo enabled. FDX means local echo disabled. When the host does not echo characters by sending what you typed back to you, you must enable a local echo on your PC or terminal to see what you typed.

The IRS in the very early days of PCs solicited automation equipment for their offices. They selected Zilog 16-bit multi-user microcomputer systems to perform spreadsheet analysis and basic word processing. The Zilog 16-bit multi-user microsystems were designed to handle from 8 to 12 active users. But in typical government fashion, when they awarded the contract, it was easier to extend that contract than to re-compete and get something better, or more likely, worse. (As I recall, Zilog was owned at the time by Exxon as one of their forays into the computer marketplace.) So the number of users on the multi-user micro zoomed from 8 to 12 to around 24. This poor Zilog system was overloaded, especially at the beginning of each day when everyone would log on and select spreadsheet or word processing software to load.

The users interfaced to the Zilog 16-bit multi-user microsystems through dumb terminals connected by Layer-1 bit serial full duplex wiring directly to the Zilog 16-bit multi-user microsystems. Their terminals were set into full duplex transmission mode so that their typing input to the Zilog 16-bit multi-user microsystems was returned to their terminal, permitting the user to verify what they typed. This verification was not needed to correct transmission errors, for after all, what errors could there be on 50 feet of wire running across the floor. There should have been none! When users logged in at the beginning of the day, the poor Zilog 16-bit multi-user microsystems were overloaded. An IRS user would log in and receive a menu of options, of which they would select, say, option "A" by typing "A" on the keyboard. In good full duplex fashion, the "A" would travel promptly into the Zilog. The poor Zilog at this time totally exasperated. It would think, "Oh no, not another."

Now our intrepid IRS employee user was sitting comatose in front of the Zilog terminal with finger on the "A" key and was beginning to drool on the keyboard because several minutes had passed. They thought nothing had happened, so they proceeded to strike "A," "A," "A," "A," "A," and "A" and thought, "Take that!" Now where did they end up in the menus? Certainly not where they expected. How could this be easily fixed? You are correct! Just set the terminals to half-duplex or local echo operation so as the IRS users typed, every character would be immediately displayed.

Simplex, half-duplex, and full duplex simply define how we and devices communicate with each other.

Brain Teaser

Applying Basic Transmission Concepts

Let's apply transmission concepts using a PC. We need any Windows 95 or 98 PC with Hyper Terminal installed. The Hyper Terminal program makes a PC behave like a simple keyboard display terminal for dial-up communications. It is used to permit any PC to function as a console device to a PBX, disk array RAID controller, etc.

1. First open a DOS window. At the prompt, enter **mode com1 300**. The PC should return:
   COM1: 300,e,7,1
which states that COM Port 1 is set to 300 bits per second asynchronous transmission and the character format is 7 data bits with even parity and one stop bit. The "-" describes the retry status for operations on the COM1 port.

2. Enter **mode com1 9600 n,8**. The PC should return:
   COM1: 9600,n,8,1
which states that COM Port 1 is now set to 9600 bits per second asynchronous transmission and the character format is 8 data bits with no parity and one stop bit.

3. Try **mode com1 9600 n,8,2**. What does this change? Can you set it to **mode com1 9600 n,8,0**? In asynchronous transmission, characters can use 1, 1.5, or 2 stop bits. Other combinations are not permitted.

4. Start the Hyper Terminal program. It should be found under **Accessories — Communications — Hyper Terminal**. Open **AT&T** or any preset configuration by double-clicking on the icon. Cancel dialing a number and get to the empty terminal screen. Open **File Properties** and ignore the port selection message. Click the **Configure** button to set or view the transmission speed.

5. Cancel modem setup and click the **Settings** tab. Notice the backspace key setting. It should say Ctrl H. Does that match our ASCII code chart in Figure 5-4?

6. Click the **ASCII setup** button. What does **echo typed characters locally** mean? Duplex or half-duplex operation?

The goal here is to see how these fundamental data communications concepts are applied and related to PC communications.

Modems and ISDN Modems

A modem (Modulator/Demodulator) is a telephone for a computer. It is simply a conversion device. Digital data from a PC is converted into analog tones of varying phases and amplitudes by a modem. The modem takes the digital data in our PC and modulates it to produce the equivalent of an analog voice signal. Older modems modulated frequencies to send data. Newer modems modulate phases and amplitudes. With analog transmission, noise detection is difficult, and amplification increases noise. Analog signal noise is a big factor in reliable data transmission using modems.

Today's modems go beyond simple data modulation into a voice-grade-equivalent analog signal. They provide data compression and special link controls to increase the effective transmission speed. We need to examine basic modem operation before reviewing newer, more sophisticated modem features. Before examining modems, we need to explain baud vs. bits per second vs. bytes per second. These are three common mechanisms for expressing communication speed.

BAUD VS. BITS PER SECOND VS. BYTES PER SECOND

Bit is short for BInary digiT. A bit is a voltage state that either is present (on, yes, mark, "1," +5 volts, or positive) or absent (off, no, space, "0," 0 volts, or negative). It is the smallest unit of data recognized by computers. All data (letters, numerals, symbols) handled by computers is digitized, i.e., expressed entirely as a combination of "0's" and "1's." A bit is the smallest unit of information (0 or 1) in a binary system of notation. As we have seen, bits are used in combination to form characters; framing bits are used for parity, transmission synchronization, and so on.

Baud is a unit of signaling speed. Speed expressed in baud is equal to the number of signaling elements per second. However, baud has been corrupted and today is most commonly used to describe data transmitting/receiving speeds that are equal to a single bit per second. Common bits per second speeds (called baud rates) are 110, 300, 1,200, 2,400, 4,800, and 9,600, 19,200, 28,800, 33,600, and 56,000.

The term "baud" was derived from a unit of signaling speed equivalent to the number of signaling elements per second, usually designating the transmission speed of systems employing Baudot code and low-speed asynchronous transmission.

Most high-speed modems communicate at lower baud rates, e.g. 2,400 baud, but send data at high bits per second speeds, e.g. 9,600 bps. Baud is the number of times per second that a modem signal can change its amplitude, frequency, and phase states.

A byte is an eight-bit unit of information equivalent to a printed character. As we saw earlier, a byte is different patterns of zeros and ones, eight at a time, representing printable characters. A byte is a group of eight binary digits (bits) processed by a computer as a unit. A byte is commonly shorter than a computer word, which can be 16 bits, 32 bits, or 64 bits. A byte, then, is eight successive bits handled as a single unit in computer manipulation or data transmission. Sometimes transmission speeds are expressed in bytes per second.

To illustrate the difference between bits per second and baud, we are going to transmit some data across a communications channel using frequencies. In the first case, we will let each frequency represent a single bit.

We need to construct a communications channel, so let me be the transmitting device and you can be the receiving device. The channel we use is a trough of water running from me to you. I make waves in the trough of water by splashing 700 times a second, 1,400 times a second, 2,100 times a second, or 2,800 times a second. I am acting like a Frequency Shift Keying (FSK) modem. Your job is to roll up your sleeve, stick your arm in the trough of water, and determine how fast (what frequency) the waves are coming down the trough. Are they 700, 1,400, 2,100, or 2,800 splashes per second? So far, so good! Now, who has the harder job, you or me? You guessed it, you have the harder job. (Everyone always thinks that they have the harder job!) In this case it is true; receiving signals is more difficult than sending them. Look, I am writing this book, so why would I pick the hardest job?

```
─────────────────────────────────────────   3,400 Cycles Per Sec
F4 = 2,800 Cycles Per Sec                    = 1
F3 = 2,100 Cycles Per Sec
F2 = 1,400 Cycles Per Sec
F1 =   700 Cycles Per Sec                    = 0
─────────────────────────────────────────   300 Cycles Per Sec
```

Case #1: Change Frequencies 100 Times Per Sec = 100 Bits Per Sec

Figure 5–14   *100 baud = 100 bits per second.*

Here are a couple of interesting thoughts. What must happen when I stop sending (splashing) and shift to receiving and you stop receiving and start transmitting (splashing)? Think for a second: What must happen to the trough of water? It must become quiescent so I do not confuse the new waves you create with the old waves I created. What would an OSI Layer-1, full duplex channel look like? It would be two separate troughs of water. Now let's move on to baud vs. bits per second.

In our first case, let's agree that a one is 2,800 cycles per second and a zero is 700 cycles per second. If I shift between 2,800 cycles per second and 700 cycles per second one hundred times each second, then I send you 100 bits per second across our communications channel. We are signaling at 100 baud and sending 100 bits per second. In this instance, baud and bits per second are exactly the same. This is illustrated in Figure 5-14.

In our second case, we will use four frequencies. Each frequency represents two bits (or a dibit). Two zeros are signaled by 700 cycles per second, a zero and a one by 1,400 cycles per second, a one and a zero by 2,100 cycles per second, and two ones by 2,800 cycles per second. What has happened to your job? You guessed it; it is now harder. If I shift between the four frequencies 100 times a second, I still signal at 100 baud. However, in this case, each signal change sends two bits so that the bits per second transmission speed is 200 bits per second. This is illustrated in Figure 5-15.

This is the true difference between baud and bits per second. We like to always use bits per second or characters per second when describing transmission speeds because it leaves no room for misinterpretation of the speed.

MODEM DATA ENCODING

Modems use amplitude, frequency, and phase changes in their analog signal to encode bits and transmit them across communications links. This is referred to as Amplitude Modulation (AM), Frequency Modulation (FM), and phase modulation. More commonly, frequency and phase modulation

```
──────────────────────────────────────────   3,400 Cycles Per Sec
F4 = 2,800 Cycles Per Sec                     = 1 1
F3 = 2,100 Cycles Per Sec                     = 1 0
F2 = 1,400 Cycles Per Sec                     = 0 1
F1 =   700 Cycles Per Sec                     = 0 0
──────────────────────────────────────────   300 Cycles Per Sec
```

Case #2: Change Frequencies 100 Times Per Sec = 200 Bits Per Sec

Figure 5–15   *100 baud = 200 bits per second.*

are called Frequency Shift Keying (FSK) and Phase Shift Keying (PSK), or Differential Phase Shift Keying (DPSK). New modems use more sophisticated encoding techniques that we will discuss shortly. For the time being, let us examine some simple modem data encoding.

In early modems bits were encoded in the analog signal by shifting between high and low frequencies for "0's" and "1's." This encoding was used by Western Electric 103/113 modems, the most commonly used 300 bits per second, or 30 characters per second, modem.

As modems moved to higher speeds, PSK encoding was employed. With PSK, bits were encoded by shifting the phase angle of the transmitted data signal. For example, a phase shift of 180 degrees signals a 0 bit as shown in Figure 5-16. DPSK uses several different phase shifts to represent the four possible combinations of two 0 and 1 bits (00, 01, 10, and 11). The Western Electric 212 modems, the most commonly 1,200 bits per second, or 120 characters per second, modems use this encoding.

Newer modems transmit at much higher speeds than these early modems. Nonetheless, it is helpful to understand how they work before tackling some of the encoding techniques used by newer high- speed modems.

QUADRATURE AMPLITUDE MODULATION • Quadrature Amplitude Modulation (QAM) is used in 28,800-bps modems. QAM combines amplitude modulation with PSK to produce unique, distinctive combinations called tokens. These tokens are assigned to four-bit groups, or quads. QAM combines 8 different angles in phase modulation and 2 amplitudes of signal modulation to provide 16 different signals, each of which can represent 4 bits.

Let's see how this works. We can create a table (Table 5-2) to determine the tokens for each 4-bit quad. Any resemblance between our table and the QAM standard is purely coincidental.

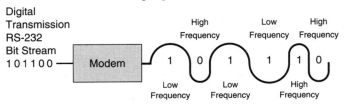

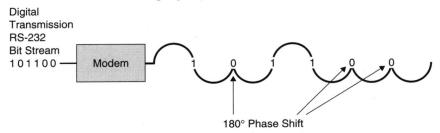

Figure 5–16 *Modem encoding.*

Table 5.2 *Quadrature Amplitude Encoding*

Decimal Value	Bit Value	Amplitude	Phase Shift
0	0000	1	No shift
1	0001	2	No shift
2	0010	1	45 degrees, or 1/8 phase shift
3	0011	2	45 degrees, or 1/8 phase shift
4	0100	1	90 degrees, or ¼ phase shift
5	0101	2	90 degrees, or ¼ phase shift
6	0110	1	135 degrees, or 3/8 phase shift
7	0111	2	135 degrees, or 3/8 phase shift
8	1000	1	180 degrees, or ½ phase shift
9	1001	2	180 degrees, or ½ phase shift
10 or A	1010	1	225 degrees, or 5/8 phase shift
11 or B	1011	2	225 degrees, or 5/8 phase shift
12 or C	1100	1	270 degrees, or ¾ phase shift
13 or D	1101	2	270 degrees, or ¾ phase shift
14 or E	1110	1	315 degrees, or 7/8 phase shift
15 or F	1111	2	315 degrees, or 7/8 phase shift

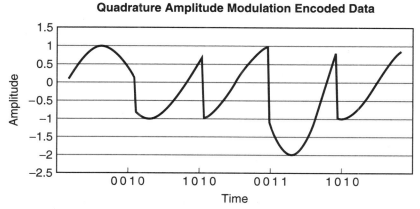

Figure 5-17 *Quadrature amplitude encoded data.*

Now we can encode the bit stream:

    0010101000111010

First, break it up into 4-bit quads:

    0010-1010 -0011-1010

Now assign the proper token to the 4-bit quad to determine what the resulting signal will look like. Each wave shifts relative to the wave before it. See Figure 5-17.

Higher speed modems use more tokens and more bits per token. Think of the different amplitudes and phase shifts needed for 28.8-Kbps and higher speed modems. QAM performs better than PSK because there are greater changes between QAM phases.

TRELLIS CODING • Trellis coding is an encoding and decoding technology that uses a large set of possible changes in amplitude and phase tokens combined with sophisticated mathematics to predict the best fit for modulating a stream of digital data. A trellis is a transition diagram for finite states (amplitude and phase change tokens) that takes time into account. Populating a trellis means specifying output symbols (like the four bits assigned to different QAM tokens) for each branch. Once complete, specifying an initial phase and amplitude token predicts an allowable set of resultant phase and amplitude tokens.

Trellis coding permits a modem to best match the data rate with the channel's electrical properties, e.g., the channel's Signal to Noise Ratio (SNR). A trellis coder, which is populated with symbols (or binary values, e.g., 4-bit patterns of data) and a beginning input, outputs the sequence of bits corresponding to the output sequence that maximizes the SNR of the

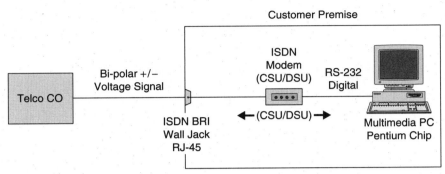

Figure 5–18 *ISDN CSU/DSU.*

encoding. The receiving modem determines, based upon the value of the preceding signal, whether or not a given signal is received in error. In this manner, trellis encoding provides a form of error detection and correction. Data transmitted over a channel can be damaged and yet a trellis decoder can rebuild the information with very high accuracy. Modems that operate at 14,000 bps and higher speeds use trellis encoding. V.34 and V.34 bis modems use multi-dimensional trellis encoding to provide higher immunity to noise and other telephone line transmission impairments.

Modems are simply conversion devices. Digital Subscriber Line (DSL) is the next generation of modems that provides megabits per second transmission speeds.

ISDN MODEMS—CHANNEL SERVICE UNIT/DATA SERVICE UNIT

In contrast to modems, digital data transmission requires a Data Service Unit/Channel Service Unit (DSU/CSU) combination. A DSU/CSU is simply a conversion device that converts one type of digital signal to another type of digital signal. ISDN provides direct digital data transmission. PCs are interfaced to ISDN BRI lines using ISDN modems. These are not really modems, but rather Channel Service Units/Data Service Units (CSU/DSUs). Marketing and advertising people label them modems because the term "modem" has come to mean a telephone for a computer.

CSU/DSU are the interface between CPE and the telephone network. The CSU side interacts with the telephone network to permit remote automated testing of the local loop connecting the CPE to the telephone network. The DSU side interfaces with the CPE using a compatible interface, e.g., RS-232 (see Figure 5-18).

CSU/DSUs are required for connecting equipment to digital transmission facilities. They are not used to connect communications equipment to analog facilities. The CSU portion examines incoming data and ensures that it is clean. If the square wave pulses are not clean, the CSU cleans up incoming data pulses. It also provides a loopback capability for network troubleshooting. The DSU portion converts the terminal equipment square waves to bipolar (+ positive or − negative) pulses, and vice versa. Bipolar pulses are just another somewhat more reliable way to represent digital signals. The DSU also inserts extra transitions into the bit stream (isochronous transmission) if there is a long string of zeroes so telephone company equipment does not become confused and as a result drop one of the zeros in the string.

The CSU loopback capability permits the telephone company to send signals from its central test equipment and loop them back to that same test equipment. It can test circuit continuity and bit error rates using the loopback capability of the CSU. Thus the CSU's loopback test facility verifies the integrity of the circuit and permits measurement of circuit electrical operating parameters.

2B1Q • ISDN BRI service is delivered full duplex as a 160-Kbps signal over existing ordinary copper wire facilities using Two Binary One Quaternary (2B1Q) data encoding. However, for 2B1Q modulation loading coils, restricting the frequency response of the line must be removed.

2B1Q transmission is simply an amplitude modulation scheme for DC pulses. The 2B1Q encoding standard in North America uses two bits assigned to a single quaternary line state. The 2B1Q two-bit patterns represent one of four amplitude levels on the line. The resultant baud rate (channel signaling rate) is 80K. 2B1Q signaling operates with a maximum frequency range of 40 KHz and at distances up to about 18,000 feet. 2B1Q transmission is shown in Figure 5-19.

DIGITAL LOOP CARRIER ISDN CONNECTIONS • ISDN and some other telephone company high-speed communications services are delivered to customer premises using Digital Loop Carrier (DLC) technology. The first DLC technology began to appear in the 1980s. These early DLC technology implementations provided a cost-effective means to connect many subscriber concentrations to a telephone CO. DLC technology is used as a service delivery tool. Early DLC network architectures were designed to deploy ISDN to all telephone subscribers. However, the widespread need for ISDN never materialized. Nonetheless, DLC was good for delivering high bit rate services such as T-1, ISDN, and DDS. (Note: Digital Data Service, or DDS, was an early private-line digital service offered at data rates of 2.4, 4.8, 9.6, and 56 Kbps.)

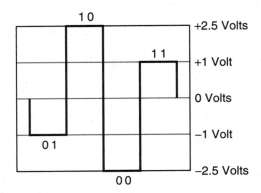

All Voltage Values Are Approximate Values, Not Exact Values.

Figure 5–19 *2B1Q encoding.*

As far as transport on the network side, most of these systems were designed for fiber. So, the key element as far as deployment of this system was concerned was making sure that fiber ran between the CO and a remote subscriber's terminal. Unfortunately, that was not always the case. Nonetheless, if fiber was in place between the two locations, this was a very good system and the intent was to serve large numbers of customers.

New DLC uses 1990s technology to take advantage of increasing computing power and new microelectronics. DLC is based more on software control and intelligence and less on fiber optic transmission. DLC is now a service delivery tool designed for mixed media transmission. DLC uses whatever OSI Layer-1 infrastructure is in place: T-carrier, analog, fiber, or coax. DLC technology running over local loops is more important for delivering the new services that customers require.

MODEM SPECIFICATION SUMMARY

Current dial-up PC modems are described by analog signaling specifications and data compression specifications. Table 5-3 summarizes the different signaling specifications used by dial-up modems. Modems typically support all specifications up to the highest specification advertised. For example, a V.32 bis modem would also incorporate V.32, V.22 bis, etc. analog signaling.

Modems also perform protocol handshaking and data compression functions separate from and in addition to their digital-to-analog encoding functions. Modems are computers that talk to each other using an OSI Layer-2 protocol. They perform on-the-fly data compression using compression algorithms built into their ROMs (see Table 5-4).

Table 5.3 *Modem Analog Signaling Specifications*

Modem Transmission Speed	Signaling Compatibility
300 Bps	WE 103/113 (WE -- Western Electric)
1,200 Bps	CCITT V.22 CCITT V.22 bis Bell 212 A (most used in U.S.)
2,400 Bps	CCITT V.22 bis
4,800 Bps	CCITT V.32
9,600 Bps	CCITT V.32
7,200 Bps to 14,400 Bps	CCITT V.32 bis
28,800 Bps	CCITT V.FAST CCITT V.34
33,600 Bps	CCITT V.34 +
33,600 Bps - up and 56,000 Bps - down	V.90 or K-Flex (USR-X2)

The protocol handshaking and data compression performed by modems is invisible to our PC while it is transmitting data. So to every PC, a modem appears as an OSI Layer-1 device when in fact they are really sophisticated devices incorporating OSI Layer-1 and Layer-2 functions with data compression. This results in a key configuration option for the interface between the modem and the PC. For these sophisticated modems to operate properly with a PC, the PC/modem interface must be configured for hardware handshaking. The XON/XOFF handshaking option should not be used.

High-speed modems sold today perform both data and facsimile transmission. They are used in individual PCs to send and receive faxes and in fax server PCs that serve a LAN. Facsimile operation requires that special setup commands (different from data transmission setup commands) be given to the modem and that special data/facsimile software be used in the PC. The modem automatically recognizes an incoming fax transmission, but must have special software in the PC to receive the fax.

HIGH-SPEED MODEM TECHNOLOGIES

Two modem technologies are used for high-speed Digital Subscriber Line (DSL) modems. These technologies are Carrier-less Amplitude and Phase (CAP) modulation and Discrete Multi-Tone (DMT) modulation.

CARRIER-LESS AMPLITUDE AND PHASE MODULATION • Carrier-less Amplitude and Phase (CAP) modulation is a variant of QAM; this modulation scheme is used for ADSL. CAP modulation is an *adaptive* form of QAM. It adjusts its

Table 5.4 *Modem OSI Layer-2 Protocol Specifications*

Link Protocol	Error Detection—Compression	Remarks
CCITT V.42 bis	Error detection and correction Data compression up to 4:1	Little compression and speed increase for compressed files such as ARC, ZIP, LZH. Some compression and speed increase for binary files such as EXE, COM, DLL, etc. Maximum compression and speed increase for text and tabular files. Transmission speed can increase as much as 400% over modem speed.
CCITT V.42	Error detection and correction	Error correction only. Uses synchronous transmission to increase effective data rate to as much as 120% of the rated modem speed.
MNP Class 5	Error detection and correction Data compression up to 2:1	Similar to V.42 bis with less effective data compression. Transmission speed can increase as much as 200% over modem speed.
MNP Class 4	Error detection and correction	This protocol includes adaptive packet sizing and data optimization, producing improved data transfer speeds. Maximum improvement on clear telephone lines is 120%.
MNP Class 3	Error detection and correction	Uses full duplex synchronous transmission to increase effective data rate. Maximum transmission speed increase is about 108%.
MNP Class 2	Error detection and correction	Uses full duplex **asynchronous** transmission to increase data rate. Maximum transmission speed increase is about 84% of modem speed.

symbol values to take account of line conditions (e.g., noise) of the channel. CAP is labeled "carrier-less" because the carrier frequency is removed from the output waveform. This makes CAP more efficient because the carrier frequency carries no useful information and wastes transmission power. CAP runs across a wider frequency range from 4KHz up to 1.1MHz as a single channel. The number of signals that CAP modulation can generate depends on the number of information bits sent over a channel.

CAP can be designed to transmit multiple bits, ranging from 2 to 9 bits per baud. This enables CAP-based transceivers to transmit the same amount of information using a lower range of the frequency spectrum than is required by ISDN's 2B1Q. This results in less signal attenuation and greater loop reach. By using different algorithms CAP can adjust the bit rate of the session in real time. This gives CAP modulation the advantages of low cost, reduced latency (delay), and data rate adaptation.

Similar to 2B1Q, CAP modulation uses an advanced encoding technique that allows multiple bits of information to be represented by a single frequency cycle or baud. CAP modulation provides T-1 (1.544 Mbps) speeds at low cost because of its simplicity. CAP is not a standard and is susceptible to interference because it uses a single channel. Discrete Multi-Tone (DMT) modulation is standardized for DSL loops and will be more widely used in the long term.

DISCRETE MULTI-TONE MODULATION • Discrete Multi-Tone (DMT) modulation and CAP modulation use the same fundamental modulation technique, a form of QAM. They apply the QAM technique differently. Both DMT and CAP use the full copper telephone wire's frequency spectrum of 1.1Mhz. This range of frequencies is used with two restrictions:

- The lower 4Khz frequency must be reserved for voice telephony.
- Signal amplification isn't the same for all frequencies.

DMT modulation divides the frequency range from 64Khz to 1.1Mhz onto 256 4-KHz channels and CAP modulation does not. In this fashion, DMT is similar to spread-spectrum communications. Instead of a bit serial transmission path, DMT creates the equivalent of a parallel channel. Each sub-frequency is an independent channel with its own stream of data. The protocol sends a pre-defined data stream to find the specific SNR for each sub-frequency. This information is then used to determine how the data is split over the sub-frequencies for transmission (see Figure 5-20).

Regular voice telephone frequencies are not affected in any way because an analog splitter circuit separates the lowest 4KHz. DMT technology in the asymmetric mode divides sub-channels into groups, one for upstream data (from the customer premise to the telephone company) and the other for downstream data (from the telephone company to the customer premise).

DMT modulation divides the available frequencies into discrete 4KHz channels and then breaks down incoming data for distribution to a specific 4KHz channel based on the channel's SNR. The SNR is a measure of the

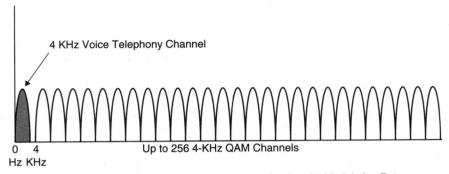

Total Data Rate = Number of Channels × Bits Per Baud × Modulation Rate

Figure 5–20 *DMT channel division.*

ability of the channel to carry the data transmission. Because high-frequency signals are more susceptible to noise, more data travels on the lower sub-frequency channels than in the upper ones. DMT modulation is faster, less prone to interference, and carries data over longer distances than CAP modulation.

Discrete Wavelet Multi-Tone (DWMT) modulation is a new variation of DMT modulation. DWMT modulation increases performance and complexity by creating greater isolation between the 4KHz channels.

In summary, modems are conversion devices that allow devices with different types of electrical signaling to communicate to one another. The conversion could be analog to digital conversion, or it could be digital to digital signal conversion. Such conversions are OSI Layer 1, physical layer, functions.

Brain Teaser

Modems

Get a Windows PC that has a modem installed and open the **Control Panel – Modem selection**.

1. Select the **Diagnostics** tab. What brand name modem is identified? To which COM port is it assigned?

2. Highlight the modem's COM port and click on **More Info…**. What is displayed? Is the Rockwell chip set identified anywhere? The chip set may not be identified. Most modems use a Rockwell chip set, but they differ in the internal ROM software controlling the modem.

3. Return to the **General** tab and click the **Properties** button. Now select the **Connection** tab and the **Advanced** button. Is **Use Error Control** selected? This enables the error control and data compression identified in Table 5-4. How is the **Use Flow Control** option set? Hardware flow control should be set

and not software (XON/XOFF) flow control. Sometimes modem operation is improved using the **Extra** setting **&F S9=1**. &F resets the modem to its default values and s9=1 is an old Hayes modem command that has the modem detect the carrier signal in one millisecond.

4. Now call an AOL modem using your telephone (not your modem) so you can listen to how a modem answers the telephone. Use an AOL 800 number like 800 716-0023. Listen while the modem cycles through its modulation cycles trying to connect to your modem.

This study break makes you more aware of Windows modem settings.

Voice, Image, and Video Encoding

Data transmission is text information encoded in ASCII characters. Typical data is electronic mail or email messages. Not all digital data transmitted is text. Images are also sent as digital data. An image is a picture or scanned document that is represented in a digital form with binary data. Images are similar to data because they are sent as blocks, chunks, or wads of information.

Video with sound or voice can be similarly encoded into a digital data stream. It is different than data traffic in that it is transmitted as a continuous stream of digital information. Video and voice transmission use the isochronous transmission mode.

Voice, Images (Pictures), and Video as Data

To send an image (still picture or scanned document) as a digital stream, the image must be converted from its analog form into a digital form. This is accomplished by sampling the analog information.

Visualize a black and white photograph. A black and white photo is not black and white, but rather shades of gray. Let us use 16 shades of gray. To digitize the photograph, we divide the 16-level grayscale photographic image into little squares. Each square is assigned a value 0, 1, 2, ... 8, 9, A, B, ... E, F according to how white (or black) the square is.

With four bits assigned to each value, e.g., 0=0000, 1=0001, 2=0010, ... E=1110, F=1111, we can produce a stream of bits representing the photo. Transmitting the bits assigned to each cell as we scan the cells from upper left to lower right in the image creates the stream.

To a communications network carrying and routing streams of bits, voice, image, video, and data traffic appear much the same. However, there are some basic differences, including:

- Voice—Requires moderate transmission speeds (64 Kbps), can have lost bits, and the bit sequence of the transmission must be maintained.
- Image or facsimile—Uses slow (9,600 Bps) to moderate (14.4 Kbps) speeds with data compression (no one is waiting hat in hand for the fax), can have lost bits, and data can arrive in any order as long as it is reassembled properly.
- Data—Can use slow (9,600 Bps) to moderate speed (128 Kbps) transmission (moderate transmission is needed when data and images are combined), no bits can be lost, and data can arrive in any order as long as it is reassembled.
- Video—Requires high speeds (128 Kbps, minimum) because it is a constant stream of images (15 per second and up), can have lost bits, and the bit sequence of transmission often must be maintained. With video, high transmission speed means that more simultaneous conversations can happen at any given time, e.g., a video conference call.

The important thing to realize here is that image, voice, and video traffic are the driving factors behind the need for increased transmission speed (or increased bandwidth). Text information alone is boring. Making it look good with interesting fonts, images, and video with sound is critical for providing future Internet services. This increased need for speed is illustrated in our Study Break exercise using Figure 5-21.

To a communications network, data, voice, and video are still a bunch of "0's" and "1's" that have different delivery requirements (regarding errors and continuous flows) that must be met by the network.

Brain Teaser

The Need for Speed

Use Figure 5-21 to answer the following questions:
1. If we were to transmit our character "Z" as an ASCII character, how many bits would be sent across a communications channel? The answer is 8 bits.
2. We could convert the "Z" to a graphic image, similar to what a scanner or facsimile machine would do, by breaking up the image area into cells. In Figure 5-21, there are 10 columns and 11 rows, for 110 total cells. Each cell could be assigned a number based upon the shading in the cell. No shading would be "0" and black would be all "1's." A cell in between would have a value like 0010. These are grayscale assignments using a 4-bit grayscale. To transmit our image, we would now scan the cells from upper left to lower right. This would produce a stream of how many bits? It

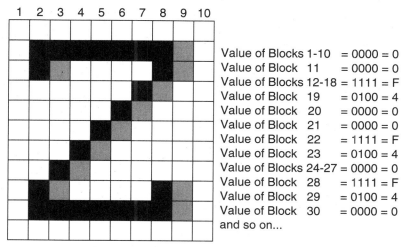

| | | | | | | | | | | |
Value of Blocks 1-10 = 0000 = 0
Value of Block 11   = 0000 = 0
Value of Blocks 12-18 = 1111 = F
Value of Block 19   = 0100 = 4
Value of Block 20   = 0000 = 0
Value of Block 21   = 0000 = 0
Value of Block 22   = 1111 = F
Value of Block 23   = 0100 = 4
Value of Blocks 24-27 = 0000 = 0
Value of Block 28   = 1111 = F
Value of Block 29   = 0100 = 4
Value of Block 30   = 0000 = 0
and so on...

Figure 5–21 *Image encoding.*

would be 110 cells times 4 bits per cell, or 440 bits. This is a 55-fold increase in the bits transmitted.

3. Now let us make a better-looking "Z" image by adding cells. We could split every cell into four smaller cells. What happens to the bits representing the image now? They increase to 110 times 4 times 4, or 1,760 bits.

4. Now let us improve the "Z" image by making more grayscales, or by using 32-bit true color. The 32-bit true color would increase the bits per cell from 4 bits to 32 bits. This is an 8-fold increase in the number of bits, so we now must transmit 14,080 bits — a lot of bits, but just think, we have a good picture of that Z!

5. Now we send our image as strobe light video at four frames per second, or robot video at 17 frames per second, or full-motion video at 30 frames per second. For full-motion video, we would create a 422,400-bps data stream. Now can you see the need for speed?

The goal here is to understand the increases in transmission speed that image, voice, and video traffic demand.

Data Communications Layer-2 Protocols

As we discussed in Chapter 2, protocols are the languages of data communications. The OSI Layer-2 data link protocols are not visible to us. They are implemented in LAN card and modem hardware, which to us appear to be cards or boxes with flashing lights. This section describes protocols. The primary objective of a (data link) protocol is error-free transfer of data from one end of an electrical communications channel to another. A protocol is equivalent to a language. If we speak English, when we answer the phone, we say "Hello." If we can't hear someone, we say, "I didn't hear you, please repeat the message." These are handshake messages used in protocols to coordinate the transfer of data across a communications channel.

Understanding protocols is important because they provide the underlying operating characteristics that impact telecommunications equipment and services. This is true for both voice and data transmission.

In data communications, protocols perform character and message synchronization functions, error detection and correction functions, coordinate sending and receiving data frames, and pace and buffer data to match transmission speed with display speed (see Figure 5-22).

Protocols play a very important role in today's voice, image, and video communications. They essentially determine the product characteristics of telephony and video communications products and services. The protocols used by such telephony equipment and services must provide robust error handling and other functionality depending upon the application. These protocols are less visible to us because they are embedded into the products and services we purchase.

Further, for products from one vendor to talk with the products of another vendor, these protocols must inter-operate. They must work exactly the same way in both vendors' equipment.

Second- and third-generation protocols are not used in voice and video communications. Fourth-generation protocols are the foundation for SS-7 and ISDN services. The fourth-generation LAPD (Link Access Protocol Data) runs on the "D" channel and carries ASCII code signaling packets. Fifth-generation LAN protocols compete with PBX switching for carrying voice, video, and data to the desktop. They compete with seventh-generation ATM protocols for that task as well. Gigabyte Ethernet may be the final winner here. Sixth-generation frame relay protocols were originally aimed at data only. However, today there is increasing interest in setting up voice connectivity over frame relay networks. Finally, underlying all of this is the Synchronous Optical Network (SONET) ring multiplexing. They are the foundation for the SONET rings that provide high-speed optical transmission facilities between telephone company COs and business campus sites with extraordinary communications loads.

An understanding of data communications protocol operating characteristics, message formats, and features helps us understand telecommunications, communications equipment, and the services built upon them.

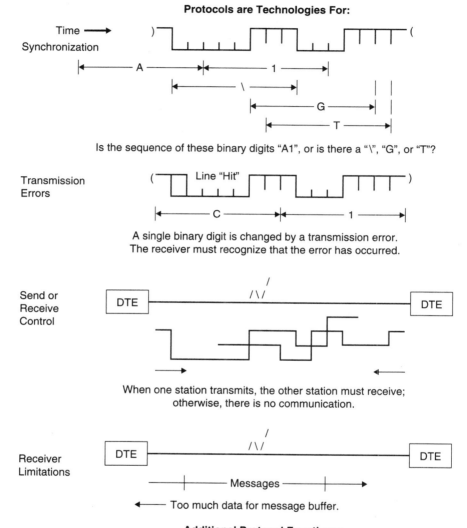

Protocols are Technologies For:

Time →
Synchronization

Is the sequence of these binary digits "A1", or is there a "\", "G", or "T"?

Transmission
Errors

A single binary digit is changed by a transmission error.
The receiver must recognize that the error has occurred.

Send or
Receive
Control

When one station transmits, the other station must receive;
otherwise, there is no communication.

Receiver
Limitations

Too much data for message buffer.

Additional Protocol Functions:
* Binary Data (Image) Transmission
* Communication Channel Sharing (Multi-point and Multiplexed Channels)
* Device Control

Figure 5–22 *Layer-2 protocol functions.*

Protocols are explained in the following section, where they are broken into different generations based upon their capabilities and evolution.

Layer-2 Protocol Generations

The Layer-2 data link protocols can be divided into generations that organize them according to their capabilities and evolution. There are in use today second- through seventh-generation protocols. A brief summary of the operating characteristics of each protocol is presented here. Figure 5-23 shows a typical data framing structure for each protocol generation.

Second-generation protocols are sometimes called Teletypewriter (TTY). They are character-based, send text information only, and end each line with a CR character. TTY protocols are used for dial-up, point-to-point connections like those used to connect to the Internet. The communications channels are full duplex physical channels; the PC or terminal device is set for echoplex, or full duplex, operation. The echoplex character transmission mode supports data verification by the PC or terminal operator.

Third-generation protocols first appeared in 1964. The IBM Binary Synchronous Communications (BSC) protocol supports file transfer and interactive keyboard–display terminals. Other asynchronous file transfer protocols including, the Xmodem protocol and Ymodem protocol, resemble the BSC protocol and belong to this generation of protocols. Third-generation protocols carry either text or binary (image) data in blocks. The beginning of a block is signaled by a special communications control character sequence. The end of a block is determined by a different character sequence or as a predetermined fixed block length.

Computing a checksum or Cyclic Redundancy Check (CRC) error code and transmitting it with each block of data performs error detection. The receiving device then recomputes the checksum or CRC and compares it with the transmitted checksum or CRC. If they match, the data is okay. When there is no match, then the data transmitted is in error and the receiving device requests retransmission of the block in error. The transmission and acknowledgement scheme is block-by-block. One block is acknowledged as received successfully before the next block can be transmitted. ASCII or EBCDIC communications control characters are used to frame each block of data.

Fourth-generation protocols came out in 1974 as an upgrade to third-generation protocols. To be sure, fourth-generation protocols did everything that third-generation protocols did, but more efficiently. They used fewer handshakes because each data frame had a control field that carried acknowledgement information in the same frames as fresh, unacknowledged data. Fourth-generation protocols were capable of full duplex message flows,

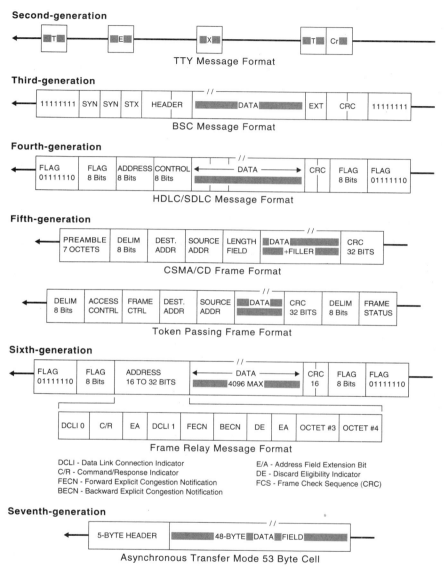

Figure 5–23 *Protocol framing formats.*

although few products implementing fourth-generation protocols exploited this capability.

A variation of the High-level Data Link Control (HDLC) protocol carries the signaling information in SS-7. IBM's Synchronous Data Link Control (SDLC) protocol is a fourth-generation protocol. Fourth-generation protocols send text or binary data in frames, perform better CRC error detection (because they use an improved CRC), and correct frames having errors by requesting retransmission of the frames with errors. However, fourth-generation protocols use a Go-Back-N error correction methodology that permits in some cases up to seven frames to be received before the acknowledgement must be received by the transmitting device. This makes them less efficient.

> The most important thing to remember here is that second-, third-, and fourth-generation OSI Layer-2 protocols were designed to work on communications channels with low transmission speeds (1,200 to 9,600 bps) and high error rates (one error in every 10,000 bits transmitted). If we had a high error rate and we transmitted a big block of data, what would be the chance of getting an error in that block? There would be a darn good chance. When there is an error, how much must be retransmitted to correct the error? The whole block of data must be retransmitted. So now let us make the block 10,000 bits. In this, every block would have an error and nothing would get across the communications channel. If this was the case, how should we design a protocol so that data could get through? You've got it! We would use smaller blocks. Now what is the chance of having an error in a single block? It is a lot less! And how much must be retransmitted in the event of an error? Right again! Only the small block with the error (a whole lot less) must be retransmitted. This is how second-, third-, and fourth-generation OSI Layer-2 protocols operate. The maximum block or frame size is 1,024 characters, with most protocols supporting 128- or 256-character blocks.

Second-, third-, and fourth-generation protocols were also designed for a central computer to control communications with dumb terminals. The central computer maintained the configuration of the communications channel. Any changes to the channel most often required software updates on the central control computer. They supported primarily computer to terminal communications with half-duplex message flows. Today, most communication is computer-to-computer or computer-to-PC communications with, when possible, full duplex message flows.

Fifth-generation protocols were LAN protocols. LANs operated at higher speeds (in the millions of bits per second range) with lower error rates. They were groups of computers or servers and PCs that needed autonomous control at OSI Layer 2. That meant no central control computer at Layer 2, but centralized network security was needed at higher layers. Fifth-generation protocols were not better than second-, third-, and fourth-generation protocols, they were just different. Their data sizes were larger (1,514 for Ethernet to 4,000 plus characters for token ring) because of the higher transmission speeds and lower error rates. Communications channels were self-configuring and added new devices as soon as they were attached to the channel and powered on. The two best-known fifth-generation LAN protocols are Ethernet's Carrier Sense Multiple Access with Collision Detection (CSMA/CD) protocol and the IBM token ring protocol. It is good to know how they operate because many newer protocols are somewhat similar in design. For example, the Universal Serial Bus (USB) protocol is somewhat similar to the Ethernet CDMA/CD protocol.

Sixth-generation protocols are the dinosaurs of protocols. Their block size is bigger because they operate on communications channels with very high transmission speeds and very low error rates. Frame relay protocols are sixth-generation protocols that are loosely based upon fourth-generation protocols. The frame size for a frame relay protocol can be 4,096 characters. Frame relay protocols are often called fast packet protocols. They concern themselves less with error detection and correction than do the fourth-generation protocols on which they were based. Frame relay protocols leave error detection up to software that operates at OSI Layer 4, the message integrity layer. Because of today's high transmission speeds and low error rates, it is faster to correct errors in messages sent across a network than to assure each frame is without error. The network overhead for frame-by-frame verification is more costly than resending an entire message or just the frame that is in error in the message.

Finally, we have seventh-generation protocols that are designed for very high-speed transmission links with very low error rates. ATM protocol is a seventh-generation protocol with a cell size of 53 characters (bytes). Wait a darn minute! It is like the comet has hit the planet, the dinosaurs are dead, and the small mammals have survived. Why instead of going larger in block size did seventh-generation protocols go to 53-byte cells, a much smaller size? The answer lies in the efficiency or effectiveness in using very high-speed communications channels. This is illustrated using Windows PCs and 16-bit File Allocation Tables (FAT-16) vs. 32-bit File Allocation Tables (FAT-32).

Figure 5-24 shows hypothetically how a disk drive would be divided using FAT-16 and FAT-32. FAT-16 would have four sectors in which to store data and FAT-32 would have twice as many sectors, but they would be half the size. A file of a single character, when stored in a large sector, would occupy the entire sector. So with the FAT-16 sectors, three-quarters of our disk drive space would be used storing file 1, file 2, and file 3. Using the smaller sectors of FAT-32 permits us to more effectively use the available disk drive space, and consequently we use less than half the available space.

Seventh-generation protocols with their small cell size can allocate and use very high-speed, low error rate communications channels most efficiently. They waste little bandwidth (the available bits per second inventory) waiting for the next chunk of data to transmit. Small, 53-byte (character)

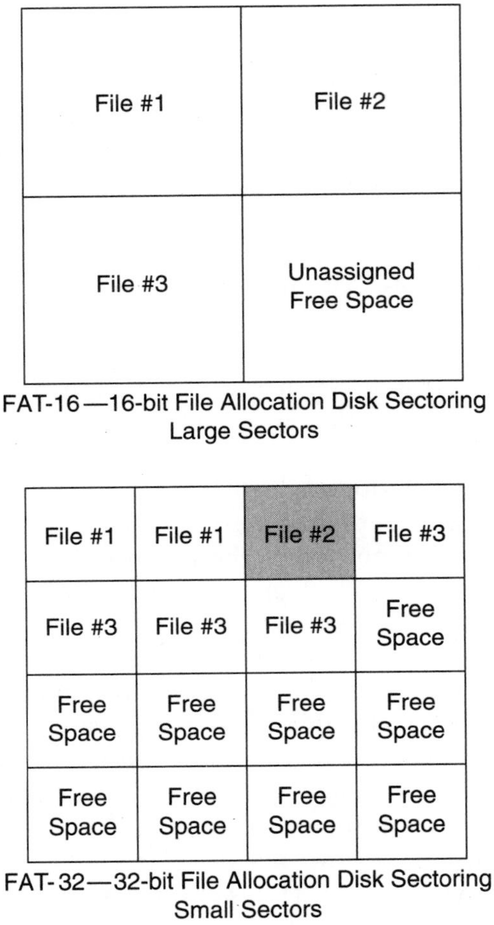

File #1	File #2
File #3	Unassigned Free Space

FAT-16—16-bit File Allocation Disk Sectoring
Large Sectors

File #1	File #1	File #2	File #3
File #3	File #3	File #3	Free Space
Free Space	Free Space	Free Space	Free Space
Free Space	Free Space	Free Space	Free Space

FAT-32—32-bit File Allocation Disk Sectoring
Small Sectors

Figure 5–24 *Storage effectiveness.*

cells make them very responsive to and effective in meeting changing demands for communications channel bandwidth. With very high-speed communications channels, wasting bandwidth is much more costly than the extra overhead imposed by small cell sizes.

As with sixth-generation protocols, seventh-generation protocols rely upon OSI Layer 4, the message integrity layer, to detect and correct errors in messages. When transporting voice or video transmission, these errors, if a relatively few bits in size, are often ignored and passed on to the destination device. Humans do not mind small errors as long as they are not frequent and of long duration.

We will examine the fifth-generation LAN protocols to get a better appreciation of just how protocols really work.

Protocols are implemented in hardware. Users never really see them working. When a protocol is working properly, some type of green flashing light may be visible.

LAN Protocol Operation Examples

The two most well-known LAN protocols are Ethernet's CSMA/CD protocol and the IBM token ring protocol. Both of these protocols are IEEE and international standards. The Ethernet protocol is the most widely implemented LAN protocol on the planet. It may be the most widely implemented protocol of any WAN and LAN protocol on this planet, period.

ETHERNET—CSMA/CD PROTOCOL

Ethernet, originally designed by Xerox with chip sets developed by Intel and marketed by Digital, uses the CSMA/CD protocol. This is part of the OSI Layer-2 protocols known as the Medium Access Control (MAC) protocol. Although CSMA/CD sounds complicated, it is really quite simple to explain.

Referring to Figure 5-25, the CSMA/CD protocol operates similar to people talking in a room. Each person has a carrier sense capability. What is the carrier they can sense? Sound or voice is correct. All persons have free and equal access (multiple access) to the communications medium. The communications medium (or Ether) is the air in the room. Any person can speak at any time. When a person has something to say, they first listen to see if the channel is occupied. If they hear nothing, they blast away with their message, "Breaker, breaker 1-9, Rubber Ducky are you there?" While they broadcast, they listen to the channel. If what they hear was not corrupted, then they assume that their message was transmitted okay.

However, we do not live in a perfect world and sometimes collisions happen. When a collision occurs, the transmitter hears their message is garbled. They back off and retry a short time later. To determine how long they wait, they flip a coin. Now both stations having the collision must flip coins to determine how long to wait. One gets heads, while the other gets tails. The one with heads multiplies the time they wait by one to get one time unit and we (the station with the tails) multiply our wait time by two to get two time units. So we wait until our time expires and listen again for anyone talking on the channel. We hear the first station blabbing away because its wait time was less than ours. Soon they stop and it looks like we have our chance to transmit. Away we go, only to have another collision with a third station. So the

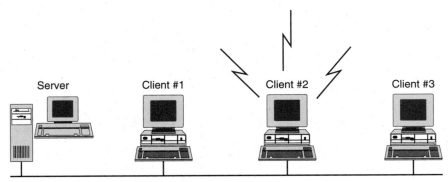

Figure 5–25 *Ethernet protocol operation.*

third station and we are forced to flip the coins again. This time we get heads and they get tails. Looks good for us, but wait, our time is determined by the "automobile theory of insurance." You know the "automobile insurance theory," don't you? When you have a fender bender, the insurance company ups your rates or yanks your policy so you cannot get out on the road again immediately. In our CSMA/CD case, we must multiply our wait time by one and then by three. We end up waiting three time units and the other station only needs to wait two time units. Is this unfair or what?

CSMA/CD operation may seem backward, but it isn't. If every device were to, upon detecting a collision, immediately retry transmitting, the result would be collision after collision and no one would get through. Consider people exiting a room. If they all rushed the door, one or two might get through, but the remainder would collide. If those that collided lunged for the door again and again, there would be even more collisions and no one would get out of the room. By forcing those people having one collision to start more or less halfway back across the room and by forcing those people having a second collision to start more or less on the opposite side of the room, all the people would soon exit the room.

The Ethernet collision detection algorithm is technically called a binary exponential back-off algorithm. It makes Ethernet particularly good at handling bursts in network activity, but not as good at constant heavy loads. Newer Ethernet protocol implementations use full duplex physical channels, so they have basically no collisions.

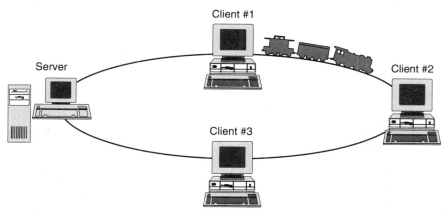

Figure 5–26   *Token ring protocol operation.*

TOKEN RING—TOKEN PASSING PROTOCOL

The token passing ring protocol operates differently from the Ethernet CSMA/CD protocol. The token ring MAC protocol is deterministic, i.e., each and every station gets its turn on the ring.

The token ring protocol operates like a train running around a track, with one boxcar carrying all the packets from PC to PC (see Figure 5-26). The train runs at either 4 Mbps (20 miles an hour) or 16 Mbps (80 miles an hour). The train never stops. The token is a green flag on the engine of the train.

Let's say Client #2 has data to send to the server. The stationmaster at Client #2 gets the bag of mail (the message) together and goes to the station platform near the tracks to wait for the train. Soon the stationmaster hears the train whistle blowing. The train zooms through town at 80 miles an hour (16 Mbps), never stopping. The stationmaster spots a green flag on the front of the train, signaling that the boxcar is empty. So when the engine passes by, the stationmaster quickly grabs the green flag off the engine and replaces it with a red flag, signaling that the train is busy carrying data (mail). When the engineer appears, the stationmaster throws the engineer the destination station address and then the station's address. When the empty boxcar rolls by, the stationmaster throws the sack of mail through the open boxcar door, where a train conductor catches it and places it on a hook. Then the train continues and roars out of town at 80 miles per hour, never stopping.

The stationmaster at Client #3 also has a bag of mail (a message) to send. This stationmaster is also waiting on the station platform for the train to arrive. Soon the stationmaster hears the train whistle blowing. The Client #3 stationmaster spots the red flag placed on the train by the Client #2 stationmaster, signaling that the boxcar is occupied. This forces the Client #3 stationmaster to wait until the train is free to send Client #3's bag of mail. So the train roars out of town at 80 miles per hour, never stopping.

The stationmaster at the server also has a bag of mail (a message) to send. The server stationmaster is waiting patiently on the station platform for the train to arrive. Soon the stationmaster hears the train whistle blowing. The server stationmaster spots the red flag placed on the train by the Client #2 stationmaster, signaling that the boxcar is occupied. So the server stationmaster thinks that he has nothing to do now but wait for the next time the train is free. But low and behold, the engineer is waving the server's address and thus signaling that the mail on the train is for the server's station. As the train roars through town at 80 miles an hour, the conductor in the train throws out the sack of mail at the server stationmaster. If the server stationmaster catches the sack of mail and doesn't lose one letter, he quickly attaches a green flag to the caboose as the train roars out of town at 80 miles per hour, never stopping.

Actually I have stretched the truth here. What really happens is that the server stationmaster quickly makes a copy of all the mail while the train roars through town at 16 Mbps, or 80 miles an hour. The sack of mail is not removed from the train yet. The train continues on at 80 miles an hour to Client #1.

The stationmaster at Client #1 has a bag of mail to send as well. But when the stationmaster hears the train whistle blowing and spots the flag on the engine, it is a red flag. The red flag signals that the boxcar is occupied. This forces the Client #1 stationmaster to wait until a train with a free boxcar passes so he can then send his bag of mail. The train roars out of town at 80 miles per hour, never stopping.

Finally, the train returns to Client #2, where the stationmaster has another bag of mail to send. When the stationmaster hears the train whistle blowing, he spots the red flag he placed on the train, signaling that the boxcar is occupied. So he thinks that he has nothing to do now but wait for the next time the train is free. But low and behold, the engineer is waving Client #2's address, thus signaling that the train has come full circle. As the train roars through town at 80 miles an hour and the engine passes by, the stationmaster quickly grabs the red flag off the engine and replaces it with a green flag, signaling the train is empty and able to carrying other data (mail). As the engineer appears, he throws the Client #2 stationmaster the destination station address and then the Client #2 station's address. When the boxcar roars by, the conductor throws out the sack of mail to empty the boxcar. Finally, as the caboose flies by at 80 miles an hour, the stationmaster grabs the flag from it. If the flag is a green flag, the mail was received okay. However, a red flag signals a mail tragedy and the sack of mail must be resent.

ETHERNET VS. TOKEN RING

How do the token ring and Ethernet's CSMA/CD protocols compare? Is one better than the other? In reality, one is not better than the other, they are just different. Ethernet came out in 1984, while the token ring arrived in 1987. (1987 was a banner year for IBM because the token ring, the PS-2, and OS 2 all were released that year.) Which is more sophisticated? I think the token ring. Does that make the token ring better? No, not that I can see. The token ring's greater sophistication is needed because of its design as a ring and its desire to keep the ring operating regardless of hardware failures. Such sophistication is evidenced by the greater operating overhead of the token ring. Diagnostic messages constantly flow on the ring.

What can you say about Ethernet as compared to the token ring because Ethernet came out in 1984? Ethernet boards are cheaper and there are more of them than token ring boards.

Which protocol do you think performs better? For me, they both perform about the same for most LANs. Figure 5-27 shows their network performance vs. network load. This diagram is not an exact representation of Ethernet or token ring performance, but a general, simplified representation of their performance.

In the diagram, the performance of both Ethernet and the token ring are the same for network loads that go from 0% load to around 40% load. A wide swing in load from say 10% to 30% produces no noticeable slowing of either network. At 40% load, Network General's Sniffer Protocol Analyzer suggests that Ethernet begins to experience saturation and starts to slow. With the token ring, according to IBM, this does not happen until around 70% utilization. The value of this diagram is that it illustrates that by simply measuring network load over time, you can get an idea if your network is overloaded and performing poorly.

Regardless, at higher than 70% utilization, both the token ring and Ethernet can slow noticeably. What a user would see at load saturation is a significant delay in response to network requests. Both token ring and Ethernet LANs would operate sluggishly. Poor performance caused by heavy loads is easy to solve in both token ring and Ethernet networks. The easiest solution is to increase network speed. A 10-Mbps Ethernet could be increased to a speed of 100 Mbps. Further, breaking the network up into different seg-

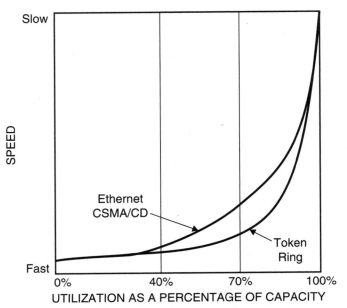

Figure 5–27 *Ethernet and token ring performance.*

ments using bridging, switching, and routing components would reduce network load and dramatically increase network performance.

Protocols are in the hardware. So to end-users, a protocol is represented by a LAN card with specific connectors.

Protocol Summary

LAN and WAN protocol characteristics are summarized in Table 5-5. Each protocol generation is summarized by:

Transmission type:
- Synchronous—Centralized circuit clock.
- Asynchronous—Clocking provided by the terminal and host computers.
- Isochronous—Data and clocking combined.

Message flows:
- Full duplex—Two-way, simultaneous transmission and reception of data.
- Half-duplex—One-way, at-one-time transmission.

Error detection:
- CRC—Cyclic Redundancy Check bytes.
- Parity—Single-bit error checking.

Table 5.5 *Layer 2 Protocol Summary*

Protocol/ Family/ Feature	TTY	BSC	SDLC	HDLC (X.25)	CSMA/CD	Token	Frame Relay	ATM
Generation	2nd	3rd	4th	4th	5th	5th	6th	7th
Synchronization	Asynchronous	Synchronous	Synchronous	Synchronous	Isochronous	Isochronous	Synchronous & Isochronous	Isochronous
Message Flow	Half	Half	Half or Full	Half or Full	Half & Full	Half	Half or Full	Half or Full
Error Checking	Parity (None)	CRC-16	CRC-16 CCITT	CRC-16 CCITT	CRC-32 CCITT	CRC-32 CCITT	CRC-16 CCITT	CRC-8 on header
Error Correction	Echoplex	Block-by-Block	Go-Back-N	Go-Back-N	Go-Back-N	Go-Back-N	Discard bad frames	None
Binary Data Transmission	No	Character insertion	Bit stuffing	Bit stuffing	Delimiter length field	Delimiters	Bit stuffing	Delimiters
Point-to-point vs. Multi-point	Point-to-point	Both, using polling	Both, using polling	Point-to-point	Bus with collisions	Ring with token passing	Point-to-point	Point-to-point
Year Introduced	1950s	1964 IBM	1974 IBM	Mid-1970s	1982 DEC	1987 IBM	Early 1990s	Mid-1990s
Estimated Equipment Cost for Hardware, Software, and Modems	$10	$200	$200	$200	$14	$100	$600, plus channel charges	$200 to $600
Terminal Emulation	DEC, VTxx, and IBM 3100	IBM 3270, 3780	IBM 3270, 3770, and APPC	None	None	None	None	None
PC Products	Many	Many	Many	Indirect	Ethernet	Token ring	Bridges and routers	ATM equipment, PBX

Error correction:

- Block by block—Checks each block before requesting another.
- Sliding window/Go-Back-N—Returns to the frame that was expected to be received next.
- Binary Data Transmission—The ability to transfer images and programs between computers as well as text information.

Circuit types supported:

- Point-to-point—One device on each end of a circuit.
- Multi-point—Several terminals sharing the same circuit via polling operations.

Other factors are also of interest beyond these basic technical features and characteristics. The cost estimates are very general and should not be used for network planning.

All we have discussed here is implemented in the OSI model Layers 1 and 2. Protocols and communications links are constantly working. What people see are PC hardware (LAN cards), or boxes with flashing lights. When the lights flash green, things are good; yellow often indicates caution, meaning there could be problems; and red lights usually denote a component failure or network error, which is bad.

Brain Teaser

Protocols

Use a Windows PC, go to **Programs – Accessories – Communications**, and start the Hyper Terminal program. Select one of the predefined options and then cancel dialing. Use the menu selections and pick **Transfer** and then **Receive File**.

1. What file transfer protocol is the default protocol? In Windows 98, it is ZMODEM with Crash Recovery.

2. What other file transfer protocol options are there? Windows 98 lists 1K XMODEM, KERMIT, XMODEM, YMODEM, YMODEM-G, ZMODEM, and ZMODEM with crash recovery.

3. Select the **Send File** option. What is the default protocol? In Windows 98, it is ZMODEM.

4. Which protocol would be better to use for file transfer when communicating with a new 33.6-Kbps modem: 1K XMODEM or XMODEM? In this case, the answer would be to use 1K XMODEM with the larger 1,024-character block sizes. XMODEM uses a block size of 128 characters, which is less efficient with the newer high-speed modems.

5. Select **Send Text File**. What protocol is used? In this case, it is a variation of the TTY protocol. The goal of this exercise is to familiarize you with Windows dial-up networking protocol choices.

Component Interfaces

The OSI Layer 1 is implemented in several different physical interfaces. These interfaces are the traditional RS-232 serial interface, the parallel port interface, the Universal Serial Bus (USB) Interface, the IEEE 1394 Fire Wire interface, and LAN interfaces. Interfaces are used to connect devices together. All end-users see for an interface is different shaped connectors. Each interface is used for different types of communications.

Parallel Port Interface

The parallel printer port is a common printer interface. It transmits data to a printer from a PC one byte at a time. Parallel ports are bit-parallel, but byte-serial ports. Parallel ports operate over 26-conductor cables that have a 26-pin male connector at one end and a 34-conductor Centronics connector at the opposite end. Newer printers use a high-density connector in place of the bulky Centronics connector. These cables typically vary from 6 to 15 feet in length. Special cables can extend the distance a parallel interface can cover to some 30 or 40 feet. Overall, though, parallel cables run short distances at higher speeds.

A PC's parallel interface can be set up to operate in several different modes. These include a compatible mode that emulates the old PC—printer interface providing output only mode—a bi-directional mode providing input and output capabilities, an Enhanced Parallel Port (EPP), and an Enhanced Capabilities Port (ECP) conforming to IEEE-1284 specifications. The ECP and EPP modes sometimes do not work with older printers. In these instances, downgrading to bi-directional or another compatible mode may resolve the printing problem. Bi-directional, EPP, and ECP modes may require IRQ and DMA channel resource assignments in addition to the standard LPT1 port I/O address resource assignment.

The port mode setting is most critical for proper device operation. The compatible mode provides output only. It operates like an old PC AT parallel port. Bi-directional mode is an AT port that uses the control lines to permit both output and input operation. This is a two-way interface, but a very slow two-way interface because input data is received a half-byte (nibble) at a time. The Enhanced Parallel Port (EPP) mode is a high-speed, bi-directional port. There are revisions to this parallel port operation specification. The BIOS supports Revision 1.7. The Extended Capabilities Port (ECP) conforms to the IEEE 1284 parallel port specification. Specific peripheral devices attached to the parallel port require a matching setting. Sometimes what appears to be a better setting for a device is not really better. Worst-case scenario is that all four settings must be tested to determine the correct or optimal setting for a specific peripheral.

RS-232 Interface

The RS-232 interface is the PC serial interface used to interconnect modems, mice, and sometimes printers to a PC. RS-232 started as a computer to modem interface. There are two sides to the interface:

- The terminal side, referred to as the Data Terminal Equipment (DTE) side.
- The modem side, referred to as the Data circuit-terminating Equipment (DCE) side.

The proper name for the interface today is the EIA-232 D interface, which stands for the Electronic Industries Association Recommended Specification Number 232 Revision D. The EIA-232 D interface is similar to the electrical power interface. For example, the electrical power interface parallels RS-232 as shown in Table 5-6.

Table 5.6   *Interface Comparisons*

	Electrical Power	**EIA-232 D**
Goal	Exchange electrical energy	Exchange low-speed data
Physical Interface	Three-prong plug	25-pin plug
	Providers = female	Data circuit-terminating (DCE) = female
	Users = male	Data terminal equipment (users) (DTE) = male
Electrical Specification	115 volts AC 15 to 20 Amps	+ 3 to + 15 volts DC = 0 − 3 to − 15 volts DC = 1

The EIA-232 D or RS-232 interface has a specific configuration. This configuration is:

- Physical—It uses "D"-shaped connectors with 9 or 25 pins.
- Electrical—It uses +15 volts and −15 volts to signal.
- Logical—It has 9 or 25 pins, with each pin assigned a specific function.

The RS-232 interface has certain operating characteristics, including:

- Protocol-transparent—It does not care about what Layer-2 through Layer-7 protocol is using it.

- Cable length—It was designed and specified to work over 50-foot cables.
- Low-speed data transmission—It was designed to transmit data at 20,000 Bps or lower.

Often, the distance and transmission speed limitations of the RS-232 interface are exceeded. It is possible to run at 115,200 Bps for short distances and at 9,600 Bps for 1,000 feet. We ran across a case that went 114 feet and 6 inches at 56 Kbps over a standard RS-232 interface. Thinking that they performed some precise engineering to calculate that exact distance, I asked how they were able to precisely determine that 114 feet and 6 inches would work at that speed. They said that they just kept shortening the cable until it worked.

Key RS-232 pin assignments are listed in Table 5-7. The table identifies the pin number and the direction of signal travel from the PC or terminal (DTE) side of the interface. For example, the Transmit Data (TD) signal travels on the 25-pin connector pin number 2 from the DTE to the DCE. Figure 5-28 shows an RS-232 DTE to DCE cable configuration.

Table 5.7   *EIA-232D (RS-232) Key Pin Functions*

Data Leads	DTE Pin # for 25-pin Connector	DTE Pin # for 9-pin Connector	Abbreviation
Transmit Data	2 -->	3 -->	TD
Receive Data	3 <--	2 <--	RD
Timing (Clock) Leads			
Transmitter signal element timing (DCE source) Synchronous Transmission Clock	15 <--		TC
Transmitter signal element timing (DTE source) Synchronous Transmission Clock	24 -->		TC
Receiver signal element timing (DCE source) Synchronous Transmission Clock	17 <--		RC

Table 5.7 *EIA-232D (RS-232) Key Pin Functions (Continued)*

Control Leads			
Request To Send	4 -->	7-->	RTS
Clear to Send	5 <--	8<--	CTS
Data Set Ready (DCE ready)	6 <--	6 <--	DSR
Data Terminal Ready (DTE Ready)	20 -->	4 -->	DTR
Data Carrier Detect (Received line signal detector)	8 <--	1 <--	CD
Ring Indicator	22 <--	9 <--	RI
Ground			
Signal Ground	7 <->	5 <->	SG
Protective Ground (Shield)	1 <->		FG

RS-232 modem cables make direct connections. There is a one-to-one matching of the signals on the DTE side of the interface and the DCE side of the interface. This is shown in Figure 5-28. For printer and null modem cables, special configurations are used which do not use straight-through (pin for pin) wiring.

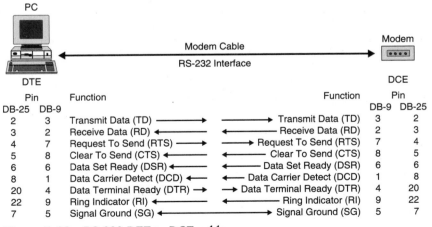

Figure 5–28 *RS-232 DTE to DCE cable.*

Here is how RS-232 works when coordinating modem and PC activities. To fully understand RS-232 operation, you need to use your imagination for a second. Imagine that on one side of a room is a PC and on the other is a modem. Next to the PC is a board that runs from floor to ceiling, and in the board are drilled holes. There are numbers painted next to the holes. The numbers are 2, 3, 4, 5, 6, 8, 20, and 22. Similarly, next to the modem is a board of identical size with identical holes and numbers. Through the holes in each board run ropes. The rope from Hole #2 in one board runs down across the floor to Hole #2 in the other board. There are eight ropes in all, one for each hole. Now we are ready to begin using our RS-232 interface.

At the beginning of the day, both our PC and modem are powered off. The user comes in and powers them both up. The modem wakes up and thinks, "This is a great day! I am ready to have some fun!" And then the modem remembers that it should let the PC know it is up and ready to go. So it reaches down, grabs the rope going through Hole #6 (Data Set Ready—DSR), gives it a hard yank, and ties it up to a peg on the wall.

Meanwhile, the PC wakes up and just like the modem thinks, "This is a great day! I am ready to have some fun!" And then the PC feels the rope through Hole #6 being yanked up tight. The PC then thinks, "This is good, there is a modem over there and it is powered on!" The PC remembers that it should let the modem know it is up and ready to go as well. So it reaches down, grabs the rope going through Hole #20 (Data Terminal Ready—DTR), gives it a hard yank, and ties it up to a peg on the wall.

The modem feels the rope through Hole #20 being yanked up tight. The modem thinks, "This is good, there is a PC over there and it is powered up and ready to go!"

The PC and the modem were powered on because our user was expecting a call from another computer. So soon the phone begins to ring. Recall that the ringing signal from the phone company is a 90-volt AC signal. Well, every time the 90-volt ringing signal hits the modem, it gets a good jolt. But as the modem recovers between jolts, it thinks that it should signal the PC that the phone is ringing, so it grabs the rope going through Hole #22 (Ring Indicator—RI), gives it a hard yank, and ties it up to a peg on the wall. The PC feels the rope through Hole #22 being yanked up tight. It then thinks, "Well that poor modem. Last week it took ten rings to answer the phone line. I wonder how many of those 90-volt jolts it is going to endure today?" The PC continues to mind its own business.

Back on the modem side, the modem thinks, "Well I have had enough of this!" so it answers the phone. Now remember in our modem Study Break exercise what a modem sounds like when it answers a phone. (Actually, we had a person call us on our radio show and do impersonation of a Kflex modem. He did it on the air and it was very good.)

The modem goes through the synchronization and channel testing functions with the calling modem on the other end of the channel. Soon they are communicating and our modem says to the other modem, "Everything all right?" The calling modem replies, "It's all right!" Now our modem signals the PC by grabbing the rope going through Hole #8 (Data Carrier Detect —DCD), giving it a hard yank, and tying it up to a peg on the wall.

Our intrepid PC notices the rope through Hole #8 being yanked up tight. It then thinks, "This is good. The modem answered the phone and is now speaking to a modem on the other end of the channel. We could have some fun today!" At that instant, the user types the letter "A" on the keyboard and there is our PC stuck holding this "A." It thinks, "What can I do?" And then it occurs to the PC that it can send the "A" to the other computer, so it quickly grabs the rope going through Hole #4 (Request To Send—RTS), gives it a hard yank, and ties it up to a peg on the wall.

Now the modem feels the rope through Hole #4 being yanked up tight. It thinks, "The PC wants to send something!" So it quickly confers with the modem at the other end of the channel, "My user wants to send something, is it all right?" The calling modem replies, "It's all right!" Our modem is still not sure, so it asks again, "Is it all right?" The calling modem replies, "It's all right!!!" Now our modem signals the PC to send data by grabbing the rope going through Hole #5 (Clear To Send—CTS), giving it a hard yank, and tying it up to a peg on the wall.

Our PC notices the rope through Hole #5 being yanked up tight, signaling it to send the "A." The PC then grabs the rope in Hole #2 (Transmit Data —TD) and yanks and yanks in a pattern that mimics the "0's" and "1's" in the ASCII letter "A." The modem feels the yanks and modulates the carrier signal to send the "A" to the other modem. The other modem gets the "A" and passes it to the computer attached to it. But it is full duplex, or echoplex operation, so the remote computer passes the "A" back to the remote modem. The remote modem then modulates the carrier signal to return the "A" to our modem. Our modem receives the "A" and grabs the rope going through Hole #3 (Receive Data—RD) and yanks and yanks in a pattern that mimics the "0's" and "1's" in the ASCII letter "A." Our PC now gets the "A" and puts it up on its screen so the user knows that the other computer received it properly. And that is how the RS-232 interface works!

If you followed the concept of the ropes, then you should understand how RS-232 and similar interfaces operate. They use specific wires to handshake and pass messages across them. The opposite of this type of interface is an interface acting similar to Ethernet's CSMD/CD protocol. In CSMA/CD,

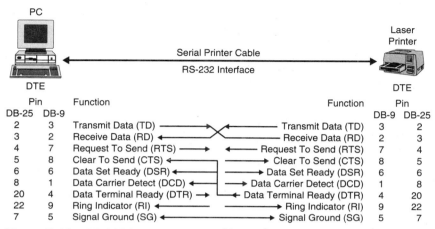

Figure 5–29 *RS-232 DTE to printer cable configuration.*

there are no handshake wires, only handshake messages exchanged across a single coaxial cable wire or a 4-wire twisted pair wire interface.

When you have communications problems, it is likely for new installations to be an incorrectly configured RS-232 interface. Straight pin for pin wiring is used only to connect a modem to a computer with a 25-pin cable. Otherwise, the interface pins are cross-connected. Figure 5-29 shows one possible configuration for a printer cable. What makes this special is the DTE to DTE connection.

Null modem cables permit PCs to be directly connected. This DTE to DTE cable is different from printer cables because each PC thinks it is talking to a modem. Printers, on the other hand, never expect to talk to a modem. What additional line would need to be added to the printer cable to make it into a PC-to-PC null modem cable? The answer is in Figure 5-30.

Sometimes terminals are connected using RJ-11 jacks and RS-232 signaling. Table 5-8 documents a common RJ-11–RS-232 cable configuration.

The USB and the IEEE 1394 interfaces are steadily replacing RS-232. These interfaces use fewer wires and are more Plug-and-Play (PnP) than is the RS-232 interface. Unlike RS-232, they do not use single wires to handshake, but rather they send control messages similar to Ethernet's CSMA/CD protocol. This permits them to use 4-wire or 6-wire interfaces, where RS-232 uses 9-pin or 25-pin connectors. Within five years, few if any PCs will be built with RS-232 interfaces. Today, legacy-free PCs have no RS-232 connections.

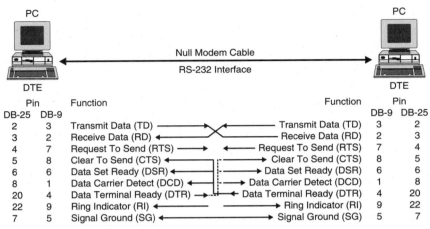

Figure 5–30 *RS-232 PC-to-PC null modem configuration.*

Table 5.8 *RJ-11 to DB-25 Pin Assignments*

Pin Number	RJ-11	DB-25
Data Carrier Detect (DCD)	1	8
Transmit Data (TD)	2	2
Receive Data (RD)	3	3
Data Terminal Ready (DTR)	4	20
Signal Ground (SG)	5	7
Data Set Ready (DSR)	6	6
Request To Send (RTS)		Request To Send—4 to 5
Clear To Send (CTS)		Clear To Send—5 to 4

Universal Serial Bus

Newer PCs generally have two USB connections. The USB is being rapidly and broadly implemented in both desktop and mobile computers. USB provides an easy way to add peripheral devices to a PC. It configures itself automatically (provided the correct drivers are loaded) and transfers data between the peripheral device and the PC at speeds of 1.5 Mbps to 12 Mbps. A USB bus in theory can support 128 devices, but practically about 10 to 20 devices is a more realistic upper limit. USB devices include scanners, printers, mice, keyboards, Web cameras, palmtop PCs, microphones, and more.

Most USB devices run into hubs, but some can be daisy-chained, permitting several devices to use the same USB port. USB devices connected to ports on a hub device are linked in a tree wiring topology. Each device tree connects to a PC USB root-hub port through which the PC communicates with the tree's USB devices. USB devices attach to all ports with standard 5-conductor cables. USB root-hub ports provide some 5-volt power for low-power devices. The root-hub ports support high-powered device attachments when they provide their own power from an AC source or from batteries. Devices sharing the same port operate at the speed of the slowest device on that port.

Windows 98 has software support for built-in USB devices, but this must often be augmented by driver software provided by the USB device manufacturer. USB devices are PnP devices.

These are compelling reasons for serial busses to replace RS-232 and PC parallel ports. USB permits easily attached and detached devices through PnP software that finds devices, assigns addresses to them, and sets them up. USB communication software sends data packets from a source to a destination using logical pipes designed to perform specific functions. There are separate packet types for data and for control information. USB supports asynchronous communication for simple devices like mice and keyboards and isochronous communication guaranteeing a set portion of the available bus bandwidth for more demanding multimedia applications that have stringent latency limits.

USB devices may control their power consumption rather than being controlled by the PC. USB devices can automatically enter a suspended low-power consumption state if the bus to which they connect becomes inactive. Suspended devices can resume operation at their pre-suspend consumption level when they awaken.

These features make USB a cost-effective and user-friendly, general-purpose attachment mechanism for many PC peripherals.

IEEE 1394

The IEEE 1394 high-speed serial bus specification covers several busses ranging in performance from about 25 Mbps to 400 Mbps. This will increase to 1.2 Gbps and higher speeds. IEEE 1394 is a general-purpose serial bus for connecting high-speed peripherals to PCs. IEEE 1394 bus connections include connections between consumer AV electronics made possible by the peer-to-peer communication supported by IEEE 1394 bus-mastering features. Similar to the USB bus, the IEEE 1394 bus attaches multiple devices to a PC, as well as supports peer-to-peer device connection like directly connecting a scanner to a printer or a PC to a PC. IEEE 1394 busses can connect multiple devices through a hub, or can connect a hierarchy of serial busses each supporting up to 63 device attachments. Bridges transfer data between busses in the hierarchical IEEE 1394 bus configuration.

Like USB, IEEE 1394 bus communication uses packet transmission between devices. IEEE 1394 transaction software services present application software with read, write, and lock services. Each service translates into packet sequences in a link software layer that are transmitted over copper wires or fiber optic cable. The IEEE 1394 provides both asynchronous and isochronous communication.

The IEEE 1394 bus has PnP capability. When IEEE 1394 devices are added or removed from a bus, all devices connected to the IEEE 1394 bus reset and then perform a self-identification and enumeration process. Unique addresses are then assigned to all devices and normal bus operation resumes. A single device functions as bus manager. It performs bus power management, optimizes performance, maintains bus connection information, and manages isochronous bandwidth allocation.

IEEE 1394 costs more than USB. IEEE 1394 bus power management depends on the power consumption of the IEEE 1394 Physical (PHY) layer. The IEEE 1394 standard specifies a device's physical layer be powered on whenever the device is connected to the IEEE 1394 bus. Devices that are not powered on can split an IEEE 1394 bus into two separate segments. IEEE 1394 devices can draw up to 1 Watt of power when attached to an IEEE 1394 bus. This can present problems in lower power consumption applications such as those of laptop PCs. Both bus-powered and self-powered devices can attach to an IEEE 1394 bus. The bus manager reads the power source for each node and each node's power requirements. Using that information, the bus manager node sends power enabling or disabling packets to individual nodes to budget IEEE 1394 bus power.

Most main logic boards include USB ports, and some include IEEE 1394 Fire Wire bus connections as well. My Sony laptop computers have both USB and IEEE 1394 interfaces. The USB ports are used for microphone inputs and the IEEE 1394 interfaces connect to my JVC digital camcorder and to my other Sony Laptop.

A rapid increase in USB and IEEE 1394 serial bus is happening because:

- They have simpler and more user-friendly connectors and cables.
- They connect multiple devices to a bus using hubs or chaining to form a tree structure.
- They have bandwidths that match or exceed parallel busses.
- They operate with low power consumption.
- They provide PnP self-configuration for connected devices.

- They provide the capability to hot-swap devices.

- They employ protocols supporting a broad range of transport services, including isochronous (guaranteed transmission bandwidth) service to multimedia applications.

Soon, older parallel port and RS-232 interfaces will be replaced by USB and IEEE 1394 high-speed serial interfaces.

All these connectors are simply hardware.

Brain Teaser

RS-232 Serial Port

Get an RS-232 9-pin or 25-pin connector. Use a bright light to look into the end of the connector.
1. Can you see the pin numbers just above each pin? What pin is in the upper left of the connector? It should be Pin 1.
2. Get a new USB cable. Examine the connector with your bright light. How many wires can you see? Generally, four are visible.
3. See if you can find a PC with an IEEE 1394 cable. How does this interface differ from the USB interface? It should be smaller and square, while the USB interface is flatter and wider. Both interfaces should be keyed so that the cable cannot be inserted backward.
This exercise should familiarize you with OSI Layer-1 physical interfaces.

Multiplexers and Multiplexing Fundamentals

Multiplexing combines several low-speed lines into a single high-speed line between two sites to make better use of limited physical channel facilities. However, the primary use of multiplexing is to save communications line costs. The cost of the single composite high-speed line is less than the combined costs of several low-speed lines (see Figure 5-31).

A good example of multiplexing would be a TV because the remote control selects one channel from many channels carried by a single wire running into the back of the TV. The remaining channels are not displayed.

There are three basic types of multiplexing performed in data communications and telecommunications. They are frequency division, time division, and statistical multiplexing.

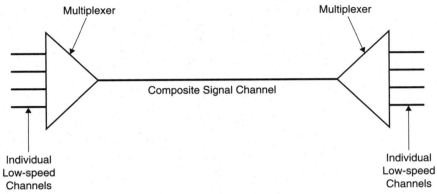

Figure 5–31 *The goal of multiplexing.*

Frequency Division Multiplexing

A frequency division multiplexer combines multiple parallel information streams into a single communications channel. Each of the information streams, or sub-channels, is assigned a separate frequency within the broader frequency range of the single communications channel interconnecting the frequency division multiplexers. In Figure 5-32, Channel 1 operates at high frequency, Channel 2 at medium frequency, and Channel 3 at low frequency. Could Channel 1 carry voice, Channel 2 HDLC data, and Channel 3 a TTY protocol all at the same time? They sure could, because at Layer 1, they are separate physical channels. Multiplexing works at Layer 1, the physical layer. Multiplexers are not concerned with Layers 2 through 7.

Each input channel resides in a separate range of frequencies. When you think of Frequency Division Multiplexing (FDM), you should think of Cable TV (CATV). CATV uses different frequencies in the same coaxial cable to carry the individual television channels to your home. All channels exist on the same cable at the same time. Think of FDM as dividing our composite channel up on a horizontal basis.

This can also be illustrated using highway systems implementing the different multiplexing techniques. If we commute using FDM, the FDM highway system would provide a separate lane for every car. No other car could use the lane except the car it was designed to carry. There would be an on ramp at our house and an off ramp at our office. We could use our lane at any time without fearing interference from any other car. As drivers we would be extremely happy. As taxpayers paying for the FDM highway, we would be much less happy because it is inefficient and costly. Since the FDM

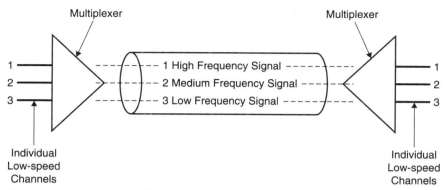

Figure 5–32 *Frequency division multiplexing.*

highway is used heavily only a few times each day, it may be completely full for only a few hours and at other times largely empty. We would pay for a costly highway that was underused. The goal of FDM is not transmission efficiency, but rather to guarantee capacity.

FDM is used by cable modems. Cable modems use CATV for their backbone transmission medium, but they are restricted to using specific frequencies. Before fiber optics and digital voice transmission, the telephone company used FDM to separate the channels carried over telephone trunks between toll offices. FDM is not very efficient and is used in cable companies, cell phones, some telephones, satellites, microwave, and fiber optic communications. FDM is the same as Dense Wave Division Multiplexing (DWDM) used in fiber optic systems.

DENSE WAVE DIVISION MULTIPLEXING (OPTICAL FDM)

DWDM uses different colors of light (different frequencies of light) to represent separate channels on a single optical fiber. This is how fiber technology is increasing fiber transmission capacity today. On a single fiber, from 4 to 128 different colors of light can be sent at the same time. Each different color represents a different wavelength of light, a different frequency of light, and a different channel. In the near future, about 1000 colors may be carried across a single fiber. Each color or channel can carry 70 Gbps of digital information for a total fiber carrying capacity of 70 terabits per second. However, such speeds may not be attained for another 10 years. The fiber itself may need to be upgraded to achieve these speeds.

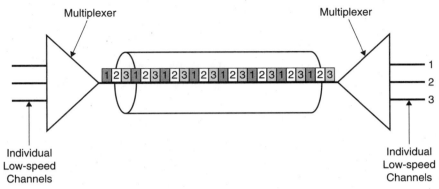

Figure 5–33 *Time division multiplexing.*

Time Division Multiplexing

Time Division Multiplexing (TDM) is a technique commonly employed in telephony equipment. It interleaves bits or bytes from multiple, independent sources into a single higher speed composite stream. At the destination site, these streams are separated back into their original individual bit or byte streams. The high-speed channel is shared because separate time slots are assigned on it for each input channel. Figure 5-33 shows a time division multiplexed channel.

If we commute using TDM, the TDM system would not be a highway, but rather a train that ran into the city. Instead of being guaranteed a lane, a separate box car would be assigned to every car. Every second, a fresh box car would come down the tracks as people arrived at their ramp. Each box car would be designated for a specific on ramp, so only we could use our box car to travel to work and back. Each morning we would get up, drive out our designated ramp, and hit a jump at the end of the ramp. We would then fly in the air, turning our car precisely 90 degrees while flying, so we landed perfectly in the box car. Individual box cars would provide transportation guarantees and prevent accidents. With TDM and this railroad configuration, we still have guaranteed box car space, so there are no delays for any drivers. However, the train is also not efficient. Each box car would be used only when the person from a specific ramp wanted to use it. If the on ramp was not used, the box car would be empty. This configuration in not the most efficient type of multiplexing, but it still provides guarantees. TDM is used by T-carrier (T-1 and T-3) channels.

Time division multiplexers (TDMs) combine multiple parallel digital streams (sub-channels) into a single high-speed digital (stream) channel.

Each of the sub-channels is assigned a specific time slot within a time frame large enough to accommodate all of the sub-channels. The frames are repeated often enough to handle the information transmission rate of every sub-channel. TDM divides up our composite channel on a vertical time-sliced basis. Thus, the high-speed channel connecting two time division multiplexers must be greater than or equal to the sum of the speeds of the input channels. The input channel bits are time interleaved on the high-speed channel in a precise scanning sequence. The receiving time division multiplexer then rebuilds the individual information streams from the composite high-speed data stream.

Time division multiplexers use the high-speed composite channel more efficiently than do frequency division multiplexers. For example, one voice-grade channel was at one time frequency division multiplexed into about 25 75-Bps channels. In contrast, time division multiplexers could divide up the same voice-grade channel into 32 300-Bps channels.

T-1 and fractional T-1 services are time division multiplexed, full-period, leased channel, high-speed digital communications links between facilities. T-1 and fractional T-1 employ TDM to combine 24 64-Kbps DS-0 channels into one 1.544-Mbps T-1 channel. In this manner, they provide multiple channels that can be combined to form one single large digital pipe or can be subdivided into lower capacity sub-channels for combined data and voice transmission between facilities. Fractional T-1 services permit organizations with lesser communications needs to contract for digital transmission capacity that fits their load as opposed to contracting for a full 1.544-Mbps T-1 channel.

Statistical Time Division Multiplexers

Statistical multiplexing is a form of TDM. A Statistical Multiplexer, or Stat-Mux, is a microcomputer-controlled device that processes data from low-speed input lines and places them in HDLC frames for transmission across a high-speed line to a companion StatMux. A StatMux processing the data from each input channel passes only live data. Idle information is not placed in packets and transmitted to the companion StatMux. Thus, StatMuxes increase communications efficiency on the high-speed channel. High-speed channel utilization may reach as high as 90% (see Figure 5-34).

Statistical multiplexing follows the familiar train scenario. In this case, efficiency is provided at the sacrifice of capacity guarantees because anyone can use any available box car at any time. The box cars are no longer assigned to specific cars and on ramps. Stoplights at the end of each ramp indicate that a box car is full or taken. The stop lights prevent accidents. The stop

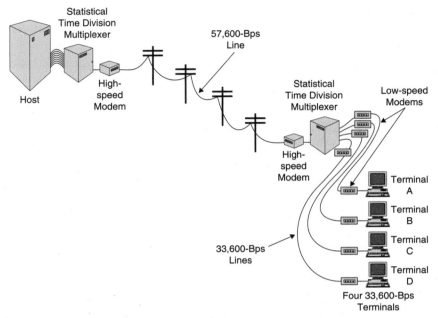

Figure 5–34 *Statistical multiplexing.*

lights prevent access when a boxcar is occupied. This no longer guarantees capacity or available space on the train. The stoplights control the flow of cars onto the train, thus permitting the train to slow down so that only one car every minute can get on the train. This increases efficiency, but causes drivers to get upset because they must wait for a free box car. We are less concerned with the driver delays and are more happy as taxpayers because our commuter train is used more efficiently.

Most multiplexers today are intelligent devices that implement some form of statistical time division multiplexing.

FDM and TDM Applications Overview

FDM and TDM are used throughout telecommunications systems. For example, cable modems run across a frequency division multiplexed system. DSLs are also frequency division multiplexed on the same pair of telephone wires used to carry a voice communications channel. T-1 channels are time division multiplexed DS-0 channels. PBXs use TDM on their voice bus to make voice circuit connections. Some cell phones use a combination of both FDM and TDM. The point here is that to understand how these devices work and to determine how to save communications costs, a fundamental understanding of TDM and FDM is very helpful.

These technologies are all OSI Layer-1 technology that is implemented in network hardware for the most part. A multiplexer looks like a box with flashing lights.

Brain Teaser

Time Division Multiplexing

Examine Figure 5-35. It shows four 300-bps, low-speed lines running into a single 1,200-bps composite channel. We will use the numbers in this figure to further illustrate TDM concepts. As stated above, our composite channel has to be greater than or equal to the speeds of the input channels. Since the multiplexed channel is 1,200 bps, it is equal to the sum of the speeds (300+300+300+300) of the input channels. So far, so good!

In the time it takes one bit to come in on a 300-bps channel, four bits go out on the 1,200-bps channel with one bit assigned to low-speed Channel A, one to Channel B, one to Channel C, and one to Channel D. The assignment sequence is fixed and does not change. The receiving TDM knows that Channel A is always first and that Channel D is always last.

1. Could Channel A run the HDLC protocol, Channel B run voice (just think that speed is not an issue here), Channel C the TTY protocol, and Channel D carry video information simultaneously? Certainly, higher transmission speeds would be required, but the channels are separate Layer-1 physical channels so they do not care about what is happening in Layers 2 through 7.

2. Can we have a mixture of transmission speeds on each of the time division multiplexers? Could we in our example have two lines at 150 bps, one at 300 bps, and one at 600 bps? Yes we could when the time division multiplexers are properly configured.

3. What percentage of the 300 bps, or 30 characters per second, of the low-speed channels is used on average over several hours to carry data to the central computer? Is it 10% - 3 characters per second, 50% - 15 characters per second, or 90% - 27 characters per second? The fastest typist in the world has a typing speed of about 16.67 characters per second. So what do you think is the best answer? The best answer is 10%, or 3 characters per second. Humans spend lots of time reading or drinking coffee, so our data rate is quite low.

4. If the utilization of the input channels is 10% (i.e., of the 30 characters per second, only 3 characters per second are actually transmitted on the average over several hours), what is the utilization of the high-speed channel? 90%? 40%? 10%? In this case, it is the same as the low-speed channels, 10%. Here is the math that verifies it. Each low-speed channel uses 10% times 300 bps, or 30 bps. Four times 30 bps is 120 bps, which is exactly 10% of the high-speed 1,200-bps channel's capacity.

The goal here was to show that TDM while saving costs, does not use high-speed channels efficiently. Much capacity is wasted sending idle bits across the channel. Newer telecommunications

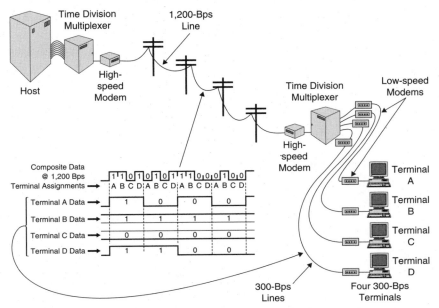

Figure 5–35   *Low-speed channel time division multiplexer configuration.*

technologies utilize high-speed channels more effectively today as we shall see in subsequent chapters.

■ Summary

This chapter explained the fundamental transmission concepts of data communications. It examined modems and modem data encoding. Sending digitally encoded image, voice, and video information demonstrated the need for increased networking transmission speeds. Data communications Layer-2 protocols were explained and their evolution from simple second-generation to modern seventh-generation protocols was reviewed. Layer-1 physical interfaces used for communications were identified and described. Finally, we discussed the important frequency division and time division multiplexing concepts. Understanding these fundamental data communications terms and concepts lays the foundation for understanding new telecommunications products and services, for they are the result of the convergence of telephony with data communications.

▲ CHAPTER REVIEW QUESTIONS

1. *Voice-grade telephone subscriber lines are "bit robbed" channels. Can modems hear the bits being robbed?*

   A. No

   B. Yes

   C. Maybe

2. *How is data transmission different from video transmission?*

   A. It can have errors.

   B. It arrives in a continuous stream.

   C. It is transferred using protocols.

   D. It is carried across the telephone network in digital form.

3. *Is an ISDN phone used only for 128-Kbps data communications?*

   A. Yes

   B. No

   C. Always

   D. Maybe

4. *What device interfaces a PC to an ISDN line?*

   A. A modem

   B. A CODEC

   C. A Channel Service Unit (CSU)

   D. A CSU/DSU

5. *What does modem stand for?*

   A. Modulate the signal

   A. Modulator/Demultiplexor

   A. More Digital Encoding

   A. Modulator/Demodulator

6. *How many possible patterns are produced by eight bits?*

   A. 128

   B. 32

   C. 64

   D. 256

7. *How many printable characters are there?*
   A. 32
   B. 96
   C. 128
   D. 64

8. *The functions of an OSI Layer-2 protocol are?*
   A. Detect errors
   B. Synchronize sender and receiver
   C. Correct errors
   D. Match the flow of data to the terminal device
   E. All of the above
   F. None of the above

9. *Second-, third-, and fourth-generation protocols were designed for _____ channels?*
   A. High-speed and low error rate
   B. Low-speed and low error rate
   C. Low-speed and high error rate
   D. High-speed and high error rate

10. *What protocol property is aimed at high-speed and low error rate channels?*
    A. Large frame size
    B. Go-Back-N error correction
    C. Half-duplex message flows
    D. CRC error detection

11. *Which serial interface will replace RS-232?*
    A. Printer
    B. COM port
    C. USB
    D. Ethernet

12. *What interface is targeted at connecting multimedia devices to a PC?*
    A. USB
    B. IEEE 1394
    C. RS-232
    D. Ethernet

13. *What is a key parameter in determining CSMA/CD performance?*
    A. Channel utilization
    B. Channel speed
    C. Error rate
    D. Server speed
    E. All of the above
    F. None of the above

14. *What is the maximum specified speed of the EIA-232 D interface?*
    A. 115,000 bps
    B. 20,000 bps
    C. 53,000 bps
    D. 64,000 bps

15. *How many 1,200-bps lines can run across a 56,000-bps time division multiplexed channel?*
    A. 54
    B. 32
    C. 94
    D. 46

16. *We have 20 DS-0 active voice channels in a T-1 circuit. How many 56,000-bps data channels can the circuit support?*
    A. 1
    B. 4
    C. 9
    D. 7

Local Area Networks

This chapter completes the foundation needed to survive telecommunications networks and develop cost-saving telecommunications applications. Telephony, WANs, and LANs form the three basic building blocks of all telecommunications networks. In this chapter, we examine LAN technologies and products that are key for building telecommunications networks. This chapter covers those products and technologies that are used to construct a LAN, but it does not cover administering server software and managing LAN users.

LAN technologies provide high-speed distribution of data around business offices and campus locations. If the local loop is the last mile for delivering telecommunications services, the LAN is the last 200 feet for delivering those services to any client PC. LANs usually occupy a single building or campus facility. Today LAN technologies are moving into the home. This leads to new business opportunities for established and innovative businesses. LANs provide the critical third component for future growth of the Internet, e-commerce, video telephony, home entertainment, and a host of new telecommunications applications. A LAN is just hardware and software.

General LAN Structure and Components

What is a LAN? A LAN is having the PCs in a facility communicate with a central server or series of servers. If we think geographically, a LAN would be in a building, on a floor, or in a room. LANs are physically small in size. LANs, like all other telecommunications networks, consist of hardware, software, and channels. The hardware is in PC clients, servers, and networking components like wiring hubs. To communicate, the PCs must be connected together by a wiring plant. Wire forms the channels that connect everything. Generally, in the past, the wire was coaxial cable, but today you'll find more Unshielded Twisted Pair (UTP) copper wire in LANs. Finally, the software is some form of Windows in the clients; Windows, UNIX, or NetWare in the servers; and specialized software in the networking components (see Figure 6-1). LANs, like any network, are composed of hardware, channels, and software.

LANs with UTP wiring connect clients and servers using wiring hubs. The wiring hubs improve network reliability by isolating wiring and component malfunctions to individual wiring runs.

Servers

Many servers in the mid-1980s (Ethernet hit the market in 1984) were beefed up PCs with a large disk drive. Large disk drives at that time were 20MB to 60MB. Beefed up meant that they had more RAM and a LAN board installed. The server software was mostly Novell NetWare that worked with DOS. Our first server was a Columbia Data Products PC with a 20MB disk drive and 128KB of RAM. Because disk drives were relatively unreliable (as compared to disk drives today), the software performed extensive testing of the disk drive before permitting it to be used as a server drive. These servers provided primarily disk sharing and file sharing functions.

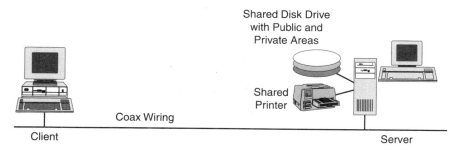

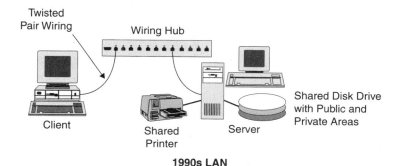

Figure 6–1 *Simple LAN configurations.*

PC servers evolved rapidly from their modest beginnings by taking steroids. They now are dual CPU systems with 512MB of RAM or more and Redundant Array of Independent Disks (RAID) storage that holds 20 to several hundred gigabytes of data.

Keep in mind that servers are PCs on steroids. Big, bad, and tough compared to a PC.

Clients

Similar to servers, early clients were PC systems running DOS and needing to share information or printers among other PCs in an office environment. Client PCs were not beefed up beyond the addition of a LAN board. Multimedia products have now impacted these clients. Most PC clients have sound and video input capabilities. Client PCs are just a little bit wimpier than server PCs.

A typical multimedia PC is shown in Figure 6-2. Multimedia PC clients depend upon high-speed LAN connections to effectively perform Voice over Internet Packet (VoIP) protocol telephony, video teleconferencing, e-com-

Figure 6–2 *Multimedia PC client.*

merce, music distribution, video news distribution, and other types of multi-media communications. LAN connections of 100 Mbps or higher are required to effectively implement the multimedia telephony applications. These must be backed-up 24 hours per day, 7 days per week (24/7) Internet connections of 100 Kbps to Mbps or higher speeds to effectively do voice and video teleconferencing planet-wide. Video teleconferencing is possible at low speeds as well, but it is not as effective for business applications.

Wiring

LAN wiring in the 1980s was either coaxial cable or the more expensive twisted pair wire used for IBM's token ring. LANs now use one of several categories of twisted pair wiring or optical fiber for connecting components. Often the network is a combination of twisted pair wires with optical fiber backbone (wiring closet to wiring closet) connections that run from wiring hub to wiring hub.

Software: Windows, NetWare, and UNIX

Early network software was Novell's NetWare. It dominated the LAN market with at one point 80% of installed servers running NetWare. This has changed with high-end office servers running Microsoft Windows NT or Windows 2000 and other special servers running UNIX. Many NetWare installations remain because it provides very solid file and print sharing services. Windows servers, in contrast, provide a wide range of functionality. Windows NT supports email, SQL, and many other types of servers. The main drawback is that Windows servers are a la carte. In other words, you purchase Windows NT or Windows 2000 and then you must purchase extra software, e.g., Microsoft Back Office server software and more, to implement special office automation server functions. In contrast, Lotus Notes and Domino provide equivalent functionality in a single software package. Operating system software comprises OSI Layers 6 and 7. This is the software we see.

LAN Characteristics

What makes a LAN a LAN? LANs are geographically compact. They cover a single building or a campus area. This means that the LAN owner runs and manages the wire to all LAN components. Since the LAN operator controls the wire, it is typically higher quality than telephone company wiring. This translates into high-speed transmission and lower transmission error rates. LAN speeds started at 4 Mbps and 10 Mbps, moved to 100 Mbps and now are moving beyond 1 Gbps. LAN protocols and components were specially designed to utilize this environment. Further, network configuration and maintenance were issues because the LAN owner had to perform those functions. LAN products evolved over several years into much more robust and reliable products. They require less effort to configure than their predecessor components, data communications, or WAN components. Many components are self-configuring with few user-settable options.

LAN Types

There are two main types of PC LANs:

- Client/server LANs.
- Peer-to-peer.

Client/server LANs have servers that provide disk sharing, printer sharing, and other special services to client PCs. Generally, one server can support from 50 to several hundred clients, depending upon client activity. Thin clients have the server perform all data and program storage. Applications are downloaded into the thin PC client and run. The applications reference data stored on the server.

Lantastic products epitomize peer-to-peer LANs. Lantastic software sets up disk and printer sharing between DOS PCs. Windows now provides a peer-to-peer networking capability for PCs. They can share disk and printer resources based upon a LAN security provider or based upon password security they set. Figure 6-3 was clipped from a Windows 98 system.

Figure 6-3 shows both Windows NT/2000 client/server and Windows 98 peer-to-peer LANs connecting to a Windows 98 PC. The Windows 98 PC connects at the same time to both the client/server LAN and the Windows 98 peer-to-peer LAN.

Peer-to-Peer

Windows 95/98/ME and Windows NT/2000 provide peer-to-peer LAN capabilities with up to 10 PCs simultaneously using resources on any peer PC. A peer-to-peer LAN can be defined as PCs working together. Every PC acts as both disk and print server and simultaneously as a client. Microsoft introduced peer-to-peer networking with their Windows for Workgroups product. This same technology is used in Windows NT/2000, allowing it to operate on a peer-to-peer LAN as well as a client/server-based network.

The peer-to-peer strategy works well for small organizations. With it, each user is responsible for managing their workstations and resources. If a user wants to share their printer, that is up to them. Additionally, if a user wishes to use multiple computers in the office, they must have a password on each machine in the network. Security authorizations can be passed from a LAN-wide user manager providing client/server security to the peer-to-peer LAN. Pass-through security for peer-to-peer networking is more secure than security administered for each peer-to-peer LAN resource.

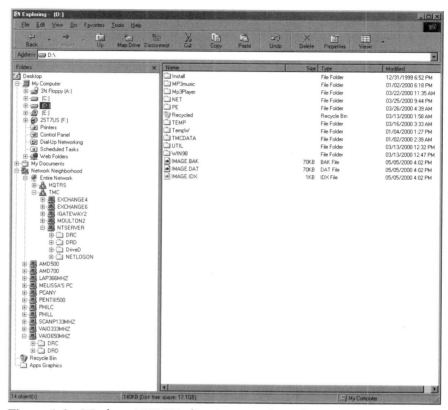

Figure 6–3 *Windows NT/2000 client/server and Windows 98 peer-to-peer LANs*

Here are some reasons why you would use a peer-to-peer strategy:

- You have a very small number of users to connect and support.
- You do not need centralized management of resources.
- You do not need centralized management of user accounts and network security.

The NetBEUI (Network BIOS Extended User Interface) protocol is excellent for peer-to-peer networks since it is not routable and these networks are small in design and complexity. NetBEUI is a protocol that extends the original PC Basic Input/Output System (BIOS) to operate with networks. NetBEUI stands for Network BIOS Extended User Interface.

Peer-to-peer networks can support some telecommunications applications, but the majority of telecommunications applications rely upon the security provided by client/server LANs.

Client/Server

Most LANs operate as client/server LANs with the server being a Windows NT or Windows 2000, UNIX, or NetWare server. The server provides central network security, and disk and printer sharing services to the attached PC clients.

Some servers implement special network functions such as Structured Query Language (SQL) database servers, office automation servers (Microsoft Exchange Servers), and fax servers.

For larger LANs, Microsoft provides a client/server-based networking approach. It does this by creating control domains to overcome the limitation of peer-to-peer connections. It provides a centralized way to control user accounts, set security rights, and provide access to network resources. All this control is provided by a domain-controlling PC. With Windows 2000, a Domain Name Service (DNS) provides a reliable, hierarchical, distributed, and scalable database to manage LAN access. Windows clients use the DNS for name resolution and for locating domain-controlling servers for logon.

Each domain can have many client types. At least one server contains a centralized security database for the domain. This Windows NT/2000 server is the Primary Domain Controller, or PDC. The administrator for the domain can alter and change security databases located there. Other backup domain controller servers in the same domain back up the domain control databases. These are known as Backup Domain Controllers (BDCs) and can be used to authenticate and log on users. The choice to be a PDC or BDC is decided initially during installation.

With Windows NT/2000, the client/server setup can be managed through the Network Control Panel. This allows adding services, transport protocols, and additional adapters. The setup for most of the networking services can be controlled or changed there as well.

User account management is handled through the User Manager. This controls login restrictions and group assignments for all user accounts.

Assigning domains to a server is done through the Server Manager. This allows you to move easily from one domain to another. You can also see other characteristics about the servers, like their TCP/IP assignment, with this tool.

Client/server LANs provide centralized network management and security functions as illustrated by the Windows NT and Windows 2000 LANs just discussed. This type of security and management is needed for moderate to large enterprise LANs. Telecommunications applications are best implemented using centralized LAN user account management to provide access to specialized LAN servers.

Thin Client/Server

There are also thin client/servers. The Citrix MetaFrame servers connect thin client PCs to powerful servers. Citrix loads Independent Computing Architecture (ICA) protocols on top of TCP/IP or any other OSI Layers-3/4/5 protocols in the thin client so that only mouse clicks, keystrokes, and screen updates are transmitted across the network. All of the application installation and execution is done on the MetaFrame server. Client and server communicate using 128-bit encryption for maximum security. A Citrix feature, Speed Screen 2, reduces transmission of frequently transmitted screens by caching them in the client. This reduces network traffic and the bandwidth applications require.

Thin client applications can be implemented using Java applets, Web browsing software under Windows, or custom software, all designed to perform specific business functions. Thin client LANs provide more control over PC-based clients because all application software is downloaded from the server as needed by the client.

Thin client/server LANs can provide rapid delivery of business-critical applications across an extended enterprise using LANs, the Internet, and other TCP/IP networks. Thin client/server LANs deliver interactive applications into any standard Web browser, and extend the reach of servers beyond the desktop to all types of devices, including UNIX, Windows, Macs, wireless terminals, and dial-in clients. See Figure 6-4, which shows a Citrix thin client/server LAN.

With thin client LANs, the central server performs all application processing. Clients do not need to be as robust as they do with other LANs. This could extend the useful operating life of older PCs.

Thin client/server LANs can support telecommunications applications with better control than a normal client/server LAN.

Different types of networks are defined by the LAN software working in OSI Layers 6 and 7. We interact with this software.

Basic Configuration for Disk and Printer Sharing

PC LANs provide basic disk and printer sharing functions. In a client/server network, the servers provide access to their disk drives and printers to groups of users. Each user group has authorization to use entire disk drives or specific areas of disk drives because a disk drive can contain critical enterprise data. Printers have fewer restrictions because they are simple LAN output devices.

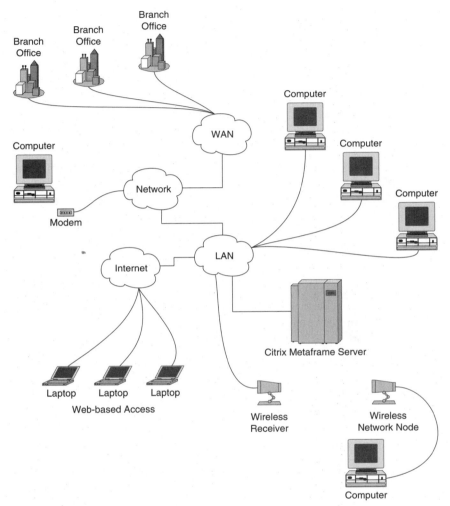

Figure 6–4 *Citrix thin client/server LAN.*

DISK SHARING BASICS

Clients share their drives based upon authorizations obtained from the LAN security provider, a PDC in Windows NT/2000 domains. The setup for other network operating system software is similar. Sharing Windows disk resources in a client/server environment requires that an administrator or user who has permission to make this change be logged on to the PC, and that the service for disk and printer sharing be operating in the PC.

Disk sharing can be set up remotely on Windows NT/2000 systems as well. In this case, a remote administrator must have the correct permissions on the server to set up the sharing. By default, the standard Windows NT/2000 Administrator and Power User groups have such permissions. Once a disk drive is shared, permissions for other users and groups are set.

Windows NT uses an advanced filesystem designed for networking and data security called NT Filesystem (NTFS). NTFS provides different file and directory permissions, including:

- No Access—Allows connection to the directory, but the user cannot access anything or see anything in the directory.
- Read—Users or groups can view sub-directories and filenames, display data attributes, run programs, and alter sub-directories.
- Change—Users and groups can create sub-directories and add files, change data and append it, alter file attributes, and delete files and sub-directories.
- Full Control—Allows user all the above capabilities as well as claim ownership of an NTFS drive and alter specific permissions for a drive, directory, or file.

NTFS partitions also offer another file directory permission called Special Access. Special Access allows a user to customize the read, write, execute, delete, change permissions, and take ownership capabilities.

Windows NT/2000 disk sharing is illustrated in Figure 6-5.

LAN users can view shared resources as mapped drives or by using the Universal Naming Convention (UNC). More discussion of this follows soon.

PRINTER SHARING

Printers attached to servers and clients are similarly shared. Sharing a printer is similar to sharing a disk drive. Installing a printer locally allows the user to use the printer locally at any time. Setting up printer sharing is easy. Install a printer and then select sharing. Similar to disk sharing, the printer permissions window pops up. Select the groups to use the printer and assign permissions to the printer. Some basic printer permissions and other printing options are:

- No Access—No printing privileges.
- Print—Users can print documents, control their job settings, and pause and restart jobs.
- Manage Documents—Same as Print, but users can control, pause, delete, and restart all print jobs.

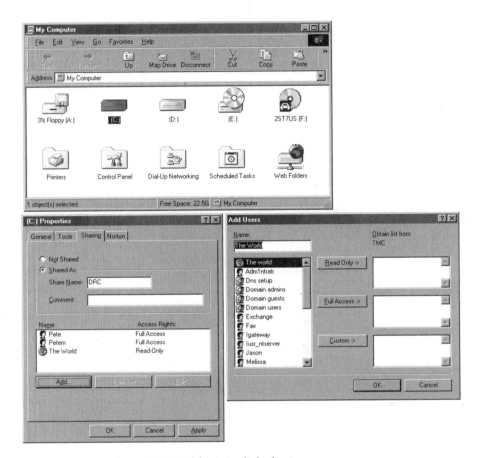

Figure 6–5 *Windows NT/2000 domain disk sharing.*

- Full Control—Same as Manage Documents, but users can also control shares and properties, and connect to and delete printers.

Figure 6-6 illustrates Windows printer sharing. Network printers like the Epson color 800 have a network symbol, indicating that they are network printers.

When using a LAN, a client station has a different view of network resources than the server or client sharing its disk and printer resources.

User's View of a LAN

Each user views the LAN as an extension of their PC. To them, it appears as though there are now extra disk drives attached to their PC. To transfer data

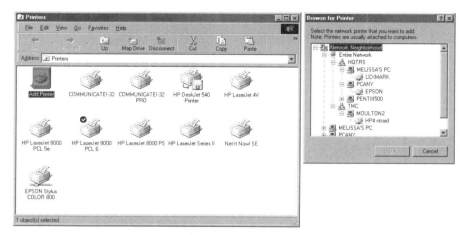

Figure 6–6 *Windows NT/2000 domain printer sharing.*

from their system to the server, the user merely copies the file from a local disk drive, C:, to a server disk drive, F:, or uses the Windows Explorer to drag and drop the files in the appropriate folders on each disk drive.

In basic LANs, client PCs can present network drives as mapped drives; for instance, drives can be assigned a drive letter or the user can connect to them using the Universal Naming Convention (UNC).

DRIVE MAPPING

Drive mapping assigns disk drive letters to network drives. Thus, drive letters F: to Z: can be assigned to network drives. Drive mapping is performed using map commands for Novell's NetWare and the Windows Explorer map drive (see Figure 6-7).

Drive mappings are convenient when using DOS applications, but they can cause real performance problems in Windows. Windows continually sends status check messages to verify that the drive mappings are okay. If the system does not respond to these messages, it slows down and waits for responses, thus degrading PC client performance.

UNIVERSAL NAMING CONVENTION

The UNC is a way to refer to network servers or clients and their shared resources by name. In our LAN, we use the convention of DRC to represent Drive C: (DRD for Drive D:, etc.) shared on a client or server. To access drive C: on server MOULTON2 using the UNC, we address the drive as \\server-

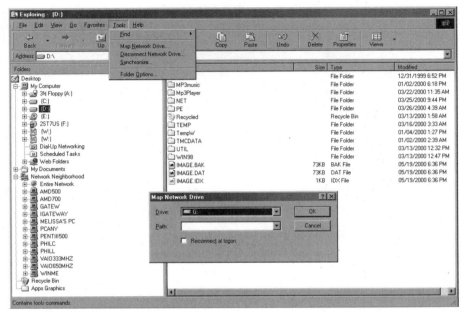

Figure 6–7 *Windows Explorer map network drive.*

name\sharedresourcename, or for our specific case, \\moulton2\DRC. Figure 6-8 shows a simple PC LAN with UNC names applied to mapped drives.

LANs are really defined by the software that works in OSI Layers 6 and 7 and is visible to us as network users.

Brain Teaser

Simple PC-Based LAN Concepts

All LANs apply the simple disk and printer sharing concepts we discussed here. Let us familiarize ourselves with the LAN connections in our work PC.

1. Open the Windows Explorer and click on the **Network Neighborhood** icon. What types of networks appear? Are a peer-to-peer network and a client/server network accessible? Peer-to-peer networks are identified as PCs with shared resources under **Network Neighborhood**. Client/server networks are viewed under the **Entire Network** icon.

2. Pick a server and map the drive letter N: to a server drive. Open a DOS window and perform the command **DIR N:** Does the directory for the server display as a DOS directory list? Try the **DIR** command using the UNC to the same drive, **DIR ***server_name**drive_name*. Did you get the same results as with the mapped drive?

3. Connect to a network printer using the **Add Printer Wizard**. Print a test page. Now try the **DIR**

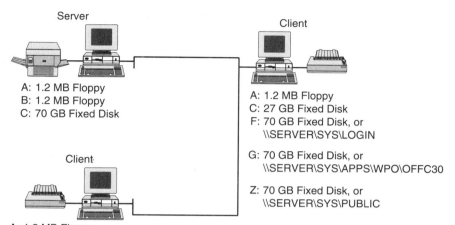

Server

A: 1.2 MB Floppy
B: 1.2 MB Floppy
C: 70 GB Fixed Disk

Client

A: 1.2 MB Floppy
C: 27 GB Fixed Disk
F: 70 GB Fixed Disk, or
   \\SERVER\SYS\LOGIN

G: 70 GB Fixed Disk, or
   \\SERVER\SYS\APPS\WPO\OFFC30

Z: 70 GB Fixed Disk, or
   \\SERVER\SYS\PUBLIC

Client

A: 1.2 MB Floppy
C: 18 GB Fixed Disk
F: 70 GB Fixed Disk, or
   \\SERVER\SYS\LOGIN

G: 70 GB Fixed Disk, or
   \\SERVER\SYS\APPS\WPO\OFFC30

Z: 70 GB Fixed Disk, or
   \\SERVER\SYS\PUBLIC

Figure 6–8 *User view of a PC LAN.*

command to the printer using the UNC, **DIR** > *server_name**printer_name*. Did the directory print?

The goal here is to understand PC LAN basics before we discuss how LANs are playing an increasingly important role in telecommunications.

LAN Market Summary

LAN products fit into three different network areas:

- Backbone LANs.
- Work area LANs.
- Voice, Video, and data LANs.

Backbone LANs interconnect the work area LANs in a facility to services and servers used by everyone in the enterprise. Work area LANs support small workgroup operations. They provide local disk and printer sharing for an individual organizational unit. Work area LANs may be more PC-based. Backbone LANs have robust servers specially designed and configured to deliver specific services to work area PC LAN clients. This is illustrated in Figure 6-9.

Voice, video, and data networks support new telephony and other multimedia LAN applications such as VoIP. They require a special design to meet voice and video delivery QoS requirements. In the long term, all LANs will support voice, video, and data traffic.

The LAN market can be viewed from the hardware, software, and wiring perspective. These are the main products purchased when implementing a LAN. The hardware (a LAN board) and wiring are inextricably tied together, while the software may be used with almost any hardware component.

Two LAN hardware boards dominate the market today, Ethernet and token ring. Ethernet uses the Carrier Sense Multiple Access with Collision Detection (CSMA/CD) protocol and token ring uses the token passing ring protocol. These protocols are the Medium Access Control (MAC) protocols at OSI Layer 2. The interface to the LAN software is performed by the Logical Link Control (LLC) component of OSI Layer 2.

Virtually all LAN adapter cards or Network Interface Cards (NICs) work with UTP wire. UTP wiring is the preferred type of LAN wiring.

Novell dominated the LAN software market with a 50% to 70% share in the early 1980s. Microsoft NT/2000 Server has now taken the lead in market share. In the long term, a battle between Microsoft and UNIX for LAN server market dominance appears to be developing. These products are becoming more important as PC LANs become the basic building block of business communications in the 21st century.

Figure 6-10 identifies the LAN hardware, software, and wiring that are likely to dominate the LAN market over the next several years. These are the main products purchased when implementing a LAN. The hardware (NIC) and the wiring are linked, while the software may be used with almost any hardware component.

In Figure 6-10, the numbers on the right-hand side identify the OSI layers covered by the products. In the left column, the LAN hardware and software components and the type of compatibility they resolve (Wire/Speed) are listed. The middle columns identify the LAN hardware and software products most commonly used to build LANs. The gray bars identify the interfaces between the LAN hardware and software products. The F: at the top left of the diagram is the mapped drive letter a network user sees when using Windows to access network disk drives. It is coincidental that the token ring card lines up with Novell. Novell, Windows, and UNIX software all work with token ring, Ethernet, and ATM PC cards.

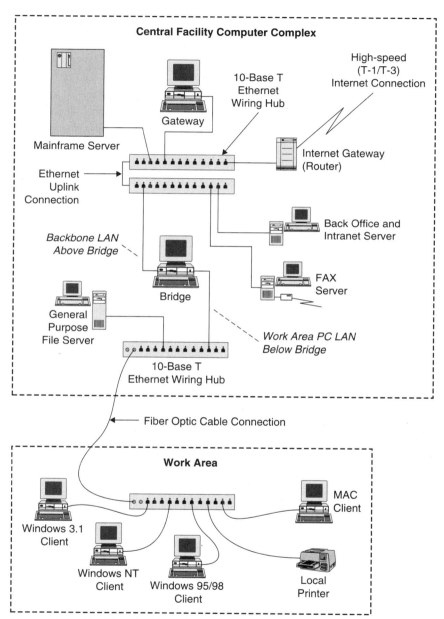

Figure 6–9   *Backbone and work area LANs.*

Two LAN hardware boards, Ethernet and token ring, dominate the market today, but ATM Cards could challenge them in the future. In the home, USB and IEEE 1394 Fire Wire are now used to interconnect devices to

PCs and to provide the mechanism to carry sound (sound = music and voice) and video between TV, VCR, DVD, PC server, and PC clients. Which of these technologies will dominate in the long term is anyone's guess.

Ethernet is most likely to be the LAN of choice because:

- Ethernet is already widely implemented.
- It is easy to migrate from a slow Ethernet to a faster Ethernet.
- Ethernet now operates at 100 Mbps, but is moving to 10 Gbps.
- Ethernet uses UTP wiring.
- Bridging and switching components can significantly enhance Ethernet performance.

In the longer term, ATM may replace Ethernet, but that is not guaranteed at this time. The token ring is an okay LAN, but is less likely to be a long-term LAN choice. USB and IEEE 1394 are not shown in the diagram because they are relatively new in providing LAN capabilities to PCs. They are most likely to be used in consumer/residential LANs.

Novell software provides very robust file and printer sharing; however, Novell has not captured the enterprise LAN market share that Windows has captured. Windows 2000 Network Directory Services (NDS) can make a big impact in the next several years because it is a standard NDS implementation with a Windows 2000 twist. UNIX provides the greatest potential competition to Microsoft Windows because it is a hugely efficient operating system as compared to Microsoft's bloated code. It will be interesting to see how the battle between UNIX and Windows develops.

Let us look at how the NICs work in more detail.

LAN Boards and Protocols

Basic LAN operation begins with the transmission media or wire, and protocols, principally Ethernet and token ring. The Ethernet CSMA/CD protocol and the token ring token passing ring protocol are the most widely used protocols in LANs.

As we saw in Chapter 5, CSMA/CD is a simple protocol. Its operation is statistical in nature, i.e., it depends upon how many stations need to be active at any given moment. CSMA/CD responds well to traffic bursts, but does not perform as well under heavy, sustained loads.

The token passing ring protocol is a more sophisticated protocol that behaves well under heavy, sustained loads. The token passing ring protocol is deterministic, with every station assured its turn on the ring. The token ring's greater sophistication requires more operating overhead. Diagnostic messages constantly flow on the ring, and whenever the ring must be reconfig-

	Application		7
F:	Windows 95/98		6

	Novell	**Microsoft**	**UNIX**	
Software	Ver 4.0 Ver 3.11 Ver 4.01 Ver. 3.12 Ver 4.02 Ver 4.1 **Ver 5.0**	**Clients** Windows 95/98 Windows NT/2000 Workstation **Servers** Windows NT Server Windows 2000 Advanced Server	UNIX SQL Servers	
	SPX/IPX **TCP/1P**	NETBEUI **TCP/IP** SPX/IPX	**TCP/IP** NETBEUI SPX/IPX	5 4 3
Interface	Board Driver Program (3C509 for 3Com Ethernet)			
Board ------ Protocol	**Token Ring** Token Passing Ring	**Ethernet** CSMA/CD	**ATM** Cell Relay	2
Interface	IBM-9-Pin "D" Non-IBM-RJ-45	BNC Bi-Conic RJ-45 or Mod-8	Bi-Conic RJ-45 or Mod-8	

	STP	**UTP**	**Coax**	**Fiber**	**UTP**	**Fiber**	**UTP**	
Wire ------ Speed	Shielded Twisted Pair	Unshielded Twisted Pair	50-Ohm Coaxial Cable	62.5-Micron/ 125-Micron Glass Fiber Cable	Unshielded Twisted Pair CAT 5 CAT 5+ Level 7	62.5-Micron/ 125-Micron Glass Fiber Cable	Unshielded Twisted Pair CAT 5 CAT 5+ Level 7	1
	4 Mbps or 16 Mbps 100 Mbps and going to 1024 Mbps		10 Mbps, 100 Mbps, 1 Gbps, and coming, 10 Gbps		25 Mbps, 155 Mbps, or 620 Mbps			

UTP = Unshielded Twisted Pair
STP = Shielded Twisted Pair
SPX/IPX = Sequenced Packet Exchange/Internet Packet Exchange
NETBIOS = Network Basic Input/Output System
TCP/IP = Transmission Control Protocol/Internet Protocol
BNC = British Naval Connector, or Barrel Neutral Connector (Push and Twist)
CSMA/CD = Carrier Sense Multiple Access with Collision Detection

Figure 6–10   *Popular LAN hardware and software products.*

ured, there is a brief but heavy period of overhead traffic that completes the reconfiguration.

With any LAN, the nature of the load is difficult to predict. There are times when it is bursty and other times when there is a normal, heavy, sus-

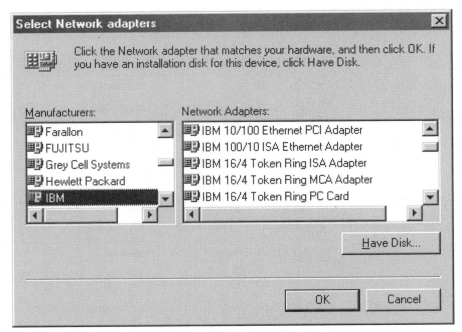

Figure 6–11 *Windows 98 IBM NIC selections.*

tained traffic period (e.g., closing the books at month's end). On top of the normal data load, servers and PCs constantly send idle data to assure that logical connections across a LAN are still valid.

Windows supports multiple network adapters. Newer Windows versions have a larger selection of supported NICs than earlier Windows versions. When Windows is installed and the PC hardware is set up, the NIC is chosen. Later, additional adapters can be added through the **Network** item in the **Control Panel** (see Figure 6-11).

LAN cards implement OSI Layers 1 and 2. They are network hardware components designed originally to carry data, but now they also carry voice and video transmissions.

Windows NT does not support PnP, but Windows 95/98/2000 and ME (Windows Millennium Edition) do. As a result, with NT, knowing board setup parameters, including the IRQ, I/O, DMA, and shared ROM address, can be important. Most NIC problems come from incorrect setup.

ETHERNET

Xerox originally designed Ethernet. Intel developed the first Ethernet chip sets. Digital Equipment Corporation sold the early Ethernet products. We

Figure 6–12 *Ethernet ISA Bus (right) and PCI Bus (left) NICs.*

Figure 6–13 *PCI Ethernet NIC LED 100-Mbps and FDX LED indicators.*

saw in Chapter 5 that although Ethernet's CSMA/CD sounds complicated, it is really quite simple to understand. The key things to understand about Ethernet NICs are the speed at which they operate, whether they support half-duplexᵢor full duplex data transfers, and the PC bus type the card supports. Most new Ethernet NICs are Peripheral Component Interconnect (PCI) bus cards. These cards are PnP cards that can share IRQs with other PCI bus cards. An Industry Standard Architecture (ISA) bus Ethernet card and a PCI bus Ethernet Card are shown in Figure 6-12. The ISA bus Ethernet NIC supports only 10-Mbps half-duplex data transfer operations over UTP wiring. This would not be the best Ethernet NIC for new multimedia LAN applications.

The PCI Ethernet NIC works with UTP wiring as well. However, it is capable of 100-Mbps transmission with full duplex data transfer capabilities. This is illustrated in Figure 6-13 by the 100-Mbps and FDX Light Emitting Diode (LED) indicators on the PCI bus Ethernet NIC.

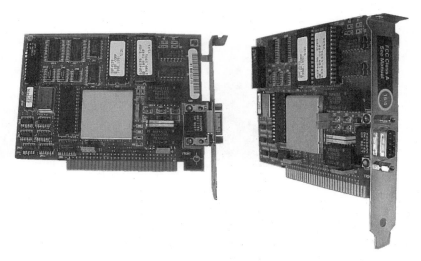

Figure 6–14 *IBM 16/4-Mbps token ring NIC.*

The PCI bus NIC is capable of supporting some new telecommunications applications over the Ethernet LAN, depending upon the backbone and work area LAN configuration.

TOKEN RING

IBM developed the token ring network in the 1980s. It was first released in 1987 as a 4-Mbps token passing ring MAC network running on Shielded Twisted Pair (STP), IBM's Type-1 and Type-2 wire. As we saw in Chapter 5, the token ring MAC protocol is deterministic; each and every station gets its turn on the ring. The token ring protocol was good for supporting heavy, sustained LAN loads. It would be better in telecommunications applications environments with constant voice and video data flows, however. The problem is that because Ethernet is now full duplex and because Ethernet networks employ switching hubs, the deterministic advantage of the IBM token ring network has largely been obviated.

The next generation IBM token ring NICs ran at 16 Mbps, or, if mandated, 4 Mbps (see Figure 6-14).

The token passing protocol requires sophisticated handshaking to recover from ring errors. Client PCs shutting down and starting up require that the token ring go through a reconfiguration cycle. A token ring monitoring station is the ring station with the lowest MAC address. The monitoring station changes each time a new client PC enters or leaves the ring. The monitoring station is responsible for recovering from minor and severe ring errors. A minor error occurs when a station enters or leaves the ring. A severe error is a broken ring. The monitoring station observes all packets traveling around the ring to assure that the station placing them on the ring properly removes them.

The token ring LAN protocol is a half-duplex (one way at one time) protocol. This may impose limitations on the token ring's effectiveness in implementing voice and video applications.

ASYNCHRONOUS TRANSFER MODE

Asynchronous Transfer Mode (ATM) is the future of broadband telecommunications networks. ATM is the first hardware designed with data, voice, and video telecommunications applications in mind. It is expensive to deploy today, but if all data, voice, and video traffic is merged across it, the cost per bit can be acceptable.

ATM networks are based upon cell relay protocol. A cell is just a small fixed-size container. Cell relay protocol transmits 53-character cells, having a 5-character header and a 48-character information field. These cells can be allocated to voice, data, or video transmission. Although the cells are sent synchronously between ATM nodes, their assignment to a connection is as needed (asynchronous). In this manner, ATM provides channel bandwidth allocation as demanded by the application. For example, a video teleconferencing call requires 384-Kbps of communications channel capacity (bandwidth). In a 1.544-Mbps channel, ATM would allocate cells to match the 384-Kbps transmission speed of the video teleconferencing connection. At the same time, it would be providing other voice connections just enough cells to meet their need for 64-Kbps transmission speed.

An ATM NIC is shown in Figure 6-15. This NIC is an Efficient Networks, Inc., ATM NIC designed to go into a network server. It uses a fiber connection to transmit data to an ATM switch at about 620 Mbps.

ATM operates at speeds of 25 Mbps, 155 Mbps, and 620 Mbps in LANs and at higher speeds in the backbone telephone network. ATM transmission speed is determined by the OSI physical layer electronics. So, ATM operating in the backbone telephone network can potentially be operating at speeds up to as high as around 39 Gbps. ATM is designed to support the following application types at the OSI Layer 2: Constant Bit Rate (CBR), Variable Bit Rate (VBR), and Available Bit Rate (ABR) applications.

CONSTANT BIT RATE APPLICATIONS • CBR applications send continuous high-speed data to ATM. A CBR application would be high-speed multiplexed data, voice transmission, or video transmission. These applications

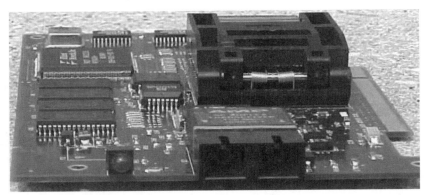

Figure 6–15 *ATM NIC.*

need a guaranteed QoS with low delays and consistent bandwidth. To them, ATM looks almost like a physically switched circuit with a guaranteed bandwidth.

VARIABLE BIT RATE APPLICATIONS • VBR applications send data chunks of different lengths or varying sizes. These use multiplexing to make maximum effective use of the ATM channel. A VBR application would be a file or image transfer, or a disk image backup. It mixes different data types. Bandwidth requirements change throughout the transmission. A VBR application would multiplex several data communications channels into a single ATM channel. VBR shrinks and grows based upon the transmission load offered. VBR applications do not get a guaranteed bandwidth like CBR applications.

AVAILABLE BIT RATE APPLICATIONS • ABR transmission uses the leftover space on the ATM link to transmit small amounts of data. Applications would be a LAN-to-LAN communication using TCP/IP or network diagnostic and status messages.

ATM service and equipment promise to provide the flexibility to support high bandwidth multimedia applications because of the high data transfer speeds, small cell sizes, and rapid switching of data between source and destination. ATM is a strong candidate for providing the type of transmission service needed for future voice, video, and data applications.

ATM is in OSI Layer 2 and implemented in a piece of hardware. ATM is designed to effectively carry data, voice, and video transmission.

LAN BOARD INSTALLATION

LAN boards installed in PCs have four key parameters:

- Input/Output (I/O) address.

- Interrupt Request (IRQ) line.
- Reserved memory area for buffers or ROMs.
- Direct Memory Access (DMA) channel.

I/O address is the most critical parameter for NIC installation. It must be unique or the card cannot talk with the PC. IRQ selection is also relatively easy to solve. Most software permits selecting about 3 to 7 specific I/O address/IRQ combinations.

Some NICs require a memory area in the PC's Upper Memory Blocks (UMBs). Sometimes exhaustive trial-and-error is required to find the best working combination of IRQ, I/O address, and UMB areas for a specific PC and its installed hardware and software.

ISA VS. PCI BUS BOARDS • PCI bus boards and PnP installation make installing most LAN boards a snap. Occasionally there is a glitch that the PnP BIOS and operating system software do not handle as they should. In this case, changing the I/O address (port) usually corrects the problem.

ISA boards need to have fixed IRQ and I/O addresses set prior to installation. The newer PCI bus cards use PnP installation so they are easier to install.

I/O ADDRESSES, IRQS, AND DMA CHANNEL REFERENCES • I/O addresses are not shared. Typical LAN board I/O port addresses range from 240h to 360h. (The small h denotes hexadecimal numbering. In hexadecimal, the numbers run 0, 1, 2, …., 8, 9, A, B, C, D, E, and F. They represent the 16 different patterns of "0's" and "1's" produced using 4 bits.) Some LAN board I/O address or port assignments are identified in Table 6-1.

Table 6.1 *Common I/O Ports Used by PCs*

Address	Description
0000 - 000F	DMA Controller 8237A
0020 - 002F	Interrupt Controller 1, 8259A
0040 - 004F	Programmable Timer
0060 - 006F	Keyboard Controller, 8042
0070 - 007F	CMOS Real-time Clock, NMI mask
0080 - 008F	DMA Page Registers
00A0 - 00AF	Interrupt Controller 2, 8259A
00C0 - 00DF	DMA Controller 2, 8237A-5
00F0 - 00FF	Math Co-processor
01F0 - 01FF	Fixed Disk

Table 6.1   *Common I/O Ports Used by PCs (Continued)*

0240 - 024F	LAN Board
0260 - 026F	LAN Board
0278 - 027F	Parallel Printer 2
0278 - 027F	Parallel Printer 1
0280 - 028F	LAN Board
02A0 - 02AF	LAN Board
02B0 - 02DF	Alternate EGA
02E1 -	GIB Adapter (0)
02E2 - 02E3	Data Acquisition
02F8 - 02FF	Serial Communications (COM2)
0300 - 030F	LAN Board
0310 - 031F	LAN Board
0320 - 032F	LAN Board or Prototype Card
0340 - 034F	LAN Board
0360 - 036F	PC Network = LAN Board
0380 - 038C	SDLC Communications
0390 - 0393	Cluster (Adapter 0)
03A0 - 03A9	BSC Communications (Primary)
03B0 - 03BF	Mono Display, Parallel Printer
03C0 - 03CF	EGA Adapter (Primary)
03D0 - 03DF	CGA Adapter
03F0 - 03F7	Floppy Disk Controller
03F8 - 03FF	Serial Communications (COM1)

PCs using ISA bus architecture are limited to basically 15 IRQs. With the PCI bus architecture, all that changed, and now IRQs can be shared. IRQs in a PC are identified in Table 6-2. NICs often use IRQ 5, IRQ 10, IRQ 9, or IRQ 3, depending upon the hardware installed in the PC.

Table 6.2   *Common IRQ Lines Used by PCs*

IRQ0	System Timer
IRQ1	Keyboard
IRQ2	[Cascade to 8259A PIC #2]
IRQ3	COM2 Serial Mouse
IRQ4	COM1 Communication Port

Table 6.2 *Common IRQ Lines Used by PCs (Continued)*

IRQ5	LPT2 Printer Port
IRQ6	Floppy Controller
IRQ7	LPT1 Printer Port
IRQ8	Real-time Clock
IRQ9	[Reserved]
IRQ10	Available
IRQ11	Available
IRQ12	Available
IRQ13	80486 Floating Point Processor
IRQ14	Hard Disk
IRQ15	Available

Most NICs do not use DMA channels because 400-MHz and higher speed PCs perform programmed data transfers faster than DMA chips can perform them. There are no typical DMA channel assignments for NICs. Table 6-3 lists common PC DMA channel assignments.

Table 6.3 *Common DMA Channel Used by PCs*

Channel 0	Available (8-bit)
Channel 1	Available (8-bit)
Channel 2	Floppy Controller
Channel 3	Available
Channel 4	[Cascade to 8237 DMA #1]
Channel 5	Available (16-bit Device to Memory)
Channel 6	Available (16-bit Device to Memory)
Channel 7	Available (16-bit Device to Memory)

Some NICs require UMB areas for buffering and data transfer operations. PnP PCI NICs have few problems today in setting up UMB areas for their use.

MEMORY ASSIGNMENTS • PC Random Access Memory (RAM) is divided into what are called paragraphs or segments. Each paragraph or segment is 64KB. Ten paragraphs make 640KB or the lower memory used by most real mode (DOS) applications. The boundary between the lower 640KB and UMBs is the address 0A000h. The next two plus paragraphs are display memory. They

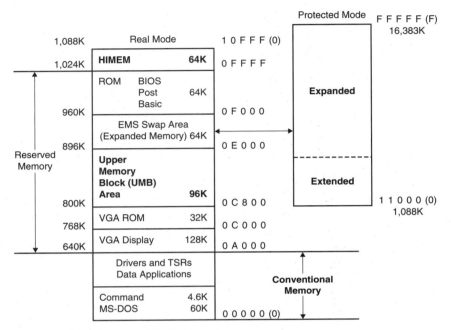

Figure 6–16 *Common PC RAM assignments.*

end at 0C000h. Video Read Only Memory (ROM) goes up to 0C7FFh, and disk ROM is sometimes at 0C800h. System ROM is at 0F000h to 0FFFFh. The Expanded Memory Specification (EMS) swap area is just below that at 0E000. Typically, EMS is not used at all anymore because Windows and PCs with megabytes of RAM made it obsolete in 1990. Figure 6-16 shows common PC memory area assignments.

Typical Ethernet NIC resource usage is illustrated in Figure 6-17. The assignments in the figure are for a PCI bus Ethernet NIC. They were made with the PnP capabilities of Windows.

This NIC was assigned IRQ 10, I/O port address DC00 to DCFF, and a memory address range for buffering. The memory address is in the 0E000 UMB area. The last four digits, 1000-10FF in each address, are ignored here.

OTHER LAYER-1 AND LAYER-2 LANS

Two other LAN technologies are evolving into robust LANs, potentially supporting telecommunications applications in the home. These work in the consumer market, supporting specific consumer multimedia PC applications.

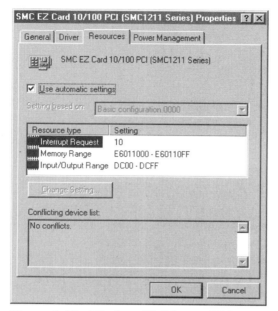

Figure 6–17 *Windows 98 Ethernet NIC resource assignments.*

Figure 6–18 *USB diskette drive.*

UNIVERSAL SERIAL BUS • As we explained in Chapter 5, USB looks to us like a physical connector. The USB is widely implemented in PCs. USB speed ranges from 1.5 Mbps to 12 Mbps, with its operating speed determined by the slowest device attached to the USB. USB with the right software becomes a LAN. A USB diskette drive is shown in Figure 6-18.

USB devices connect to ports on a hub device linked in a tree wiring topology. Each device tree connects to a PC USB root-hub port through which the PC communicates with the tree's USB devices. USB devices attach to all ports with standard 5-conductor cables. Most PC main logic boards include two USB ports. Some newer PCs have as many as six USB ports.

Figure 6–19 *USB male and female connectors.*

Figure 6–20 *Sony VAIO IEEE 1394 (iLink) 400-Mbps and USB connections.*

USB root-hub ports provide some 5-volt power for low-power devices. When using USB as a LAN, the PC USB root-hub ports have adequate power so that the hubbing device can be a passive USB hub. USB drivers that work with the USB PnP firmware are needed to find other USB networked PCs. USB connectors are shown in Figure 6-19.

These features make USB a cost-effective and user-friendly, general-purpose attachment mechanism for many PC peripherals and a low-speed and low-cost LAN alternative.

IEEE 1394 FireWire. • As we explained in Chapter 5, Fire Wire, similar to USB, looks to us like a physical connector. IEEE 1394 is a general-purpose serial bus for connecting high-speed peripherals to PCs. However, with the right software, the IEEE 1394 bus can function as a LAN. Sony's VAIO computers run NetBEUI or TCP/IP across IEEE 1394 links to transfer files using Windows peer-to-peer networking software. Sony's IEEE 1394 serial bus operates at 400 Mbps. Figure 6-20 shows both IEEE 1394 400-Mbps and USB bus connections on a laptop PC.

Similar to the USB, the IEEE 1394 bus attaches multiple devices to a PC, as well as supports peer-to-peer device connection like directly connect-

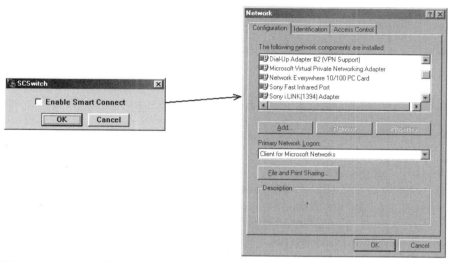

Figure 6–21 *Enabling Sony's Smart Connect driver software.*

ing a scanner to a printer. IEEE 1394 busses can connect multiple devices through a hub, or they can connect a hierarchy of serial busses, each supporting up to 63 device attachments. Bridges transfer data between busses in the hierarchical IEEE 1394 bus configuration.

The Sony VAIO PCs come with Smart Link software that supports peer-to-peer networking of PCs using the IEEE 1394 bus. The Sony Smart Connect driver is enabled, permitting the standard built-in Windows peer-to-peer networking software to use the 400-Mbps IEEE 1394 connection to network PCs. The beauty of this approach is that the IEEE 1394 networking is set up like any other LAN NIC with just a simple driver program. It supports networking with the same TCP/IP or NetBEUI protocols that are used with any other NIC (see Figure 6-21).

Most PCs use add-on PC adapter cards to implement IEEE 1394 Fire Wire connections. In the longer term, IEEE 1394 is most likely to have the greatest impact on telecommunications applications in the consumer-residential market. Because of its ability to work with a variety of data types and its high speeds, IEEE 1394 is most likely to become the transmission medium of choice for consumer multimedia PC applications. USB is used primarily to connect peripherals into the PC, in spite of its increased speed and the software implementing peer-to-peer networking functions using it. Both the IEEE 1394 and USB are OSI Layer-1 and Layer-2 hardware devices.

Brain Teaser

LAN Boards

What type of LAN board connections does your PC have? Check the rear of the PC.

1. Can you find an RJ-45 connector with a wire connected to it? This is likely an Ethernet connection.
2. Does your PC have any USB ports? Is anything attached to them? Use Figure 6-19 to help spot the USB ports.
3. Can you find any 4-wire IEEE 1394 ports? These are less likely to be found on your PC.
4. Now verify what you found using the Windows **Control Panel**. Open **Control Panel**, then **System**. Now check the **Network Adapters**. Is an Ethernet NIC listed as installed? Can you find an IEEE 1394 port listing?
5. A USB serial bus controller should be listed at the bottom of the list. Can you find a USB root hub? Does it list power properties? The goal here is to help identify the typical LAN and high-speed networking options installed on PCs.

LAN Internetworking Components

LAN internetworking components are the tolls used to connect LANs to one another and to the Internet. Building a LAN requires a good understanding of the function of the hardware components used in constructing the LAN and how they can be used to interconnect to other networks, improve LAN performance, expand the LAN's area of coverage, and make the LAN more reliable. Different basic LAN internetworking components work in several of the OSI model layers. Inter-networks are built using hubs, repeaters, bridges, switches, routers, and gateways. These devices permit physical, electrical, data link, and network layer connection of LANs and WANs.

OSI Model vs. Basic LAN Components

LAN networking components work in specific OSI layers. Other layers above the networking component are untouched by the component. Table 6-4 associates basic LAN networking components with the OSI layers in which they work.

Layer 1 simply connects everyone together. Layer 2 adds some intelligence so information is transferred from LAN card A to LAN card B without

Figure 6–22 *Ethernet active UTP hub with coax connection.*

error. Layer 3 moves information in the right direction through the network. Performance is improved by restricting information flows to specific logical paths or routes from source to destination. Layers 4-7 look at different software information for security purposes, translation purposes, and performance purposes.

Table 6.4 *OSI Model Layers vs. Basic LAN Components*

OSI Layers	Internetwork Device
Extends distance LAN covers in OSI Layer 1	Repeater/Hub
Layers 1-2 worked upon, 3-7 generally ignored	Bridge/Switch
Layers 1-3 worked upon, 4-7 generally ignored	Router
Layers 1-6 worked upon, 7 generally ignored	Gateway

HUBS AND REPEATERS

The lowest layer LAN network component is a hub. Most all hubs are active hubs (see Figure 6-22). Active hubs perform a repeater or signal regenerator function. Hubs work at OSI Layer-1 to extend the physical distance a LAN covers or to electrically isolate parts of the LAN and thus increase overall network reliability. Some hubs are more intelligent than others so that they can support simultaneously a mix of 10-Mbps and 100-Mbps Ethernet connections. Therefore, the auto-sensing speed translation hubs buffer Ethernet CSMA/CD packets to match speeds between different parts of the network. Hubs are OSI Layer-1 devices connecting everyone together.

Hubs only care about OSI Layer 1, the physical layer. They do not work with any Layer-2 MAC or any software in OSI Layers 3 through 7.

BRIDGES AND SWITCHES

Bridges and switches are OSI Layer-2 devices that are more intelligent than hubs. They can improve performance and segment traffic based upon the MAC address identification of the specific LAN hardware. Bridges break a LAN into separate LANs at OSI Layer 2. They isolate Layer-2 traffic on each side of the bridge. A switch is a high-performance LAN device that, like a bridge, works at OSI Layer 2. Bridges and switches work equally well with TCP/IP and SPX/IPX, or any higher layer LAN software.

There are three basic types of LAN bridges, including:

- Filtering bridges are the simplest and most common bridge. They isolate traffic on each side of the bridge through address monitoring. Filtering bridges are highly effective in small LANs.

- Spanning tree bridges are sophisticated bridges that talk with each other. They exchange information on the structure and loading of the network. They set up dynamically preferred routes through the network based upon the loading of communications links interconnecting them. Spanning tree bridges are self-configuring, based upon observing network traffic and addresses. They are highly effective and useful in large Ethernet networks.

- Source routing bridges are used in token ring networks. They are simple in design because they need only to pass traffic based upon routing information contained in the token ring address field. The actual routing is set up by the workstation based upon route discovery messages exchanged between it and the server. These bridges are effective in large token ring networks.

Switches are high-performance LAN components. Switches, like bridges, operate at OSI Layers 1 and 2. Switches have the intelligence of an intelligent hub and more. Each RJ-45 (MOD-8) port has its own individual path for data. Any port can be connected to any other port at full transmission speed. Ports can operate at 10 or 100 Mbps (see Figure 6-23).

Switches perform Ethernet switching functions, making several separate Ethernet segments look like a single 10- or 100-Mbps LAN. Switches connect clients on several separate Ethernet segments to servers on several other separate segments. When a client talks to a specific server, the switch connects the client and the server segments together. For that brief instant, there is a single 10-Mbps connection between that client and that server. Switching significantly improves Ethernet performance.

Figure 6–23 *Ethernet 5-port 10/100-Mbps switch and auto-sensing 16-port 10/100 active hub.*

Store-and-forward switches speed-buffer (translate from one speed to another). They must receive an entire packet at one speed before it can be transmitted out at the other speed. This means that their latency is greater than that of a switch that does no speed translation.

Cut-through switches minimize latency. They can perform the switching function once the destination address has been decoded. In this case, the packet is passed on to the destination before it is entirely received. Figure 6-24 illustrates the difference between store-and-forward and cut-through switch operation.

While cut-through switches also improve performance, their impact is not nearly as great as that of store-and-forward switches. Store-and-forward switches are more commonly used in networks today. This is especially true when migrating from a slower 10-Mbps LAN to a faster 100-Mbps or 1-Gbps LAN.

Switches isolate LAN traffic and implement full duplex data transmission between LAN servers and clients that have NICs providing full duplex transmission capabilities. This greatly increases Ethernet performance, virtually eliminating the performance load saturation of the half-duplex CSMA/CD MAC protocol.

Using TCP/IP subnet masks and switches assigned to each subnet, it is possible to create virtual LANs. Each virtual LAN is a single subnet isolated by switches from other subnets. Domain Name Servers (DNSs) or routers are needed to route LAN traffic between subnets (virtual LANs).

Bridges and switches are OSI Layer-2 hardware components of a LAN. Sometimes manufacturers label their devices switches even though they may work a little into OSI Layer 3.

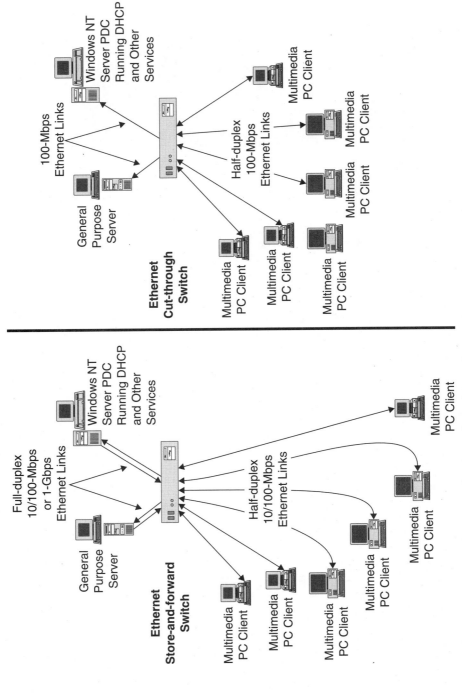

Figure 6–24 *Store-and-Forward and cut-through switch operation.*

ROUTERS (INTERNET GATEWAYS)

Routers connect two or more networks. They are OSI Layer-3 devices that are more intelligent than switches. A Layer-3 device looks at a software-assigned address, known as an IP address, instead of the LAN board hardware address, the MAC address. With software, there are configuration options that can increase network security and performance. A router would link a LAN to the Internet or to other LANs. Routers decide which way to send packets based on the router's current knowledge of the status of the LANs or networks to which it connects. In connecting LANs to the Internet, a router is a network component or software in a PC that determines the next network point to which a packet (TCP/IP packet) is forwarded so that the packet can reach its final destination.

Routers create or copy a table of available routes through a network and maintain their status. Routers use this information and combine it, according to routing algorithms with distance and cost data, to calculate the best route for a packet to follow to reach its final destination. Typically, packets travel through several routers to reach their final destination.

Routers work in OSI Layers 1, 2, and 3. Routers that work at higher layers are under development because routing network traffic based upon higher layer software-provided information is more efficient for the network. They must know something about TCP/IP or SPX/IPX to work properly. An Internet gateway is a router. Some new routers are a combination of switch and router as illustrated by the LinkSys cable modem/DSL four-port switch router in Figure 6-25.

Routers provide increased network capacity by reducing excess network traffic. They send data from source to destination based upon network routing information contained in the packets. This is more than just the address information that switches or bridges use. The tradeoff here is that routers handle fewer packets per unit of time than do switches or bridges.

Multi-protocol routers are more sophisticated than simple routers because they route packets for multiple protocol stacks. Multi-protocol routers support IBM's source routing and spanning tree routing operation. They talk to each other to route packets through a network based upon traffic observation. These sound too good to be true, but there are limits. Typically, a single vendor throughout a network provides multi-protocol routers. Multi-protocol routers have become much less important as more LANs switch from other OSI Layer-3, Layer-4, and Layer-5 protocols to just TCP/IP.

Figure 6–25 *DSL/cable modem router and four-port Ethernet switch.*

FIREWALLS • A firewall performs routing and packet filtering functions. Firewalls provide more functionality than routers by protecting the resources of a private network from unauthorized users and sometimes limiting network users in how they can access the public Internet. An enterprise with employees accessing the public Internet installs a firewall to prevent unauthorized outsiders from accessing its private data and for controlling the specific Internet resources (no colorful or racy Web sites permitted. Bummer!) its users can access.

These are the basic components of most LANs. As LANs carry more voice and video traffic, switches and routers are becoming more common because they have the ability to provide better LAN performance and security.

Functions Firewalls route data and filter all network packets to determine whether to forward them to their desired destination. They are the security guards for the network. Firewalls represent a network as a single IP address to the Internet just as a proxy server or a NAT (Network Address Translation) server would, but the firewall provides more security. Sometimes a firewall is a specially designated computer separate from the rest of the network. It may use a separate router and perform only packet filtering functions. The firewall may physically separate the Internet from a LAN. In this case, no packets can directly access the LAN without going through the firewall first.

Firewall packet filtering includes screening packets to assure they come from previously identified domain names and IP addresses. From this information, they make logs that your network administrator examines. Every network event can be tracked and cataloged at an office. Firewalls can also scan packet headers and contents for key words and phrases. These can be used to discard unauthorized packets.

Firewalls allow laptop users access into a LAN through secure logon procedures and authentication certificates. Firewall features include logging and reporting, automatic alarms at given thresholds of attack, and a Windows user interface for managing and configuring the firewall.

Limitations   Because Internet traffic patterns and attacks change so often, it is hard to make a firewall totally impervious to external attacks. Firewalls require constant maintenance to keep filtering effective. Sometimes firewalls filter too well and block LAN access from sites that are authorized to connect to a LAN.

Security Issues   While firewalls can prevent unauthorized LAN access from the Internet, they typically cannot effectively filter viruses from packets passing through the firewall. LAN users must use virus scanning programs, must not blindly open files with Visual Basic Script (VBS) macros, and must delete mail from unknown users to keep their chance of getting a virus infection low.

Firewalls do not effectively protect against Trojan horse software that gathers passwords and user account information. HAPPY99.exe was one such program that captured password information and sent it to an Internet account in China. At one time, Microsoft in its update and registration process was capturing Ethernet NIC MAC addresses and storing them.

When surfing authorized Web sites, cookies are exchanged between the surfing PC and Web site. These cookies and other information are used to track Internet usage. Firewalls do not effectively protect against this information-gathering activity on the Internet.

PROXY SERVERS • Many proxy servers act as an intermediary between a PC client and the Internet. Proxy servers perform some security, administrative control, and data caching functions. A proxy server receives a request for an Internet Web page from a client PC. The proxy server filters the request similar to a firewall. If the Web page request is okay to service, the proxy server searches for the Web page in a local cache of previously downloaded Web pages. When the proxy server finds the page, it returns it to the client PC

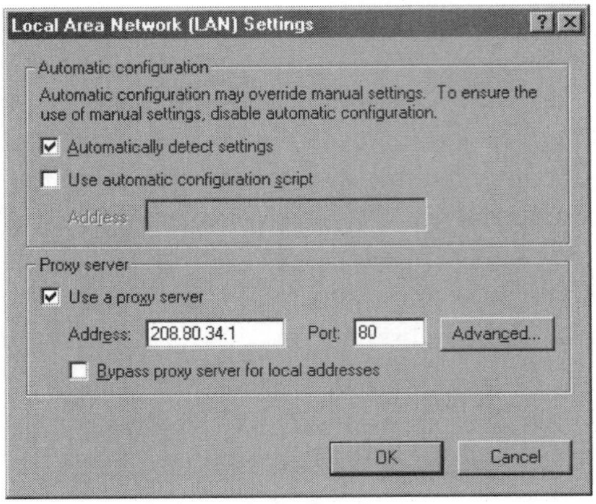

Figure 6–26 *Internet Explorer proxy server settings.*

without needing to retrieve the Web page from the Internet. If the requested Web page is not in the cache, the proxy server acts as a surrogate for the client PC and requests the Web page from the server on the Internet. When the requested Web page is returned, the proxy server matches it to the original request and forwards it on to the client PC. It then stores that page in its local cache.

To client PCs, proxy servers are transparent. Internet requests and responses appear to be direct services by the Internet Web page server. The proxy server is not totally invisible to PC clients because its IP address has to be specified as a configuration option for the PC networking software. Further, Web browsers and other programs need to know the specific proxy server ports they use to access the Internet (see Figure 6-26).

A proxy server's cache serves all LAN PC clients. If an Internet site's Web pages are frequently requested, these are likely to be stored in the proxy server's cache and retrieved from there rather than the Internet Web site. This can greatly improve Internet response time. Proxy servers can log Internet request and response activity.

Proxy servers can be associated with a gateway server separating a LAN from the Internet and with a firewall server protecting a LAN from Internet intrusion. The functions of the proxy server and firewall can be in separate server programs or combined in a single package. Firewall and proxy server programs can run in different computers. For example, proxy server software may run in the same machine with firewall software, or it may run in a separate server and forward requests through a firewall server.

NETWORK ADDRESS TRANSLATION • Network Address Translation (NAT) is mapping an IP address used in one network to a different IP address in another network. NAT designates one network as the inside network and the other network as the outside network. An internal LAN can use NAT to map its local inside network addresses to one or more global outside IP addresses.

Packets are sent from a LAN inside network address to the Internet using the global Internet IP address. Packets returned to the global Internet IP address are then translated back into local IP addresses.

The mapping process helps ensure security since each outgoing or incoming request goes through the mapping process. Mapping provides the ability to qualify or authenticate requests by matching them to previous requests. NAT reduces the number of global Internet IP addresses needed by representing a LAN to the Internet using a single IP address.

NAT is part of a router and is often part of a firewall. LAN administrators create NAT tables that map global-to-local and local-to-global IP addresses. NAT can be static using few addresses, or it can be dynamic, translating from and to a pool of IP addresses. NAT can support mapping:

- A local IP address to one global IP address.
- A local IP address to any global IP addresses in a rotating pool of global IP addresses.
- A local IP address plus a specific TCP port to a single or pooled global IP address.
- A global IP address to a pool of local IP addresses.

NAT is described in RFC 1631. It discusses the NAT relationship to Classless Inter-Domain Routing (CIDR) as a means to reduce the global IP address depletion. NAT reduces the need for publicly known IP addresses by mapping publicly known to privately known IP addresses. CIDR aggregates publicly known IP addresses into blocks as opposed to the previous hierarchical class IP address structure so that fewer IP addresses are wasted. The goal is to extend the use of IP Version 4 addresses for a few more years before the new IP Version 6 is generally supported on the Internet.

FRAME RELAY ROUTERS • Frame relay routers are special routers that work up to Layer 4, the message integrity layer. Frame relay, or fast packet networks, do not correct errors while the data is traversing the network. They detect errors and signal that data is potentially corrupt. It remains for the routing equipment at each end of the frame relay network to correct the errors by retransmitting data at OSI Layer 4, the message integrity layer. A discussion of frame relay follows in Chapter 8, "Packet-switched Networks."

OTHER ROUTERS • Brouters, an early LAN component, are a combination bridge and router. A Brouter functions as a router when it understands the routing information contained in the packet received; otherwise, it acts as a simple filtering bridge, passing data between networks based upon the address information in the packet.

Edge routers are used to interface with ATM networks. Leading router manufacturers include 3Com, Ascend, Cabletron, and Cisco.

GATEWAYS

Gateways provide access to mainframe computers and other networks. A gateway is needed to connect an IBM legacy SNA network to a TCP/IP LAN. There are different protocol stacks on each side of the gateway. When connecting a legacy SNA network to a TCP/IP LAN, the legacy SNA network uses Physical Unit (PU) 2.1/Logical Unit (LU) 6.2 and the TCP/IP LAN uses TCP/IP. Gateways work in Layers 1 through 5.

CLIENTS

Clients are most often Windows-based PCs. They provide user access to network resources and services. Clients work in all seven of the OSI model layers.

SERVERS

Servers share disk and printer resources on the network. In some cases, they perform special networking functions. Servers sharing resources only work on OSI Layers 1 through 6, while special function servers can work on all seven ISO layers.

An enterprise LAN configuration with added LAN components is shown in Figure 6-27. In this figure, we can see some more specialized LAN servers and other components we may find in an enterprise LAN. This LAN connects all PCs to several specialized servers and the Internet. The specialized server is a fax server that acts as a facsimile transmission and storage point. Any PC needing to send a fax would pass that fax to the facsimile server. The server would transmit the fax to its destination at a time that would save the most money. Incoming faxes would be stored there until retrieved by the client PCs. When a fax is received, the facsimile server may send an email message to the fax recipient to notify them that a fax is waiting for them. Alternatively, each network user could check their fax mailbox periodically for fax messages received for them.

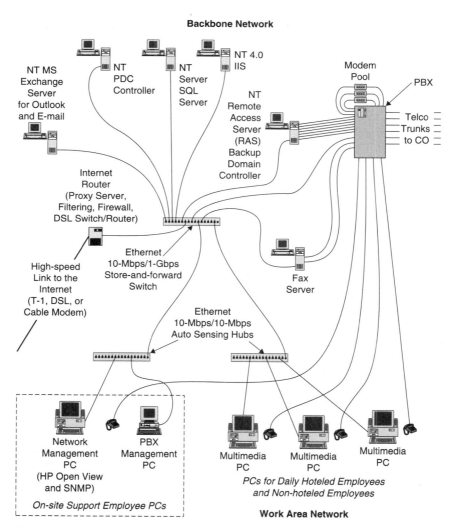

Figure 6–27 *Enterprise LAN components.*

The Remote Access Server (RAS) permits PCs with WAN access at remote locations to connect into the enterprise LAN and use it as though they were directly attached to the LAN. The Internet Information Server (IIS) sets up an internal intranet for publishing internal information in an electronic browseable HTML format. The SQL server implements key enterprise applications such as order entry, inventory management, billing, and other centralized financial functions. The Windows PDC is the security manager for the LAN. It manages user accounts and provides authorizations for each user to access specific network resources. Generally, resources are managed using group designations, e.g., accounting, marketing, and engineering groups have access to different resources. The MS Exchange Server is used to implement Microsoft email and pass those nasty VBScript email worm programs to hapless Outlook users on the network. The Internet router (proxy server or firewall) provides high-speed access to the Internet for all LAN-attached PCs. This is key for e-commerce, business research, communications with customers, downloading Napster files, and other business and non-business activities.

This LAN has the enterprise PBX directly attached to it. A PBX management PC can now sit anywhere on the LAN and manage PBX features and functions. More advanced PBX systems would support Web browser management. The menus would be displayed and manipulated using HTML code by any Web browser running on a PC that had logged on to the PBX management system.

A network management PC would also reside on the network. This PC monitors all network components and configures them using Simple Network Management Protocol (SNMP). HP Open View is generalized network management software that works with SNMP to talk with and manage network components that have SNMP agents (software programs using SNMP that monitor and control the component) in them.

Mapping the OSI layers and compatibility functions to LAN components working in those layers is provided in Figure 6-28. This summary diagram includes the specialized servers and network management components in our enterprise network above. The basic LAN internetworking components are highlighted in bold in the diagram.

Relating these networking components to the OSI layers provides us with a mechanism to understand the functions they perform. Figure 6-28 presents a generalized roadmap to LAN component functionality; individual products may fit this road map or they may differ from it. Whether they fit or do not fit is not as important as using the OSI model layers to understand the role each component plays in any specific LAN. Figure 6-28 helps determine overlaps and potential conflicts in functionality between different LAN components.

The enterprise LAN in Figure 6-27 sets up Internet access, an intranet, and provides extranet capabilities to an enterprise. These will be discussed next.

Layer 7 -- Application Layer --	Operational Compatibility ---	Clients SQL Application Server Fax Server LAN Management Console	Operating system & application software
Layer 6 -- Presentation Layer --	Feature/Code Compatibility ---	Message Filtering Firewall Disk and Print Servers	
Layer 5 -- Session Layer --	One to One Logical Connection --	Gateway	Network software
Layer 4 -- Transport Layer --	Message Integrity		
Layer 3 -- Network Layer --	Routing --	Router (Internet Gateway) Packet Filtering Firewall	
Layer 2 -- Data Link Layer --	Protocol Compatibility --	Bridge Switch	Hardware
Layer 1 -- Physical Layer --	Speed Compatibility --	Hub Repeater	

Figure 6–28   *Enterprise internetworking hardware vs. OSI layers.*

The Internet, Intranets, and Extranets

We will now look at how LANs provide high-speed access to the Internet, intranets, and extranets. The Internet is a planet-wide interconnected system of computer networks that permits users at any one computer to view published information from any other computer. The Internet is a public, cooperative, self-sustaining group of computer networks. It is accessible to hundreds of millions of people worldwide. The Internet uses a portion of the facilities of the existing public telecommunications networks. The Internet is distinguished from other legacy networks by its use of TCP/IP. Adaptations of Internet technology produce intranets and extranets. Figure 6-29 shows the relationship between the Internet and these adaptations of Internet technologies.

An intranet is a private enterprise-wide network consisting of LANs linked to other LANs using high-speed leased lines. An intranet includes

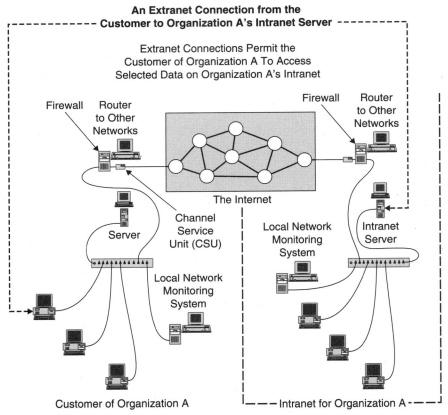

Figure 6–29 *Intranets, extranets, and the Internet.*

connections to the Internet. An intranet shares enterprise information and computing resources among employees of the enterprise.

An extranet is a private network using Internet protocols and public telecommunications networks to securely share specific business information with suppliers, vendors, consultants, and other business partners. An extranet is an intranet that is partially accessible to authorized outsiders. An intranet resides behind a firewall and is accessible only to employees of the same organization. An extranet provides various levels of accessibility to the intranet to non-employees. Extranet access is permitted only for users with valid usernames and passwords. The username determines which parts of the extranet can be viewed. Extranets are a very popular means for business partners to exchange information.

Internet communications technologies hold the promise of revolutionizing tomorrow's telecommunications networks. High-speed, 24/7 services are needed by consumers to propel the Internet into becoming the telephone, video-on-demand, shopping, and telecommuter communications network of the next millennium. Internet technologies like HTML, Dynamic HTML (DHTML), HTTP, and more will reshape the way individuals work and live. This section examines future telephony-incorporating Internet technologies.

LAN to Internet Connectivity

Connecting a LAN to the Internet permits it to support extranet communications, Internet access, and cost-effective intranet connections between an enterprise's central and remote locations. All LANs may directly or indirectly connect to the Internet at one time or another. All large LANs are connected to the Internet 24 hours a day, 7 days a week (24/7). Connecting to the Internet or some other high-speed TCP/IP backbone network sets up a LAN for being the final dissemination point for all communications entering or leaving an enterprise.

Enterprises access the Internet through an Internet Service Provider (ISP). An ISP is an organization offering access to the Internet for a fee. It may be an Internet feeder network or a server farm organization reselling high-speed Internet access to smaller ISPs. Smaller ISPs in turn sell Internet access to individual Internet users. The Moulton Company purchases Internet access from AOL, MDconnect.net, and Comcast@home. All provide access to the Internet. Comcast@home provides high-speed cable modem access for our facilities. Our Web site information resides on MDconnect.net's Internet servers. Both are local to Baltimore, Maryland. For worldwide and nationwide email service, we use AOL.

LAN-based intranets connect to the Internet using cable modems, DSLs, frame relay, and ISDN communications links. As we have just discussed, routers, firewall servers, proxy servers, and NAT servers make a LAN-based intranet appear to the Internet as a single IP address.

The following devices connect us to the Internet at high speed. They are an important key to future planet-wide telecommunications as the need for bandwidth grows.

CABLE MODEMS

A cable modem connects a PC to a local CATV coaxial cable line, permitting the PC to receive data at speeds of 400 Kbps to about 1.5 Mbps. Cable modems are typically separate from the CATV set-top box connecting TVs to the CATV network. Cable modems have two connections: one to the CATV coaxial cable and the other, a 10-Mbps Ethernet connection, to the PC. Cable modems modulate digital signals in specific analog frequency ranges. Cable modems attach to a CATV company coaxial cable. They communicate with a Cable Modem Termination System (CMTS) at the local CATV company head-end office. All cable modems receive from and send signals to the head–end CMTS. They do not communicate directly with other cable modems on the same coaxial cable. Some cable modem services return upstream signals by telephone rather than the coaxial cable. This is called a telco-return cable modem.

Cable modems can receive data from the Internet over the TV cable at speeds up to 30 Mbps, and can transmit data at speeds up to 2.5 Mbps. Other links between the cable modem subscriber and the Internet can restrict cable modem speeds to 64 Kbps to 1.5 Mbps.

In addition to the faster data rates, the advantage of cable modems over telephone Internet access is that cable modems provide continuous high-speed Internet connectivity with either a variable or a fixed IP address 24/7. There is no phone line sharing with the computer required.

Cable modems have an early lead in providing residential users with high-speed Internet access. Cable modems are discussed more in Chapter 9. Time-Warner and @Home are two leading companies using cable modems to provide homes and businesses with high-speed Internet access.

DIGITAL SUBSCRIBER LINE

DSL (Digital Subscriber Line) technology brings high-speed Internet access to residences and small businesses using existing copper wire telephone lines. xDSL represents all variations of DSL, such as ADSL, HDSL, and RADSL. When a home or small business is within 18,000 feet of a telephone company CO offering DSL service, it may be able to receive data at speeds up to 6.1 Mbps. This can support transmission of motion video, audio, and simulated 3-D images using Virtual Reality Modeling Language (VRML). More commonly, connections operate at 1.544 Mbps to 512 Kbps downstream and 128 Kbps upstream.

A DSL carries data and provides at the same time a regular voice telephone connection. The data connection is continuous, 24/7. DSL installations began in 1998. They are expected to continue at an increased rate over the next decade in the U.S. and elsewhere. DSL is replacing ISDN in many areas and competes with cable modems in bringing voice, multimedia video, and 3-D imaging to residential customers and small businesses.

FRAME RELAY

Frame relay service is designed for cost-efficient data transmission between LANs and other networks. A frame relay puts data in a variable-size frame. Frame is a container for information that is usually large and varying in size. Error correction is provided by data retransmission. Frame relay end-points determine whether error correction is required, which speeds up data transmission through the frame relay network. Frame relay provides a Permanent Virtual Circuit (PVC), giving the customer 24/7 continuous connection.

An enterprise can select a QoS prioritizing specific frames and making other frames less important. LECs and IXCs/IECs offer frame relay, including AT&T.

Frame relay provides transmission speeds up to 1.544 Mbps. This is competitive with cable modems and DSL channels for businesses. Frame relay is typically too expensive for residential users.

INTEGRATED SERVICES DIGITAL NETWORK

ISDN provides special telephone services using digital transmission over ordinary telephone lines. Home and business users install ISDN to speed up Internet access to 128 Kbps. ISDN is generally available from the LEC in most areas of the U.S.

ISDN provides BRI (Basic Rate Interface) and PRI (Primary Rate Interface) services. BRI service is equivalent to a dial-up modem that can provide twice the speed of an analog modem (128 Kbps vs. 56 Kbps). For Internet access, ISDN is more predictable because it is a digital service. ISDN can always provide the user a 128-Kbps channel to the Internet, whereas the dial-up modem speed depends upon the varying quality of an analog connection. Two ISDN B (Bearer) channels must be bound together to provide a 128-Kbps connection to the Internet.

The major drawback of ISDN service is that Internet access is initiated with a phone call. ISDN connections use telephone company CO switch facilities when connecting to the Internet. ISDN connections are not like leased line, cable modem, or DSL connections that provide Internet connectivity 24/7.

These services connect LANs to the Internet through routers, firewalls, proxy servers, and network address translation servers.

Intranets

Intranets use the technologies developed for the Internet and the graphical application of the World Wide Web (WWW) to bring corporate information in an easily digestible form to corporate employees. This means that reports generated as paper documents can now be created electronically using HTML editors and Web browsing tools. Employees are armed with Web server programs and browsers to create and access an organization's information. The goal is to improve organization communications and make business run more smoothly.

In basic terms, an intranet is your organization's existing enterprise network with client and server software that lets it display and link HTML documents. This is the same HTML linking and graphics displaying software that is used to access the Web. An intranet uses TCP/IP and HTTP Internet protocols to permit Windows Web browsers to view information published on internal servers. Intranets generally look like a private in-house version of the Internet.

Some of Microsoft's products used to implement Intranets are: Windows 95/98/ME clients, Windows NT/2000, the Internet Information Server (IIS), and Microsoft Exchange Server.

Intranets use Web servers that are UNIX or Windows NT/2000 server systems, PC clients running Windows or Windows NT/2000, and Web browsing software to surf their intranet. Intranets may be configured to support working in groups and teleconferences. An intranet may only support the employees at a single site. In this case, their LAN and its clients and servers become the intranet computers.

In other cases, an intranet may support employees both at a central site and at remote sites. The remote sites are commonly connected to the central site with high-speed digital circuits, or they could use protocol tunneling to send private messages through the public Internet. Tunneling uses the Internet and special encryption/decryption and other security safeguards to connect a remote site to the enterprise intranet. Both intranets are secure because only organization employees have access to them.

Some intranets are connected to the Internet to permit information exchange and research. In this scenario, a firewall would be used to protect the intranet from unauthorized intrusion and prevent employees from visiting sites for recreation rather than research. Firewall servers screen messages in both directions so that company security is maintained.

When an intranet is made accessible to customers, partners, suppliers, or others outside an enterprise, that outside extension of the enterprise intranet becomes an extranet.

Extranets

Extranets are intranets with a twist. They permit outsiders access to specific intranet information. For example, the Social Security Administration would have an extranet because it links its internal intranet to the Internet so that anyone can query their social security account information. Similarly, large organizations permit customers and collaborators to access their internal intranet for specific types of shared information.

Brain Teaser

LAN Internet Connectivity

Routers and other internetworking components are assigned specific IP addresses on a TCP/IP network. This exercise is to see if you are using routers or firewalls on your network. On a Windows 95/98/ME system, open and then right-click on **Network Neighborhood** and select **Properties** from the drop-down menu. Scroll down to the TCP/IP setting for your NIC. Highlight it and click the **Properties** button. The **IP address** tab should pop up.

1. Do you use a fixed IP address or is the IP address assigned automatically? When an IP address is assigned automatically, it means routers must handle dynamic IP addresses.

2. Click on the **Gateway** tab. Are any installed gateways listed? Generally, gateways have nnn.nnn.nnn.1, nnn.nnn.nnn.2, nnn.nnn.nnn.3, nnn.nnn.nnn.4, or nnn.nnn.nnn.5 IP addresses. Does your gateway fit this pattern?

3. Open the Internet Explorer and select the **Tools** and **Internet Options** menu items. Click on the **Connections** tab, then the **LAN Settings** button at the bottom. Is anything set in the **Proxy Server** box? If not, you are likely not using a proxy server in your network.

The goal here is identify and illustrate the router and proxy server components used in your LAN.

IEEE Standards

The Institute of Electrical and Electronic Engineers (IEEE) is a technical professional society promoting the development and application of electronic related technologies. When thinking of the IEEE, hardware and power standards quickly come to mind. However, the IEEE is today creating software standards. The IEEE develops standards that often become national and international standards. The organization publishes journals, and has many local chapters and several large societies in special areas, such as the IEEE Computer Society.

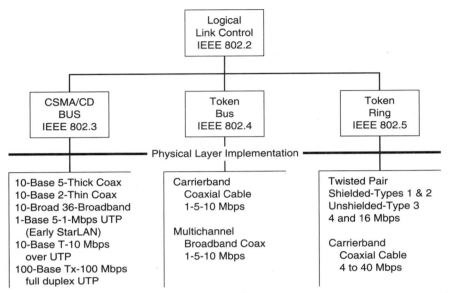

Figure 6–30 *Original IEEE LAN standards.*

The IEEE 802 LAN/MAN Standards Committee develops LAN standards and MAN (Metropolitan Area Network) standards, with the most widely used standards covering the Ethernet family, the token ring, Wireless LANs (WLANs), bridging and virtual bridged LANs. Individual Working Groups (WGs) provide the focus for each standard development area. The standards help assure that the LAN components purchased work together as long as they all conform to the same standard.

IEEE LAN Standards

IEEE standards influence the development of new LAN hardware, cabling, and software products. IEEE LAN standards fall under the IEEE 802 committee. The original LAN standards were all under IEEE 802.3, IEEE 802.4, and IEEE 802.5 designations. IEEE 802 standards have a much broader scope of coverage today. The early IEEE LAN standards for LANs are identified in Figure 6-30. When you see IEEE 802, just think LAN products.

Of the original standards, the 802.3 is the most active today, with Ethernet being extended to WANs and 10-Gbps transmission speeds. Token ring 802.5 development continues as well with 100-Mbps and Gbps token ring specifications being worked on. The 802.4 token bus network never really took off, and there is little standards activity there today.

The IEEE 802 LAN/MAN Standards Committee is organized into a number of WGs and Technical Advisory Groups (TAGs) working on specific standards. The current IEEE 802 standards development and study groups are:

- 802.0—The Sponsor Executive Committee (SEC).
- 802.1—High-Level Interface (HILI) or Higher Layer LAN Protocols Working Group.
- 802.2—Logical Link Control (LLC) Working Group (currently inactive).
- 802.3—Ethernet or CSMA/CD MAC Working Group.
- 802.4—Token Bus Working Group (currently inactive).
- 802.5—Token Ring Working Group.
- 802.6—Metropolitan Area Network (MAN) Working Group (currently inactive).
- 802.7—Broadband Technical Advisory Group (BBTAG) (currently inactive).
- 802.8—Fiber Optic Technical Advisory Group (FOTAG).
- 802.9—Isochronous LAN or Integrated Services LAN (ISLAN) Working Group.
- 802.10—Standard for Inter-operable LAN Security (SILS) Working Group.
- 801.11—Wireless LAN (WLAN) Working Group.
- 802.12—Demand Priority Working Group.
- 802.13—This designation is not used. It is like buildings not having a 13th floor for good luck.
- 802.14—Cable Modem or Cable-TV-Based Broadband Communication Network Working Group.
- 802.15—Wireless Personal Area Network (WPAN) Working Group.
- 802.16—Broadband Wireless Access (BBWA) Working Group.
- RPRSG—Resilient Packet Ring Study Group.

The IEEE 802.3 WG develops standards for CSMA/CD (Ethernet)-based LANs. This WG has several active projects, including the following:

- IEEE 802.3ae (standardization of 10-Gbps Ethernet)—This project extends the 802.3 CSMA/CD protocol to operate at 10 Gbps and expands the Ethernet application space to include WAN links. The goal is to provide a significant increase in bandwidth while maintaining maximum compatibility with the installed base of Ethernet 802.3 networks, 802.3 network operation, and 802.3 network management.
- IEEE 802.3af (Data Terminal Equipment (DTE) Power via Media Dependent Interface (MDI))—This project defines a methodology

for providing electrical power to equipment via balanced cabling to attached DTE with 802.3 interfaces. The amount of power is limited by cabling physics and regulatory considerations. The project also considers compatibility with existing 802.3 components.

- IEEE 1802.3rev (Conformance Test Maintenance #1)—This project cleans up the 802.3 specifications by merging front matter from 1802.3 with technical data from 1802.3d 10-Base T Conformance Test. The process will remove obsolete material, e.g., the AUI Cable Conformance Test.
- IEEE 802.3 (Maintenance Requests)—This is ongoing maintenance of the 802.3 standards, including such tasks as updating 100-Base T to reference the CAT-5 specification and listing physical layer signals.

The IEEE 802.5 WG develops token ring standards. It is currently working on the following:

- IEEE 802.5t (100 Mbps Token Ring)—This specification draft was conditionally approved by the IEEE, pending resolution of patent issues. Patents for 100-Mbps Ethernet physical layer may apply to the 100-Mbps token ring as well. All patent issues were to be resolved by mid-December 1999 with publication of the 802.5t standard by January 2000.
- IEEE 802.5v (Gigabit Token Ring)—An 802.5 re-circulation ballot completed with no negative comments. An LMSC sponsor ballot was scheduled to start in December 1999.
- IEEE 802.5z (Link Aggregation)—A first draft standard was presented at the November 1999 plenary meeting and adopted by the task force.

Work on these LAN specifications and other specifications continues.

New IEEE Standards Development

A new Ethernet standard for 10 Gbps is in development. The P802.3ae standard extends the 802.3 CSMA/CD protocol to operate at 10 Gbps. It expands the Ethernet application space to include WAN links. The goal is to provide a significant increase in bandwidth while maintaining maximum compatibility with the installed base of Ethernet 802.3 networks, 802.3 network operation, and 802.3 network management

This development work defines 802.3 MAC parameters and minimal augmentation of CSMA/CD operation, physical layer characteristics, and management parameters for transfer of LLC and Ethernet format frames at 10 Gbps using full duplex operation as already defined in the 802.3 standard.

In addition to the traditional LAN space, new parameters and mechanisms are being added to support deployment of Ethernet over WANs operating at data transmission speeds compatible with Synchronous Optical Network (SONET) Optical Carrier-192 (OC-192). This is about 9.953 Gbps.

A second hot IEEE standards development area is Wireless LANs (WLANs). Current activity is focused on extending the 802.11b standard to operate at data rates higher than 20 Mbps while maintaining compatibility with the existing IEEE 802.11 standard.

Additional work is aimed at enhancing the current 802.11 MAC to provide expanded support for applications with QoS requirements. Further work is targeted at improving security and the efficiency of the protocol. Such enhancements combine improvements in PHY capabilities from 802.11a and 802.11b, increase overall system performance, and expand the application space for 802.11.

IEEE 802.11 is developing recommended practices for an Inter-Access Point Protocol (IAPP). The objective is to realize multi-vendor access point inter-operability across a Distribution System (DS) supporting IEEE 802.11 WLAN Links. IAPP is being developed for a DS consisting of IEEE 802 LAN components supporting Internet Engineering Task Force (IETF) networks. IETF defines standard Internet operating protocols such as TCP/IP, the IP networking environment, and protocols for other networks as it deems appropriate.

The resultant Recommended Practices Document must support the IEEE P802.11 MAC and PHY layers of a WLAN system and must include the basic architecture of such systems, including the concepts of access points and DSs.

Initial implementation of WLAN concepts were purposely not precisely defined by P802.11 because there are many ways to create WLAN systems. Many implementation approaches involve concepts from higher network layers. This provides great flexibility in DS and access point design. However, physical devices from different vendors are unlikely to inter-operate with this approach.

As WLANs have grown in popularity, this limitation has become an impediment to WLAN market growth. This standardization project is to specify the information that needs to be exchanged between access points to support the P802.11 DS functions. The information exchanges required for one or more DSs will be standardized to enable implementation of DSs containing access points from different vendors.

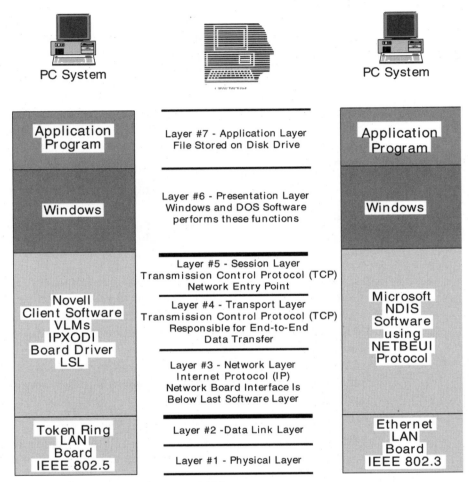

Figure 6–31 *LAN products vs. OSI layers.*

Matching PC LAN Products to Layers

The difficulty with understanding the OSI layers and IEEE 802 LAN standards is that we do not purchase an OSI layer, but rather we purchase a PC LAN product. LAN products match up with several layers. For example, LAN boards cover Layers 1 and 2; the network software performs its functions in Layers 3, 4, and 5; and the application programs, or Windows today, perform their functions in Layers 6 and 7. Figure 6- 31 illustrates how PC LAN products match up with the OSI layers and IEEE standards for Ethernet and token ring networks.

When a LAN is implemented, we purchase Ethernet products that conform to IEEE 802.3 standards and perform the functions defined in OSI Layers 1 and 2. IEEE can extend the Ethernet specifications to 10 Gbps by changing Layer 1, the physical layer, and adjusting Layer 2, the data link layer, to accommodate the changes in Layer 1 while maintaining inter-operability with existing IEEE 802.3 LAN components.

Layer 3, the network layer, Layer 4, the transport layer, and Layer 5, the session layer, specifications cover TCP/IP protocols. IEEE does not specify these protocols, but rather the Internet Engineering Task Force (IETF) specifies them. The IETF is developing new TCP/IP protocols that incorporate an expanded IP addressing scheme to accommodate the explosive growth of the Internet.

Brain Teaser

IEEE Standards

This exercise is designed to familiarize you with the latest IEEE LAN standards activities.
Use the link http://grouper.ieee.org/groups/802/dots.html to go to the IEEE standards Web site and view the IEEE 802 Committee's standards activity.
1. Review the current status of the IEEE 802.5 (Gbps Token Ring). Is the standard finalized?
2. Is there any activity to increase token ring speed to more than 10 Gbps?
3. Is the IEEE 802.3 enhancement going to support speeds higher than 9.9 Gbps on WAN Ethernet links? Will OC-768 (39.8 Gbps)? Our guess is that at some point it will, if it does not now support it.

LAN Media (Cabling)

One item every network needs is cable. Cable is some type of medium to transmit across. The medium could be the air, copper wire, or fiber optic cable. These are all OSI Layer-1 network components. When air is used as the transmission medium, different broadcast frequencies carry the data. If copper wire is used, it is likely to be either coaxial cable or twisted pair wire. Fiber optic transmission medium is either multi-mode or single-mode fiber optic cable.

Setting up a LAN for telecommunications applications requires selecting the appropriate LAN cabling system. Cabling determines the LAN speed, flexibility to expand, area of coverage, and network reliability. Using an incorrect cable type or violating a manufacturer's wiring rules are invitations to LAN disaster.

Three types of cable dominate today's LANs: fiber optic cable, twisted pair wiring, and coaxial (coax) cable. While coax cable was used on large Ethernets by DEC, and it is still used as cheaper-net cable for small LANs today, it has lost popularity. Unshielded Twisted Pair (UTP) wiring dominates LAN media today. Twisted pair wiring comes in both shielded and unshielded varieties, and in various gauges (thicknesses).

Fiber is used primarily for backbone network connections, high-speed connections, or connections between buildings or floors. Fiber is preferred for linking different physical facilities because of its security, life expectancy, bandwidth potential, and the ability to work in damp and high RF interference environments.

Coaxial Cable

The first LANs were broadband LANs built in the early 1980s. They used 75-ohm coaxial cable—TV antenna cable. In 1982, the first Ethernet products developed from a Xerox, Intel, and Digital alliance were marketed by Digital. These early Ethernet LANs used 50-ohm coaxial cable. This antenna cable was different electrically from the broadband network 75-ohm cable. The primary drawback of coaxial cable in a LAN is that if the cable breaks at any location, the entire LAN fails to operate. At one time, disgruntled employees used to crash an entire Ethernet by sticking a pin in the coaxial cable, shorting the coaxial cable center conductor to the outside cable ground. This was a particularly nasty and difficult cable fault to locate.

Coax cable is used with cable modems. It is the cable connecting the cable modem to the CATV company fiber transmission facilities. Typically this fiber operates as a frequency division multiplexed transmission facility. The coax cable used by a cable modem is generally not the same cable as was used to initially implement the CATV network. Early CATV coax carried a maximum of 500MHz of transmission frequencies. The newer cable used for cable modems carries typically 1GHz of transmission frequencies, so it has twice the capacity of the older coaxial cable. Digital Satellite Service (DSS) for satellite-based direct broadcast television sometimes uses 2GHz coax cable to carry signals from the rooftop antenna to the satellite receiver box next to the TV. Figure 6-32 identifies some different types of coax cable.

In the figure, the electrical characteristics identified are the capacitance of the cable expressed in Pico Farads per Foot (PF/FT) and the signal propagation speed expressed as a percentage of the speed of light (VP 65%). Coax cables come in thick (lower loss) and thin varieties. Physically, the thick cable

```
RG-58C/U   50 OHMS   30.8 PF/FT    VP 65.5% - ETHERNET
                    Attenuation Freq. In MHz
                      10   50   100   400   1000  3000
          dB/100 ft   1.4  3.3   4.9  11.0   20.0  41.0


RG-59B/U   75 OHMS   20.6 PF/FT    VP 65.5% - BROADBAND
                    Attenuation Freq. In MHz
                      10   50   100   400   1000  3000
          dB/100 ft   1.1  2.3   3.3   6.7   11.5  25.5


RG-62A/U   93 OHMS   13.5 PF/FT    VP 84.0% - ARCNET
                    Attenuation Freq. In MHz
                      10   50   100   400   1000  3000
          dB/100 ft    .9  1.9   2.8   5.2    8.5  18.4
```

Figure 6–32   *Coaxial cable types and characteristics.*

is about .5" diameter and the thin cable is around .25" diameter (see Figure 6-33).

The coax cable at the top left of Figure 6-33 is 1GHz 75-Ohm thin coaxial cable used to connect cable modems to the CATV network. It uses screw-on F-type connectors. The connectors are crimped onto the coax cable itself. The center conductor is a single strand of wire protruding from the dielectric insulator in the center of the cable.

On the bottom right is a cross-section of antenna tower coax cable. This cable is about one inch in diameter. The center conductor is hollow to make the cable lighter (no use dragging a really heavy cable up a radio or TV tower). Thick coax cable is very difficult to work with and to bend.

Coax cable provides an excellent transmission environment with signals traveling down a single conductor in the center of the cable surrounded by an insulating dielectric, and finally sheathed by an outside cable ground of wire mesh, or wrapped aluminum foil for thin coax cables.

Twisted Pair Wiring

Twisted pair wire is easily identified by pairs of wires twisted together. Twisted pair wire is used for voice, data, and video communications. To overcome the problems associated with coax cabling, twisted pair cable and wiring hubs were used. All clients and servers were wired to a hub using UTP wire. In this case, if one cable broke, only that link to the hub was impacted. The demands for higher LAN transmission speeds required reduced signal

Figure 6–33 *Thin and thick coaxial cable.*

crosstalk (signal crossover interference from one pair of wires to another, sometimes referred to as Near End Crosstalk—NEXT) within the cable. A cable grading scheme, or category level, was developed.

The Telecommunications Industry Association/Electronic Industries Association (TIA/EIA) published the TIA/EIA-568 Commercial Building Telecommunications Wiring Standard. This standard specifies minimum requirements for telecommunications wiring within a building. The standard covers cabling systems with a recommended topology and recommended distances, wire and associated parameters that determine transmission speeds, and connectors with pin assignments to ensure devices can be interconnected.

Figure 6-34 illustrates the difference between T-568a and T-568b. Pair 2 and Pair 3 reverse positions. This means that whenever a facility is wired with the T-568a or T-568b wiring specification, additional wiring must follow the original wiring specification, or the LAN transmit and receive paths get crossed in the network, causing problems.

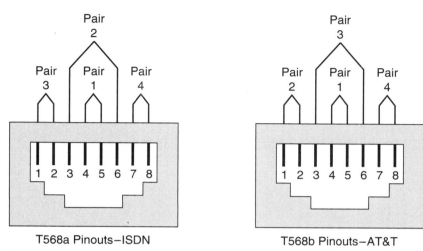

Figure 6–34 *T-568a and T-568b MOD-8 connector pair pin assignments.*

Cabling systems include the wire and other components such as punchdown blocks and connectors. The categories are related to the data transmission speeds that the cabling systems can support. The specifications cover wire, connectors, and punch-down blocks to be used to meet the requirements of a specific category. Table 6-5 lists different wiring categories or levels, the supported transmission speeds, and the common applications of a wiring category.

Technical Service Bulletins (TSBs) have been published to clarify various points in the T-568 standard. Some of these are:

- TSB-36: UTP Categories 3, 4, and 5 Defined.
- TSB 40A: UTP Connecting Hardware for Category 3, 4, 5.
- TSB-53: Additional Specifications for STP (Shielded Twisted Pair) Hardware.
- TSB-67: Transmission Performance Specification for Field-testing UTP Network Cabling.
- TIA/TSB-72: Centralized Optical Fiber Cabling Guidelines.
- TSB-75: Defines "zone distribution systems" for horizontal wiring.

Like all standards, T-568 is continuously reviewed and updated to reflect major changes in technology and marketplace conditions. It is leading to new wiring categories like CAT-5+ and Level 7, and is supporting higher LAN transmission speeds.

Table 6.5 *Wiring Categories/Levels vs. Transmission Speed vs. Applications*

Cabling System Classification	Data Transmission Speed Supported	Typical Applications
CAT-1	Less than 1 Mbps	Telephones—Analog voice transmission ISDN BRI Doorbells
CAT-2	4 Mbps	Used in token ring networks—See Table 6-6.
CAT-3	16 Mbps	Telephones—Analog voice 10 Mbps data on 10-Base T Ethernet 16 Mbps data on IBM token ring
CAT-4	20 Mbps	Used in 16-Mbps token ring
CAT-5	100 Mbps	100 Mbps on Ethernet
UL Level 5	200 MHz	More stringent specification than CAT-5
CAT-5+ (Data Grade High-end) UL Level 6	155 Mbps (350 MHz)	155 Mbps on ATM networks
UL Level 7	400 MHz	Data speeds up to 1.2 Gbps

The most widely used cabling today is UTP cable in Category 5, or CAT-5 with data grade CAT-5 (CAT-5+), rated to support transmission at speeds up to about 155 Mbps. This CAT-5 cable is used extensively in both telephony and LAN wiring.

CAT-3 CABLING

Category 3, (CAT-3) twisted pair cable was the original telephone-style cable. CAT-3 twisted pair cable came with two to four pairs in each cable. It worked for low LAN transmission speeds of 10 Mbps. Higher categories have special cable designs that carefully match pairs of wire with more twists in each pair. Figure 6-35 shows CAT-3 UTP 3-pair cable used for standard telephones. The cable has red-green, yellow-black, and blue-white pairs. The red-green pair is for the primary telephone line; the yellow-black pair is for a second telephone line; and the blue-white pair on the left carries electrical power for lights on a telephone, like the lighted dial of the Princess phone.

The difference in pair twisting between CAT-3 and CAT-5 UTP wire is illustrated in Figure 6-36.

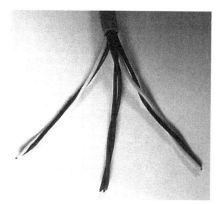

Figure 6–35   *CAT-3 telephone wire.*

In the figure, CAT-5 wire pairs are on the left. Only three of the four pairs are visible. On the right is the CAT-3 UTP wire. The sizes are relatively accurate in the composite photograph, illustrating that CAT-5 is twisted about four times more than CAT-3 wire.

CAT-5

While CAT-3 and CAT-5 cables may look identical, CAT-3 is tested at lower transmission speeds. If CAT-3 wire is run at higher speeds, it can cause network transmission errors. CAT-3 cabling is NEXT certified for only 16-MHz signals, while CAT-5 cable must pass a 100-MHz signal test permitting it to carry data at 100-Mbps speeds. Figure 6-37 shows two round CAT-5 cables.

There are more differences between CAT-5 and CAT-3 cable beyond CAT-5 twisted pair cable having more twists per foot than CAT-3 cable. I cannot quote you chapter and verse on the differences between CAT-3 and CAT-5 cabling, but I can give you an idea of how detailed the differences are between cable types.

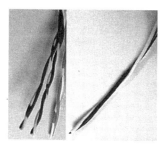

Figure 6–36   *CAT-3 vs. CAT-5 pair comparison.*

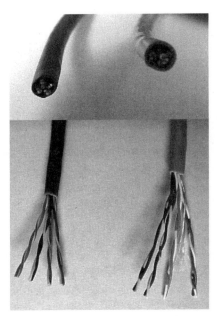

Figure 6–37 *CAT-5 round cable.*

First, guess how many words there are in Eskimo language for snow. I do not know the exact number myself, but there are a lot of Eskimo words for snow because snow is much more important to Eskimos than it is to us. Okay, now how many ways can a wiring engineer describe wire? As many ways as Eskimos can describe snow. There are simple parameters like the gauge (thickness) of the wire, the twists per foot, the copper purity, the capacitance per foot, the resistance per foot, the thickness and type of insulation, the metallic content of the paint coloring the wire pairs, the wire pair coloring— green-green/white, blue-blue/white, orange-orange/white, brown-brown/ white, and many more parameters. Now do you have a feeling for the differences between wiring types?

When wiring a LAN or a facility, most vendors will specify CAT-5 or CAT-5 data grade wiring. They will wire according to the TIA/EIA-568a or TIA/EIA-568b wiring scheme. The most current scheme is T-568a. These schemes determine how the pairs are laid out in the RJ-45 or MOD-8 con- nectors (refer back to Figure 6-34).

The pairs in both cables use the standard green-green/white, blue-blue/ white, orange-orange/white, and brown-brown/white coloring scheme.

There are different styles of CAT-5 wire. The styles illustrated so far have been round wire, but data grade CAT-5 wire (CAT-5+) has a flatter design, placing specific pairs next to one another to reduce crosstalk of elec-

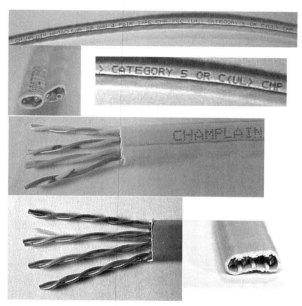

Figure 6–38 *CAT-5+ cable.*

trical signals between pairs. Figure 6-38 shows CAT-5+, or CAT-5 data grade wire.

In the figure, the top four images are of one cable and the bottom two images are of another cable. The top cable has, like most all LAN cabling, the cabling system specifications that it meets printed on the outside of the cable. On the top right, there is a close-up of the CAT-5 designation printed on the cable. Figure 6-39 shows a TIA/EIA-568a CAT-5 cable label.

Although both top and bottom cables are specified as CAT-5 data grade cables (CAT-5+), they are not the same design and quality. The top cable has two separate sheaths, each carrying two of the four twisted pairs found in the cable. While this separates the pairs just fine, it is possible for pairs to bunch up in one or both of the sheaths. This could alter the data transmission speed characteristics of the cable.

The bottom cable has each individual pair isolated in a specific position in the cable. This prevents bunching of the pairs, resulting in higher data transmission speeds. High-speed networks should use the best cable available. The cable should be certified for the transmission speed used in the net-

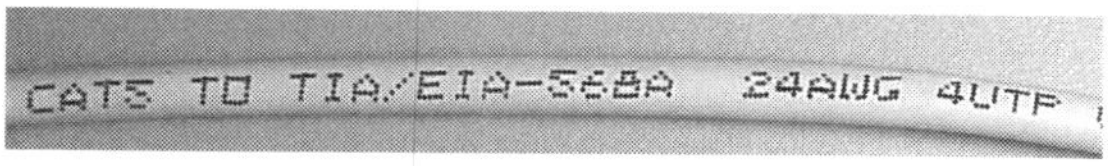

Figure 6–39 *CAT-5 cable labeling.*

work and other transmission criteria, including SNR, pair signal propagation delay skew, and signal attenuation characteristics.

High-speed LAN cabling standards generally meet SNR and maximum noise threshold standards. But pair signal propagation delay skew and overall signal propagation delay characteristics are important for LANs transmitting data above 100 MHz. Pair signal propagation delay skew applies to components using more than one twisted pair to send data. In this case, transmission is divided between pairs, requiring the receiving component to reassemble the data. When data sent on each separate pair arrives at different times because the signal propagation delay on each pair is different, skew transmission errors result.

Overall propagation delay, the time it takes for the signal to travel to the receiver, may also determine LAN performance and area of coverage. Propagation delay is expressed as the electrical signal speed relative to the theoretical speed of electricity (light). This is sometimes called the velocity of propagation. The LAN speed is measured in Megabits per second, not in signal propagation speeds. Propagation delays cause delays in conversational handshaking (like talking on a satellite link). Once transmission reception begins, data arrives at the designated LAN at a Mbps speed.

Some network component manufacturers resolve electrical loss across cable distances by incorporating signal equalizers into their receivers. The signal equalizers attempt to amplify the received signal based on an anticipated attenuation or electrical signal loss from transmission across the cable. The received signal must be distinguishable from electrical noise picked up during its transmission. Some noise is always present in any cable and is re-amplified along with the data signals. If an incorrect interpretation is made, the original data results in a bit error. Bit errors are detected by LAN components and are corrected by retransmission of the data in error.

In the case of 155-Mbps transmission on CAT-5 cable, signaling errors can occur above the CAT-5 maximum signal frequency of over 100 MHz, and as high as 200 MHz. These signaling errors, when processed by the equalizer, can be amplified as if they were part of the signal. This may cause an unacceptably high bit error rate.

Gigabit Ethernet could use CAT-5 for short-distance wiring to the desktop. This would save costs by preserving the CAT-5 twisted pair wiring most organizations already have in place. Longer runs of Gigabit Ethernet will use optical fiber.

BEYOND CAT-5 CABLING

Higher speed transmission is fast becoming a necessity for new multimedia LAN applications to meet new creative and competitive business challenges. These applications are continuing to consume more and more LAN bandwidth. The Gigabit Ethernet Alliance concluded that high-speed gigabit technology significantly impacts LAN cabling. Gigabit Ethernet pushes cabling speed capabilities to its limits. Regardless of product and installation quality, Gigabit Ethernet leaves no room for error when implemented on CAT-5 cabling systems.

New specifications and guidelines for electrical bandwidth in excess of 100 MHz are now required. The Level-5 specification from 1992 was modified to cover the performance requirements for existing CAT-5 cables. Stringent requirements for data grade, high-end CAT-5, or CAT-5+ cables are referred to as Level-6 (see Table 6-5). New-generation products that support twice the CAT-5 bandwidth requirement are referred to as Level-7. Level-5 is different from the standard CAT-5 because it must meet the new stringent requirements included in the international standard ISO 11801. This ISO 11801 standard for cable performance creates a "super-set" of the original CAT-5 requirements. Cable that meets Level-7 standards attains performance that has over twice the actual usable electrical bandwidth of the current CAT-5 cable. Level-7-compliant cable extends the data bandwidth to 1.2 Gbps, permitting it to be used in Gigabit Ethernet networks.

Fiber Optic Cable

Fiber cable carries pulses of laser light from one end to the other. Two fiber strands are used for one communications pathway, a transmit strand and a receive strand. Figure 6-40 illustrates how fiber optic transmission works.

Both glass and plastic fiber is composed of a core and a cladding. The standard core and cladding diameters for multi-mode glass fiber are 62.5 microns/125 microns, and for single-mode glass fiber they are 8.3 microns/125 microns. Plastic fiber core cladding diameters are larger than glass fiber diameters. There are other fiber configurations as well.

Multi-mode fiber is commonly used in LANs. It works on refraction, or the bending of light. Single-mode fiber is used in telephony. It works on reflection like a mirror. Single-mode fiber carries signals much longer distances than multi-mode fiber for two reasons. The light in single-mode cable is more concentrated in the small diameter core, so, similar to a rifle bullet, it is soaked up less by impurities in the fiber. In multi-mode fiber, the light is

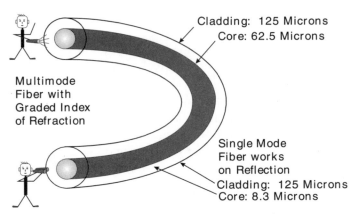

Figure 6–40 *How fiber optic transmission works.*

spread over a larger core area, like a shotgun blast, so it is soaked up more by the impurities in the cable.

In single-mode fiber, the light reflects off the boundary between the core and cladding, much like a mirage is created in the desert between two layers of air with different densities. Reflection soaks up less light than the refraction, or the bending of light, in a multi-mode cable.

Fiber operates by having a person at one end of the fiber with a flash-light use a laser emitting diode to blink the light on and off. At the other end of the cable, a person with binoculars records the flashes of light and converts them into digital electrical signals. In multi-mode fiber, the index of refraction (how much the glass bends the light) changes from the center of the core to the outside of the core. In the center, the index of refraction is one-to-one (no bending of light). As the light travels to the outside of the core, the index of refraction increases to one-to-two, one-to-ten, one-to-one hundred, one-to-one thousand, one-to-ten thousand, and maybe more. As a result, the light is bent back towards the center of the core. It can only escape the core onlyat the end of the cable, where the person with the binoculars sees it.

Single-mode fiber operates similarly. The light is reflected like a mirror (or a mirage in the desert) off the boundary between the core and the clad-ding. Consequently, it only escapes the core of the cable at the end where the person with the binoculars sees the light and converts it back into electrical signals.

What happens to the flashes of light in the fiber if the fiber is sub-merged in water? They go right on to their destination without disruption. Water submersion shorts out electrical signals. If a fiber cable is left under water for a long time and the water has a specific acidic chemical content, the chemicals can leach into the glass of the fiber cable and cause it to become cloudy. In this case, the fiber becomes useless. However, this is only after years of submersion in water.

What happens to the flashes of light if the cable passes through a high-intensity RF field? Generally, they are unaffected. If the electronics at each end of the fiber cable are near the high-intensity RF field, they may have their electrical signals scrambled, but the flashes of light in the fiber cable get through okay.

What happens if the cable is close to a person with a jackhammer? Nothing happens to the flashes of light unless the mechanical movement of the fiber is so violent that the fiber cracks. In that case, communication across the fiber is disrupted.

What happens when the person blinking the flashlight on and off is struck by lightning and fried to a crisp? The person with the binoculars gets to see one last brilliant flash of light, then total darkness. However, they are alive and ready to go when another person with a flashlight shows up at the other end of the fiber optic cable.

My example here highlights the benefits of fiber cable over copper cable. One benefit of fiber cable and optical transmission over copper cable and electrical transmission is that fiber operates in harsh physical environments. This means that water or strong electrical fields do not significantly impact light wave transmission on fiber. A second benefit is that optical transmission and fiber electrically isolate receiving devices from transmitting devices. This eliminates problems caused by ground loops and electrical storms. The third and most obvious benefit is that fiber is capable of much higher transmission speeds at much longer distances than is copper cable and electrical signaling.

As LAN transmission speed demands increase to support video transmission on multimedia LANs, fiber optic cabling plays an increasingly important role. However, fiber is not likely to be routed to each desktop anytime soon. The preferred wiring from wiring closets and the repeaters therein to the desktop is likely to remain UTP wiring.

Fiber with 1-Gbps transmission speed is most likely used to interconnect wiring closets and the LAN switches in them to one another. Such a fiber backbone supports high transmission speeds and provides electrical isolation of one wiring closet from another (see Figure 6-41).

In Figure 6-41, the fiber connectors are shown on the left and the actual fiber itself is protruding from the cable component with the white sheath. A close-up of the fiber is in the inset on the right. The actual glass fiber by itself is very small. It is encased in PVC (Polyvinyl Chloride) plastic, surrounded

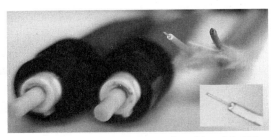

Figure 6–41 *Fiber optic patch cable with ST-style connectors.*

by fiberglass, and further encased in PVC plastic. This makes the patch cables very flexible and strong. Regardless of their flexibility, they cannot be bent at right angles or the glass fiber breaks. All cables (fiber or copper) have a specific bend radius beyond which they fail to carry signals properly.

SIGNAL LOSS IN FIBER CABLE

Attenuation is a decrease in signal power. During transmission, fiber optic light pulses lose some photons, reducing their brightness and diminishing their signal power. Fiber attenuation is specified in dB/km ranges, from around 1 dB/km for premium small-core glass fibers to over 2000 dB/km for large-core plastic fibers. The larger the dB/km figure, the greater the loss.

Fiber attenuation, or signal loss, is caused by absorption, scattering, and reflection. For instance:

- Impurities in the fiber cable absorb light energy, turning photons to heat. Optical fibers must be made of ultra-pure glass that can exceed the purity semiconductors. Nonetheless, impurities remain as residues in the glass after processing, causing signal attenuation.
- Scattering of the fiber signals is caused by the molecular structure of the glass and by density variations produced during manufacturing. Variations in core diameter, micro bends, and small incongruities in the core to cladding interface also cause scattering loss.
- Reflection losses occur as light reflects off internal fiber surfaces. Reflection is caused by differences in refractive indices of the core and other materials at their interface.

Fiber only experiences high signal loss when there are poor splices, sharp bends, or cable breaks. Because optical fiber has low attenuation, signals can be sent over longer distances without using repeaters. Fiber optic repeaters may be as far apart as 60 miles. Bell Labs once demonstrated transmission of readable optical pulses at 3,700 miles without repeaters.

Fiber attenuation is related to light wavelength. Careful matching of light sources and fibers is required. Most fibers have a low loss window in the 800 nm to 900 nm wavelengths. Longer wavelengths, 1300 nm to 1500 nm, give lower losses, but matching fibers and semiconductors is more restricted.

DENSE WAVELENGTH DIVISION MULTIPLEXING

Fibers can operate using multiple wavelengths of light. This is a form of frequency division multiplexing (FDM), with each wavelength being a different color of light. At first, only two colors were used, but this has increased to 16 colors, 32 colors, and up to 256 colors (wavelengths) of light. This is used on telephone network fiber. It is called Dense Wavelength Division Multiplexing (DWDM).

DWDM is a fiber optic transmission technology that multiplexes (combines) different digital transmission streams together on a single optical fiber. Each signal is carried on its own separate light wavelength (frequency). DWDM can multiplex up to 256 separate wavelengths, or digital transmission streams, into one optical fiber. If each digital transmission stream was 2.5 Gbps (billion bits per second), then a fiber could carry up to 640 Gbps. DWDM is sometimes labeled Wave Division Multiplexing (WDM).

DWDM is needed to increase fiber capacity; otherwise, many fiber runs would be totally saturated with data, necessitating costly installation of new optical cable. DWDM is becoming a central technology in all-optical fiber networks. DWDM systems are being deployed now. DWDM is one of the key technologies used to provide high-bandwidth communications links.

FIBER OPTIC CABLE SYSTEM COMPONENTS

The components of a fiber optic link are cable, connectors, splices, cabinets, and mounting hardware. The cable contains and protects optical fibers. Cable is selected by fiber type, fiber size, fiber grade, fiber count, sheath strength, strength member material, and flammability.

Connectors join optical cables to electronics or to other optical cables. Connectors permit cables to be mated and unmated repeatedly without damage. Connectors are usually located at a cross-connection box and on electronic equipment. There are several standard types of fiber optic connectors, including Biconic, SC, ST, ESCON, FC, FSD, and SMA connectors, among others.

Splices are permanent or semi-permanent devices joining two fiber ends from separate cables.

Cabinets and mounting hardware include cross-connection boxes, closures, and outlets. Cross-connection boxes, located in wiring closets, mount connectors for flexible and easy rearrangement of optical circuits while protecting the cables. Cross-connect boxes also isolate cable segments, making system testing easier.

Closures are sturdy plastic or metal cases housing and protecting splices and securing cables during splicing. Closures are typically found in wiring closets or riser shafts.

Outlets are termination points close to network terminals. Outlets are located on walls.

SINGLE-MODE FIBER

The fiber cable used in telecommunications for telephony transmission is commonly single-mode cable. Single-mode optical fibers are used in long-haul telephone network interchange and feeder loop installations because they easily span between 50 and 100 kilometers and have capacities exceeding 20,000 voice channels. Single-mode is easily identified by its yellow color and the single-mode label on the cable. As we discussed in the how fiber works analogy, single-mode fibers have a small core, concentrating the laser light signal. This signal concentration results in reduced signal loss in the cable, providing longer cable runs between repeaters and higher bits per second transmission speeds.

Single-mode fibers operate similar to microwave RF wave-guide. The wave-guide's physical dimensions approach the wavelength of the electromagnetic radiation being transmitted. This prevents microwaves from traveling through the wave-guide to escape the wave-guide. The same principal is used to construct see-through door panels on microwave ovens. The wire mesh in the door prevents the microwaves from escaping the microwave oven.

Because core diameters of single-mode fiber are small—8.3 microns or less—their light wave propagation path is nearly straight. The nearly straight path permits the light to travel through the fiber, efficiently giving single-mode fiber a higher signal bandwidth (more bits per second capacity). Single-mode fiber core diameters range from 6 to 10 microns. Cladding diameter for these fibers is 125 microns (about 0.005 inch). Single-mode fiber cables constructed using 8.3/125 micron fiber are identified as 8.3/125 single-mode fiber cables (see Figure 6-42).

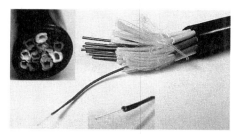

Figure 6–42 *Exterior fiber cable.*

MULTI-MODE FIBER

The fiber optic cable most frequently used in LANs is multi-mode with a graded index of refraction. This bends the light so much as it travels though the glass fiber that the light cannot escape the fiber during its journey. Multi-mode cable is orange and is labeled "multi-mode."

Multi-mode fiber is the standard for campus LANs. AT&T developed a 62.5/125 micron fiber that has become a de facto standard. The 50/125 micron fiber is also popular. Both fibers afford users the greatest range of features and flexibility at an economical price. Multi-mode fiber features and benefits include:

- Large core size, making installation relatively easy.
- Larger fiber size, requiring less costly interface connections and splices.
- Less costly electronics.
- Less expensive cable cost per foot than single-mode fiber.
- Supports data rates up to 1 Gbps.
- Carries data up to five kilometers without repeaters.

Because single-mode fiber supports higher transmission speeds, it may become the fiber of choice for backbone LANS.

PLASTIC FIBER

Plastic optical fibers were marketed in the early 1980s with mixed success. Mechanical, optical, and heat sensitivity problems marred their performance. Improved plastic fiber products are used in short data links, illumination, and sensing.

Plastic fiber durability and flexibility make it useful in factory robotics and automotive applications, and in other applications where fiber flexing and vibration make glass fiber unusable. Plastic fiber core diameters range from 100 micrometers to 1000 micrometers in 100-micrometer steps. Because plastic fiber cores are large splicing, connector tolerances are less precise. Splices typically take about one minute to complete. Easy splicing and termination can dramatically reduce plastic fiber installation costs.

Plastic fiber is used in short runs that tolerate high signal loss such as those used for some process control devices. Plastic fiber costs the least of all fiber. A 150-foot plastic fiber cable ran around $25, as compared to a similar single-mode glass fiber cable costing around $200. Plastic fibers have significant signal attenuation and therefore must be matched to an application. They also operate with shorter wavelength light than glass fibers. This means that they use different optical components than glass fiber cable.

Some plastic fiber systems transmit 80 Kbps at a distance of 250 feet, 1 Mbps at 90 feet, and 5 Mbps at 30 feet.

WORKING WITH FIBER

When fiber is installed in a LAN, it must first have connectors attached to the fiber cable ends so that they can plug into network equipment. Sometimes fiber requires splicing. Testing fiber is necessary to determine if it is functioning properly. There are different splicing technologies, with the easiest being simple mechanical splices and the most effective being fusion splicing. Testing fiber is done with an Optical Time Domain Reflectometer (OTDR) and optical power meters.

CONNECTORIZATION • Connectorization is the physical attachment of fiber optic connectors onto the ends of a fiber run to interface the fiber to network hardware. Standard connectors terminated are commonly ST and SC styles. Other connectors may also be used.

SC and ST connectors precisely mate finished fiber ends. ST connectors use straight ceramic tips to align the fiber ends. The tips slide into a plastic sleeve contained in a metallic barrel coupler. The tips are held firmly in place with a spring. The spring pressure holds the fiber ends at exactly the required facing distance for a multi-mode connection, no more than 0.0006 inches apart. The ST connector has been the most widely used connector for fiber optic cabling. It continues to be widely used.

ANSI TIA/EIA-568A standardizes SC connectors for use in structured wiring installations. Many single-mode applications are now only available in the SC-style connectors.

FUSION/MECHANICAL SPLICING • Mechanical splicing connects optical fibers with mechanical connectors. The fiber is installed into the mechanical connectors and the connectors plugged together to complete the splice. Early mechanical splices required that the fiber ends be highly polished to minimize signal loss. This required a lot of time to make a mechanical splice. Newer mechanical fiber couplings use an optical gel and tight mechanical tolerances to minimize signal losses. These mechanical couplers can have a signal loss of as low as 2 dB. They require only a short time to make a splice.

Other fiber splicing procedures require more time and special fusion splicing equipment. A fusion splicer is ideal for long-haul telephone and CATV single-mode fiber splicing where accuracy is imperative. A fusion splicer first aligns fiber cores. It then fuses the fibers together, forming the splice. Some fusion splicers monitor light injected into the core of the fibers to provide the lowest splice loss possible.

Fusion splicer software stores programs with user-defined splicing parameters for different types of fibers. They also have predefined programs for standard and specialty single-mode fibers and multi-mode fiber. Fusion splicers precisely evaluate the cleaved fiber ends—a prerequisite for good splices.

Fusion splicing is extensively used in long-haul communication backbones where fiber runs are measured in miles and kilometers rather than feet and meters. Examples of this are long-distance telephony and CATV systems.

OPTICAL TIME DOMAIN REFLECTOMETER • An Optical Time Domain Reflectometer (OTDR) measures transmission characteristics by sending a short pulse of light down a fiber and observing the backscattered light. An OTDR measures the elapsed time and intensity of light reflected on optical fiber to compute the distance to breaks in the fiber and to determine if a given fiber has attenuation problems.

An OTDR measures distance and loss of optical fiber and components like splices, connectors, etc. An OTDR is similar to radar in that it sends a short pulse of light down a fiber strand and observes a small fraction of light that is reflected back. The reflected light identifies fiber breaks and other points of discontinuity. Further, the light scattered back gives an overall measure of end-to-end fiber loss. Traces showing signal strength as a function of the distance along the fiber are displayed and stored. The graphically displayed physical slope of the trace shows fiber discontinuities. The trace shows for each discontinuity its precise distance from the OTDR to the meter as well as the dB loss at that discontinuity.

Once I was teaching for an enterprise in Richmond, Virginia. They showed me their token ring fiber backbone that interconnected their office with other company offices. This token ring fiber backbone was run to the other offices on telephone poles that were on a very busy street. The street had frequent auto accidents during peak traffic periods. My hosts stated to me that they had contracted with the LEC (Bell-Atlantic) to have an OTDR on-call in the event that there was an automobile accident and a car ran up one of the telephone poles that carried their fiber backbone cable. They wanted the OTDR to test and precisely locate any break in the cable caused by a car running up one of the telephone poles carrying their fiber optic cable. Keep in mind that an OTDR can locate a cable break to the meter. So they felt confident that they could locate any cable break caused by a car running into a telephone pole carrying their cable. I thought, "Why use an OTDR to locate the break, when you can just walk out the front door and look for the car up the pole to precisely determine where the break is?" In reality, you do need to precisely identify with an OTDR where to begin splicing the broken cable and where to end splicing the cable to bypass the damage.

Fiber Applications

Because of fiber's ability to support high-speed digital transmission, it will be used more and more in telecommunications networks. In telephony networks, fiber provides the foundation for all other communications services. It will increasingly be deployed to provide terabits per second transmission channels between major telephone company facilities. These links will carry voice, video, and Internet traffic. LANs will use gigabit fiber for campus backbone network connections and slower speed fiber links to connect wiring closet LAN components to central facility switches. Fiber connections will run from these LANs into ISPs to connect the LANs to the Internet. New fiber channel technology will be used to connect LAN servers to remote facilities housing huge networks of disk drives providing servers with access to terabytes of disk storage and more.

Everything we just discussed is in OSI Layer 1.

Brain Teaser

LAN Cabling

Look at the cable connecting to the LAN board in your PC.
1. Is there labeling on the cable? If so, read the labeling.
2. Does the labeling state that the cable meets CAT-5 standards?
3. Is the cable a CAT-5+ or data grade cable? Is it flat like the cable in Figure 6-38, or is it round cable like that in Figure 6-37?

The goal here is to understand how to identify different LAN cabling from the label and from its physical appearance.

LAN Wiring Hardware

Now that we have the wire, something must connect it to our PC clients and servers following some basic wiring layouts and rules. Our emphasis here is on twisted pair wiring because it currently dominates the wiring used in facilities today for both LAN and telephone wiring. UTP wire in wide use is typically 19-gauge to 26-gauge. Older telephone premises wire is 24-gauge to 26-gauge (AWG) with commonly two twists per foot, while newer wiring is CAT-5 or CAT-5+.

Twisting wire pairs cancels out radiated energy from current flowing in any one wire by the radiated energy from the same current flowing back in the return wire of the same pair. Radiated energy is called Electromagnetic Radiation (EMR). Twisting effectively and inexpensively minimizes crosstalk between adjacent pairs in a multi-pair cable. Twisting also makes the wire pairs less susceptible to external noise. The noise is coupled equally into each wire in a pair, causing the noise to cancel out when the wires are properly terminated. At voice frequencies, each pair appears to be balanced, e.g., equal electrical energy is emitted from each wire within the pair to any point outside the pair of wires.

Wire can be either plenum or non-plenum cabling. Plenum cable uses Teflon or other high-temperature material for outside electrical insulation as opposed to non-plenum wire that uses PVC material. LAN wiring hardware is designed to work with specific cabling from both the electrical and mechanical viewpoints.

UTP MOD-8/RJ-45 Connectors

UTP cabling is tricky to use because Ethernet and token ring use different hubs to NIC cable configurations and different schemes to cross-connect cables. Token ring and Ethernet use four wires, with each using a different combination of four wires in the hub to the NIC cable. Most NIC and hub concentrator or Multi-station Access Unit (MAU) vendors use MOD-8/RJ-45 connectors for UTP connections. This standardization allows a common cable pin configuration that works with Ethernet, token ring, and other networks. To determine the pin configuration for UTP, hold the MOD-8/RJ-45 connector by the wire with the clip down and the insertion end pointing

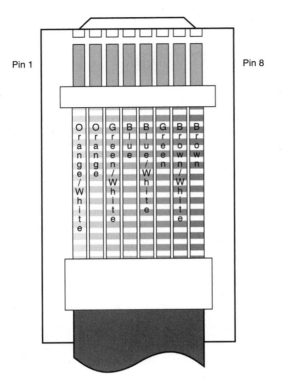

Bottom View of the Connector

Figure 6–43 *MOD-8/RJ-45 connector wiring—bottom view.*

away from you. The pin on the left is Pin 1. A standard MOD-8/RJ-45 connector has eight pins. UTP CAT-3 cable uses a solid and striped wire color scheme (see Figure 6-43).

The wire pairs are colored:

- Orange and orange/white.
- Blue and blue/white.
- Green and green/white.
- Brown and brown/white.

The solid/striped combination identifies pairs of wires that must be twisted together in a specific sequence to provide good electrical signals. The pairs must match at the remote end of the cable to transfer the signal. Common cabling pin-outs are:

Ethernet 10-Base T connections use Pins 1 and 2 and 3 and 6. Token ring UTP connections use Pins 4 and 5 and 3 and 6. Creating a cable that works with token ring and Ethernet NICs requires the following pin-outs:

Figure 6–44 *Cable stripper and modular jack crimping tools.*

Pin 1 - Orange/White.

Pin 2 - Orange.

Pin 3 - Green/White.

Pin 4 - Blue.

Pin 5 - Blue/White.

Pin 6 - Green.

Pin 7 - Brown/White.

Pin 8 - Brown.

To create a CAT-5 cable, it is important to have the twists in the cable as close to the connector pins as possible. The outside cable insulation and twists should extend into the MOD-8/RJ-45 connector beyond the cable stress relief clamp. Crimping the cable is critical for CAT-5 performance. Equal crimping pressure on all cable pins provides the best electrical performance. Each cable should be tested to assure that it is functioning properly. Tools for cabling are shown in Figure 6-44.

A cable tester determines that all pairs are functioning properly and that the cable has acceptable NEXT so that it can carry data at 100 Mbps (see Figure 6-45).

This cable tester uses devices at both ends of the cable to test the signal loss and NEXT between all cable pairs. The central unit is programmed with different standard wire types, including TIA/EIA-568 UTP CAT-3, CAT-4, and CAT-5.

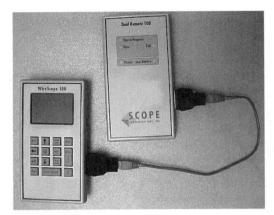

Figure 6–45 *Cable tester.*

Hubs and Intelligent Hubs

In a UTP wiring scheme, the wiring hubs perform the key functions. The most basic functions performed are the repeater (signal regenerator) function, and electrically isolating each wiring run from the other wiring runs. Wiring hubs may be a simple wiring hub or a switch.

Most hubs have intelligence, or some microcomputer monitoring capability. Hub intelligence is focused on monitoring network activity, alerting network operators to wiring problems, and providing additional network physical connectivity features.

The three types of wiring hubs are:

- Active and passive hubs—Passive hubs just connect wires, while active hubs perform signal regeneration functions. Hubs provide a shared bus to all individual connections. The individual lines are isolated electrically from the devices attached to an active hub.

- Intelligent hubs—These hubs perform signal regeneration functions, traffic monitoring, media diagnosis, and transmission speed translation. Similar to a basic hub, intelligent hubs provide a shared bus to all client connections with individual lines isolated electrically from one another. Newer hubs perform speed translation between 10 Mbps and 100 Mbps as well.

- Switches—These are high-performance network wiring components. They perform all the functions of an intelligent hub and more. Each MOD-8/RJ-45 port has its own individual path for data such that any port can be connected full duplex to any other port at 10 Mbps, 100

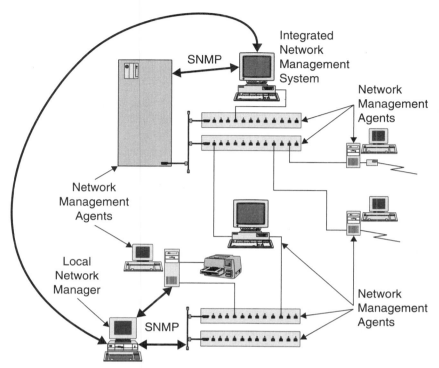

Figure 6–46 *LAN management with SNMP.*

Mbps, or 1 Gbps. Switches are software configured and controlled, making it possible to construct virtual LANs (i.e., logical groupings of PC clients using IP addresses).

Most wiring hubs monitor themselves and their functioning in the network. Additionally, each wiring hub and network component communicates with a network management system using SNMP (see Figure 6-46). Standards-based, open systems are very flexible since they can often control devices based on the same standards. The SNMP has been a primary focus in the rise of standards-based management systems. Integrated management systems help users manage networks by establishing a single location to control network operations, regardless of the type and source of devices on the network.

As LANs grow larger and are connected to one another and to other resources, the need to control these interconnected systems increases. One successful approach is the three-tiered management system. Network nodes and devices constitute the first tier. Individual standalone management systems form the second tier and control various resources. An enterprise network manager occupies the third tier and provides a single enterprise-wide management interface.

LAN hubs typically have an SNMP agent that monitors network activity and alerts a central management system to cable outages. The central system and hub exchange messages using TCP/IP and SNMP. Hubs that are more sophisticated permit active testing of the cabling and disabling of cable segments from the central management system.

TOKEN RING WIRING

Table 6-6 identifies different types of wire that work with the IBM token ring network. Many token ring LANs use CAT-5 UTP wiring today instead of the IBM wiring scheme.

Table 6.6 *IBM Token Ring Twisted Pair Wiring*

IBM Cable Type	Data Pairs	Voice Pairs	Optical Fibers
Type 1 Cable	2 Pairs 22 AWG (American Wire Gauge) Solid Conductor Both Shielded	None	None
Type 2 Cable	2 Pairs 22 AWG Solid Conductor Individually and Both Shielded	4 Pairs 22/24 AWG Solid Conductor Unshielded	None
Type 3 Cable (Originally CAT-3, but now CAT-5 for high speeds)	2 Pairs 24 AWG Solid Conductor Unshielded	None	None
Type 5 Cable	None	None	Two Fibers 100-micron Core 140-micron Cladding Multi-mode
Type 6 Cable	2 Pairs 26 AWG Stranded Conductor Both Shielded	None	None
Type 9 Cable	2 Pairs 24 AWG Solid or Stranded Conductor Both Shielded	None	None

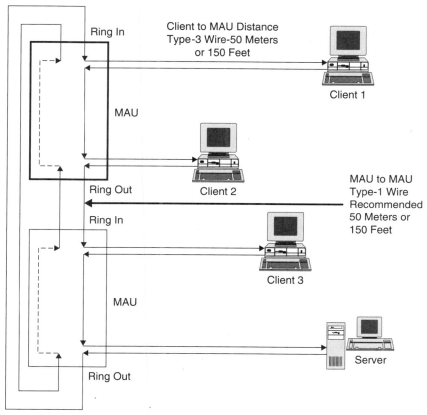

Figure 6–47 *IBM token ring general wiring rules.*

The token ring runs over UTP pair wiring at 4 Mbps, 16 Mbps, or higher speeds. The IBM token ring employs wiring hubs called MAUs. These wire the token ring in star-type topologies using IBM Type-1 wire between MAUs and permitting IBM Type-3 UTP wiring to run from the MAU to the PC client (see Figure 6-47).

To run at 16 Mbps or higher speeds over UTP, active hubs that perform signal re-timing are required. IBM's active hubs have two components: a Controlled Access Unit (CAU), which is the intelligent part of the hub, and a Lobe Access Module (LAM). Each LAM connects up to twenty devices (PC clients or servers); each CAU supports up to four LAMs. You must use a CAU/LAM combination for the token ring to work. A single CAU with fully populated LAMs supports 80 devices. The maximum token ring size is 255 devices. Other token ring vendors build intelligent hubs, incorporating all functions into a single hub unit.

Although the token ring is a ring of wire, on the surface, the wiring topology does not seem to be a ring but rather a star, wired from each of the MAUs. Wiring topology for LANs today is star wiring from network hubs. This star wiring prevents common Ethernet and token ring PC wiring glitches from disabling the entire network.

ETHERNET WIRING

Ethernet started with coaxial cable wiring. This proved to be an unreliable approach to wiring up Ethernets because one break in the coax cable disabled the entire network. To overcome the problems associated with coax cabling, twisted pair cable and wiring hubs were used to implement Ethernet in the late 1980s. All clients and servers were wired to a hub using UTP wire. This increased network reliability because one cable breaking only impacted that link to the hub. As Ethernet increased the transmission speeds, reduced signal crosstalk (signal crossover interference) from the cable was required. The cable category levels were developed. Most Ethernets are implemented with CAT-5 cable supporting 100-Mbps transmission speeds. This CAT-5 cable is also used for telephony wiring today. With the demand for higher and higher Ethernet transmission speeds, new switching components are added to the Ethernet wiring scheme to increase network performance.

Wiring Rules

Every LAN technology has specific wiring rules. These rules are based upon signal attenuation in the wire and signal propagation delays in the network. Signal attenuation was discussed in Chapter 5. Propagation delays have a different impact on wiring rules. Let me illustrate with a simple example.

In half-duplex Ethernet, the sending device detects collisions only while it is actually sending data. Once it stops transmitting, it stops detecting collisions as well. In a bus-style half-duplex Ethernet, it would take some time as determined by the signal propagation delay for a station's signal to reach the most remote end of the network. If a station at the remote end transmitted, causing a collision without the original station knowing it, then the Ethernet would not function properly.

Think of it this way: You and I are at opposite ends of a 1,000-foot-long room. We use sound as our carrier to send data among the stations in the room. When I am speaking, I am also looking to assure there are no collisions. If I began transmitting a message, how long would I need to transmit to assure that I never missed a collision? Since sound travels at 1090 (1000 feet is close enough for government work) feet per second, it would take one second for my signal to propagate across the room to you. However, if I stopped transmitting at one second, I could miss detecting a collision. Because you might start transmitting a message just an instant before my signal propagated to you, a collision would occur. However, it would take a second for that collision to propagate across the room for me to detect it. Consequently, I must transmit two full seconds, or enough time for the signal to reach you at the most distant end of the network and return to me, to detect the collision. The problem would be impacted if my signal had to run through a repeater because each repeater adds a half-bit time of propagation delay to the transmission.

Early half-duplex Ethernets used a 5-4-3 rule to account for repeaters and propagation delays to assure all collisions were detected. The 5-4-3 rule worked something like this:

- An Ethernet could have five segments.
- The segments could be connected using four repeaters.
- Three segments could be active (have attached PCs or servers), and two segments would only extend the physical distance that the LAN covered.
- A client was separated from its server by no more than two repeaters.

This is changed now with Ethernet switching. However, there are now new wiring rules that must be followed with switches based upon signal propagation delays and signal attenuation.

The wiring rules for a LAN must be followed precisely for the LAN to function; if not, bad things will happen. Such wiring problems are very difficult to pinpoint. They will cause you to want to kick the living "bad word" out of your network (as my granddaughter, Jenna, says).

Preventing Common Cabling Problems

Several guidelines help in preventing and avoiding cabling problems. These guidelines are:

1. Buy the best wire that fits your budget. Get the best UTP CAT-5+ wire you can afford.
2. Use wiring blocks, modular connectors, etc., that exceed the quality of the cable used.
3. Keep wire twisted for all pairs to within 0.5 inch of the termination for CAT-5 installations.
4. Avoid running voice and data in the same cable, unless, of course, it is VoIP.

5. Terminate voice and data to separate punch-down blocks and racks. Label the racks.

6. Keep the minimum bend radius for cables to 10 times the cable diameter.

7. Do not over-tighten cables.

8. Strip cable sheaths back no more than 0.5 inch.

9. On cables that are 75 feet or less in length, check the remote terminations. They can significantly affect NEXT for such short lengths.

10. Avoid 66 blocks unless they have been specifically designed for CAT-5 wiring. They attenuate high frequencies and deliver poor NEXT. Short connections can have more NEXT.

11. Watch terminations carefully. Maintain a tight twist up to the termination point at the punch-down blocks, wire plates and connectors.

12. Do not route cables near RF sources, e.g., motors, fluorescent lights, and power lines.

13. Use short patch cables because patch cables have more NEXT.

14. Do not use untwisted cables (Station Wire—Red/Green/Black/Yellow) or flat telephone cables (Silver Satin wire) from the wall plate to the PC's NIC.

Correctly cabling your LAN is vital to get the desired performance from LAN components. Proper cabling becomes more critical as LAN transmission speeds increase. Every LAN connection must be tested to assure it meets the rated speeds. Anything less begs for cabling problems to crop up unexpectedly.

In this section, we discussed the network wire that fits into OSI Layer 1, the physical layer.

Brain Teaser

LAN Wiring

Go back to the LAN cable coming into your PC's NIC.

1. Look at the underside of the RJ-45/MOD-8 connector. Does the wiring follow the T-568a scheme described in this chapter in the "UTP MOD-8/RJ-45 Connectors" section?

2. Fire up a Web browser and go to www.AMP.com. Select **Products** from the top menu, then **Fiber Optic Products**, and finally **Fiber Optic Interconnects & Cables**. Do they sell ST and SC connectors? What other types do they sell?

3. Try selecting a connector type. How are the fiber cables described?

The purpose of this exercise is to become familiar with twisted pair and fiber cabling components.

LAN Servers

Servers (or PCs on steroids) are the central LAN component. Without them, resource sharing, and more importantly, LAN-centric applications, could not be implemented. Once users begin to rely on the LAN and its servers to perform their daily work functions, the network and the servers must be highly reliable. If the network or a server is unavailable, then users at PC clients cannot work. If a server loses a user's data, then months of effort can be lost and may have to be recreated by the irate user. Since most users rely on the LAN and Prayer-Based Backup (what we label PBB) to preserve their critical work, implementing reliable and robust servers is not a luxury, it is a necessity for most LANs. Servers must be extremely reliable and robust to implement VoIP and other specialized telecommunications applications. Understanding what makes a reliable and powerful LAN server is as important as having good LAN wiring.

In our network at Moulton Company, we are using Microsoft Outlook and Microsoft Exchange Server to manage user contact lists. The server hardware died at one time and we thought the Exchange server's data was all lost. Now we run two Microsoft Exchange servers on our network, with each server containing the exact same database and synchronizing itself frequently with the other companion Microsoft Exchange server.

Reliable servers require several key features and technologies including:

- Redundant CPUs.
- Error detecting correcting memory.
- Hot-swappable components.
- Redundant Array of Independent Disks (RAID) data storage.

This section examines these special server features.

REDUNDANT CPUS • Most servers use from two to eight CPUs. Windows or UNIX software spreads the processing load evenly across all CPUs. This is called symmetric multi-processing. When one CPU fails, the server slows but keeps on running. Multiple CPUs must be matched with each other for the software to run properly. This is described as matching the stepping level of the Intel CPU chip (see Figure 6-48).

Intel CPUs designed specifically for servers are:

- Pentium Pro.
- Pentium III Xeon.

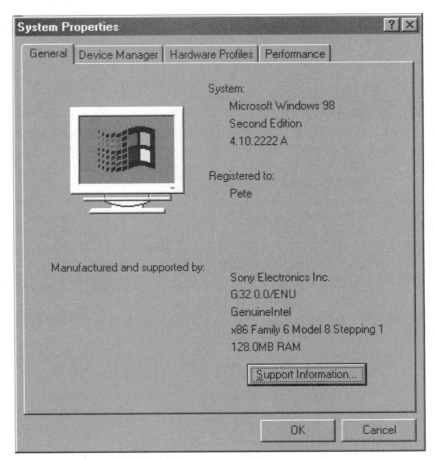

Figure 6–48 *Intel CPU stepping.*

Other Intel Pentium and Celeron chips can be used as server CPUs, but the Pentium III Xeon and Pentium Pro have an extra large Level-2 (L2) cache on the chip. This L2 cache can be 256KB to 2MB in size. The Pentium III Xeon is likely to continue as the preferred chip for servers because of its internal L2 cache. It is reasonable to expect the size of this L2 cache to increase in the future. Pentium III and Celeron chips are aimed at the largest PC market, consumer PCs. The Multimedia Extension (MMX) technology is incorporated into the Celeron chips, and the Single Instruction Multiple Data (SIMD) technology is in the Pentium III chips. MMX technology enhances multimedia performance and SIMD technology enhances Internet performance for sites that take advantage of it. Pentium III chips mount to the main logic board using Slot-1 technology, and Pentium III Xeon chips mount to the main logic board using Slot-2 technology.

The Pentium mounting technology is called Single Edge Contact (S.E.C.) cartridge technology. It uses Slot-1 and Slot-2 mounts. Multiple Pentium configurations support Symmetric Multi-Processing (SMP) systems, facilitating improved performance with Windows NT, Windows 2000, and UNIX.

AMD and others make competing CPUs. The principle competing CPU chips from AMD are the AMD K6 and AMD K7. AMD has an equivalent mounting technology to Intel's S.E.C. used with its Athlon (K7) CPU. The Athlon mount is a Slot-A or socket 462 mount. AMD and Intel CPUs have similar capabilities (see Table 6-7).

Table 6.7 *Server CPU Chip Comparisons*

Chip/Feature	Internal L1 CPU Cache Size	Multimedia Extension Technology (MMx)	Internal L2 Cache Size	Chip Speed	Bus Speed
Pentium Pro Dual/Quad Processors	16Kb Total ========= 8Kb Data and 8Kb Instructions	None	256KB to 2GB (Socket 8)	166MHz to 500MHz	66MHz
Xeon Pentium III Dual/Quad Processors	32Kb Total ========= 16Kb Data and 16Kb Instructions	Yes and SIMD Instructions	512 KB to 2 GB (SEC – Slot 2).	400MHz to 500MHz	66MHz
Pentium II Dual Processors	32Kb Total ========= 16Kb Data and 16Kb Instructions	Yes	In S.E.C. Cartridge, Slot 1 operates at one-half CPU speed.	233MHz to 500MHz	66MHz
Pentium III Dual Processors	32Kb Total ========= 16Kb Data and 16Kb Instructions	Yes and SIMD Instructions	In S.E.C. Cartridge, Slot 1 operates at one-half CPU speed.	400MHz to 1GHz	66MHz, 100MHz, 133MHz, and RAMbus
AMD K6	64Kb Total ========= 32Kb Data and 32Kb Instructions	Yes	External (Socket 7)	166MHz, 200MHz, 233MHz, and up	60MHz and 66MHz
AMD K7	128Kb Total ========= 64Kb Data and 64Kb Instructions	Yes	In S.E.C. Cartridge, Slot A operates at one-half CPU speed. In socket 462 operates at CPU speed.	166 MHz, 200 MHz, 233 MHz and up	66MHz, 100MHz, and 133MHz

CPU chips differ in their structure and capabilities, making it impossible to predict upon specifications alone the performance of any LAN server using those chips. Only when tests are performed with each chip side by side with precisely the same hardware and LAN software can their performance be compared. A 20% or lower increase in performance is not noticeable to human beings. However, this can be significant for LAN servers.

The server design, CPU chip used, and LAN software running on the server determine whether multiple CPUs can be used in a server. Windows NT Server and Windows 2000 Server software can run on up to four CPUs out of the box. Special configurations permit Windows to work with up to eight CPUs. Pentium II, Pentium III, Celeron, and Xeon CPUs can be installed in multiple CPU systems. AMD chips should work in multiple CPU configurations, but the supporting electronics may not be available yet.

RAM AND ERROR CORRECTING CIRCUITRY RAM • Dynamic RAM (DRAM) has been used for PC main memory for years. The Dynamic page mode (DPM) RAM was predominantly used. This was replaced by another form of DRAM Fast Page Mode (FPM) RAM. However, CPU performance increases made these RAM types obsolete. They restricted CPU performance, keeping computers at slower speeds than necessary.

Memory bank interleaving was first used to speed up RAM access. Next, caches were introduced in the CPUs and on the motherboards to offset RAM speed restrictions. Now, new RAM types have been developed and employed, to let server main memory keep up with CPU speeds.

The RAM types used in servers may be:

- Fast Page Mode (FPM)—obsolete.
- Extended Data Out (EDO)—obsolete.
- Burst Extended Data Out (BEDO)—obsolete.
- Synchronous DRAM (SDRAM).
- RAMbus® DRAM (RDRAM).

RAMbus® memory, or RDRAM®, operates differently from all previous versions of RAM. RDRAM® is a general-purpose, high-performance, packet-oriented DRAM. The memory modules use RAMbus® Signaling Level (RSL) technology to achieve 356MHz or 400MHz clock speeds using differential clocks. The architecture of RDRAM®s allows high sustained bandwidth memory transactions for multiple, simultaneous, semi-random addresses. The 32 banks can support up to four simultaneous transactions (within bank restrictions). This type of memory, in the long term, is ideal for LAN servers.

Error correcting codes are used to correct single- and multiple-bit errors in server disk and memory operations. Error correcting codes use multiple bits to detect and correct errors. For server RAM to use Error Cor-

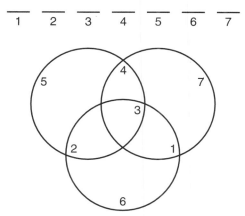

Figure 6–49   *ECC exercise.*

rection Circuitry (ECC), each byte of data must be stored in RAM with nine-bits. This is specified by RAM Dual In-line Memory Modules (DIMMs) being 9 by 36 bits, or four 9-bit bytes. Non-ECC RAM DIMMs are 8 by 32 bits, or 4 8-bit bytes per DIMM. Operation of ECC RAM is illustrated in the next Brain Teaser.

Brain Teaser

ECC RAM Concepts

To illustrate the operation of error correcting codes, we will use a simple example. Using three extra bits, we can detect and correct single-bit errors in four bits. Use Figure 6-49 to write down any four bits in positions 1 through 4. Next, write these bits down in the circle areas 1 through 4. Then, using the rule of even parity, create the bits encompassed by Circle 5, Circle 6, and Circle 7. Write these bit values in positions 5, 6, and 7. Now alter a bit position. Any bit position. Using the altered bit value, recalculate bits 5, 6, and 7.

1. Which bits do not match the originally created bits? The circle area unique to only those mismatched bits is the bit that is in error.

2. Which bits do not match when the center bit is changed? This should be all bits, e.g., 5, 6, and 7.

3. Which bits do not match when a parity bit 5, 6, or 7 is changed? This should be only the changed parity bit.

This is the simplest illustration of the operation of error correcting codes. Real ECC operation uses 3 bits to detect and correct single bit errors in 16 bits or 4 bits to detect and correct single bit errors in 32 bits. The goal here is to understand the basics of how bit error detection and correction work.

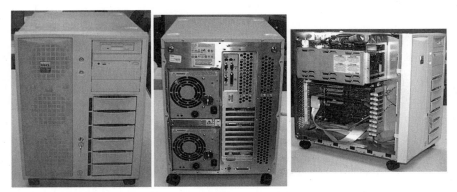

Figure 6–50 *Server with hot-swappable, redundant power supplies.*

HOT-SWAPPABLE COMPONENTS • Servers have hot-swappable components. Redundant hot-swappable power supplies to insure reliability in the event that one failed were the first hot-swappable server component. This has been expanded to include other server components that may fail, such as cooling fans, fixed disk drives (RAID drives), and PCI bus cards (see Figure 6-50). When the failed component is a power supply or fan, a service person just pops out the old, dead unit and replaces it with a new or refurbished unit. During this process, the server continues to operate normally.

LAN servers have active monitoring capabilities built into hardware and software. Servers constantly monitor heat and fan operation to assure that internal component failures are prevented. When a failure is detected, it is displayed on the server's Control Panel. Software may send error notification to a central management system as well.

REDUNDANT ARRAY OF INDEPENDENT DISKS • RAID is Redundant Array of Independent (or Inexpensive) Disks. Servers use RAID to provide reliable data storage and improved performance.

RAID is implemented using SCSI bus-attached disk drives or storage arrays. The Small Computer System Interface (SCSI) is an industry-standard interface, allowing servers to communicate with peripheral hardware. Thirty disk drives may be connected to a dual-port SCSI controller. SCSI is also used to connect to tape drives, CD-ROM drives, printers, and scanners. SCSI is more flexible than earlier parallel data transfer interfaces and operates at higher data rates. The Ultra-2 SCSI for a 16-bit bus can transfer data at up to 80 Mbps. SCSI allows up to either 7 or 15 devices to connect to a single SCSI port in daisy-chain fashion. RAID drives are implemented using SCSI interfaces to connect multiple drives to a single server.

RAID configurations are numbered. Some are standard, while other configurations are non-standard. Regardless of how hardware RAID drives are configured, they just look like a single fixed disk to the software. Figure 6-51 illustrates the basic RAID configurations.

RAID-0 RAID-0 stripes data across multiple disk drives. This makes all disks appear to the server as one large disk. RAID-0 can improve performance on reads and writes because the information is spread across all the disks. RAID-0 commonly uses from 2 to 8 SCSI bus-attached drives. RAID-0 provides **NO** protection against disk failure. Sometimes RAID-0 is called JBOD (Just a Bunch Of Drives, or Disks). JBOD means lots of drives look like a single disk drive. In Figure 6-51, for RAID-0—Data Striping, you see *"Data Goes Here"* spread across all drives in the RAID array.

RAID-1 RAID-1 is mirroring data by two disk drives. The data on one drive is duplicated on the other drive. Mirroring minimally requires two drives. Data is protected in the event that one drive fails. RAID-1 is quite expensive because each drive storing data needs a twin to store the backup data. Write performance is slower than with RAID-0 because data must be written to both drives before writing data is complete. Read performance can be good because data can be read from either drive using multiple controllers (sometimes called duplexing) and SCSI buses. In Figure 6-51, for RAID-1—Mirroring you see *"Data Here"* mirrored on each separate set of eight drives in the RAID array. The first two drives mirror the "D's," the second the "A's," and so forth.

RAID-0+1 RAID-0+1 is striping mirrored drives. Data is mirrored on pairs of drives. The mirrored pairs are then added to a RAID-0 stripe set. A minimum of three or four drives is required, depending upon how the controller implements the RAID-0 stripe set. This is striping mirror sets because you mirror first, then stripe. It provides excellent reliability, but at a high cost. Since twin drives are required for each mirror set, RAID-0+1 is expensive to implement. However, in this configuration, multiple drives could fail and your data could be okay. If both drives in a single mirror set fail, then all data is lost. The ultimate in data integrity is mirroring three drives in each mirror set, then striping the mirror sets. Then you would need to lose all three drives in a single mirror set to lose all the data in the stripe set. Write performance is not the best, but read performance is excellent. In Figure 6-51, for RAID-0+1—Striping Mirrored Drives, you see *"Data Here"* mirrored on pairs of drives, and then each pair of mirrored drives is striped to store all the data.

RAID-5 RAID-5 is striping both data and parity on multiple disk drives. RAID-5 needs a minimum of three drives. The capacity of one drive is con-

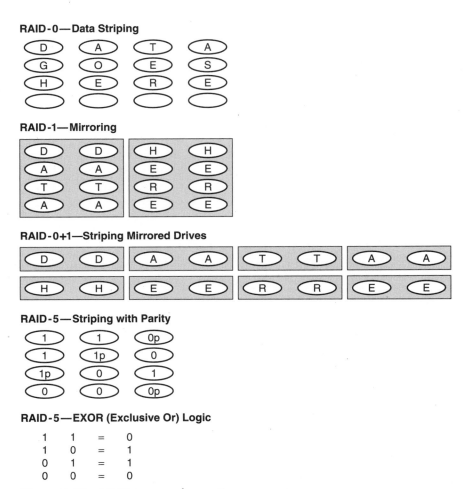

Figure 6–51 *RAID types and operation summary.*

sumed with the parity information. Hence, three 4GB drives in a RAID-5 set yield 8GB of usable data storage. If more than one RAID-5 drive fails at the same time, all data is lost. The position of the drive in the RAID set can be important for some servers. For example, if Drive 2 failed and Drive 4 was moved into its position, then the RAID recovery could try to rebuild Drive 2 using what data it could find on Drive 4. This process would destroy any data on Drive 2.

Brain Teaser

How RAID-5 Works

Use the RAID-5 illustration to understand how RAID-5 works. RAID-5 is based upon Exclusive Or (EXOR) logic. The truth table for EXOR is shown at the bottom of Figure 6-51.

EXOR is the logic used when you are confronted with that age-old dilemma of choosing between two doors, one leading to instant and hellacious death in the volcano and the other to the prince or princess and a kingdom of riches. Two huge guards guard the doors. One guard never lies and the other guard always lies. You get to ask one question of either guard. What is the question? I have forgotten what the answer is, but it contains a query of whether they are telling the truth and what is the correct door to choose.

In the diagram, block out any one column of RAID-5 drives and use the bits on the remaining drives and the EXOR logic table to create the bits on the missing column of drives.

1. Did the missing data get created correctly?
2. Use a different column. Does the EXOR logic recover it as well?

This illustrates RAID-5 operation. Real RAID-5 operation uses from 3 to 8 drives. The goal here is to understand the basics of RAID-5.

NEAR FUTURE STORAGE AREA NETWORKS • RAID storage is becoming a back-end service to LAN servers. RAID storage is moving into Storage Area Networks (SANs) using fiber and SCSI channels to transfer data to and from RAID array disk drives. Storage is becoming a basic LAN service and may become a utility-like service to any organization. Storage service, repair, and maintenance are performed separate from the user of the storage service, so to the user, the storage is always there.

Storage can now be purchased from a storage service company. The storage service company uses a fiber link to connect you to their Storage Area Network (SAN). The SAN uses SCSI channels to connect disk drives to RAID array controllers. SCSI channel commands are sent across the fiber cable to the RAID arrays to retrieve and store data on the RAID array disk drives.

A SAN is a dedicated, high-speed network providing a direct connection between storage elements and servers. A SAN frees general-purpose LANs from storage-related activities. A SAN helps to minimize contention between applications and storage for the same network bandwidth. SANs alleviate logistical and maintenance tasks and outages associated with direct-

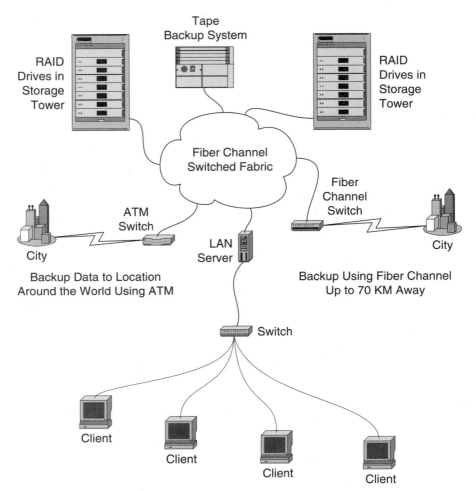

Figure 6–52 *A SAN.*

attached and network-attached storage. SANs are based upon fiber channel technology (see Figure 6-52).

Fiber channel is an industry standard. It interconnects using a high-speed serial I/O protocol that is media-independent and supports simultaneous transfer of many other different protocols.

Fiber channel was developed in 1988 as an extension to the Intelligent Peripheral Interface-Level 3 (IPL-3) work. Fiber channel supports both channels and networks. In fact, it combines some of the attributes of a channel with some of those of a network. It is the foundation for future SANs (see Figure 6-53).

An ANSI/ISO Open Standard

Data Speeds Range from 133 Mbps to over 4 Gbps

Distances Range from 2 M up to 70 KM

Data Duplexing

Serial Data

Multiple Protocols Are Supported, Including:

   Small Computer System Interface (SCSI)

   Intelligent Peripheral Interface (IPI)

   High-Performance Parallel Interface (HIPPI) Framing Protocol

   Internet Protocol (IP)

   ATM Adaptation Layer (AAL5) for Computer Data

   Single-Byte Command Code Set (SBCCS) Mapping

   IEEE 802.2

Figure 6–53   *Fiber channel characteristics.*

Channels are host to peripheral interfaces that operate in a master/slave fashion. SCSI is a channel interface. Channels have low processing overhead and are configured in advance, identifying the exact peripherals connected. There is little software required to operate a channel and the distance covered is short – a few meters at best.

In contrast, networks use host-to-host interfaces that operate in a peer-to-peer fashion. They have high processing overhead and dynamically self-configure. Networks are software-intensive and the geographic area of coverage can be a campus or larger area.

A very important characteristic of fiber channel is that channel and network protocols can share the same physical media because the I/O protocols (software) are separated from their I/O interfaces (hardware). This separation makes it possible to use multiple protocols via the same physical hardware transport mechanism, which in turn makes SANs feasible.

In SANs, backing up data can be done independently of server processing. So both normal database processing activity and data backup activity can occur simultaneously without degrading server performance. Since the tape backup device runs on a server separate from the normal LAN servers, and since there is little network blockage on a SAN, backups can be processed without impacting normal server operation.

SERVER CLUSTERING

LANs requiring extraordinary server reliability employ server clustering. Clustering has several servers working on the same application. The server software splits the processing load more or less evenly between all servers in the cluster. If a server fails, the remaining servers pick up its load. In this fashion, heavy application loads can be reliably handled by clustered LAN servers. This is referred to as fail-over clustering.

LAN Software

LAN servers perform general and specific network functions as determined by the capabilities of the software installed on them. Some LAN servers can be assigned database operation; others network management functions, while still others can act as fax and email servers. Each special server requires server software and then additional network application software for the specific function they perform. For example, a SQL server would need the basic Microsoft Windows NT or Windows 2000 Server software and then the Microsoft SQL Server software as well. Similarly, an email server would need the Microsoft Windows NT or Windows 2000 Server software and the Microsoft Exchange Server software.

Microsoft

Windows NT was one of the most significant products to be introduced to networking in the 1990s. The reason for this is the fact that networking components are neatly integrated into the operating system. Additionally, Windows comes with a broad set of client software for most of the popular network operating systems. This allows Windows to operate as a client or a server on your network. Windows can also work in a peer-to-peer networking system. Windows provides inter-operability to the following networks:

- Microsoft networks, including Windows for Workgroups and MS LAN Manager.
- Novell NetWare.
- TCP/IP hosts, including UNIX hosts.
- Remote access clients, talking to remote access servers.
- Apple Talk (NT 3.5).

Windows supplies this flexibility though modularization of the network components. This means that network components can be added, removed, or updated, in some cases without disturbing the other network components. A reboot may be required to activate a component before its change takes effect. The downside here is that Microsoft software products are very much "a la carte." You must buy Windows server software and then add modular Windows application software to support key enterprise activities. Once added, Microsoft application software intertwines with Windows; it cannot be easily removed.

Windows NT/2000 uses the OSI layer approach in its LAN server and network software. Microsoft divides the seven layers up into three areas. The various filesystem drivers loaded by Windows handle OSI Layer-6 and Layer-7 functions. These would be for the different types of filesystems that Windows supports. Layers 3, 4, and 5 are controlled by the transport protocols supported by Windows. These are TCP/IP, SPX/IPX, and NetBEUI. Layers 1 and 2 are handled by the various network adapters and their supporting drivers, as well as NDIS. NDIS 3.0 allows multiple adapter types and protocol types to exist in one machine.

Between these different layers resides what Microsoft calls boundary layers. These layers provide communication between the different network module layers, like the filesystems and transport protocols.

Windows LAN server software provides basic LAN client/server disk and file sharing capabilities. It supports user management through domains and a variety of LAN boards (NICs). Virtual private networking software permits connecting central and remote facilities via secure links.

Windows NT/2000 provides gateway services for network clients to access NetWare resources. A 32-bit software system allows users to access NetWare files and printers across the network. It also functions as a non-dedicated gateway for any SMB (Server Messaging Block) clients. It is able to access resources on any server running the older NetWare bindery services. Newer NetWare servers not running bindery will be inaccessible for resources.

This design was intended for the occasional need of users to access a NetWare resource. If you use this as a primary interface for users to access these resources, you will see significant performance degradation.

For the gateway to work, the server installing the gateway services must have a group named NTGATEWAY. Users intending to use the gateway must be part of this group.

Once the service is installed and users and groups have been set, then you must configure the service. You need to set a server, enable the gateway, and then make a connection to shareable resources. Like other resources and Windows NT/2000, permissions can be set to control security access. By default, all users will have full control of the resource.

Windows 2000 is Microsoft's latest client/server operating system. It comes in several flavors, the most powerful being the Windows 2000 Advanced Server software. Windows 2000 in a single integrated Network Operating System (NOS) provides a Web application platform, Internet performance and scalability, and security based on the latest standards and technologies. Windows 2000 is designed to provide integrated Web and application development services, scalability and flexibility, and security services to extend enterprise operations using the Internet.

Windows 2000 Server can:

- Connect employees, customers, and suppliers using the Web, spanning geographic or corporate network boundaries.
- Build internal line-of-business applications.
- Share select enterprise information in an extranet without compromising confidential data.
- Allow mobile users to connect securely to corporate resources from anywhere in the world.
- Increase performance as application load increases.
- Integrate Web and application services.

Windows 2000 implements Active Server Pages (ASPs) similar to other servers, allowing the Web to become dynamic and highly personalized. With Windows 2000, ASPs run on cutting-edge, high-end multi-processor hardware. Windows 2000 supports Extensible Markup Language (XML). XML integrates data from multiple sources, reduces network traffic, and supports searches that are more useful. Windows 2000 supports streaming media. This allows development and distribution of real-time presentations and rich multimedia content to both internal and external audiences. Streaming media can send full-screen video to PC clients on demand and provide CD-quality audio.

Windows 2000, like Windows NT, is designed to increase performance through Symmetric Multi-Processing (SMP) support. SMP means that Windows takes equal advantage of multiple microprocessors on the same machine. Although microprocessors get faster and faster, real scalability is achieved by adding more processors or by adding more machines to a cluster of servers, sometimes referred to as "scaling out." Windows 2000 allows demanding high-end applications to access and use more memory. Windows 2000 Server supports four CPUs and Windows 2000 Advanced Server supports eight.

A Windows 2000 Network Load Balancing (NLB) service is part of Advanced Server. With NLB, an Internet site grows by adding more Windows 2000 servers. NLB directs traffic on the site, spreading the traffic across multiple Windows 2000 servers without requiring new application development or reengineering.

Enterprise LANs support intranets, Internet sites, and extranets, all of which require increased system security. Confidential information may be stored on mobile computing devices, which can be stolen or lost. Windows 2000 has end-to-end security that integrates systems both inside and outside an enterprise into the enterprise LAN while controlling LAN access and protecting data. Security includes identifying who is accessing systems, including digital "keys" used to access selected data. A single ID permits users to access their own computer and other shared resources on the enterprise LAN, the Internet, or on an extranet. Windows 2000 Server has comprehensive, standards-based security services, including flexible authentication, data encryption, flexible and secure network access, and protection of VPNs. Windows 2000 uses core Internet standards such as IP Security (IPSec) and secure transaction processing.

Novell NetWare

For almost a decade Novell claimed the lion's share of the NOS market. For nearly as long, they enjoyed little competition. They provided an easy-to-implement solution for connecting PCs together. NetWare ran on many network types, including Ethernet and token ring. Originally, NetWare used a flat bindery database approach to user management, providing easy-to-use, menu-driven tools for DOS-based PCs. This was the most successful NOS package for small DOS-based PC LANs for many years.

NetWare's primary competitor is the Microsoft Windows NT operating system. Novell redesigned NetWare to work as part of larger and heterogeneous networks, including the Internet. NetWare adopted domain management and a hierarchical network management database structure to support enterprise-wide LANs. This jump from a simple DOS menu-driven network management system to hierarchical network management was very difficult for most NetWare users because the network management paradigm was so different. At that time, it was easier to use the Windows network management paradigm to manage enterprise-wide LANs with Windows PC clients.

Today Novell offers its NetWare 4.X and 5.X products. They provide a very good enterprise-wide network management solution. They are also designed to meet the DOD C-2 level of security. NetWare has abandoned the flat bindery approach to managing users and has pursued the NetWare Directory Services (NDS) hierarchical approach to user and LAN management.

The latest version of NetWare is NetWare 5. NetWare 5 supports both Novell's own IPX network protocol and the Internet's IP protocol. NetWare 5.1 is a Web-based NOS with the following new servers included:

- NetWare Enterprise Web Server—Provides fast, reliable Web page hosting.
- NetWare News Server—Enables threaded discussion groups.
- NetWare FTP Server—Offers simplified file downloads.
- NetWare Multimedia Server—Supplies audio and video feeds over the network in .mpeg, .ra, .rm, and .wav file formats.
- NetWare Web Search Server—Indexes Web sites to simplify searches.

NetWare 5 integrates NDS with the industry-standard Domain Name System (DNS) and Dynamic Host Configuration Protocol (DHCP). NetWare 5 supports Java applications and the Common Object Request Broker Architecture (CORBA) Object Request Broker (ORB). Netware 5 has a multi-processing kernel. Additional NetWare 5 features include a next generation filesystem, printing services, and advanced security that has public-key cryptography and Secure Authentication Services (SAS).

NetWare 5.1 simplifies administration tasks with the NetWare Management Portal™ (NMP). NetWare 5.1 servers and filesystems are managed through a Web browser from any location in a network. Some tasks performed through the Web browser connecting with a NetWare 5.1 server running the NMP include mounting and dismounting volumes, monitoring system resources, browsing the NDS tree, and many other routine management tasks.

NetWare 5.1 supports all open Internet standards, including LDAP V3. LDAP accesses directory information from many different directories. NetWare 5.1 contains expanded support for HTTP and WebDAV (WWW Distributed Authoring and Versioning). The WebDAV protocol integrated into NetWare 5.1 permits you to serve files from Microsoft Office 2000 Web folders. WebDAV builds Web-based administration tools for specific network functions such as printing.

Novell software is predominantly client/server LAN software. Novell's NetWare provides both server and client software. The server software is licensed for a specific number of active client stations. Novell's NetWare is high-performance disk and print serving LAN server software. NetWare has always been robust server software. Until Novell's failure to bundle TCP/IP protocols with both NetWare 3.x and early 4.x servers and clients, and its migration to the more complex NDS LAN management, it led the market in LAN server (NOS) installations. Today, Windows and UNIX are more dominant in the high-end enterprise LAN market.

UNIX

UNIX is an operating system that was developed at Bell Labs in 1969 as an interactive time-sharing system. UNIX has evolved into many different variations. Different companies wrote their own versions of UNIX, such as HP UNIX, Sun Solaris UNIX and even Linux. Linux is freeware with different extensions that may someday compete with Microsoft. Businesses, universities, and individuals developed these UNIX versions. Because UNIX was not a proprietary operating system owned by a single computer company and because UNIX is written in the standardized C programming language, UNIX became the first standard open operating system. As an open operating system, UNIX could be improved or enhanced by anyone.

IEEE standardized the C language and UNIX user command interfaces as the Portable Operating System Interface (POSIX). POSIX interfaces specified in the X/Open Programming Guide 4.2 became known as UNIX 95, or the Single UNIX Specification. Version 2 of the Single UNIX Specification is labeled UNIX 98. The Open Group, an industry standards organization which certifies and brands UNIX implementations, owns the "official" trademarked UNIX.

UNIX operating systems are used in workstations produced by Sun Microsystems, Silicon Graphics, and IBM. UNIX and its client/server program model played a key role in Internet development and in reshaping computing to center it in networks of computers rather than in individual computers.

Other companies also have their own proprietary version of UNIX. Linux is a UNIX derivative. Linux has both free software and commercial versions. Linux is increasing in popularity as an alternative to proprietary operating systems.

UNIX software is used heavily in Internet servers and databases because of its performance, security features, and reliability. It is server software but has been adapted to perform client operations as well. Client UNIX requires an easy-to-use GUI to front-end the cryptic command level interface. The availability of hardware driver programs for UNIX software may also be an issue. The best things about UNIX software are:

- Some versions of UNIX are free. The Linux version of UNIX can be downloaded off the Internet.
- UNIX is very efficient. UNIX running on an old, tired 486 CPU can handle communications loads that would stress Windows NT running on a 400MHz CPU.
- UNIX has very good security features if you know how to effectively implement them.

- UNIX supports TCP/IP, SPX/IPX (Sequenced Packet Exchange/Internet Packet Exchange), and NETBEUI.
- UNIX software is very reliable and robust. Many high-performance Internet servers run some version of UNIX.

Linux is free and available for download over the Internet. However, the easiest way to install Linux is to use CD-ROMs because installation from CD-ROM is automatic. Internet installations are done manually. CD-ROM collections, known as distributions, can be purchased for a small fee. A standard distribution typically includes more than just the necessary Linux OS software. A distribution includes programming languages, editors, hardware drivers, window managers, and other CD-ROMs of software that may contain well over 1,000 individual programs.

The primary benefits of Linux as an operating system are its reliability and performance and also the cost (Windows and NetWare licenses can cost into the hundreds of thousands of dollars for a large enterprise). A difficulty with UNIX is learning the interface because it is very cryptic. This means that a Windows-like shell needs to be added to make UNIX usable by humans. Windows shells for UNIX have been around a long time. Hardware driver support may also be limited. This is not good if you want to play Quake using the latest Voodoo 3 graphics card on your UNIX system. UNIX is one of the most reliable and oldest operating systems used. We see Linux software interfaces at OSI Layers 6 and 7.

LAN Protocol Suites

Now let's look at OSI Layers 3, 4, and 5, the communication software layers.

LANs and computer networks use several protocols that together comprise the overall structure of the network. The set of protocols used within a network is called a protocol suite—the protocols that must work together seamlessly to provide network services. Protocol suite software is one set of functions found in the OSI reference model. It involves OSI Layer 3, network, OSI Layer 4, transport, and sometimes the OSI Layer 5, session.

The OSI model explanation of how each layer is applied to the LAN marketplace today gives us a good basis for understanding how OSI-compliant protocols are key to today's LANs and how they apply to NOSs. In particular, it describes how the NOS protocol stack uses the OSI model.

The most common protocol suites are:

- TCP/IP.
- SPX/IPX

- NetBEUI.

NOS and Windows client software implement these protocol suites. It is a matter of choosing one protocol suite and configuring the NOS and clients to use that protocol suite. It is possible to run all protocol suites on a LAN simultaneously. However, some protocol suites are more efficient than others, resulting in lower network traffic.

Protocol suites, or stacks, are implemented in software. They exchange data across multiple LANs and can deliver data to remote computers via the Internet.

The software above protocol suites is middleware. Middleware translates and manages information exchange between applications residing on different computers. Middleware software is in the OSI session and presentation layers. Middleware functions are handled through separate protocols. In the Internet, middleware functionality is divided between TCP software (part of the networking software) and application software (see Figure 6-54).

The software on the top of the OSI stack is the network applications. They use printer, disk, and file sharing to support distributed computing functions. The applications are the sources and destinations for network data. Network applications are for email (for example, cc:Mail, Microsoft Mail, X.400), file transfer, and document exchange.

TCP/IP

The TCP/IP protocol stack dominates LAN and enterprise communications because the Internet established it as a de facto standard and because Windows standardized the interface to the TCP/IP protocol suite software for Windows applications. The Windows standardized TCP/IP application interface is known as Winsock32—the 32-bit Windows software socket for TCP/IP communications. UNIX systems, NetWare, and mainframe computers use TCP/IP as well. TCP/IP is the most universal protocol stack.

Let's briefly examine both the services and applications associated with the TCP/IP suite. Following is a list of some TCP/IP services:

- The Internet Protocol (IP).
- The Internet Control Messaging Protocol (ICMP).
- The Address Resolution Protocol (ARP).
- The reverse ARP.
- Datagrams, and the User Datagram Protocol (UDP).
- Virtual circuits, and the Transmission Control Protocol (TCP).

These transport services are used by TCP applications to establish internetwork links and to transfer data between systems attached to those

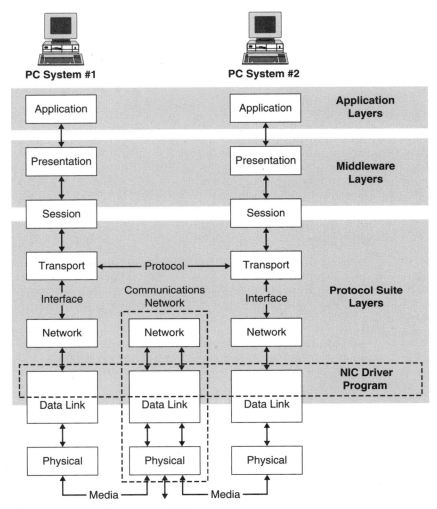

Figure 6–54 *Software vs. OSI layers.*

links. The TCP/IP protocol suite provides extended network services. The following are the software applications operating in the upper OSI layers:

- Simple Mail Transport Protocol (SMTP).
- File Transfer Protocol (FTP).
- Standard terminal access application—level network (TELNET) protocol.
- Programming interfaces.
- The AT&T Streams Transport Layer Interface (TLI).
- UNIX 4.3 BSD sockets.

- NFS.
- Trivial file transfer protocol.

Other TCP/IP networking services involve external data representation, remote procedure calls, and security. TCP/IP software today runs on Windows 95/98/ME and NT/2000 using a Windows 32-bit TCP/IP API called Winsock-32. Similar TCP/IP capabilities are available for UNIX and NetWare applications (see Figure 6-55).

TCP/IP is a routable protocol because each network end-point is assigned a four-number (32-bit) numeric address at the IP layer—OSI Layer 3. These addresses are used to route IP traffic across multiple networks, including the Internet. A typical IP address is 208.80.34.0. This is similar to a country (208), state (80), city (34), and street (0) address structure.

IP address numbers vary from 0 to 255. A 0 address identifies a network and 1 address a network gateway. So, the 208.80.34.0 address represents a network, and 208.80.34.1 would be a router to that network. Networks use subnet masks to communicate between network components in the same network. A subnet mask is 255.255.255.0. This means that the first three address numbers remain the same for communications within a given subnet.

IP addresses can be assigned as required to LAN clients using DHCP. With DHCP, a client sends out a general broadcast message requesting an IP address. A DHCP server leases or loans an IP address from a pool of IP addresses it manages to that client for a predetermined period of time. When the time expires, the client releases the IP address.

TCP/IP is a very efficient protocol stack. At the TCP layer, it is connection-oriented. It establishes fixed logical channels from client to server. At the IP layer, it is connectionless, with IP packets routed dynamically by routers using routing algorithms based upon network connectivity and cost factors. When a network link fails, IP packets are immediately routed over alternate links to their destinations. The routing algorithms assure that IP packets are routed consistently to their destinations. Routes only change when a link becomes congested or fails.

Virtually all LANs run the TCP/IP protocol stack. In the near future, TCP/IP is likely to become the protocol stack used exclusively on every LAN.

SPX/IPX

NetWare uses the Sequenced Packet Exchange/Internet Packet Exchange (SPX/IPX) protocol. It is a very chatty protocol, requiring lots of handshaking to transfer data across the LAN. Windows supports SPX/IPX for commu-

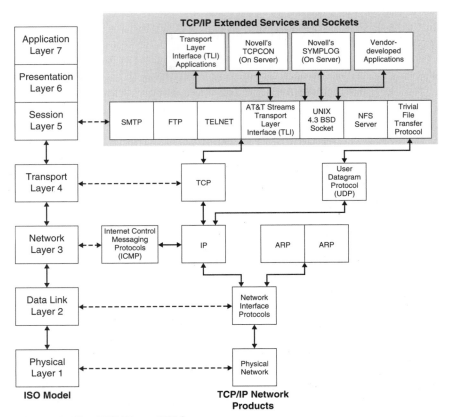

Figure 6–55 *TCP/IP vs. OSI layers*

nications to NetWare servers. SPX/IPX is also a routable protocol because network components have numeric addresses. SPX/IPX is mostly found in Novell NetWare-based LANs and TCP/IP is used in most other LANs.

NetBEUI

Microsoft originally used the NetBIOS Extended User Interface (NetBEUI) protocol in its products. NetBEUI identifies LAN components by a name and numeric address. This worked fine for small LANs, but not well for large ones because without numeric addresses, NetBEUI cannot be routed. Without a numeric address, NetBEUI does not provide sufficient routing information in each frame to easily route packets from source to destination.

Others

IBM's LU6.2/PU2.1 is a protocol stack that evolved from IBM's original SNA terminal to host protocols. Because the products implementing this protocol use centralized network control, its use is primarily in IBM SNA networks, and not in most LANs today.

The Microsoft 32-bit Data Link Control (DLC) protocol can establish multiple connections to different IBM mainframe and AS/400 computers using the same network adapter. The 32-bit DLC protocol software lets a network administrator add support for Windows-based 32-bit programs that use the Command and Control Block 2 (CCB2) interface and 16-bit programs that use the Command and Control Block 1 (CCB1) interface.

The 32-bit DLC protocol provides connectivity to local area printers connected directly to the network. For example, the DLC protocol can be used to print to a printer that uses an adapter to connect directly to the network rather than to a port on a print server. DLC must be installed and running on the print server for the printer, but it does not need to be installed on the PCs sending print jobs to the print server. To use the DLC protocol device driver, a network printer must be created in the **Printers** folder on the PC.

Brain Teaser

Network Software and Protocol Stacks

Use a Windows PC and open the **Network Properties** window using the **Control Panel** and **Network** selections. In the **Network Properties** panel, scroll down to see what protocol stack software is installed in the Windows PC.
1. Is TCP/IP installed?
2. Are other protocol stacks installed as well?
3. Check out the TCP/IP stack by highlighting it, binding to the PC's NIC, and then clicking the **Properties** button. Is a fixed IP address specified or is "**Obtain an IP address automatically**" selected? What subnet mask is used?
4. Is a gateway identified under the **Gateway** tab? Does it have a 1, 2, 3, 4, or 5 address?
This exercise is to help you understand the implementation of TCP/IP protocol suites in LANs and Windows clients.

LAN Telecommunications Applications

This is the payoff for building and operating an enterprise LAN. The applications are what users in the organization rely on to accomplish their daily work. For our researching and writing for seminars and consulting activity, we need a LAN that has excellent and reliable disk storage and high-speed Internet access. Without these capabilities, our work would be many times more difficult than it is.

Other key applications for enterprise LANs are groupware, Voice over IP (VoIP), video teleconferencing, and client/server applications. Now let's examine OSI Layer 7, or the applications that run on our LAN.

Groupware

"Groupware" is a term used to identify collaborative software. This goes beyond simple email. Groupware programs help people work together collectively while located remotely from each other. Groupware services include sharing calendars, collective writing, email handling, shared database access, and electronic meetings. Each person using the groupware can see and display information with others.

With groupware, groups of people share a common database of information and interact with that information to produce reports, coordinate business activities, and more. Lotus Notes is groupware software that runs on a variety of LANs.

Lotus Notes lets an enterprise develop communications and database applications so that users at different geographic locations can share files with each other and exchange comments on them publicly or privately. Lotus Notes keeps track of development schedules, work projects, guidelines and procedures, plans, white papers, and other documents. Lotus Notes works with multimedia files. Notes tracks changes to the database and updates copies of any database replicas in use with the changes.

A Lotus Domino Server extends the capabilities of Lotus Notes to include integrated messaging and a Web application software development and implementation platform. A Domino Server is special software that runs as an application on Windows, NetWare, and UNIX servers. Replicated Notes databases on Windows servers are updated using Remote Procedure Call (RPC) requests. Notes coordinates with Web servers and applications on a company's intranet.

Basic email and calendar applications come with Notes. In addition, Notes provides capabilities for users to create their own document-oriented applications. Notes is not transaction-oriented. Notes was designed to handle large work projects. Microsoft Exchange is a comparable product, but lacks the application development tools that Notes provides.

Voice Over IP

VoIP is voice communications delivered using IP. VoIP sends voice information digitally in IP packets rather than in circuit-switched 64-Kbps digital streams used in the switched telephone network. VoIP and Internet telephony are compelling because they avoid the common telephone toll charges for long-distance and international calls and consolidate voice and video over the same network.

VoIP equipment providers are promoting the use of ITU-T H.323 through the VoIP Forum. H.323 is a standard for sending voice and video using IP on the Internet and within intranets. The VoIP Forum also promotes directory service standards so that callers can locate the parties they want to call. VoIP directory services use touch-tone signals for automatic call distribution and voice mail.

VoIP uses the Real-Time Protocol (RTP) to deliver packets with sufficient speed, to ensure good voice quality, and to meet a specific QoS level. With public networks, QoS is difficult to guarantee. Better QoS is attainable over private IP networks. Another technique that helps ensure fast packet delivery is pinging all network gateway computers accessing the Internet and then using the fastest path for a VoIP connection to the called LAN component.

VoIP routing is incorporated into the LAN Internet gateway. It receives packetized voice transmissions from users within an enterprise. The VoIP-enabled gateway then routes the packetized voice to intranet components or sends them over the Public Switched Telephone Network (PSTN) using T-1 or E-1 interfaces.

VoIP vendors include Cisco, VocalTec, Lucent, Nortel, 3Com, and Netspeak.

Video Teleconferencing

Video teleconferencing is interactive video communications between people in separate locations. Simple video teleconferencing transmits static images and text between two locations. More sophisticated video teleconferencing transmits full-motion video images and high-quality audio between multiple locations.

Video teleconferencing software and high-speed LAN connections are turning PCs into universal communications appliances. Microsoft's Net-

Meeting combined with an inexpensive Webcam (a PC-attached camera) provide easy and cheap live connections to remote friends or family. The audio and video quality in this case is not high. Regardless, the benefits of a video link and long-distance savings are compelling.

For businesses, video teleconferencing lowers travel costs. Better customer service can be provided using video teleconferencing. Other video teleconferencing benefits include facilitation of group work among geographically distant teammates and developing a stronger sense of community among day-to-day business contacts. Video teleconferencing users chat, transfer files, share programs, send and receive graphic data, and operate computers from remote locations. Face-to-face connection adds non-verbal communication to the exchange and allows participants to develop a stronger sense of familiarity with individuals they may never physically meet.

A videoconference is a phone call with video that someday is most likely to become the primary mode of distance communication for business and consumer communications.

Client/Server Applications

In client/server applications, a client computer program requests service from a server program, which fulfills the request. Clients are best at displaying information. Servers are designed to perform background database query and response processing functions. In LANs, the client/server interconnects programs distributed across multiple locations. For example, a client/server computer transaction to check a bank account from a client program in a PC creates a request. The request is sent to a server at a bank. That server in turn passes the request to its own client program. The server's client program now sends a request to a database server in another bank computer. That computer retrieves the account information and prepares a response. The response is returned back to the first server's client, which in turn passes the response back to the original PC client, which displays the information.

In the Internet, a Web browser is a client program that requests Web pages or files from a Web server. A Web server is Hypertext Transport Protocol (HTTP) server software running in a computer somewhere on an IP network or the Internet. Similarly, computers running TCP/IP make client requests for files from FTP servers.

Today's business applications are written using the client/server model. The newest twist is that these client/server applications are accessed using Web browser clients. These client/server applications run in intranets, extranets, and the Internet. E-commerce applications are an example of Web browser-accessible client/server applications.

Brain Teaser

LAN Applications

Use the Web to go to the Lotus Notes Web site (www.Lotus.com) and select products.
1. Notes is a product that does what?
2. Lotus Domino Servers provide what?
3. Is there a Lotus product equivalent to Microsoft's NetMeeting product?
This exercise illustrates some software supporting LAN applications.

■ Summary

This chapter has completed the basic information that lays the foundation for examining and discussing ways to save costs and increase business by using telecommunications. Three areas of knowledge comprise this foundation: voice communications, or telephony; data communications, or WAN communications; and LANs. LANs cover the last few feet of the communications channel to the PC—the universal communications appliance.

In this chapter, we discussed LAN types, including peer-to-peer and client/server LANs. Most LANs are hybrids having both peer-to-peer and client/server connections. A LAN market summary identifying popular LAN wiring (media), NICs, and NOS software was presented. Then a tour of LAN internetworking components and their functions was conducted. The IEEE specifications were identified.

LAN media (cabling) and cabling hardware were examined in some detail, along with servers and server features that make them reliable and robust. Windows, NetWare, and UNIX LAN software and LAN protocol suites were explored. Finally, we concluded with a preliminary discussion of LAN applications. More detailed discussion of these applications follows when we look at saving costs and expanding business capabilities.

Now you have seen all the items needed to build a LAN. At OSI Layer 1 is the wire, like CAT-5 UTP wire. At OSI Layer 2 is the hardware protocol, like Ethernet's CSMA/CD, which we pick by selecting a PC LAN card. At OSI Layers 3, 4 and 5 is the LAN protocol suite software, like TCP/IP. Finally, at OSI Layer 6 is the operating system, like Windows 98/ME/2000, and at OSI Layer 7 is the application program, like NetMeeting. As you can see, our network is composed of just a few hardware, wiring, and software components.

▲ Chapter Review Questions

1. *How many active peer-to-peer connections can Windows 95/98/ME and NT/2000 support?*

   A. 100

   B. 10

   C. Unlimited

   D. None

2. *What are popular LAN NICs?*

   A. Token ring, ArcNet, Ethernet

   B. Ethernet, ArcNet, ATM

   C. Ethernet, ATM, token ring

   D. None of the above

3. *What is the most widely used NIC?*

   A. Ethernet

   B. Token ring

   C. ArcNet

   D. None of the above

4. *What wiring can Ethernet use?*

   A. Fiber

   B. Twisted pair

   C. Coaxial cable

   D. All of the above

   E. None of the above

5. *What is the most popular LAN wiring?*

   A. Fiber

   B. Twisted pair

   C. Coaxial cable

   D. UTP CAT-3

   E. CAT-5

6. *What features make servers robust and reliable?*
   A. Hot-swappable power supplies
   B. Multiple CPUs
   C. Error detecting and correcting RAM
   D. Hot-swappable fans

7. *What is the IEEE designation for Ethernet?*
   A. IEEE 802.5
   B. IEEE 802.11
   C. IEEE 802.2
   D. IEEE 802.3
   E. IEEE 802.4

8. *The Universal Naming Convention (UNC) designates servers how?*
   A. \
   B. \\
   C. First
   D. Last

9. *How fast is Ethernet?*
   A. 10 Mbps
   B. 100 Mbps
   C. 1 Gbps
   D. 10 Gbps
   E. A, B, and C
   F. All of the above

10. *What internetworking components work in OSI Layers 1 and 2?*
    A. Repeaters
    B. Switches
    C. Gateways
    D. Routers

11. *What internetworking components work on the same layers?*
    A. Switches and bridges
    B. Repeaters and bridges
    C. Routers and gateways
    D. Clients and servers

12. *What is an Internet gateway?*

    A. A switch

    B. A bridge

    C. A gateway

    D. A router

13. *What are the hottest LAN applications?*

    A. VoIP and disk serving

    B. Groupware and printer serving

    C. VoIP and Web-based client/server applications

    D. Disk and printer sharing

14. *What RAID level is the most expensive to implement?*

    A. 0

    B. 1

    C. 0+1

    D. 5

15. *What RAID level requires only one disk to back up three other disks?*

    A. 0

    B. 1

    C. 0+1

    D. 5

16. *Ethernet uses what MAC protocol?*

    A. Token passing

    B. DLC

    C. Bus collision

    D. CSMA/CD

17. *TCP/IP runs on?*

    A. Ethernet

    B. Token ring

    C. ArcNet

    D. ATM

    E. All of the above

    F. A, B, and D

18. *What software is most likely to be Microsoft's biggest competitor?*
    A. NetWare
    B. UNIX
    C. DOS
    D. POSIX

19. *What wiring specification covers premises wiring?*
    A. IEEE 802.3
    B. EIA RS-232 D
    C. TIA/EIA-568
    D. CAT-5

20. *Single-mode fiber is described by* _____
    A. 125/62.5
    B. T-568a
    C. 125/8.3
    D. CAT-5

Saving Telecommunications Costs

This chapter describes telecommunications networking technology products that can be used to reduce telecommunications communications costs. There are two general networking choices today: packet-switched or circuit-switched. Circuit-switched technologies are ISDN, T-1, and SONET. When you think of circuit-switched technologies, what should come to mind is a pipe that makes a point-to-point connection. Circuit-switched technologies carry voice, video, and data. They provide excellent Quality of Service (QoS), but are not the most efficient form of networking. Circuit-switched technologies are sometimes priced on distance, the longer the circuit the more costly it becomes. Circuit-switched technologies fit largely in OSI Layer 1.

Packet-switched technologies are X.25, frame relay, SMDS, and ATM. These technologies were originally used for data and not voice. Now, packet-switched technologies are used to carry data, voice, and video. When you think of packet-switched technologies, you should see information chopped up and placed in buckets and sent across a common network. The advantage of packet-switched is lower overall costs in many situations because facilities are more efficiently used and distance does not influence pricing. There are charges to connect to a packet-switched network (often illustrated as a cloud) at both data source and data destination. There are no distance charges with packet-switched networks, however, there may be bandwidth or usage charges for packet-switched networks. Packet-switched technologies provide a lower QoS than circuit-switched technologies because information can require more time to traverse the network. Such delays are not good for voice and video traffic. In contrast, data traffic has few problems with such delays.

Now it is time to examine several cost-saving services and technologies, including Integrated Services Digital Network (ISDN), packet-switched networks, digital networking technologies, RF and satellite communications, and cellular communications. The first service examined is ISDN. The chapter covers basic ISDN technology and services and then examines the status of current ISDN service offerings. ISDN drawbacks and cost saving applications are described.

Integrated Services Digital Network

We touched on the Integrated Services Digital Network (ISDN) in the last two chapters. As mentioned, ISDN is a telecommunications networking architecture using digital transmission for integrated voice, data, video, and image services over standard twisted pair telephone wire. Think of ISDN as an intelligent pipe. ISDN is defined by CCITT/ITU standards, which specify digital transmission over ordinary telephone copper wire and other media.

ISDN as a digital phone connection has been available for over a decade. It is widely available throughout the U.S.; however, in some areas, ISDN remains quite expensive. ISDN is a service supporting low-end video conferencing, branch office LAN-to-LAN interconnection, and Internet access. ISDN meets international standards that define interfaces between telecommunications equipment and intelligent telephone networks.

ISDN uses a separate Data channel (D channel) for supervisory signaling. It sends information about a call along with the call. An ISDN network configuration is shown in Figure 7-1.

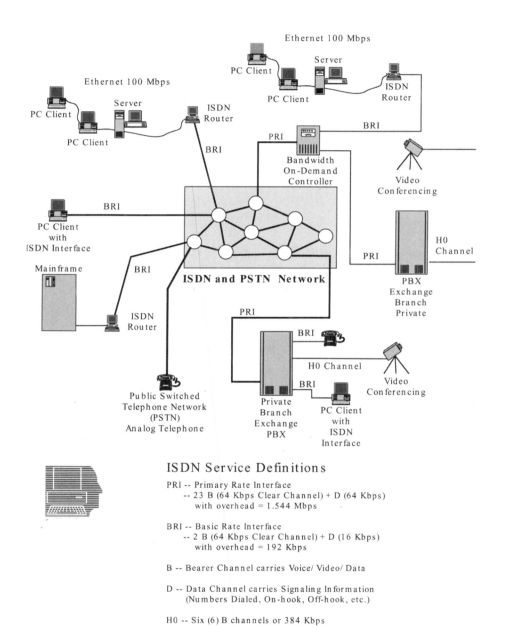

Figure 7–1 *ISDN networking architecture.*

Services and Applications

ISDN services can be narrowband or broadband services. Current ISDN narrowband offerings are Basic Rate Interface (BRI) and Primary Rate Interface (PRI). They differ in aggregate transmission capacity and channel configuration. Narrowband ISDN has aggregate speeds from 128 Kbps to 1.544 Mbps for the U.S. and up to 2.038 Mbps in Europe.

BEARER CHANNELS, OR B CHANNELS

An ISDN channel carries voice, data, image, or facsimile information over Bearer (B) channels at 64 Kbps. The B channels allow voice or data to be transmitted digitally around the planet. A 64-Kbps B channel is the equivalent of a single phone line. These B channels are clear channels, with the full 64 Kbps being available to handle voice, image, or data transmission.

While ISDN carries voice and data over 64-Kbps B channels, sometimes CO switches limit B channels to a capacity of 56 Kbps. B channels are provided two to 24 for basic ISDN services.

DATA OR DELTA (SIGNALING) CHANNELS, OR D CHANNELS

The B channels are combined by ISDN with a separate channel for signaling transmission. This is the Data or Delta (D) channel. The D channel carries signaling at 16 Kbps to 64 Kbps using HDLC (High-Level Data Link Control protocol)—LAPD (Link Access Protocol Data). The D channel may also carry other packet-switched data to and from an intelligent telephone network.

The two basic types of ISDN service are: BRI and PRI.

BASIC RATE INTERFACE—2B+D

The BRI consists of two 64-Kbps B channels and one 16-Kbps D channel for a total of 144-Kbps usable bandwidth. This basic service is intended for residential users. A BRI is sometimes referred to as 2B+D.

The B channels carry circuit-switched voice and other digital transmissions. Control signaling for call establishment, call monitoring, call termination, and enhanced telephone features use common channel signaling on the D channel. The D channel's speed of 16 Kbps is more than adequate to handle the signaling information for the two B channels in a BRI.

To get BRI service, a customer must be within 18,000 feet (about 3.4 miles, or 5.5 km) of the telephone company Central Office (CO). Beyond that distance, repeaters are required, or ISDN service may not be available at all. Customers also need special equipment to communicate with the phone company switch and with other ISDN devices such as ISDN Terminal Adapters (TAs), which are sometimes called ISDN modems.

PRIMARY RATE INTERFACE—23B+D

The PRI has 23 B channels and a full 64-Kbps D channel for an aggregate transmission capacity of 1.536 Mbps available to the user. The PRI is provided over a T-1 specification communication link of 1.544 Mbps with 8 Kbps used for transmission overhead. In Europe, PRIs consist of 31 B channels plus one 64-Kbps D channel for a combined speed of 2048 Kbps. PRIs interconnect medium and large PBXs, ISDN multiplexers, and mainframes to each other or to a telephone company CO.

PRI is targeted at business users with greater capacity requirements. It is possible to cover multiple PRIs with one 64-Kbps D channel using Non-Facility Associated Signaling (NFAS). Telephone companies like PRI customers to have at least two PRIs with D channels before they provide a PRI with no D channel. In this manner, the customer has a D channel backup in the event of a network outage.

ISDN PRI call-by-call service allows PRI channels to support different mixes of services as needed such as 800, 900, or WATS. Customer PBXs perform service reconfigurations automatically using the D channel ISDN interface to negotiate the changes with the ISDN network.

H channels aggregate B channels. They are defined as:

- H0=384 Kbps (6 B channels).
- H10=1472 Kbps (23 B channels).
- H11=1536 Kbps (24 B channels).
- H12=1920 Kbps (30 B channels)—international (E1) only.

H channels carry high-speed circuit-switched traffic like video teleconferencing calls.

BROADBAND ISDN SERVICES

Broadband ISDN (B-ISDN) is designed to provide transmission capacity suitable for high-quality television, video teleconferencing, video telephony, image, and high-bandwidth data communications. B-ISDN channels can provide aggregate bit rates around 155 Mbps and 622 Mbps. B-ISDN is intended for widespread use in five years. Defined B-ISDN service categories are interactive services and distributive services.

Interactive services are:

- Conversational services, including video telephony, video teleconferencing, and high-speed data transmission. Conversational services are typically bi-directional, real-time data transfers between users or between a user and a host.
- Message services provide communication using intermediate data storage such as a mailbox. There are speech, video, and high-resolution image message services.
- Retrieval services provide access to centrally stored information. Data is accessed on demand. Retrieval services include video and high-resolution images combined with audio.

Distributive services are services with user presentation control, like broadcast services for TV and radio.

B-ISDN's high bandwidth enables different types of information to be delivered by a service. For example, video telephony might include audio, video, and text as well as icons and other graphics.

Broadband services, such as video signal transmission, require on-demand variable bandwidth. This is best delivered by cell switching technology. For this reason, the European International Telecommunications Union (ITU) picked ATM as the transfer mode for B-ISDN.

ISDN VOICE SERVICES

ISDN voice services include simple, one-touch activation voice features such as:

- Call transfer.
- Call forwarding.
- Conference calling.
- Call pickup.
- Intercom.
- Caller ID.
- Multiple call appearances.
- Shared call appearances.

Call transfer, call forwarding, conference calling, call pickup, and intercom services are basic services provided by ISDN in combination with Central Office Exchange switching (CENTREX). Other services are less focused on CENTREX. Caller ID service presents the number for each incoming call and potentially the caller's name. ISDN caller ID uses an Incoming Line Identifier (ICLID) to provide the number of the calling party to the called party. Multiple call appearances permits making or receiving multiple calls simultaneously on the same phone number. The phone number appears on separate buttons, with each button functioning like a separate line. The subscriber is charged only for a single ISDN line. This cuts down on busy signals and calls that roll over into voice messaging. Shared call appearances permit a phone number be assigned to multiple telephones throughout an office. When there is no one to answer the phone at a specific desk, calls are answered by a live person at another desk. ISDN is compatible with current analog telephones, permitting easy migration to ISDN.

ISDN HIGH-SPEED DATA

ISDN supports special transaction services. Transaction services enable the processing of electronic transactions faster by eliminating time-consuming dial-ups for modem-based transaction processing. This is aimed at retail stores electronically verifying credit card transactions. Typical transaction time drops from 20-30 seconds to just six seconds.

ISDN transaction services are best for businesses processing 15 to 200 electronic transactions a day. These businesses include retailers, gas stations, medical service providers, restaurants, insurance companies, travel agents, banks with ATMs, and many others. With ISDN, the lines used for transaction services can also be used for phones, faxes, computers, and even video monitoring and surveillance applications.

Using an ISDN BRI, the two B channels carry voice, data, and image communications while the D channel handles packet data and call management. Transactions are fast and reliable because the D channel interfaces the transaction processing terminals to a telephone company's X.25 packet data network. The telephone company's X.25 packet data network simultaneously switches millions of data packets to and from locations across the U.S. It can connect into the ISDN transaction support service providers directly.

Faster transactions improve customer satisfaction, while less time online can result in lower usage fees and most certainly higher productivity. ISDN supports telephone calls, fax calls, computer Internet access, and transaction processing all with the same line.

ISDN permits BRI lines to bind both B channels into a single high-speed (128-Kbps) channel for connection to the Internet or any other backbone data network. ISDN PRIs can bind together six B channels to form one H0 channel for switched video teleconferencing calls between facilities. H10 and H11 B channel aggregations are possible for even higher speed circuit-switched transmission between facilities.

ISDN Service Implementation

ISDN requires new telecommunications hardware components. Special interface cards (sometimes called ISDN modems) are required for multimedia PCs to interconnect with ISDN channels. Digital ISDN phones are needed to make voice calls over the ISDN network. The good news is that no special software beyond a driver program for special ISDN interface boards is required to use ISDN.

PBXs and Hybrid-Key systems do require ISDN interfaces for either the BRI or PRI to work with ISDN. They may also require software upgrades to function fully with the intelligent phone network.

Because ISDN is defined as an international standard there are differences between the U.S. and international implementations. In the U.S., telephone companies provide a BRI to customers using a U interface running over a 2-wire (single pair) loop from the telco Branch Exchange (BX) switch. Because the single pair of wires (2-wire) provides full duplex data transmission, only a single device is connected to a U interface. The device is Network Termination 1, or NT-1 (see Figure 7-2).

The NT-1 converts the 2-wire U interface into a 4-wire S/T interface. The S/T interface supports up to seven devices on an S/T bus. It is also a full duplex interface with a separate pair of wires for receiving data and for transmitting data. Many devices have NT-1s built into their design, making them less expensive and easier to install. However, this reduces flexibility by preventing additional devices from being connected. Internationally, the PTTs supply the NT-1 and customers supply an S/T interface.

To conform to standards, ISDN devices must connect through a Network Termination 2 (NT-2). An NT-2 converts a T interface into an S interface. S and T interfaces are electrically equivalent. Virtually all ISDN devices include an NT-2. These NT-2 interfaces communicate with Terminal Equipment (TE) and handle Layer-2 and Layer-3 ISDN protocols. Components attached to an ISDN line most commonly expect either a U interface because they have a built-in NT-1, or an S/T interface connection.

Inside the telephone switch the U interface connects the telco BX switch to the CPE. This local loop connection is called a Line Termination (LT) function. Connection to other telco BX switches within the phone network is called an Exchange Termination (ET) function. LT and ET functions communicate via a V interface.

The BRI–U interface from the telco is a 2-wire, 160-Kbps digital connection. Echo cancellation reduces noise and data encoding schemes (2B1Q

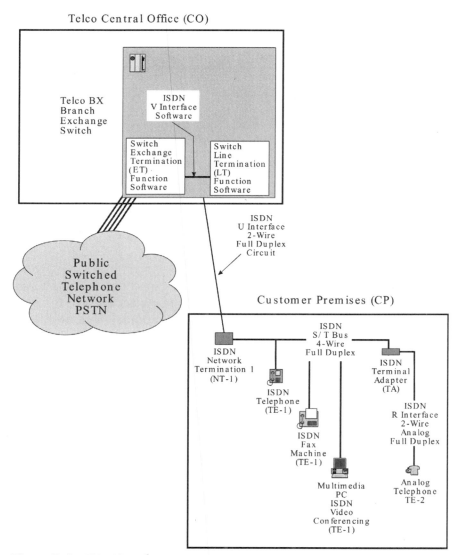

Figure 7–2 *ISDN interfaces.*

in North America, 4B3T internationally) permit this data rate over ordinary single-pair local loops.

The 2 Binary 1 Quaternary (2B1Q) encoding scheme is the most common signaling method for U interfaces. This protocol, defined in ANSI spec T1.601, provides two bits per baud, 80K bauds per second, and a transfer rate of 160 Kbps (see Table 7-1).

Table 7.1   *2B1Q Data Encoding Voltages*

Bits	Quaternary Symbol	Voltage Level
00	−3	−2.5
01	−1	−0.833
10	3	2.5
11	1	0.833

In 2B1Q, the voltages can have four distinct levels, with 0 Volts not being a valid voltage level. These levels, or quaternaries, represent two data bits; so four unique voltage levels cover all combinations of two bits. Additional information on 2B1Q was in Chapter 5.

ISDN TERMINAL ADAPTERS

ISDN-capable telephones and fax machines, video teleconferencing equipment, bridge/routers, and TAs all expect the S/T (or S) interface. Devices designed for ISDN are designated Terminal Equipment 1 (TE-1).

All remaining communication devices are designated Terminal Equipment 2 (TE-2). These components are not ISDN-capable, but have a normal analog 2-wire telephone interface called an R interface. They include analog telephones, fax machines, and modems.

Terminal Adapters (TAs) connect a TE-2 component to an ISDN S/T bus.

CONSTRUCTING A CIRCUIT

The ISDN U interface uses a single twisted pair to carry full duplex transmission from the CO BX switch to the NT-1 component. From the NT-1 component, the S/T interface provides 4-wire, full duplex connections to ISDN TE—TE-1 and TAs, to be specific.

To convert an analog telephone local loop to ISDN operation, circuit construction is often required. The construction process removes loading coils from the local loop and tests the local loop end to end to assure that sufficient signal levels are present for accurate digital transmission. If not, repeaters may need to be added to the local loop.

ISDN LAN routers provide routing between ISDN BRI and the LAN by dialing up other routers based upon traffic demands from the LAN. An ISDN LAN router automatically establishes and releases circuit-switched calls as required to connect to remote sites based on internetworking traffic. The

ISDN LAN router controls establishing and releasing secondary B channels based on load thresholds.

Multi-link PPP provides bandwidth aggregation when using multiple ISDN B channels.

PC Terminal Adapters (PC-TAs) connect to PCs using internal adapters, or external adapters connecting the RS-232 serial ports to ISDN circuits. They are used like an analog internal and external modem. PC TAs provide a PC direct control over ISDN session initiation and release. This is identical to using an analog modem. Automated mechanisms must be provided to permit binding and unbinding the second B channel to achieve 128-Kbps connectivity.

NATIONAL ISDN-199X, OR NI-X

ISDN, in spite of being an international standard, is anything but homogenous. National ISDN (NI-x) is a mechanism for unifying ISDN services. There are three NI specifications, NI-1, NI-2, and NI-199X (NI-x) with each one building on the previous specification. ISDN devices meet NI-x compatibility, therefore they are more compatible with different ISDN CO switches.

SERVICE PROFILE IDENTIFIER NUMBER

National ISDN-2 (NI-2) uses SPIDs (Service Profile Identifiers). SPIDs are free-formatted numeric strings between 3 to 20 characters in length. The Local Exchange Carrier, or LEC (ISDN service provider), assigns SPIDs when the customer places an order for a BRI. The customer typically enters the SPID into the terminal before the terminal can initialize at Layer 3. SPIDs are used only inside North America.

The SPID number assigned to a fully initialized ISDN terminal enables the Stored Program Control Switching System (SPCS) to uniquely identify the ISDN terminal at Layer 3 of the D channel signaling protocol. There is no standard format for SPID numbers. As a result, SPID numbers vary depending on the switch vendor and carrier. Typical SPIDs are 0835866201 8358662 or 0835866401 8358664. Some ISDN switches require only one SPID per line, while others require one for each channel. The telephone service provider in your area should be able to tell you which SPIDs to use and how many SPIDs are required.

Each fully initialized ISDN terminal must be uniquely identified at Layer 3 for the SPCS to provide terminal-dependent features. When a terminal sends its SPID during Layer 3 initialization, the SPCS uses the SPID to associate the terminal with a specific set of terminal services (that have been previously provisioned in the SPCS). The telephone directory number of the terminal is not sufficient for this purpose because telephone directory numbers may not uniquely identify a terminal on an interface. Multiple terminals on a single BRI can use identical telephone directory numbers.

SPIDs simplify switch-based troubleshooting when multiple terminals are assigned to a BRI. Abnormality logs kept by the SPCS show SPIDs of terminals experiencing problems. For example, different terminal-dependent features need to be assigned when two phones are served by a single BRI. The phones share the same telephone directory number, but only one phone has call hold and conference calling features. In this case, separate sets of characteristics or profiles are provisioned in the SPCS for each phone. One profile includes call hold and conference calling; the other profile does not. When each phone initializes, the SPCS uses the terminal's SPID to provide the correct features and button assignment to the phone.

BONDING B CHANNELS

Bonding is a protocol that allows both B channels to combine and transmit a single data stream. The user places a single B channel call in the normal fashion, then the bonding protocol dials the subsequent calls needed to achieve the desired data rate, synchronizing the network delay between the respective B channels and aggregating the bandwidth to present a single data stream to the DTE (Data Terminal Equipment). A single BRI line with bonding can aggregate both 64-Kbps B channels to accommodate near 128 Kbps data throughput.

RFC (Request For Comment)-1717 is the Multi-link PPP protocol and it is not bonding. RFC-1717 is from the Internet Engineering Task Force (IETF). Bonding is used by ISDN to provide an aggregated link speed. Similarly, Multi-link PPP (MP) bundles multiple B channels for data rates over 64 Kbps. These bundled links can use different physical links such as ISDN, X.25, or frame relay, and work with synchronous and asynchronous transmission. MP is negotiated within the PPP protocol as a transmission option. A key difference is that MP supports dynamic bandwidth allocation, while bonding does not.

ISDN Costs

Connection and installation fees vary widely depending on the city where ISDN is installed (see Table 7-2).

Table 7.2   *ISDN Costs in Selected U.S. Cities*

City	Installation	Added Costs	Monthly	Per Minute
Memphis Nashville Knoxville (Bell South)	$41.50 to $59.50	Taxes Extra Jacks Inside Wiring	$29.50 to $40.50	None
Baltimore Richmond Charlestown, WV (Bell Atlantic)	$125 + $48.00	Inside Wiring	$30.35	$0.02/minute Peak $0.01/minute Off Peak
Hartford (SNET)	$265	$15 per additional number Extra Jacks	$50 + $7.50 per additional number	$0.035/minute Peak $0.015/minute Off Peak
St. Louis (SBC)	$400	Inside Wiring	$92	None
Dallas and Houston (SBC)	$78.60 to $328.60	Taxes Extra Jacks Inside Wiring	$58	None
San Francisco San Jose Los Angles (SBC)	$125	New Line $34.75	$29.50	$0.03 for first minute and $0.01/minute thereafter

Only one thing is certain, for widespread ISDN implementation, the access fees must come down. Flat-rate pricing must be offered, otherwise ISDN use is not practical.

The costs for a BRI for a business are higher than the costs of an ISDN BRI for a residence. Both the installation cost and monthly fee are greater for business BRIs.

PRI COSTS

Getting ISDN PRI pricing from a telephone company is like getting the price on a car that you want to buy. They really do not publish pricing that anyone can see. They charge so much that they are embarrassed by their prices. The prices presented here should be considered ballpark prices only. To do a detailed pricing analysis, a precise quote from the local telephone company is needed. These quotes include factors for installation costs and recurring charges for the mileage run.

Ballpark costs for as ISDN PRI service only using an existing T-1 facility are:

- Configuration Package 1: 23B+D $750 installation, $220 per mont.
- Configuration Package 2: 24B $750 installation, $220 per month.
- Configuration Package 3: 23B+backup D channel $750 installation, $270 per month.

These charges are probably in addition to T-1 charges. The backup D channel is available in case the facility with the main signaling channel goes down.

T-1 channel pricing and tariffs vary substantially. T-1 costs for a general PacBell T-1 channel according to the California Public Utility Commission (CPUC) 175-T tariff pricing of November 1, 1999 are:

- One-time installation—Channel terminations: $1001.38.
- Recurring monthly costs—Channel terminations, multiplexing, and fixed mileage recurring charges plus $23.71 per mile recurring charges: $663.76.

Channel termination charges are for terminations at the customer site and the IEC POP site. Each T-1 line requires CPE. For non-channelized service, the customer provides a Channel Service Unit (CSU) that costs from around $800 to $2500, depending on features and capabilities.

In Houston, an ISP published ballpark ISDN costs for connecting to them as $300 installation for a 384-Kbps ISDN channel and $755/month. For 512-Kbps ISDN channels, the costs were $400 installation and $977/month. The same ISP published a $1,250 installation cost and a $1,499/month charge for a full T-1 connection.

Similarly, our ISP, MDconnect.com, published this ballpark pricing for ISDN and T-1 channels:

T-1 point-to-point channel service charges are mileage-sensitive. All T-1 service is calculated on a circuit-by-circuit basis. Point-to-point T-1 pricing starts at $1,250/month. T-1 frame relay pricing for a 1,544-Kbps (T-1 channel equivalent) is $1,200 installation and $1,205/month. ISDN 24/7 connections require an $800 installation fee and $350/month for a 128-Kbps speed connection.

Saving Costs with ISDN

Because of its high price, ISDN is sometimes known as I Smell Dollars Now. There is no rationale to the published or quoted ISDN pricing from different telephone companies. The illogical pricing is a monument to regulation of the telephone industry. Fortunately, competition is coming with its favorable lowering of ISDN pricing.

ISDN does provide businesses with ways to save costs. Telecommunications costs are saved by using ISDN to back up mission-critical circuits, providing temporary connectivity for video teleconferencing and anticipated network overloads, and connecting remote workers. Further, ISDN provides better PBX integration with the telephone network, thus supporting advanced calling features.

Because it is a dial-up service where charges are incurred by the call, it provides excellent opportunities to save an enterprise money where they need a high-speed communications channel for short-duration connections.

BACK UP MISSION-CRITICAL CIRCUITS

You should back up circuits for mission-critical sites. By providing an ISDN dial-up capability for backup, an organization saves the money it would normally spend for a separate alternately routed dedicated backup circuit. Because ISDN call establishment times are short (less than analog call establishment times), a backup connection is completed quickly in the event a primary dedicated link fails.

SAVING TELECONFERENCING COSTS

Video teleconferencing performed using dedicated circuits between sites can be done using ISDN connections. A site's PBX initiates an H0 call to a remote site with video teleconferencing facilities that can accept an H0 call. This saves the cost of leasing 24/7 T-1 channels between sites to support the video teleconferencing.

PREDICTED DATA OVERLOADS

Data overloads can be handled by combining backup ISDN links with normal dedicated channels to provide added transmission capacity during peak periods. his is only effective when overloads can be predicted in advance, e.g., month-end closing activities.

TELECOMMUTER COST SAVINGS EXAMPLE

Because ISDN is available where other high-speed transmission technologies are not yet available, it can be used to connect remote workers into a central facility. The cost savings here is in lowering personnel costs because with ISDN connectivity to an enterprise's central facilities, workers can work from virtually anywhere. This means that talent can be recruited where labor costs are lower than in expensive areas, like Silicon Valley or Silicon Valley-East (Northern Virginia).

PBX TELEPHONE NETWORK INTEGRATION

ISDN provides better PBX integration with the telephone network because the D channel carries SS-7 signaling data directly to an ISDN PRI-attached PBX. This permits PBXs to use advanced SS-7 features and capabilities when acting like a call director, handling voice mail, routing calls outside the primary facility, and more. Keep in mind that ISDN is just an intelligent pipe.

Brain Teaser

Windows ISDN Support

Select **Network Neighborhood** on a Windows 98 system. Right-click and select **Properties**. Select **Add adapter** and see if you can find any ISDN adapters.
1. Did you find a Digi-International manufacturer listed? Were there any ISDN adapters listed for them? Did their adapters support S/T and U interfaces?
2. Are there other ISDN manufacturers? Did you find ISDN adapters from EICON Technology?
3. Are there ISDN adapters from Philips? US Robotics?
The purpose of this exercise is to illustrate the software support built into Windows for ISDN adapters.

Packet-switched Networks

Packet-switched networks are X.25 packet networks and fast packet (frame relay) networks. Cost savings and performance benefits can be realized by using packet networks in place of full-period, leased channel facilities. Let us examine first how packet-switched networks operate and then look at how they may be used to save telecommunications costs.

Packet-switched services were first aimed at data communications. These services were offered as Value Added Networks, or VANs. VANs first appeared in the mid 1970s. At that time, AT&T and other telephone companies could only sell communications services to end-users. Communications services could not be purchased from AT&T and the telephone companies and then resold. To act as a data communications carrier, Telenet petitioned the FCC to permit the resale of VANs. They claimed that Telenet used regular high-speed communications channels and packaged them with computer systems that added value to the basic communications channels. The added value was error-free, end-to-end transmission of data at a cost savings. Consequently, they should be permitted by the FCC to resell these value-added services. The rest is history.

My first publication was on the Telenet packet-switched network in the mid 1970s. It described how packets filled with only a few characters dramatically drove up the Telenet usage charges. The article included a fantastically fancy declining exponential curve. It was really awesome. At the time I worked as a consultant for a small communications consulting firm that no longer exists. But, I thought, "It is happening now baby! There will be consulting jobs galore. I am on my way." But nobody called. Not a soul. Humbling. The reason was that I missed the point with my publication. Certainly, what I described was true, but most all Telenet packets were packed to the rafters with data. Only a very, very small percentage had less than five characters in the packet (five was the number where packet costs began to rocket upward). Consequently, connect time charges comprised the major cost component in any Telenet bill and packet charges were of minor consequence.

Packet switching technology developed from those first VAN offerings. Soon VANs offered nationwide public network access. Telenet and Tymnet were early public packet network providers with access in 400 to 600 metropolitan areas nationwide. America Online (AOL) at one time used these public packet networks to support their subscribers nationwide. AOL used the Sprint network to connect to the public packet network originally created by Telenet. Today, Worldcom has largely acquired this AOL network access.

These public packet network vendors offered to set up private packet networks through the packet switching software used in their networks. Essentially, these private networks ran over public facilities, but kept the data private through definitions in the packet switching network software.

For some users, this was not enough. They demanded to purchase their own packet switching computers so they could establish a physically private packet-switched network. Banks were some of the types of organizations desiring physically separate packet networks. The most obvious reason for a physically separate packet network is increased security. The packet switching also lowered network costs because channels formerly dedicated to a single application that were redundant with other channels dedicated to different applications could now be combined into a single channel shared by all applications.

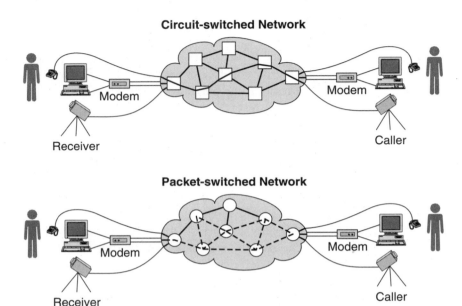

Figure 7–3 *Circuit vs. packet-switched network.*

Today the biggest public packet-switched network is the Internet. Further, any network employing TCP/IP software and HDLC Level-2 protocols is a private packet-switched network.

Circuit vs. Packet Switching

Dial-up connections are circuit switched because an exclusive physical electronic path between the calling and receiving end of a dial-up telephone call is established. Originally, the path was formed by two wires completing an end-to-end electrical circuit for communications, hence the term "circuit-switched." Today, there is not just one circuit between communications caller and receiver, but rather many physical electrical circuits. In circuit-switched connections, a fixed communications channel is established between the caller and the receiver (see Figure 7-3).

Packet switching takes data and breaks it into chunks, or packets. These packets are transmitted from caller to receiver over the network. However, they do not necessarily follow a fixed, rigid pathway (or channel) from source to destination, but rather may travel over many different channels (or paths) and may arrive at the destination out of sequence. In a packet-switched network, routing algorithms are used to direct the packets from caller to receiver. These algorithms assure consistent routing through the packet network. The only time a route changes is when a path is blocked or for some similar reason the routing algorithm selects a different path. Routing algorithms can change packet routing dynamically on-the-fly to adjust for sudden network outages or load increases.

With circuit switching, the full capacity of the channel is available to carry data from caller to receiver. With packet switching, the backbone network forces many users to share channels. This could mean that when the network was heavily loaded, the full channel capacity would not be available to carry packets from caller to receiver. The result would be slow network performance. However, with today's high-speed backbone networks, such overloads are truly non-existent. The only congestion occurs when there is only one route to use into the receiver's site or from the caller's site. These on and off links can sometimes be congested.

When a channel fails in a circuit-switched network, communications are disrupted. In contrast, packet-switched networks may experience outages that do not impact caller communications because data is re-routed dynamically on-the-fly over the remaining communications channels.

CIRCUIT-SWITCHED OR CONNECTION-ORIENTED SERVICES

Circuit-switched networks are referred to as connection-oriented networks because communications are completed with fixed channel connections. In the voice telephone network, there is a point-to-point fixed connection (time division multiplexed 64-Kbps channel) between the called party and the calling party.

In TCP/IP networks, at the TCP layer there is a connection-oriented path between the client and the server on the network. This is a logical one-to-one communications path between them.

PACKET-SWITCHED OR CONNECTION-LESS SERVICES

Packet-switched networks are referred to as connectionless services. They have no fixed path and no guarantee of packet delivery between source and destination. This works fine for data, but is not so good for voice.

Voice must arrive in sequence. There has to be a guaranteed delivery time for voice communications, often expressed as QoS. High service quality in this case does not mean low errors, but rather a guaranteed bit per second delivery rate.

The way to deliver voice over a connectionless service is to buffer the delivery. When there is sufficient transmission speed, voice comes into the buffer in chunks. The buffer then feeds it out at the constant prescribed transmission speed. TCP/IP networks at the IP layer are connectionless networks. There is no guaranteed delivery time for IP packets. Soon IP will be enhanced to permit priority traffic that meets a specific QoS transmission delay.

The X.25 Networks

X.25 networks use the X.25 standard to transfer data between nodes in the network. They support X.25 direct interfaces and terminal devices without X.25 interfaces. Non-X.25 terminals use TTY, BSC, and SDLC protocols, among others.

X.25 (LAYER 2) VS. FAST PACKET (LAYER 4) OPERATION

An X.25 network checks the data transmitted for accuracy as the data traverses each link. So when a packet is sent between two X.25 packet-switched network nodes, it cannot move on through the network to the next node until the receiving node has verified its accuracy. This was good for the original packet-switched networks because they operated using low transmission speed and high error rate communication channels. Recall our protocols from Chapter 5. HDLC, the X.25 protocol, was designed with small packet sizes that worked best with low transmission speeds and high error rates.

Fast packet networks work on high-speed, low error rate communications channels. So their protocols do not verify the packets crossing each link, but rather they leave it up to Layer 4, the message integrity layer, to verify that an entire message traversed the network without error.

Figure 7-4 illustrates this.

Fast packet network flag packets signal Layer 4 at the end of the network that a transmission error is likely to have happened, but they do not request retransmission of any packet to correct the error. The nodes merely pass along the packet with an error indication and leave it to Layer 4 at each end of the network to verify data accuracy and to request retransmission of any data in error from the transmitting device.

In the top of Figure 7-4, a traditional X.25 packet network acknowledges data packets as they travel across each link. OSI Layer 2, the data link layer, performs this verification.

In the bottom of Figure 7-4, we see a fast packet network. Each node starts routing the packet as soon as it determines the destination address from the packet header. Error detection is performed, but error correction through retransmission of the data is not performed. OSI Layer 4, the mes-

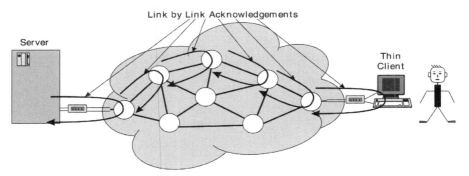

X.25 Packet Switched Network

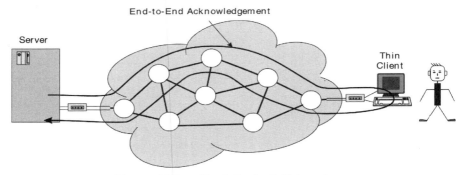

Frame Relay (Fast Packet) Network

Figure 7–4 *X.25 vs. fast packet network operation.*

sage integrity layer, performs error detection on the entire message and if an error is found, requests retransmission of the message in error. This is faster than link-by-link error correction because few errors occur and the transmission speeds are so high that little time is wasted correcting errors. Frame relay routers are different from regular routers, as was discussed in Chapter 6, because they incorporate this Layer-4 error correction functionality.

THE X.25 STANDARD

X.25 is the interface specification for connecting computers and terminals to packet-switched networks (see Figure 7-5).

X.25 covers the bottom three OSI layers:

- **Layer 1, the physical layer,** is a full duplex synchronous connection to the network.

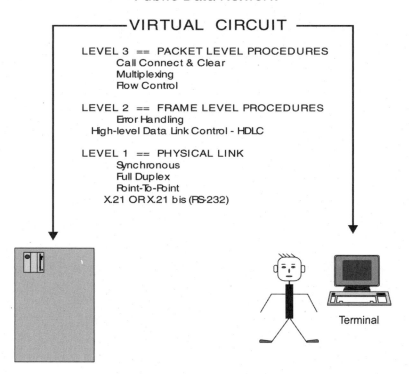

Interface Between Terminal (Computer) And Packet-Switched
Public Data Network

VIRTUAL CIRCUIT

LEVEL 3 == PACKET LEVEL PROCEDURES
  Call Connect & Clear
  Multiplexing
  Flow Control

LEVEL 2 == FRAME LEVEL PROCEDURES
  Error Handling
  High-level Data Link Control - HDLC

LEVEL 1 == PHYSICAL LINK
  Synchronous
  Full Duplex
  Point-To-Point
  X.21 OR X.21 bis (RS-232)

Terminal

Figure 7–5 *X.25 interface specification.*

- **Layer 2, the data link layer,** uses the HDLC protocol to provide a full duplex data transfer with the packet-switched network.
- **Layer 3, the network layer,** performs routing. In this layer, packet-level procedures are performed such as call (virtual circuit) connecting, call (virtual circuit) clearing, and multiplexing data.

Packet networks use X.25 internetworked computers by encapsulating data at the Layer-3 level. Whatever Layer 3 and above protocols are used by the transmission end and the reception end equipment are encapsulated into an X.25 data stream and transported from source to destination across a packet-switched network.

Terminals and PCs are interfaced to an X.25 packet-switched network through a Packet Assembler and Disassembler (PAD). The PAD is defined in an X.3 specification. It receives data from the terminal or PC and translates it into an X.25 data stream for transmission across the packet-switched network.

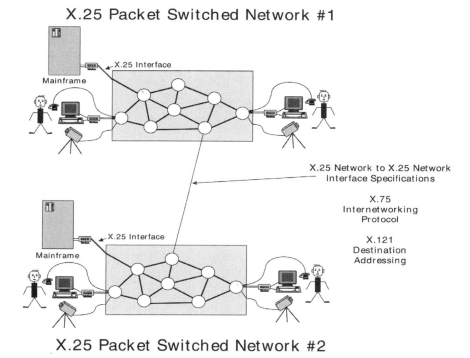

X.25 Packet Switched Network #1

X.25 Interface

Mainframe

X.25 Network to X.25 Network
Interface Specifications

X.75
Internetworking
Protocol

X.121
Destination
Addressing

X.25 Interface

Mainframe

X.25 Packet Switched Network #2

Figure 7–6 *X.75 and X.121 standards.*

Data is delivered to the PAD in an X.28 format that includes specifications on procedures for the break signal, end-of-line character, echo, and other terminal-related functions.

The PAD sends commands to the host computer using the X.25 interface via an X.29 specification. These commands cover functions for handling breaks, etc.

X.75 AND X.121 STANDARDS

The X.75 and X.121 specifications describe the interface between two separate X.25 packet-switched networks. These interfaces are concerned with routing and addressing between X.25 networks (see Figure 7-6).

X.75 is a signaling protocol used to connect X.25 packet-switched networks on international circuits. X.75 defines how X.25 packet-switched networks allow international links to be established, even where some incompatibilities exist. X.75 is a gateway interface protocol at network

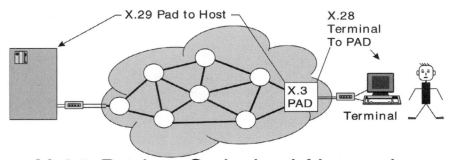

X.25 Packet Switched Network

Figure 7–7 *Packet assembler-disassembler (PAD) specifications.*

boundaries. X.75 supports call and network control information and user traffic transfers between X.25 networks.

X.75 uses X.25 as a foundation, but adds new internetworking facilities that are needed to pass alien traffic through to a final destination point. X.75 is needed because X.25 has undergone many modifications such that no two X.25 networks are the same. For example, X.75 allows X.25 packets to vary from the original standard of 128 bytes. When longer packets need to traverse an X.25 network that only permits smaller packets, X.75 provides segmentation and reassembly.

X.75 handles packets from the 16-byte control message standard to the 4096-byte long packet formats used to encapsulate Ethernet.

X.121 is an international standard for data destination codes or addresses used by X.25 networks. Destination codes or addresses are composed of a four-digit Data Network Identification Code (DNIC) followed by a Network Terminal Number (NTN). The DNIC consists of a Data Country Code (DCC) and a network digit. For example, Tyment's DNIC is 3106 and Telenet's is 3110. The country code is "31" for both networks. Canadian networks have a "30" country code. So the Canadian Data Pac network is 3020 and Infoswitch network is 3029.

PACKET ASSEMBLERS AND DISASSEMBLERS (X.3, X.28, AND X.29 SPECIFICATIONS)

Three related specifications for X.25 packet-switched networks are X.3, X.28, and X.29 (see Figure 7-7).

The X.3 specification defines a Packet Assembler-Disassembler, or PAD. This software receives data from a non-X.25 terminal and converts it into X.25 packets for transmission through the X.25 packet network. The X.3

PAD communicates with the terminal using an X.28 command language specification. The X.28 specification covers terminal setup and other communications features such as line wrapping for lines longer than 80 characters, a procedure to follow when a break signal is sent, etc. The X.29 specification governs PAD-to-PAD and PAD-to-packet mode terminal interfaces.

Some X.3 PAD Parameters are:

- Escape from data transfer (shift in talker).
- Echo
- Data forwarding signal (CR, etc.).
- Idle timer.
- Ancillary device control (XON-XOFF flow control).
- PAD service signals.
- Procedure on break.

PADs are implemented as hardware boxes or as software on packet-switched network routers.

Packet Network Performance

Packet-switched network performance is determined by in-transit delays and packet sizes. Congestion at network entry and exit points also impacts overall network performance. Packet size impacts performance in different ways. Large packets are good for high transmission speeds and low error rates. They use a channel with the least amount of packet overhead. The drawback with large packets is that the channel is occupied with a single task for as long as it takes to transmit the large packet. Channels today must carry digital information for many tasks simultaneously. Small packets are better at providing this flexibility.

PACKETS VS. CELLS VS. FRAMES

What packets, cells, and frames all boil down to are that they are chunks of data. The differences in the data chunks determine the operating characteristics of the communications services that use them. The differences are mainly in the size of the data chunk and in the error detection capabilities associated with the data chunk.

FRAMES • These are typically the largest size data chunks. They are used to send larger amounts of data over high-speed, low error rate communications links. Frames are about 2,000 to 10,000 characters in size. Further, even though they have error detection capability, the data is not corrected link by link because of the low error rate of the link. The impact of link-by-link error checking would cause a slower overall operation of a frame relay-based network.

PACKETS • Designed to transfer chunks of data across low-speed, high error rate communications links. Consequently, they are relatively small in size, typically 128 to 256 characters (bytes), assuring a low chance of error in each packet and small amounts of data retransmitted.

CELLS • These are very small chunks of data with sometimes no error checking. They are designed to operate over highly reliable optical fiber links that have virtually no errors. The benefit of using such small cells on these high-speed links is that the links can now quickly respond to changes in load, e.g., switch from many voice cells to many video cells then to many data cells as the need to service voice, video, and data interfaces changes.

EXAMINING IN-TRANSIT DELAYS

To better understand the differences between X.25, frame relay, and other packet-switched network services, we need to examine in-transit (or store-and-forward) delays. An in-transit delay occurs when data is transmitted into a component, retained in memory for some short time period, and then retransmitted on to the final destination. Such in-transit delays are very short in duration, but the in-transit process can result in a significant overall delay, as we shall see. In-transit delays are experienced with packet-switched networks, Ethernet switches, ATM switches, and just about any network component that takes in data, holds it in memory, and then passes the data on to its destination.

In-transit delays are most important for interactive applications, and somewhat less important for broadcast and file transfer applications. With interactive applications, an operator is waiting for a response from a server or some other computer system. An operator expects short response time. Extra delays in transmission can be noticeable with every query, especially if the queries and responses are short (transfer small amounts of data). In contrast, file transfers or digital broadcasts (such as television or music off the Web), once they are set up and the digital stream is flowing (at an acceptable speed for TV and radio broadcasts) to the destination and properly buffered, in-transit delays have little noticeable impact.

In-transit delays in packet-switched networks are the delays experienced by packets as they travel from node to node. To see the impact of in-transit delays, we examine four cases:

Transmission delay for terminal to host trip of a 10-character message.

TD = 10 Characters / 10 cps (the transmission speed) =   1 SECOND

Figure 7–8   *Case #1: Direct.*

- Case 1: Direct point-to-point transmission—no packet-switched network.
- Case 2: Packet-switched network.
- Case 3: High-speed host access channel.
- Case 4: Character-at-a-time transmission.

These cases examine the delays encountered by a 10-character message as it travels from a PC to a host computer. We are going to send this to a server over 10 characters per second links that run on to and off of a packet-switched data network. The message also runs through the packet-switched data network to get to its destination. The numbers used here make calculations easy and over-dramatize the impact of in-transit delays. In the real world where transmission speeds are 56 Kbps and over, in-transit delay impact is not as dramatic as portrayed here.

Case 1: Direct—In this case, the message travels directly into the host computer over a 10 characters per second link. Figure 7-8 shows the baseline comparison of direct transmission between the client and the server. The direct case (no delays) requires one second for the data to be received by the host computer.

Case 2: Packet-switched network—Here the message must travel from the terminal onto the packet-switched network, through the packet-switched network, and then off of the network into the server system. All packet network services have these same three performance components and cost components as well. The three performance and cost components are:

1. ON (data must get on the network)—There are monthly access charges for packet-switched networks.
2. THROUGH (data must travel through a packet-switched network)—There are monthly charges for transmitting a specific volume of data or using a specific capacity of a packet-switched network.

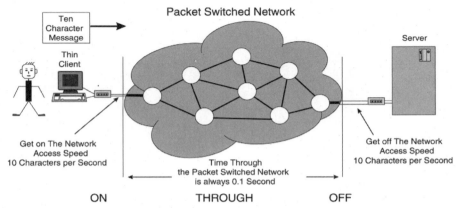

Transmission delay for terminal to host trip of a 10-character message.
TD = Time on to PSN   + Time through PSN + Time off of PSN
   = 10 characters/10 cps + 10 ch / 100 cps*   + 10 ch / 10 cps
   = 1 second   + 0.1 Second   + 1 second   = 2.1 SECONDS
   (* 100 cps is an approximate average internal transmission speed for a
   Packet Switched Network. Most PSN's use much higher transmission speeds.)

Figure 7–9   *Case #2: Packet-switched network.*

3. OFF (data must get off the network)—There are monthly access charges for packet-switched networks at the destination sites.

Generally, cost factors are billed for each site accessing the packet-switched network as access fees and channel fees. The cost of the host site access channel is billed separately (see Figure 7-9).

The total time to traverse the network is then:

Total Time = Time to get ON + Time to travel THROUGH + Time to get OFF

The cumulative impact of the in-transit delays is 1 second + .1 second + 10/10, or 1 second, making the total transfer time in Case #2 2.1 seconds. This is more than double the time in Case #1. Our example here really over-dramatizes the impact of in-transit delays. However, if a doubling of the in-transit time was the case, there would be many unhappy packet-switched network users.

Case 3: High-speed transmission—In this case, the speed of the link connecting the server to our path is increased to 1,000 characters per second (see Figure 7-10).

Here, the high-speed link reduces the in-transit delay impact dramatically. Out-transfer time is 1 second + 0.1 second + 10/1,000, or 0.01 seconds making the total transfer time in Case #3 a total of 1.11 seconds. This is about a 10% increase from the direct transfer case.

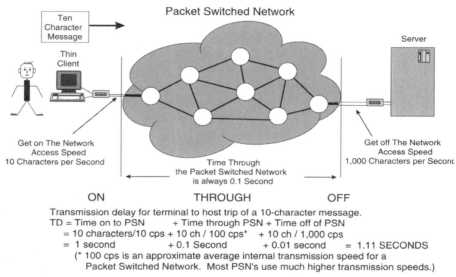

Figure 7–10 *Case #3: High-speed server link.*

This example is straight from Communications Network Design 101. The first rule of network design is the closer you get to the target server or host computer, the faster you want your transmission speed to be. This has two beneficial impacts. The first impact we have already seen, in-transit delays are dramatically reduced. The second impact is that the high-speed link at the target server or host computer can now provide (in theory) that same performance to 100 thin clients, all sent in a 10-character message (100 times 10 equals 1,000 characters per second).

Case 4: Character-by-Character—In the character-by-character case, our "ON" and "OFF" packet-switched network speeds are again returned to 10 characters per second. The main difference in Case #4 is that we do not wait for the entire message to be received before sending it on to the destination (see Figure 7-11).

The first character is transmitted on to the packet-switched network. It is then transmitted immediately through the packet-switched network. While the first character is traveling through the packet-switched network, the second character is being transmitted onto the packet-switched network. Next, the third character is transmitted on to the packet-switched network, the second character travels through the packet-switched network, and the first character travels off the network into the target server or host computer. The process continues with the fourth character to the tenth character. This means that some of the transmission times overlap and cancel each other out

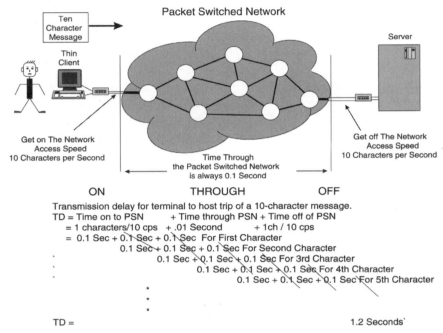

Figure 7–11 *Case #4: Character-at-a-time transmission.*

as shown in Figure 7-11. They are essentially the same time, making the overall time to transfer the frame 1.2 seconds.

Alternatively think of it this way, it takes one second to sent the full 10-character message to the packet-switched network. All the time, the characters are also moving through and off the packet-switched network. So when the last character enters at the end of one second, it only has to travel through (0.1 second) and off (0.1 second) for the entire 10-character message to arrive in full at the target server or host computer system. This means that the total time required is 1 +0.1+0.1, or 1.2 seconds.

Once we understand the impact of in-transit delays, we can examine in closer detail the differences between traditional X.25 packet-switched networks and frame relay, etc.

X.25 networks perform traditional packet switching behaving like Case #2. X.25 networks send data through a network packet-by-packet, verifying that each packet has crossed each link without error before passing the packet on to the next link. This places the responsibility for reliable packet delivery upon the packet-switched network. Operating in this fashion was good for early packet networks because often functions assuring reliable packet delivery were not implemented in higher OSI layers.

Further, communication across links between pack nodes was not so reliable. It was dependent upon high-speed analog transmission facilities. Finally, the transmission speed between packet nodes was relatively slow. Top speed in many cases was 56 Kbps. These factors combined placed the responsibility for reliable packet delivery with the packet-switched network.

On X.25 packet links, when errors occurred, the link-by-link checking caused the network to quickly resolve communications problems rather than pass indications to higher layers that would not react so quickly because they would need to analyze the entire message received. Higher layer (end-to-end) reaction time was much longer due to the slow 56-Kbps transmission speeds across the packet network.

Packet networks established virtual circuits between calling and answering systems. These virtual circuits stayed in place for the duration of the call. Private packet networks could be set up using software.

Fast Packet Vs. X.25 Packet Networks

Frame relay networks behave like Case #4. They do not wait to receive an entire frame before sending a packet on to its destination. As soon as they see the header information, the frame is routed on to the next link. Frame relay networks rely on high-speed transmission over low error fiber optic links to operate effectively. They can push the error detection and correction responsibility up to higher ISO layers because they transmit the data at high speeds—T-1 speeds or greater between nodes—minimizing end-to-end delay. This permits the higher layers to react quickly to high error conditions and respond accordingly. Further, the error rate on the fiber links is very low. Consequently, high error conditions rarely occur on frame relay networks.

Frame relay links use Cyclic Redundancy Check (CRC) error detection to flag the receiving end that a potential error has been detected. It is up to the receiving end to request retransmission of the data in error. Frame relay routers perform speed buffering to match different transmission speeds on different communications links.

Frame relay networks behave like Case #3 as well. The high-speed links reduce the effective delays through the frame relay network while servicing data traffic from many sources simultaneously.

Frame Relay Networks

One of the hottest and fastest growing areas in telecommunications today is the implementation of frame relay, or fast packet, networks. Frame relay networks were originally targeted at providing high-speed data services between facilities. Their usefulness today has been expanded to incorporate both voice and video transmission across these fast packet networks. Special configurations and equipment have been developed to accommodate voice and video transmission.

BASIC CONFIGURATION

Figure 7-12 shows a general frame relay network configuration. A LAN at one site is connected to a LAN at a second site through a frame relay network. The first site has a local access channel connecting to a frame relay network Point Of Presence (POP). This is a zero mileage digital channel operating at one of several transmission speeds up to T-1 channel speeds of 1.544 Mbps. The local access channel speeds are dependent upon the frame relay service provider's offerings. A Channel Service Unit/Data Service Unit (CSU/DSU) connects a frame relay router to the frame relay service digital access channel. This same configuration is repeated at the destination site. Between the two sites, the frame relay user contracts for Permanent Virtual Circuits (PVCs) with a Committed Information Rate (CIR).

VIRTUAL CIRCUITS

Frame relay networks support Permanent Virtual Circuits (PVCs) and Switched Virtual Circuits (SVCs).

PVCs are software-defined logical connections between two end-points in a frame relay network. PVCs permit users to define logical connections and required transmission speeds (bandwidths) between frame relay network end-points. The frame relay network determines how the physical network is used to make the PVC connections and how the PVC traffic is managed. The end-points and a stated bandwidth, called a Committed Information Rate (CIR), constitute PVCs.

PVCs are similar to a leased line channel between two sites because they guarantee a specific transmission speed (bandwidth) between those sites. However, since the PVC runs across shared facilities, it costs the frame relay subscriber substantially less than an equivalent leased channel facility would cost. Once a site connects to a frame relay POP, it can connect to many other sites with PVCs.

SVCs are temporary virtual circuits established and maintained only for the duration of a data transfer session between frame relay network endpoints. An SVC is a circuit that appears to be a discrete, physical circuit available only to a single user. However, the SVC is actually a shared pool of circuit resources used to support multiple users, as they require the

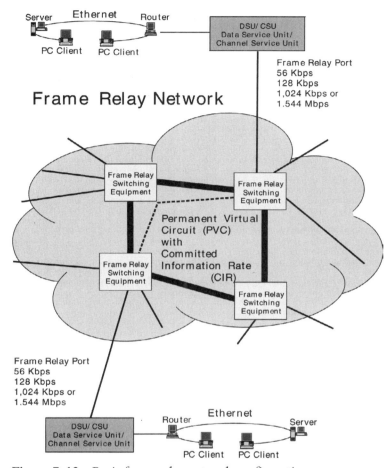

Figure 7–12 *Basic frame relay network configuration.*

connections. SVCs were originally defined for X.25 packet-switched networks. Frame relay networks can also implement SVCs.

COMMITTED INFORMATION RATE

The CIR is the transmission speed or bandwidth expressed in bits per second assigned to PVCs or SVCs. In frame relay networks, different logical connections share the same physical path. Some logical connections are assigned higher transmission speeds or more bandwidth than others. A PVC carrying video would require 384-Kbps CIR while a LAN-to-LAN connection may only need a 128-Kbps CIR. Both logical connections could run across a frame relay network backbone link operating at say 1.544 Mbps. A CIR is

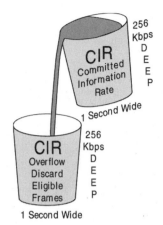

Figure 7–13 *Committed Information Rate (CIR) operation.*

defined in software, permitting a frame relay network's mix of traffic bandwidths to be quickly and easily redefined as requirements change. However, it makes no sense to define a 128-Kbps CIR for a site that has a local connection speed of 64 Kbps.

The CIR is implemented with software buffers. These buffers are like glasses of water. They are one second wide and for a 256-Kbps CIR, 256,000 bits deep. Figure 7-13 illustrates generally how the CIR works. The glass that is the CIR can hold one second's data, or in our example, 256,000 bits. When data arrives at a faster rate than 256 Kbps, the CIR buffer overflows into an equivalent glass that is also one-second wide and 256,000 bits deep.

Each frame header has a Discard Eligibility (DE) bit. The frames below CIR (those that fit in the CIR glass) are not eligible for discard (DE = 0).

The bits falling into the CIR overflow buffer are marked as DE by the frame relay router. The DE bit in those frames is set to one and the frame is eligible for discard. In the event of network congestion, they can be discarded (spilled on the floor, never to return). Most frame relay vendors say that discarded frames in their networks are much less than one percent. This is true if you measure them as a percentage of the total data sent through the network; but what really counts is that during periods of data congestion, what percentage of the active frames are discarded. This is more a true measure of frame relay network performance.

Frame relay network frames are larger in size then X.25 network packets. X.25 packets vary in size to a maximum of 128 characters. In frame relay networks, the information field size is negotiated between users and networks, and between networks. The maximum size can be as small as 262 characters and as large as several thousand characters. LAN-to-LAN connections generally use a frame size around 1,600 characters. Some frame relay services support sizes of 4,096 characters or more, frame relay frames have low frame overhead. The frame overhead is two flag characters, two CRC-16 frame check characters, and from two to four characters of frame addressing information, resulting in about eight characters of overhead for several thousand characters transmitted.

FRAME RELAY ACCESS DEVICE

A Frame Relay Access Device or Frame Relay Assembler/Disassembler (FRAD) is a telecommunications network component that formats outgoing data for transmission across a frame relay network. It strips the data back out at the other end, presenting it to the target system as if it were the original data stream. A FRAD is the frame relay network counterpart to an X.25 PAD (see Figure 7-14).

Similar to HDLC-based packet networks, frame relay networks pass data using OSI Layer 1, Layer 2, and Layer 3 by encapsulating the data into frame relay frames. A FRAD provides an interface to LANs and the frame relay network. FRADs can provide simple data encapsulation functions, or they can be more sophisticated and interact with the transmission and receiving devices to spoof them. FRADs performing spoofing do not transmit overhead messages such as polls and acknowledgments across the frame relay network.

In Figure 7-14, the FRAD at the host computer system would respond to terminal polling messages as though it was a terminal control unit with many attached terminals. The remote FRAD would poll the terminals or terminal control units, aggregating the data for transmission across the frame relay network. Once a message or messages were accumulated in the remote FRAD, it would send them in frames to the host-attached FRAD. These messages would be passed to the host computer in response to its polling messages. Responses would be aggregated by the host-attached FRAD and sent to the remote FRAD. The remote FRAD would in turn pass the response messages to the appropriate terminals. In essence, the FRADS would make the frame relay network transparent to the host computer system and terminals.

VOICE AND VIDEO OVER FRAME

Since fast packet services operate over shared facilities, substantial cost savings can be realized by combining voice, video, and data communications on these shared backbone links. Because this voice and video are isochronous transmissions requiring a constant bit rate, they must be handled differently

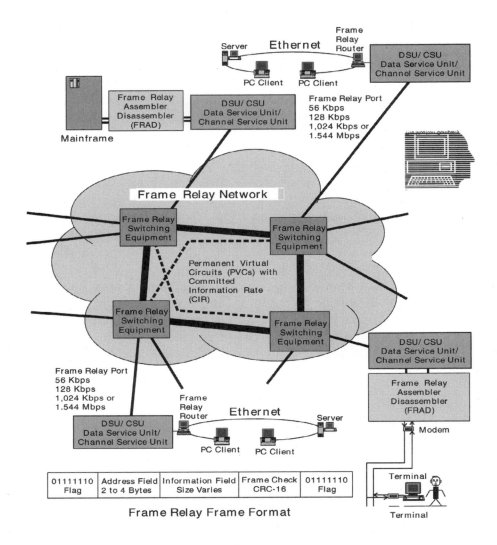

Figure 7–14 *Frame relay network FRAD configuration.*

than data transmission running across a frame relay, or fast packet, network. In the case of voice and video transmission, a minimal QoS or a guaranteed bits per second transmission speed must be provided. This generally translates into voice and video running across links without exceeding the CIR.

In contrast, data is transmitted across a fast packet network as quickly as it can be accommodated. If it exceeds the CIR and some frames are discarded as a result, then it is up to the FRAD or frame relay router to assure that the data is eventually passed end to end through the frame relay network.

Saving Costs Using Frame Relay and Packet Network Services

When an organization has leased channels between facilities, it can potentially save communications costs by replacing those leased facilities with frame relay network PVCs or packet-switched network facilities. This is particularly true when many facilities are connected using leased line circuits. Typical frame relay network pricing is provided in Table 7-3.

Table 7.3   *Frame Relay Pricing from Public Service Commission Tariffs*

			Recurring Charges	
Service Level	**One-time Installation Charges**	**Monthly**	**with 3-year commitment**	**with 5-year commitment**
56-Kbps/64-Kbps Network Access CIR per PVC	$800	$175 $5	$160 $5	$150 $5
1.536 Mbps Network Access	$1,000	$435	$400	$380
CIR per PVC from 56 Kbps to 768 Kbps		$2 to $28	$2 to $28	$2 to $28

Frame relay and packet-switched networks use virtual circuits to connect locations. A frame relay network user contracts for a specific capacity virtual circuit between two locations. This capacity is based upon the amount of data being transferred regularly between the two sites. The actual frame relay network backbone transmission speed is much greater than the virtual circuit capacity. This combination of high-speed backbone, minimized in-transit delays, large packet sizes, and lower communications costs for PVCs makes frame relay networks a popular solution for transporting data between facilities.

Frame relay and packet-switched networks save costs over full-period lines by charging for access rather than the capacity used. Some frame relay networks provide PVCs with CIRs equal to zero. This means that the customer pays for the packets of data transmitted, but not a fixed CIR. Also, all data transmitted is DE. A frame relay network and packet-switched network vs. private leased line network strategy summary is provided in Table 7-4.

Frame relay and packet-switched networks are best for networks that have small data loads with wide geographic coverage. They must service

Table 7.4   *Packet-switched Network Applications*

Network Characteristics	Private Network	Frame Relay or Packet Network
Networks with Large Data Volumes	Good Strategy	- - -
Networks with Low Data Volumes	- - -	Good Strategy *Especially when remote network sites are near frame relay or packet-switched network POPs.*
Wide Geographic Coverage	- - -	Good Strategy *Especially when remote network sites are near frame relay or packet-switched network POPs.*
Dial-up Communications	- - -	Good Strategy
Special Terminals and Protocols	Good Strategy	- -.-
Short Implementation Lead Time	- - -	Good Strategy
Continued Network Changes	- - -	Good Strategy
New Network	- - -	Good Strategy
Network Data Load Overflows	- - -	Good Strategy
Mainframe Computers and Servers from Different Manufacturers	Gateways	Good Strategy *When the hosts support X.25 networking.*

many cities in the U.S. and internationally as well. When a network must be expanded or built quickly, frame relay and packet-switched networks are already in place. To connect to them requires implementing local channels to the frame relay or packet-switched network POPs. Frame relay and packet-switched networks provide all network management and troubleshooting technical support, alleviating the user of these requirements. This can make implementing a new network much easier than constructing an equivalent private network. Further, since the CIR can be exceeded, frame relay and packet-switched networks adjust dynamically to data load overflows. Fixed network facilities do not as easily accommodate network data load overflows. Finally, frame relay and packet-switched networks can translate between host computer systems of different manufacturers, providing the manufacturers both have frame relay network interfaces or that FRADs exist to interface with their networking systems.

Brain Teaser

Packet-switched Networks

Compare hypothetical network costs for a leased channel network and frame relay network to connect Washington, D.C. to remote sites in Boston, New York, and Los Angeles. The connections must be up 24/7. The network loads are:

1. LA to Washington load is 256 Kbps.
2. Boston to Washington load is 256 Kbps.
3. New York to Washington load is 512 Kbps.

Leased T-1 circuits between the cities cost:

1. LA and Washington is $2,750 per month.
2. Boston to Washington is $1,550 per month.
3. New York to Washington is $1,260 per month.

Frame relay access channels in these cities cost:

1. LA: 256 Kbps — $250 per month;   1.544 Mbps — $500 per month.
2. Boston: 256 Kbps — $250 per month;   1.544 Mbps — $500 per month.
3. New York: 512 Kbps — $350 per month;   1.544 Mbps — $500 per month.
4. Washington: 256 Kbps — $250 per month;   1.544 Mbps — $500 per month.

PVCs run $15 per month for 256 Kbps, $20 per month for 512 Kbps, and $28 for 1.544 Mbps.

1. What is the total monthly cost for a private network of leased lines connecting all sites to Washington? The cost should be $2,750 + $1,550 + $1,260, or $5,560 per month. Each channel has excess capacity.

2. What is the lowest cost frame relay network connecting the remote sites to Washington. Its cost is:

LA connection: $250 plus $15, or $265 per month.
Boston connection: $250 plus $15, or $265 per month.
New York connection: $350 plus $20, or $370 per month.
Washington connection: $500 plus $15+$15+$20, or $550 per month.

Total monthly frame relay network cost is $1,450 per month, which provides a $4,110 per month savings.

3. Does the lowest cost frame relay network provide equivalent performance to the private network? No, it is lower performance because the access links in LA, Boston, and NY are 256 Kbps, 256 Kbps, and 512 Kbps, respectively. Review the in-transit delay analysis to see why.

4. Can we provide better frame relay performance for slightly increased cost? Yes, its cost would be:

LA connection: $500 plus $30, or $530 per month.
Boston connection: $500 plus $30, or $530 per month.
New York connection: $500 plus $30, or $530 per month.
Washington connection: $500 plus $30+$30+$30, or $590 per month.

Total monthly frame relay network cost is $2,180 per month, which provides a $3,380 per month savings.

5. Why does the network in Question 4 increase performance? All access speeds are 1.544 Mbps, permitting the CIR to be exceeded when needed.

The goal here is to illustrate with a hypothetical example how frame relay and packet-switched network services can be used to reduce network costs.

All Digital Network Technologies

Digital networking technologies support other telecommunications cost-saving products and services. It is important to understand how these technologies work and their role in telecommunications networks. Digital networking technologies consist of T-carrier channels, Switched Multi-megabit Data Services (SMDS), ATM services, and SONET.

T-Carrier Channels and Services

The T-carrier system supports digitized voice transmission. AT&T first used it in the 1960s. The basic T-carrier line is a T-1 channel with a transmission speed of 1.544 Mbps. T-1 channels are commonly used today to connect to Internet Service Providers (ISP) and the Internet. A T-3 channel is another common channel that operates at 44.736 Mbps. Fractional T-1 channels break the 24 channels in a T-1 line down into fewer 64-Kbps DS-0 voice channels for which the customer is charged, with the other DS-0 channels in the T-1 channel going unused.

The T-carrier system is digital, using Pulse Code Modulation (PCM) and Time Division Multiplexing (TDM). The T-carrier channels are full duplex capability using 4-wire service with two wires for receiving and two for transmitting. The T-1 digital stream consists of 24 DS-0 64-Kbps channels that are time division multiplexed. T-1 channels were originally delivered using 2-pair twisted pair copper wires. Coaxial cable, optical fiber, digital microwave, and other media may also deliver T-1 channels.

T-1 services are typically used to provide high-speed digital transmission channels to a business. They can support both voice and data transmission circuits with a transmission rate of 1,544,000 bits per second and higher on two pairs of wires.

In T-1 channels, voice signals are sampled 8,000 times using PCM with an 8-bit byte representing the voice signal at that instant in time. This sampling produces a 64,000 Bps digital stream representing the voice signal

| Signal=8 bits | Signal=8 bits | 22 Signal Frames | Framing=1 bit |

Figure 7–15 *T-1 Frame structure.*

known as Digital Signal Level – Zero or DS-0. To compute T-1 speed, we multiply 24 DS-0 voice channels using PCM by 64 Kbps then add 8,000 synchronization/framing bits, resulting in a DS-1 (Digital Signal Level – One) transmission speed of 1.544 Mbps.

DS-0 CHANNELS AND T-1 FRAMING

Telephone companies think of T-carrier channels in terms of framing. A frame is what is sent 8,000 times each second across T-channels. The universal number here in telephony is 8,000. Everything in the telephone network happens 8,000 times a second. In some cases, smaller frames are sent 8,000 times a second and in other cases much larger frames are sent 8,000 times a second. Regardless, everything happens 8,000 times a second.

Each T-1 channel frame carries 24 voice channels, each represented by an 8-bit byte and a single control bit, giving a total frame size of 193 bits. DS-0 specifies that data be carried in 192-bit frames followed by the framing bit. The framing bit synchronizes clocks in both user and telephone company equipment (see Figure 7-15).

These frames are sent 8,000 times a second. This yields a total T-1 transmission speed of 1,544,000 bits per second. Signaling bits are robbed from each DS-0 channel in a T-1 span. These signaling bits are the least significant bits in each DS-0 channel.

MULTIPLEXING HIERARCHY (T-1, T-1C, T-2, AND T-3)

The T-carrier system is the North American telephone industry standard for interconnecting digital communication systems. T-1 circuits are defined as any digital communication system operating at a synchronous data rate of 1.544 Mbps. Data can be transmitted over a T-1 circuit at 56 Kbps to 1.544 Mbps. Voice channels use 64 Kbps. Twenty-four simultaneous digitized voice signals are time division multiplexed on one T-1 circuit. T-1 circuits transport data or voice using a framing format called DS-0.

T-carrier channels are time division multiplexed DS-0 channels. They are combined together to provide multiple DS-0 channels, depending upon the customer requirements. T-carrier channels form a hierarchy of digital transmission and TDM standards ranging from T-1 to T-3. The multiplexing and channel hierarchy is:

Digital Signal Level Designation	Voice Channel Equivalence	T-Carrier Equivalence	Transmission Speed
DS-1	24 voice channels	1 T-1 channel	1.544 Mbps
DS-1C	48 voice channels	2 T-1 channels	3.152 Mbps
DS-2	96 voice channels	4 T-1 channels	6.312 Mbps
DS-3	672 voice channels	28 T-1 channels	44.736 Mbps

T-carrier circuits were defined and implemented for speeds faster than DS-3. However, any circuit with bandwidth greater (higher transmission speed) than a DS-3 circuit is sold today as most typically a SONET ring OC (Optical Carrier) circuit.

This hierarchy was set up just to bug Pete. Why didn't the telephone companies make two T-1 channels a DS-2 channel rather than a DS-1C channel? And why for a DS-1C channel is the speed not 2 times 1.544, or 3.088 Mbps? Of course the telephone companies took one T-1 frame and added it to another T-1 frame and then added 8 more bits of overhead bits to make a new DS-1C frame of 394 bits, which is sent across the network 8,000 times a second.

And if this was not enough, why weren't 4 T-1 channels called DS-4 and not DS-2? Also, why is it not two times DS-1C speed, or 6,304 Mbps? The same technique applies. The telephone companies took one DS-1C frame and added it to another DS-1C frame and then added one more bit of framing overhead to make a new DS-2 789-bit frame, which is sent across the network 8,000 times a second.

Now by this time, Pete doesn't care anymore. DS-3 only makes sense to the most dedicated telephone company personnel. As far as I am concerned, it is 44.736 Mbps, or equivalent to 28 T-1 channels. A DS-3 or T-3 frame is seven DS-2 frames plus another 69 framing bits, or 5,592 bits per frame. Sending this king-size frame across a channel 8,000 times a second produces a 44.736-Mbps channel capacity. Because these channels are time division multiplexed, the true capacity is equal to the number of voice-grade-equivalent (DS-0) channels they carry. A DS-3 or T-3 channel really delivers only 43.008 Mbps for voice and clear channel data. With "bit robbed" DS-0 channels for data, the effective capacity is 37.632 Mbps.

FRACTIONAL T-1, DIGITAL ACCESS, AND CROSS-CONNECT SYSTEMS

Fractional T-1 and T-3 divide a full T-1 or T-3 channel into multiples of DS-0 channels. The user pays for the portion of the channel capacity used and not the full T-1 or T-3 channel.

Fractional T-1 and T-3 connections use Digital Access and Cross Connect Systems (DACS) to rearrange DS-0 channels without requiring that the T-1 channels be de-multiplexed, cross-connected, and re-multiplexed. The DACS can break out channels with speeds as low as 2.4, 4.8, 9.6, and 56 Kbps. A DACS is located on customer premises where the fractional T-1 or T-3 channel is terminated. A telephone company typically owns DACS. DACS are used to switch, groom, and route DS-0 channels. Grooming data traffic combines, consolidates, and segregates network traffic. As a telephony term, "grooming" typically refers to managing high-capacity channels between COs, carriers, ISPs, and very large corporations (see Figure 7-16).

"DACS" is a common telephone term that one hears time and time again. It is a telephone network component that rigidly breaks a T-1 or higher speed T-carrier channel into individual DS-0 channels. It is different from a T-carrier multiplexer in that a T-carrier multiplexer not only divides a T-carrier channel into DS-0 channels, but can reconfigure those channels to adjust to changing load requirements through software. DACS systems are not typically adjustable.

ALTERNATE MARK INVERSION AND BIPOLAR 8-BIT ZERO SUBSTITUTION

In 1988, clear channel transmission became an option for T-1 service from AT&T. Users could now transmit DS-0 or DS-1 signals without restricting the consecutive zeros.

T-1 channels are encoded using Alternate Mark Inversion (AMI). AMI encodes each "1" bit as a positive then a negative voltage. The receiving device on a T-1 channel detects dropped bits because it receives two positive or two negative voltage signals back to back when it should always receive a positive then a negative then a positive signal. With digital encoding, there tends to be more "0's" transmitted than "1's" transmitted. The ratio is something like 53% "0's" to 47% "1's." Thus, with AMI, there can be long strings of "0's," which means no positive to negative signal changes. This makes AMI more vulnerable to transmission errors. To overcome this potential problem,

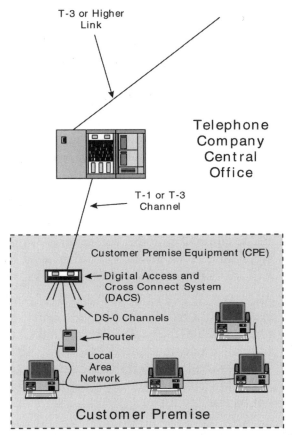

Figure 7–16 *Digital Access and Cross-connect System (DACS) and fractional T-carrier channels.*

Bipolar 8-bit Zero Substitution (B8ZS) is used to augment T-channel AMI signal encoding.

Technically, T-1 bit streams should not contain more than 15 "0's" in a row. B8ZS solves this problem. Further, B8ZS can provide a full 192-Kbps bandwidth on a T-1 channel. B8ZS augments the normal T-1 AMI encoding by violating AMI bipolar encoding rules when strings of eight consecutive "0's" are found. When eight consecutive "0's" are encountered, a unique coding violation pattern replaces them (see Figure 7-17). This B8ZS coding violation provides sufficient timing pulses to maintain synchronization across the T-1 channel.

B8ZS does not create errors, but rather its coding violations guarantee the minimum pulse state changes needed for synchronization without adding bits into the data stream. B8ZS sidesteps the 15 consecutive "0's" restric-

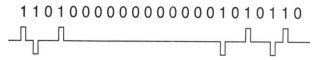

1 1 0 1 0 0 0 0 0 0 0 0 0 0 0 0 1 0 1 0 1 1 0

Normal T-1 Encoding -- Alternate Mark Inversion

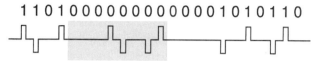

1 1 0 1 0 0 0 0 0 0 0 0 0 0 0 0 1 0 1 0 1 1 0

B8ZS - Bipolar Eight Bit Zero Substitution

Figure 7–17 *B8ZS vs. AMI.*

tion and supports clear channel signaling. On B8ZS channels, all T-1 bandwidth can be used for data transmission supporting clear channel, or full 64-Kbps DS-0 channels.

To use this clear channel signaling, a Channel Service Unit (CSU) conforming to B8ZS signaling must be placed at each end of the T-1 link. A B8ZS transmitter in the CSU watches the data stream for excessively long strings of "0's." When detected, the long strings of "0's" are replaced by a bipolar encoding violation before being passed to the network. A compatible receiving CSU spots the bipolar encoding violation and converts the violation back into its original string of "0's."

EXTENDED SUPERFRAMES FORMAT

To insert framing bits across 24 consecutive T-1 standard 192-bit data frames, a CSU uses Extended Superframe Format (ESF). These additional 24 framing bits form the extended superframe and create three supervisory channels. These channels are:

- The first channel is a six-bit pattern synchronizing the entire T-1 data stream.
- The second channel uses a six-bit CRC code to provide error checking. The six-bit CRC is created in the transmitting unit based upon the 4,608 data bits within an extended superframe. The receiving unit compares the CRC transmitted with a CRC computed from the data received and identifies when errors have occurred. This pinpoints the links in an end-to-end circuit causing errors.
- The last 12 bits of the 24 frame bits create a 4-Kbps link, a Facilities Data Link (FDL), which exchanges maintenance information. The FDL is available to both carriers and users for exchanging channel

performance and supervisory information. An end-to-end T-1 circuit is usually segmented to monitor for errors without disrupting normal data traffic.

The interface device between terminal equipment and carrier facilities is the ESF CSU. At this interface, performance information is collected from both the CPE and the channel. With this data, problems between terminal equipment and carriers can be identified. The ESF CSU provides raw data to telecommunications network management software, which uses it to evaluate network performance, analyze traffic, and present alarms.

CONNECTING SITES WITH T-CARRIER CHANNELS

A typical T-1 site-to-site connection is shown in Figure 7-18. The T-1 channel between the two sites connects to CSUs/DSUs that implement B8ZS and ESF transmission on the T-1 channel. T-1 multiplexers attach to the CSU/DSU and split the T-1 channel into DS-0 channels with some routed to the PBX and others routed to the data network. The T-1 multiplexer permits the DS-0 channels assigned to voice and data to be varied such that during the daytime, most of the DS-0 channels handle voice communications between the two sites. At night, the bulk of the DS-0 channels are moved over to the data side to facilitate computer-to-computer data file backups and other file transfers between the sites.

T-1 channels are not such cost-saving services unless there is sufficient call and data transfer volume between the two sites. In this case, the cost of the T-1 full-period leased channel would reduce the long-distance telephone charges between the sites and provide for data transfers. Alternatively, frame relay service with voice channels having priority or meeting a specific QoS delay could be less costly than a T-1 channel.

T-1 channels are time division multiplexed. This means when DS-0 channels are assigned to voice traffic and there are few calls to carry, the capacity of those channels is wasted. What networks would prefer is to dynamically allocate T-1 bandwidth to voice or data traffic as needed with voice traffic having the highest priority. As we shall soon see, ATM technology promises to deliver such capability.

Add/Drop Multiplexers (ADM) are used when multiplexing T-1 channels to several different sites. They permit dropping and adding individual or combinations of individual DS-0 channels out of the T-1 channel bit stream without de-multiplexing and re-multiplexing the entire T-1 channel.

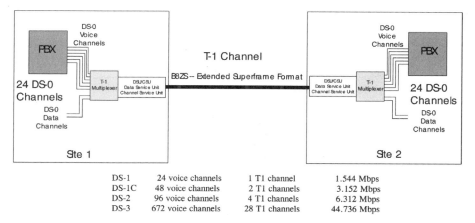

DS-1	24 voice channels	1 T1 channel	1.544 Mbps
DS-1C	48 voice channels	2 T1 channels	3.152 Mbps
DS-2	96 voice channels	4 T1 channels	6.312 Mbps
DS-3	672 voice channels	28 T1 channels	44.736 Mbps

Figure 7–18   *T-1 channel configuration.*

Brain Teaser

T-1 Channels

AT&T's T-1 service is described as terrestrial, 1.544-Mbps local channel service capable of simultaneous, two-way transmission of serial, bipolar, return-to-zero isochronous digital signals on a two-point basis only. This terrestrial, 1.544-Mbps local channel service is furnished between a customer's premise and an AT&T CO, or between two or more customers' premises. Customers are responsible for providing CSU functionality at each local channel service termination on the customer's premise. The terrestrial, 1.544-Mbps local channel service is a framed DS-1 signal format (D-4 or ESF). Customers are required to select either D-4 format or the ESF, if it is available.

This tariff is published at: http://www.att.com/tariffs/state/in/docs/inp6s4m.doc.

We have a network of six sites that all communicate both voice and data extensively with one another. Using T-1 channels to build a private communications network, answer the following:

1. How many T-1 channels would be required to connect every site to every other site? In this case, a fully connected T-1 network would require five T-1 lines at each site to connect that site to every other site. Is this an effective network configuration? Effective, perhaps? It is certainly costly.

2. The network carries both voice and data on the T-1 links. Are there any alternate approaches using T-1 channels that could reduce network costs? Any technology that reduces the number of T-1 channels lowers network costs. Deploying packet switching technology, or IP networking technology in the form of packet switches or IP routers installed at all five sites connecting and interconnecting them with the T-1 spans would do the job.

3. What would need to be checked to build this T-1-based packet-switched or IP routed network? Does the equipment interface with T-1 spans? Does the equipment have a CSU that works with D-4 or ESF?

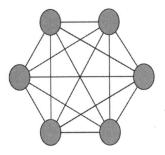

Initial T-1 Network

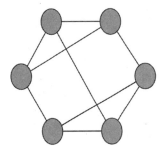

Packet Switched
or
IP Routed
T-1 Network

Figure 7–19   *Network configurations.*

4. What reduction in T-1 lines might a packet-switched or IP-routed network implementation produce? To effectively route and create a mesh network, probably three T-1 links would be terminated at each site, saving the cost of two T-1 links per site (see Figure 7-19).

The goal of this exercise is to illustrate how T-1 channels could be used to build a private network.

Switched Multi-megabit Data Service

Switched Multi-megabit Data Service (SMDS) is a packet-switching service that provides LAN-like performance and features over a metropolitan area. SMDS transports data over wide areas at speeds up to T-3 speeds of 44.735 Mbps. SMDS services include group addressing, connectionless transport, and fixed packet delays. SMDS is based upon the IEEE 802.6 MAN Standard.

SMDS uses cell relay switching technology at Layer 2, the data link layer, similar to ATM networks. Cell relay breaks Layer 3, the network layer, frames into 53-character cells, with 48 characters of data and 5 characters of

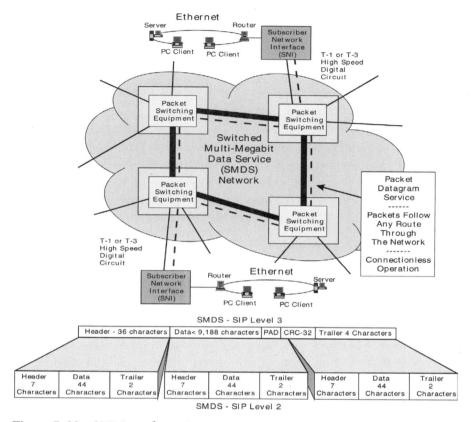

Figure 7–20 *SMDS configuration.*

overhead. Similar to frame relay, it relies upon high-speed, 44.735-Mbps or higher, and low error rate fiber optic links to carry the data from one SMDS node to another. Cells are reassembled into SMDS Layer-3 Protocol Data Units (PDUs) at the destination SMDS node. The Layer-3 SMDS PDUs may be large, with information fields of up to 9,188 characters (see Figure 7-20).

Access to SMDS is determined by SMDS Interface Protocols (SIPs). SIP functions cover addressing, data framing, and physical data transport. Protocol framing differs for Layers 3 and 2. The SIP protocols are connectionless. This means that each frame, or PDU, is independently routed to its destination using least loaded links. No connection establishment handshakes are needed, since each PDU can follow a different path from source to destination. In contrast, connection-oriented services require that a connection be established, the data transferred, and the connection terminated. These functions must be completed in sequence for data transmission to occur. During data transfer, connection-oriented services must sequence the data frames, pace the flow of data between transmission and receiving devices, and detect and correct transmission errors. With SMDS, similar to frame relay, these functions are shifted up to the Layer-4 software.

SMDS has SIP protocols for Layer 1 that describe bit-level transmission across mainly fiber optic facilities.

The Subscriber Network Interface (SNI) is the component that the SMDS user installs at the user's site. It interfaces T-3 and SONET transmission facilities to the user's LANs.

Typical SMDS costs are shown in Table 7-6. These prices do not compare favorably with the costs for other digital transmission services such as cable modems and Digital Subscriber Line (DSL) connections.

Table 7.5 *SMDS Pricing from Public Service Commission Tariffs*

Service Level	One-Time Installation Charges	Monthly	Recurring Charges	
			With 3 Year Commitment	With 5 Year Commitment
56-Kbps Subscriber Network Access Line	$600	$225	$210	$190
1.17-Mbps Subscriber Network Access Line	$1,000	$570	$525	$500
4-Mbps Subscriber Network Access Line	$2,000	$1,900	$1,900	$1,900
34-Mbps Subscriber Network Access Line	$2,000	$4,000	$4,000	$4,000

SMDS has not really sold effectively. It is a good idea, but because of high pricing, it has lost its way in the wilderness of telecommunications.

Asynchronous Transfer Mode

ATM is a broadband ISDN service. There are many ATM cell relay products aimed at making high-speed communications links more effective in carrying voice, video, and data loads.

ATM technology covers ISO Layers 1 and 2. It implements cell relay protocol at ISO Layer 2, the data link layer. ATM can be implemented with a variety of Layer 1, physical layer, transmission media. Typically, it operates at 25 or 155 Mbps over UTP, and at 622 Mbps over fiber optic links. It is possible to deploy ATM technology over SONET links that operate in the gigabits per second speed range.

Implementing ATM requires that each device have an ATM card installed as well as Windows software supporting LAN, as well as voice and video transmission. All devices are connected through ATM switches. LAN setup requires that a portion of the ATM bandwidth be allocated to LAN data transfers. Voice and video transmission are commonly set up as circuit-switched calls.

ATM can support both local area communications as well as wide area communications networking. While there is little competition for ATM technology in the wide area communications market, gigabit Ethernet poses significant competition in the LAN marketplace.

CELL RELAY OPERATION

ATM technology carries multiple traffic types, including:

- Constant Bit Rate (CBR).
- Variable Bit Rate (VBR).
- Available Bit Rate (ABR).

CBR is for video and voice applications requiring fixed bit rate circuits. Voice transmissions use the standard 64-Kbps speed, while standard TV requires 384 Kbps.

VBR supports high-priority data applications such as inter-LAN traffic. Most all data transmission arrives in chunks or wads. Sometimes there is no data to transmit, while at other times buffers are crammed full. VBR can easily provide increased transmission capacity for this type of traffic.

ABR makes use of spare bandwidth that is not being used by CBR and VBR traffic. Network diagnostics fit into this category. They operate in the background, using whatever cells are left over after the CBR and VBR applications have used all the cells they need. ABR information is the lowest priority data transmitted unless a network failure happens.

The mechanism for ABR does not guarantee availability of bandwidth. It does however provide fair access to the available bandwidth using a flow control feedback mechanism. This notifies end-nodes in the network that the network is becoming congested, allowing the end-nodes to react accordingly by reducing the ABR traffic entering the network.

The real key to understanding ATM cell relay is that it acts like a conveyor belt with 53-character buckets. The conveyor belt is constantly running whether the buckets contain any information to transfer or not. Full or

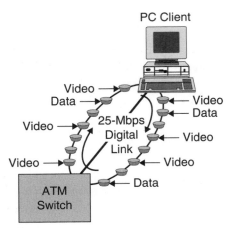

Figure 7–21 *ATM conveyor belt.*

empty, the buckets whip around the belt at 25 Mbps, 155 Mbps, or 622 Mbps (see Figure 7-21).

In Figure 7-21, our PC client is performing both a video telephony link and a data transfer to a server simultaneously. At the ATM board in the PC, both a video bit stream and chunks of data arrive. The video has priority and requires one cell in every three (in this example). The ATM board stuffs the video bits into every third cell, leaving many cell left empty to carry other information. In this case, the data transfer requires one cell in every six (again in this specific example). So the ATM board stuffs data into every sixth cell. Still more cells remain to carry more video, voice, or data streams across the 25-Mbps ATM link to the ATM switch. It is the conveyor belt operation that makes ATM very effective at utilizing the capacity of the high-speed links in an ATM-based network.

The ATM switch now unloads and transfers the contents of every conveyor belt bucket to the next conveyor belt that carries the data streams onto their final destinations. Figure 7-22 shows the video stream being switched to the conveyor belt connecting to the other PC. At the same time, the data stream must travel to the facility-wide ATM switch, then down to the switch connecting to the server, and finally over the link into the server.

ATM Layer-3, Layer-4, and Layer-5 software sets up the connections and the data routing through the switch when the logical point-to-point connections are first established. On each link, ATM allocates the bandwidth to match the CBR/VBR/ABR priorities, data load mix, and the bits per second speed (bandwidth) of the link. So on the video connection to the other PC, the video stream gets every third bucket. On the faster links into the ATM

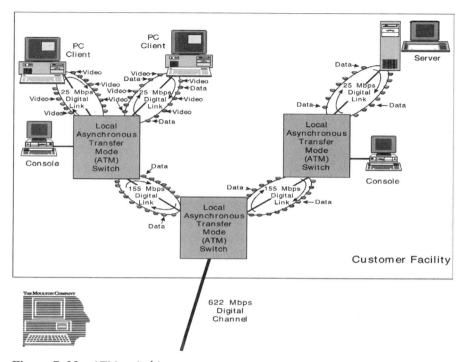

Figure 7–22 *ATM switching.*

facility switch, the data streams only get one bucket in every eight buckets. (Yes, I know the math does not compute exactly, but I need a little artistic license to make this fit the figure.) Every eighth bucket in the 155-Mbps ATM channels contains data, but this reverts back to one bucket in every six on the 25-Mbps ATM channel connecting to the server.

Figure 7-23 shows how our facility network could be connected to ATM WAN switches. These switches could carry ATM cells at 39-Gbps speeds to facilitate planet-wide connections. Any ATM traffic (video, voice, or data calls) could be switched out of our facility onto the ATM backbone WAN and then to a remote facility as needed to make video, voice, or data calls.

Cell relay and the conveyor belt operation is a very powerful technology because it effectively allocates each channel's bandwidth (bits per second speed) to handling the load offered at any instant in time.

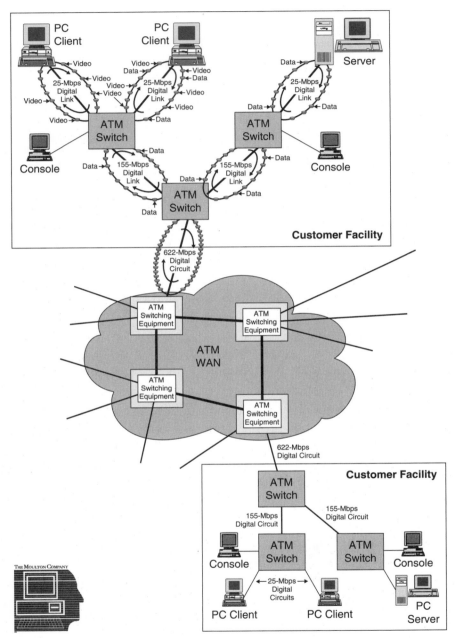

Figure 7–23 *ATM networks.*

CELL FORMAT AND ADAPTATION LAYERS

ATM uses 53-byte cells with no data error checking to transfer voice, video, and data across high-speed communications links. The few voice and video errors that occur are passed on to the receiving equipment. Data errors are corrected by ISO Layer 4, the transport layer.

ATM networks are based upon cell transmission with a 5-character header and 48-character information field. These cells can be allocated to voice, data, or video transmission. Although the cells are sent synchronously between ATM nodes, their assignment to a connection is as needed (asynchronous). Thus, ATM provides bit rate allocation as demanded by the channels.

ATM supports data, voice, and video channels at the Adaptation Layer (AAL). These channels are assigned to Virtual Channels (VCs) and Paths (VPs). The ATM header in Layer 2 contains a Virtual Path Identifier (VPI) and a Virtual Channel Identifier (VCI). An error detection field protects the header information. No error detection is provided at Layer 2 for the ATM data. Data error detection is shifted up to Layer 4. The AAL assigns ATM cells as needed by the higher layer channels. The VCI permits ATM to associate a specific QoS or priority with a higher layer channel.

The ATM AAL supports three classes of channels:

- Type 1—Channels that provide CBR services to ATM. This would be a high-speed multiplexed data or a video channel.
- Type 3 and Type 4—Channels supporting transport of variable-length data frames with error detection and multiplexing. This classification fits when the AAL multiplexes several channels into a single ATM channel. SMDS channels would also fit these classifications.
- Type 5—Channels providing low overhead transport of variable-length frames, but without multiplexing identification. A LAN-to-LAN channel using TCP/IP would fit into this class.

ATM service and equipment promise to provide the flexibility to support high-bandwidth multimedia applications because of their high data transfer speeds, small cell sizes, and rapid switching of data between source and destination.

ATM SWITCHING AND MULTIPLEXING

ATM is a connection-oriented service that buffers information and then places it into cells. When data fills a cell, the cell is then sent across the network to the destination specified.

ATM is similar to packet-switched networks with some important differences:

- ATM links provide no error and flow control—these functions must be provided by the transport layer. The low error rate transmission links permit omission of error correction, maximizing transmission efficiency. Packet-switched networks are aimed at high error rate links, so they provide link-by-link acknowledgements.
- ATM cells are of fixed length. There is no provision for accommodating variable data size in ATM cells because ATM cells are 53 bytes and ATM cells carry 48 characters of data all the time. These cells are smaller than standard packet-switched networks, thus reducing transmission delay variability. In this manner, ATM is able to carry timing-sensitive, isochronous data streams like voice and video. Packet-switched networks use varying size packets, with the maximum size being from 128 characters to 4,096 characters.
- ATM provides a connection-oriented service—all information is transferred over virtual channels for the duration of the ATM call.
- ATM maintains cell sequence. Cells arrive at the destination in the same order as they left the source. This is not necessarily the case with other packet-switched networks.
- Cells are continuously transmitted like buckets on a conveyor belt. When the network is idle, empty cells are transported. Packet-switched networks send packets only when there is data to transfer.
- The ATM header provides limited Layer-2 capabilities. This permits rapid switching and information transfer.

These techniques allow ATM to be more flexible than Narrowband ISDN (N-ISDN). ATM is the broadband access for ISDN. The ATM's high-broadband capacity transports data from different types of services using the same format. ATM is ideal for integrating voice, data, and video on a single network. Consolidation services simplify network management and operation. Network administration is required to match billing rates to QoS agreements.

The ATM's small cell size allows it to match the rate at which it transmits data to the rate that data is produced by the source. High bit rate services, such as video, are VBR because compression creates bursty data. This is easily transmitted using ATM cells.

VIRTUAL CIRCUITS

ATM is connection-oriented. ATM transports information across the network using "virtual" connections for information transport. Connections are called virtual because although users logically connect end-to-end, a connection is only made when a cell is sent and received. Connections are not dedicated, with several exchanges using a connection at the same time. Connections are divided into two levels:

- Virtual Channel (VC), or Virtual Channel Connections (VCCs), are essentially a VC carrying a single stream of cells from end-user to end-user.
- Virtual Path (VP), or Virtual Path Connections (VPCs), are collections of VCs bundled together. A VPC may run end-to-end across an ATM network. An ATM network in this instance does not route cells belonging to particular VCs, but rather all cells belonging to a VP are routed the same way through the ATM network. This is to provide fast recovery from major ATM network failures.

A VCC connects ATM network end-points. The VCC is several VC links extending between VC switches. A Virtual Channel Identifier (VCI) identifies a VC. Routing translation tables change VCIs as they pass through ATM switches. Between two ATM switches in a VC link, the VCI does not change. The VCI and VPI (Virtual Path Identifier) ensure that ATM switches route channels and paths correctly. There are several VCCs, including:

- User-to-user applications—VCCs between customer equipment at each end of a communications link.
- User-to-network applications—VCCs between customer equipment and network nodes.
- Network-to-network applications—VCCS between two network nodes that exchange traffic management and routing information.

VCCs:

- Have a QoS, specifying the Cell Loss Ratio (CLR) and Cell Delay Variation (CDV).
- Are switched or semi-permanent.
- Maintain cell sequencing (Cell 1 arrives before Cell 2, etc.).
- Negotiate traffic parameters using Usage Parameter Control (UPC).

VPCs and VCCs allow cell multiplexing with a complication. Cell switching requires only the value of the VPI to be known.

ATM networks use VPs internally to bundle VCs between switches. Two ATM switches with different VCCs between them belonging to different users can bundle these VC paths into a VPC. This creates in effect a virtual trunk between the two ATM switches. This virtual trunk may in turn be handled as a single entity by intermediate cross-connects between the two ATM VC switches.

VCs can be static Permanent Virtual Circuits (PVCs) or dynamically Switched Virtual Circuits (SVCs). VCs make point-to-point or point-to-multi-point connections.

ATM BROADBAND INTERFACES AND ROUTING

ATM User Network Interface (ATM UNI) standards specify how users connect to ATM networks. Several standards are defined for T-1/E-1 (1.544 Mbps/2.048 Mbps), 25 Mbps, T-3/E-3 (44.736 Mbps/34.368 Mbps, OC–3 (155 Mbps), OC–12 (622.08 Mbps), and OC–48 (2.488 Gbps). Higher speed interfaces are also being developed.

OC–3 interfaces are specified for single-mode fiber supporting wide area applications and for UTP or multi-mode fiber for lower-cost LAN applications.

Two ATM networking standards define connectivity between network switches and between networks:

- Broadband Inter-Carrier Interface (B–ICI).
- Public Network-to-Network Interface (P–NNI).

P-NNI has more features. P-NNI supports Class of Service (CoS) routing and bandwidth reservation. CoS manages traffic in a network by grouping traffic like streaming video, voice, and large document file transfer together and handling each class with its own distinct level of priority. Different from QoS traffic management, CoS does not guarantee bandwidth and delivery time, but rather provides "best-effort" delivery. CoS is simple to manage and very scalable as network traffic volume grows. CoS is less sophisticated than QoS.

CoS includes:

- 802.1p Layer-2 Tagging.
- Type of Service (ToS).
- Differentiated Services (DS or DiffServ).

The 802.1p Layer-2 tagging and ToS use three bits in the Layer-2 packet header to specify priority. While three bits can specify priority, they do not provide traffic management capabilities. In contrast, the DS or DiffServ uses information on how a packet is to be forwarded to manage ATM traffic. Called Per Hop Behavior (PHB), the packet forwarding information describes service levels by bandwidth, queuing, and packet discard decisions.

The P-NNI routes and distributes traffic over an ATM network topology based on advertised link parameters, attributes, and bandwidth (bits per second link speed). Some parameters used in path computation include the destination ATM address, traffic class, traffic contract, QoS requirements, and channel constraints. ATM connection path determination includes over-all network impact assessment, avoidance of loops, minimization of rerouting attempts, and policies for inclusion/exclusion in rerouting, diverse routing, and carrier selection. Connection Admission Controls (CACs) define procedures used by switches at the edge of an ATM network, whereby a call is accepted or rejected based on the ability of an ATM network to support the requested QoS. Once a VC has been established, ATM network resources are held and QoS is guaranteed for the duration of the connection.

All ATM traffic carried in cells requires definition of how the data is placed into the cells, thus permitting a receiver to reconstruct the original bit stream. Three important schemes are:

- RFC-1483—Specifies inter-router traffic encapsulation using ATM Adaptation Layer-5 (AAL–5). AAL–5 is similar to HDLC framing like that used by frame relay, SDLC, and X.25.
- ATM LAN Emulation (LANE) and Multi-Protocol Over ATM (MPOA)—Designed to support dynamic use of ATM Switched Virtual Circuits (SVCs) primarily for TCP/IP. LANE, a subset of the MPOA standard, is widely deployed.
- Voice and video adaptation schemes using AAL–1 for high efficiency—Voice and video streams have no breaks. They are circuit-switched connections carrying bits at fixed bits per second speeds.

Voice and video transmission using circuit switching and multiplexing are mapped ATM CBR PVCs using circuit emulation and AAL-1. The disadvantage with circuit emulation is that the bandwidth is dedicated whether useful information is transmitted or not. A T-1 1.544-Mbps circuit, when transmitted in circuit emulation mode, uses 1.74 Mbps of ATM bandwidth. This is an easy to implement but inefficient ATM interface.

ATM VBR connections can exploit the burstiness of voice and many real-time applications using sophisticated compression schemes to increase ATM efficiency. During all voice communication, there are periods of silence that can be used to service other calls and thus increase transmission efficiency. Some of these silent periods are:

- When a trunk is idle during off-peak hours.
- When one person is talking at a given time (half-duplex).
- When no one is talking during a call.

A further enhancement to voice over ATM is voice switching over SVCs. This requires interacting with PBX signaling and then routing voice calls to the appropriate destination PBX. The ATM Forum, which sets ATM standards, is focusing efforts on voice handled over CBR SVCs and Variable Bit Rate-Real Time (VBR–RT) circuits.

APPLYING ATM PRODUCTS TO SAVE COSTS

Customer equipment capable of using ATM networking technology such as routers, switches, and PC adapter cards is now available in many communications vendors' product lines.

ATM products integrate multiplexing and switching functions. They can save costs when handling bursty traffic in contrast to traditional circuit switching and T-1 channel multiplexing. ATM is good at handling communications between devices that operate at different speeds. ATM designed for high-performance multimedia networking is implemented in a range of networking devices, including:

1. PC NICs.
2. Switched Ethernet and token ring hubs.
3. Campus ATM switches.
4. Enterprise ATM network switches.
5. ATM multiplexers.
6. ATM edge switches.
7. ATM backbone switches.

These devices support construction of private ATM networks that handle traffic between sites efficiently. This is shown with a hypothetical example in Figure 7-24.

At the top of Figure 7-24, a T-1 link is run between two facilities. The T-1 creates 24 separate time division multiplexed channels. If one of these channels is idle, its capacity is wasted. The T-1 channel capacity is parceled out in big, wasteful chunks. In the middle of the diagram, running frame relay frames across each of the 24 channels uses the T-1 span more effectively. Now all channels are in use at any given time, but the frames are large and inefficient, resulting in significant idle capacity. By deploying ATM on each channel the channels are now used more effectively. They are broken down into ATM cells that minimize wasted idle capacity. Because ATM can make a communications channel use more effective, it saves telecommunications costs.

The example in Figure 7-24 was set up artificially to illustrate ATM efficiency. In reality, frame relay and ATM would not be broken up into individual 64-Kbps channels. Both frame relay and ATM would use the entire T-1 1.544-Mbps bandwidth. Frame relay frames carrying 4,096 characters would occupy 21.22 milliseconds on the T-1 channel with 41.7 4096-character frames being available to carry all offered traffic. Each 53-byte ATM cell passes across the T-1 channel in 274.6 nanoseconds. This means that each

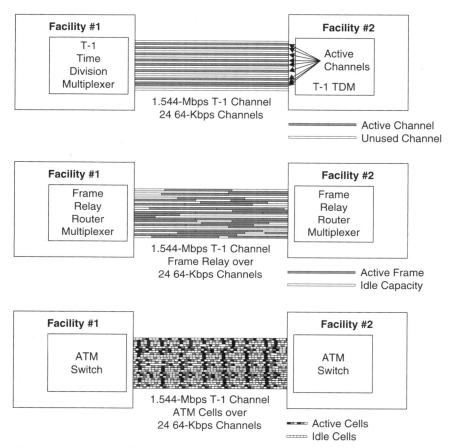

Figure 7–24 *T-1 vs. frame relay vs. ATM.*

second, a T-1 channel has 3,641.5 cells to assign to voice, video, or data transmission. So our information carrying efficiency is:

- T-1 multiplexed channel—24 data links, fixed 64-Kbps capacity.
- Frame relay on T-1—41.7 frames a second at 1.544 Mbps, or 21.22-millisecond delay.
- ATM on T-1—3,641.5 cells a second at 1.544 Mbps, or 0.2746-milliseconds delay.

ATM is offered as an end-user service. ATM service providers such as Cable & Wireless and MCI WorldCom, among others, offer ATM tariffed services.

The basic service building block is the ATM VC. ATM switches are placed at customer sites. The switches implement ATM VCs end-to-end connections with defined end-points and routes. The ATM VCs do not have bandwidth dedicated to them, but rather, bandwidth is allocated on demand by the network as required. In this manner, different traffic streams can be organized into separate VCs. Just the network resources required to handle this traffic is assigned to it, or the ATM network allocates resources based on varying traffic needs. Because multiple traffic streams are multiplexed on each physical facility between the end-user and the network or between ATM network switches, and because ATM can direct traffic streams to many different destinations, costs are saved by reducing the interfaces and the facilities required to construct a private network.

PC ATM PRODUCTS • ATM PC products are PC cards. PC adapter cards were among the first products offered. ATM adapter card vendors include IBM, Sun, Fore Systems, and Efficient Networks, Inc.

The most widely used set of standards in local ATM environments is ATM LAN Emulation (LANE). Windows 98 software implements LANE. ATM LANE makes an ATM SVC network appear to be an Ethernet (IEEE 802.3) or token ring (IEEE 802.5) LAN. LANE duplicates LAN characteristics, enabling existing LAN applications to run over ATM transparently. In ATM LANE, unicast LAN traffic travels over direct ATM SVCs from clients to servers. Servers use multicast LAN traffic to respond to some client requests. Bridging interconnects real LANs and emulated LANs running on ATM, and routing interconnects ATM emulated LANs to other WANs or LANs.

The ATM Forum LANE implementation agreement specifies two types of LANE network components connected to an ATM network:

- LANE clients such as PCs with ATM interfaces, operating servers, or PCs; Ethernet or token ring switches supporting ATM networking; and routers and bridges in an ATM LAN.
- LANE servers supporting ATM LANE service for configuration management, multicast support, and address resolution.

The LANE service is implemented in clients or in other ATM network devices. The LAN Emulation User-Network Interface (LUNI) sequences and packages messages to clients in IEEE 802.3 or IEEE 802.5 formats. The LAN Emulation Configuration Server (LECS) initializes the PC on the ATM LAN by emulating plugging the PC ATM NIC into a LAN hub. Clients use it to connect to a LAN Emulation Server (LES) that performs LAN address registration and resolution. The LES maps IEEE 48-bit MAC addresses and token ring route descriptors to ATM addresses. A very important MAC address for clients is the MAC-layer broadcast address used to send traffic to all locations on a LAN. The Broadcast and Unknown Server (BUS) performs this function in LANE. ATM LANE is a comprehensive set of capabilities that has been

Layers 3 & 4

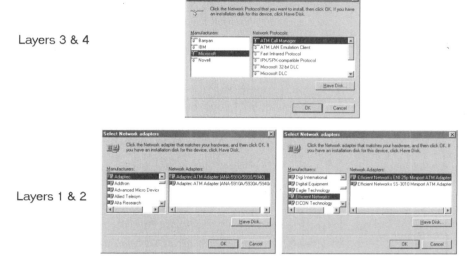

Layers 1 & 2

Figure 7–25 *Windows and ATM.*

widely deployed in ATM networks. Some Windows 98-supported ATM NICs and Windows 98 LANE software are identified in Figure 7-25.

ATM NETWORKING PRODUCTS • ATM networking products include switches and gateways (routers). The switching products interconnect ATM with other networks like Ethernet IP networks. Some switches use indirect connections to ATM services through standalone gateways (routers). Standalone ATM gateways (routers) often provide ATM interfaces directly to customer equipment. Router vendors are now moving away from standalone gateways to lower costs and improve performance.

ATM LAN switches drive the U.S. market. LAN switches have encroached into WANs, using WAN interface support designed to interconnect ATM LANs. This is more economically feasible because high-speed T-3 circuits are more available and economically priced. Some ATM networking product vendors are 3Com and Cisco, among others.

ATM SERVICE EXAMPLE OFFERINGS • The European approach to Broadband Integrated Services Digital Network (BISDN) services is defined by the ITU-T. The concept is for BISDN to deliver a spectrum of Telecommunications Operator (TO) services to customer premises using an ATM infrastructure. The services to be delivered include SMDS, frame relay, leased circuits, voice, and raw ATM cell relay services. IEEE 802.6 MAN also specifies providing SMDS services based upon SMDS surrounding an ATM infrastructure.

The approach in the U.S. is less packaged. ATM products are oriented towards data communications or private networking. Delivery of ATM Permanent Virtual Circuit (PVC) and frame relay PVC support is aimed at private WANs, at ATM PVCs, and at ATM SVCs in LANs. Vendors developed ATM products supporting UNI 3.0, UNI 3.1, as well as proprietary LANE schemes. Proprietary LANE schemes are often faster than the ATM Forum's definition of LANE.

Cable & Wireless' ATM service provides a complete, end-to-end transmission delivered over Cable & Wireless' global digital highway. The Cable & Wireless backbone network is a highly reliable self-healing fiber optic transmission network. Cable & Wireless supports one-stop ordering, circuit provisioning (configuring), billing, and account management. ATM service access speeds range from T-1/E-1 to T-3/E-3. VBR service accommodates all major networking protocols in an efficient and cost-effective architecture. Voice, data, and video circuits are available within the U.S., and to the U.K. and other major European cities. The backbone network has proactive 24/7 network monitoring and support. Service prices are often half the cost of a comparable E-1 or higher speed international private line.

Cable & Wireless' ATM service is cell relay protocol and ATM switching, providing seamless, managed broadband network services for WAN and LAN solutions. ATM enables integrating data, voice, and video services on a single-cost, efficient network. ATM's low-latency (in-transit delay) characteristics are ideal for streaming video, voice, and other types of high-priority, time-sensitive traffic.

Cable & Wireless services are:

• CBR for demanding real-time video and multimedia applications.
• Variable Bit Rate-Non-Real Time (VBR-NRT) service for critical but lower bandwidth applications.

Both services are available globally. An ATM switch connects to a high-speed ATM backbone network. This ATM backbone in turn links the ATM switches to deliver a uniform level of performance, maintenance support, and end-to-end network management.

Similarly, MCI WorldCom's ATM service supports voice, video, data, and other multimedia applications using a single network access interface. MCI WorldCom's ATM service is available nationwide and planet-wide. MCI WorldCom's ATM is a cell relay, connection-oriented, data transmission service that integrates all types of traffic. It decreases the number of access lines needed and greatly simplifies technology management.

MCI WorldCom's ATM service provides several options to meet data transport requirements. Access speeds range from slower than 1.544 Mbps over DSL access to 622 Mbps, or OC-12 speeds. ATM provides the ability to prioritize service to support multiple types of traffic. MCI WorldCom's ATM service supports all five ATM service classes, as defined by the ATM Forum.

MCI WorldCom's ATM service implements the latest ATM Forum specifications and international standards. Some advantages of ATM service are:

- Local to global to local connectivity (one bill/one provider/one contact).
- Supports scalable access/port speeds from less than 1.544 Mbps to 622 Mbps.
- Supports all five major service classes as defined by the ATM Forum.
- Internetworking with frame relay and the Internet.
- Industry-first Service Level Agreements (SLAs).

ATM continues to be based upon international interface and signaling standards defined by the International Telecommunications Union-Telecommunications (ITU-T) Standards Sector (formerly the CCITT). The ATM Forum plays a pivotal role in the ATM market since its formulation in 1991. The ATM Forum is an international voluntary organization composed of vendors, service providers, research organizations, and users. The goal of the ATM Forum is to expand the use of ATM products and services through rapid convergence of inter-operability specifications, promote industry cooperation, and develop multi-vendor implementation agreements.

ATM services save network costs over leased line services by reducing network interfaces and channels, by providing variable-speed VCs to multiple locations, and by efficiently using physical channel bandwidth. ATM services can integrate with Windows and other LANE products to provide planet-wide facility connectivity for video, voice, multimedia, and data applications.

Brain Teaser

ATM Networking

Using the T-1 network we constructed in the previous Brain Teaser, replace the T-1 links with an ATM service like that sold by MCI or Cable & Wireless.

1. What is required to move our T-1 network onto an ATM service? High-speed links into the ATM service provider's network combined with ATM switching/interfacing equipment on our network

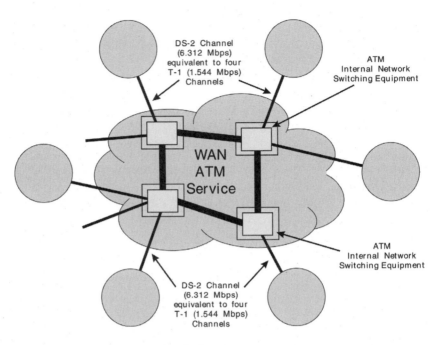

Figure 7–26 *ATM network solution.*

sites. VCs (circuits) would need to be logically configured to connect all sites.

2. What would be a good speed to run the ATM network access channels at? It is best to match speed with load. However, without knowing the load, choosing a speed that is equal to or higher than the current aggregate T-1 speed is a reasonable guess. In Figure 7-26, channels were used.

3. What would happen if the access speeds chosen were too low? You would finish your network planning using the scream approach to sizing capacity. When a link lacks capacity, everyone on that link screams until the capacity is increased. It works, but leaves some unhappy users.

4. What cost savings are realized? Lower physical interconnection costs and most likely lower networking costs as well.

The goal here is to understand how ATM service can reduce network costs.

Synchronous Optical Network

Synchronous Optical Network, or SONET, is a transmission system technology for use on fiber optic cable networks. SONET is not only a high-capacity digital transport service directly provided to organizations, but it is also the technology forming the foundation for future high-speed multimedia telecommunications networks and services.

In the U.S., SONET is an ANSI standard for synchronous data transmission on optical media. Internationally, SONET's equivalent is the Synchronous Digital Hierarchy (SDH). These standards together ensure that planet-wide digital telecommunications networks can interconnect. They also ensure that existing telecommunications transmission systems can use optical media by attaching to them as tributary or feeder channels.

ATM, frame relay, and telecommunications services run as a layer on top of SONET. Essentially, SONET forms the foundation for building networks and delivering telecommunications services. SONET is considered to be the foundation for the physical layer of Broadband ISDN (BISDN).

SONET systems carry traffic called the payload with overhead blocks called section, line, and path overheads. The section and line overheads together are identified as the transport overhead. The path overhead is an end-to-end overhead, while the line and section overheads help move data from one SONET component to another.

SONET CONFIGURATIONS

SONET specifies a digital hierarchy based on Optical Carriers (OCs). SONET specifies transmission channel speeds up to the maximum transmission speed of 39.81312 Gbps. SONET defines a base rate of 51.84 Mbps, and a set of multiples of the base rate called Optical Carrier (OC) levels. Unlike T-carrier channels, the OC levels are all direct multiples of the base 51.84-Mbps transmission speed.

SONET defines Synchronous Transport Signals (STSs), which are electrical interfaces used as the multiplexing mechanisms within SONET. SONET Network Elements (NEs) multiplex (or aggregate) STS-1 signals into STS-N signals where needed. The N in STS-N is the number of STS-1s that form the STS-N. SONET provides high-bandwidth connections by concatenating STS-1s up to the aggregate speed required. The concatenated STS-1s are designated with a "c." An STS-3c is therefore three STS-1s and the STS-3c speed is 155 Mbps.

SONET is multiplexed at the byte level, permitting dynamic mapping of services into the broadband STS for transport. The DS-0 speed of 64 Kbps is the basic building block of SONET frames. This easily integrates current digital services into the SONET optical hierarchy.

OC MULTIPLEXING HIERARCHY • SONET uses OCs that operate at the following speeds:

Optical Carrier Level Designation	Transmission Speed	Digital Signal-1 Channel Equivalents	Digital Signal-3 Channel Equivalents
OC-1/STS-1	51.84 Mbps	28 DS-1 Channels	1 DS-3 Channels
OC-3	155.52 Mbps	84 DS-1 Channels	3 DS-3 Channels
OC-12	622.08 Mbps	336 DS-1 Channels	12 DS-3 Channels
OC-48	2,488.32 Mbps	1,344 DS-1 Channels	48 DS-3 Channels
OC-192	9,953.28 Mbps	5,376 DS-1 Channels	192 DS-3 Channels
OC-768	39,813.12 Mbps	21,504 DS-1 Channels	768 DS-3 Channels

SONET is fundamentally a sophisticated multiplexing technology at the frame level combined with high bit rate optical physical transmission facilities.

FRAME FORMATS • Similar to T-1, SONET bit streams are divided into frames. The frames are 810 characters in size, with 36 characters of overhead and 774 characters of payload. As on every other telecommunications link, SONET carries 8,000 frames per second. These frames are 125-microseconds duration (1/8000=125 microseconds). Frames contain 810 8-bit characters, resulting in a basic SONET transmission speed of 51.84 Mbps (8000 X 8 X 810 = 51.84). This is the basic SONET OC-1 channel (see Figure 7-27).

Removing all overhead characters results in a payload data rate of 49.536 Mbps (774 characters X 8,000 frames/second X 8 bits/character = 49.536 Mbps).

Section overhead includes STS-N channel performance monitoring, data channels for management, and framing bits. Management functions include channel monitoring, channel administration, maintenance functions, and channel provisioning. The section overhead is used to perform channel functions between SONET components such as repeaters, Add Drop Multiplexers (ADMs), terminal equipment, and Digital Access and Cross-connect Systems (DACS).

Line overhead functions are STS-1 performance monitoring, management data channels, payload pointers, protection switching information, line

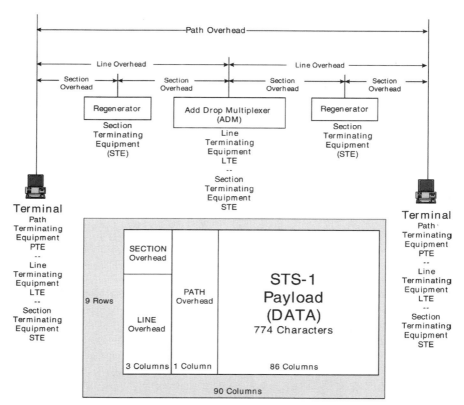

Figure 7–27 *SONET frames and overhead.*

alarm signals, and far-end failure to receive indicators. The line overhead supports channel functions between SONET terminals and ADMs.

Path overhead functions are STS and Synchronous Payload Envelope (SPE) monitoring, signal labels, and path and trace status information. Virtual Tributary (VT) path overhead functions are VT performance monitoring, signal labels (equipped or unequipped), path status, and pointers. These support channel functions from one SONET terminal to another SONET terminal end-to-end across a SONET network.

The SONET framing and functions supported by the framing are primarily confined to OSI Layer 1, the physical layer. Individual channels feeding a SONET network are brought on and split off of the SONET network using SONET networking components, including: ADMs and DACS.

SONET NETWORK COMPONENTS

SONET transport networks use a number of different networking components and topologies to satisfy objectives for network simplicity, cost containment, bandwidth efficiency, and survivability. Optical hubs remove the need for an expensive and complex arrangement of several back-to-back network elements. Similarly, self-healing rings assure survivability through redundancy and geographically diverse paths.

POINT-TO-POINT TERMINAL • A point-to-point configuration is a traditional topology that terminates an entire SONET payload at each end of a fiber span. Point-to-point topologies are typically used in basic transport applications needing a single route solution. Point-to-point configurations are not specifically designed to be completely survivable. Using geographically diverse paths can enhance reliability of a point-to-point configuration. When the path exceeds optical transmission limits, regenerators or optical amplifiers are used to reconstitute the signal. In Figure 7-28, an optical repeater at an intermediate node eliminates the need for an expensive SONET back-to-back terminal configuration at that node.

1:N PROTECTION CHANNEL-SHARING • The 1:N channel-sharing configuration is a multi-network element point-to-point configuration that conserves fiber pairs. Multiple systems share a common protection channel. In applications with growing traffic, the 1:N protection arrangement can defer some new fiber deployment.

When a failure occurs on a working optical channel, traffic is automatically rerouted over a protection channel via an inter-component protection loop and dedicated protection components. Working components are equipped with mixed electrical and optical tributary types.

If desired, the 1:N protection configuration's protection components and the normally empty protection bandwidth can transport unprotected extra traffic. In Figure 7-28, a single (the 1) diversely routed fiber channel acts as the backup for two SONET fiber channels. In the event of failure of one or both active channels, the backup channel carries the load (in degraded mode when both active channels fail).

MULTIPLEXING OVER FIBER

SONET physical channels are multiplexed to increase network capacity (overall aggregate speed). The multiplexing performed is Frequency Division Multiplexing (FDM), with frequencies represented by different colors of

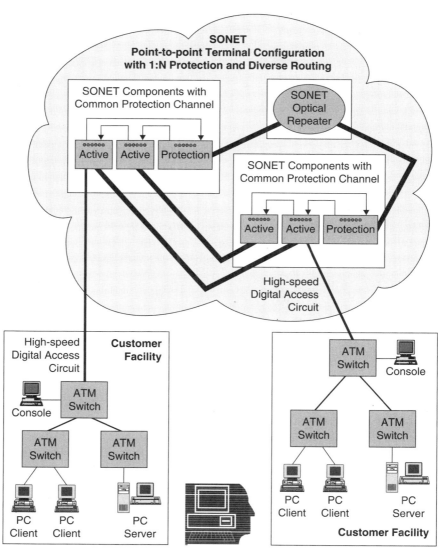

Figure 7–28 *SONET point-to-point terminal on 1:N protection configuration.*

light. This is referred to as Wave Division Multiplexing, Wavelength Division Multiplexing (WDM), or Dense Wave Division Multiplexing (DWDM). Chapter 6 contained a brief explanation of DWDM.

Since SONET is all fiber optics, multiplexing schemes are based on the possible wave variants. This is sort of like cable TV—one cable with sixty channels, and each channel at a different frequency so they do not interfere with one another. With fiber, essential multiple channels use different wavelengths of light.

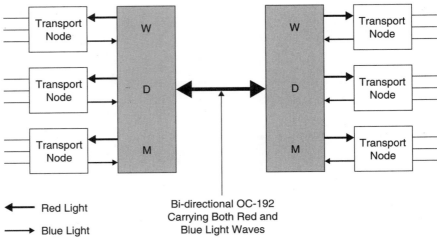

Figure 7–29 *Wave Division Multiplexing (WDM).*

WAVE DIVISION MULTIPLEXING OR WAVELENGTH DIVISION MULTIPLEXING (WDM) • WDM multiplies (up to 32 or more times) the capacity of existing fiber spans by combining two or more optical signals of different wavelengths on a single fiber. Because WDM avoids the large capital outlays and long lead times often associated with deploying new fiber cable, WDM is a practical solution for crucial SONET capacity growth.

In WDM, an external coupling device performs the multiplexing of different optical signals. These communications can be both unidirectional as well as bi-directional. Unidirectional WDM makes the multiple wavelengths travel in the same direction on an optical fiber. Bi-directional allows multiple signals to pass in opposite directions. Bi-directional WDM is often the preferred approach, especially in applications employing two wavelengths due to the one-to-one association of an individual transport system to an individual optical fiber (see Figure 7-29).

WDM is classified as wideband (cross-band), narrowband, or dense, depending on the wavelengths involved. WDM provides multiple channels by using lasers at slightly different wavelengths. It is a form of FDM requiring very stable lasers at very specific and narrow frequencies. An optical grating separates the optical frequencies at the receiving end of a link, permitting them to be detected.

WDM is an inexpensive way to get more capacity out of fiber trunks by sending multiple signals down the same fiber filament. Unfortunately, the glass used to make the fibers has a very large range of frequencies where its transparency is best. This means that the lasers must be highly coherent and relatively close together in wavelength. It is not like sending red and blue light down the same cable, but rather like sending several shades of red and blue light across the same fiber.

Wideband WDM doubles the capacity of a fiber span by combining the 1310 nm wavelength with a second wavelength in the low-loss window of optical fiber, between 1528 nm and 1560 nm. As with wideband WDM, the narrowband method provides a two-fold increase in fiber span capacity. It employs two low-loss wavelengths, typically 1533 nm and 1557 nm. On long-haul routes, narrowband WDM is usually a better choice relative to wideband WDM.

DENSE WAVE DIVISION MULTIPLEXING • DWDM once signified using more than eight wavelengths of light per fiber. This is less meaningful today, as channel counts per fiber have zoomed from 16 wavelengths to hundreds of wavelengths. DWDM still generally refers to high channel count fiber links.

DWDM technology employs as many as 100 wavelengths to increase fiber span capacity up to 100-fold. These wavelengths fall within different bands: a blue band between 1529 nm and 1541 nm and a red band between 1549 nm and 1557 nm. Each band is dedicated to a particular direction of transmission. For example, an eight-wavelength system uses:

- Red waves: 1550 nm, 1552 nm, 1555 nm, and 1557 nm.
- Blue waves: 1529 nm, 1530 nm, 1532 nm, and 1533 nm.

Vendors have DWDM systems that can support more than 100 wavelengths with each wavelength being a single channel. Each channel can carry up to 10 Gbps. DWDM optical transmission links can carry more than a terabit per second digital transmission. Current DWDM technology is supporting 256 colors of light.

LITE TERMINATING EQUIPMENT • In SONET, Lite Terminating Equipment (LTE) terminates a SONET communications channel using the Lite Transmission Convergence (TC) layer in an ATM network component. This type of termination is more commonly used for end-user or LAN equipment because the SONET Lite TC layer does not implement some path, line, and section overhead functions used in long-haul networks.

SONET SELF-HEALING RING OPERATION

SONET rings are self-healing to provide extraordinary network reliability. SONET's self-healing ring architecture protects against cable cuts and node failures by providing duplicate, geographically diverse paths for each SONET channel. To assure end-to-end survivability for services traversing multiple rings, adjacent rings may be interlocked using redundant matched-node inter-ring gateways. These configurations provide linear add/drop route cost savings and improved reliability in comparison to back-to-back SONET terminal configurations.

TWO- AND FOUR-FIBER RINGS • A SONET ring is generally one of three types: a Unidirectional Path-Switched Ring (UPSR), a two-fiber Bi-directional Line-Switched Ring (BLSR), or a four-fiber Bi-directional Line-Switched Ring (BLSR). While each type of ring features fully self-healing operation, differing characteristics may make each ring architecture preferable for specific applications. UPSRs are good for linking remote offices to a CO where most traffic terminates (see Figure 7-30).

The UPSR in Figure 7-30 has data entering the single fiber ring at the left and exiting the single fiber ring at the top. At the source node, the data is split into two identical streams. One stream is sent clockwise around the ring (the shortest path) and the other identical stream is sent counter-clockwise around the ring (the longest path). At the destination node, the data traveling counter-clockwise (the longest path) is passed on to the destination. The data traveling clockwise is discarded into the proverbial bit bucket, or write-only memory. Each path (clockwise and counter-clockwise) uses a single fiber that is fully occupied with SONET transmission traffic. In the event the most common fiber cable locating tool (a backhoe) locates and breaks the fiber on the clockwise fiber segment, the destination node senses darkness from that path and immediately switches the clockwise bit stream into the outgoing bit stream path. In this manner, the UPSR self-heals.

A two-fiber BLSR is a good choice for inter-office networks with a highly distributed mesh traffic pattern. Four-fiber BLSRs are good for high-traffic applications and where multiple fault protection is required.

SUBTENDING RINGS • A subtending ring is a dual-ring configuration where a node's tributary optics support a secondary ring. This arrangement offers substantial capital savings and network simplification at a CO hub by allowing a single network element to serve in place of multiple co-located shelves. A subtending ring may be either a UPSR or a BLSR (see Figure 7-31).

FOLDED RINGS • In a folded ring configuration, a UPSR or BLSR can be implemented even where infrastructure does not support route diversity. The folded ring functions in exactly the same manner as a UPSR or BLSR, but the fibers on each side of the ring share a common physical path. This solution enables conversion from a linear topology to a SONET ring topology, and then upgrades to a route diversity configuration when additional fiber routes are constructed.

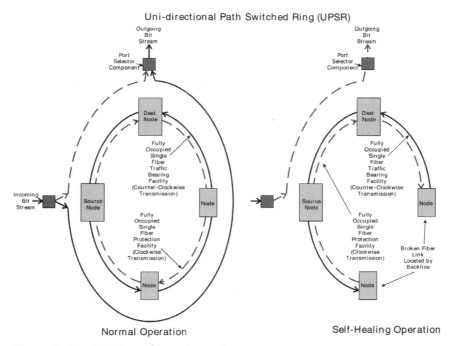

Figure 7–30   *UPSR configuration and operation.*

OPTICAL HUBS • Optical hubs consolidate traffic from multiple spur routes onto an optical channel extending to a remote site. This configuration eliminates the cost and complexity of multi-component arrangements that would otherwise be required to pass traffic from several lower rate fibers to a single higher rate fiber. The advantages of optical hubs apply equally to point-to-point, linear add/drop, and ring systems.

REGENERATORS • A regenerator extends ring coverage by reconstituting the optical signal at intermediate points between two service-terminating locations. If necessary, multiple cascaded regenerators are used to extend a ring hundreds of miles. Unlike optical amplifiers, regenerators use the SONET overhead section bytes for greater flexibility of operation and improved malfunction isolation.

Regenerators are generally one of two types. A non-route diverse regenerator supports two bi-directional optical channels in each direction to reconstitute the optical signal on both the working and protection fibers of a 1+1/1:1 protected point-to- point or linear system without route diversity. A diverse route regenerator works on single bi-directional optical channels for two-fiber BLSRs and other route diversity arrangements.

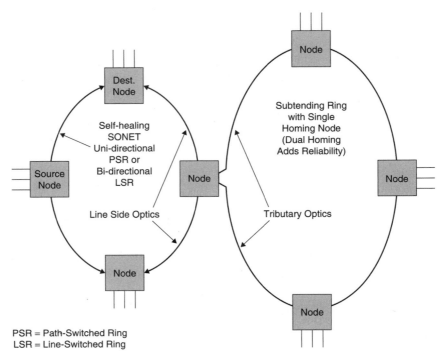

PSR = Path-Switched Ring
LSR = Line-Switched Ring

Figure 7–31 *Subtending rings.*

TRAFFIC GROOMING • Traffic grooming is consolidating or segregating traffic to make more effective use of the SONET ring. Traffic grooming functions that are consolidated combine fractional T1 links into full T1 circuits. Segregation separates traffic and routes it more directly to its final destination.

USING PROTECTED FACILITIES • Traffic features offered by SONET facilitate new services. These traffic features provide additional data carrying capacity for new services, such as Internet access and distance learning, without increasing telephone company fiber facilities.

Extra traffic support is the ability to use normally idle protection bandwidth built into today's point-to-point and self-healing ring SONET networks. This bandwidth's primary function is to assure SONET ring survivability. Most times it is unused and fully capable of supporting high-quality services (see Figure 7-32).

Some SONET products take advantage of this to maximize traffic flow. The unprotected status of extra traffic at first appears to seriously diminish its value, but several factors can substantially lessen the impact of a preemptive loss of the extra traffic capacity because facilities are switched during a cable cut or other fault condition. These include:

- Diverse routing—A redundant, geographically diverse route may protect extra traffic so no single source of failure causes an outage.
- Service discounting—During a trial period, a service provider could choose to offer an innovative, extra traffic-based service at a substantial discount to compensate for the possibility of a service interruption. After the service has proven its value to the customer, the service provider offers a fully protected service.
- Degradable services—Multiple protected and unprotected service channels may be provisioned for certain data services such as Internet access and packet-switched data. Loss of any unprotected extra traffic channels result in degraded performance (e.g., reduced throughput) during times of peak usage rather than a total service interruption.

In Figure 7-32, the unused time slots in each fiber could provide degradable service. In the event of a SONET outage, the unused time slots carry the primary SONET traffic and the degradable services wait until the ring is restored. The BLSR in Figure 7-32 has one link configured (provisioned) to connect Client #1's channels from the left-most node to the right-most node, Client #3's channels from the right-most node to the top node, and Client #2's channels from the top node to the left-most node. If the bottom node were to fail, the channels for Client #1 would be re-routed using the protection time slots on the inner (clockwise) fiber from the left-most node to the right-most node. This assures that Client #1's channels are not broken in the event of failure. Degradable services using the protection time slots would use any time slots remaining after the primary provisioned (configured) channels for Client #1 used all time slots needed to assure service without interruption.

SYNCHRONIZATION • SONET line overhead applies to the multiplexing and switching functions as well as ring synchronization. SONET overhead is in three layers that match the section, line, and path segments of a telephone network. This layered approach allows specific equipment to be built to support different functions. The section layer defines the network segment between regenerators, an optical repeater. The section layer's job is to transport overhead traffic for both line and path layers and the actual network traffic. Framing, scrambling, error monitoring, and order wiring—installing or removing service—are done in the section layer.

The line is that portion of a network between line-terminating equipment where STS-1 signals are multiplexed to higher rates. It performs syn-

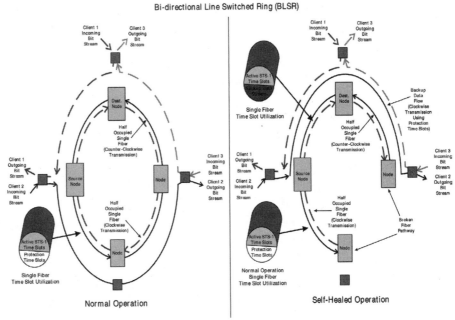

Figure 7–32 *BLSR configuration.*

chronization, multiplexing, automatic protective switching, and additional error monitoring. It also provides a data communications channel, a channel for priority installation or removal of a service, and room for growth. Automatic protection switching is intended to facilitate the automatic switching of traffic from a primary to a backup circuit if the quality of the primary circuit drops below a certain threshold. Line overhead is intended to ensure that the path payload, whether data, video, or voice, is reliably transported.

SONET uses Bit-Interleaved Parity (BIP), a 1-byte code consisting of 8 bits to furnish parity for SONET frames. The section BIP furnishes parity from regenerator to regenerator. If section parity is correctly transmitted, the other layers are also correctly transmitted. Parity between terminating devices is done by line BIP, which covers line, path, and traffic segments of a frame. Path BIP sets up parity between line termination equipment, and it covers path and traffic sections of a frame.

EQUIPMENT INTERFACES • SONET interfaces with channels connecting to customer network components. DACs and Add/Drop Multiplexers (ADMs) support these interfaces. SONET network components must also interface with one another.

Connecting optical multiplexers with DACS requires matching low-speed channels with the OC channel digital hierarchy. Lower transmission speed channels, such as DS-1, DS-1C, and DS-2, are mapped into SONET using pointers. SONET pointers do away with bit stuffing and buffering. This eliminates signal slips at multiplexers. Pointers provide easy access to actual traffic. By using pointers to mark the beginning of a frame, SONET makes breaking a higher rate signal into a DS-0 signal an easy task.

ADD/DROP MULTIPLEXERS

An ADM that allows one channel (or a group of channels) to be added to, or dropped from, a broadband digital time division multiplexed data stream. ADMs add a channel to, or extract a channel from, a multiplexed stream without disrupting transmission of other channels in the same multiplexed stream. A channel exists as a single-bit number in streams of data divided into frames. ADMs identify which bits belong to a channel. Then, at a precise time in the multiplexed data stream, they add (alter) or remove bits without de-multiplexing the data stream.

In the past, adding or removing a single channel was only possible by de-multiplexing the entire multiplexed data stream to the lowest level, adding or extracting a channel, then re-multiplexing the data stream. ADMs make this process simpler and less expensive.

Drop-and-insert multiplexers are ADMs. Drop-and-insert multiplexers are smaller units that generally extract or add one or more data channels in a multiplexed n x 64 Kbps channel to a multiplexed bearer carrying many 64-Kbps multiplexed channels between major installations. The remaining 64-Kbps channels are unaffected.

Linear ADMs provide direct access to individual clockwise or counterclockwise Virtual Tributary (VT)/Synchronous Transport Signal (STS) channels at intermediate sites along a fiber route without multiplexing/de-multiplexing pass-through traffic. ADMs save costs and improve reliability in comparison to intermediate sites equipped with complex back-to-back terminal arrangements.

Survivability of linear add/drop routes is enhanced through geographically diverse protection paths. Alternatively, survivability is achieved using a hybrid linear ADM/subtending ring configuration (path-protected, linear ADM route).

A SONET ADM drops a low-speed channel from a gigabit-speed trunk at a lower cost than a DS-0 dropped from a DS-3 trunk. This enables telephone companies to deploy high-speed trunks closer to subscribers and reduces overall networking costs. Adding and dropping of channels is achieved by using complementary ADMs. Rather than terminating all traffic received as asynchronous DS-1 and DS-3 multiplexers do, SONET ADMs transmit traffic on to other ADMs or locations. This capability facilitates the formation of the SONET ring configuration. The ADM inserts and deletes low-speed (i.e., sub-line rate) channels within a single piece of transmission equipment, thereby significantly saving costs over conventional multiplexing schemes requiring two multiplexers in a back-to-back configuration.

DIGITAL ACCESS AND CROSS-CONNECT SYSTEMS

DACs are devices used to prepare digital streams for inclusion into SONET OC channels. DACS mesh network applications requiring switching, grooming, and routing functions.

"Cross-connects" refers to connecting many channels at network cross points to many more channels. Originally, cross-connects used patch cords and sockets. Telephone companies still use passive cross-connects wherever large bundles of wires connect with other large bundles of wires. A passive cross-connect connects 1,200 wire pairs at the end of a large cable to numerous smaller cables which carry wire bundles into surrounding streets. Such a passive cross-connect uses short jumper wires to link wire bays on the incoming side to wire bays on the outgoing side.

Most cross-connects are active, many-to-many electronic switching units. Such active cross-connects are electronic multiple switching devices handling more than one circuit at a time. Active cross-connects switch links under the control of an electronic signal usually in the header of a packet. No physical wires or patches are used. Cross-connects can switch any connection on one side of a wiring frame to any connection on the other side of a wiring frame. Multiple simultaneous connections can usually be made on a cross-connect.

Digital cross-connects, including DACS, are computers with memory and many channel connections. Switching is implemented in silicon to handle high-speed and real-time voice (isochronous—CBR) channels.

SONET NETWORK COMPONENT INTERFACES

SONET interfaces conform to SONET specifications covering optical interface wavelengths and power levels for single-mode fiber. Other SONET specifications cover maintaining fiber systems and interconnecting fiber optic network elements. The most common SONET interface is an ITU-compliant OC-48/STM-16 short-reach optic interface. It is supported by virtually all network equipment that operates at 2.5 Gbps. The standardized 10-Gbps interface is the SONET/SDH serial interface. These 10-Gbps interfaces have high component costs. To reduce costs, leading SONET suppliers are developing an ultra-low-cost interface known as OC-192/STM-16 Very Short Reach (VSR). The OC-192/STM-16 VSR interface provides low-cost interconnection of optical network elements residing in the same CO. It supports distances up to 400 meters over 62.5-micron multi-mode ribbon fiber.

The OC-192/STM-16 VSR incorporates low-cost technologies developed for Gigabit Ethernet and an array of 12 low-cost 850-nm lasers. Each laser runs at 1.25 Gbps over one of the fibers in the 12 fiber ribbon cables. Complete OC-192/STM-16 VSR transceivers should cost substantially less than SONET/SDH 10-Gbps serial optics. This reduces interconnection costs for high-speed optical elements within a telephone company CO. OC-192/STM-16 VSR transceivers are smaller than OC-192/STM-64 short-reach transceivers, making optical equipment denser and more compact.

SONET PROVISIONING • Provisioning is configuring circuits over SONET facilities. SONET permits circuits to be remotely enabled and disabled. This remote configuration flexibility permits dynamic reconfiguration of a SONET network. This provides the benefits of faster circuit installation, less need to have personnel physically install circuits, easy reconfiguration to bypass outages, and increased responsiveness to changing traffic loads.

Effective provisioning of SONET traffic is an important function in every telecommunications network. Traffic routing, grooming, and consolidation functions must be easily performed to manage ever-increasing network operational costs, congestion, and expansion. To more effectively provision bandwidth reasonably for small to medium-capacity metropolitan-sized networks, many providers use a cross-connect hub architecture. This solution allows a single DACS at a hub site to handle all bandwidth management needs for an entire network that may contain numerous small offices.

Traffic grooming and consolidation are back-hauled to the DACS site before being routed to a final destination. However effective, there are drawbacks to this solution, including increased operational complexity and the requirement for additional bandwidth to support the back-haul channels. Cost efficiency decreases as office size decreases.

SONET VENDORS, PRODUCTS AND SERVICES • All large telephone equipment manufacturers sell some SONET components, including Lucent, Nortel, Ericsson, and others. Other SONET suppliers come from the Internet equipment manufacturing community, most notably Cisco Systems.

A list of SONET product vendors is also given at:

http://www.sonet.com/vendor/vendor.htm

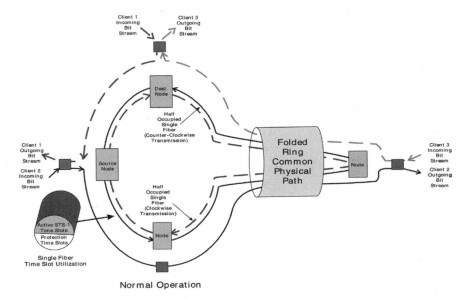

Figure 7–33 *Folded ring configuration.*

SONET Networks

Answer the following questions using Figure 7-33.

1. If the folded ring common physical path were damaged, which SONET communications channels would be inoperative? The channel for Client #2 and Client #3 would not operate because there is no backup for them on the folded path.

2. What channel would continue to operate? The channel for Client #1 would remain operational.

3. If the link between the left-most source node and the top destination mode were to fail as well, would Client #1's channel remain operational? No, because it could not be re-routed through the folded ring common physical path.

The goal is to understand SONET ring self-healing properties and limitations.

Applying Digital Network Services

Table 7-6 presents differences between digital transmission services. With older packet network services, packet sizes were small because data traveled across low-speed, high error rate links. Frame relay service went to larger blocks because transmission speeds increased and error rates became lower. Frame relay, similar to X.25 packet network services, was focused on data communications from facility to facility. X.25 packet network services supported mostly terminal to host traffic. Frame relay supports primarily LAN-to-LAN traffic, but also supports voice and video transmission across frame relay links. Voice and video over frame relay networks must not exceed the CIR. SMDS is a BISDN delivery mechanism. So far, SMDS offerings in the U.S. have been aimed at LAN-to-LAN data communications.

ATM serves different needs. It supports data communications, voice, and video communications. ATM effectively uses communications links by responding quickly to changes in a voice, video, and data traffic mix. At one time, there may be predominantly video traffic. At another time, there may be more voice and data. Switching between these traffic types is rapid and invisible to the ATM network user. ATM solves the problem of flexibility with small data cells, no link-to-link error checking (supported by low error rates), and extremely high transmission speeds.

Digital network services are aimed at future multimedia communications, e.g., video telephony. While these high-speed digital services are expensive today, they are fast becoming more affordable for businesses in general. Only five years ago it was unheard of for an organization to use more than a T-3 channel. Now Bill Gates has an OC-12 channel feeding his house. Internet access providers (those service providers selling digital transmission connectivity to local ISPs) are using OC channels to form their backbone network links. As prices decline usage continues to dramatically increase.

Figure 7-34 shows the hierarchy of digital transmission services. Businesses buy T-1 channels and ISDN PRIs for data and voice communications between facilities. These services separate voice and data links on the same physical channels, wasting communications capacity. Frame relay services support high-speed data and voice and video communications using shared facilities. This saves interconnection and recurring channel costs. There still remains significant wasted communications capacity, however. SMDS service is targeted at LAN-to-LAN communications even though its high speed permits SMDS to deliver a variety of multimedia communications services. ATM represents the best opportunity for an enterprise to create an integrated telecommunications network supporting data, voice, and video communications seamlessly over network communications channels. ATM service can

Table 7.6 *Digital Transmission Service Summary*

Feature/ Network	X.25 Packet	T-1 TDM	Frame Relay	SMDS	ATM
Transmission and Switching Unit	Packet	Framed Digital Bit Stream	Frame	Cell	Cell
Facilities Used Only When Data is Sent	Yes	Always Used (Assigned)	Yes	Yes	Yes
Permanent Virtual Circuits	Yes	Leased Physical Channels	Yes	Yes	Yes
Switched Virtual Circuits	Yes	Circuit-switched	Yes	No	Yes
Error Detection and Correction	Link-by-link	End-to-end Protocol	Network Detects, Layer 4 Corrects	Link-by-link	Detection on Routing Information Only Layer 4 Detects and Corrects
Data Bursts	Yes with PAD	Yes Buffering Required	Yes with FRAD	Yes	Yes
LAN-to-LAN Connection	Very Slow	Yes Expensive	Yes Cost Effective	Yes	Yes Shared Facilities
Image	Very Slow	Yes	Yes	Yes	Yes
High-speed Isochronous Data	No	Depends upon End-to-end Connections	Yes	Yes	Yes
Voice	No	Yes	Yes Cannot Exceed CIR	No	Yes
Video	No	Requires High-speed Channel	Yes Cannot Exceed CIR	No	Yes
Transmission Speed	19.2 Kbps	1.544 Mbps	1.544 Mbps	Up to 44 Mbps	Up to 39 Gbps
In-transit Delays	High	Low	Low	Low	Lowest
Saves Telecommunications Costs	Shared Low-speed Facilities	Only with Heavy Traffic between Fixed Facilities	Shared High-speed Facilities	Shared High-speed Facilities, But Expensive	Shared High-speed Facilities with Effective Utilization

be delivered directly to customer sites or it can be the technology underlying T-1, ISDN, frame relay, or SMDS network services.

At the base of our telecommunications food chain hierarchy is SONET. Organizations with heavy campus-wide transmission loads can implement

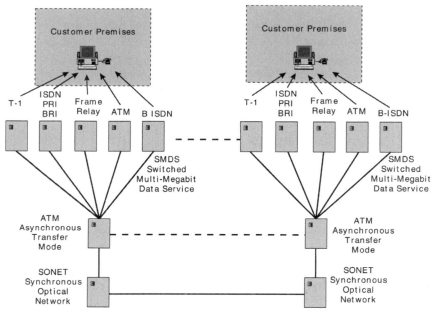

Figure 7–34 *Digital transmission service food chain.*

erwise, SONET is the foundation on which all other telecommunications services rest. SONET implements most high-speed (high-bandwidth) channels between telephone company and Internet access provider facilities.

SERVICE SELECTION AND INTERCONNECTION

The telecommunications services most readily affordable and available to most organizations are frame relay, T-1, and some ISDN. Selection of the appropriate type of service depends upon the communications load (in Mbps) and types of traffic (voice, data, image, or video) carried between locations. The different high-speed digital services need specific types of interconnection equipment to interface with the CPE sending and receiving voice, data, image, or video information. The types of interconnection equipment and its ability to sub-divide the services into DS-0 or smaller channels is dependent upon the service used.

COSTS AND GEOGRAPHIC COVERAGE

Most high-speed digital services are available in major U.S. metropolitan areas. Services may not be so easily accessed in rural areas. An enterprise operating in Nebraska to save overhead probably pays more for the communication services they need to operate from there, than it would have cost to get the same communication services in Chicago or St. Louis. This is because the facilities for high-speed digital transmission are not as prevalent in Nebraska as they are in St. Louis or Chicago. Often when a type of service (e.g., frame relay or SMDS) does not have an access point (or POP) geographically close to a remote facility, the installation and access fees are likely to be much higher than a service with a local access point (e.g., T-1 service).

EQUIPMENT INTERFACES

High-speed digital services must be broken down into channels usable by our existing voice, data, facsimile, and video teleconferencing equipment. This means that interconnection equipment must support the physical interfaces to the high-speed digital channel (most often a fiber optic link) as well as provide DS-0 or ISDN interfaces to the existing CPE.

MANAGING DIGITAL NETWORKS

High-speed digital networks are high-cost. Managing and monitoring operation is key to successful implementation. A central monitoring system needs to be implemented that talks to every network component using high-speed digital channels. This network management and monitoring system instantly alerts operating personnel to problems so that service can be maintained. Service maintenance may require use of temporary alternate routes, or switching to redundant backup equipment. Automated network monitoring is essential for managing high-speed digital network services.

Brain Teaser

Applying Digital Network Technologies

Use the Internet to determine what digital networking services your Local Exchange Carrier (LEC) sells. This is a daunting task because most of them organize their sites around business solutions and not around products and prices. Their goal is to get you to request a price quote for specific services.

1. Your LEC most likely sells T-1, frame relay, and ISDN connections. Do they offer ATM service? What companies would offer ATM networking services? We already mentioned MCI WorldCom and Cable & Wireless.

2. What other companies would provide ATM service? Check out AT&T and Qwest using their Web sites. We do not know the answer here as yet, but we guess that they will provide ATM services.

Notice that each telecommunications service provider has their special brand name for ATM services. Bewildering, isn't it?

3. How does the SMDS pricing compare to frame relay pricing from the LEC? Our guess is that SMDS pricing will be higher than frame relay.

The goal here is to better identify telecommunications services that can be purchased from your LEC and to visualize the cost tradeoffs between these services.

■ Summary

This chapter examined digital transmission services, or ways to connect us together that save telecommunications costs. It discussed ISDN as a mechanism to replace costly fixed video teleconferencing leased line facilities with switched ISDN H0 channels. ISDN also represents a better mechanism to interface PBX switches with the PSTN. Packet-switched network services, particularly fast packet or frame relay services, offer potential cost savings by replacing leased line data communications channels with PVCs. These PVCs run across shared packet-switched network resources, which cost less than full-period leased line facilities. All network services running over shared facilities save telecommunications access charges because only a single access line is needed to interface to the shared network facilities. Once connected to any shared facility, many VCs can be configured for that single connection. T-1 channels were the original leased line channels that saved costs between two facilities if there was high traffic volume between those facilities. SMDS was a high-speed packet network aimed at providing BISDN service to facilities. It has been largely ineffective because of its comparatively high tariffs. ATM technology now promises to provide high-speed telecommunications channels that carry integrated video, voice, and data traffic. This traffic is efficiently transferred from ATM component to ATM component using cell relay protocol. ATM technology supports delivery of other digital services across the telephone backbone network today. Finally, SONET was examined. SONET is the foundation for delivering all other services. In campus areas with heavy traffic between buildings in the campus, SONET technology provides a super high-speed transmission facility to service the traffic. ATM and all other digital telecommunications services are more and more carried by high- speed SONET facilities in telephone company and Internet access provider networks.

▲ Chapter Review Questions

1. *What ISDN service is similar to a T-1 channel?*

   A. Basic Rate Interface (BRI)

   B. Primary Channel Interface (PCI)

   C. Primary Rate Interface (PRI)

2. *What high-speed digital service is seldom sold directly to end-user organizations?*

   A. ISDN

   B. SONET

   C. T-1

   D. SMDS

3. *What digital transmission service operates at the highest speeds?*

   A. T-1

   B. Frame relay

   C. ATM

   D. X.25 packet networks

4. *What T-carrier circuit is twice the speed of a T-1 channel?*

   A. T-1c

   B. T-3

   C. T-2

   D. T-4

5. *What does a DACS do?*

   A. Switches T-1 channels

   B. Multiplexes T-3 channels

   C. Cross-connects DS-0 channels

   D. Cross-connects DS-4 channels

6. *What does CIR stand for?*

   A. Committed Interface Rate

   B. Committed Information Reduction

   C. Continual Inter-hop Rate

   D. Committed Information Rate

7. *What technology uses CIR?*

    A. X.25 packet-switched networks

    B. Fast packet networks

    C. ATM

    D. SMDS

8. *What should not exceed CIR?*

    A. LAN-to-LAN data traffic

    B. FRAD traffic

    C. Voice and video traffic

    D. Terminal to host traffic

9. *What technology uses cells?*

    A. SONET

    B. Fast packet networks

    C. ATM

    D. SMDS

10. *How large are cells?*

    A. 53 characters

    B. 47 characters

    C. 128 characters

    D. 4,096 characters

11. *Do cells have error checking?*

    A. No

    B. Header only

    C. Yes – all cells have it

    D. Payload only

12. *What transmission technology uses payloads?*

    A. Frame relay

    B. SMDS

    C. ATM

    D. SONET

13. *What technology functions in OSI Layer 1?*

    A. Frame relay

    B. SMDS

    C. ATM

    D. SONET

14. *What is the top SONET speed?*

    A. 51.84 Mbps

    B. 39.813 Gbps

    C. 622.08 Mbps

    D. 9.9 Gbps

15. *What is the base SONET speed?*

    A. 51.84 Mbps

    B. 25 Mbps

    C. 1.544 Mbps

    D. 6.312 Mbps

16. *What is a frame relay frame size?*

    A. 128 characters

    B. 106 characters

    C. 4096 characters

    D. 810 characters

17. *LANE is important with* _____?

    A. Frame relay

    B. X.25 packet networks

    C. The Internet

    D. ATM

18. *Can ATM be run over copper wire?*

    A. No

    B. Yes - always

    C. At speeds of 25 Mbps and 155 Mbps

    D. At speeds up to 9.9 Gbps

19. *How many fibers in a SONET ring?*

    A. 2

    B. 4

    C. 8

    D. 6

20. *A T-1 span runs between two facilities. The average data load is 256 Kbps. To replace it with frame relay service and get the best performance, what access speed should be used?*

    A. 256 Kbps

    B. 1.544 Mbps

    C. T-1C access

    D. 512 Kbps

RF, Satellite, and Cellular Communications

This chapter examines Radio Frequency (RF) communications used in telecommunications. RF communications can be divided into line-of-sight RF communications, satellite, and cellular technologies. These technologies meet specific communications needs, as we shall see as we examine them in this chapter.

Radio Frequency Communications

Dramatic changes in the way RF communications is used have taken place over the last several years. However, RF communications is equivalent to any other communications channel or pipe, like fiber optic cable or copper wire. The physics of RF communications remains the same as always, but the electronics implementing it have been combined with data communications technologies to radically enhance and alter RF applications. Today RF communications provides anywhere cellular phones, paging, Internet access, television distribution, data communications, and more.

Everyone is familiar with radio because of the radios in our cars. They work by receiving transmitted electronic waves and converting them into sound. RF communications is the same, but the radios use both transmit and receive radio signals. These signals are low-power signals so that receiving and transmitting hubs need to be placed close together. All radio communications share one immutable resource, the electromagnetic spectrum. Two basic pieces of knowledge are needed to put RF communications in perspective. One has to do with the physics of radio communications and the other with the regulation of radio communications. RF telecommunications are governed by:

- The properties of RF transmission.
- Government and international regulations.

First, let's examine the properties of RF communications. When I was in college and first married, every appliance was a big expenditure. My first wife, Mary, and I purchased a TV, but we lacked the money to buy a TV antenna. Some TVs came with rabbit ears at the time, but ours did not. So I proceeded to make an antenna. I went to my general physics textbook and looked up the RF spectrum. Then I selected the frequency right in the middle of the VHF TV band and divided it into one to arrive at the wavelength. It calculated out to be 6 feet. To make a half-wave antenna, I cut 3 feet of 300-ohm (the wide TV cable that is difficult to find anymore) cable, twisted the ends together to get a reasonably precise 3-foot length, and soldered them. Next I nailed the cable to a board, and in the exact center, I tapped another 300-ohm cable into the side to form a "T." This was the antenna. It worked, but not very well.

Good TV antennas, you see, have many elements (the spikes) that run perpendicular to their length. Each spike or element is a very precise length. The length matches the wavelength of a single broadcast TV channel. In that manner, the antenna filters the signal received and maximizes it for the broadcast TV channel frequencies. The antenna elements range from about 4 inches to about 3 feet in length.

This illustrates that each RF frequency has a wavelength that can be physically measured. There are very long waves (miles in length) that can penetrate the earth and ocean. They are used to communicate with submarines. As the broadcast RF gets higher and higher, the physical wavelengths get shorter and shorter until they reach the size of a raindrop. At this point, when they travel through the air and it is raining, three things can happen:

- The radio wave hits the raindrop head-on and gets soaked up—it heats the raindrop slightly—being soaked up is bad for us.

- The radio wave hits the raindrop obliquely, bounces off, and goes someplace that we do not want it to go—this is also bad for us.

- The radio wave misses all raindrops and is received correctly by the radio receiver. This is good for us because our message gets through.

You can see that rain and water are the enemies of radio communications. Of course, radio waves that are 3 feet long do not need to worry much about raindrops. As broadcast radio frequency increases more, getting higher and higher, the physical wavelengths get shorter and shorter still until they reach the size of a molecule of water in the air. Water molecules are always in the air (it is called humidity), they are much more prevalent than rain drops, but they are mostly invisible to us. At this point, when radio waves travel through any air, three things can happen:

- The radio wave hits a water molecule head-on and gets soaked up—it heats the water molecule slightly—being soaked up is bad for us.

- The radio wave hits a water molecule obliquely, bounces off, and goes someplace that we do not want it to go—this is again bad for us.

- The radio wave misses all water molecules and is received correctly by the radio receiver. This is the good thing for which we hope, because our communications get through.

What is illustrated here is that the higher the broadcast frequencies, the more susceptible to attenuation (absorption) are the radio waves. To overcome this absorption, transmitters and receivers must be closer to one another at the higher frequencies, or much more power must be used to burn through the atmosphere. The strength of a radio signal drops quickly as the distance from the broadcast antenna increases. So, high-frequency radio waves need more power or short distances between transmitting and receiving devices to get through (see Figure 8-1).

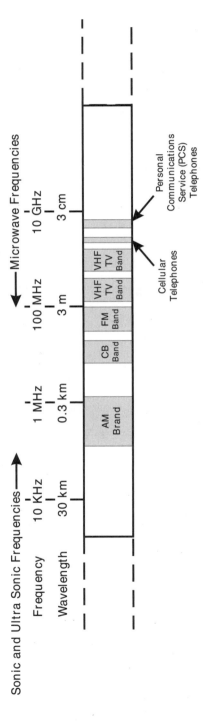

Figure 8–1 *RF broadcast spectrum.*

Remember from Chapter 4, "Voice Communications," that higher frequencies can send more bits per second. Therefore, high frequencies have a higher digital information carrying capacity than lower frequencies.

Our second point deals with the regulation of RF broadcasts. In the U.S., the Federal Communications Commission (FCC) regulates RF. The FCC divides up the frequencies into bands and specifies how the frequency bands must be used. The AM (Amplitude Modulated) and FM (Frequency Modulated) bands are used to broadcast music, news, and public information. Use of the RFs is regulated through licensing. Originally, licensing was to assure no broadcasting conflicts between stations. Licensing was intended to prevent problems like the problem one man had replacing his storm windows. He neatly propped them against his half-opened garage door, only to have the door open unexpectedly, which caused the windows to fall on the driveway and break. When the replacement windows arrived, they were neatly laid on the driveway, beneath the fully-opened garage door. You guessed it! The garage door unexpectedly closed, crushing all the windows. The cause was a neighbor's wireless TV controller.

Most recently, licensing has become a revenue source for the federal government. Unfortunately, the FCC auctions selling off licenses to the RF spectrum for perpetuity did not generate the revenues expected. It would have made better sense for the federal government to lease the frequencies and be paid periodic usage fees instead of a one-time charge for a section of the RF spectrum. An RF spectrum license gives the license owner the right to use specific frequencies as described under license guidelines.

Basic RF Technology

RF communications sends signals at specific frequencies measured in cycles per second or Hertz (Hz). The relationship between broadcast frequency and wavelength is shown in Figure 8-2. In Figure 8-2 there are four complete sinusoidal waves in one second, so our frequency is 4Hz. Each wave has a specific length from start to finish, that is the wavelength of the signal. In the figure, to have higher frequencies, we must have more cycles per second and conversely shorter wavelengths.

AM radio signals are broadcast in a range of frequencies from 540KHz to 1620KHz. FM radio broadcasts operate in a higher frequency band, from 90MHz to 108MHz. Cellular phones broadcast in frequency bands around 800MHz.

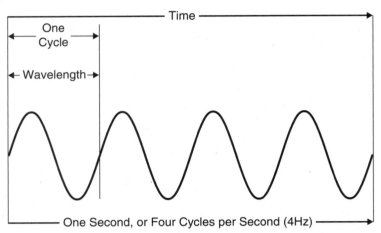

Figure 8–2   *Frequency and wavelength.*

Wireless Services Categories

Wireless communications can be categorized as:

- Broadcast services.
- Two-way radio communications.
- Point-to-point services.

Broadcast services are voice and video broadcast services, better known as radio and television broadcasts. Broadcast services are one-way transmission of information to all receiving devices in a specific geographic area. Most RF broadcasts have limited coverage to one city or extended metropolitan area. Radio and TV broadcasters do not know who receives the information broadcast, so there are limits on what can be publicly broadcast. Radio and television have dominated entertainment and information delivery for the last 50 years. New broadcast applications promise to dramatically change RF broadcasting, including High-Definition Television (HDTV), Digital Audio Broadcasting (DAB) satellite broadcast delivery, and FM High-Speed Sub-carrier (FM HSS) data services.

A radio station broadcasting with a signal of 50,000 Watts and a 300-foot-high antenna can cover a 100-mile-diameter circle. Most radio stations broadcast with power levels ranging from 500 Watts or 50,000 Watts. I remember as a child listening to music broadcast by WKBW in Buffalo, New York at night. WKBW broadcast at 50,000 Watts. Their signal was able to make the 160-mile trip to Elmira only at night because radio signals travel better at night.

Two-way radio communications range in capabilities from simple CB band walkie-talkies to more sophisticated mobile radios with trunks and repeater towers. These are sometimes called Land Mobile Radio (LMR) systems. There are both public and private systems. A local company would run a private system for its own use, like an electric power company communicating with service and maintenance crews. A public system would provide communications services to taxis in a metropolitan area. In these systems, a base station sends signals out to broadcast towers over wired links. The broadcast is sent on one frequency and the mobile radios respond using a separate frequency (CB radios, in contrast, broadcast and receive on the same frequency). The central office shares its broadcast frequency with no other radios. However, the mobile radios must take their turn using the single frequencies assigned to them, otherwise their broadcasts collide. Systems with repeater towers have the mobile radios broadcast using one frequency and receive on a separate frequency. The repeater towers shift the frequency broadcast by the mobile radios (and received by the repeater towers) to the frequency on which the mobile radios receive. Most mobile radios can tune into one or more frequencies to communicate with the base system or one another.

Point-to-point systems are generally private systems connecting facilities belonging to an organization. The telephone companies used point-to-point RF systems extensively to carry voice channels from Central Office (CO) to CO in the 1950s through the 1980s. At its peak, around 1980, AT&T had constructed and operated about 500,000 miles of point-to-point microwave systems. These point-to-point systems used 4GHz and 6GHz frequencies, with each telephone channel frequency division multiplexed into the frequency band. Guard bands separated each voice channel. The original frequency division multiplexed point-to-point systems were converted to all-digital transmission systems operating at the same frequencies. This provided better transmission quality and increased capacity. Many still operate today.

Line-Of-Sight Microwave Transmission

The RF and satellite communications that promise to make high-speed digital planet-wide networks a reality are based upon Line-Of-Sight (LOS) microwave technology. Most RF communications uses RFs classified as microwave frequencies. Microwave frequencies provide a significant advantage for voice, video, and data communications. A single microwave radio channel can carry 6,000 voice channels in a 30-MHz bandwidth. This capac-

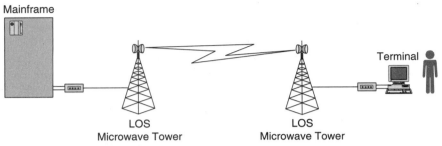

Figure 8–3 *LOS microwave channel.*

ity is increasingly important as needs for voice, data, and video communications rise.

LOS means literally that the transmitter and receiver must be in a direct line of sight with one another. There can be few if any obstructions between them. Higher frequencies in the microwave frequency range (frequencies above 800MHz are generally considered microwave frequencies—microwave ovens use 2.5GHz—the upper-most RFs are 300GHz) need the broadcast power more focused into a narrow beam for the signal to travel long distances (see Figure 8-3).

Microwave communications was first used after World War II. It is RF communications using high-frequency (800MHz to 40GHz) signals. Equipment operating at microwave frequencies includes cellular broadcast transmission, LOS microwave transmission, and satellite communications. LOS microwave transmission using 4GHz and 6GHz frequencies is still widely used in private and public networks. A single microwave channel can have up to 38MHz of bandwidth for digital transmission and introduces much less noise into transmissions than many copper lines. Microwave transmission is limited to LOS paths and it can suffer serious signal degradation in heavy rain.

The components required to build a microwave network are multiplexers, analog modems, digital interfaces, RF transmitter/receivers, and antenna equipment. Both time division multiplexers and frequency division multiplexers are used in microwave systems. Time Division Multiplexing (TDM) is more prevalent today in digital T-carrier systems. Radio transmission is typically AM or FM using Frequency Shift Keying (FSK) or Quadrature Amplitude Modulation (QAM) to encode the information being sent.

Operation involves generation of an RF signal that is then modulated, amplified, and passed to a transmitting antenna system. The resultant signal travels through free air to a receiving antenna, where it is sampled, amplified, and demodulated. In general, microwave transmission characteristics are similar to low-frequency radio transmission characteristics, except that microwave is considerably more efficient. For example, the wavelength for a Very High Frequency (VHF) channel is around 20 feet. A VHF receiving antenna needs to be about 10 feet long for maximum signal efficiency. In contrast, a 4 GHz microwave signal has a three-inch wavelength that reduces antenna size and cost.

LOS microwave networks are somewhat simple to implement. However, microwave signals used in these networks tend to fade from signal-based interference, from multiple path reflection, or from heavy rain. Signal interference includes overreach (the flashlight beam effect), where a signal feeds past a repeater to the receiving antenna at the next station. Overreach is controlled using a zigzag signal path or by using different frequencies between receiving stations. Another anomaly is adjacent channel interference, which can be controlled with band pass filtering. A multi-path reflection happens when a main signal traveling LOS between antennas is reflected over a secondary path by a temperature inversion layer or a heavy ground fog. The secondary signal travels a longer distance to the antenna than the main signal and arrives slightly out of phase. This causes phase canceling, thus reducing the signal level. Rain absorbs signal power at frequencies higher than 10GHz. Fading is a phenomenon of microwave or radio transmission, where atmospheric, electromagnetic, or gravitational influences cause a signal to be deflected or diverted away from the target receiver.

The impact of atmospheric interference on an LOS microwave signal is minimal when it travels only short distances. The primary restriction to providing service is having an unobstructed LOS between the subscriber antenna and the LOS microwave provider's antenna. This may be very difficult to achieve in high-density urban areas. In such cases, a hybrid wired/LOS microwave configuration could be used to interconnect with subscribers. Further, higher frequency microwave transmission similar light waves can be focused. Short-haul signals can be aimed to maintain LOS using intermediate antennas or passive reflectors. Over long distances, secondary transmission/receiving systems or repeaters maintain signal levels. Cell phones operating at microwave frequencies operate with reflected signals as well. This is particularly true inside buildings.

TRANSMISSION FREQUENCIES AND CHARACTERISTICS

Different RF systems operate in distinct frequency bands. These bands are:

- Telephone network RF links use 4GHz and 6GHz frequencies. These frequencies are relatively unaffected by rain when applied by telephone companies to build point-to-point channels between facilities.

The typical distance between repeaters is around 20 miles, with the longest channel running 90 miles somewhere in Wyoming or Montana.

- Cellular RF frequencies in the U.S. are in the 800MHz band for the original cellular carriers and Nextel and 1.8GHz for newer Personal Communications Services (PCS) phones. International cellular frequencies are 900MHz for original cellular services and 1.9GHz for PCS phones. In the U.S., cordless phones use the 900MHz frequencies.
- Private RF network frequencies can run a wide range of frequencies, depending upon RF congestion, channel length, data speed, and atmospheric interference. Typical frequencies used are 2.1, 6, 7, 8, 10, 11, 13, 15, 18, 23, 24, 26, 28, 29, 31, and 38 GHz. These frequencies are used to construct digital channels operating at DS-1 to OC-3 speeds.

Many factors influence frequency selection for any given LOS channel in any given RF network.

RF NETWORK ADVANTAGES AND DISADVANTAGES

The advantages of RF networks are that frequencies in the MHz and GHz ranges are used to facilitate high channel capacities. Digital channel speeds carried by these frequencies range from 1.544 Mbps to 155 Mbps. Channel distance can be 20 miles or more depending upon the physical environment and transmission tower height. Generally, short-haul channels are 38GHz and run up to 5 miles; 2GHz channels run 20 miles or more.

LOS microwave is an exciting technology for providing enhanced capacity in cellular telecommunications infrastructures. LOS microwave using high transmission frequencies can deliver cable television, telephony, and high-speed Internet access services to consumers. Because high frequencies are very susceptible to atmospheric interference, the area of coverage for each cell is small, but at the same time, these high frequencies mean that each signal has a substantial digital transmission capacity to carry voice, video, and data. High frequency (GHz) systems are less vulnerable to interfering and conflicting signals from other systems, but more susceptible to atmospheric interference. Channel transmission is digitally encoded voice, data, and video. These LOS microwave systems use proven technology that has been further improved by incorporating data communications technologies.

LOS microwave systems have some disadvantages. They do require FCC licensing. Further, signal congestion and conflicts at 4GHz and 6GHz frequencies occur in many urban/suburban areas, but using higher frequencies mitigates this congestion. Weather degrades performance, and power lines or other RF sources may interfere with transmission. The LOS microwave transmission beam has the flashlight effect going from a small focused beam, to a wider beam, making it less secure. When working at the Senate, we looked at several alternatives for connecting the Senate's computer center to the senators' offices. The alternative technologies included fiber cable, telephone cable, special telephone services, LOS infrared transmission, and LOS microwave transmission. When making the final decision, LOS microwave transmission was easily removed from consideration because the direct LOS between the two microwave antennas connecting the Senate offices to the Senate's computer center was in line with the Russian embassy. An LOS microwave system implementation would definitely not have been a politically correct move.

LICENSING

Because microwave communications channels broadcast RF signals at high power levels, the FCC licenses them. The FCC divides the RF spectrum up into different frequency bands, licenses the frequency bands to users, and specifies how the frequencies are to be used. Companies holding a license have a legal right to use very specific frequencies or a range of frequencies.

Illegal RF frequency band use is subject to prosecution, license suspension, and stiff financial penalties (if caught). CB radio fanatics often boosted the power output of their radios. This was definitely an illegal move, but it was also very difficult to catch and prosecute offenders.

There are unlicensed sections of the radio frequency spectrum. In this case, manufacturers of general-usage RF equipment are regulated by the FCC to manufacturing devices that operate in specific frequencies, to emitting a maximum transmitted power, and to the methods used to control the RF signal. By manufacturing devices such as garage door openers, radio-controlled toys, CB radios, and cordless phones within these guidelines, the amount of RF interference with other RF devices is minimized.

RF Networks that Save Costs

Public and private RF networks save communications costs by bypassing the local telephone company. They reduce the need for local telephone company facilities and thus reduce network costs. Whenever there are sufficient traffic volumes, it is always cheaper to construct a private network than to purchase communications services from the telephone company.

Private LOS microwave networks have a central communications room in each facility that splits a communications channel into separate pathways for video distribution, voice communications, and high-speed data connections. Public LOS microwave providers use techniques similar to cellular telephony to connect subscriber facilities into a central facility. The public LOS microwave provider establishes cell-like areas servicing subscriber neighborhoods. Each LOS microwave subscriber has a special antenna and distribution box to split the received channel into its separate video, voice, and Internet access components. These all feed channels back to a central distribution facility where the video, voice, and high-speed Internet access are split into separate digital streams and routed to the appropriate destination. Some of these services are Local Multi-point Distribution Service (LMDS) and Wireless Local Loop (WLL).

Local Multi-point Distribution Service

Local Multi-point Distribution Service (LMDS) is broadband microwave wireless transmission service direct from a local antenna to residences and businesses within an LOS of a microwave broadcast facility. LMDS is aimed at both cable television distribution and voice communications. LMDS operates over a super high-capacity wireless system using the 28GHz frequency range. At this frequency range, LMDS capacity rivals that of fiber optic cable. Such a system also employs repeaters to assure adequate coverage.

LMDS is targeted at economically bringing high-bandwidth services to residential and business customers. LMDS, because of its high capacity, presents an alternative to installing optical fiber to residential and business facilities and to cable TV providing Internet service. LMDS can operate at 1.5 Gbps from the service provider to the customer (downstream) and 200 Mbps from the customer to the service provider (upstream). The typical service provider to customer (downstream) speed is 38 Mbps. Some LMDS services offer symmetric and asymmetric services. Symmetric service provides the same speed each way, while asymmetric service is typically higher speed down from the service provider and lower speed up to the service provider. In asymmetric service, the upstream link may be a telephone network connection as well. This service requires investment by both service providers for transmitters and by subscribers, who pay about $100 to $250 for transceiver equipment installed on their premise.

LMDS services are used for:

• High-speed digital services for businesses.
• Television distribution (in competition with local cable TV).

- High-speed Internet access supporting streaming multimedia Web applications.
- Telephone or voice services as an add-on to provide a full service offering.

LMDS is not a replacement for or alternative to mobile cellular wireless technologies because LMDS requires more costly and larger transceivers than cellular devices. LMDS provides much higher data rates than cellular because it uses higher frequencies (in the 28GHz band) and supports fixed locations.

LMDS frequencies vary slightly in the U.S., Canada (where it is called Local Multi-point Communication Service (LMCS)), and Europe. Similar to cellular technologies, LMDS has a central broadcast facility communicating with multiple subscriber facilities (point-to-multi-point). The LMDS system uses Ethernet, ATM, or T-1/E-1 network interfaces at the subscriber facility. ATM interfaces allow subscribers to receive different QoSs at different costs.

LMDS can provide two-way digital communications between residential and commercial facilities and a central distribution facility of the LMDS provider. In Figure 8-4, LMDS delivers voice, video, and high-speed Internet access to a subscriber facility. LMDS provides Gigabits per second transmission speeds along LOS distances of several miles.

Multi-channel Multi-Point Distribution Service (MMDS) is defined by ITU-T recommendation J.150. MMDS delivers digital multi-program television, sound, and data services over wireless links in the 2.0 to 2.7 GHz frequency range. It uses different frequencies than LMDS.

Wireless Local Loop

Wireless Local Loop (WLL) connects telephone subscribers to the Public Switched Telephone Network (PSTN) using RF transmission as a substitute for copper wire local loops between subscriber premises and the CO telephone switch. WLL includes cordless access, proprietary fixed radio access, and fixed cellular technologies.

Global WLL products are projected to service millions of subscribers in the 21st century. Many of these subscribers live in emerging economies like China, India, Brazil, Russia, and Indonesia, where WLL technology is an efficient way to deploy telephone service for millions of subscribers without the expense of burying tons of copper wire. In the U.S., WLL enables Competitive Local Exchange Carriers (CLECs) to bypass existing copper wire local loops controlled by the Incumbent Local Exchange Carriers (ILECs) and to deliver services directly to subscribers.

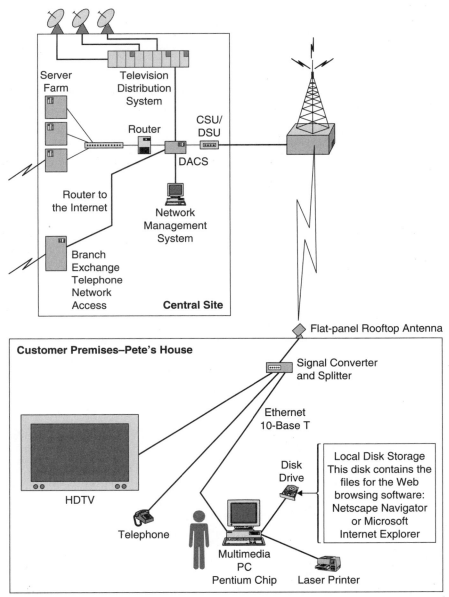

Figure 8–4 *LMDS/MMDS network configuration.*

WLL technology's low deployment and maintenance costs make it a competitive bypass solution and a viable alternative to copper wire local loops for telephone and low-speed data access. WLL implementation depends upon cost and the bandwidth it delivers to subscribers.

The exorbitant service access charges currently levied by telephone companies provide CLECs incentive to implement their own WLL networks. WLL deployment costs are expected to be around $200 per subscriber installation. The CLEC investment must be carefully balanced against the LEC's capability to lower subscriber access charges. Growing demand for high-bandwidth 24/7 Internet access places additional requirements on WLL networks. CLECs must evaluate different WLL technologies based on providing high-speed digital transmission in excess of Integrated Services Digital Network (ISDN) speeds. The ability to support such high-speed transmission may relegate WLL networks to emerging economies in developing countries.

Vendors can implement WLL networks using a choice of fixed-access, mobile, and digital cordless technologies because there aren't definitive WLL network standards. The WLL network technology deployed depends on an application's considerations such as rural area vs. urban area, residential vs. business services, and Plain Old Telephone Service (POTS) vs. Internet access services. WLL can be implemented using analog cellular, digital cellular, PCS/Personal Communications Network (PCN), Cordless Telephones-Second generation (CT–2)/Digital European Cordless Telecommunication (DECT), or proprietary technologies. Each technology has its own unique strengths and weaknesses for WLL applications.

Analog cellular technology is widely available because it has been implemented to serve mobile telephones for the past 20 or more years. The three main analog cellular technologies planet-wide are:

- Advanced Mobile Phone System (AMPS).
- Nordic Mobile Telephone (NMT).
- Total Access Communications System (TACS).

AMPS and its cousin, Narrowband Advanced Mobile Phone System (NAMPS), implemented in North America, service 69% of cellular subscribers, while TACS services 23% and NMT services only 8%.

Analog cellular has capacity and functionality limitations. However, widespread deployment and excellent geographic coverage make analog cellular systems a major WLL technology for the immediate future. The drawback is that analog cellular is best suited to serve low-density to medium-density markets that don't require high-speed Internet access.

Digital cellular systems are growing rapidly. Worldwide digital cellular standards include:

- Global System for Mobile (GSM) communications.
- Time Division Multiple Access (TDMA).
- Enhanced TDMA (E–TDMA).
- Code Division Multiple Access (CDMA).

These standards are discussed in more detail later in this chapter. GSM serves around 71% of the digital cellular market. This percentage is diminishing. Digital cellular, like analog cellular, is widely available. However, digital cellular can provide high-speed digital transmission links to subscribers and at the same time offer all the functions provided by current copper wire loop telephone networks.

Although GSM currently dominates mobile digital cellular, it was designed to handle international cellular roaming. GSM's design has significant communications overhead, making it inefficient and costly for WLL applications. In spite its drawbacks, GSM WLL products are likely to be developed and marketed.

CDMA is the standard best suited for WLL applications. CDMA technology is discussed further later in this chapter. CDMA uses spread-spectrum modulation with a low-power signal spread across wide-frequency bands. CDMA offers 10 to 15 times greater network capacity than analog cellular, relatively high-quality voice, and a high degree of privacy. The disadvantage of CDMA is that it is only now being deployed on a wide scale.

PCS/PCN combines parts of digital cellular and cordless phone standards with newly developed RF protocols. In North America, PCS is a wireless service using low-power antennas and lightweight, inexpensive handsets. PCN is primarily seen as a metropolitan communications system with more compact geographic coverage than cellular telephone networks. PCS is intended to provide a broad range of individualized telecommunications services. PCS lets people or devices communicate, regardless of where they are geographically. PCS services include caller ID, text messaging, direct phone Internet access, call completion regardless of location, calling party pays (calls to the PCS customer are charged to the caller), and other call management services. PCS was designed specifically to provide WLL by public wireless operators. The main weakness of PCS is that its deployment is still somewhat limited.

Second-generation Cordless Telephones (CT-2—Cordless Telephones 2nd generation)/Digital European Cordless Telecommunication (DECT) telephony was developed to provide wireless access within a residence or business between base stations and handsets. About 60 million cordless telephones are used in the U.S., with sales of about 15 million units per year. Cordless technology uses low-power transmission and is limited to short ranges.

If a cordless base station is hard-wired to the PSTN, it is not a WLL. If a public telephone network provides wireless service directly to a subscriber/user via CT-2 technology, it is a WLL.

Digital cordless standards include CT-2 and DECT, with the DECT system more closely resembling cellular system architecture than classical cordless telephone system architecture. DECT uses TDMA with 12 slots per carrier in each direction. DECT can allocate multiple time slots to a single call, thus increasing the data rate. DECT is a potential basis for a future, low-cost, micro-cell or pico-cell telephone system.

Cordless telephone technology is not ideal for rural or low-density applications, it provides some advantages in medium-density to high-density areas. Cordless telephony has advantages in terms of scalability and functionality. Similar to cellular technology, DECT technology can carry substantial traffic loads, provide better voice quality, and offer higher data rates. DECT's micro-cell or pico-cell architecture permits deployment in smaller steps, more closely matching subscriber growth and thus minimizing capital investment (see Table 8-1).

Table 8.1 *WLL Service Requirements*

Service Geography	Developed Countries Telephone Company Bypass	Emerging Countries Basic Voice Telephone Service
Urban/Suburban	• High-speed data • Enhanced services • Limited mobility • High traffic • High subscriber densities	• Voice-quality telephone service • Low-speed modem data • Minimal mobility • High traffic • High subscriber densities
Rural	• High-speed data • Enhanced services • Limited mobility • Low subscriber densities • Wide coverage	• Voice-quality telephone service • Low-speed modem data • Minimal mobility • Low subscriber densities

Motorola has WLL products. This is a fixed cellular phone system employing RF technology to replace traditional wired telephones. There are two implementations. The first connects Customer Premise Equipment (CPE) over RF links to telco COs. The second is aimed at cellular operators desiring to add fixed subscribers to their existing cellular networks. The Motorola products are compatible with most existing analog and digital cellular standards using the 800MHz to 900MHz, the 1.5GHz, the 1.8GHz, and the 1.9GHz frequency ranges. They also employ both TDMA and CDMA technologies.

Wireless Office and Personal Area Networks

The wireless office is based upon implementing a Wireless Private Branch Exchange (WPBX) and Wireless LANs (WLANs). The new products operate in the 2.4GHz Industry, Science, and Medicine (ISM) band. Spread spectrum is typically employed to reduce interference and more effectively utilize the bandwidth. This band is also used for WLANs and soon for Personal Area Networks (PANs).

WIRELESS PRIVATE BRANCH EXCHANGE

New 2.4GHz wireless phones are used in WPBX systems. These WPBXs provide PBX features between a base station and wireless handsets, permitting workers to move throughout an office area. Some typical 2.4GHz wireless PBX features include:

- Operation at 2.4GHz—Cordless units operate at a frequency of 2.4GHz, which is faster, clearer, and more secure than 900Mhz.
- Frequency Hopping Spread Spectrum (FHSS) operation—This operation thwarts eavesdroppers by changing frequencies over 100 times per second.
- Excellent range—Depending upon power, they can operate from 10 to 100 meters (30 to 300 feet).
- Expandable from two to eight cordless handsets.
- Adaptive Digital Pulse Code Modulation (ADPCM)—Voice digitizing at 32 Kbps for unsurpassed cordless voice quality.
- Two-line capability with auto line selection.
- Caller ID/caller ID on call waiting.
- Digital answering machine.
- Smart fax/modem port that eliminates the need for data line.
- Simultaneous internal/external calling.
- Conference/group calling.
- Transfer/intercom/paging/forwarding.
- System features are accessible from cordless handsets.
- Customizable ring tones for each handset.

The first five features are demanded by 2.4GHz wireless operations. The remaining features could be found on any PBX system.

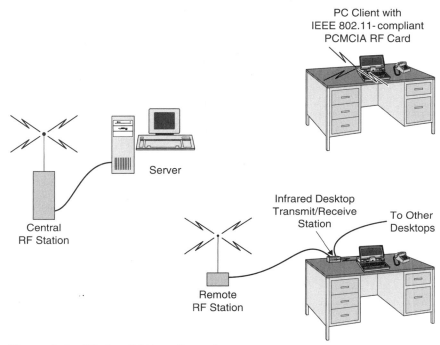

Figure 8–5 *Wireless LAN configurations.*

WIRELESS LOCAL AREA NETWORKS
AND PERSONAL AREA NETWORKS

WLAN products conforming to the IEEE 802.11 standard WLAN protocol are sold as PCMCIA (Personal Computer Memory Card International Association) cards to network laptop computers throughout a facility.

A popular WLAN is Apple's AirPort product for wirelessly networking Apple computers in a facility. It connects devices at speeds up to 11 Mbps with a range of around 150 feet, depending upon building construction. AirPort is compatible with IEEE 802.11HR Direct Sequence Spread Spectrum (DSSS) 11 Mbps and 5.5 Mbps draft standard and IEEE 802.11 DSSS 1 and 2 Mbps standards (see Figure 8-5).

Such IEEE 802.11-compliant products consume power and more range than is needed for PAN devices. An IEEE special interest group, Wireless Personal Area Networks (WPAN), has formed to modify the IEEE 802.11 standard for PAN application. Other groups developing radio specifications for 2.4GHz PAN are HomeRF and Bluetooth. The HomeRF Working Group is a consortium of several major consumer electronic and computer companies.

The HomeRF group's focus is developing specifications for wireless communications in the home to interconnect PCs, peripherals, and remote displays. The Bluetooth Special Interest Group is an industry group of major cell phone and computer companies. Bluetooth is developing a global specification for wireless technology. Bluetooth technology was initially developed to connect cell phones to laptop computers.

Each of these 2.4GHz RF technologies is very similar and yet incompatible. All of the technologies use the 2.4GHz frequency band and Frequency Hopping Spread Spectrum (FHSS) technology. They support data rates of 1 Mbps and higher. Differences in the technologies are hop rate and signal power or coverage area (refer to Table 8-2).

Table 8.2 *2.4 GHz Personal Area Network (PAN) Characteristics*

Operating Parameter	IEEE 802.11- WPAN	HomeRF	Bluetooth
Distance	Not determined	50 meters	10 meters
Hop Rate	2.5 hertz	50 hertz	1600 hertz
Transmit Power	<1 watt (100 milli-watts)	100 milli-watts	1 milli-watt

IEEE 802.11 WPAN specifications are closer to the HomeRF specification than Bluetooth. Incompatible HomeRF and Bluetooth specifications could easily split wireless networks into home and business markets. If both markets were to adopt one standard, a broader customer base would develop. Users would benefit by having seamless connections that were independent of environment, and manufacturers would benefit from higher volumes and lower costs for radio components.

WLANs offer significant potential for cost savings. A key application is inventory tracking in large warehouses. Typical warehouse operations track shipments, log deliveries, count stock in inventory, and more. When these activities are performed by hand or even electronically captured by bar code scanning devices, they can be time-consuming and prone to errors. Instead of overseeing critical tasks, warehouse personnel can be chained to their desks or busy ferrying data from storage areas to data entry terminals. Using WLAN technology and laptop or Personal Digital Assistant (PDA) computing devices connected to hand scanners, warehouse personnel could capture data and interact with the inventory database while roaming throughout the warehouse facility. This capability would increase worker productivity and effectiveness in most all inventory or asset tracking applications.

BLUETOOTH

Bluetooth technology enables consumer electronics devices to communicate with each other over short distances by 2.4GHz RF signals automatically. The first devices allow mobile headsets to communicate with cell phones, permitting hands-free and untethered operation while a caller drives or does other tasks. Soon thereafter Bluetooth technology should turn up in business and personal communications devices, ranging from desktop and laptop PCs to pagers and PDAs. Automobile manufacturers could install hands-free car kits that work with any Bluetooth-compliant mobile telephone. Because Bluetooth automatically and cordlessly connects a PC and a mobile telephone, the mobile phone could communicate with a PC in a briefcase. Users would be notified of incoming e-mail via the telephone, and then could read the titles of e-mails on the telephone screen. Eventually Bluetooth devices will be built into cars, refrigerators, and an array of electronic components and home appliances.

Information exchange and synchronization is the initial Bluetooth-enabled product's application. Updating information in Personal Information Manager (PIM) software or exchanging a business card from a PDA to a PDA, cellular phone, or business/home PC is very important to many PC users. Money is saved when less time spent transferring files. This means that a user can spend more time on another project. Eliminating time to interconnect devices makes life more convenient as well as increases time that can be used for other work.

Bluetooth is designed to create PAN that are always operating and exchanging data in a way that simplifies our lives. Potential applications include cell phones that automatically check palm computer schedules to automatically switch into vibrate mode during meetings or cars that recognize your cell phone so that they adjust the seats and radio to your personal preferences as you walk towards the car.

Bluetooth communicates via a 2.4GHz RF signal for about 10 meters, or 30 feet, but distances can increase to 100 meters, or 300 feet. The transmission speed is 720,000 bps, or about 72,000 characters per second. This speed is more than adequate for simple text transfers between devices. It may also handle voice and graphics. Slow-motion video transmission is also possible. FHSS technology makes the RF signal robust to minimize data loss and encryption provides communications security.

Bluetooth technology is based upon a microchip containing a radio module capable of communicating point-to-point or from one point to several. Equipped with this chip, a laptop PC could talk to several other hand-held devices. Bluetooth developers eventually envision places in commercial establishments where Bluetooth-enabled devices receive signals carrying dining menus, store sale information, games, and the Internet automatically.

Bluetooth was originally pioneered by Ericsson in 1994, and was named for a 10th century Danish king who unified Denmark and Norway. Since then, many leading communications equipment makers, including Lucent, IBM, Compaq, Motorola, Ericsson, Nokia, Toshiba, and others, are preparing to offer Bluetooth products.

As notebook computers, PDAs, and cell phones have become vital working tools for even non-PC users, enterprises have tried to simplify connectivity. Bluetooth is the most likely candidate to solve the connectivity problem, provided price and chip size both get smaller. Bluetooth devices and notebook computers will ship this year, but Bluetooth-enabled devices will not be widely used until after 2002 because two years is needed to reduce chip size and cost. To see widespread implementation, Bluetooth needs be a single inter-operable chip sold for under $10.

One problem looming on the horizon is as Bluetooth proliferates, competing radio signals within the various devices could cause signal interference.

The dream of instant information access could be realized using such RF networking technologies.

Brain Teaser

RF Communications

Locate LOS microwave antennas carrying telephone communications. In cities, most large buildings have LOS microwave antennas installed on the top. Telephone company buildings usually have several antennas. Scan the rooftops of all the large buildings you can see.

1. What shape are the antennas you spot? LOS microwave antennas are often shaped as half a sphere, but some are "L"-shaped horns with the active components shooting signals straight up. The "L"-shaped horn then reflects the signals sideways to their destination.

2. How big are the antennas? Smaller antennas typically operate at higher frequencies and channels run shorter distances.

3. Can you spot the target antennas? This is much more difficult because LOS microwave links can run several miles.

This exercise illustrates how much LOS microwave transmission is used in telecommunications networks.

Satellite Communications

Russia launched the first satellite that transmitted a simple Morse code signal over and over in the late 1950s. Modern satellites receive and retransmit thousands of signals simultaneously. These signals carry digital data to complex television programming.

Satellite communications use special wireless receivers/transmitters in orbit around the earth. Orbiting satellites receive radio signals from an earth station on one frequency (the uplink) and transmit them back at a different frequency (the downlink) to other earth stations. Most communications satellites operate in geo-synchronous or geo-stationary orbits above the equator. Geo-synchronous or geo-stationary orbits require the satellites to be 22,500 miles from earth at the equator. In this manner, they revolve or rotate at the same rate as the earth, so the satellite is always in the same position over the earth's surface.

The communications satellite receivers/transmitters are transponders. A satellite consists of transponders and antennas. The transponders amplify end-user signals received from sending earth stations and then retransmit them to receiving earth stations. Signals at a transmitter are much stronger than signals at a receiver. Since signals at the same frequency interfere with one another, satellite transponders convert signals they receive to a different frequency before transmission back to earth.

Satellite communications networks have a space segment, a signal component, and a ground segment. The space segment is a leased satellite transponder. The signal component includes the frequencies used for communicating with the satellite, the effects of distance on communications, the sources of signal interference, and the modulation schemes and protocols used to ensure proper transmission and reception. The ground segment includes placement and construction of earth stations, the antennas used for different applications, and the multiplexing and multiple access schemes that efficiently access and use satellite transponders.

Hundreds of satellites are currently in operation for various purposes. They are used for weather forecasting, television broadcast distribution, amateur radio communications, Internet communications, and global positioning (the Global Positioning System, or GPS).

Satellite Orbits and Constellations

Satellites operate in three major types of earth orbits as shown in Figure 8-6. These orbit types are:

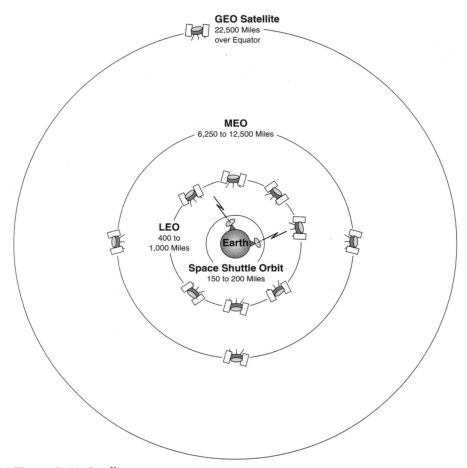

Figure 8–6   *Satellite*

- GEO (Geo-synchronous Earth Orbit or Geo-stationary Earth Orbit) —22,283 miles at the equator—used by most communications satellites today.
- MEO (Medium Earth Orbit)—6,250 to 12,500 miles. No longer geo-stationary—used by the Global Positioning System (GPS).
- LEO (Low Earth Orbit)—400 to 1,000 miles. This is the area where new cellular and Internet satellite services are positioned. Minimal propagation delays and low-power transmitters/receivers are the compelling features of these applications.

Figure 8–7   *East coast GEO satellite image.*
(Image courtesy of NASA—Global Hydrology and Climate Center in Huntsville, Alabama)

Satellites are positioned in geo-synchronous orbit around the equator. They are separated by about 1.5 to 3 degrees of arc, so signals sent from earth do not interfere with each other.

A geo-synchronous or geo-stationary satellite orbit is directly over the equator, approximately 22,500 miles above the earth's surface. At this altitude, a complete trip around the earth takes 24 hours. As a result, GEO satellites remain over the same location on the earth's surface. From the earth's surface, a GEO satellite remains fixed in the sky from any point on about one-third of the earth's surface. All weather satellites are GEO satellites, providing images of specific areas of the planet. There are two U.S. weather satellites, one East coast satellite and a West coast satellite. In the 1980s the East coast satellite failed, so the West coast weather satellite was moved into the East coast position to provide coverage for hurricane season. The replacement East coast weather satellite was destroyed when the Challenger space shuttle crashed in 1986. Two weather satellites are now again in operation, with a spare satellite in the event one satellite fails. NASA's Global Hydrology and Climate Center in Huntsville, Alabama publishes weather satellite images on the Web (see Figure 8-7).

While this image gives the impression that the weather satellites fly really close to Earth, they do not. This is a zoomed-in shot of the planet from the satellite. If we were to see a normal, un-enhanced image, the earth would appear as a small dot in the middle of the image. A single GEO satellite view or broadcast signals to about one-third of the planet's surface. Three GEO satellites spaced at equal intervals (120 angular degrees apart) are needed for complete planet coverage. Satellites that cover North America occupy the same geo-stationary/geo-synchronous equatorial orbit positions (slots) as do those that serve all South and Central American nations. Similarly, satellites that serve Europe would occupy some orbital positions (slots) as those that serve African nations.

A GEO satellite is accessed using a dish antenna aimed at the spot in the sky where the satellite hovers. Digital Satellite Service (DSS) has small receive-only dish antennas pointed at GEO satellites. These satellites have 32 transponders. The dishes must be precisely aimed at the satellite for the signal to be received with acceptable strength. The TV controller has a signal measuring function that can be used to view the strength of the received satellite signal on the TV. Each satellite has a broadcast footprint that has different received signal strengths for different longitude and latitude locations on the earth's surface.

When my DSS was first installed, it was February and everything worked just super. About June, the signal kept dropping. TV reception would be on then off, then on again. It was very annoying, so I went out to the rear deck and looked at the satellite receive-only dish. It looked okay, but when I followed where it pointed to in the sky, I discovered that a tree branch with lots of leaves was in the path. Whenever the wind blew, the tree branch would block the satellite signal. So the satellite repair person came out and moved the antenna up on the roof 20 feet and away from the tree branch. Then the roof was replaced, and the roofers ripped the antenna off and just stuck it back on again. Everything worked pretty well. The received signal strength, while not in the 90 percent range, was close at 86 percent. Then one cold and rainy fall day, the signal reception became real marginal (TV reception was on then off, then on again as before) so I knew that the dish had to be re-aimed. It was one of those damp, wet, cold fall Saturdays—just an ideal time to line up the old satellite dish. So I got my second ex-wife, Cindy, to look at the signal meter on the TV while I adjusted the antenna 30 feet up on the roof. We communicated using cordless phones. There are only two adjustments on the satellite antennas, up/down and right/left. Up/down was easiest to adjust, so I marked it with a magic marker and moved the dish upward. Out of the phone in the cheeriest voice ever came the word "ZERO!" I now had no signal. The number "ZERO!" was cheerily sung out no matter how the antenna was adjusted. I was beginning to think that my signal power meter reader could not read. So I set the antenna back where it was marked with the magic marker. Still more "ZERO!" announcements. Then I moved it right/left to suddenly hear "84, 90, 92, and finally, 94!" The antenna aim was quite precise. Anything off-axis saw no signal. This is true for all GEO satellite signals.

MEO and LEO satellites use a group of satellites called a constellation to provide continuous coverage because their location relative to the earth's surface is constantly changing. There may be from 24 to as many as several hundred satellites in a constellation.

The best-known Medium Earth Orbit (MEO) satellites are the Global Positioning System (GPS). GPS is a constellation of 24 satellites, with eight satellites always visible at any time from the earth's surface. Special GPS receivers are used to provide precise location plotting.

A Low Earth Orbit (LEO) satellite system uses larger constellations of satellites. Each satellite is in a circular orbit at a constant altitude of a few hundred miles. These satellite orbits are polar orbits and not equatorial orbits. Polar orbits take satellites nearly over the geographic north and south poles. Each orbital revolution ranges from 90 minutes to a few hours. Satellite constellations are arranged so that from any point on the earth's surface at any time, one or more satellites are in a line of sight with the earth station receiver. Satellite constellations operate in a manner similar to the way cellular telephones function. In satellite networks, both the transponders (equivalent to cellular radio towers) and phones are moving rather than fixed. Further, the transponders are in orbit rather than on the earth. When earth antennas are in fixed positions and not on mobile phones, they must pick up signals from moving satellites. The fixed antennas cannot effectively be physically rotated to point at the satellite, so they must be solid-state, phased array antennas that function as though they are pointed at the satellite as it moves in space. A phased array antenna is composed of several small antennas. The received signal from these small antennas is combined to form a composite signal that in effect is equivalent to pointing the antenna at the satellite as it travels across the sky.

What makes new satellite networking services interesting is that using satellites running in LEO, they can deliver high-speed Internet access to just about any location on the planet. Broadband satellite distribution is a powerful, cost-effective technology for providing rural locations with high-speed Internet access.

Satellite Signal Propagation Delay

Satellite communications uses geo-synchronous or geo-stationary satellites to broadcast from one earth station to multiple earth stations, or to relay microwave frequency RF signals from one earth station to another. Newer satellite systems can relay signals from satellite to satellite as well to complete connections around the planet.

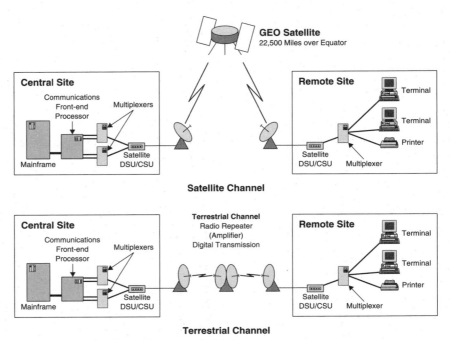

Figure 8–8 *Satellite vs. terrestrial channels.*

For GEO satellites, signal propagation delays are significant. How long at the speed of light does it take a microwave RF signal to travel to a satellite 22,500 miles above the earth and back? The speed of light is 186,000 miles per second. So the time is 45,000 miles/186,000 miles per second, or one-quarter second. A round trip to a remote station and back with electronic processing delays added in consumes around one-half second. While this doesn't seem like a lot of time, it is when you are trying to talk with someone over a satellite phone link. Terrestrial links have virtually no delays because they are relatively short (at most 25,000 miles but more like several hundred to 10,000 miles—see Figure 8-8).

MEO and LEO satellites have much lower propagation delays than those from GEO satellite communications. Although MEO and LEO satellite propagation delays induce potentially more latency in communications signals than terrestrial communications links, the propagation delays fall within a very acceptable performance range for two-way voice and Internet communications. Even the half-second GEO delay in Internet communications does not present the same propagation problems as it does for interactive voice communications.

Satellite RF Bands

Satellites use different microwave frequency bands to carry communications. These frequency bands have different operating characteristics. Many satellites use C-band, because C-band transmissions have a broad footprint that makes them especially useful for signals that must be broadcast over a wide area. C-band signals are relatively weak and often require large and somewhat expensive earth station antennas, but they are relatively immune to atmospheric interference. The earth's atmosphere is nearly invisible to signals in the 6/4GHz range, permitting C-band signals to pass through fog and rainstorms without interference. This property also makes C-band signals ideal for terrestrial point-to-point microwave transmissions causing terrestrial C-band signals to interfere with or to jam weaker C-band satellite signals. Since 6/4GHz microwave signals are used for many LOS microwave networks in major metropolitan areas, C-band earth stations are located away from city centers in satellite earth station farms, sometimes called teleports. The teleports are connected to sites within cities by fiber, cable, or other microwave facilities. Table 8-3 identifies communications satellite frequency bands.

Ku-band transmission complements C-band signals. Ku-band is best used in strong, narrow spot beams ideal for point-to-point or point-to-selective-multi-point applications. Unlike C-band, Ku-band signals are higher frequency and more or less immune to interference from terrestrial microwave networks. Thus, Ku-band receivers can be located in the centers of cities. Ku-band signals are stronger than C-band signals and use smaller less expensive earth station antennas. However, Ku-band signals are more sensitive to atmospheric interference, especially from heavy fog or rainstorms. Although stormy weather usually covers only a small area for a brief time, the outage caused by atmospheric interference can be serious when it occurs during a period of heavy data traffic, or during a special broadcasting. Ka-band signals are similar to Ku-band signals, but because of their higher frequency, they are even more susceptible to atmospheric interference.

The most practical way to compensate for losses due to attenuation from any source is to increase the signal power. Attenuation is more pronounced at higher frequency Ka and Ku-bands. However, higher receiver gains possible at these higher frequencies can compensate for this effect.

UPLINK/DOWNLINK TRANSMISSION DIFFERENCES

The uplink is the satellite circuit extending from an earth station to the satellite, while the downlink is the circuit extending from the satellite to an earth

Table 8.3 *RF and Satellite Bands*

Band	General Uplink/ Downlink Frequency Range (GHz)	Available Bandwidth (MHz)
L	1.6/1.5	15
S	3/2	15
C	6/4	500
Xc	7/5	500
X	8/7	500
Ku	14/12	500
Ka	30/20	2,500

station. In satellite transmission, uplink frequencies are higher because they are the most susceptible to atmospheric interference. Since increased broadcast power can compensate for atmospheric interference, it is easy for terrestrial stations to increase signal power during rain or foggy weather. Terrestrial stations have access to the earth's power grid, which can provide them with plenty of power. Satellite transmission downlinks use lower frequencies because satellite power is limited to the power generated by the solar panels. When a satellite is in the earth's shadow, it must run on batteries. Using a lower frequency helps the limited power signal from the satellite get through rain and fog.

Because of uplink and downlink frequency differences, the frequencies used for satellite communications are identified in frequency pairs. Each pair of frequencies is called a band. Satellite circuits now operating use several frequency bands: the C-band, with uplinks in the 6GHz range and downlinks in the 4GHz range; the Ku-band, with uplinks in the 14GHz range and downlinks in the 12GHz range; and the Ka-band, with uplinks in the 30GHz range and downlinks in the 20GHz range. Each frequency band has special characteristics that make it useful for certain applications. Higher frequencies, while being more susceptible to atmospheric interference also carry more information, than do lower frequencies.

SATELLITE LIFE EXPECTANCY

Satellites are built with a usable life of 7 to 12 years. A satellite's useful life depends upon the fuel on board. The fuel is consumed performing constant station keeping. GEO satellites can fly in a "figure 8" pattern. Other satellites must stay within specific orbital plane boundaries. The satellite fuel is consumed maintaining these orbital positions. Since satellites cannot pull up at a gas station and conveniently refuel, they eventually run so low on fuel that they must be moved to a different orbital position where they can gradually slow down and crash into the earth's atmosphere.

Why don't we use the space shuttle to refuel satellites? The answer is simple: How high up does the space shuttle fly? Space shuttles fly from 150 miles to 250 miles above the earth. This is well below the orbits of GEO satellites and even MEO and LEO satellites. So there is little chance that the space shuttle could refuel any satellite.

Positioning satellites must be done carefully to conserve on-board fuel. This is illustrated by a story I once heard about a NASA telecommunications satellite launched for India. The satellite was turned over to the Indian satellite technicians for final positioning. Not fully understanding what a delicate procedure positioning is, the Indian technicians drove the satellite like a car or a truck into position only to run it out of fuel. Oops! They ended up with a $100 million useless telecommunications satellite.

SPACE SHUTTLE LAUNCHES

If this is true, how can the space shuttle launch GEO communications satellites? The most difficult part of any satellite trip is the first 150 miles. Once in orbit, it is relatively easy to then fly out to a 22,500-mile geo-synchronous or geo-stationary earth orbit. The space shuttle flies up to 150 miles (the hard part), opens the cargo bay doors, kicks the satellite out, and says, "See ya!". A rocket engine on the satellite then fires and carries the satellite up to its designated geo-synchronous or geo-stationary earth orbit. One GEO satellite's rocket motor failed and it was left in low orbit. The insurance companies then owned this useless $100 million (GEO communications satellites cost about $100 million each) communications satellite. Hughes Aircraft, the manufacturer of most all GEO satellites, purchased this satellite from the insurance companies for $25 million with a plan to salvage the satellite and position it in geo-synchronous or geo-stationary orbit by shooting it around the moon. There was some 3,970 pounds of fuel on the spacecraft. While this amount of fuel was not enough to directly position it in the proper geo-synchronous or geo-stationary orbit and still have its working life be 7 or 8 years, there was enough fuel to shoot the satellite around the moon and then position it in the proper geo-synchronous or geo-stationary earth orbit. Hughes accomplished this successfully, as I recall.

VERY SMALL APERTURE TERMINAL

Very Small Aperture Terminal (VSAT) is a satellite communications system serving mainly business users. A VSAT user has a special satellite network interface unit that supports a wide variety of interfaces for a user's network equipment. These interfaces range from T-1 channel interfaces supporting voice and video transmission to Ethernet IP networking interfaces. The satellite network interface unit connects with an outside satellite dish antenna to perform the necessary data encoding. In this sense, it acts as a very high-speed, sophisticated modem. VSAT antenna dish diameters range from usually 1.2 m (about 4 feet) to 2.4 m (about 8 feet) across. Many VSATs are receive-only or receive/transmit terminals installed at geographically dispersed sites. The network topology is commonly a star because most VSATs communicate through a Master Earth Station (MES) or network hub. The antenna and its transceiver receive or send signals to a satellite that relays the signals to the earth station acting as a hub. Each user connects through the hub earth station via satellite in a star topology. To communicate, each user's transmission goes first to the hub earth station and then is retransmitted via satellite to the other end-user's VSAT.

VSAT carries IP data, voice, and video transmission. VSAT changed from a low-rate data transmission medium to a multimedia solution for handling high-speed data, file transfer, voice, facsimile, imaging, business TV, video conferencing, terrestrial backup, CAD, LAN connectivity, and digitized video and audio. Multi-rate bandwidth makes VSAT less expensive and more reliable by increasing bandwidth on the satellite transponder.

VSAT allows businesses to operate or lease private satellite networks. VSAT permits companies to have total control of their own communication network without depending upon any telephone companies. Business and home users have high-speed data reception as compared to ordinary telephone service or even ISDN service. The cost of a VSAT hub can run upwards of $1 million or more. Remote stations can cost from several thousand to around $100,000, depending upon capabilities. This can make a fully private VSAT network impractical for many organizations. However, VSAT is available to users through full-service, shared hub network offerings from satellite carriers.

Advances in earth station technology permit full mesh networks with higher power VSATs to communicate directly through the satellite with each other.

SATELLITE NETWORK TECHNOLOGY

Satellite services originally used two one-way channels to connect earth station sites. This satellite channel usage was very inefficient and could at best provide service to a few users. In the 1980s Satellite Business Systems (at that time an IBM subsidiary) started a new satellite service based upon Time Division Multiple Access (TDMA) technology. With TDMA, many stations shared the same transponder because each station was assigned a time slot when it could transmit into the central satellite network hub. The hub then resent the packets it received out over a few channels as a continuous stream that all earth stations received. This is a form of Time Division Multiplexing (TDM) specifically tailored to satellite network operation. TDMA as an access method is still used in satellite networks today.

The latest satellite technology is Demand Assigned Multiple Access (DAMA). DAMA technology provides reliable digital telecommunications connectivity by controlling satellite bandwidth use. A DAMA satellite network assigns an earth station that demands the service of a pair of available channels from a pool of satellite channels. Those channels service the earth station for the duration of its communications. When a channel connection becomes free, the pair of channels is returned to the satellite channel pool for reassignment as needed. Since DAMA satellite networks use satellite channels on an as-needed basis instead of permanently assigning them; there are no dedicated point-to-point channels that waste satellite capacity. DAMA reduces the satellite bandwidth needed to service the entire network. The reduction in satellite bandwidth may be as high as 80 percent. This bandwidth reduction combined with lower equipment requirements result in dramatically lower satellite network operating costs.

A variation of DAMA is Single Channel Per Carrier-Demand Assigned Multiple Access (SCPC-DAMA). SCPC-DAMA satellite systems support voice, fax, and point-to-point high-speed data applications. SCPC-DAMA can provide full-mesh connectivity between thousands of remote satellite VSAT terminals.

Other aspects of satellite communications have advanced dramatically over the last decade. Both the ground segment and the space segment have changed. On the space side, increased transponder power results in improved signal strength. Signal quality is now acceptable when smaller and less expensive earth stations are used to capture that signal.

Another improvement in satellite communications is transmitting the satellite signal in scanning spot beams more accurately to cover specific sites. Thus, the smaller dishes that receive signals from a broader area than large antennas now receive fewer interfering signals from satellites close to the satellites at which the smaller antennas are pointed.

TRANSMISSION SECURITY AND DATA ENCRYPTION

Gaining access to private telephone conversations is relatively easy. Wiretapping extends beyond copper wire phone line interception to include all types of communications media. All communications technologies—including satellite, microwave, infrared, and even fiber optics—can be intercepted. Wiretapping and other electronic equipment needed to intercept and interpret telephone conversations is inexpensive. The technical knowledge is provided by electronics hobbyist organizations and Internet publications. There are few if any cost-effective, commercially available products to detect electronic eavesdropping on satellite communications links.

Signal scrambling or digital data encryption is the only way to prevent satellite transmissions from being intercepted and disclosed to unauthorized parties. Signal scrambling prevents satellite video and voice signals from being intelligible to unauthorized parties. Analog scramblers are used where low cost is the primary factor in device selection. Digital signal encryption is used when higher levels of security are needed. Digital encryption devices are incorporated into satellite equipment using Digital Encryption Standard (DES) public and private key as well as secret key encoding to assure information security.

Secure satellite networks use point-to-point extensions to build hub-and-spoke-style networks, or they use static configuration tables to build multi-point networks. Type 1 inline network encryption devices provide secure VPNs. They must support satellite network full-mesh connectivity to improve network performance and reliability, while reducing network management costs.

Satellite Services

There are a wide variety of satellite services sold today. These services fit into two general categories: broadband satellite services and low-speed voice/messaging satellite services.

Typical satellite services are:

• Digital Satellite Service (DSS) providing DirecTV broadband service competing with CATV for distributing high-quality video to homes.

• DirecPC providing 400-Kbps residential Internet access.

- Broadband satellite services designed to build private enterprise-wide and planet-wide communications networks without using telephone company facilities.
- Voice services for business and residential use.
- Geo-location services for locating mobile equipment.

New broadband services use LEO satellites and Ka-band frequencies to deliver broadband transmission services supporting video telephony, high-speed data, and Internet access to any location on this planet.

DirecTV uses an 18" mini-dish to deliver digital broadcast television to residential users throughout the U.S. DirecTV provides access to more than 210 TV channels with digital quality picture and Dolby digital sound. DirecTV offers a wide selection of basic channels, premium movie channels, pay-per-view, and audio music choice.

DirecPC is a satellite network that gives home users high-speed Internet access as shown in Figure 8-9. DirecPC can become your ISP or it can work with your existing ISP using high-speed links from the Internet to a satellite connected to your PC. This service uses telephone connections to send information requests into the DirecPC central site. The Web pages and downloads requested are then sent to the PC over the satellite link at kilobits per second speeds.

When a PC user surfing the Web requests a Web site URL, the request is sent by modem to their ISP. With DirecPC, before that request leaves the customer's PC, DirecPC software attaches a tunneling code to the URL request. This tunneling code is an electronic addressing mask that instructs the PC user's ISP to forward the URL request to the DirecPC Network Operations Center (NOC). When the DirecPC's NOC receives the PC user's request, the tunneling code is stripped off. Then the request is send using T-3 channels to the target Web site and the desired Web page is retrieved. The DirecPC NOC then uploads the information to the DirecPC satellite that in turn transmits it at about 400 Kbps to the PC user's DirecPC dish. The direct PC box converts the signal into an Ethernet connection that feeds into the user's PC.

Other broadband services are based upon new satellite technologies. Some are aimed at voice communications, while others are focused on providing cheap high-speed global Internet access. Table 8-4 lists several satellite services aimed at providing high-speed telecommunications services.

Such satellite services provide instant access to a broad range of applications. Data rates are selectable and easily matched to specific user needs, with satellite networking charges based on the satellite resources used by the customer. This gives enterprises and consumers worldwide, affordable access to

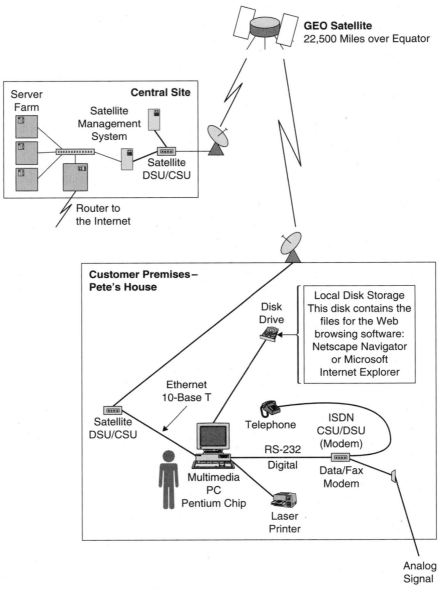

Figure 8–9 *DirectPC satellite internet service.*

a wide range of interactive, high-speed, and high-quality broadband tele-communications applications, including:

- Enterprise networking interconnecting corporate LANs and WANs— Multiple locations anywhere in the world can link LANs and WANs

Table 8.4 *Broadband Satellite Services General Information*

Vendor	System	Availability	Satellites	Web Site URL
Hughes	Spaceway	2002	9 GEO	hns.com/spaceway/ spaceway.htm
Teledesic	Teledesic	2004	288+ LEO	teledesic.com
Lockheed	AstroLink	2003	9 GEO	astrolink.com/welcome.html
Loral	Cyberstar	1999/2003	3 GEO	cyberstar.com
Alcatel	SkyBridge	2003	80 LEO	skybridgesatellite.com

into a single, unified, high-speed enterprise network. Private satellite networks offer increased security and faster data transfer than many terrestrial telephone company-based networks.

- Multimedia applications in enterprise intranets—High-speed satellite networking can distribute internal communications to all corporate facilities efficiently and effectively.

- Electronic commerce (e-commerce) and extranets—Electronic Data Interchange (EDI) between businesses and suppliers and commerce between businesses and customers can be implemented globally.

- High-speed Internet access and file transfer—Business and residential users can access the Internet at high speed, sending and receiving large amounts of data in seconds. Broadband satellite access offers a competitive advantage by speeding up Internet data transfers. Data files and monstrous program downloads for business, home office, and residential consumers require less than a minute to complete as opposed to hours.

- Distance learning—High-speed satellite networks make possible interactive education and training programs, bringing together students at multiple sites with an instructor on the other side of the country or the world. Satellite broadband transmission supports exchanging graphics, images and video to all locations.

- Video telephony and video teleconferencing—ISDN-class communications supports desktop PC and high-end videoconferencing between facilities.

- Telecommuting—Satellite network, high-speed, interactive data transfer capabilities make the telecommuter feel like they are sitting in an office at work, sharing information on the office LAN.

- Information broadcast (multi-cast)—Global broadband access is essential for network applications that broadcast multimedia information simultaneously to many Internet users.

- Telemedicine—Physicians can transmit and receive high-resolution X-ray and ultrasound images, allowing specialists to work with patients at remote locations.
- Voice communications replacing POTS—Providing T-1/E-1 voice network channels bypassing telephone company facilities and lowering voice network costs.

- Satellite networks support such applications in urban and rural areas very cost-effectively. Table 8-5 provides more detailed data on broadband satellite networks.

Table 8.5 *Broadband Satellite Service Networks*

Name	AstroLink	Cyberstar	SkyBridge (Cyberstar)	Spaceway	Teledesic
Sponsors	Lockheed	Loral	Alcatel Loral	Hughes	McCaw Gates Boeing
Use	Voice Data Video Multi-cast Multimedia	Voice Data Digital Video Broadcast (DVB) IP Multi-cast	Voice Data Digital Video Broadcast (DVB) IP Multi-cast	Voice Data Video Multi-cast Multimedia	Voice Data Video Multi-cast Multimedia
Altitude	GEO	GEO	LEO 911 Miles	GEO	LEO 435 Miles
Band	Ka	Ka	Ku	Ka	Ka
Antenna	33-47 inches	16 inches	--	26 inches +	10"
Speed	16 Kbps to 9.6 Mbps	400 Kbps to 30 Mbps	16 Mbps to 20 Mbps	16 Kbps to 6 Mbps	16 Kbps to 64 Mbps
Cost	$1,000 to $2,000	$1,000	$500	$1,000 +	--
Investment	$4B	$1.6B	$4.1B	$3.5B	$9B
Operational Date	2003	1999/2003	2003	2002	2004
Satellites	9	3	80	9	288
Access	FDMA TDMA	FDMA TDMA	FDMA TDMA CDMA WDMA	FDMA TDMA	MF-TDMA ATDM
Satellite-to-satellite Links	Yes	No	No	Yes	Yes

The Teledesic satellite network, touted to be the "Internet in the Sky," is targeted at providing high-speed digital links to the Internet. The Teledesic system uses satellite-to-satellite cross-links, switching to route connections from their source to the destination. Ka-band frequencies can provide a wide range of digital transmission services to subscribers. The Teledesic concept is illustrated in Figure 8-10.

Some broadband satellite services employ narrow spot beams, facilitating frequency re-use and providing greater satellite transmission capacity. Other broadband satellite services plan to support satellite-to-satellite switching similar to Teledesic. Satellite-to-satellite switching requires on-board storage and processing capabilities in the satellites to implement this functionality. Finally, some systems use Error Correcting Codes (ECCs) so that transmissions are accurately received.

Teledesic will most likely in congested urban areas utilize a hybrid wired/satellite communications infrastructure to deliver services to individual subscribers. Teledesic was originally planning to use about 1,000 satellites to provide the requisite coverage and bandwidth. Today that number has been reduced to 288 satellites. These orbit in a precise polar orbit constellation. Teledesic is representative of satellite broadband services. They all provide similar capabilities and are based upon similar technology. Small variations in technical characteristics can make one satellite system better for a specific network application than another.

Satellite Voice Services

There are several new telecommunications services on the horizon aimed at voice communications such as the Ellipso and GlobalStar. An early LEO voice communications satellite system was Iridium. Iridium came on-line November 1998. Unfortunately the business plan was not well thought out and Iridium failed. It is included in the chart here for comparison purposes only. Iridium was a planet-wide cellular communications system. The Iridium hand-held cell phones utilized either terrestrial cellular links or satellite links with satellite-to-satellite call routing.

These satellite-based systems typically use satellites in LEOs ranging from about 400 miles to 800 miles above the earth. Some use circular orbits, while others employ elliptic orbits. Because they are LEOs, all these systems require multiple satellites for continuous service. Ellipso and the new ICO employ the fewest, with full constellations of 17 and 12 satellites, respectively. Other LEO networks require more satellites, with OrbComm and Globalstar anticipating 48 satellite constellations. (The 72 satellites of Iridium were equal to the number of electrons orbiting an iridium atom—hence the name.

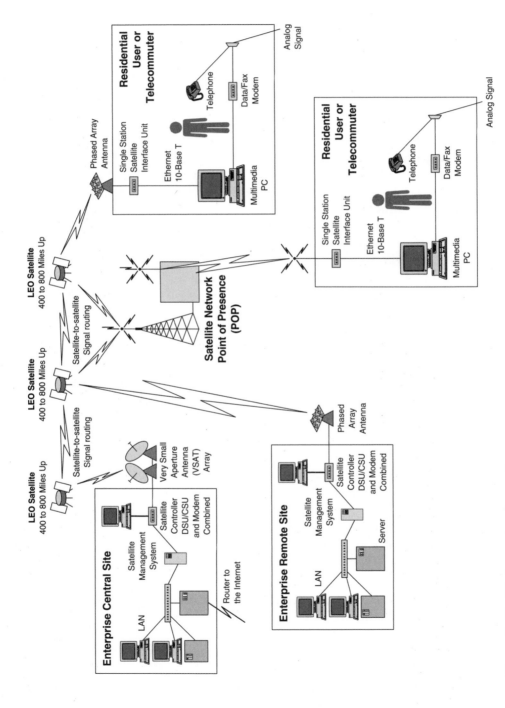

Figure 8–10 *Teledesic network operation.*

When the required number was reduced to 66 satellites, it became equivalent to the number of electrons orbiting a different, less glamorous, element—say like lead because it failed to fly.)

Table 8-6 presents brief summaries of current and planned telephony satellite communications systems.

Table 8.6 *Telephony Satellite Systems*

Name	Ellipso	Globalstar	New ICO (Teledesic)	OrbComm	Iridium (defunct)
Sponsors	Westinghouse	Loral Alcatel	Hughes	Teleglobe Orbital Sciences Corp.	Motorola Raytheon
Use	Voice Data Fax Paging Geo-location	Voice Fax Data	Voice Paging	Data messaging Paging Geo-location	Voice Fax Data
Band	UHF	L, S, and Xc	Xc	VHF	L and Ka
Speed	2,400 bps (voice) 28.8 Kbps (data)	2,400 bps (voice) 9,600 bps (data)	2,400 bps	2,400 bps	2,400 bps
Approximate Terminal Cost	$1,000	$750	$300	$1,000 to $3,000	$3,000 at the end
Investment	$1.5 M	$3.8B	$4.3B	$1+B	$4.4++B
Operational Date	2002	2000	2003	1998	1998
Satellites	17 MEO	48 (8 spares) MEO	10 (2 spares) MEO	48 (8 spares) LEO	66 (6 spares) LEO

SATELLITE PAGING SERVICES

Paging delivers text or voice messages to a specific person in a general geographic area. The person's exact location in that area is not precisely known. Paging subscribers carry a small receiver that receives phone number text, short message text, or a voice message. Paging services can be one-way, or receive-only, or two-way, permitting confirmation that the message was received. Satellite paging services use a combination of terrestrial network in major metropolitan areas and satellite links to interconnect them. When a page goes out from one city, it travels across satellite links to remote cities, where it is sent to the pager using a local RF link. OrbComm sends paging data directly from the satellite to the pager unit, but most paging networks rely on local RF links for final paging delivery.

GLOBAL POSITIONING SYSTEM

The Global Positioning System (GPS) is a system in MEO that was originally developed for military applications. It is a constellation of 24 satellites orbiting at about 11,200 miles. At any given time, a GPS receiver can see eight of the 24 satellites from its position on the earth.

Each GPS receiver gets timing and positioning signals from the satellites it sees. It then uses them to compute its precise location relative to the satellites. This permits identifying a terrestrial location by longitude, latitude, and height above sea level to within a meter of the actual location.

GPS is designed to treat military and civilian applications differently. Military applications are given more precise positioning than are civilian applications. However, a Presidential ruling has now permitted civilian GPS applications to have the same precise positioning as military applications.

One GPS application is in agriculture. New tractors that pull harvesters and fertilizing equipment come equipped with GPS systems. As a farmer harvests a crop, he or she enters crop yield information into the GPS located in the tractor. This status is then plotted on a precise map of the field being harvested. In the next, year when a new crop is being planted and later fertilized, the data obtained through the GPS is used to regulate the amount of fertilizer applied to the field. Areas with lower yield are given more fertilizer, while areas with higher yield are given less fertilizer. In this manner, the crop yield for that year will be more uniform and predictable across the entire field. This also optimizes fertilizer use.

At any electronics store, GPS receivers can be purchased for any PC. These are combined with travel map software to plot street addresses and routes from one location to another. Once I was teaching at a Holiday Inn in Jacksonville, Florida. I arrived at the airport and got a rental car, but had absolutely no idea where the hotel was. So I fired up the laptop, started the travel software, put in the hotel's address and the address of the Jacksonville airport, and plotted a from/to route. Next, I attached the GPS receiver to the laptop and placed it on the dash of the rental car. Then I started driving. Within several minutes, the laptop started plotting my progress on the from/to route. I could see when turns were approaching and which way to turn. The GPS receiver and travel map software guided me to the front door of my hotel. The newest GPS receiver is a handheld, color unit containing road maps of all major U.S. highways. It is fun to use on an airplane. Pick a hapless victim sitting in the window seat, and explain to him or her that placing the GPS unit's antenna against the window, they are able to view exactly where they are on the color display. In this manner, you can tell that you are flying at 42,000 feet, going 618 miles per hour over Wyoming, and that there are rest rooms directly below you.

Saving Costs by Using Satellite Communications

Satellites have unique advantages over other communications technologies. The advantages of satellites include the following:

- Stable costs—The cost of satellite transmission over a single link is the same regardless of the distance between the sending and receiving stations. Further, all satellite signals are broadcast, making the cost of a satellite transmission the same regardless of the number of stations receiving that transmission.
- High bandwidth—Satellite signals are at very high transmission speeds capable of carrying large amounts of data.
- Low error rates—Bit errors in a digital satellite signal are almost completely random. Therefore, statistical systems for error detection and correction can be applied efficiently and reliably.

Other attributes are inherently restrictive, making satellites impractical or unusable for other applications. Among the restrictions to satellite use are:

- Signal propagation delay—The great distance from an earth station to a GEO satellite causes any one-way transmission over a satellite link to have an inherent propagation delay of roughly 250 ms (a quarter of a second = 45,000 mi/186,000 mi). This delay is noticeable in voice communications and can make satellite links inefficient when used with data communication protocols that have not been adapted to satellite use. Most fourth generation protocols should be okay, and satellite interface boxes often buffer data to compensate for propagation delays.
- Earth station size—Two-degree orbital spacing for satellites, low-power satellite signals in some frequency bands, and the great distances satellite signals span produce weak signals at receiving earth stations. These factors can keep earth station antenna diameter large, making installation difficult. New higher frequency, higher power, spot beam satellites overcome these difficulties.
- Security—All satellite signals are broadcast and therefore insecure unless the signals are encrypted. Any receiving station within sight of

the satellite can receive any signal transmitted over the satellite if it is tuned to the proper frequency.

• Interference—Satellite signals operating at Ku- or Ka- band frequencies are highly susceptible to interference from bad weather, especially rain or fog. Satellite networks operating at C-band experience interference from terrestrial microwave signals. Bad weather can provide sporadic, unpredictable performance in the K bands. Terrestrial interference in C-band limits the earth stations in major metropolitan areas, where users are concentrated more heavily.

These advantages and limitations of satellite systems influence the decisions regarding types of satellite systems selected for private networks. Users with satellite-compatible network requirements (e.g., networks with geographically dispersed locations and large bandwidth requirements within the network) find a satellite network saves costs over a terrestrial network.

Cost savings are realized when organizations build private satellite networks to bypass telephone company facilities and their related costs. This can be especially true for international communications. Telephone companies and Post Telephone and Telegraph (PTT) ministries tend to charge high prices for communications services.

In some cases, telecommunications loads are unbalanced or asymmetric with more information flowing out of a site than comes into the site. This is especially true of Internet sites. By using DAMA satellite technology, these sites can reduce communications costs by paying only for the communications services used.

EARTH STATION EQUIPMENT
AND SATELLITE CHANNEL SERVICE SUPPLIERS

There are several satellite earth station and NOC center vendors. U.S. companies have dominated the VSAT market. Some U. S. vendors are Orbital Sciences Inc., Hughes, AT&T, GTE, and Scientific Atlanta (now ViaSat). Hughes Network Systems owns and operates the most private satellites (C-band and Ku-band). It offers a comprehensive range of satellite telecommunications products, including the Integrated Satellite Business Network (ISBN), Telephony Earth Station (TES), and a TDMA network of data, voice, fax, and video applications embracing its video conferencing system, teleconferencing delivered over VSAT terminals to remote sites. ViaSat (Scientific Atlanta) has installed over 45,000 VSAT terminals worldwide. ViaSat provides all the components needed to install and operate private satellite networks.

Satellite Communications

Locate a satellite dish used at a hotel to receive television broadcasts. It is usually installed in the rear of the hotel in the parking lot.

How big is the satellite antenna? Generally, these are VSAT antennas that measure about 8 feet across.

1. Go to an electronics store and examine the Digital Satellite Service (DSS) components sold, especially the antenna. Is it smaller? This typically means that DSS operates at higher frequencies and that it is a receive-only antenna.

2. If it is possible, use the active DSS-connected TV to switch to dish-pointing mode. If the store will not let you go to the dish-pointing mode, go to a friend's house and have them demonstrate it to you. What signal strength do they receive?

This exercise illustrates the differences between some GEO satellite systems.

Cellular Telecommunications

Cellular telephone uses microwave analog or digital signals to connect subscriber wireless mobile telephones to transmitter stations within miles of the wireless mobile phone. Each transmitter station's area of coverage is a single cell. Cellular telephone service is readily available in most all urban areas and along virtually all major highways. When mobile cellular telephone users move from an area covered by one cell to an area covered by another cell, the wireless mobile telephone connections pass from one local transmitter station to the other local transmitter station.

Cellular telephones, while wireless, are not the same as cordless telephones that use around a 150-foot wireless connection to a local cordless base station. The base station has a wired connection to a telephone CO. Similar to cellular telephones are Personal Communications Services (PCS) phones. PCS phones operate like cellular phones, but use higher RF frequencies so that more cells are required. PCS phones are all-digital phones. Most urban cellular systems are digital, but some rural cellular systems remain analog.

PCS includes automatic number identification and text mail as part of its basic service package. PCS was also the first service that removed the one- or two-year term contract. PCS subscribers purchase their phones, thus removing phone payment subsidies used to pay for subscriber cellular phones.

Cellular communications has competition from traditional cellular telephony service providers, PCS, and Nextel. Nextel service is cellular telephony that spun out of Enhanced Specialized Mobile Radio (E-SMR) service. Both Nextel and PCS have text messaging and calling number identification (new digital cell phones provide such features as well). Because Nextel evolved from the E-SMR two-way radio network, Nextel has an additional intercom-like push-to-talk feature that is unique in cellular communications.

Cellular telephony services are now offering a single rate for nationwide service. These service plans calculate cellular charges based upon airtime used and not on the distance called. This makes every phone call within the contracted minutes look like a local call to the cellular subscriber.

Mobility increases productivity in many cases, so making workforces increasingly mobile is good business. New mobile communication systems like cellular telephones, PCS, and Nextel are contributors to the rapid growth in telecommunications services. Cellular telephones are used everywhere today. They are rapidly becoming the phone of choice for everyone. It is easy to incorporate cellular technologies where needed to handle a wide variety of mobile communications requirements.

Cellular Communications Evolution

Early mobile phone services had a big radio mounted in the trunk of an automobile. When the driver wanted to place a call, they picked up the microphone and requested a mobile operator to dial the desired telephone number. When the called party answered, the mobile operator connected the telephone line to the mobile radio channel. The call proceeded in a half-duplex "over to you" or "push-to-talk" fashion because the mobile RF link was half-duplex.

Today cellular mobile telephone service operates like normal telephone service used at home and in the office. Traditional telephone service is referred to as wire-line telephone service. Telephone service is full duplex (two-way, simultaneous transmission) over voice-grade channels. A telephone number identifies every phone line uniquely. To act like normal telephones, mobile telephones interconnect with the public telephone network and with one another directly. Each mobile phone is identified by a unique binary address (an OSI Layer-2 address) that is assigned a telephone number (an OSI Layer-3 address).

Cell phones originally operated in the 800MHz frequency band. The wire-line and non-wire-line providers split the available frequencies in the

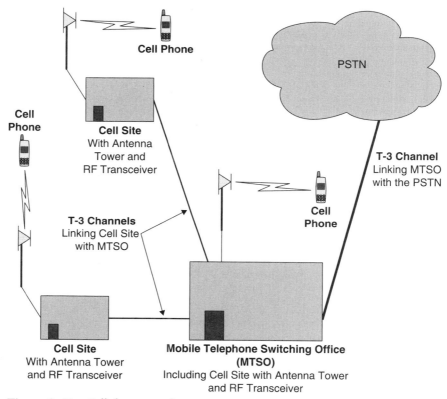

Figure 8–11 *Cellular network components.*

800MHz frequency band. PCS operates in North America in a 1.8GHz frequency band. Nextel operates in the 800MHz frequency range. International cellular frequencies, 900MHz for cellular and 1.9GHz for PCS, are just slightly different than North American frequencies. This means that cell phones in the U.S. will not function with European cellular systems.

CELLULAR NETWORK COMPONENTS

Figure 8-11 identifies the four major components of a cellular telephone network. These four components are:

- A Mobile Telephone Switching Office (MTSO)—A specially designed telephone CO that services mobile telephones and connects them to the PSTN.
- Cell sites with a controller and transceiver—These are the ubiquitous cell towers we see most everywhere. The 800MHz systems space these every 25 miles, and the 1.8GHz systems space them every 12 miles.

- System interconnections—T-1 or higher speed links connecting cell sites to the MTSO.
- Mobile phones—the hand-held analog or digital phones almost everyone has today.

The cell site with the strongest measured signal strength connects to the mobile telephone. The cell site then sends telephone call requests to the MTSO, which establishes, maintains, and disconnects all mobile phone calls. The MTSO connects to the PSTN to complete telephone calls to other wire-line phones. Because cells overlap, frequencies must be re-used, and because RF frequency coverage depends upon geographic terrain, the area each cell covers is difficult to precisely determine. As a mobile phone moves outside the range of one cell and into the range of a new cell, the new cell picks up the phone call and continues handling the call. When external RF signals are strong enough in a cell to disrupt mobile phone signals, then an adjacent cell may take over handling the call. Cells switch automatically and invisibly for the user. Switching cells is coordinated through the MTSO.

There are different cellular protocols used to establish and control telephone calls. These protocols must all uniquely identify the mobile telephone handset by a numeric identifier in its Non-Volatile Random Access Memory (NVRAM). This identifier is assigned a telephone number. The assigned telephone number and NVRAM telephone identifier (for Nextel, it is an IMEI—Internal Mobile Equipment Identifier number) are used by the MTSO to originate, terminate, and bill for calls from the mobile telephone. The assigned telephone number and NVRAM telephone identifier are communicated to the MTSO using different protocols. One protocol, GSM (Global System for Mobile Communications), has the unique mobile phone identified by a personality module or NVRAM chip in the phone. This chip can be moved from a North American mobile telephone to a European mobile telephone, permitting the user to make calls in both North America and Europe. Some cell phones in North America use N-AMPS (Narrowband Advanced Mobile Phone Service or North American Advanced Mobile Phone Service) RF signaling. N-AMPS is not GSM. There is more on GSM and AMPS later in this chapter.

WIRE-LINE VS. NON-WIRE-LINE CARRIERS

Originally, in metropolitan areas, there were two cellular service providers: a wire-line (or Group A) provider and a non-wire-line (or Group B) provider (see Figure 8-12). Wire-line providers are cellular phone companies that are owned or were started by an RBOC (Regional Bell Operating Company) or LEC (Local Exchange Carrier). In contrast, non-wire-line providers connect

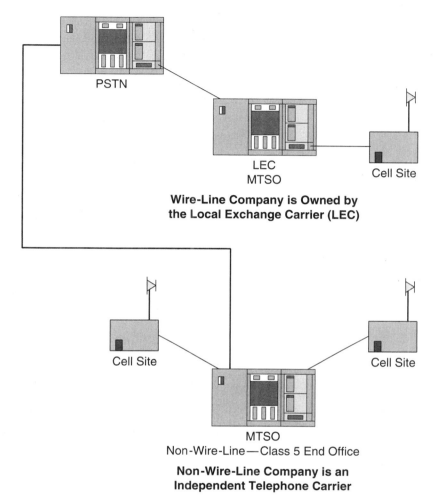

Figure 8–12 *Cellular wire-line vs. non-wire-line providers.*

to the existing wired telephone network by leasing facilities from a LEC. In the Baltimore-Washington metropolitan area, the wire-line provider is Verizon wireless. The non-wire-line provider for the same area is Cellular One. Wire-line and non-wire-line providers compete on price and coverage.

The main differences between wire-line and non-wire-line providers are the area of local coverage and the cost to access the PSTN. For example, with our original analog cell phones from Cellular One and our current Nextel phones, we can make local calls from almost Richmond, Virginia to near the Susquehanna River. With Cellular One, there are no toll charges or roaming fees associated with these calls. With Nextel, all calls nationwide are local calls. We are only assessed airtime up to the limit of our plan (about 600 minutes) and then we pay by the minute for each minute over 600. This is a good deal for Nextel, because our monthly usage is only 200 to 300 minutes. The optimal usage for a Nextel 600-minute subscriber would be just 600 minutes. At that usage level, the cost per airtime minute is a little less than $0.15 per minute.

Any overage is billed at around $0.25 per minute. That means the cell bill increases rapidly after 600 minutes.

There are many cellular market participants today. These generally include new PCS services, the traditional wire-line and non-wire-line carriers, and Nextel.

CELLULAR TECHNOLOGIES

Cellular services are described in terms of the technology used to implement them. These technologies vary in the RF transmission frequencies, the base RF protocol operation, and the cellular system protocols used. Transmission frequencies are in the 800MHz band for original cellular telephone services, and 1.8/1.9GHz for PCS cellular services in North America. The base RF protocols are Time Division Multiple Access (TDMA) and Code Division Multiple Access (CDMA). Analog cell phones still use simple frequency division multiplexed channels to support voice communications. Digital cell phones use TDMA (a form of TDM) or CDMA technologies, which permit supporting more phones with the same cellular RF bands.

CELLS AND FREQUENCY RE-USE • The frequency used determines how much information or data can be carried. To carry information, electromagnetic radiation is modulated. Generally, higher frequencies can carry more information because the information-related modulation of the electromagnetic wave is tied to its frequency. Thus, a signal at 1,000 cycles carries less information than a signal at 10,000 cycles. Bandwidth refers to the information carrying capacity of a communications link. Higher bandwidth means more information is sent in a specific time period.

When two devices use the same frequencies, there are conflicts and interference. What it simply boils down to in the case of a conflict on the same frequency is the device with the most radiated power wins. Frequencies are re-used by different cellular systems as long as the cellular base stations are sufficiently separated to eliminate interference (see Figure 8-13). Certainly, frequencies are re-used between Tampa and Orlando, but with increased cellular traffic, more frequency re-use is required in very small geo-

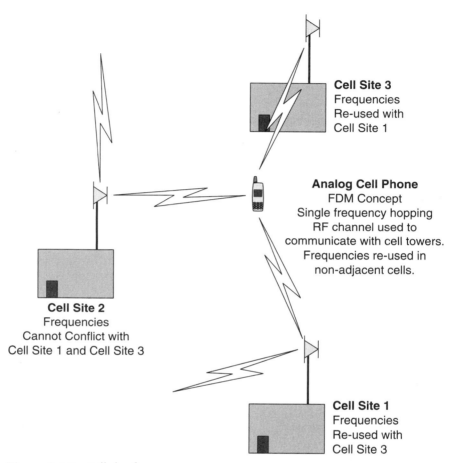

Cell Site 3
Frequencies
Re-used with
Cell Site 1

Analog Cell Phone
FDM Concept
Single frequency hopping
RF channel used to
communicate with cell towers.
Frequencies re-used in
non-adjacent cells.

Cell Site 2
Frequencies
Cannot Conflict with
Cell Site 1 and Cell Site 3

Cell Site 1
Frequencies
Re-used with
Cell Site 3

Figure 8–13 *Cellular frequency re-use concept.*

graphic areas. As cell phones and sites use lower power radios, the ability to re-use frequencies increases.

Even with frequency re-use, there are not enough frequencies to support the demand for cellular communications. Consequently, new technologies for frequency sharing must be employed to support continued subscriber growth.

CALL DENSITY • Call density has become a problem with many cellular systems. The analog systems have reached maximum caller capacity in some urban areas (e.g., Los Angeles, where even movie star dogs get cell phones). To increase capacity, cellular systems are converting to digital transmission technologies. The digital technologies make it possible for the same frequencies to be used simultaneously by more than one phone through digital multiplexing techniques. The cellular 800MHz band provides about 800 total available channels for cell phone calls. These 800 channels are divided between wire-line and non-wire-line carriers, with each using 400 channels. A cell phone call requires a minimum at two channels, which means that 400 channels can support a maximum of 200 calls. Since each cell site's channels (frequencies) must not conflict with adjacent cell site channels, each cell site can support around 40 to 100 simultaneous calls.

MICRO-CELL AND PICO-CELL SYSTEMS • Micro-cell and pico-cell systems create private cellular systems for campus facilities using low-power RF signals broadcast from special antennas that limit their coverage area to the campus facility. Micro-cells use RF frequencies in the 800MHz band and pico-cells use RF frequencies in the 1.9GHz band.

CELL TOWER SPACING • Cell phones originally operated in the 824MHz to 896MHz frequency range. The 800MHz frequencies provide good geographic coverage using 25-mile spacing between cell towers and excellent structure penetration. Wire-line and non-wire-line providers share the frequencies. PCS systems operate in North America in a 1.8GHz frequency band. This higher frequency means that there is more capacity available in PCS systems, but at the same time it reduces building penetration by PCS signals and cuts tower spacing to about 12 miles. Nextel operates in the 800MHz frequency range, so it has good signal penetration into buildings and the wider 25-mile tower separation. International cellular frequencies are 900MHz and PCS frequencies are 1.9MHz, just slightly different than North American frequencies. This means that cell phones in the U.S. will not function with European cellular systems, but international cellular systems use similar tower spacing.

DEAD SPOTS • In any cellular system, there are dead spots. A dead spot is where the RF signal is weak and can barely be received. When this happens calls get dropped. Most cellular systems are designed so that as you travel down major highways, there are no dead spots. However, when you are in a building or off the major highways and there are lots of trees and hills blocking the signal, dead spots happen. Cellular network designs, while very good, are not perfect because signals cannot be tested at every point in the cellular network coverage area. Most cellular and PCS service providers do perform continuous and extensive testing to assure that there are no signal dead spots, but they cannot test every location and in buildings. When a signal is lost in a dead spot, just move to a different location nearer the outside or away from trees and buildings to correct the problem.

MIGRATION TO DIGITAL CELLULAR • Most urban cellular systems are digital. Digital equipment can provide better service and more features to customers, including increased security, better quality transmission, and more features (e.g., text messaging and caller ID). We have used analog cell phones that at the time required a one-year contract, and then switched to digital cellular with phones costing from $400 to $700 dollars at that time. Next we moved to Sprint PCS, and finally today we use Nextel's *i*DEN network with its push-to-talk intercom-like feature. The quality of every digital phone was better than the analog phones. However, every phone had dead spots in the network where reception dropped. Further, the Nextel *i*1000 phones and some of the early digital cell phones malfunctioned. In spite of these problems, we used the Nextel *i*1000 phones because of the push-to-talk feature and the voice signal quality. Soon virtually all cell phone networks will use digital cellular phones to permit more phones to be serviced and to provide additional cellular phone features.

ANALOG CELL PHONES

The original cell phones were analog cell phones. When an analog cell phone was powered on, it would immediately communicate with the cellular phone system to identify itself as active in that mobile calling area. To do that, the phone transmits its Electronic Serial Number (ESN), Mobile Identification Number (MIN), and its station class mark in a short stream of data to the cellular network. Some channels are used to support signaling and coordination of RF channel use by the mobile cell phones. Each phone has a Number (Numeric) Assignment Module (NAM) that associates the Mobile Identification Number (MIN) with the Electronic Serial Number (ESN). Dual NAMs permit a phone to have more than one telephone number. Analog cell phones are frequency division multiplexed (see Figure 8-14).

The original standard for analog cell phones was Telecommunications Industry Association/Electronic Industries Association (TIA/EIA) IS-3. This standard has been replaced by American National Standards Institute (ANSI) EIA/TIA-553 and TIA interim standard IS-91. The ANSI EIA/TIA-553 Revision A standard is just behind IS-91 and does not support Narrowband AMPS (NAMPS). The TIA/EIA/IS-88 Narrowband Analog Cellular standard came from a Motorola-developed system that squeezed three telephone calls into one cellular channel using analog FDM. The TIA/EIA/IS-94 In-building Cellular standard addresses in-building operation of analog cellular systems using extremely low power (micro-cell and pico-cell networks). Finally, the TIA/EIA/IS-91 Analog Cellular standard is the TIA analog cellular standard

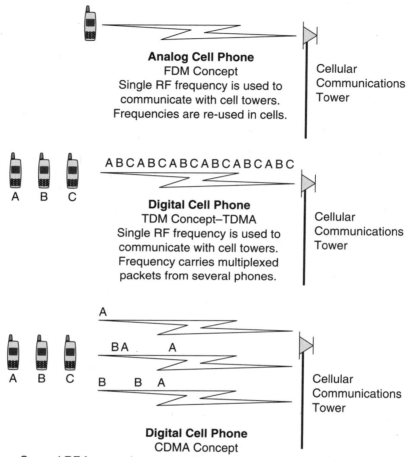

Figure 8–14   *Cell phone transmission technologies.*

version incorporating IS-3, IS-88 narrowband analog, and IS-94 and authentication functions.

DIGITAL PHONES

The rapidly increasing number of pocket and transportable cellular telephones requires network equipment that handles the low-power phones and more simultaneously active subscribers. Digital cell phones are needed to more effectively share frequencies. These digital cell phones employ two

Figure 8–15 *Nextel iDEN i1000 TDMA 800MHz cell phone.*

technologies to meet these needs, Time Division Multiple Access (TDMA) and Code Division Multiple Access (CDMA).

TIME DIVISION MULTIPLE ACCESS • The Cellular Telecommunications Industry Association promoted TDMA technology as a solution to the increasing number of active low-powered phones. The cellular industry adopted TDMA technology as its industry standard. TDMA routes calls simultaneously over one channel. Nextel and some other digital cellular telephone networks currently use it (see Figure 8-15).

TDMA was originally used in satellite communications to increase capacity of satellite transponders. TDMA divides a channel up into time slots. Each separate channel or frequency now has many time slots in which to carry digital data to and from each remote transmitter/receiver. A mobile phone making a call is assigned a frequency and time slot in a given cell. It uses the frequency and time slot assignment while it is in that cell. When it shifts cells, a new frequency and time slot in that frequency are assigned to that call. The digitized call is broken into packets that are transmitted during the time slot assigned to that call.

Compatibility between radio system parameters and call processing procedures are resolved by the TIA/EIA/IS-54 TDMA Digital Cellular standard. The TIA/EIA/IS-54 TDMA Digital Cellular standard squeezes three telephone calls into one cellular channel using TDMA technology. The plan is to squeeze six telephone calls into one channel using digital speech interpolation. This would double capacity. Next up is the TIA/EIA-136 TDMA Digital Cellular standard with digital control channel. This enhances IS-54 TDMA by specifying a more advanced control channel, the Digital Cell phone Control Channel (DCCH), to distinguish it from the analog cell phone control channel. The latest version of IS-136 is ANSI standard TIA/EIA-136 Revision C.

CODE DIVISION MULTIPLE ACCESS • A technique developed by the military for secure communications helps solve conflicting transmission problems. Spread Spectrum Technology (SST) spreads digital transmission across a range of frequencies rather than sending information in a single frequency, making it more difficult to intercept an entire transmission. SST is used in Ultra High Frequency (UHF) wireless communications, especially the UHF range around 900MHz e.g., cordless telephones. Frequency Hopping Spread Spectrum (FHSS) divides the radio spectrum into many specific frequency channels. Transmitters use subsets of these channels, hopping from channel to channel during transmission, following a designated pattern.

With CDMA protocol, the receiver follows the transmitter as it hops from frequency to frequency. While one transmitter/receiver pair hops around some channels, other transmitter/receiver pairs are doing the same thing across the same channels. Everyone shares the frequencies, but SST and CDMA greatly reduce frequency interference.

CDMA uses a spread spectrum approach for digital transmission. CDMA digitizes conversations and tags them with a code. The mobile phone is then instructed to monitor transmissions containing a specific code identifier to receive the desired call. This is like an English-speaking person picking the only other English conversation in a room full of conversations in other languages.

CDMA may provide a 20-fold improvement in capacity over analog cellular network technology. CDMA also allows Personal Communication Networks (PCNs) and other wireless services to work simultaneously within the allocated cellular spectrum. CDMA is used by Sprint PCs, Verizon Wireless, AT&T, and other wireless networks. TDMA technologies were deployed ahead of CDMA technologies, but today, CDMA is more widely used than TDMA.

The original cellular and PCS systems employed TDMA technology. New systems use CDMA technology. CDMA makes better use of the available RF transmission links than does TDMA. The technology is also less susceptible to atmospheric interference and other RF transmission impairments. Because of the code identifying each telephone conversation, CDMA phones do not have the same frequency hopping problems when moving between cells, as do TDMA phones. Using the codes to identify each cellular call, no phone interferes with the communications from any other CDMA phone.

Whatever they use, service providers know it must support increased capacity while providing good voice and data quality. More powerful error correction and easy hand-offs between connections are also required to meet voice quality objectives.

ADVANCED MOBILE PHONE SERVICE • Advanced Mobile Phone Service (AMPS) is a standard for analog signal cellular telephone service in the U.S. and in some other countries. AMPS is based on the initial FCC frequency spectrum allocation for cellular service in 1970. AT&T initially implemented AMPS in 1983. Today, AMPS is the most widely used cellular system in the U.S.

AMPS is now a family of cellular standards. Because AMPS has increased cellular network capacity by supporting low-power hand-held cellular phones, about half the cellular phones worldwide operate using AMPS standards. Since 1988, the Telecommunications Industry Association (TIA) maintains and develops AMPS standards. AMPS first set the standard for 800MHz analog cell phones. It was then expanded to support digital cell phones using TDMA and CDMA digital technology, narrowband (FDMA) analog operation (NAMPS), and TDMA and CDMA 1.8GHz PCS frequencies. The AMPS enhancements have maintained compatibility with the original AMPS. This is critical for cellular companies offering nationwide cellular service. Unless the cell phone can operate with the older analog AMPS networks, the cellular service cannot be provided in more rural geographic areas like Fairfield, Iowa. AMPS compatibility bridges the gap between advanced digital cellular networks and older analog cellular networks. AMPS for the 900MHz frequency band is Total Access Communications System (TACS) or Extended Total Access Communications System (ETACS).

AMPS allocates frequencies in the 800MHz and 900MHz bands to cellular telephones. Wire-line and non-wire-line service providers share 800MHz frequencies. They are each given half the 824-849MHz band for receiving signals from cellular phones and the 869-894MHz band for sending signals to cellular phones. Each frequency band is divided into 30kHz channels. Reverse 30kHz channels are receiving channels from cell phones and forward 30kHz channels are sending channels to cell phones. AMPS uses a form of FDM to divide the 800MHz frequency bands into 30kHz channels. This is called Frequency Division Multiple Access (FDMA).

AMPS specifies how signals received from a cell site are handed off as cell phones move from the area covered by one cell site to another. As a phone moves out of one cell site's area into an adjacent cell, the phone picks up the new cell site's signals without any noticeable transition. Signals in the adjacent cell are sent and received on different frequencies than the signals from the previous cell, preventing interference.

The analog service of AMPS has been updated with digital cellular service by adding to FDMA a further subdivision of each channel using TDMA. This service is known as Digital-AMPS (D-AMPS). The TIA IS-136 standard specifies Digital AMPS (D-AMPS), widely used throughout the Americas,

Asia Pacific, and other areas. D-AMPS services use TDMA in both 800MHz and 1900MHz frequency bands. Although AMPS and D-AMPS came from the North American cellular telephone market, they are now used worldwide with over 74 million subscribers.

GLOBAL SYSTEM FOR MOBILE COMMUNICATIONS • Global System for Mobile (GSM) communication is a digital mobile telephone specification widely used in Europe and other parts of the world. GSM uses TDMA. GSM digitizes and compresses a telephone conversation and sends it down a channel shared with two other telephone conversations. Each telephone conversation uses a specific time slot. GSM phones operate in either the 900MHz or 1.8GHz frequency bands.

GSM was developed from a 1982 Conference of European Posts and Telegraphs (CEPT) that formed a study group called the Groupe Spécial Mobile (GSM). The goal was to develop a European public land mobile system that met specific communications criteria:

- It must provide good subjective speech quality.
- The terminal and service costs must be low.
- It must support international roaming to permit calling from different countries.
- It must support hand-held cellular phones.
- It must be capable of delivering new services and facilities.
- It must use the communications spectrum efficiently.
- It must be compatible with ISDN.

GSM's basic service is voice communications. Speech is digitally encoded and transmitted through a GSM network as a digital stream. GSM mobile phones can contact emergency services by dialing three digits (e.g., 911).

GSM users can send and receive data at rates up to 9600 bps. This data can be sent to dial-up ISPs, ISDN ISPs, packet-switched public data networks, and circuit-switched public data networks using different access methods and protocols. GSM is a digital network, so no true modems are used. There are laptop devices called PCMCIA GSM modems. Another GSM digital service is Group 3 facsimile (ITU-T recommendation T.30). This requires a special fax adaptor. GSM provides a Short Message Service (SMS). SMS is a bi-directional service for alphanumeric messages of 160 bytes or less. Messages are sent to and received from a central post office server similar to the way email operates. SMS has a broadcast mode for sending traffic or news updates. Messages can also be stored in the GSM Subscriber Identification Module (SIM) card for later retrieval.

Basic supplementary services include call forwarding when the mobile subscriber is unreachable by the network and barring of outgoing or incoming calls when roaming in another country. Additional supplementary services include caller identification, call waiting, and conference calls.

GSM is the de facto wireless telephone standard in Europe. GSM has over 120 million users worldwide and is available in 120 countries. Users often use their mobile phones when they travel to other countries because many GSM network operators have roaming agreements with other foreign operators. The initial Sprint PCS used GSM cell phones made by Ericsson. The cell phones supported text pager, caller ID, and voice mail.

WIRELESS APPLICATION PROTOCOL • The Wireless Application Protocol (WAP) is a set of communication protocols standardizing Internet access for wireless devices. This is how new cell phones get Internet email, surf the Web, peruse news groups, and perform Internet relay chat. Cell phone Internet access has always been possible, but manufacturers each used different technologies. The goal is for devices and service systems using WAP to interoperate.

The WAP layers are:

- Wireless Application Environment (WAE).
- Wireless Session Layer (WSL).
- Wireless Transport Layer Security (WTLS).
- Wireless Transport Layer (WTP).

WAP promotes convergence of wireless data and the Internet. Both wireless data and the Internet have explosive growth. Most technology developed for the Internet is designed for desktop and laptop computers and medium- to high-bandwidth communications channels provided by reliable networks. Mass-market, hand-held wireless devices present a more difficult networking environment because of power and form factor limitations. Such hand-held wireless devices have:

- Less powerful CPUs.
- Less ROM and RAM.
- Highly restricted power consumption.
- Small displays.
- Strange input devices such as touch screens.

Wireless data networks are much more constrained communication environments compared to wired networks because of limited power, available spectrum, and mobility. Wireless data networks have:

- Less bandwidth.
- More latency.

- Less connection reliability and stability.
- Unpredictable availability.

As cellular networks grow in size and complexity, the cost for provisioning more value-added services is increasing. To meet the service needs of cellular network operators, solutions must be:

- Inter-operable—Devices from different manufacturers communicate with each other to provide services in cellular networks.
- Scalable—Cellular network operators need to easily grow in size to meet customer needs.
- Efficient—Provide QoS suited to cellular networks.
- Reliable—Provide a predictable platform for deploying services.
- Secure—Enable services to be provided over unprotected cellular networks while preserving user data security, and protect devices and services from security problems such as denial of service.

Many current cellular networks include advanced services offered to end-users. Cellular network operators strive to provide advanced Internet services to promote increased cellular airtime usage and decrease customer turnover. Standard cellular network features like call control may be enhanced by using WAP to provide customized user interfaces. WAP could add to the call forwarding service by prompting a user to choose between accepting a call, forwarding the call to another telephone, or forwarding the call to voice mail. WAP addresses cellular network characteristics and operator needs by adapting existing Internet technology to the special requirements of mass-market, hand-held wireless data devices.

THIRD-GENERATION WIRELESS • The International Telecommunications Union (ITU) has a task group developing concepts and standards for Third-Generation (3G) wireless networks. This is intended to be a global system, meeting consumer needs. 3G technology lays the foundation for future land mobile (cellular) telecommunications systems by identifying suitable frequency bands and by determining the required characteristics, features, and compatibility between systems from different manufacturers.

The second-generation digital radio transmission technologies CDMA, TDMA, GSM, and AMPS compete for the 3G wireless limelight to protect imbedded investment and expand market share. A critical 3G question is should the ITU should approve separate CDMA-based radio transmission technologies and cause networks to proceed along separate tracks, or press for a harmonization (a single universal standard for wideband CDMA) of the proposals.

The 3G wireless networks are not an effort to establish one, single, global radio transmission technology. The ITU's goal is to have high data rate communications with universal coverage and handsets capable of seamless roaming between multiple networks. At least one TDMA-based standard is likely to be included in the ITU's 3G specification.

A harmonization vs. non-harmonization debate is about universal communications coverage and seamless roaming. These goals are not necessarily achieved by converging Wideband CDMA (W-CDMA) and Qual-Com's cdma2000. Some manufacturers doubt global roaming is possible without a global spectrum allocation. However, roaming among incompatible CDMA-based systems can be achieved via multi-mode handsets. Eventually, the wireless industry will compromise somewhere between the business interests of the participants and the original 3G concept.

CELLULAR NETWORKING SUMMARY

Table 8-7 summarizes cellular systems by frequency characteristics.

Table 8.7 *Cellular Summary*

Frequency	Protocols	Frequency Hopping	Tower Spacing	Service
800 MHz	AMPS (NAMPS)	Yes	25 Miles	Cellular Telephony
800 MHz	AMPS TDMA	Yes	25 Miles	Digital Cellular Telephony
800 MHz	CDMA	No	25 Miles	Digital Cellular Telephony
800 MHz	Nextel TDMA	Yes	25 Miles	Nextel
900 MHz	GSM *(TDMA)*	Yes	25 Miles	European Digital Cellular Telephony
900 MHz	Spread Spectrum	Yes	0.2 Miles	Cordless Phones
1.8 GHz	GSM *(TDMA)*	Yes	12 Miles	Early Personal Communications Service (PCS)
1.8 GHz	CDMA	No	12 Miles	Personal Communications Service (PCS)
1.9 GHz	GSM *(TDMA)*	Yes	12 Miles	European Digital Cellular Telephony
1.9 GHz	CDMA	No	12 Miles	European PCS
2.4 GHz	CDMA	No	12 Miles	European PCS
2.4 GHz	Spread Spectrum	Yes	0.4 Miles	Cordless Phones
L-Band	Satellite - SIMs (like GSM)	Yes	NA	Iridium (now defunct)

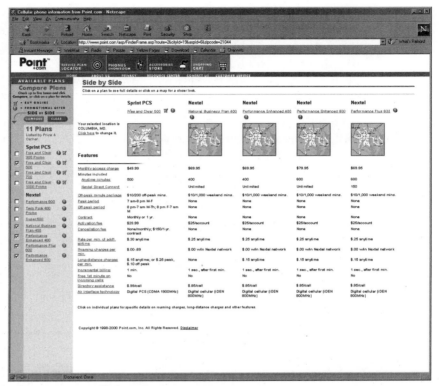

Figure 8–16   *Cellular service comparison*
(Courtesy of Point.com).

Cellular Services

Traditional cellular services are mobile analog and mobile digital voice communications. New services are emerging based upon digital cellular and PCS communications. Cellular and PCS are analyzed at the http://www.point.com/ and http://www.GetConnected.com Web sites as shown in Figure 8-16.

PERSONAL COMMUNICATIONS SERVICES

PCS systems are newer cellular-like services based upon 1.8MHz/1.9MHz RF bands. PCS provides users with one telephone number wherever they travel. They can carry a portable telephone or even a complete portable office anywhere. To use PCS, you just dial a telephone number wherever you are located. PCS was first implemented in the Baltimore-Washington area as

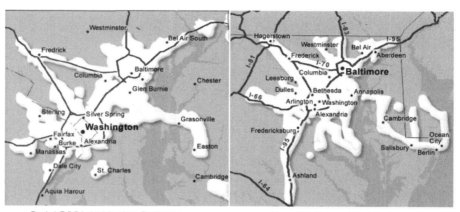

Sprint PCS Washington-Baltimore   Nextel Baltimore-Washington

Figure 8–17 *Sprint vs. Nextel coverage*
(Courtesy of Point.com).

Sprint Spectrum service. This service was a 1.8GHz TDMA-GSM service. Ericsson provided the PCS phones. The initial offering included caller ID and voice mail. There were no service contracts. Rates varied upon the number of minutes purchased. Today Sprint PCS in Baltimore uses CDMA phones from several vendors.

Sprint PCS uses CDMA now. The 1.8GHz PCS networks require towers that are a maximum of 12 miles apart because of signal attenuation in the atmosphere. Geographic coverage is more limited than cellular service (see Figure 8-17). Signal structure penetration is also lower for PCS systems. To provide high-quality communications, PCS systems must have many more cell sites. Limited PCS cell site manufacturing capacity hindered early PCS system rollout.

The figure shows both Sprint 1.8GHz PCS and Nextel 800MHz geographic coverage for the Baltimore-Washington area. Notice that Nextel covers a slightly greater geographic area. On the right side of the Sprint diagram, Sprint has a gap between Easton, MD and Cambridge, MD where Nextel does not. This is because 800MHz towers can service a slightly larger geographic area than 1.8GHz PCS towers. Sprint Spectrum service is nationwide, providing coverage in most major U.S. cities. Nextel has similar nationwide coverage.

Our PCS phones were upgraded to use other Sprint Spectrum networks by a software download over the PCS RF link. One of our consultants teaching with me on the West coast demonstrated his new Sprint PCS phone's networking option. My PCS phone, being an original Sprint PCS phone, did not have that option. Upon returning home, I called Sprint and asked where I should take the phone for an upgrade? They replied, "What signal strength do you have?" I replied, "2." They said that I needed at least 3. So I held up the phone and started wandering all around outside to find a spot where the signal strength was 3. I must have looked like the Statue of Liberty with my hand in the air holding the PCS phone aloft. Finally, in the front yard, the signal strength reached 3. I said to them, "It is 3 now." They replied, "Don't move!" Next thing I knew, the new software was downloaded into the phone and I was instructed to power off then back on to activate it. Sure enough, it worked. Way cool!

PCS systems operating at 1.8GHz have inherently higher bits per second carrying capacity than do equivalent cellular systems operating at 800MHz. The higher the frequency, the faster bits can be sent by switching the RF carrier because the carrier is more responsive. This higher capacity has yet to be fully exploited by current PCS phones. Only now are new phones that support Internet browsing making effective use of this inherent higher data carrying capacity. Next will come more PDA-like phones with video cameras and color displays. Higher data carrying capacity translates into more active phones as well.

PCS systems differ from older cellular telephony systems because they are digital systems using CDMA. Most cellular systems are now converting to digital CDMA operation except Nextel. Nextel phones are digital phones, but they use TDMA operation. There was more on CDMA and TDMA earlier in this chapter.

Personal Communications Services vs. Cellular

Although analog cell phones can transmit and receive data, analog cell phones are not PCS technology. PCS only refers to digital cell phone technologies. PCS, because of its digital implementation, has several advantages over analog or even digital cellular phones (see Table 8-8). These advantages include better voice transmission quality, digital technology, enhanced service features, and lower service costs to the user.

The advanced digital technology combined with encryption provides a secure wireless communications network. Cell sites that are smaller and closer together provide a stronger signal for cellular phones and lower power requirements. This results in better building penetration and fewer dropped calls provided there are sufficient cell sites. Broadband PCS will have smaller, lighter handsets and longer battery life.

Table 8.8   *PCS VS. Cellular Comparison*

PCS	Cellular
Digital voice	Analog voice with noise and static
Higher capacity	Limited capacity
Increased privacy	Susceptible to signal interception and eavesdropping
Increased security	Fraud possible
Long battery life	Shorter battery life
Extended services	Limited services

LOCAL AND NATIONAL CELLULAR SERVICE PROVIDERS

There are many cellular service providers that now compete viciously for the growing cellular market. This results in improved services for cellular customers. Think of the Sprint commercial for the PCS-combined beeper, phone, answering machine, and voice mail product. One piece of equipment does it all. Let's look at a couple of major cellular service providers.

Bell Atlantic Mobile and NYNEX Mobile are now Verizon Wireless. Verizon Wireless is a new company formed by the merger of Bell Atlantic Mobile, Airtouch Cellular, and PrimeCo®. Verizon is also used as the name for the new merger of Bell Atlantic and GTE. Verizon is a nationwide cellular service provider competing with AT&T and Nextel. Verizon uses CDMA digital technology throughout the company's cellular joint network. This increases fraud protection, enhances privacy, and adds new messaging services. Additionally, CDMA technology allows up to ten times more customers to use the system at a time without any interference. CDMA technology is described earlier in this chapter.

Nextel provides two-way push-to-talk (intercom-like) communications and cellular services on its *i*DEN network. The *i*DEN frequencies are in the 800MHz band. Motorola builds the Nextel phones. Unfortunately, there was a run of misbehaving *i*1000 and *i*1000 plus phones that during the middle of a call would suddenly start looking for a cell site to connect with. This caused dropouts in the call. It at first seemed like dead spots in the Nextel network, but it was the Motorola *i*1000 phones causing the problem. The Nextel *i*DEN phones are digital phones communicating using TDMA.

Some cellular companies still charge for long-distance toll access when you make toll calls from your cell phone. The newer cellular and PCS rate plans pioneered by AT&T provide one number nationwide local calls. AT&T offers one of the most aggressively priced PCS systems. It is a combination of

PCS and analog cell phones providing nationwide coverage. Some AT&T service plans advertise, "Every call is a local call." Flat-rate nationwide plans charge a single rate for 500 to 1600 minutes. You can call anywhere in the continental U.S. toll-free. Making the most of these plans means using exactly the minutes in the plan and no more. Otherwise, every minute over the monthly plan minutes is billed at a premium per minute rate.

FACTORS DETERMINING NETWORK PERFORMANCE

Cellular networks use CDMA or TDMA to support more subscribers. CDMA distributes messages using a unique code identifying each active telephone call. After reception, the signal is decoded or de-spread by combining the received signal with the unique telephone call identifying code. During this process, other signals with different codes are not decoded or de-spread. Other signals cause only a minimal interference in the message bandwidth. Analysis of TDMA systems shows as much as 30% to 40% of the analog frequencies must be reallocated to TDMA to achieve acceptable trunking efficiency. In contrast, CDMA needs a reallocation of 10% of the analog system capacity, resulting in about a 200% capacity gain.

From a subscriber's perspective, a cell phone's antenna, given equal power levels, determines cellular performance most. The better the antenna, the more stable the connection. Hand-held antennas are not very good. Fixed automobile antennas, especially those mounted in the center of the roof of the car, are best. Of course only us nerds would mount an antenna there.

Finally, the location and number of cell sites servicing a calling area determines cellular network performance. When the terrain is flat, cellular signals can travel long distances to reach receivers. However, trees and hills can easily kill cellular transmission. They create some serious dead spots, but more cell sites reduce these dead spots.

SECURITY AND PRIVACY ISSUES

Generally, analog cell phone transmissions are not private and secure. Anything transmitted via RF signal can be intercepted and consequently is not absolutely secure. The newer digital cell phones provide a greater measure of security and privacy because they encrypt the signal being sent. Intercepted signals must now be decoded to listen in on intercepted calls. In most digital phones, digital encryption is always on.

CELLULAR DIGITAL PACKET DATA

Cellular Digital Packet Data (CDPD) is a digital data service transmitting data packets over the idle capacity of an analog cellular network. CDPD rides on top of existing analog cellular service. This makes it cheaper to implement than an all-new technology. To run CDPD, cellular operators must deploy new hardware and software throughout their network base stations rather than building a new network.

CDPD is fast—response times are often less than five seconds. Since CDPD is a packet-switched service, there is almost no call setup. Normal switched cellular connections are set up in about 30 seconds. CDPD runs at 19.2 Kbps, which provides a higher throughput than the CDPD chief competitor, private packet radio. Private packet radio generally transmits at 2.4 to 4.8 Kbps. CDPD is based on TCP/IP, thus simplifying communications with networks running that protocol.

CDPD subscribers access the network using an IP address. CDPD providers sometimes charge by the kilobyte. CDPD offers built-in security, including authentication and signal encryption data is transmitted in packets over different cellular channels, making eavesdropping virtually impossible.

CDPD works well for applications with short, bursty messages such as credit card verification, vehicle dispatch, package tracking, telemetry, and short email exchanges. CDPD service providers generally charge by the kilobyte and not by connect time. Charges range from 12 cents to 19 cents per kilobyte. CDPD service providers offer a bewildering number of rate plans. Each must be carefully analyzed to determine which fits your specific application.

Verizon Wireless offers mobile 24/7 Internet access at 9.6 Kbps for a flat fee of about $40 per month based on CDPD.

Cellular phones have become more versatile by supporting text and facsimile transmission. Data transmission can be provided by special services or for laptop PCs by modems specially designed to communicate across cellular links. These modems are connected into a cell phone and the data connection is made over a cellular call.

Special systems use cellular telephony and special equipment to carry packet data. They are CDPD systems. Such CDPD systems are good when you have mobile stations that transmit small quantities of data. Tariffs are such that large data loads are prohibitively expensive to be carried by CDPD.

PC Cellular Communications

Mobile terminals provide access to central databases, record information (deliveries) and events, and provide a means of delivering written instructions to personnel in the field. These terminals rely upon cellular data communication to function. Laptop PCs have been linked to communications networks by modems since they first appeared in the market. A laptop that cannot communicate is not much of a laptop. More often today, the on-site use of laptops often makes access to a phone line impossible. Modems designed to operate over cellular links fill the gap here. These cellular modems are designed specifically to operate over cellular networks with high transmission error rates and lost carrier signals. Some modems are specifically designed to operate with GSM networks as well. Personal Digital Assistants (PDAs) are pocket computers. They are increasingly provided with cellular modem options that permit email and facsimile transmission. They are anticipated to play an increased role in PCS networks. The PDA of the future will become our own personal video telephone.

Saving Costs Using Cellular Communications

RF networks save costs by coordinating the activities of mobile workers, thus minimizing their travel. Microwave communications systems are particularly useful in communicating across difficult natural terrain, in urban areas with signal obstructions (e.g., buildings or bridges), and as a means of continued communications during natural disasters.

Brain Teaser

Cellular Communications

> Fire up a cellular phone. Hold it vertically.
> 1. Use the signal meter to note the signal strength.
> 2. Now hold the phone horizontally and rotate it around in a circle. Does the signal strength vary as you rotate? A higher strength signal may be pointing more directly towards a cell site.
> 3. Extend the antenna while holding the phone vertically. Does the signal strength increase or decrease?
> 4.Now again hold the phone horizontally and rotate it around in a circle. Does the signal strength vary?
> The purpose of this exercise is to illustrate the effectiveness of cell phone antennas.

▇ Summary

This chapter examined RF communications, satellite communications, and cellular telecommunications. It illustrated some of the cost savings and untapped potential that exist in each of these microwave frequency wireless technologies. RF or wireless communications have a great potential to deliver a variety of services to mobile and fixed location subscribers. The subscribers could be both urban and rural because satellite communications can deliver cost-effective high-speed digital links to most any location on the planet. As RF frequencies increase and cells proliferate, the capability to deliver high-speed digital data, image, voice, and video to wearable computers comes closer to reality. RF communications offers the most exciting promise for the future.

▲ Chapter Review Questions

1. *What is CDMA?*
   A. Code Divided Multiplexing Access
   B. Code Division Multiplexing Access
   C. Code Division Multiple Access
   D. Code Divided Multiple Access

2. *What frequencies communicate with satellites?*
   A. 800/900MHz
   B. 12/14GHz
   C. 200/300GHz
   D. 1400/1600KHz

3. *What is a characteristic of microwave networks?*
   A. Frequencies are in the KHz range.
   B. Rain and weather do not affect transmission.
   C. They have limited transmission capacity.
   D. They use Line of Sight (LOS) transmission.

4. *What is a bad characteristic of satellite transmission?*
   A. Satellite antennas must shoot up in the sky.
   B. Satellite uses microwave frequencies.
   C. All satellite antennas are big.
   D. Some satellite links have significant propagation delays.

5. *Why would one use private microwave or satellite networks?*

   A. They do not pay telephone companies for point-to-point channels.

   B. It is fun.

   C. They put cool dish antennas on your roof.

   D. They have the highest security.

6. *What general type of multiplexing is similar to the operation of standard analog cellular phones?*

   A. FDM

   B. CDM

   C. TDM

   D. TDMA

7. *What helps wireless phones communicate with the Internet?*

   A. FDM

   B. CDMA

   C. GSM

   D. WAP

8. *What will follow GSM?*

   A. 3G

   B. WAP

   C. AMPS

   D. N-AMPS

9. *Which frequency sharing technique is most effective, TDMA or CDMA?*

10. *Which is more widely used, CDMA or TDMA?*

11. *About how far apart are PCS cell sites?*

    A. 24 miles

    B. 300 Km

    C. 12 miles

    D. 25,000 feet

12. *What frequency range does Nextel use?*

    A. 900MHz

    B. 1,600MHz

    C. 24GHz

    D. 800MHz

13. *Weather satellites use what orbit?*
    A. LEO
    B. MEO
    C. GEO
    D. Stationary EO

14. *The Global Positioning System (GPS) uses what orbit?*
    A. LEO
    B. MEO
    C. GEO
    D. Non-stationary EO

15. *What do most North American cell phones use?*
    A. AMPS
    B. TDMA
    C. FDM
    D. PCS

16. *Do cellular plans where all calls are local calls really save money?*
    A. Absolutely
    B. Maybe
    C. Only if you use exactly all the minutes of the plan each month
    D. No

Telecommunications Technologies Providing New Business Opportunities

This chapter describes the technologies that are supporting development of new business opportunities. These technologies make new business development possible by providing high-speed digital transmission facilities to consumers in their homes at reasonable cost. Such high-speed Internet access is vital for home shopping, maintaining PC software, and communicating with business associates, friends, and family. We are shifting from text-based communications to image and video communications. This increased and enriched information flow is transforming our work and our personal lives.

While writing this book, I called a company to purchase a new Main Logic Board (MLB) for my computer. I was increasing its speed up to 1.1 GHz. The speed increase requires a new MLB. First I went to pricewatch.com and looked for "AMD K7 Slot A" MLBs without the CPU chip. Then I visited, using links at pricewatch.com, several MLB manufacturer sites to compare specifications. I discovered that only one board matched my requirements. Next I called the vendor with the lowest price for that MLB board to order it. The salesperson at the distributor politely directed me to order it through the distributor's Web site. Their rationale was that errors in ordering were less likely when ordering the MLB off the Web as opposed to ordering it over the phone and having them transcribe a verbal conversation into an order. Amazing! This is what the world is becoming. And ordering was so easy. Using a secure link, I entered my personal address information, gave them a credit card number, selected the type of shipping, and zoom, I was done. This took all of two minutes because I cannot type (I flunked typing in high school—my final grade was in negative numbers).

And just imagine, the president of the United States is decided by a manual hand count (which is more accurate and less biased than a computer count)!

The technologies examined in this chapter make such shopping and other commercial activity possible. Further, they reduce operating costs significantly, making any enterprise more profitable. This is not only for consumer purchasing, but also for business purchasing as well. The Internet is not just a network, but rather it is an evolving set of technologies facilitating planet-wide communications for everyone.

The Internet

The Internet is the fastest growing entity on this planet today. The growth rate is about a 55% increase in Web sites each year. In 1999, there were an estimated 85 million sites on the Internet. Business and personal use of the Internet has skyrocketed and continues to skyrocket. It was estimated recently that around 4% of the people on this planet (and probably numerous space aliens) have Internet access. What has contributed to this growth and the Internet's success? We can understand by looking at the evolution of the Internet.

What does the Internet represent to everyone? It is an opportunity to have access to large amounts of current information at your fingertips. Examining Internet technologies shows us what the current and future impact of the Internet will be on our lives. Windows 95 heralded in the Inter-

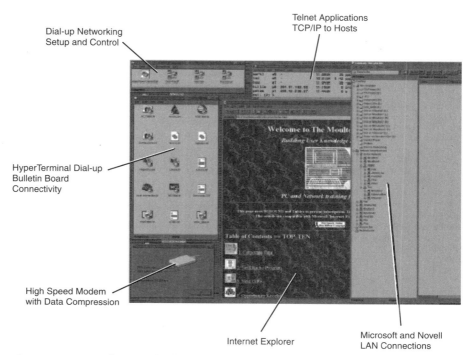

Dial-up Networking
Setup and Control

Telnet Applications
TCP/IP to Hosts

HyperTerminal Dial-up
Bulletin Board
Connectivity

High Speed Modem
with Data Compression

Internet Explorer

Microsoft and Novell
LAN Connections

Figure 9–1 *Windows 95 built-in communications software.*

net revolution on PCs because it incorporated many of the Internet technologies into a single operating system platform for the masses (see Figure 9-1). Internet technologies like HTML, DHTML, HTTP, and more are reshaping the way individuals work and live.

Dot COM companies are springing up every day. The Internet is business and business opportunities. Like most businesses, many of these companies will fail or will become small parts of much larger companies. This section describes new Internet services and the potential they provide for developing new business using the Internet.

Internet communications technologies hold the promise of revolutionizing tomorrow's telecommunications networks. High-speed 24/7 services are needed by consumers to propel the Internet into becoming the telephone, video-on-demand, shopping, and telecommuter communications network of the next millennium. This section examines future telephony incorporating Internet technologies.

The Internet Evolution

The Internet was originally conceived of as a global network of computers acting as information providers, communicators, and consumers. The idea of interconnecting dissimilar computers worldwide sprang from the Defense Advanced Research Projects Agency (DARPA). DARPA developed the original TCP/IP protocols and used them in 1969-1970 on the Advanced Research Projects Agency network, or ARPAnet. The ARPAnet was a packet-switched network using Internet Packet (IP) protocol designed to interconnect thousands of networks. The Defense Department incorporated dynamic re-routing—the ability to find and use the next operating and available route to the destination during transmission—into the TCP/IP protocols. This feature was incorporated into the ARPAnet to enable it to survive an atomic attack. This dynamic routing feature is called connection-less service—one not requiring a fixed route or connection.

The Defense Department IP network evolved over 20 years into the Internet we use today. In 1981, computers changed forever with the introduction of the PC. Soon dumb terminals attached to large mainframe computers found in Digital's DECnet and IBM's SNA networks were transformed into powerful UNIX workstations and into less powerful DOS PCs attached to LANs. LANs interconnected PCs to servers, mainframes, and other information services. Suddenly, instead of having a few computers attached to the ARPAnet, universities and other organizations had hundreds interconnected. In the mid 1980s, the National Science Foundation (NSF) built supercomputers at strategic sites across the U.S. called the National Centers for Supercomputing Applications (NCSA). The NSF originally used the ARPAnet to connect the computers. This did not work effectively, so the NSF built a new faster network called, appropriately, NFSnet, which linked these centers using T-1, 1.544-Mbps lines. The resulting hierarchical network had regional networks feeding into this NFSnet high-speed backbone network. NFSnet focused on traffic related to research and education. This collection of NCSA T-1 lines was the backbone network into which colleges and universities connected their computers for research. These computers provided primarily text information to their users.

I can vividly remember teaching a data communications course at the State University of New York in Syracuse, New York, where the students (all university employees) were thrilled to death with the Internet as it was then. They were searching and finding research information on computers at universities worldwide. They used Veronica and Archie programs to perform their searches. All the results came back in pica type text. This was very boring to me, but very exciting to them. The Internet at that time worked mainly with text information.

Non-government ISP networks supporting commercial traffic began to attach to the regional networks. Thus, NCSA is widely recognized as the creator, or source, of the backbone communications network for the World Wide Web.

Today's Internet really began in 1987 with an NSF grant to Michigan State Networking Organization (Merit), MCI, and IBM for developing a national 1.544-Mbps backbone network with access points around the country. (This infant Internet had nothing to do with Al Gore as he proudly proclaimed.) Merit contributed networking expertise, IBM contributed equipment, and MCI contributed telephone lines. The resultant organization, Advanced Networks and Services (ANS), developed into a non-profit enterprise serving the NSF and a for-profit enterprise sold to America Online (AOL). Because of the ANS for-profit/non-profit split, the NFS regional networks began creating commercial counterparts. New York's NYSERNet became Performance Systems International (PSI). Soon the remaining non-profit NSF networks became overloaded with university traffic and were facing an NFS funding cutoff by 1998.

The NFS grant to ANS ran out in 1992. During its years of operation, there was much debate over how to make ANS a profitable company. Meanwhile, the Internet grew very fast, making it clear that the backbone network had to be upgraded. NSF experienced conflict as it watched commercial usage grow, yet wanted to continue funding experimental high-speed networks. To resolve this conflict, NSF decided to set up NAPs—Network Access Points. The NAPs tie together Internet backbone networks from the major communications companies like MCI WorldCom, PSInet, and AT&T. They also connect to regional feeder networks such as Capital Area Internet Service (CAIS) in Washington, D. C. These feeder networks fan out to lower tier ISPs in each geographic region. Some ISPs have nationwide reach like Comcast@home. They lease their own backbone network links from telephone companies and other communications providers. However, most often all network traffic hopping between networks like AT&T, PSInet, and Cable & Wireless's Internet backbone passes through a NAP.

Many new companies focused on the Internet sprang up in northern Virginia near Washington, D.C. and elsewhere. Today, there are hundreds of companies in the top U.S. metropolitan areas providing Internet access. Cable TV (CATV) companies, entertainment companies, telephone companies, and utility companies now sell Internet access and high-speed Internet access. The Internet backbone speed has increased from its modest T-1 transmission speed to SONET OC-192 and OC-768 speeds.

The Internet Today

The Internet today connects several hundred million computers and PCs. The Internet uses TCP/IP to communicate between all computers. TCP/IP addresses are 32-bit addresses issued to primary Internet access points. Primary Internet access points are organizations interfacing directly to the Internet or are ISPs.

INTERNET PROTOCOL ADDRESSES

IP addresses represent each device attached to the Internet. Duplicate IP addresses cause one device not to function. IP addresses are four numbers separated by three dots that represent a 32-bit binary pattern of "0's" and "1's." The numbers vary from 0 (all "0's") to 255 (all "1's"). Originally, IP addresses were assigned in a hierarchical fashion with large organizations such as IBM and AT&T getting Class A addresses that supported millions of sub-addresses and smaller organizations getting Class B and Class C addresses. A Class C address supported 256 sub-addresses. The Internet growth and this wasteful hierarchical structure quickly exhausted IP addresses. Consequently, the hierarchical structure was abandoned in favor of a structure that issued Class C address blocks to organizations directly connecting to the Internet or supporting domain names.

Each domain name requires its own unique fixed IP address. Domain names are linked to these IP addresses by Domain Name Servers (DNSs) sprinkled throughout the Internet. The DNSs exchange information on IP addresses constantly with each other. Any new domain name takes hours to cascade through all the Internet DNSs and become actively accessible.

Some IP addresses are used for special functions. The "0" address represents a single IP network. For example, our internal IP network is represented by the address 208.80.34.0. The "1" through "5" addresses are assigned to gateways (IP routers) to other IP networks. The Internet would have run out of IP addresses if it were not for Internet gateways or routers. A router connects a network of hundreds of IP addresses to the Internet using a single Internet IP address.

DOMAIN NAMES

On the Internet, Web sites are identified using the UNIX Domain Name System (DNS). A domain name locates an organization or other entity on the Internet. Each domain registered its name originally with the InterNIC. The InterNIC placed the name in a searchable database of Web site names. This

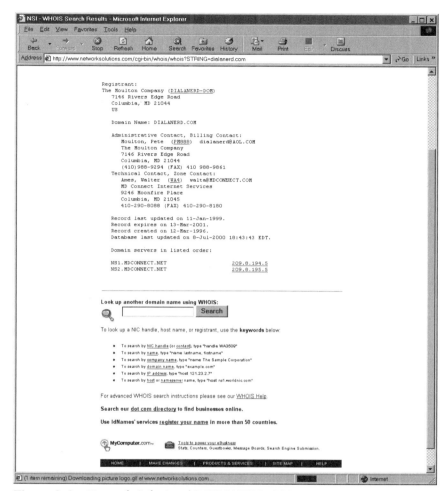

Figure 9–2 *Network Solutions' DIALANERD.COM registration.*

database is available for searching at http://www.networksolutions.com/ (see Figure 9-2).

Each Web site name has a suffix designating the type of organization owning the name. The first domain name suffixes were:

- COM—Designates COMmercial enterprises in business to make money (e.g., for-profit).
- NET—Designates networking enterprises.
- EDU—Used by 4-year degree-granting colleges/universities.
- GOV—Used in U.S. federal government agencies. A good joke is to say that you hacked Whitehouse.COM (a porn site) when everyone thinks you mean Whitehouse.GOV.

- ORG—Designates miscellaneous common non-profit organizations.
- MIL—Is for the military.

New domain name extensions are being added to the list and domain name registrations. These domain name suffixes include:

- FIRM—Designates businesses or firms.
- STORE—Identifies stores or companies offering goods to purchase.
- WEB—Enterprises with activities focused on the Web.
- ARTS—Identifies cultural and entertainment groups.
- REC—Enterprises providing recreation and entertainment.
- INFO—Designates organizations that are information suppliers.
- NOM—These sites are personal or family sites.

Registering domain names is a painless process performed using any of several domain name registration services today. Typical cost of domain name registration is around $30 to $40 per year.

An Internet link to a domain name is:

HTTP://WWW.DIALANERD.COM

This Internet link describes HTTP://, WWW, sub-domain names, and domain name suffixes.

HTTP://—Hyper-Text Transfer Protocol (HTTP) is a protocol for exchanging text, graphic images, sound, video, and other multimedia files on the World Wide Web. HTTP is an application protocol working in OSI Layers 6 and 7. HTTP runs over TCP/IP networks with TCP/IP performing the work in OSI Layers 3, 4, and 5. HTTP permits files to reference other files. These references, when selected, request transfer of the other files to the PC. HTTP gives the Internet its point-and-click capability. This point-and-click capability is essential to making the Internet and PCs usable to everyone from the most experienced PC user to the most novice PC user. Web servers contain HTML files, other image and sound files, and an HTTP server program or daemon. The HTTP daemon program waits for HTTP requests and services them by sending the requested files. PC Web browser programs like Microsoft's Internet Explorer or Netscape's Communicator are HTTP clients. These Web browser programs send requests to Web server machines. When a user requests a file by clicking on a hyperlink in an HTML document or by typing in a Uniform Resource Locator (URL), the Web browser program creates an HTTP request and sends it to the IP address in the URL. The HTTP daemon in the destination Web server receives the request and returns the requested file to the Web browser. HTTP is continually being enhanced with the latest version being HTTP 1.1.

WWW—The World Wide Web is basically the servers and PCs with Web browsers on the Internet using the HTTP to send text, image, sound, video, and other files to one another.

Sub-domain names—A sub-domain name may identify a particular part of a domain. So, a possible address is http://www.moulton.dialanerd.com. This example address leads nowhere. The sub-domain name may point to information on our parent organization, The Moulton Company.

Domain name suffix (the dot COM identifier)—Designates the goal of the organization or entity. The DIALANERD name is the second-level name identifying the enterprise creating the site. The top-level name is the domain suffix – the dot COM part. The second-level domain name maps to a specific IP address in DNS servers throughout the Internet.

User-created second-level domain names must be unique on the Internet and registered by the Internet Corporation for Assigned Names and Numbers (ICANN), accredited registrars for the COM, NET, and ORG top-level domains. Top-level domain names may also be geographic such as UK and JP designating names in Britain and Japan, respectively.

There has been some controversy over domain name registration. The two controversial areas are the organizations registering domain names and squatting on trademarked domain names. The first issue has been resolved with the expansion of the domain name registering organizations. The original InterNIC spun off Network Solutions (www.networksolutions.com). However, a search on domain name registration can produce as many as 40 or more domain name registering services with pricing varying from $17 to $255 per year per domain name.

ICANN arbitration resolves squatting issues. They have a Uniform domain name Dispute Resolution Policy (UDRP) that all domain name registrars in the .com, .net, and .org top-level domains must follow. The Uniform Domain-Name Dispute-Resolution Policy is referred to as the UDRP. The policy requires most types of trademark-based domain name disputes to be resolved by agreement, court action, or arbitration before a domain name registrar cancels, suspends, or transfers a domain name. Some disputes alleged to arise from abusive registrations of domain names called cybersquatting get expedited through administrative proceedings when the holder of trademark rights files a complaint with an approved dispute resolution service provider.

To resolve trademarked name issues, a trademark owner should either (a) file a complaint in a court of proper jurisdiction against the domain name holder, or (b) in cases of abusive registration, submit a complaint to an approved dispute resolution service provider including:

Internet Backbone

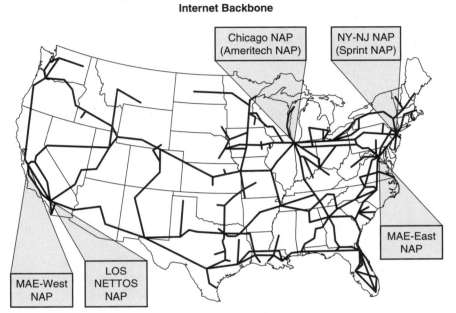

Figure 9–3 *Typical Internet backbone network and NAPs.*

- CPR Institute for Dispute Resolution (CPR).
- Disputes.org/Resolution Consortium (DeC).
- The National Arbitration Forum (NAF).
- World Intellectual Property Organization (WIPO).

INTERNET ARCHITECTURE

The Internet remains a hierarchy of networks with a large backbone network and many second-level and third-level feeder networks. Most users access the Internet through a dial-up connection; also, most users use Windows 95 with a Web Browser from Netscape or Microsoft. They call into an ISP. The ISP is a third-level feeder network to the Internet. The ISP connects to a second-level feeder network that in turn connects to the Internet backbone network through a NAP (see Figure 9-3).

Internet users surf the Web, downloading images and text. Popular applications include shopping, playing games, monitoring investments, chat rooms, travel, downloading software, research for specific answers (e.g., health issues), career management, reading sports and news, and surfing. Live video and audio feeds provide direct access to news and other programming.

The commercial Internet backbone—the basic infrastructure needed to access the Web—is currently composed of networks from several large companies, including WorldCom (uuNET), AT&T, PSInet, GTE Corp (now Verizon), and Cable & Wireless. WorldCom had to sell off some of its Internet backbone as it acquired MCI and Sprint. Cable & Wireless was the primary beneficiary of this sale. The FCC requested the divestment to ensure healthy competition. Although WorldCom is an American company, the FCC has jurisdiction over any merger involving companies with combined worldwide turnover of more than five billion euros ($4.81 billion) and European sales of at least 250 million euros each.

The backbone network consists of high-speed government networks, private networks and commercial networks connected together at NAPs. Today some backbone links operate at OC-192 speeds. ATM technology is being deployed on Internet backbone links to efficiently utilize the high-speed digital transmission capacity.

Figure 9-4 illustrates what networks are connected at the Network Access Points (NAPs). This diagram reflects NAP connectivity in the late 1990s. Today there would be many more networks connected to each NAP. The Chicago NAP has around 116 networks that interconnect to it using a variety of OC-3 and DS-3 channels. Similarly, the Metropolitan Area Exchange (MAE) NAP has around 128 network connections that it services. In the diagram, the interconnections between the NAPs are to conceptually illustrate that they are interconnected by high-speed links to one another.

NAPS

The Internet was transformed into a global information highway by the NAPs. NAPs are exchange points where ISPs as well as experimental research networks meet and exchange traffic. In February 1994, NSF funded three NAPs that were operational by 1999.

These early NAPs were:

- The New York NAP, located in NJ, awarded to Sprint.
- The Chicago NAP, awarded to Ameritech and Bellcore.
- The San Francisco NAP, awarded to Pacific Telesis and Bellcore.

Starting in 1994, through the beginning of 1995, regional networks moved their traffic onto new ISP backbone networks. Some NFS-sponsored NAPs weren't fully ready at that time. The first commercial NAP was created in Washington, D.C. by Metropolitan Fiber Systems (MFS). It is best known as Metropolitan Area Exchange-East (MAE-East) and is today owned by WorldCom. It interconnects most of the ISP backbone networks. MAE-East

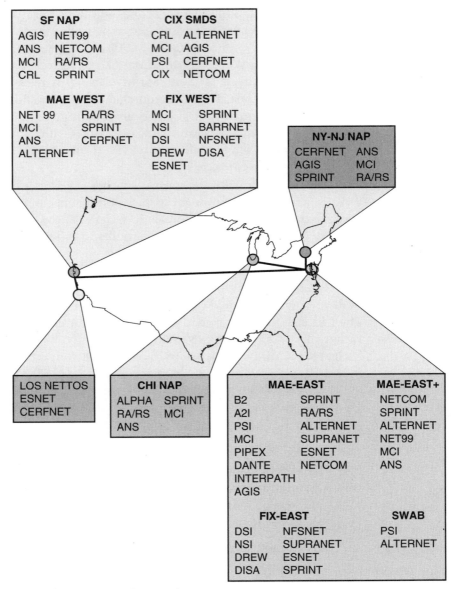

Figure 9–4 *NAP and network connections.*

has become a key Internet hub. It has evolved from a 10-Mbps Ethernet LAN to a 100-Mbps FDDI traffic-routing LAN and to high-speed ATM switching. MAE-East's FDDI traffic is over 1 Gbps and its ATM traffic ranges from 750 Mbps to 1.35 Gbps.

There are many NAPs today. They include:

East Coast
ATL-NAP—Atlanta
BMPX—Boston Metropolitan Exchange Point
BNAP—Baltimore NAP
MAE-East—Vienna/McLean, VA
MAGPI—Mid Atlantic Giga-Pop for Internet2
NNAP—Neutral NAP
NYIIX—New York International Internet Exchange
Philadelphia Internet Exchange
Pittsburgh Internet Exchange
Research Triangle Park
Sprint NAP—Pennsauken, NJ

West Coast
AMAP—Anchorage Metropolitan Access Point
AIX—Ames Internet Exchange
CIX—Commercial Internet Exchange
COX—Central Oregon Internet Exchange
HIX—Hawaii Internet Exchange
LAP—Los Angeles Exchange, including MAE-LA.
MAE-West—San Francisco NAP
OIX—Oregon Internet Exchange
PAIX—Palo Alto Internet Exchange
SD-NAP—San Diego
SIX—Seattle Internet Exchange
SNNAP—Puget Sound Regional Interconnect

Middle States
New Mexico Network Access Point
TTI—The Tucson Interconnect
AMAP—Austin
DFWMAP—Dallas-Ft Worth—MAE-Central
MAE—Houston
SAMAP—San Antonio
Ameritech NAP—Chicago, IL NAP
CMH-IX—Columbus Internet Exchange
DIX—Denver Internet Exchange
IndyX—Indianapolis Data Exchange
Mountain Area Exchange (Denver)
Nashville CityNet
Ohio Exchange

STAR TAP (12 Giga-POP)
The Arch—St. Louis, MO
Utah REP—Salt Lake City

There are also about nine or more Canadian NAPs. Sometimes NAPs are called POPs, or Points Of Presence, similar to telephone company POPs.

We can see the MAE-East NAP in a trace route command to my ISP, MDConnect.com. The trace is:

```
C:\WINDOWS>tracert mdconnect.com
Tracing route to mdconnect.com [209.8.194.2]
over a maximum of 30 hops:
  1    18 ms    17 ms    18 ms    10.74.122.1
  2    27 ms    29 ms    31 ms    r1-fe0-0.twsn1.md.home.net [24.3.0.3]
  3    27 ms    29 ms    27 ms    10.0.236.5
  4     *       31 ms     *       c1-pos5-0.bltmmd1.home.net [24.7.72.93]
  5    43 ms    22 ms    32 ms    c1-pos2-0.washdc1.home.net [24.7.65.89]
  6   213 ms   296 ms   317 ms    bb1-pos2-1-0.mae-e.nap.home.net
[24.7.72.54]
  7    58 ms    55 ms    56 ms    mae-east.cais.com [192.41.177.85]
  8    62 ms    52 ms    63 ms    fe1-1.brdr2.east-fddi.mae.cais.net
[209.8.159.29]
  9    48 ms     *       51 ms    h2-0.edge1.dc.cais.net [209.8.159.34]
 10    54 ms    69 ms    54 ms    s6-1.edge1.balt.cais.net [209.8.159.37
 11    68 ms   119 ms    82 ms    fe0-0.edge1.balt.cais.net
[207.226.208.1]
 12    63 ms    74 ms    68 ms    ABS-Mdconnect-512K.abs.net
[207.114.7.38]
 13    61 ms    68 ms    70 ms    mdconnect.com [209.8.194.2]
Trace complete.
```

Hops 6 and 7 pass from my @home cable modem network connection through MAE-East to the Capital Area Internet Service (CAIS).

Brain Teaser

Network Access Points

Use the iWon.com search engine and search for NAPs. Find the Globix network Web page (http://www.globix.com/network_naps.html) and identify the U.S. and international NAPs that it lists.
1. Which U.S. NAPs match up with the NAPs listed above? They should be the Sprint NAP, Ameritech NAP, PAIX — Palo Alto Internet Exchange, MAE — West, MAE — East, and NYIIX — New York International Internet Exchange.
2. What are some international NAPs identified by the Globix network? Globix identifies a London NAP (London Internet Exchange (LINX)), Paris (SFNIX), Geneva (CERN-IXP), Milan Internet

Exchange (MIXITA), Vienna Internet Exchange (VIX), Frankfurt (De-CIX), Amsterdam Internet Exchange (AMS IX), and Stockholm (D-GIX).

3. What country has more NAPs than any other country on the planet? The U.S., obviously.

The goal of this Brain Teaser is to illustrate how many NAPs are really in the Internet. There are probable around 50 major NAPs planet-wide in the Internet. Most NAPs and other Internet hubs are located in the U.S.

BACKBONE NETWORKS

Every telecommunications company has an IP backbone network that carries Internet traffic between Web sites serviced by that company and other Web sites on the Internet. Another typical IP backbone network is shown in Figure 9-5. This network has a SONET OC-192, or 9.95328-Gbps link, connecting Boston to New Jersey, and 2.48832-Gbps links between other major U.S. cities, including:

- Washington, D.C.
- Atlanta
- Orlando
- Philadelphia
- Pittsburgh
- Detroit
- Chicago
- Minneapolis
- Omaha
- Kansas City
- St. Louis
- Dallas
- Austin
- Houston
- Denver
- Phoenix
- San Diego
- Los Angles
- San Francisco
- Denver
- Salt Lake City
- Sacramento
- Seattle

AT&T's Internet Backbone Network Showing Major Links and Nodes

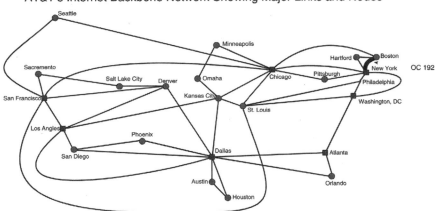

Figure 9–5 *Typical IP backbone network.*
(Courtesy AT&T)

These high-speed connections are typical of the backbone networks carrying IP traffic. They are being upgraded to higher speeds constantly as IP traffic increases. Expect to see OC-768 links implemented soon.

These backbone networks are fed IP traffic by feeder networks.

FEEDER NETWORKS

Regional feeder networks provide the link between ISPs and the backbone networks. These feed into the backbone networks typically through NAPs. Figure 9-6 shows a general picture of a regional feeder network covering New York to Washington, D.C.

From a functional view, the Internet is a hierarchy of interconnected mesh networks using high-speed links to route and deliver traffic between Windows and Macintosh Web browsing clients and UNIX or NT-based Web site servers. Backbone and regional feeder networks tend to grow in capacity and connectivity. Capital Area Internet Service (CAIS) was a regional feeder network that now has national connections, and AboveNet has both national and international connections. Continued growth for both backbone and feeder networks can be expected to continue as Internet traffic increases.

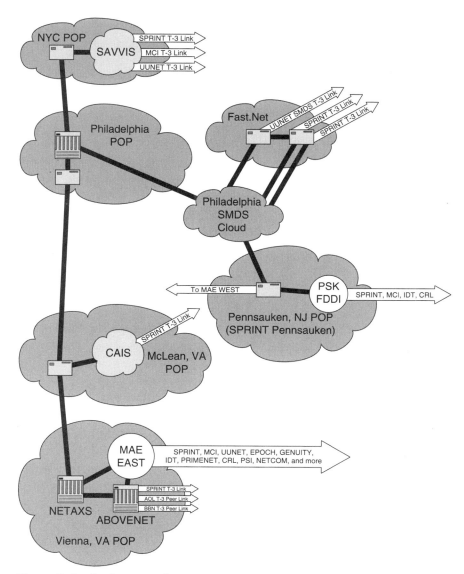

Figure 9–6 *Feeder network.*

INTERNET PERFORMANCE CONSIDERATIONS

Metropolitan Area Exchanges (MAEs) and NAPs are often congested, producing latency (transmission delays and lags) and packet losses. To improve performance, some feeder networks implement private NAPs directly, connecting to the largest Internet backbones, Sprint, Cable & Wireless, and UUNet. These private NAPs are not like POPs, which are only transfer points for data traffic. The private NAPs are points where peering relationships with other ISPs are implemented. Multiple DS-3/OC-3 circuit connections and peers at private NAPs improve Internet performance. Customers a few hops from a private NAP have less distance to travel to interconnect with an Internet backbone. Fewer hops and shorter interconnection distances make connections faster and more reliable. To insure maximum reliability, most networks install redundant circuit connections throughout. If a network component fails, data traffic is not disrupted because of the redundant connections.

INTERNET II, OR INTERNET2

The Internet II/Internet2 goal is to develop networking and advanced applications for learning and research. Because teaching, learning, and collaborative research requires real-time multimedia and high-speed communications, the Internet II/Internet2 work involves deploying sufficient network communications infrastructure to support these applications. Internet II/Internet2 research also investigates and develops new ways to use the Internet and the Internet II/Internet2 infrastructure. Internet II/Internet2 is not specifically intended to be a future replacement for the Internet. However, Internet II/Internet2 developments will most certainly spill over into the Internet.

Internet II/Internet2 includes further development of the NSF's very high-speed Backbone Network Service (vBNS). The vBNS currently interconnects research supercomputers in the U.S. One hundred or more universities in the U.S. collaboratively do most Internet II/Internet2 work. These universities continue using the Internet for email, personal Web access, and newsgroups.

The Internet II/Internet2 uses QoS to reserve and use network bandwidth for special events or at specific time periods. Possible Internet II/Internet2 uses include:

- Distributed learning allows teachers and students to share materials using the Internet. Students learn in a self-directed manner under supervision of a teacher. Internet II/Internet2 extends this concept with tools that make it easy to create teaching materials (called LearningWare) using object-oriented programming. Internet II/Internet2 tools also further develop Instructional Management Systems (IMSs). IMSs use the Internet to develop and deliver learning packages and to track learning assessments.

- New ways to retrieve and present information replace text and image information with interactive video. This would be analogous to replacing a table of contents or a menu with interlinked and interactive three-dimensional video (the virtual reality concept). With high-speed connections, such information visualization is possible. Where up-to-date information is critical, that information can be pushed as it changes to users that request it.
- Virtual environment sharing referred to a tele-immersion has teleconferencing participants perceiving that everyone is in the same room. Virtual work objects such as building models, virtual meeting rooms, or multimedia storyboards would permit participants to see themselves and others in a conference room, talking and working on objects in the room.
- Virtual laboratories allow scientists at different physical locations, with unique expertise, computing resources, and/or data to collaborate on research. This is a not a video teleconferencing meeting, but ongoing collaboration. These projects extend and pool resources among participants. Virtual laboratories would facilitate communication and progress towards a shared research goal. In this manner, researchers could share experiments and knowledge on research and suggest new experiments and research alternatives. Virtual laboratories could be used to design and manufacture complex systems such as supersonic transport vehicles, space shuttles, space stations, satellites, and more, and to study and forecast global weather.

A current Internet limitation is the IP address space. IP addresses are currently 32-bit addresses. While this is a large number of addresses, they were originally issued in an A-B-C-D-E scheme that wasted significant portions of the address space. Portions of the A-B-C-D-E scheme have been reclaimed and IP addresses are now issued in blocks of 256 addresses (C Class-like addresses). Further, modern routing algorithms make a single C Class address capable of servicing an entire network of computers using their own isolated scheme of IP addresses. A proxy server can isolate an entire network of IP addresses behind a single Internet-direct IP address.

The Internet II/Internet2 work solves these and other pending Internet problems. The Internet II/Internet2 vBNS solves the IP addressing and other infrastructure problems.

The Internet II/Internet2 effort sponsored by universities, the federal government, and industry partners initially accelerates Internet development for educational and academic work. In 1987, the NSF network supporting academic research was unequaled anywhere. However, privatization of the

NSF network deprived universities of network capacity needed for network and other academic research.

The Internet II/Internet2 provides universities a high-speed network free of congestion to support research activities. The Internet II/Internet2 enables new applications like media integration and real-time collaboration that fully exploit broadband network capabilities. Such applications are essential for higher education to support national research objectives, distance education, and life-long learning.

Lastly, integrating Internet II/Internet2 with other ongoing efforts improves existing Internet services. A major goal of the Internet II/Internet2 project is to transfer new network services and applications to other areas of educational use and to the broader national and international Internet community.

The Internet is always a work in progress. As these high-speed applications and new multimedia technologies are developed, the privatized Internet will evolve quickly to deliver those capabilities to everyone connected to the Internet. Two words, "holographic email," will give you an idea of where the future of Internet communications is headed.

THE WORLD WIDE WEB

The World Wide Web (WWW, or Web) is a standardized way for representing information as interesting text and graphics linked together on computers. It uses the Hyper-Text Markup Language (HTML) and Hyper-Text Transfer Protocol (HTTP) to send information from servers to client PCs for display across TCP/IP-based networks. The information is referenced through hyper-links to other documents on the Web. The hyper-links employ Universal Resource Locators (URLs) to identify and connect to other information on the Web. We will discuss URLs in more detail later.

Tim Berners-Lee, a researcher at CERN, the European Particle Physics Laboratory, created the Web in 1989. He specified tags that linked one document (or page) to another, making navigation of the Internet easier for researchers. Such links, called hyper-text links, are used in other applications such as the Windows help system.

Prior to the Web, information on the Internet was presented primarily in ASCII text. Such text information was searched using VERONICA software. Some was set up in an indexed, more searchable form. One such form was called the GOPHER space. However, the free-form hyper-text links of the Web have now become the dominant form for presenting information on the Internet.

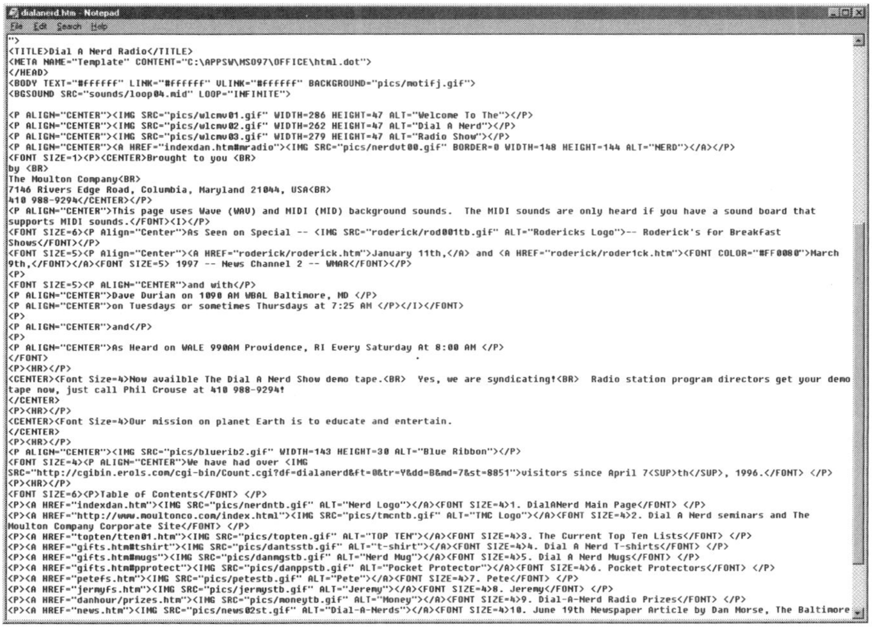


```
">
<TITLE>Dial A Nerd Radio</TITLE>
<META NAME="Template" CONTENT="C:\APPSW\MS097\OFFICE\html.dot">
</HEAD>
<BODY TEXT="#ffffff" LINK="#ffffff" VLINK="#ffffff" BACKGROUND="pics/motifj.gif">
<BGSOUND SRC="sounds/loop04.mid" LOOP="INFINITE">

<P ALIGN="CENTER"><IMG SRC="pics/wlcmv01.gif" WIDTH=286 HEIGHT=47 ALT="Welcome To The"></P>
<P ALIGN="CENTER"><IMG SRC="pics/wlcmv02.gif" WIDTH=262 HEIGHT=47 ALT="Dial A Nerd"></P>
<P ALIGN="CENTER"><IMG SRC="pics/wlcmv03.gif" WIDTH=279 HEIGHT=47 ALT="Radio Show"></P>
<P ALIGN="CENTER"><A HREF="indexdan.htm#mradio"><IMG SRC="pics/nerdvt00.gif" BORDER=0 WIDTH=148 HEIGHT=144 ALT="NERD"></A></P>
<FONT SIZE=1><P><CENTER>Brought to you <BR>
by <BR>
The Moulton Company<BR>
7146 Rivers Edge Road, Columbia, Maryland 21044, USA<BR>
410 988-9294</CENTER></P>
<P ALIGN="CENTER">This page uses Wave (WAV) and MIDI (MID) background sounds.  The MIDI sounds are only heard if you have a sound board that
supports MIDI sounds.</FONT><I></P>
<FONT SIZE=6><P Align="Center">As Seen on Special -- <IMG SRC="roderick/rod001tb.gif" ALT="Rodericks Logo">-- Roderick's for Breakfast
Shows</FONT></P>
<FONT SIZE=5><P Align="Center"><A HREF="roderick/roderick.htm">January 11th,</A> and <A HREF="roderick/roder1ck.htm"><FONT COLOR="#FF0080">March
9th,</FONT></A><FONT SIZE=5> 1997 -- News Channel 2 -- WMAR</FONT></P>
<P>
<FONT SIZE=5><P ALIGN="CENTER">and with</P>
<P ALIGN="CENTER">Dave Durian on 1090 AM WBAL Baltimore, MD </P>
<P ALIGN="CENTER">on Tuesdays or sometimes Thursdays at 7:25 AM </P></I></FONT>
<P>
<P ALIGN="CENTER">and</P>
<P>
<P ALIGN="CENTER">As Heard on WALE 990AM Providence, RI Every Saturday At 8:00 AM </P>
</FONT>
<P><HR></P>
<CENTER><Font Size=4>Now availble The Dial A Nerd Show demo tape.<BR>  Yes, we are syndicating!<BR>  Radio station program directors get your demo
tape now, just call Phil Crouse at 410 988-9294!
</CENTER>
<P><HR></P>
<CENTER><Font Size=4>Our mission on planet Earth is to educate and entertain.
</CENTER>
<P><HR></P>
<P ALIGN="CENTER"><IMG SRC="pics/bluerib2.gif" WIDTH=143 HEIGHT=30 ALT="Blue Ribbon"></P>
<FONT SIZE=4><P ALIGN="CENTER">We have had over <IMG
SRC="http://cgibin.erols.com/cgi-bin/Count.cgi?df=dialanerd&ft=0&tr=Y&dd=B&md=7&st=8851">visitors since April 7<SUP>th</SUP>, 1996.</FONT> </P>
<P><HR></P>
<FONT SIZE=6><P>Table of Contents</FONT> </P>
<P><A HREF="indexdan.htm"><IMG SRC="pics/nerdntb.gif" ALT="Nerd Logo"></A><FONT SIZE=4>1. DialANerd Main Page</FONT> </P>
<P><A HREF="http://www.moultonco.com/index.html"><IMG SRC="pics/tmcntb.gif" ALT="TMC Logo"></A><FONT SIZE=4>2. Dial A Nerd seminars and The
Moulton Company Corporate Site</FONT> </P>
<P><A HREF="topten/tten01.htm"><IMG SRC="pics/topten.gif" ALT="TOP TEN"></A><FONT SIZE=4>3. The Current Top Ten Lists</FONT> </P>
<P><A HREF="gifts.htm#tshirt"><IMG SRC="pics/dantsstb.gif" ALT="t-shirt"></A><FONT SIZE=4>4. Dial A Nerd T-shirts</FONT> </P>
<P><A HREF="gifts.htm#mugs"><IMG SRC="pics/danmgstb.gif" ALT="Nerd Mug"></A><FONT SIZE=4>5. Dial A Nerd Mugs</FONT> </P>
<P><A HREF="gifts.htm#pprotect"><IMG SRC="pics/danppstb.gif" ALT="Pocket Protector"></A><FONT SIZE=4>6. Pocket Protectors</FONT> </P>
<P><A HREF="petefs.htm"><IMG SRC="pics/petestb.gif" ALT="Pete"></A><FONT SIZE=4>7. Pete</FONT> </P>
<P><A HREF="jermyfs.htm"><IMG SRC="pics/jermystb.gif" ALT="Jeremy"></A><FONT SIZE=4>8. Jeremy</FONT> </P>
<P><A HREF="danhour/prizes.htm"><IMG SRC="pics/moneytb.gif" ALT="Money"></A><FONT SIZE=4>9. Dial-A-Nerd Radio Prizes</FONT> </P>
<P><A HREF="news.htm"><IMG SRC="pics/news02st.gif" ALT="Dial-A-Nerds"></A><FONT SIZE=4>10. June 19th Newspaper Article by Dan Morse, The Baltimore
```

Figure 9–7 *Raw HTML.*

HYPER-TEXT MARKUP LANGUAGE • HTML is the ASCII text command codes that are used by Web browsing software to translate plain text files with embedded HTML commands into the interesting text and graphics displays presented on our client PCs.

An HTML view of Web page text is shown in Figure 9-7.

Anyone who can use Microsoft Word can create HTML documents. With the HTML extension, Word automatically creates the HTML tags that are required by Web browsing software to display your document or link it to other documents. Most HTML tags have a beginning and an ending entry. Ending entries are most always the same as the beginning entry preceded by a slash (/). Boldface type is produced using <B> to start and </B> to end. Internet (or intranet) browsers display the words between these tags in boldface characters.

The next generation of HTML is Dynamic HTML, or DHTML. DHTML identifies a combination of new HTML tags and options, style sheets, and programming. DHTML supports development of Web pages incorporating more animation, permitting them to respond to user requests. HTML 4.0 specifies much of what is considered DHTML. DHTML pages support changing text heading color when a mouse passes over the header and dragging and dropping images to other places on Web pages. DHTML makes Web documents behave like desktop application programs.

DHTML features are implemented in Netscape's Navigator 4.x Web browser and in Microsoft's Internet Explorer 4.x and 5.x browsers and above. Because many Internet Web surfers use older versions of browser software, Web sites create separate versions of each page and send them to the appropriate browser version. Simpler HTML pages for IE version 3.x are sent to IE 3.x browsers, and DHTML pages are sent to IE 4.x and 5.x browsers.

DHTML features supported by both Netscape and Microsoft are:

- Object-oriented Web pages and Web page components.
- Cascading style sheets (CSSs).
- Content layering.
- Programming addressing page elements.
- Dynamic fonts.

Object-oriented Web pages and Web page components view each page component, including sections, headings, paragraphs, and images, and lists them as objects. This is Microsoft's "Dynamic HTML Object Model," Netscape's "HTML Object Model," and the World Wide Web Consortium (W3C's) "Document Object Model." In an object-oriented Web page, a heading on a page can be named (e.g., Heading23), assigned text style and color attributes, and addressed by its name in programs or scripts sent with the page. The heading could then be changed by the script or program when a mouse passed over it. Images identified as objects can be dragged and dropped using a mouse as defined by a script sent with the Web page. Changes are immediate because all allowable object variations have been sent as part of the Web page and the client PC Web browser performs the changes.

Cascading Style Sheets (CSSs) link to or specify different style sheets with specific precedence within the same Web page or within a set of related Web pages. Style sheets describe the default page layout, the font type style, and font size for headings and body text in a document or a portion of a document. Web page style sheets also describe a default background color or image, hypertext link colors, and possibly Web page content. Style sheets ensure consistency across all or a group of pages in a document or a Web site. DHTML permits specifying style sheets in a cascading fashion so user interaction changes style sheets and Web page appearance. DHTML permits multiple style sheet layers within a Web page, e.g., a style sheet embedded within a style sheet embedded within a style sheet. New style sheets can vary just a single element from the style sheet preceding it in the cascade of style sheets.

Content layering uses alternate style sheets or other techniques to vary Web page content. Content layers overlay or replace existing Web page content. Content layers can appear as timed presentations or as the result of user interaction. Netscape implements a style sheet approach and offers a new HTML LAYER tag set. Microsoft implements style sheet layers, but does not support the HTML LAYER tags in Internet Explorer. The W3C Working Committee is determining the recommended layering approach.

Programming permits JavaScript, Java applets, and ActiveX controls to alter Web pages. Such programming is already used on Web pages, but DHTML increases the Web page elements addressed by programs.

Dynamic fonts are downloaded with the Web page so that the font choice no longer depends on browser-provided fonts. Web pages can include font files containing specific font styles, sizes, and colors.

In addition to DHTML, normal HTML has been augmented by Java programming and Visual Basic programming extensions for the last several years. These extensions permit small programs to run on your PC and perform interesting visual and data manipulation tasks on Web pages.

Brain Teaser
_____

HTML Tags

Start the Windows NOTEPAD program. Write your name on a line. Save the file as braint.htm. Use the Windows Explorer and double-click on the filename.

1. This should launch your default Web browser and display your name in a simple text window. Your name should appear in the upper left cornet of the Web browser window.

2. Surround your name with the HTML tags **<center>**_your name is here_**</center>** using the open file in NOTEPAD and then save the file. Click the **Refresh** or **Reload** button on your Web browser. What happens to your name? It should now be centered. HTML tags generally follow the format _<tag command>_text that tag applies to_</tag command>_. The "/" designates stop applying the tag command.

3. Type in your address after the **</center>**, save the file, and refresh/reload the page in the browser. The address should appear on a line below your name left-justified.

4. Place the **
** (break) tag after your name and delete the **</center>** tag. What happens when the page is refreshed/reloaded? The center tag applies to all text. The break tag makes the address appear on the line below your name.

The goal of this exercise is to illustrate what HTML tags are and how HTML tags function in Web page documents.

UNIVERSAL RESOURCE LOCATORS • A Universal Resource Locator (URL) is the text string that precisely specifies the location of information on the Web (e.g., the Web pages posted on Internet or intranet servers). URLs most commonly identify a server in a DNS database. The DNS database links domain names to fixed IP addresses. URLs begin with HTTP://WWW, signifying Hyper-Text Transfer Protocol://World Wide Web.

The elements of a URL are separated from one another by periods. Web browsers automatically add the HTTP://WWW and appropriate "period" separators to domain name requests. For example, if I just enter themoultoncompany.com into Microsoft's Internet Explorer, it links me automatically to HTTP://WWW.themoultoncompany.com. URLs to Web site domains automatically launch an INDEX.HTML file from that domain server. Thus, the same information is displayed for both HTTP://WWW.themoultoncompany.com and HTTP://WWW.themoultoncompany.com/index.html.

In contrast, HTTP://WWW.themoultoncompany.com/radio.htm produces a different Web page display. A typical URL specifying an exact Web page is:

http://www.moultonco.com/notes.htm

Note that this URL jumps you immediately to a document in our Web page. URLs can be used to jump directly to any information displayed on the Internet, providing you know exactly where that information is stored. The Internet and World Wide Web are most often surfed using INDEX.HTML files as entry points to every Web site.

TCP/IP NETWORKS • TCP/IP is central to all networks today. Most LAN and enterprise communications use the TCP/IP protocol stack as well as the Internet. Windows helped standardize interfacing applications to the TCP/IP protocol suite software. Since UNIX systems, the Internet, and mainframe computers use TCP/IP, the most universal protocol stack is TCP/IP. Novell's NetWare 5 is more TCP/IP-centric for both NetWare servers and clients.

The services and applications associated with the TCP/IP suite are:

- Internet Protocol (IP) and Transmission Control Protocol (TCP).
- Internet Control Messaging Protocol (ICMP).
- Address Resolution Protocol (ARP) and Reverse Address Resolution Protocol (RARP).
- Datagrams and User Datagram Protocol (UDP).
- Virtual Circuits (VCs).

These transport services are used by TCP applications to establish internetwork links and to transfer data between systems attached to those links.

The IP is an Open Systems Interconnection (IOSI) Layer-3 protocol that routes data from one computer to another on the Internet. Each computer or host on the Internet has an IP address uniquely distinguishing it from all other Internet computers or hosts. When email or Web pages are transmitted between computers, the transmission is divided into chunks or wads of data called packets. Each packet contains the sender's and the receiver's Internet (IP) address. Packets are sent to Internet gateway computers (routers) that understand a small part of the Internet. Gateway computers (routers) read destination addresses and forward packets based upon a specific routing algorithm to an adjacent gateway (router). This process continues until a gateway (router) recognizes the destination address as an address belonging to a computer within its immediate neighborhood or domain. That gateway (router) then delivers the packet directly to the destination computer.

Dividing messages into packets permits sending packets by different routes across the Internet. Packets routed across different routes may arrive in a different order than the order in which they were sent. The IP just delivers packets without regard to their order in the message sent. The TCP, operating at OSI Layer 4, reassembles them in the proper order.

IP is a connection-less protocol. It does not require a fixed path between source and destination. Packets traveling through the Internet are transmitted as independent data units unrelated to any other data units. In the Internet, routing algorithms route the packets consistently across the same route. If you run the TRACERT command from a Windows PC DOS prompt to a Web site several times, the route followed is the same because routing algorithms cause the packets to follow the same route. Only when traffic load or network component malfunctions change the parameters used by the routing algorithms, does the route followed by the packets change. In this manner, the packets sent through the Internet are consistently, and also as needed, dynamically routed.

TCP is a connection-oriented protocol. It keeps track of packet sequencing in messages. This means that the Internet is a connection-less service at OSI communication model Layer 3—the networking layer with the IP. However, at OSI Layer 4, TCP makes the Internet a connection-oriented (a point-to-point channel) service between the Web server and PC client browser.

The most widely used IP version is Internet Protocol version 4 (IPv4). IP version 6 (IPv6) is beginning to be implemented in the Internet. IPv6 increases the IP address size from 32 bits to 128 bits. One hundred twenty-eight-bit addresses are sufficient to assign a unique IP address to every square foot of the planet's surface. IPv6 incorporates IPv4 capabilities. Servers supporting IPv6 packets can also support IPv4 packets.

ICMP is a message control and error and status reporting protocol between a server and an Internet gateway (router). ICMP sends messages using IP packets. The IP is not designed to be absolutely reliable. ICMP control messages provide feedback on IP packet transmissions. ICMP does not make IP reliable because it cannot guarantee that IP packets are delivered or control messages are returned. IP packets may not be delivered and their loss may go unreported. The higher layer protocols using TCP must provide data integrity procedures for reliable communications. ICMP messages typically record errors in packet processing. The ICMP error messages are:

Number	Message Type
0	Echo reply
3	Destination unreachable
4	Source quench – Permits discarding packets
5	Redirect
8	Echo
11	Time exceeded
12	Parameter problem
13	Timestamp
14	Timestamp reply
15	Information request
16	Information reply

ICMP data is processed by IP and some network management software. Application users are unaware of ICMP data traffic and network management software.

ARP and RARP map an IP address to an OSI Medium Access Control (MAC) physical address. ARP and RARP map 32-bit IP addresses to the 48-bit ROM addresses of the LAN board. An ARP or RARP cache table maintains the associations between each MAC address and its corresponding IP address. ARP makes the IP to MAC address associations and provides address conversion for packets sent to and from other systems.

As incoming packets destined for a computer in a specific IP LAN arrive at an IP gateway (router), the IP gateway uses ARP to find the physical MAC address matching the IP address. ARP searches its ARP cache table, finds the MAC address, and provides it so that the packet is sent to the destination computer. When no ARP cache table entry exists for an IP address, ARP broadcasts a request to all computers on the LAN to find a computer with the requested IP address. A computer recognizing the ARP-requested IP address returns a reply. ARP updates the ARP table cache and forwards the packet to the MAC address of the computer that responded to the ARP broadcast. OSI Layer-2 protocols differ for Ethernet, ATM, FDDI, HIPPI, and token ring networks, causing different ARP handshakes for each type of network.

RARP helps computers not knowing their specific assigned IP address request their IP address assignment from an Internet gateway's ARP table cache. When new computers are set up, RARP requests a RARP server program running on the IP gateway (router) to send its assigned IP address. RARP is used on Ethernet, FDDI, and token ring LANs.

Datagrams are self-contained, independent data-carrying packets having sufficient information to route from the source computer to the destination computer in an IP network. This routing does not rely on information exchanges between source and destination computers and the transporting network. "Datagram" is used often synonymously with "packet." Datagrams (or packets) are message units that the Internet transports using the IP. Because no fixed connections (circuit-switched or VCs) exist at ISO Layer 3, the IP layer between source and destination computers, datagrams (packets) are self-contained and do not rely on information exchanges between source and destination computers.

UDP is an alternative to TCP. UDP provides more limited message exchange service between computers in an IP network. UDP sends all data as packets (datagrams) without any reassembly or sequencing information. This leaves the responsibility for message reassembly up to the application program using UDP. The application program must determine that an entire message has arrived and its packets are in the correct order. Applications reducing processing overhead because they send very small amounts of data often use UDP rather than TCP. Trivial File Transfer Protocol (TFTP) uses UDP instead of TCP.

UDP is in OSI Layer 4, the transport layer. It provides port numbers to help distinguish different user requests and an optional error checking capability to verify the data arrived intact.

VCs are paths between source and destination computers in a network. VCs appear to be circuit-switched physical paths, but they are constructed as logical pathways from pools of network resources. IP network physical circuit resources are assigned as needed to construct VCs and to support VC traffic loads.

Permanent virtual circuits (PVCs) are permanently assigned to users, just as though they were dedicated channels. PVCs continuously reserve IP network physical resources for a specific user, although the physical resource assignments may change depending upon network loads and network component malfunctions. Switched virtual circuits (SVCs) are set up for temporary use like dial-up phone line connections. SVCs are assigned IP network resources as long as the SVC connection is needed. IP network resources are released when an SVC connection is terminated.

The OSI Layer 4, the message integrity layer, and Layer 5, the session layer, implement VCs. TCP transfers information over VCs.

The TCP/IP protocol suite provides extended network services. These are application software programs operating in the upper OSI layers:

- Simple Mail Transport Protocol (SMTP) for sending email.
- File Transfer Protocol (FTP) for transferring files from computer to computer.
- Standard Terminal access application-Level Network (TELNET) protocol, which permits terminals to interact and control UNIX computers.
- Programming Interfaces (the AT&T streams Transport Layer Interface (TLI) UNIX 4.3 BSD sockets).
- Network Filesystem (NFS) for managing files.
- Trivial File Transfer Protocol (TFTP) for performing some file transfers.

These TCP/IP networking services permit higher layer software to interface to TCP/IP and implement email, computer control, file transfers, Web browsing, and other user application programs. These TCP/IP interfaces provide external data representation, remote procedure calls, and security functions to applications software written to use them.

TCP/IP software today runs on Windows using Window's 32-bit TCP/IP API called WINSOCK-32. Similar TCP/IP capabilities are available for UNIX and NetWare applications. TCP/IP protocol elements are shown in Figure 9-8.

INTERNET SERVICE PROVIDERS

ISPs typically offer access to the Internet for a fee. Some ISPs provide free Internet access in exchange for viewing advertising or for gathering information on Internet use.

ISPs can be large or small. They may be a regional network provider, reselling high-speed Internet access to smaller ISPs. The smaller ISPs in turn sell Internet access to individual Internet users. The Moulton Company, for example, purchases Internet access from MDconnect.com, PSINet, and MCI. All offer direct unfiltered access to the Internet. Both PSINet and MCI provide nationwide service, while MDconnect is local to Baltimore, Maryland. Our Web site information resides on MDconnect.com's Internet server. We

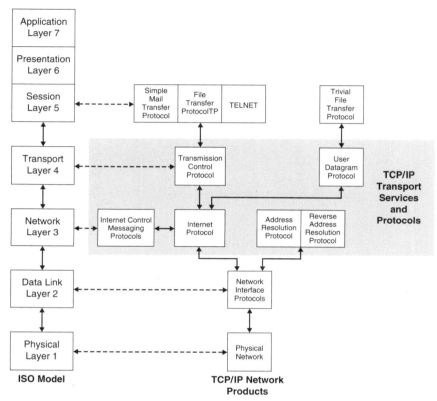

Figure 9–8 *TCP/IP transport services and protocols.*

also use AOL for Internet access while traveling around the planet. I have had Internet access and email capabilities from AOL while traveling in Ghana.

In Figure 9-9, an Internet user sits at a home PC and connects through a dial-up line using a modem to the ISP. The dial-up call is placed to the ISP phone number using telephone company-switched network facilities. When accessing Web pages posted at the ISP, the data is routed from the customer premise to the telephone company switching equipment and then to the ISP office. The ISP office connection is a high-speed digital link terminating in a multi-line controller that performs modem functions. The multi-line controller converts the incoming call's 64-Kbps digital voice channel stream into a 33.6-Kbps modem data stream and sends it to a router. The router connects to an Ethernet and the ISP's servers. The data coming from the customer site follows the dashed line route from the customer site to the ISP's server. Web pages requested from the server follow the same path back to the customer's PC.

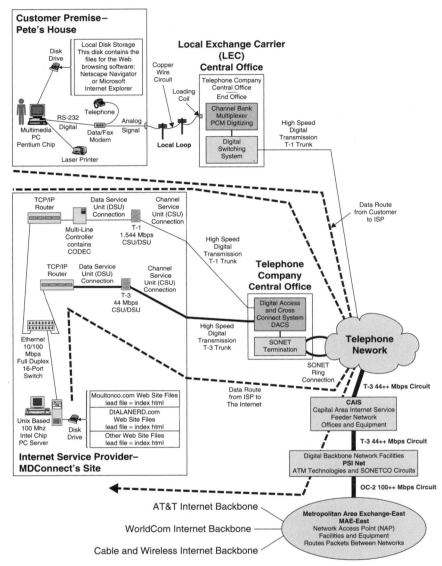

Figure 9–9 *Internet connectivity.*

The major problem with dial-up Internet connections is that telephone company switching equipment routes Internet access calls to the ISP's site. These calls average 20 minutes or more in duration. Typical voice calls average three minutes. When many ISP calls are made through the same switching equipment, the telephone company switch can become blocked. Since the heaviest Internet usage is between 6 PM and midnight, this is the period where telephone switch blocking is encountered. At those times, customers placing calls may get a fast busy signal indicating trunk lines are all occupied. High-speed Digital Subscriber Line (DSL) and cable modem access get around this problem, as we shall see later in this chapter.

At the ISP, the server containing the Web page files is an Intel CPU chip 100MHz or faster PC that runs the UNIX operating system. On its fixed disk drives reside the files for the MOULTONCO.COM and DIALANERD.COM Web pages. The kickoff file for each Web page is the INDEX.HTML file. When someone on the Internet accesses those pages, they come into the server off a high-speed Internet backbone through the MAE-East NAP. Their route travels through MAE-East to PSInet, then to CAIS, and finally through a T-3 channel into the MDconnect ISP UNIX server. The Web page files are returned via that route (the data route from the ISP to the Internet) to their Web browser.

Web pages requested from the Web server are sent across the Ethernet to the Internet gateway (router). The Internet gateway (router) tells the requesting user that the MOULTONCO.COM and DIALANERD.COM Web pages are IP addresses 209.8.195.52 and 209.8.194.68, respectively. It is connected to the CAIS via a T-3 high-speed link. CAIS in turn feeds the data to PSInet, which connects to MAE-East and the Internet backbone networks.

Data flowing from the customer premise into the ISP facility and data flowing from the Internet into the ISP office facility both travel through telephone company facilities. However, the paths followed are different. Further, ISPs could connect to the Internet without using telephone company facilities if they were connected directly to a backbone network.

The Internet is literally millions and millions of Web index pages and related information pages located on ISP server disk drives accessible to everyone connected to the Internet.

Some ISPs provide both access to the Internet and a place to visit on the Internet. Such places are America Online (AOL), CompuServe, Prodigy, and the Microsoft Network (MSN). Places to visit want "you-all to come back real soon now, you hear" because of their content. They usually charge a basic access fee plus connect time charges when your time exceeds a monthly minimum. AOL and other Internet places to go also filter access to the Internet. For example, The Moulton Company Web sites feature graphics, sounds, and moving graphics. These are not always viewable and audible when viewed from ISP places to go like AOL.

Other ISPs are the mom-and-pop stores of the Internet. They provide dial-up access to subscribers charging them a flat monthly fee varying from $8 to $24 per month. Connect time is unlimited for the flat monthly fee. This means, however, that sometimes during peak periods, you may find all their access lines busy. The mom-and-pop store ISP do not filter Internet data for their subscribers. Unfortunately, like the mom-and-pop video stores, the mom-and-pop ISPs are rapidly disappearing as well.

All ISPs provide the ability to set up and display Web pages. As part of their service, they provide 10MB to 50MB of disk space for Web page content.

Making Money with Web Sites

Internet Web sites make money for enterprises by providing useful information to people surfing the Web, by selling products, or by providing specialized services. There are several classes of revenue-generating Web sites:

- Web sites providing information and charging money for access to information services. Many newspapers and some magazines make money in this fashion. The WASHINGTONPOST.COM is one of these sites. If you find an article in their archives, they request that you pay to view it. Many of the standards body sites provide access to their published standards for a fee. The IEEE site is one of these.
- Web sites providing information to build traffic and charging advertisers for advertising on their Web pages. These pages are cluttered with advertising banners and have tracking data monitored by DOUBLECLICK.COM. The ZDnet.COM site is one of these sites.
- Web sites selling products by supporting external product sales with up-to-date, readily available information on their products and services. This information ranges from software driver and patch downloads to providing technical installation and operating manuals on products. Such sites support sales that are made by other advertising and sales efforts. Cisco and 3COM sites generally operate this way.
- Web sites selling products that can be ordered directly from the Web site. This type of sale is an e-commerce operation. Product orders are taken from the Web, credit cards are billed, and the products are sent directly to purchasers. LLBean.COM and BUY.COM fall into these categories.
- Web sites providing services over the Internet and charging for those services. The stockbroker Web sites are examples of such sites. They provide stock sale and account services that make money by charging sales commissions on stock transactions. PAYTRUST.COM provides bill-paying services for a fee.
- Some sites offer prizes to generate traffic and charge advertisers for advertising on their Web pages. The iWON.COM search site is one of these sites.

These sites and others all seek to make money by building significant traffic so advertisers will pay to advertise on their sites, charge for services, sell products, or support company sales. Most sites use a combination of these approaches so they are not purely one approach or another.

Regulating the Internet

The growth of the Internet is driven by commercial applications and technology. The governments of the world would like to regulate and tax the Internet. The regulation of the Internet is aimed at restricting access to the information published on it. Like it or not, every type of information is available on the Internet. The Internet is the ultimate mechanism for free speech. The Internet should remain as unfettered as possible because the free flow of ideas helps the population of the world work more for good and less for evil purposes.

Notwithstanding the doomsday warnings that machines might finally inherit the earth, every attempt at government regulation of the Internet and telecommunications has been met by a technological solution that obviates that regulation. We certainly should proceed with prudence as we develop and implement new computer and communications technologies, because like the atomic bomb, they could potentially harm mankind. The doomsday warnings should not be taken lightly or flippantly. There should be guidelines and safeguards for implementing new microelectronic, Internet, and communications technology and artificial intelligence. But guidelines and safeguards do not mean regulation or taxation. Added government revenues are created by the resultant traditional economic activities that explode because of the impacts of new telecommunications technologies. If the Internet is to realize its full potential, everyone on the planet should oppose government regulation and taxation.

Brain Teaser

Internet Free Speech

Use the iwon.com search engine and search for Internet free speech to locate a Blue Ribbon Campaign for Online Freedom of Speech, Press, and Association. One page we found was http://mindspring.yahoo.com/eff/blueribbon.html.
1. This was a campaign mounted to counter the threat to prosecute sites that placed sexually offensive information on the Internet. It was passed into law, but the censorship provision was subsequently ruled unconstitutional by the Supreme Court.

2. Check out the other Blue Ribbon icons at http://www.eff.org/pub/Graphics/Icons/BlueRibbon/. (The capitalized letters are important here. If the exact capital letters are not used, then the correct Web page will not be found.)

3. Go to the EFF home page. What is EFF all about? EFF's mission is to protect the interests and civil liberties of netizens (Internet Citizens).

The goal of this exercise was to illustrate some of the political issues surrounding the Internet and freedom of speech.

New Internet Capabilities

The Internet provides new ways for enterprises to save money through deploying intranets and extranets. The concepts of the Internet, intranets, and extranets were discussed briefly in Chapter 6. They are expanded upon here to highlight how Internet technologies provide enterprises new capabilities to save money and expand business.

The Internet (politically labeled the "Information Superhighway"), with more than 374 million users worldwide, is the planet's largest computer network. Internet technologies are designed to bring vast amounts of information in an easily digestible form to everyone's PC. Organizations use the Internet technologies (TCP/IP, HTML, HTTP, etc.) to implement internal Internets called intranets.

Intranets

Intranets use the technologies developed for the Internet and the graphical application of the World Wide Web to bring corporate information in an easily digestible form to corporate employees. This means that reports generated as paper documents can now be created electronically using HTML editors and Web browsing tools. Employees are armed with Web server programs and browsers to create and access an organization's information. The goal is to improve organizational communications and make businesses run more smoothly.

Intranets bring the concept of a "paperless office" closer to reality. While we still deal with about the same amount of paper in the office everyday, the amount of information we examine has increased exponentially. This is because electronically, we can examine more information and handle it quicker than if we were required to handle it on paper. The speed at which business operates has increased again because we now handle much of our information electronically with greater efficiency than when we handled it using paper.

In basic terms, an intranet is your organization's existing enterprise network with client and server software that lets it display and link HTML documents. This is the same HTML linking and graphics displaying software that is used to access the Web. Some of Microsoft's products used to implement intranets are: Windows 95/98/ME clients, Windows NT/2000, the Internet Information Server (IIS), and Microsoft Exchange Server.

HARDWARE CONFIGURATIONS

Intranets use Web servers that are UNIX or NT Server systems, PC clients running Windows or Windows NT, and Web browsing software. Intranets can be configured to support a variety of employee usage scenarios. An intranet may only support the employees at a single site. In this case, their LAN and its clients and servers become the intranet computers. In other cases, an intranet may support both employees at a central site and employees at remote sites. In this case, the remote sites are commonly connected to the central site with high-speed digital circuits. The network is relatively secure because only organization employees have access to it.

Some intranets could be connected to the Internet to permit information exchange and research. In this scenario a firewall would be used to protect the intranet from unauthorized intrusion and prevent employees from visiting sites for recreation rather than research.

Extranets

Extranets are intranets with a twist. They permit people outside the enterprise to access specific intranet information. For example, the Social Security Administration would have an extranet because it links its internal intranet to the Internet so that individuals can query their Social Security account information. Similarly, large organizations permit customers and collaborators to access their internal intranets for specific types of shared information.

In these cases, all extranet users would have multimedia Windows or Macintosh PCs with TCP/IP. They would connect to their local LANs, send data through routers to the Internet, and log their PCs onto Intranet servers. Their connections would travel into enterprise LANs through Internet routers and firewall security. Their login authorization would give them access to specific servers and data on the enterprise intranet.

Most intranet and extranet applications provide simple access to HTML data and images. Newer applications are VoIP and video teleconferencing applications.

Key Internet Telecommunications Applications

Three key Internet telecommunications applications are Voice over IP (VoIP), video teleconferencing, and Virtual Private Networks (VPNs). These applications permit enterprise employees to work more effectively together regardless of where they are located.

Voice over IP, or Internet Telephony

VoIP is voice carried between telephony clients using the IP. In IP telephony, VoIP represents the networking hardware and software components for managing delivery of voice communications using IP. This covers transmitting voice in digital form in discrete packets rather than over circuit-switched connections in the PSTN. One advantage of VoIP and Internet Telephony (IT) is that toll charges by ordinary telephone companies can be avoided. The VoIP Forum promotes VoIP telephony. The VoIP Forum is an effort by major VoIP hardware and software vendors, including Cisco, VocalTec, 3Com, and NetSpeak, among others, to promote the use of ITU-T H.323. This H.323 standard specifies how to send voice and video using IP on the public Internet or in a private IP intranet. Directory service standards permitting users to locate other users and use touch-tone signals for automatic call distribution and voice mail are also promoted.

VoIP uses the IP and Real-Time Protocol (RTP) to deliver voice and video packets. With the Internet and other public networks, QoS is difficult to guarantee. IP networks managed by an enterprise or by an Internet Telephony Service Provider (ITSP) can provide better quality service.

Transmitting VoIP networks are an exciting technology because of the cost savings that they promise. There are two general approaches to implementing VoIP technology in business, the internal approach and the external approach. The most comprehensive approach is to implement VoIP, or IT, internally. This means deploying VoIP gateway devices to convert between VoIP and traditional telephony. These gateways are deployed internally to provide external interfaces to both private IP networks and the Internet as well as the PSTN. External VoIP maintains traditional telephony internally but uses VoIP technology and the Internet to deliver voice to similarly VoIP-equipped external facilities. Both approaches provide enterprises the opportunities to save significantly on telecommunications costs and to integrate voice and data communications into a single unified network.

Since most large organizations have high-speed access to the Internet from their central and remote locations, long-distance and international costs of voice IP calls to VoIP equipped facilities costs almost nothing. The major impediments to such configurations is that each facility must be similarly equipped and that priority needs to be given to VoIP traffic if QoS criteria are to be met. Once an enterprise pays to equip a facility with VoIP network components and pays for high-speed Internet access for the facility, that facility can make VoIP calls to similarly equipped intranet and extranet facilities that it is told exist on the Internet or on a private IP network.

Products sold by Cisco and Lucent implement the two VoIP networking approaches. The internal approach uses VoIP router/gateway devices to interface to both voice and data networks. All internal communications may run across an internal IP network, or traditional voice communications may interface to the VoIP router/gateway device. The external approach integrates VoIP technology into the enterprise PBX, making it the focal point for VoIP communications. The first approach is implemented using components sold by Cisco Systems, while the second approach is a Lucent Technologies approach.

The internal VoIP approach encodes VoIP voice calls at a PC or at a VoIP telephone. The VoIP router/gateway then routes the voice calls via a private IP network or via the Internet to the destination PC or a VoIP telephone to be decoded and transmitted to the user. With this approach, all internal and external communications can travel across IP networks or the router/gateway can convert VoIP calls to switched network calls at any location to complete them using the PSTN. Some difficulties may arise in establishing the initial connection if there are traffic delays on the IP network or the Internet.

The quality of the voice signal may vary depending upon the encoding products and algorithms used. However, today most VoIP products provide very acceptable signal encoding and decoding and QoS. QoS is related to the bandwidth guarantee established through the IP network. Many IP backbone networks are implementing new routing algorithms that provide priority to specific traffic types requiring dedicated bandwidth. Data transmission comes in wads and chunks, so its need for dedicated bandwidth is much less than voice or video transmission. Data traffic gets a lower priority and a lower QoS than voice or video traffic. VoIP networks that utilize a private backbone IP network to establish the connection between calling and called PCs have better control over the calling process. The Internet and more public IP networks have unpredictable congestion that makes them much less effective for VoIP communications.

Figure 9-10 provides a general overview of the internal VoIP network implementation approach. Routers/gateways convert voice traffic to VoIP traffic and route the IP data traffic over the IP network to their respective destinations. A VoIP router/gateway, such as Cisco's AS5300 access server with a VoIP feature, receives digitized voice transmissions in IP packets from users within the company and then routes them to other parts of its LAN or WAN intranet or, using T-carrier links, sends them to the PSTN. The router/gateway is the key component for both data and voice traffic. A PBX may send some connections to the VoIP router/gateway and others to the PSTN. Calls to non-VoIP-equipped facilities are routed to the PSTN, while those to intranet and extranet VoIP-equipped facilities are sent to the VoIP router/gateway. The VoIP router/gateway would pocketsize the voice calls and connect them to the desired destination phone or PBX. Calls placed would use regular phone numbers. The VoIP router/gateway would translate these phone numbers into destination IP addresses, connect to the target VoIP router/gateway servicing the destination PCs or VoIP telephones, and cause it to ring, indicating an incoming call.

Functions performed by VoIP router/gateway devices are identified in Figure 9-11. On the telephony side, the VoIP router/gateway would likely interface to a T-1 channel connected to traditional PSTN facilities. The VoIP router/gateway would interface to a telephony G.711 specification audio Coder Decoder (CODEC) to provide a traditional Pulse Code Modulation (PCM)—64-Kbps DS-0 voice channels. The G.711 specification is an ITU-T recommended algorithm for transmitting and receiving PCM voice over 64-Kbps channels. This specification is used for digital telephones on digital, PBX, and ISDN channels and is needed for ITU-T-compliant video conferencing. Normal T-1 call supervision functions, framing, and Channel Service Unit/Data Service Unit (CSU/DSU) interfaces would be supported by the VoIP router/gateway.

A technique that helps ensure faster packet delivery is to have all possible network gateway computers having access to the public Internet select the fastest path before establishing TCP sockets connection with the target clients.

On the IP telephony client side of the router/gateway would be devices operating with the H.323 specification. H.323 is the ITU-T umbrella standard defining real-time multimedia communications over packet networks (IP networks). H.323-compliant devices can set up calls, exchange compressed voice and video information, conference with other H.323 devices, and interface to VoIP router/gateway devices connecting to the PSTN. H.323 devices incorporate:

• The G.723.1 specification to encode voice as compressed digital audio that can run over the PSTN. This encoding specification provides high-quality voice output over low bps channels.

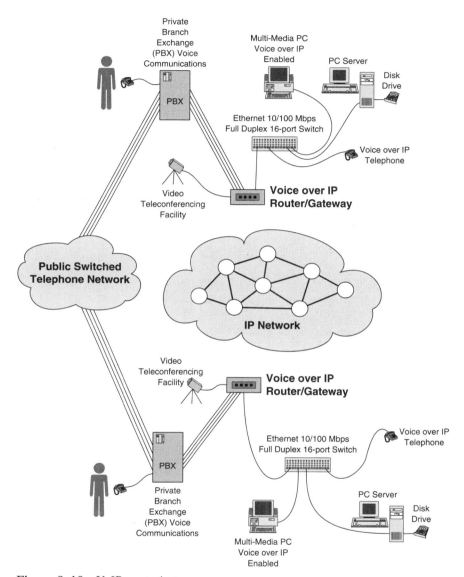

Figure 9–10 *VoIP router/gateway.*

- The H.245 specification to open and close logical channels on a network.
- The H.225 specification to define messages for call signaling and progress negotiations. Q.931 is the ISDN D-channel signaling protocol covering call setup and call termination, called party number,

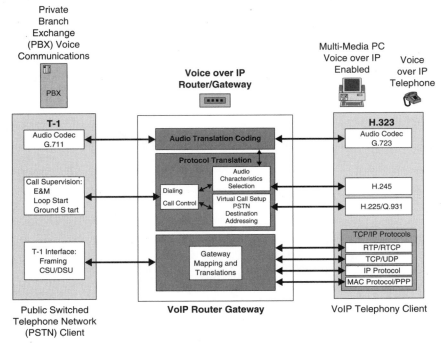

Figure 9–11 *VoIP router/gateway interfaces and functions.*

calling party number information, access and interfacing to the PSTN, and integration of voice and circuit-switched traffic.

- The Real-time Transport Protocol (RTP) for sending real-time multi-media information using IP packets. Also the Real-Time Conferencing Protocol (RTCP) to implement conferencing of groups of clients on IP networks.

- The TCP as a connection-oriented end-to-end protocol for sending data across IP networks. The UDP as a connection-less end-to-end protocol for sending data across IP networks.

- The IP as the OSI Layer-3 protocol to communicate with other IP devices.

- The LAN-MAC protocol to transport data across the OSI Layer-2 connection, or the Point-to-Point Protocol (PPP) to connect through dial-up connections to the Internet.

The VoIP gateway device provides the translation and mapping required to map the H.323 protocol functions into the T-1 voice network operation, and vice versa.

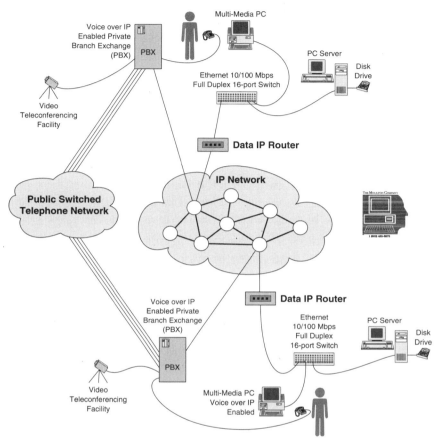

Figure 9–12 *VoIP PBX configuration.*

Telephony switches that encode voice calls in IP packets and route them over the Internet to identical switches in remote locations are the key component in the external approach to VoIP networking. This is shown in Figure 9-12. In this case, substantial telecommunications cost reductions can be realized while making maximum effective use of voice IP communications and the existing telephone company networks. The appeal here is that no internal voice networking changes are needed to take advantage of external VoIP networking. The existing telephone PBX and its designed-in reliability remain unchanged. Cost savings result from calls placed between facilities employing other VoIP-enabled PBXs or VoIP router/gateways. The VoIP PBX must be configured with IP addresses of the remote facilities for it to route VoIP traffic to those remote facilities.

In this case, a user would place a call with a conventional telephone connected to a PBX incorporating a special VoIP router/gateway component. The PBX with the internal VoIP router/gateway would complete the call and perform the voice encoding, sending the call through a high-speed connection across the Internet or any IP network to an identical PBX with a VoIP router/gateway near the destination of the telephone call. If the PSTN were used to complete the call, the PBX with a VoIP router/gateway component would be needed. The dialing digits would also be used to route the call through the Internet to the PBX or VoIP router/gateway closest to the destination phone. Once the receiving PBX with a VoIP router/gateway got the VoIP call off the Internet, it would then ring the target phone and complete the call. In this case, no long-distance toll charges would be incurred for the call. While such features are not integrated into PBXs today, we will see them appear within the next several years.

The quality of the voice call can vary depending upon the encoding products, algorithms used, and transmission speed. However, today's standardized encoding and compression schemes provide acceptable signal quality for most all VoIP products.

VoIP networks or IP telephony can deliver significant cost savings over conventional telephony. Because large organizations generally use high-speed access to the Internet from both central and remote locations, the cost of VoIP calls transported by the Internet is almost zero. Further, VoIP technology can be implemented to provide PBX capabilities using a LAN and multimedia PCs. Table 9-1 compares internal vs. external VoIP approaches.

HOW HOME PC IP TELEPHONY WORKS • Home PC users have been using VoIP communications capabilities for several years. Initially, they loaded VoIP software into their PCs and connected to special network servers that linked calling and called PCs for voice calls. Soon Web cameras were attached to the PCs and the calls became video calls. The only difficult part was that these calls required that the voice and video be compressed and sent over a 24,000 bps to 33,600 bps dial-up phone connection to Internet voice IP servers. The Internet voice IP servers provided by Vocaltech were used to make voice IP calls. Such Internet voice IP servers had at one time undesirable public chat rooms and frequent heavy congestion, making them less effective for business voice IP communications.

Internet voice IP servers provide both public and private chatting areas. Public areas are like chat rooms with just anyone connecting to anyone else using the server. Public chatting areas bring a new dimension to the typical flasher.

Table 9.1   *VoIP Internal vs. External Summary*

Characteristic	Internal VoIP	External VoIP
Wiring	Most all communications is VoIP with one set of wiring carrying data, voice, and video communications. LAN communications to each client PC and VoIP telephone should be at 100 Mbps. LAN switches with full duplex channels would be required to connect VoIP components to client PCs and telephones. Redundant Gbps Ethernet backbone networks may be required to insure voice and video QoS.	Requires separate wiring for voice and LAN communications. Separate connections route data to the Internet and voice to the PSTN.
Facilities Utilization	Most efficient – IP packets intermix data, voice, and video traffic. QoS function guarantees bandwidth for voice and video transmission	Inefficient – DS-0 channels use 64-Kbps capacity for duration of the call.
Reliability	Requires installation of redundant components and redundant network pathways to VoIP router/gateways. Uninterruptible power must be provided to all VoIP components.	Existing PBX reliability remains in effect.
Cost Savings	Substantial initial investment would pay off in longer term as long-distance charges, network wiring maintenance, and telephone administration costs are reduced.	Lower initial investment saves in long-distance communications costs between VoIP-enabled facilities.

On one occasion, Jeremy and I were trying to get my PC working with the VoIP software using a public chat room on an Internet voice IP server. Jeremy was on the other end of a normal dial-up voice phone call so we could iron out my incorrectly configured software settings. The VoIP connection was using a separate phone line at each of our houses. We were working along on a public server trying to make a voice IP connection between our PCs when I first heard some sort of strange music coming out of the phone and then Jeremy shouting "Oh my God!!!!" in response to what he was seeing. Now normally he would just laugh, but at his home were two young sons that he did not want seeing the video feed from the public server.

The software client for a home PC conforms to the H.323 specification like any other VoIP PC client.

Brain Teaser

VoIP Products

VocalTec offered early Internet phone software. Use the Internet and connect to the VOCALTEC.COM Web site to see what products and services they now offer.

1. What VoIP services are offered? They offer calling card VoIP solutions to reduce calling card costs, PC to telephone calling, VoIP for mobile telephones providing alternate routing and backup trunks, VoIP VPNs, and Web-to-phone-enabling Web pages to connect surfers to a service representative at a telephone. Which type of VoIP product or service is the most innovative? My vote goes for the Web-to-phone products and services.

2. Connect to the page http://www.vocaltec.com/consumer/products/conproducts.htm. What has happened to the original VocalTec Internet phone products? They are no longer offered by VocalTec, but are now provided by a VocalTec subsidiary, Truly Global.

3. Connect using the icon to the Truly Global Web site. Look at the Frequently Asked Questions (FAQs). Is Truly Global compatible with Internet phone? No, it is not. It is a new service.

4. Check out the other VocalTec VoIP solutions and products to get a feel for how VoIP telephony is evolving. NetSpeak.com is another VoIP vendor that offers products competing with VocalTec. Check out their Web site at www.netspeak.com.

The goal of this exercise is to illustrate how VoIP products for consumers have evolved to serve both consumer and business needs.

TELECOMMUNICATIONS SERVICES PROVIDER • A telecommunications service provider is a company implementing VoIP over the Internet for commercial purposes. These would be large companies like AT&T. They would sell voice IP long-distance at lower prices than conventional long-distance. Any telephone company could implement VoIP technology in their Central Office (CO) branch exchange switches. They could connect these VoIP-enhanced switches to a private high-speed IP network or the Internet and route voice calls across that network. Such VoIP calls would use the network facilities, as well as calls routed across traditional T-carrier based facilities, since IP packets are only sent as needed and they carry compressed digital voice informa-

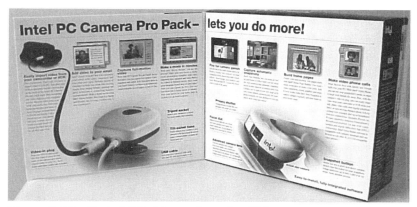

Figure 9–13 *Typical PC videoconferencing Web cam.*

tion. Expect to see the traditional voice telephone network become a VoIP network in the next ten years.

PROBLEMS AND LIMITATIONS • VoIP promises dramatic telephony cost savings. Conversely, VoIP networks present issues to be resolved, including security and access, reliability and performance, and scalability. The IP backbone network a corporation chooses directly impacts these issues. How IP service providers design and implement their backbone networks is key to the effectiveness of voice IP applications. New networks implement QoS routing capabilities designed to accommodate VoIP traffic.

Video Teleconferencing, or Videoconferencing

A video teleconference, or a videoconference, connects people in separate locations using video, voice, and data communications. The simplest video teleconferences transmit static images and text between facilities. The most sophisticated video teleconferences transmit full-motion video, high-quality audio, images, and data between multiple facilities.

Video teleconferencing software is standard PC software. Microsoft's NetMeeting runs on Windows 98 and Windows 2000. It can be downloaded from the NetMeeting homepage for free.

Think of a video teleconference as a video telephone call, often referred to as a Web phone. This implies that videoconferencing products today are transforming the PC into our video telephone of the future (see Figure 9-13).

NetMeeting provides a typical set of videoconferencing, or video teleconferencing, features. Such features permit using a PC and the Internet to hold face-to-face conversations with friends and family, or to collaborate with co-workers around the world. Such NetMeeting features include:

- Video conferencing—NetMeeting's video conferencing lets you send and receive video and audio communications with anyone on the Internet. NetMeeting supports communicating concepts, information, and applications over video links. A video camera instantly captures pictures of people and different items, has an automatic microphone sensitivity level setting to adjust for optimal sound quality, and the software adjusts the size of the video window sent. Users can remotely adjust for faster video performance or better image quality. NetMeeting PCs can send and receive real-time video images to similarly equipped PCs and to PCs that do not have video input hardware.
- Whiteboard—A whiteboard function supports multiple people in real time creating, reviewing, and updating graphic data. Clicking, dragging, and dropping information with the mouse manipulates whiteboard contents. Data from any Windows application can be cut, copied, and pasted into the whiteboard. Colored pointers differentiate participants' comments and whiteboard contents can be saved for future reference. The NetMeeting whiteboard conforms to T.126 whiteboard and conferencing protocol specifications and inter-operates with other T.126-compatible whiteboards.
- Chat—Chat supports real-time text conversations with many people simultaneously. Text messages are typed to communicate with other people in a chat room, either one person or a group of people. A whisper mode sends private messages to another person during a group chat session. Chat session contents can be saved for future reference.
- Internet directory—A Microsoft Internet Directory Web site locates people to call on the Internet. The Internet Directory is viewable from a Web page. A list of people currently running NetMeeting is displayed on the Internet Directory Web page. NetMeeting users can connect to one or more of the active NetMeeting sessions listed on the Internet Directory Web page.
- File transfer—One or more files can be sent in the background during a NetMeeting conference to all conference participants, or to one or more selected participants. NetMeeting users can accept or reject transferred files.
- Program sharing—Multiple programs can be shared during a conference. Shared programs are viewed in separate windows, making it easy to distinguish between shared and local applications. Minimize a shared program frame to work on other things, switch between shared programs using a shared program taskbar, and allow

or prevent others from working in shared programs using the Sharing dialog box.

- Remote desktop sharing (RDS)—RDS lets you operate a computer from a remote location. Operate your office computer from home, and vice versa. Use a secure connection and a password to access the remote desktop, files, and programs. Protect your computer while using RDS with a password-protected screensaver.
- Security—All shared program data, transferred files, chat text, and whiteboard data is encoded for transfer. Secure conferences encrypt data and disable audio and video. NetMeeting uses two user authentication measures to protect conference privacy.

  User authentication:
  - Verifies participant identity by requiring authentication certificates.
  - Generates NetMeeting certificates automatically during Net-Meeting setup.
  - Uses personal certificates issued by an external certifying authority or by an intranet certificate server.
  - Schedules secure conferences, requiring participants to have certificates.

  Password protection:
  - Permits hosting meetings that require a specific password to join.
  - Permits controlling an office computer from home, and vice versa.
- Advanced calling—Supports sending messages to NetMeeting users or initiating a NetMeeting call directly from your mail address book. Call people from corporate directory servers, the Windows address book, a list of people who have called you, or from the Microsoft Internet Directory. Place calls directly from the NetMeeting user interface or place calls using NetMeeting's address book if your network uses a gateway or gatekeeper.

NetMeeting videoconference software and a digital (Web cam) camera afford users easy and cheap live connections to distant friends and family. Although the audio and video quality of these setups is not great, the combined benefits of a video link and long-distance savings are quite persuasive.

An obvious benefit for businesses using video teleconferencing, or videoconferencing, is lower travel costs. Videoconferencing can also be used to provide customer service. This is an enhancement of the VocalTec Web to phone Web site product. Other benefits include group work among geographically distant teammates, and promoting a stronger sense of community among business contacts. The video face-to-face connection provides non-verbal communication to the exchange and allows participants to develop a stronger sense of familiarity with individuals they may physically never meet.

Continued rapid advances in PC and communications technologies make high-quality video telephony possible today. The multimedia PC we use at home or in the office is the video telephone of the future. Appropriately equipped, it can perform high-quality video telephony utilizing high-speed access to the Internet.

The most limiting feature to video telephony and videoconferencing is slow dial-up communications connecting PCs to the Internet. Without high-speed 24/7 connectivity by the PCs, it is not practical to place a direct video telephone call to a specific, targeted PC today. As the percentage of households with installed PCs approaches 95 percent, and as the number of them with high-speed, full-time Internet access (such as provided by cable modems, DSL connections, and other technologies) approaches the same percentage, then direct PC-to-PC video telephony will replace voice telephony.

Switched direct PC-to-PC video telephony can also be performed with some vendors' products using ISDN communications links. In this case, an ISDN call is placed to the target PC. The target PC is set up to answer incoming calls automatically and activate the video telephony application software. When the called party is at the target PC, the call is completed successfully. Otherwise, an electronic message is left, identifying the caller and the time of the call.

PC TELECONFERENCING SOFTWARE AND SERVICES • Several vendors provide PC video teleconferencing products and services using private IP intranets or the Internet. Such vendors include PictureTel Corporation (www.picturetel.com), PolyCom (www.polycom.com), and CuseeMe Networks (www.cuseeme.com).

Instant messenger software permits private and public chats between users. Instant messenger software now delivers other types of audio and video feeds. One early instant messenger package was ICQ (www.icq.com). ICQ supports video teleconferencing when a PC has an attached Web camera. ICQ was at one time unique because it provided the capability to call a specific target PC. The target PC had to be registered in ICQ's database. If the PC was on-line and active, the call was completed. When the PC was not on-line, an email message was left for the recipient, notifying them of the call.

AOL has also implemented instant messaging and video teleconferencing in its software.

Virtual Private Networks

A Virtual Private Network (VPN) is a data network exclusive to an organization that is implemented using the components of a public Internet or private IP network infrastructure. Tunneling protocols and security procedures maintain network privacy. A VPN is similar in operation to a physically private network of owned or leased channels that can only be used by one enterprise. A VPN provides private networking capabilities at much lower cost because it is implemented by software and protocols running on shared public network channels.

A VPN makes it possible to share public network resources securely for data, voice, and video communications. Enterprises use VPNs for both extranet and wide-area intranet communications.

A VPN encrypts data before sending it through the public Internet or a private IP network. At the receiving end, the data is decrypted when delivered to the destination client PC. Additional security encrypts both the data and also the originating and receiving IP addresses. The point-to-point tunneling protocol tunnels through the public network facilities, establishing a private, secure, point-to-point link between the sending and receiving endpoints. The VPN tunnel is maintained by encryption and decryption at each end of the network. Windows NT supports the point-to-point tunneling protocol and VPNs. VPN software is sometimes installed on firewall servers.

An Internet-based VPN uses the open, distributed infrastructure of the Internet to transmit data between corporate sites over secure, virtual, point-to-point channels.

VPNs can extend a LAN to a remote facility over the Internet or a private IP network. With a VPN, remote users connect to a central site LAN using the Internet and virtual point-to-point channels. Remote connected PCs act as though they are physically connected to the central site LAN. VPNs support some client/server applications. Microsoft Exchange Server and Microsoft Outlook are supported by Windows virtual private networking.

BENEFITS • VPNs offer direct cost savings over leased lines and long-distance calls because they use shared communications facilities. VPNs also offer indirect cost savings such as reduced personnel training, increased flexibility, and network scalability.

Traditional corporate networks are built using leased T-carrier channels. T-carrier channel charges are based upon tariffs that include installation fees, monthly fixed costs, and mileage charges. Leased connections to the public Internet at the same speed typically cost less because the mileage charges are much less. Leased Internet lines offer added cost advantages because prices are often tiered according to usage. Many businesses require a full T-1 or T-3 channel only during peak activity periods during the day. They do not need the full T-1/T-3 bandwidth most of the time. Sometimes burstable T-1 channels are offered. A burstable T-1 channel provides on-demand bandwidth up to T-1 capacity with flexible pricing. Customers signing up for a full T-1 but having an average traffic load of 512 Kbps pay less than a T-1 customer whose average traffic load is 768 Kbps.

Because many VPN virtual, point-to-point links can be made using a single Internet access channel, companies do not have to support multiple physical connections to remote sites, thus reducing equipment and support costs. Traditional corporate networks use dial-up modems and ISDN to service branch offices, telecommuters, and mobile workers. This requires additional equipment connecting into the corporate headquarters network. With virtual private networking, T-carrier channels connect the corporate network to the public Internet or a private IP network. Branch offices and mobile workers connect to the public Internet using dial-up modems, or ISDN channels as appropriate. VPN channels then carry their data to the corporate network without installing any added equipment. Thus, an enterprise can reduce WAN connection setup and maintenance by replacing modems and ISDN connections with T-carrier channels that carry remote user, LAN–to–LAN, and Internet traffic at the same time.

VPNs may also reduce the need for technical support personnel because connectivity is standardized on IP and VPN security. Outsourcing VPN implementation and operation to an ISP can reduce internal technical support requirements, because the ISP takes over many network support tasks.

VPN Deployment Issues • The two primary VPN deployment issues are security and performance. TCP/IP and the Internet were not originally designed with either issue as a primary concern. Initially the number of Internet users and the types of Internet applications did not require security or guaranteed performance.

VPNs running on the public Internet must act as reliable substitutes for dedicated leased lines or other WAN links. This requires adding technologies for guaranteeing security and network performance to the Internet. Standards for network data security on IP networks permit creating VPNs using

IP networks. Work on guaranteed performance is under development. Service providers have not yet deployed network performance technologies.

VPNs provide four critical functions to ensure data security:

- Authentication—Ensuring that data accurately identifies its source.
- Access control—Restricting unauthorized users from using the network.
- Confidentiality—Preventing reading or copying data as it traverses the Internet.
- Data integrity—Ensuring that no data tampering occurs on the Internet.

Different password-based, remote authentication, and digital certificates are used to authenticate users on a VPN and to control access. Encrypting data that traverses the VPN guards information privacy.

ENCRYPTION • Virtual private networking software employs data encryption to assure security while communications are in progress. This encryption process is invisible to the user. Data is encrypted and decrypted using known public encryption algorithms with special keys assigned to the VPN session. While such encryption can be broken, it would require more time than the session duration to break the data encryption.

TUNNELING • Tunneling is encapsulating data, protocol framing, and IP packets that travel through an IP network. This encapsulation forms a tunnel through the IP network directly from the remote PC to the central site LAN. Communications traveling through this tunnel are encrypted.

Originally private networks used leased hard-wired channels between sites. These channels were dedicated to carrying voice and data traffic from a single enterprise. To extend such a private network concept to the Internet, where the traffic from many users passes over the same channels simultaneously, tunnels are created. Tunneling encapsulates data in IP packets, hiding the underlying routing and switching infrastructure of the Internet from both senders and receivers. These encapsulated packets are also protected against snooping by outsiders using data encryption.

VPNs are dynamic, with channels set up and torn down as communications needs dictate. A VPN is formed logically, regardless of the physical structure of the Internet. Unlike leased lines used in traditional networks, VPN channels do not maintain permanent links between end-points. When a VPN channel between two sites is needed, it is created. When the VPN channel is no longer needed, it is torn down, making the Internet resources available for other users.

Tunnels have either an individual computer or a LAN with a security gateway as an end-point. LAN-to-LAN tunneling has a security gateway at each end-point serving as the interface between the tunnel and the private LAN. Users on either LAN connect to the tunnel transparently to communicate with each other. Client-to-LAN tunnels are usually set up for mobile users needing to connect to the corporate LAN. The remote mobile user initiates creation of a tunnel to exchange traffic with the corporate network. Special VPN client software runs on the mobile user's computer to communicate with the gateway protecting the destination LAN.

Windows has VPN software for creating and managing tunnels between a remote client and a security gateway. Other software creates tunnels between a pair of security gateways. Such VPN software provides good low-cost choices for small networks that do not have a heavy traffic load. Such software runs on existing servers and share resources with them. The Windows VPN software is good for client–to–LAN connections.

Developing New Business Using the Internet

The Internet Tool Box, as advertised on television, is all that you need to start an Internet-oriented business. Or, should you pay IBM $500 to set up a Web site for you, including domain name registration and Web page development. These products and services make it seem easy to set up Internet business and have money sent to you in buckets.

Business reality is harsher. The Internet does not make a business any easier to set up. The Internet is a new way to extend the reach of a business to customers planet-wide. The Internet is a mechanism to provide 24/7 sales support, customer service, and order entry. But a Web site and a catchy domain name alone do not make a business. Domain names that have been registered and not used, or have been used and the business has failed, are sold at:

- greatdomains.com
- 1stedomain.com
- hotwebnames.com
- domain-4sale.com
- thedomainauction.com
- domainbook.com

In the next few years, many Internet startups without good funding and sales will fail. It should be interesting to see what Internet domain names come up for sale.

Some of the most successful Internet businesses have not-so-obvious Internet names, e.g., Yahoo, Amazon, and eBay. Wouldn't Search, Books, and Auctions be more descriptive of the services they initially offered? So more memorable names are not common, descriptive words, but simple words that are heavily promoted as being the Web destination for specific products.

THE BETTER MOUSE TRAP MISCONCEPTION

The appealing business concept with the Internet is that no fixed facilities are required to open a business. Bricks and mortar are not needed to open shop. Further, a Web page can be very impressive, making a business appear more substantial to the Internet customer. The Internet is one of the most cost-effective ways to deliver information. It certainly is cheaper than printing stacks of brochures and paper (the Internet customer prints them for you). However, if you are selling products on the Internet, don't those products have to be manufactured, inventoried, delivered, invoiced, and supported? The behind-the-scenes Internet business functions require bricks and mortar facilities for manufacturing, inventories, etc. The major benefit is that one relatively small bricks and mortar facility can service a planet-wide Internet business. This might make an Internet-based business a better mousetrap than a bricks and mortar business.

However, you might build the best Internet business and have no one come to your store. Having a clever and spectacular Web site does not generate sales by itself. Being listed in lots of Internet search engines does not guarantee customers will be directed to your Internet store Web site. Becoming a link exchange (http://www.bcentral.com/?leindex) member is not necessarily a solution to generating high Web site traffic and Internet sales. The real key to Internet success is becoming a viable business first and then an Internet business second. While it is possible to be an Internet business first, there must be a business before it can be an Internet business. If information services are alone provided, they must be researched, published, and tested before an Internet business can be created.

SERVICE ORIENTATION

The Internet is an opportunity to expand and provide better customer service. Businesses can automate parts of customer service, saving costs. Virtually all computer product vendors have Web pages that permit downloading the latest hardware driver programs or program service packs from the Web. Unfortunately, the Web page location for such customer service updates is often hidden within the larger Web site. Help pages and sales documentation pages should be readily accessible (they should be "slap you in the face" visible) at any Web site.

When we think of purchasing anything today, our first research into the type of product and its features is done using the Internet. These purchases range from hot tubs and automobiles, to computer and electronics equipment, to clothes. The Internet makes shopping easy. All kinds of information on special or specific products lie literally at your fingertips. However, many Web sites and businesses do not have a good perspective and service orientation presented at their Web site. Our Web sites are included in that category. Customers surf the Web for information. The content and easy access to information (the content) is most important. A Web site provides customer service first and then sells second. Sites that make the service they provide complex and difficult to find do not have a good customer service orientation.

REAL WORLD DELIVERY

Businesses that advertise with traditional television, radio, and print media as well as on the Web are likely to be more successful than those that advertise on the Web alone. Businesses that deliver good cost-effective products and services in tune with customer needs will flourish regardless of the Internet. However, the Internet represents a new mechanism for providing cost-effective customer service. It permits customers to have the latest information on the products and services you offer. An Internet Web site lets customers know that you are an active business and can give them helpful information for free.

An interesting site is www.repairnow.com. How is their customer service orientation? You can immediately point to the problem area to find helpful information. They can make money by referring you to qualified service professionals when repairs are beyond your capability (or desire) to perform. In this case, customer service orientation is linked to real world delivery. Further, there are no busy advertisements that distract you from the information that you need.

DOT COM (.COM) BUSINESS OPPORTUNITIES

What are some Dot COM (.COM) business opportunities? Actually any idea that provides good information to potential customers and links to delivering real world products and services is a good .COM business idea. I just checked one of my ideas out and it is available. So if you do this idea, you owe me. How about setting up a fraud clearinghouse Internet business? It could be called report-a-fraud.com. (Yup, I did register the name and it is for sale.) A database of scams would be built. State, person's name, company name, type of scam, etc. queries would access fraud descriptions. Persons reporting a fraud or checking out legitimate business solicitations could call the business on the phone or go to the Web site to report a fraud or seek information. The database would build itself from customer queries and reports. People uncertain of fraudulent behavior would have instant access to reports on fraudulent businesses or businesses that treated customers poorly. Report-a-fraud would only report what is reported to it. So a business with several or many angry customers is likely a fraudulent operation. However, it is up to the caller to decide about the business because report-a-fraud makes no recommendations to people asking about frauds. Finally, the real world link would be to lawyers that could sue the fraudulent business. They would be local to the defrauded person or to where the fraudulent business operated.

This is just an idea that requires real world information services, advertising, customer service representatives, and more to make it a viable business.

RETAIL/WAREHOUSE BUSINESS MODEL • The Internet can make retail organizations more competitive. Most retail outlets in the 1960s kept significant inventories of products for their customers. The investment in inventory was a significant business cost. Companies like WalMart reinvented the retail business. WalMart reduced inventories by having a minimum inventory at each store (what you saw on the shelf was it) that was replenished based upon sales. When an item sold, it was reported immediately to a warehouse facility that loaded a replacement item on a truck for delivery the next day. In this fashion, items that sold were tracked closely, and store inventories were reduced, making WalMart a cost-competitive retailer. Today most all retail businesses follow this model.

Amazon.com took this one step further by setting up a book sales business that was only a Web store. They could succeed because a book is a book is a book. There is no difference in quality on books sold off the Web or sold in stores. Bookstores permit you to see the books before you buy (a kind of try before you buy), but if you know what book you want, trying before buying is unnecessary. The cost of selling books in volume from a single warehouse site (they have more than a single warehouse now) is much less than warehousing the books and selling them in retail stores. However, how are returns handled? When purchases are made from a warehouse facility, the buyer must pay for the shipping cost of the return. There are other steps involved as well that make customer service not as good as the customer service provided by a bookstore.

RETAIL BUSINESS MODEL • Many companies are still experimenting with their retail model to find the optimal combination of Internet warehouse sales and local storefront customer support. It will be very interesting to see how Dell, Compaq, and Gateway fare in the future. Dell is all Internet sales, Gateway has new company-run Gateway Country stores, and Compaq sells through its existing retail outlets and also off the Internet. The most interesting retail combination is Compaq. They sell PCs off the Internet at higher prices than in local stores. The lowest cost PCs in Compaq retail outlets are special configurations that are designed to be loss leaders to bring customers into the retail outlet. Those loss leader PCs have the exact same configuration as the higher priced PCs sold on the Compaq Web site. However, the Web site information easily misleads one into thinking that the Web site PC has better features. Some features that the loss leader PCs have are not listed at the Compaq Web site.

Other types of businesses cannot sell their most important products using warehouses. Think of restaurants and movie theaters. They require local facilities. How will the Internet impact them? As home theater systems become more sophisticated, expect to see Blockbuster Video and many movie theaters disappear. Movie distribution will be by the Internet. You will purchase the movie from a Sony or CBS (Turner-MGM) Web site and have it downloaded to your PC-controlled entertainment system for viewing at your convenience.

Service businesses should fare well, but will need to register with Internet service business directories as a new form of advertising (e.g., www.repairnow.com). Newspapers and magazines are moving to the Internet. Why keep paper when one can have electrons instead? Some newspapers and magazines charge for information access while others make money off advertising. Of course, you cannot read your newspaper on a commuter train. Not easily just yet, but soon with new PDAs and wireless communications.

Brain Teaser

Service Orientation

A helpful Microsoft program is REGCLEAN. There are two versions of the program — one works and one does not. They can be downloaded from the Microsoft.com Web site. Go to Microsoft.com and try finding REGCLEAN.exe to download.

1. How are you going to find REGCLEAN.exe? It certainly is not on the entry page. What information does Microsoft (and most other large companies having Web sites) want you to reveal so they

can then provide more information? They want to know what type of customer you happen to be: home and personal, business, developer, education, IT professional, or partner/reseller? And they want to know the product family: Servers, Developer Tools, Office, or Windows?

2. Do we care what type of customer we are? No. What do we want? REGCLEAN.exe. So we use search and search to find REGCLEAN.exe. What do we find? A list of documents that contain references to REGCLEAN. Some sites give you a list of documents that have little information about what you are seeking. You might test one of the Microsoft documents.

3. At the top of the search page, three best bets are listed. These appear above the document listings. One best bet is **RegClean 4.1a Description and General Issues**. This should link to http://support.microsoft.com/support/kb/articles/Q147/7/69.asp. Clicking on this link should get you to a place to download the 12/30/97 version of REGCLEAN.exe.

The goal here is to illustrate how Web sites can be more or less service-oriented. Dell is another Web site that wants information from you before providing the information you seek. Try configuring a Dell PC. Which selection permits you to configure the most kick-butt laptop — home user or business? Again, do we care? I would prefer a simple link to configure a kick-butt laptop myself. Try some links at Amazon, eBay, and other Web sites. What do you think of their service orientation?

Accessing the Internet

Many of the new Internet business opportunities and uses will depend upon high-speed access to the Internet. As I write, my high-speed link is down and I am relegated to dial-up Internet connectivity. This is like withdrawing from drugs. Yesterday, I uploaded pictures for this book to our Web site so they could be downloaded by Prentice Hall. The file size was 58MB. AOL does not permit sending files any larger than 16MB via email. Using my high-speed cable modem Internet access, I was able to post the 58MB file in about nine minutes. This is an upload speed of over 6MB per minute. Awesome! Today it took over 39 minutes to post an 8MB file using a dial-up link. As I said, using low-speed Internet access is like withdrawing from drugs.

Access to the Internet is provided by:

1. Dial-up Internet access:

    a. Using analog telephone lines or Plain Old Telephone Service (POTS).

    b. Using ISDN Basic Rate Interface (BRI) service.

2. Cable modems provided by the Community Antenna Television service, or better known as cable TV (CATV).

3. Digital Subscriber Lines (DSLs) sold by the Local Exchange Carrier (LEC) or by other competitive telephone service companies.

4. Radio Frequency (RF) access using Local Multi-point Distribution Service (LMDS) or satellite-based service.
5. Electrical power distribution services.

Some of these approaches offer high-speed access and continued high-speed access bandwidth growth. Others are more universally available planet-wide. This section generally addresses all these Internet access technologies, but focuses on cable modems and DLSs. These are the technologies that are in the front of the battle for telecommunications market dominance between LECs, long-distance companies, CLECs, and enterprises vying for a position in the telecommunications marketplace. In the next two or three years, RF technologies will join the battle as well.

An old hackers saying is, "The person owning the wire rules the world." That is why the number one target of hackers (including Steven Jobs and Stephen Wosniak) was the telephone company. The wire that helps companies rule the world is now changing. It can be telephone wire, CATV cable, the airwaves, or maybe the electrical power grid. The companies providing high-speed 24/7 Internet access will have the greatest opportunity to capture the money people will spend on communications, information, and entertainment services.

Dial-up Access

Dial-up access using normal telephone lines is the most universal form of Internet access. A PC uses a modem to send commands to and receive information from the Internet. The principal benefits of dial-up Internet access are:

- Dial-up access is available planet-wide using conventional wired phones and cellular telephones.
- Travelers can call into an ISP from most any location to access the Internet. In February 2000, I got my email while traveling in Ghana using AOL.
- Windows and Macintosh PCs support dial-up Internet access with low-cost modems.

The not-so-good things about dial-up Internet access are:

- Dial-up Internet access is slow. The maximum speed to analog modems is 56 Kbps and ISDN dial-up access is 128 Kbps. At these speeds, many minutes are required to transfer large files. Simple software updates that require 20MB downloads would take more than 30 minutes.

- Telephone company facilities supporting dial-up communications work on contention. Dial-up users contend for trunk lines to telephone toll offices and Internet users contend for access to ISP dial-up ports. This means that during peak activity periods, both voice and Internet calls could be blocked (no available trunk lines to complete the call). In some Silicon Valley towns, telephone service was effectively shut down from 6 PM to 1 to 2 AM by telephone subscribers surfing the Web. CO switches were designed to service telephone calls with holding times averaging four minutes. Internet access calls are much longer duration, with the average call being around 22 minutes or more. LECs complain that they now have to invest in new facilities to support such dial-up Internet access.
- Dial-up Internet access calls are costly unless they are non-toll calls. This means that calling a Baltimore ISP from the road can be quite expensive. Actually any hotel room phone call can be quite expensive, especially if it is a hotel near New York City or Boston. The local calls are all metered and the hotels often add extra fees, so surfing the Web for several hours every night can easily run more than a good dinner out and a movie. One solution is to use AOL (or Prodigy), because they provide worldwide local access to the Internet. Also, hotels often do not charge extra for 800-number (toll-free number) calls. Although AOL tacks an access fee on 800-number calls to it, this is often much less than the charges incurred if you were to make a local metered call. (Yes, long-distance interstate charges are lower than intrastate toll charges. The higher prices will be erased by local telephone market competition.)
- Dial-up lines are noisy and prone to error. Each call can use different telephone facilities that vary greatly in signal quality.
- Advanced telephone features such as call waiting can interfere with dial-up connections.

The main drawbacks of dial-up access are its slow speed and the connections are only for the duration of the call. This limits its ability to transfer large files, to view video, and to act as a universal communications appliance.

High-Speed Access

High-speed, 24/7 Internet access is provided by cable modems, DSLs, and by RF access. These approaches all support communications speeds ranging from several hundred Kbps to over one Mbps. Such speeds can support the large file transfers that are needed to maintain and upgrade Windows software, quickly surf image-intensive Web pages, and receive moderate-quality video transmissions. Our current high-speed Web use is mostly for maintaining and upgrading PC software and surfing image-intensive Web pages. We are soon to embark on video telephony between locations. One person telecommuter to work. On the telecommuting days, it would be nice to be able to carry on video telephone conversations whenever there are important business matters to cover. We plan to use Microsoft NetMeeting and virtual private networking to provide such video telephony.

Cable modems and DSLs in the Baltimore metropolitan area provide high-speed Internet access today. The same is true of most metropolitan areas throughout the U.S.

RF high-speed Internet access is likely to become available in the next few years. RF Internet access was discussed in Chapter 8. The benefits are similar to the high-speed Internet access benefits provided by both cable modems and DSLs. The only difference is that RF uses radio frequencies in the microwave range to carry high-speed digital transmission between the subscriber residence and the ISP providing Internet access. This is a different kind of pipe from coaxial cable and telephone cable.

Similarly, electrical power distribution systems can be used to provide high-speed Internet access. Again the benefits are similar to those provided by cable modems and DSLs. However, electrical power distribution, like RF, uses different technologies stemming from combinations of data communications and telephony technologies to transport high-speed digital data from subscriber residences to ISPs providing Internet access. The medium (in our analogy, the pipe or wire), the electrical signaling, and the protocols used to transport the data between the residence and an ISP are different for each of these approaches providing high-speed Internet access. Differences in these approaches are summarized in Table 9-2.

Electrical power distribution is a less promising approach to providing high-speed Internet access in the U.S. because digital transmission equipment must be deployed to bypass the transformers. Transformers reduce electrical power distribution voltage levels to the 110 volts used in the home. A transformer from an electronic viewpoint is similar in function to a loading coil. Transformers filter out high-frequency components, turning digital square waves into round waves. To utilize the electrical power distribution wire for high-speed Internet access, each electrical transformer must be bypassed by the digital signals. In the U.S., we use lower voltage levels in the home than they do internationally (110 volts vs. 220 volts). This translates into a transformer servicing fewer homes in the U.S. than Internationally. Thus, more bypass equipment is needed in the U.S. to service customer homes with high-speed digital transmission using electrical power lines. This makes electrical power distribution less economically feasible in the U.S. than internationally.

In the next 10 to 20 years, the type of high-speed Internet access connection used by residential subscribers will become fiber optic cable. We will soon need transmission speeds that are significantly above what can be delivered by DSLs and also above the speeds that coaxial cable can provide as well. Think of DSLs as a band-aid that the LECs can use to satisfy residential demand for high-speed Internet access. It is only a temporary solution to what residential users will demand within five years. If DSL is a band-aid, then cable modems are a patch. Cable modems are capable of supporting significantly higher transmission speeds (40 Mbps and higher) because coaxial cable has better electrical properties than telephone cable. However, in the long term, residential users will demand speeds above 100 Gbps. Such speeds will most likely be provided by fiber optic cable.

Table 9.2   *High-speed Internet Access Summary*

Type of Service	Medium	Availability	Transmission Speed	Supporting Vendor
Cable Modems	Coaxial cable and fiber optic cable	Now Not all cable systems offer these	200 Kbps to 1+ Mbps (today) Speeds significantly higher than DSL speeds are possible	CATV companies and AT&T
Digital Subscriber Lines (DSLs)	Telephone cable	Now All LEC areas are not covered	128 Kbps to 6 Mbps	LECs and CLECs
Radio Frequency (RF) via LMDS or Satellite	Microwave radio frequencies	1–5 years	Mbps each way, depending upon frequency	CLECs, Sprint, and other PCS companies
Electrical Power Distribution	Electrical wiring	Sometime, maybe Less economically appealing in the U.S.	Speeds similar to DSL	Electrical Power Companies

All these high-speed Internet access technologies are similar in that they provide 24/7 Internet connectivity. The interface at the user end is most often a 10-Mbps Ethernet LAN connection. Transmission speeds to the ISP are often asymmetric with speeds up to the ISP being slower than speeds from the ISP to the subscriber. Most subscribers using the Internet (surfing the Web) receive much more data than they send to the Internet. Mouse clicks select Web site URLs that are a few hundred characters tops to transmit from the subscriber PC to the ISP. The ISP responds by retrieving graphics-intensive Web pages that are several hundred thousand characters in size.

It is possible using a router to share a connection with other computers on the same Ethernet. In the future, residences will share these high-speed connections between multiple devices connected to a LAN. Devices on the LAN will be various televisions and electronic entertainment devices, appliances, and PCs.

The remainder of this chapter examines cable modems and DSL technologies. These technologies are currently the most widespread technologies offering high-speed Internet access. Cable modems are first because they have the early residential deployment lead. DSL connectivity should catch up to cable modem deployment soon. At this instant in time, I wish that both were available to me as opposed to using my laptop's dial-up modem. (The gas company construction cut the coaxial cable to my neighborhood, so the cable modem is down for the count.) Additionally, Verizon DSL is not available to me at this time. I checked by entering my phone number at the Verizon DSL Web page.

Cable Modems

Cable modems have the early lead in delivering high-speed digital transmission to consumers. This section describes cable modem network components and services.

Cable Television (CATV) subscribers are provided high-speed Internet access using cable modems attached to the CATV infrastructure. A cable modem is a modem that works using the Megahertz frequencies used in CATV. With a cable modem, the CATV subscriber is provided a 24/7 connection to the Internet as well as a standard CATV feed using the coaxial cable from the CATV service provider. Telephony, or voice telephone service, is not generally offered today with cable and cable modem service. Cable has the capability of providing high-quality voice service, but only a few CATV companies have entered the competition in that arena so far.

CATV systems have evolved over the years to accommodate new subscriber needs. Early CATV systems used coaxial cable that had a maximum frequency carrying capacity (or bandwidth) of 500MHz.

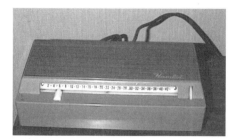

Figure 9–14   *Old cable TV tuner.*

CABLE TELEVISION NETWORK EVOLUTION

A single television channel broadcast across coaxial cable requires a bandwidth of 6MHz. This means that 6MHz of frequencies in the total range of frequencies broadcast across a coaxial cable are needed for every TV channel the coaxial cable carries. Because it makes calculations easy in this book, we are going to use 10MHz as the bandwidth required for a single TV channel. Original CATV systems supported the 12 broadcast channels with pushbutton tuners (see Figure 9-14). These tuners used a total of 10MHz times 12 channels, or 120MHz, to carry VHF (Very High Frequency) television channels to subscriber homes.

Soon 38-channel and then 50-channel tuners having infrared remote controllers replaced these tuners. Each new tuner configuration used more of the coaxial cable bandwidth. The 38-channel tuners used about 340MHz and the 50-channel tuners used nearly all the 500MHz that the CATV cable plant could carry. This cable plant could service millions of CATV subscribers because it was a broadcast signal from the CATV company head-end facility to all the subscriber terminals. (Broadcast is one-way, simplex transmission.) Pay-per-view movies on these systems were ordered using the telephone to call the CATV service provider so they would enable your decoder to unscramble the signal for the particular pay-per-view program selected. These cable systems did not typically support two-way communications across the coaxial cable.

To support two-way communications, the CATV companies would need to use two or four separate frequencies for each channel. When two-way communications were to the CATV head-end facility alone, only two frequencies would be needed. To communicate between remote sites, four frequencies would be required to establish a full duplex channel between the sites. The CATV head-end facility crosses the transmit and receive frequencies of each remote site so that the transmit path for one site is attached to the receive path for the other site, and vice versa. Because so many frequencies are required to implement remote site to remote site two-way communications on CATV systems, the first CATV systems were simplex broadcast only.

To send data over the CATV infrastructure, most CATV service operators upgrade their cable plane and use cable modems. A few cable companies do provide high-speed Internet access of sorts by having subscribers dial up an uplink connection to the Internet and then provide the downlink connection from the Internet using their 500MHz coaxial cable infrastructure.

To provide bi-directional high-speed cable transmission services, CATV operators generally upgrade their existing cable plant from 500MHz to 1GHz coaxial cable. This upgrade is also required to support the shift from standard television to the newer HDTV (High Definition Television). HDTV channels require roughly four times the digital transmission capacity of standard television channels. Because HDTV requires more bandwidth per channel, HDTV can use a substantial portion of the 1GHz coaxial cable bandwidth.

CABLE MODEM OPERATING FREQUENCIES

What makes cable modem operation possible and two-way communications possible on the new 1GHz cable plant is that the cable modems use OSI 802.2 and TCP/IP protocols to carry data from many subscribers back to the CATV head-end facility that contains a Cable Modem Termination System (CMTS). The CMTS talks to all attached cable modems, but cable modems can only talk to the CMTS. When two cable modems need to talk to each other, the CMTS relays messages between them. The cable modem takes the 802.2 data received from the modem OSI Layer 1, physical layer, and repackages it into 10-Mbps Ethernet CSMA/CD packets for delivery to the subscriber's PC.

Most cable modems have a 10-Mbps Ethernet data port interface. One might think that a 100-Mbps Ethernet port is needed to match the maximum 27-Mbps to 56-Mbps downstream speed of a cable modem. This is not true because many users share the downstream link.

The U.S. Multimedia Cable Network System (MCNS) cable modem standard specifies 10-Mbps Ethernet as the only data interface. The newer European standard is more open, allowing other interface types. Intel has announced that they are working on cable modems with a USB (Universal Serial Bus) interface. USB interface modems should make self-installation easy for novice users. U.S. cable modems now conform to the DOCSIS standard. DOCSIS is the Data Over Cable Service Interface Specification. It is the dominating U.S. cable modem standard defining technical specifications for both cable modems and the CMTS.

General 1GHz cable frequency assignments are shown in Figure 9-15. The first 500MHz of frequencies have the standard CATV assignments to assure backward-compatibility with existing cable tuners. CATV companies do not want to replace all their existing subscriber equipment when they upgrade to 1GHz cable plant on a wholesale basis. About 100 new digital TV channels and the downlink to the cable modems will be implemented in the frequencies ranging from 500MHz to 850MHz. At the same time, the uplink channels to the Internet will be implemented using a band of frequencies around 50MHz. HDTV channels will reside in the upper-most frequency band, between 850MHz and 1GHz.

There is room for growth in capacity on the 1GHz coaxial cable. After cable services expand and utilize all the new capacity afforded by the 1GHz cable, they can require that the old subscriber equipment be replaced by new subscriber equipment that no longer supports the original analog TV channel assignments that make CATV backward-compatible with older set-top boxes and television components. In the longer term, CATV companies will most likely need to scavenge capacity by using the lower frequencies currently maintaining compatibility with existing cable set-top boxes. This will no doubt raise cries of foul play from those who still watch their old black-and-white televisions. If the 1GHz coaxial cable does not provide sufficient long-term growth in transmission speed capacity, it can be upgraded again to 2GHz coaxial cable. Because coaxial cable is a better transmission medium and has the capability to carry higher frequencies, it is a patch-like solution that can provide high-speed (up to gigabits per second) Internet access for more than the next 10 years. In contrast, DSLs are a band-aid solution enabling the telephone companies to provide high-speed Internet access on their existing facilities. However, DSL is not capable of providing the higher speeds that are possible for coaxial cable. The telephone companies will need to run fiber into the home to compete with CATV telecommunications providers in about 10 to 15 years.

Cable modem uplink speed is less than downlink speed because less information flows from subscriber PCs into the Internet. General operating parameters for cable modems are listed in Table 9-3.

HIGH-DEFINITION TELEVISION

Digital TV (DTV) or Advanced TV (ATV) sets can display terrific 16:9 ratio, wide-screen, high-definition pictures with 720 or 1080 scanning lines. This contrasts with the 480 visible lines on current TVs using the old National Television Standards Committee (NTSC) analog television broadcast standards. ATVs can also receive up to six channels of Dolby CD-quality sound.

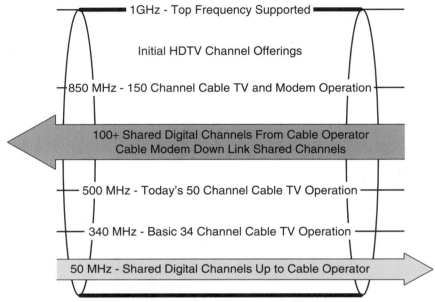

Figure 9–15 *CATV 1GHz cable frequencies.*

Table 9.3 *Cable Modem Operating Parameters*

Link Direction	Frequencies Used	Bandwidth	BPS Speed	Encoding
Upstream to CATV Head-end	5MHz to 65MHz	2MHz	3 Mbps	QPSK/16-QAM
Downstream from CATV Head-end	65MHz to 850MHz	6MHz to 8MHz	27 Mbps to 56 Mbps	QPSK/256-QAM

High-Definition Television (HDTV) is part of ATV. HDTV is new television technology providing wide-screen picture quality similar to movies and surround-sound quality equivalent to a Compact Disc (CD). Some television stations on limited channels are transmitting HDTV technology. HDTV uses digital rather than analog signal transmission. So, signals producing crystal-clear pictures and sound are received or you get nothing. There is very little in between.

The FCC has assigned broadcast channels for ATV, including HDTV transmissions. ATV also permits using channels for four, six, or more Standard-Definition Television (SDTV) program streams simultaneously (and/or various data and audio channels), instead of one HDTV signal. Commercial and public broadcast stations are deciding how to implement ATV and

HDTV. HDTV can be and increasingly will become available on CATV systems. HDTV uses MPEG file format and compression standards when sending video signals.

CABLE MODEM NETWORK COMPONENTS

Cable modems provide low-speed (typically 200 to 400 Kbps) uplinks to the Internet and high-speed (typically 800 to 1,200 Kbps) downlinks from the Internet. The cable modem's up- and downlinks are on shared channels. This means that performance can vary depending upon loading from other subscribers. In our experience with COMCAST cable modems, this has not been the case.

In Figure 9-16, the Internet user, Pete, sits at his office PC and connects through his local Ethernet to a cable modem. Not shown in the figure is an Ethernet hub that permits several PCs to be on the same Ethernet as the cable modem. In some cases, a router/switch is used to attach the cable modem's 10-Mbps Ethernet port to a 100-Mbps LAN. The switch permits high-speed LAN devices to run at 100 Mbps full duplex between one another while the cable modem access runs half-duplex at 10 Mbps.

The cable modem takes the 802.2 data received from its Ethernet port, encodes it using Quadrature Amplitude Modulation (QAM), and sends it across the CATV coaxial cable to the CMTS at the CATV head-end facility. The cable infrastructure consists of coaxial cable and fiber optic cable. This is referred to as a hybrid fiber coax system. The coaxial cable feeds into each subscriber residence while the fiber (which maybe a SONET ring or point-to-point connection) carries data from multiple cable terminations back to the CMTS at the head-end facility. The CATV head-end facility puts both TV signals that it receives from satellite broadcasts and other sources and the cable modem data onto the hybrid fiber coax distribution system.

The CATV head-end facility is the central distribution point for a CATV system. Video signals received from satellites and other sources are converted to appropriate TV channel frequencies, combined with locally broadcast channel signals, and then transmitted over the cable plant to subscriber residences. The CMTS is normally located at the head-end facility.

The CATV physical distribution system is a hybrid fiber coaxial cable network. Older CATV systems used only coaxial cable. New CATV systems use fiber transport from the head-end to optical nodes located in neighborhoods. This reduces noise and picture distortion. The fiber forms a high-speed backbone, distributing both broadcast video and two-way Internet communications around major geographic areas. The fiber plant may be a

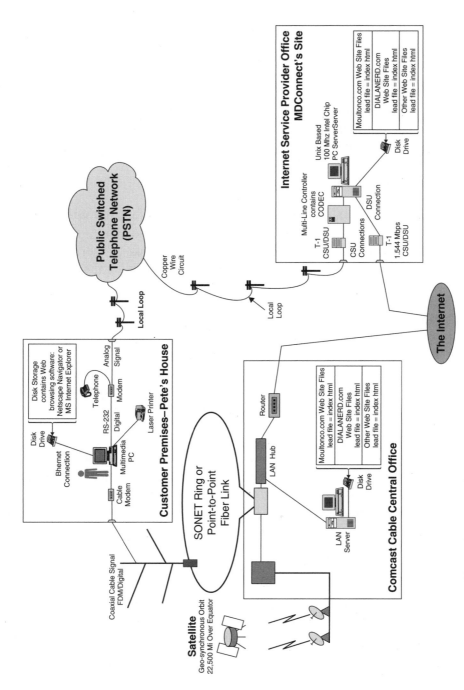

Figure 9–16 *Cable modem network components.*

Figure 9–17   *CATV neighborhood coax distribution node.*

SONET ring, but it is more often a star configuration with all optical node fibers terminating at a head-end facility.

The coax acts as the local distribution mechanism for individual CATV subscribers. Coaxial cable runs from the optical node to the subscriber residence. The coaxial cable part of the system is a trunk-and-branch configuration, like a tree (see Figure 9-17). The coax is attached to the fiber backbone to service neighborhoods from as few as 50 subscribers to as many as 1,000 subscribers, depending upon geography, communications load, and CATV services provided.

At the CATV central facilities, the fiber connection is split into a broadcast television feed and a LAN connection. The cable modem data then runs to the LAN and then into the Internet via routers and other networking components.

The shared networking facilities that may limit cable modem performance are the coaxial cable distribution facilities between the optical node and the subscriber residence and the LAN back at the CATV head end facility. Often data is cached on special servers, Web site space is provided, and email servers reside at the CATV head-end facility. These networking components are designed to reduce Internet delays for cable modem subscribers because the shared cable modem facilities are rarely a bottleneck when communicating with the Internet.

For example, I may be using the CUTEFTP program to upload 58 MB of images for this book to my Web site at speeds ranging from 900 Kbps to 1.1 Mbps while at the same time sending an email file using AOL at 64 Kbps. What causes the AOL file to go so slow? It is not the cable modem or the shared cable connection, but rather AOL limiting the transfer speed on its connections to the Internet. In virtually every case where cable modem performance was slow, testing revealed that it was the remote site that was slow, not the cable modem.

Because cable modems form a large network that uses TCP/IP, disk drives and printers shared on a PC can be shared with anyone on the cable modem network or the Internet. My ISP set up our Web server with Windows Server message block protocol. This permitted me to log on to the ISP's server and transfer files as though my PC and our Web server were on the same LAN. Cable modem companies view the ability to share disk drives and printers as a security risk for their subscribers. They recommend disabling Windows file and printer sharing features. There should be no problem with Windows file and printer sharing as long as resources are assigned a security password or a Windows NT domain controller controls access to them.

The cost of cable modem Internet access is similar throughout the U.S. In our area, COMCAST provides cable modems for $39.95 per month. Each residence can have two additional cable modem IP addresses for an additional $9.95 per month.

CABLE MODEM SERVICES

Cable modem subscriber fees cover rental and complete installation of a high-speed cable modem. The services also provide easy access to multimedia-rich national and local content such as news and weather using a customized Netscape browser. CATV services offering cable modems generally provide more than just high-speed 24/7 Internet access. They host Web pages for their subscribers, provide email, newsgroups, and chat rooms. When there are questions, there are customer support representatives available 24/7.

MAJOR MARKET VENDORS AND COMPETITION

There are several major players in the cable system market. They intend to provide both Internet access and entertainment for their subscribers. However, in the not-so-distant future, expect them to offer a total package of information, entertainment, and telephony services. Some major players are:

- Time Warner is a major player in the cable industry and provides the Road Runner high-speed on-line cable modem service. Time Warner Cable serves 21.3 million homes and more than 12.6 million customers. It has 34 cable clusters with 100,000+ subscribers. Time Warner and AOL are merging.
- AT&T acquired Tele-Communications Inc. (TCI), North America's largest cable operator. This aggressive maneuver could fundamentally alter the cable and communications industries, creating an enterprise that can offer voice, video, and data services to consumers nation-

wide. In acquiring TCI, AT&T potentially gains access to 33 million cable homes, or one-third of all homes in the U.S. TCI's owned and operated cable systems serve 17 million homes and TCI's joint venture partners serve another 16 million homes. This deal also highlights the central role cable can play as a conduit for competitive telecommunications services.

- Cox Communications is among the nation's largest broadband communications companies, serving over 6 million customers in more than 20 states. Cox provides an advanced broadband network of coaxial and fiber optic cables that delivers digital video, local and long-distance telephone, and high-speed Internet access services. Cox is rapidly evolving into a full-service provider of advanced video, voice, and data services for homes and businesses. Cox was first to deliver all these services using a single broadband network.
- Charter Communications serves approximately 6.2 million customers with a full range of traditional CATV services and now digital CATV services in some of its cable systems. Charter has introduced interactive video programming and high-speed Internet access services. They are also exploring telephony services.
- Cablevision Systems Corp. is one of the nation's leading telecommunications and entertainment companies that provides high-speed multimedia cable modems and CATV services to more than 3.4 million customers in three core markets: New York, Boston, and Cleveland.

Cable modems and digital cable technology make CATV systems a strong contender for the single source of all our entertainment, information, and communications needs.

Brain Teaser

Cable Modems

Go to a modem speed test site at: 1) http://www.datajett.com/modem.html or 2) http://homepage.tinet.ie/~leslie/testpage.htm. Run the modem speed tests there.

1. How does your modem stack up? My cable modem tested out at 78,100 characters per second for the large graphics image transfer at Site #1. At around 10 bits per character (used here to make computations easy,) that calculates out to be 781-Kbps transmission speed. Not too shabby.

2. Check out the exact same test at Site #2. My cable modem did 76,420 characters per second, or about 764 Kbps.

The goal of this exercise is to illustrate cable modem transfer speeds.

Digital Subscriber Lines

This section examines the final high-speed Internet access area, DSLs. DSL network components and architecture are presented and contrasted with cable modem networks for delivering high-speed digital communications to residential subscribers. DSL is just a pair of modems running over existing telephone wiring in a broader range of frequencies than is used for voice communications alone. Thus, DSL signifies a modem pair, and not a type of telephone line. This means that two modems attached to a line create a DSL. When a telephone company buys xDSL, it buys modems and attaches them to the lines they already own. Thus, DSL is really a new type of modem and not a line.

Employing the modem's DSL service provides a dedicated digital circuit from your home to the telephone company CO, over the existing analog telephone line. DSL overlays the existing networks so it also provides a separate channel for voice phone communication. This means voice and fax calls are carried at the same time high-speed data is flowing across the line. DSL uses the frequency spectrum between 0KHz–4KHz for analog voice, and 4KHz–2.2MHz for data. xDSL is a generic acronym for a family of dedicated services. The "x" designates:

Service Type	Down Speeds	Up Speeds
ADSL (Asymmetric Digital Subscriber Line)	1.544 to 8 Mbps	64 Kbps to 1.544 Mbps
ADSL (Lite)	1 Mbps	512 Kbps
HDSL (High-bit-rate Digital Subscriber Line)	1.5/2.048 Mbps	1.5/2.048 Mbps (4-wire)
SDSL (Single-line Digital Subscriber Line)	1.5/2.048 Mbps	1.5/2.048 Mbps (2-wire)
VDSL (Very-high-bit-rate Digital Subscriber Line)	13 Mbps - 52 Mbps	1.5 Mbps- 2.3 Mbps
IDSL (ISDN Digital Subscriber Line)	128 Kbps	128 Kbps
RADSL (Rate-Adaptive Digital Subscriber Line)	1.544 to 8 Mbps	64 Kbps to 1.544 Mbps
UDSL (Universal Digital Subscriber Line) (Also called "splitter-less" DSL, as it doesn't require a splitter)	1.0 Mbps	300 Kbps

DSLs are the telephone company's answer to cable modems. DSL technology provides high-speed data transmission and a single telephone voice channel over existing local loop wiring. In this manner, they preserve the telephone company's investment in its wiring infrastructure while answering the need for high-speed Internet access.

DSL requires equipment to be installed at both the customer premise and in the telephone company CO. This equipment uses analog transmission over a wider range of frequencies than the standard 4,000-cycle voice channel combined with sophisticated modem encoding and decoding algorithms to provide transmission speeds typically ranging between 640 Kbps to 13 Mbps.

DSL equipment is limited to operating within 18,000 feet of the telephone company CO. Higher speeds require that the customer premise be within 12,000 feet of the telephone company Class 5 CO.

DSL equipment connects to a telephone at the customer premise as well as directly to the PC using (typically) Ethernet. Similarly, the telephone voice channel is split at the telephone company CO and routed into the branch exchange switch, while the PC connection is routed to a LAN. This telephone company CO LAN is then connected via high-speed digital channels to the Internet.

DSL availability and rates vary. For a 128 Kbps/384 Kbps channel, Pac-Tel charges $89 per month. If the speed is increased to 384 Kbps/1.5 Mbps, the cost increases to $279 per month. These costs are substantially higher than cable modem costs. At one time, Verizon was offering Infospeed DSL service with a top speed of 680 Kbps/ 7.1 Mbps for a monthly fee of $189 per month. It currently has limited availability.

DIGITAL SUBSCRIBER LINE TECHNOLOGY

Transmission speed limitations of voice band lines come from the installed telephone company network. Filters at the edge of the telephone company network limit voice-grade bandwidth to 3.3KHz. Without these filters, copper lines can carry MHz frequencies with substantial attenuation (signal soak-up). Attenuation increases with line length and transmission frequency. It constrains transmission speed over 24-gauge twisted pair wire imposing practical limits like:

Service Type	Service Speed	Effective Distance
DS-1 (T-1)	1.544 Mbps	18,000 feet
E-1	2.048 Mbps	16,000 feet
DS-2	6.312 Mbps	12,000 feet
E-2	8.448 Mbps	9,000 feet
One-quarter STS-1	12.960 Mbps	4,500 feet
One-half STS-1	25.920 Mbps	3,000 feet
STS-1	51.840 Mbps	1,000 feet

Local loop configurations vary tremendously worldwide. In some places, 18,000 feet covers virtually every subscriber, while in the U.S., 18,000 feet may cover less than 80% of local loops. Most local loops have loading coils that must be removed to install any DSL service as well as ISDN. Telephone companies have programs to shrink average loop length largely to increase the capacity of existing COs. This typically involves remote installation of access nodes from COs. These create distribution areas with maximum subscriber loops of 6,000 feet from an access node. Remote access nodes are connected to the CO by T-1/E-1 lines using HDSL or fiber. In suburban communities, a distribution service area averages about 1,500 homes, and in urban areas, about 3,000 homes. The number of homes connected diminishes as transmission speeds increase. Fiber To The Curb systems (FTTC) offering STS-1 rates may only reach 20 homes in some suburban areas.

DSL transmits digitally compressed video that includes error correction to reduce errors from impulse noise on the video signal. Such error correction adds about 20 ms of delay to the signal transmission. This is fine for LAN and IP-based wide area data communications applications. However, for interactive video conferencing, the end-to-end delay must be kept to less than 150 ms.

DSL supports circuit-switched, packet-switched, and in the future, ATM-switched data. DSL must connect to PCs and TV set-top boxes at the same time. These applications create a complicated protocol and installation environment for DSL modems, moving them beyond simple data transmission and reception functions.

DIGITAL SUBSCRIBER LINE OFFERINGS

There are several DSL offerings. These offerings vary in up-line and down-line speed. We discuss these different types of DSLs including ADSL, RADSL, SDSL, HDSL, and VDSL. They are different technologies and services aimed at providing high-speed digital transmission over conventional telephone wiring (using existing telephone company wiring plant) to consumer premises.

ASYMMETRIC DIGITAL SUBSCRIBER LINES • ADSL transmits an asymmetric data stream, with higher speed downstream to the subscriber and much lower speed upstream. The reason for this has to do with the installed cable. Twisted pair telephone wires are bundled together in 50-pair cables. Cables coming out of a CO have hundreds to thousands of pairs bundled together. Thus, individual lines from a CO to a subscriber are spliced together from several cable sections as they spread out from the CO. Bellcore claimed the average telephone subscriber had 22 splices in their line. Twisted pair wiring is designed to minimize interference between signals caused by radiation or capacitive coupling. The process is not perfect and signals do couple. The coupling effect increases as frequencies and the length of line increase. This requires ending the DSL assigned local loop at the customer premise. (Analog local loops are usually run through a neighborhood, and then tapped into to deliver analog telephone service.) Thus, if you try to send symmetric signals in many pairs within a cable, the data rate and length of line you can attain are significantly limited.

ADSL downstream speeds depend on distance as follows:

Distance	Speed
18,000 feet	1.544 Mbps (T-1)
16,000 feet	2.048 Mbps (E-1)
12,000 feet	6.312 Mbps (DS-2)
9,000 feet	8.448 Mbps

Upstream speeds range from 16 Kbps to 640 Kbps

Individual offerings today offer a variety of speed arrangements, from a minimum set of 1.544/2.048 Mbps down and 16 Kbps up to a maximum set of 8.448 Mbps down and 640 Kbps up. These arrangements operate in a frequency band above basic telephone service. Thus, basic telephone service remains independent and undisturbed, even when a premise's ADSL modem fails.

ADSL focuses on two applications, interactive video and high-speed data. Interactive video covers movies on demand, other video on demand (delayed TV segments), video games, video catalogs, and video information retrieval. Data communications covers Internet access, telecommuting (remote LAN access), and specialized network access. ADSL's strength is that it can run across existing telephone lines, which are potentially 750 million connections. New cabling needed for cable modems or Fiber To The Neighborhood (FTTN) reaches comparatively few homes and almost no small businesses.

In the mid 1990s, Bell Atlantic (now Verizon) ran an ADSL trail in Northern Virginia. They connected employee homes via ADSL to a CO to test the ability of ADSL to deliver video on demand to employees' homes (see Figure 9-18). The test was successful in demonstrating that ADSL could deliver video on demand similar to CATV. This video distribution was not like CATV because it delivered only a single movie on demand. It was a single

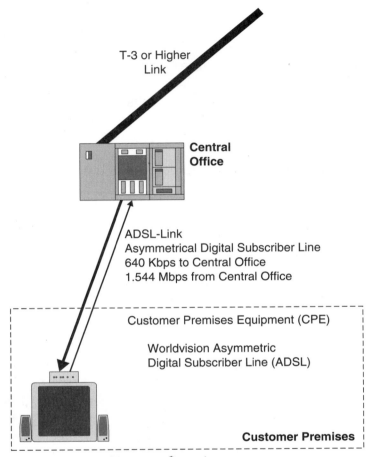

T-3 or Higher
Link

**Central
Office**

ADSL-Link
Asymmetrical Digital Subscriber Line
640 Kbps to Central Office
1.544 Mbps from Central Office

Customer Premises Equipment (CPE)

Worldvision Asymmetric
Digital Subscriber Line (ADSL)

Customer Premises

Figure 9–18 *ADSL test configuration.*

video channel or a two-video channel distribution system, not a 200+ channel distribution system. Delivering 200+ video channels with DSL would necessitate special video switching equipment at telephone company COs.

ADSL LITE • ADSL Lite (sometimes called splitter-less DSL) is a low-speed version of ADSL that eliminates the installation of a remote premise splitter. Elimination of the POTS splitter simplifies DSL installation and reduces costs. ADSL Lite can work over longer distances than full-rate ADSL, making it more widely available to mass market consumers. ADSL Lite supports both data and voice and provides an upgrade path to full-rate ADSL.

The Universal DSL Working Group leads the effort to introduce ADSL Lite. The Universal DSL Working Group worked to develop a worldwide G.Lite standard within the International Telecommunications Union (ITU)

Study Group 15. The ITU standard G.992.2 was approved in October 1998. Additional standards work can be expected in ANSI TIE1.4, the ATM Forum, and the ADSL Forum to address issues such as compatibility with home wiring and network interfaces.

HIGH-BIT-RATE DIGITAL SUBSCRIBER LINES (HDSLS) • HDSL is a better way of transmitting T-1 or E-1 over twisted pair copper lines. It requires lower bandwidth and uses no repeaters. The more advanced modulation techniques of HDSL transmit 1.544 Mbps or 2.048 Mbps in bandwidths from 80KHz to 240KHz rather than the 1.5MHz required by the T-1 Alternate Mark Inversion (AMI) scheme. HDSL supports these speeds on 24-gauge wire up to 12,000 feet in length. This is accomplished by using two lines for T-1 and three lines for E-1, each operating at one-half or one-third speed.

Typical HDSL applications include PBX network connections, cellular antenna stations, digital loop carrier systems, interexchange POPs, Internet servers, and private data networks. Because HDSL is the most mature DSL technology and has speeds greater than a megabit per second, it can be used for premises Internet and remote LAN access.

SINGLE-LINE DIGITAL SUBSCRIBER LINES (SDSLS) • SDSL is a single-line version of HDSL. T-1 or E-1 signals are transmitted over a single twisted pair. In most cases, it operates over existing telephone service, permitting a single line to support both an existing voice phone and T-1/E-1 transmission simultaneously. SDSL has an important advantage over HDSL because it fits the market for individual subscriber premises that are often equipped with only a single telephone line. SDSL is desired for applications requiring symmetric transmission speeds (e.g., servers and remote LANs). SDSL does not extend beyond 10,000 feet.

RATE-ADAPTIVE DIGITAL SUBSCRIBER LINES (RADSLS) • RADSL provides the same up- and down-link speeds as ADSL, but RADSL adjusts dynamically to different lengths and qualities of twisted pair local loops. RADSL connects over different lines at varying speeds. Transmission speed can be selected when the line synchs up, during a connection, or as the result of a signal from the CO. RADSL runs up to 18,000 feet, but 12,000 feet is the limit for the highest transmission speeds.

VERY-HIGH-BIT-RATE DIGITAL SUBSCRIBER LINES (VDSLS) • VDSL is asymmetric transceivers at data rates higher than ADSL but over shorter lines. While there are no general standards for VDSL, the following downstream speeds are generally proposed:

12.96 Mbps	(1/4 STS-1)	4,500 feet of wire
25.82 Mbps	(1/2 STS-1)	3,000 feet of wire
51.84 Mbps	(STS-1)	1,000 feet of wire

Upstream rates range from 1.6 Mbps to 2.3 Mbps. A symmetric variation of VDSL supports speeds up to 34 Mbps on both up- and down-links.

Shorter lines impose fewer transmission constraints, so the basic transceiver technology is much less complex, even though speeds are ten times faster with VDSL than ADSL. VDSL targets ATM networks, removing the channelization and packet handling required by ADSL. VDSL has passive network terminations, enabling more than one VDSL modem to be connected to the same premise line similar to extension phones connecting into home wiring.

VDSL still provides error correction. As public-switched network ATM is now beginning to be deployed, VDSL is likely to transmit conventional circuit- and packet-switched traffic. Passive network terminations have some technical and regulatory problems. This is likely to make VDSL look identical to ADSL with inherent active termination and the capability for higher data rates. VDSL operates over POTS and ISDN, with both separated from VDSL signals by passive filtering.

UPGRADING DIGITAL LOOP CARRIERS

Digital Loop Carriers (DLCs) comprise the LEC's local loop infrastructure connecting subscribers located more than 18,000 feet (about 3.5 miles as the wire runs) to a CO. DLC systems are physical pedestals containing line cards that concentrate residential traffic onto digital circuits. To provide end-users with xDSL capability, telephone companies retrofit the line cards in the DLC systems. The problem is that some cards physically do not fit into the DLC pedestals. When the new line cards fit into the DLC pedestals, retrofitting is a cost-effective solution for telephone companies because they do not need to update their infrastructure to provide xDSL services. About 30% of U. S. telephone customers are estimated to be on DLC systems. Such systems are concentrated in suburbs where more affluent people reside. A major target market for xDSL is this affluent residential suburban population.

DIGITAL SUBSCRIBER LINE COMPONENTS

DSL has several key components installed at the telephone company CO and in the subscriber residence. These components are shown in Figure 9-19.

At the subscriber residence, an ADSL or DSL Network Interface Device (NID) is installed. This device is essentially the bandwidth splitter that splits off a voice-grade analog channel from the DSL channel that runs over the telephone wire into the telephone company CO. Connected to it are an analog telephone and an ADSL Network Termination (ANT) device. The network termination device is the DSL modem that converts the DSL data signal into 10-Base T Ethernet.

The DSL signals travel over the telephone lines into the CO where they terminate in a Digital Subscriber Line Access Module (or Multiplexer), or DSLAM. The DSLAM is or contains the DSL modem at the telephone company CO. It splits the analog telephone channel from the signal and routes it to the telephone company CO switch. It also converts the data signal to 10-Base T Ethernet and routes that to a LAN that in turn connects to the Internet.

Both cable modems and DSL connections have an Ethernet connection (which are shared facilities) at some point in the path from the subscriber's PC to the Internet. This Ethernet connection is in addition to the Ethernet connection at the subscriber's facility. What I am driving at here is that both DSL and cable modems have similar shared facilities. One is not superior to the other in that regard. The typical sales allegation is that many users potentially cause it to become overloaded and slow performance shared by the cable transmission path. The bandwidth there is much larger than the bandwidth delivered by DSL over existing telephone wiring. As a result, it is highly unusual to experience any performance degradation due to the shared cable modem facilities. The shared Ethernet in the DSL and cable modem COs represents a greater potential for causing performance degradation than does the shared cable facilities.

BENEFITS FOR TELEPHONE COMPANIES

While based upon similar technology, ISDN and ADSL are not the same. ISDN provides two voice channels or a 128-Kbps data channel, while ADSL is a data pipe with an asymmetrical bandwidth of up to 8 Mbps downstream and 1 Mbps upstream. ADSL is an overlay network providing high-speed data along with an existing voice-grade connection that does not require the expensive and time-consuming switch upgrades required to implement ISDN.

ISDN provides only limited video and high-speed data transmission capabilities. It is more flexible when it comes to advanced telephone services than is DSL. So users needing more telephone functionality and no high-speed video are better candidates for ISDN. Anyone with high-speed data and video transmission requirements would most certainly choose DSL over ISDN if it were available.

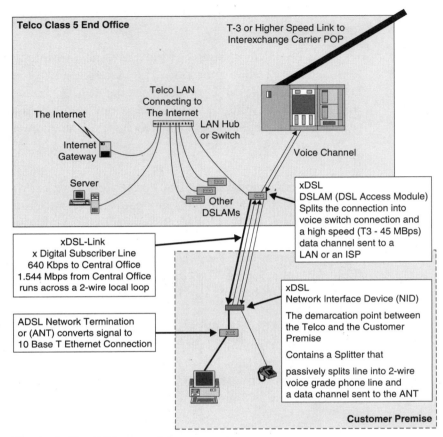

Figure 9–19 *DSL network components.*

NEW FCC RULINGS

The FCC has recently attempted to promote more competition in the high-speed Internet access arena. In late 1999, the FCC ruled that LECs must allow competitors to sell DSL services on the same phone lines that the local carriers are using to carry voice services. This is called line sharing. This ruling means that CLECs and other telephone company competitors no longer have to wait to get separate lines installed to offer DSL service. This should get DSL services expanded faster.

The ruling also means CLECs won't need to lease separate lines to offer DSL service, saving them money that can reduce DSL prices. Installation fees are also likely to drop. When a new line is installed, the LEC sends a technician to the subscriber's house. The resulting installation costs get passed on to customers.

The CLECs complain that LECs, which own the local phone lines in the U.S., overcharge them for leasing local loops. Such local loop leasing charges range from $3 to $40 per month. The FCC ruling says LECs can't charge competitors more than they charge their own subsidiaries that sell DSL via line sharing for the local loops. LEC FCC filings state that there is no additional cost to them to use existing phone wires to simultaneously carry DSL.

This should result in more widespread DSL implementation and lower DSL costs.

Brain Teaser

DSL Availability

Go to the Verizon Web site. Select **Products and Services**, then **Home and Family**. Pick **Maryland** as the state for former Bell Atlantic customers. Find the InfoSpeed DSL service offering and check availability by entering my phone number, **410 988-9294**.
1. Do you get the "We are sorry message?" or is DSL now available in my neighborhood. If it is available, drop me an email at help@dialanerd.com.
2. Check some other phone numbers like 301 596-9206 and 410 531-3423. Are any of those numbers in areas where DSL is available? Guess it is lucky that I have a Comacst@Home cable modem.
The goal of this exercise is to illustrate DSL availability.

■ Summary

This chapter has focused on telecommunications technologies providing new business opportunities. These technologies are centered mainly on the Internet. This chapter described the Internet and Internet technologies. It then examined some key Internet telecommunications applications that help enterprises work more effectively regardless of where they are located. Finally, the chapter described the telecommunications technologies providing high-speed internet access, including cable modems and DSLs.

▲ Chapter Review Questions

1. *What technology is at the core of the Internet?*
   A. HTML
   B. WWW
   C. TCP/IP
   D. DSL

2. *What technology is used by the World Wide Web?*
   A. DSL
   B. Cable modems
   C. HTML
   D. TCP/IP

3. *What is closely related to HTML?*
   A. HTTP
   B. FTP
   C. RADSL
   D. Gnutella

4. *What is a key Internet architectural feature?*
   A. HTML
   B. DSL
   C. Cable modems
   D. NAPS

5. *How many major NAPs are in the Internet today?*
   A. 5
   B. 15
   C. 50
   D. 100

6. *Domain name suffixes are?*
   A. .ac, .uk, and .nz
   B. .com, .org, and .mil
   C. .rec, .web, and .net
   D. All of the above
   E. None of the above

7. *What type of service is the Internet at OSI Layer 3?*
   A. TCP
   B. Connection-less
   C. Connection-oriented
   D. Circuit-switched

8. *What type of service is the Internet at OSI Layer 4?*
   A. IP
   B. Connection-less
   C. Connection-oriented
   D. Circuit-switched

9. *What is the top cable modem speed?*
   A. 56 Mbps
   B. 10 Mbps
   C. 27 Mbps
   D. 1.544 Mbps

10. *What are different types of DSL?*
    A. ADSL, RADSL, VDSL
    B. xDSL, nDSL, uDSL
    C. SDLS, ODSL, KDSL
    D. DSL Lite, MDSL, HDSL

11. *What component is used in a VoIP network?*
    A. Gateways
    B. Ethernet cards
    C. Switches and routers
    D. PCs
    E. All of the above
    F. None of the above

12. *Which technology has the best long-term capacity growth potential?*
    A. DSL
    B. Cable modems
    C. Dial-up lines
    D. None of the above

13. *What technology uses existing telephone lines?*
    A. DSL
    B. T-1
    C. E-1
    D. TCP/IP

14. *A major cable modem market player is?*
    A. MCI
    B. Verizon
    C. Sprint
    D. AT&T

15. *What range of frequencies are carried on cable modem CATV systems most typically?*
    A. 340MHz
    B. 50KHz
    C. 10GHz
    D. 1GHz

16. *What is the typical maximum distance of a DSL link?*
    A. 12,000 feet
    B. 5,000 feet
    C. 20 miles
    D. 18,000 feet

Looking Down the Road . . .

This chapter discusses the evolution to one device, one provider, one network, and one bill for converging telecommunications services. Use the information presented here to improve your personal and business life.

Convergent Technology Evolution

The evolution of telephony, data communications, LANs, and PC technologies sheds light on the issues that we are facing today as well as helps us to understand where we are going in the future. It is quite possible that one device will serve as our interface into a single network provided by one telecommunications service company. (There may be about 15 telecommunications-information-entertainment companies planet-wide that compete to be our single source for telecommunications.) This single source will deliver services that meet all of our telecommunications needs. Our adventure begins here, with a look at the evolution of telephony, or voice communications.

Telephony focuses on voice communications between humans. When Alexander Graham Bell first developed the telephone, he had no idea that we would use telephone lines for other types of communications. The development of the telephone was a milestone in the evolution of telecommunications as we know them today because it was one of the first devices that allowed everyone to communicate cheaply across great distances. The difficulties encountered in deployment and acceptance of telephony as a viable commercial enterprise help us understand similar difficulties we face today as our planet begins to change and evolve beyond the telephone. (Yes, today we are dealing with our planet. Soon we may be dealing with other planets as well.)

At the turn of the century, when the telephone was first being deployed, it was considered a luxury and not a necessity. The telephone was for the rich and interested academics and scientists, but not your average person. It was expensive and the telephone networks springing up were not interconnected. The early deployment of the telephone was fine, but a viable national telephone service would have been very slow to develop if the U.S. government had not recognized the potential of this new technology.

With the telephone, and a government-mandated monopoly of AT&T, daily lives changed in ways people never envisioned. We went from a country of telegraphs and letters to live voice communication. This increased the speed at which information traveled, and the increased speed at which we could communicate added fuel to the fire of business throughout the U.S. People were no longer tied to a small geographic area. Human interaction is a key to the growth of any society, and the telephone helped enable our growth. Still, the cost of communication was high and in the early 1980s, the government stepped in again to help the growth of our communications network.

In 1984, divestiture was finalized and AT&T was separated from its local carriers. We now had a separation of local and long-distance carriers for the purposes of encouraging long-distance competition and lowering communication costs. We strongly believe that the prosperity we enjoyed through the 1990s and today is, in part, attributable to reduced telecommunications costs and improved services. Thanks to extremely low long-distance rates for traditional telephone service and free phone calls through the Internet, people are communicating at an unparalleled rate planet-wide. The next question to consider is how long will providers be able to charge for long distance?

The current trends indicate that telephone service is becoming a flat-rate commodity. Telecommunications charges will not be based on metered use, but will be a flat rate (plus extra pay-per-view charges) for a monthly set of services. We are likely to pay $20 for 1,000 minutes of long-distance service to a single telecommunications provider (the provider really makes money when you do not exactly use the 1,000 minutes). The change in the telephone long-distance market has shown that such competition is indeed good for the consumer.

In the U.S., the Telecommunications Act of 1996 opened up the communication market to increased competition. This act erased the lines drawn classically between local and long-distance telephone, power, cable television, water, and wireless communications. The local telecommunications market opened up to new players as well as the traditional incumbent service providers. Cable television providers are now able to carry voice traffic and telephone carriers can provide pay-per-view TV. We can choose between multiple providers for our voice, video, and data needs. These changes in the short term are sure to result in a bit of chaos in the marketplace. However, someday you will be able to call up your provider of local, long-distance, cable, and data and say, "I want to switch." Then magically, a switch between providers will happen. You will have a new provider giving you everything for one flat fee. The next piece of the equation is the data, LAN, and PC evolution.

Data, LAN, and PC evolution go hand-in-hand. We sometimes refer to these technologies collectively as data communications. In the 1960s and 1970s, PC users were thrilled to send information at 75 to 300 bits per second. This was equivalent to 7.5 to 30 characters per second. At such high speeds, you could watch characters pop up on your green screen as they were transmitted. People would sit in front of their terminal, do basic data entry, and also have fun playing with a deck of cards. This was an incredible improvement compared to working with mechanical adding machines or pen and paper; however, the real breakthrough came with the introduction of the IBM Personal Computer in 1981.

Before the PC, all the pieces needed for large-scale networking existed, but the idea of a worldwide data network for personal and wide-scale business use was not widely envisioned. The cost of such a venture was prohibitive for a single enterprise. Further, computers were business tools that manipulated data and text. In spite of a Honeywell 316 computer being offered in the Neiman-Marcus Christmas catalog, computers were not then practical for home use. The first computers, much like the early telephone, were only affordable for the rich and not purchasable by the average person. The Neiman-Marcus Christmas catalog computer cost $10,000, used keyboard input and printed paper output, had no disk storage, and was programmable in BASIC. Computer use has changed significantly with the development of software that can accomplish a wide variety of tasks. Today's software goes well beyond making computers a typewriter or creating spreadsheets. Computers that made writing and business spreadsheet calculations easy became tools every business needed to achieve maximum productivity and remain competitive in the marketplace. Then Xerox, Apple, and Microsoft made computers user-friendly through the use of graphical user interfaces (GUIs) such as Apple's OS and Windows. With the help of Banyan Vines and Novell NetWare, it became much easier to connect computers together and share information. We believe that this was the beginning of a most significant change in the evolution of computing.

When people realized that information could be shared more easily and that this would translate into greater productivity with less effort, the excitement surrounding computing exploded. In about 10 years, we have gone from barely seeing a desktop computer at the office to having one on every desk.

The wide and rapid acceptance of the Internet was inevitable when you consider the extensive use of PCs and our desire to communicate with others. Now we are entering the next stage of data evolution. PCs, or other intelligent devices, are beginning to play a greater role in every facet of our lives. Factors such as affordable video conferencing, enhanced e-mail, and affordable high-speed Internet access allow us to use our computers in ways that we haven't as yet envisioned. It is conceivable that we might hang small flat screen video panels all around the house and use this array, and the associated computers, for 24-hour-a-day access to the Internet. These systems would quite obviously be networked and would probably respond to verbal commands rather than keyboard input. These computers would provide the window into the telecommunications network that will be called the Internet. We will depend less on cable and the classic telephone network because all communications will be merged across the Internet. The Internet will also transform to accommodate the increased usage and will grow into an IP-based telecommunications network that is much more powerful than the Internet we know today.

The future will present incredible opportunities as the world becomes one big data communications network that is connected 24/7. This network will provide us with voice, video, and data, all through one connection and one network run by one provider. In the long term, we are likely to pay $200 per month for access to a wide range of services and information such as long-distance and local video telephony, pay-per-view movies, news and information services, and more delivered by one service provider that connects to this future Internet.

Brain Teaser

Telecommunications Evolution

Have you done any of the following?
1. Called your home on your cell phone after leaving work to see if anyone was home?
2. Ordered pizza using your PC and the Internet?
3. Purchased tickets for a Saturday night movie using the Internet and then picked them up at an ATM at the movie theater?
These simple tasks can be done today using telecommunications. They are only a precursor of the types of things we may do in the future using telecommunications facilities and networks.

Universal Communication Appliance

The universal communication appliance or tool is the microcomputer. Microcomputers are becoming the only device that you use to communicate with someone. The classic telephone will remain in use for about 10 more years because it is ubiquitous planet-wide; we are familiar with it, and with competition, its cost will remain low. We feel extremely confident in forecasting that suggests that the telephone will be replaced by a microcomputer telecommunications device that delivers features and functions beyond voice communication. Such microcomputer devices will use the Internet to full advantage in delivering voice, information, and entertainment services.

The foundations of such microcomputer communications appliances are found today in the latest cellular telephony products and Personal Digital

Assistant (PDA) products. Such microcomputer-driven universal communications appliances will come in a variety of forms, from home-based networked systems to wearable-networked computers powered by body heat.

Computer technology pushes convergence because as computer speeds, storage capacities, and communications speeds to the Internet improve, all devices will expand their use from desktop publishing, Web surfing, and email to voice and video communications. The common applications that we will run in the future include video/voice conferencing, voice recognition, graphic editing, news and video entertainment feeds, and more. As we increase our use of multimedia applications on the computer, as well as basic data applications, the cost of these devices will continue to decline. This decline will be due to the large volumes of devices sold each year. Because they are powerful and disposable, we will purchase them in greater volumes than anyone imagines. PCs will be purchased to match our blue or green suit, for example. Many microcomputer-centric universal communication appliances will be used by virtually everyone, everyday.

Brain Teaser

Microcomputer Evolution

Think of what has happened to PCs in the last 15 years.
1. How much would you pay for a 1995 computer in 1995? $3,700.
2. How much would you pay for the 1995 computer today? Nothing.
3. How much would you pay for a 2000 computer in five years? Nothing.
4. What will you pay for a 2005 computer in 2005? Maybe nothing, because it is likely to be bundled with services.
The goal here is to understand what telecommunications is going to do to our everyday lives.

High-speed Networking Service Delivery

As we have discovered here, new high-speed networking technologies such as ATM, DSL, cable modems, and SONET are being widely implemented. These technologies provide businesses and residential customers with the keys to providing new services. These new services that we have not yet seen all depend upon high-bandwidth video conferencing, or let's say video-tele-communications.

Video-telecommunications places a significant demand on traditional communications links if you want truly high-quality video. High-speed networking delivers the bandwidth needed to support video-telecommunications. With video-telecommunications, telecommuting will have a whole new look because telecommuters will finally be able to see and interact with co-workers. A new dimension will be added to where we live and work. Large cities will no longer be needed as centers for commercial activity. Today this vision is beginning to be realized. Using video-telecommunications, our lives will be greatly enhanced.

Brain Teaser

Video Conferencing

> Review the video conferencing material in Chapter 9.
> 1. What will change video conferencing in the future? High-speed Internet access.
> 2. What is needed for good-quality video conferencing? More bandwidth.
> 3. Who will it benefit? Everyone, because there will be no long commutes to work or to visit family. The goal here is to start thinking about and anticipating how our lives on this planet will change. It is helpful to understand how telecommunications is changing every aspect of our lives.

The Internet Conquers All

The Internet is becoming the single communications network that connects everything. Even with today's relatively slow access speeds, the Internet has been well received and widely used to gather information, send messages, and even purchase commodity products.

All kinds of information have become available on Internet Web sites. We can use the Web to view and write email, listen to music, video conference, check schedules, and watch movies. It is becoming a fully interactive experience for all of the senses and a part of our everyday routine like drinking coffee in the morning and reading the newspaper. There is no reason to believe that this trend will ever change.

The cost and time savings that we are achieving with the Internet are significant. The amount of time that we save as a result of using the Internet for research alone allows us to be much more productive. If it were not for the Internet, we would have to travel hundreds of times to the library and peruse tons of material to write this book. The time to accomplish that would have been easily a year or more. Today, using the Internet, we research purchases and acquire products and services on-line in a fraction of the time that would be required using traditional shopping methods. The down-side seems to be that the Internet takes a little away from the human interaction during the shopping process. I believe that as the Internet and technology evolves, we will put the human touch back into such shopping. This will attract the part of our society that is not already using this resource.

The big challenge is to make the Internet a more effective and affordable communications medium than the current alternatives. This will happen as everyone attaches to it. The Internet is replacing the classic telephone network as we all connect into it 24/7.

Telecommunications Network Management

As a final thought, we want to leave you with a call for action that makes use of what you have learned in this book. We have presented as best we know at this instant in time what the past, present, and future of telecommunications offers for you. In many places around the planet, people still live in the past of telecommunications; in other places, they live very much in the present of telecommunications; and a lucky few get to experience the future of telecommunications.

I remember vividly back in the 1950s seeing an AT&T television advertisement for video telephones suggesting these devices were just around the corner. I was beside myself with anticipation of being able to make videophone calls to Grandma and Grandpa within the next year. This never materialized because at that time, the computational horsepower and telecommunications bandwidth did not exist to practically implement video telephony. This experience vividly underscored the need for technology to mature over time and reach the point where such capabilities were available to everyone as these capabilities are today.

On a trip to Germany a couple of years ago, I sat next to a PictureTel videophone development manager. He had a videophone at work and at home. He wanted not to travel, but rather to video telephone his contacts in Germany. They insisted that he come, so he was on the plane with me. During the course of our conversation, he said that his son would video telephone him in the afternoon at work and ask questions like: "How are things going, Dad?", "When will you be home?", and "Can we play ball tonight?" I thought to myself at the time; this kid lives in the future. He may never know a world without videophones. This is like children born today never knowing what life was like without a planet filled with PCs to serve them.

Everyone needs to formulate a general plan for their technological future. This should be a plan for both your personal and business life.

Life Cycles

Every technical system has a life cycle. These life cycles follow the system from "breath" to "death." A typical life cycle starts with defining a need (e.g., a new HDTV for the 2001 Super Bowl game between the Redskins and the Broncos), developing a plan (How do I convince the spouse that this is an important telecommunications need?), implementing the plan (purchase TV and DSS), operating the system (viewing programs using the system October, November, and December 2000), then upgrading to enhance and fine-tune capabilities (get the chips and salsa delivered using a Web TV connected to the Internet). This life cycle applies to all technology, including computer and communications systems.

Life cycle management encompasses:

1. Defining requirements—When you first think of telecommunications networking, you need to evaluate your basic needs as a business or home. Your analysis should include the following concerns for the entire network life cycle:

   a. Set goals for this network to meet or capabilities for it to deliver.

   b. Roughly determine the communications load or bandwidth requirements. Do you need to send data, voice, and video? How often? What are the peak activity periods?

   c. How much money do you have to spend?

   Once you have written down this basic information, you need to determine the technically feasible alternatives for meeting these network needs.

2. Defining alternatives—This step defines general strategies for building a network that meets your specific telecommunications requirements. Some questions to answer are:

   a. How much time do you have to deploy the new network?

   b. What vendors do you wish to use?

   c. Would you like outside help or will you do it yourself?

   d. Do you think this network will last three years, until a major upgrade is needed?

   e. What resources are you going to need to accomplish this task?

   f. Is this a local or planet-wide communications network?

3. Designing the network—This step gets the detailed data, including the costs, necessary to implement the network. Potential network providers and component vendors are invited to respond to Requests For Proposals (RFPs). These RFPs cover network services and components. They may specify that one vendor assume total responsibility for implementing and operating the network. In responding to RFPs, vendors should suggest ways to solve networking problems and how much those solutions cost. All recommendations should be submitted in writing with a complete technical and financial justification. This forms tangible design documentation for your network. Once you receive all of the recommendations, you should research the options carefully and challenge any assumptions to fully understand the proposed network options.

4. Acquiring components and services—Acquisition of products and services requires becoming an educated consumer. There are no "standard deals." Virtually every facet of proposed network implementation is negotiable. Whether a lower price, a longer service contract, faster deployment, free upgrades, or other enhancements are desired, you need to negotiate aggressively and never accept the first offer.

   When making a final evaluation, at least three alternatives should be evaluated. More than three competitors may make the process unnecessarily cumbersome and time-consuming. Make sure the final three alternatives include at least one of the established leaders in the market, and an aggressive new company that is anxious to gain new clients. A respected and established provider that has successfully competed against everyone else could also be included. The presence of at least three competitors assures that you are getting their best offering at the most competitive price.

   Finally, always talk to other companies who have purchased from the potential providers. It is quite common for vendors to provide the names of satisfied clients. You should speak to these clients at length. It is equally important, however, to speak to at least one dissatisfied client and analyze their complaint and how the vendor responded to their problems. It may be harder to find a dissatisfied client, but it is important to hear complaints as well as praise.

5. Implementating the solution—This is when you discover everything that was overlooked or oversimplified in the network design, when the telecommunications network is built.

6. Operating and managing the network—This is the life cycle stage where business operations are migrated onto the new network. Now the old network goes away and the new network takes over. If there are operating problems, this stage reveals them, so it is wise to move small seg-

ments of the business over to the new network and not perform a single, wholesale, weekend-business cutover.

7. Evaluating and upgrading the network—Once cutover operation is completed and business has settled into using the new network, then slow performance areas are identified and tweaked as needed to deliver the reliability and network performance needed. Complex technological systems need significant fine-tuning to deliver their promised performance.

These are the tasks that network management performs continually. Just when the life cycle of one network winds down, the life cycle of its replacement fires up and the entire process begins anew. Each life cycle today is from two to five years. Shorter life cycles would have networks always being replaced, without earning enough of a return on the investment made by the enterprise. Longer life cycles permit the network to become technologically stale and obsolete. An obsolete network or stale technology invites competitors to implement new technology that lowers costs, improves service, and increases their market share at your expense.

Brain Teaser

Planning

You have arrived at the end of this book. It is time to reflect on what you have read and learned.
1. Based upon the concepts presented here, what will you do differently to make better use of telecommunications technology in your personal life?
2. What will you do differently to make better use of telecommunications technology at work?
The goal here is to help you put some of the knowledge in this book to use in a way that directly benefits you.

■ Summary

This chapter pointed us toward the telecommunications future of one device, one network, and a single provider delivering information, voice, and video services over high-speed networking to homes and businesses. The key to future telecommunications services will be high-speed network connectivity through DSL, cable modems, ATM, and SONET technologies. With more bandwidth available at a lower cost, communication will move toward full-fledged video conferencing. The questions you must answer for yourself are: "How will these technologies fit into my communications needs?" and "When is it necessary to deploy them to increase communications capacity and lower costs?" We are now at a very interesting point in time. As the classic voice network slowly dissolves and is replaced by a planet-wide Internet (just imagine an inter-planetary Internet!), we are presented with unique opportunities to use telecommunications technologies more effectively than ever before. The future will be built upon a foundation of high-speed Internet communications carrying voice, video, and data anywhere on the planet 24/7.

Following are the answers to Chapters 1-9 review questions.

Chapter 1: Telecommunications Evolution and Future

1. What ways will not provide high-speed access to the Internet to the home?
A. Cable modems
B. Water pipe
C. Cellular radio
D. Telco DSL connections
E. Satellite communications
F. Power lines
Answer: A,C,D,E, and F.

2. DSL stands for
A. Digital Subscription Line
B. Data Subscription Line
C. Digital Subscriber Line
D. Data Subscriber Line
Answer: C.

3. What units of measure are used to represent transmission speeds to the home?
A. Bps
B. Kbps
C. Mbps
D. Gbps
Answer: A and B.

4. Cable modems operate at what speeds?
A. Bps
B. Kbps
C. Mbps

D. Gbps

Answer: B.

5. *Analog modems operate at what speeds?*

A. Bps

B. Kbps

C. Mbps

D. Gbps

Answer: A or B.

6. *What technologies are converging?*

A. Voice, WAN, LAN, video, image, and wireless with microelectronic technologies

B. Voice, WAN, LAN, video, and wireless with microelectronic technologies

C. Voice, data, LAN, video, and wireless with microelectronic technologies

D. Voice, data, LAN, image, and wireless with microelectronic technologies

Answer: A.

7. *What kind of company is promoting DSL?*

A. Electric power company

B. Retailer

C. Wholesaler

D. Cable television company

E. Satellite company

F. Telephone company

Answer: F.

8. *Which provides the highest speed?*

A. Cable modems

B. DSL lines

C. RF links

D. Satellite communications

E. Power lines

Answer: None—it depends upon the design of the hardware and the communications media.

Chapter 2: Telecommunications Standards

1. *What does OSI stand for?*
   A. Open System Internetworking
   B. Open System Interconnection
   C. Open System Internet-architecture
   D. Open Service Interconnection
   Answer: B.

2. *What does TCP/IP stand for?*
   A. Transmission Control Protocol/Internet Packet protocol
   B. Transaction Control Protocol/Internet Protocol
   C. Transmission Control Protocol/Intranet Protocol
   D. Transmission Control Protocol/Internet Protocol
   Answer: D.

3. *How many layers are in the OSI model?*
   A. Three
   B. Five
   C. Seven
   D. Nine
   Answer: C.

4. *An Ethernet card covers which OSI layers?*
   A. Layers 1 and 3
   B. Layers 2 and 3
   C. Layer 2 only
   D. Layers 1 and 2
   Answer: D.

5. *What is the function performed by OSI Layer 3?*
   A. Message integrity
   B. Electrical signaling
   C. Error-free transmission
   D. Routing
   Answer: D.

6. *What layer(s) implement the IP?*

   A. Layer 1

   B. Layer 3

   C. Layer 2

   D. Layers 3, 4, and 5

   Answer: B.

7. *What layer(s) is responsible for message integrity?*

   A. Layer 4

   B. Layer 3

   C. Layer 2

   D. Layers 4 and 5

   Answer: A.

8. *ATM is*

   A. A PC card

   B. Layers 1 and 2

   C. Asynchronous Transfer Mode

   D. All of the above

   E. None of the above

   Answer: D.

9. *Telecommunications networks are built using what?*

   A. The OSI layers

   B. Hardware, software, and channels

   C. PC boards

   D. Layers 1, 2, 3, 4, and 5

   Answer: B.

10. *Network cabling is in which layer(s) of the OSI model?*

    A. Layer 4

    B. Layer 3

    C. Layer 2

    D. Layers 1 and 2

    E. None of the above

    Answer: Answer: E. because cable is in Layer 1 only.

Chapter 3: Voice Basics

1. *What is a difference between analog and digital signals?*

   A. Analog signals are soaked up (attenuated) by wire and digital signals are not.

   B. Analog signals are tones and frequencies and digital signals are pulses.

   C. Analog signals are electrical signals and digital signals are not.

   D. Analog signals travel slower than the speed of light and digital signals do not.

   Answer: B.

2. *What are the operating frequencies in a voice-grade channel?*

   A. 0Hz to 3400Hz

   B. 300Hz to 4000Hz

   C. 300GHz to 3400GHz

   D. 300Hz to 3400Hz

   Answer: D.

3. *What device is placed in a telephone line to provide constant signal loss across the voice-grade channel frequencies?*

   A. Repeater

   B. Amplifier

   C. Loading coil

   D. Coder/Decoder

   Answer: C.

4. *What is the line running from the customer premise to the local Telephone Company Central Office called?*

   A. Copper Wire

   B. Subscriber Loop

   C. Local Loop

   D. 4-wire analog circuit

   Answer: C.

5. *What type of transmission requires the ability to transmit and receive high frequencies?*

   A. Digital Transmission

   B. Analog Transmission

   C. Voice Transmission

   D. Data Transmission

   Answer: A and in a stretch D because it could be digital. However, if you think modems D is not correct.

6. *What device terminates subscriber lines in a local Telephone Company Central Office?*

   A. Branch Exchange Switch

   B. Channel Bank Multiplexer

   C. Wiring Distribution Frames

   D. A Coder/Decoder

   Answer: B.

7. *What speed is DS-0?*

   A. 1.544 Mbps

   B. 3,400 Hz

   C. 10 Mbps

   D. 64 Kbps

   E. 53 Kbps

   Answer: D.

8. *What channel operates at the same speed as a T-1 channel?*

   A. DS-0

   B. H0

   C. PRI

   D. DS-3

   Answer: C.

Chapter 4: Telephony Today

1. *In 1985, how many RBOCs were there?*

    A. 7

    B. 6

    C. 5

    D. 4

    Answer: A.

2. *What connects the IXC/IEC networks to the LEC networks?*

    A. Branch exchange switch

    B. POP

    C. Router

    D. Class 4 toll office

    Answer: B, but a POP may be in a Class-4 toll office. There is no guarantee, however.

3. *What led to the breakup of the AT&T telephone monopoly in 1984?*

    A. Judge Harold Green

    B. MCI

    C. Advancing technology

    D. The RBOCs wanting freedom from AT&T

    Answer: C.

4. *What has happened to long-distance rates since 1984?*

    A. They have risen

    B. They declined 50%

    C. No change

    D. They declined more than 70%

    Answer: D.

5. *Are there any true 5¢ per minute rates?*

    A. Yes

    B. No

    C. Yes, for businesses

    D. Maybe

    Answer: C or D is our best guess.

6. *How are communications costs computed?*

   A. Based upon distance

   B. Based upon time

   C. Depends upon the service

   D. Based upon data volume

   E. All of the above

   F. None of the Above.

   Answer: E.

7. *Automatic Route Selection software is more sophisticated than Least Cost Routing software.*

   A. True

   B. False

   C. They are the same

   D. Don't care

   Answer: B or D, but we really do care so, B.

8. *A universal PBX features is?*

   A. Least cost routing

   B. Voice mail

   C. Hunt and pickup groups

   D. Cell phone and pager routing

   Answer: C.

9. *What feature permits the subscriber to control the CENTREX switch directly?*

   A. CLASS

   B. CLAS

   C. PBX

   D. PC software

   Answer: B.

10. *What makes CENTREX a cost-effective alternative to a PBX?*

    A. Nothing

    B. CLAS

    C. VPN

    D. Reliability

    Answer: C, nut one could argue D as well.

Chapter 5: Data Communications and WAN

1. *Voice-grade telephone subscriber lines are "bit robbed" channels. Can modems hear the bits being robbed?*

   A. No

   B. Yes

   C. Maybe

   Answer: A.

2. *How is data transmission different from video transmission?*

   A. It can have errors.

   B. It arrives in a continuous stream.

   C. It is transferred using protocols.

   D. It is carried across the telephone network in digital form.

   Answer: C.

3. *Is an ISDN phone used only for 128-KBps data communications?*

   A. Yes

   B. No

   C. Always

   D. Maybe

   Answer: B.

4. *What device interfaces a PC to an ISDN line?*

   A. A modem

   B. A CODEC

   C. A Channel Service Unit (CSU)

   D. A CSU/DSU

   Answer: D.

5. *What does modem stand for?*

   A. Modulate the signal

   B. Modulator/Demultiplexor

   C. More Digital Encoding

   D. Modulator/Demodulator

   Answer: D.

6. *How many possible patterns are produced by eight bits?*

    A. 128

    B. 32

    C. 64

    D. 256

    Answer: D.

7. *How many printable characters are there?*

    A. 32

    B. 96

    C. 128

    D. 64

    Answer: B.

8. *The functions of an OSI Layer-2 protocol are?*

    A. Detect errors

    B. Synchronize sender and receiver

    C. Correct errors

    D. Match the flow of data to the terminal device

    E. All of the above

    F. None of the above

    Answer: E.

9. *Second-, third-, and fourth-generation protocols were designed for
    _____ channels?*

    A. High-speed and low error rate

    B. Low-speed and low error rate

    C. Low-speed and high error rate

    D. High-speed and high error rate

    Answer: C.

10. *What protocol property is aimed at high-speed and low error rate channels?*

    A. Large frame size

    B. Go-Back-N error correction

    C. Half-duplex message flows

    D. CRC error detection

    Answer: A.

11. *Which serial interface will replace RS-232?*

    A. Printer

    B. COM port

    C. USB

    D. Ethernet

    Answer: C.

12. *What interface is targeted at connecting multimedia devices to a PC?*

    A. USB

    B. IEEE 1394

    C. RS-232

    D. Ethernet

    Answer: B.

13. *What is a key parameter in determining CSMA/CD performance?*

    A. Channel utilization

    B. Channel speed

    C. Error rate

    D. Server speed

    E. All of the above

    F. None of the above

    Answer: E.

14. *What is the maximum specified speed of the EIA-232 D interface?*

    A. 115,000 bps

    B. 20,000 bps

    C. 53,000 bps

    D. 64,000 bps

    Answer: B.

15. *How many 1,200-bps lines can run across a 56,000-bps time division multiplexed channel?*

    A. 54

    B. 32

    C. 94

    D. 46

    Answer: D.

16. *We have 20 DS-0 active voice channels in a T-1 circuit. How many 56,000-bps data channels can the circuit support?*

    A. 1

    B. 4

    C. 9

    D. 7

    Answer: B.

Chapter 6: Local Area Networks

1. *How many active peer-to-peer connections can Windows 95/98 and NT support?*

    A. 100

    B. 10

    C. Unlimited

    D. None

    Answer: B.

2. *What are popular LAN NICs?*

    A. Token ring, ArcNet, Ethernet

    B. Ethernet, ArcNet, ATM

    C. Ethernet, ATM, Token ring

    D. None of the above

    Answer: C.

3. *What is the most widely used NIC?*

    A. Ethernet

    B. Token ring

    C. ArcNet

    D. None of the above

    Answer: A.

4. *What wiring can Ethernet use?*

   A. Fiber

   B. Twisted pair

   C. Coaxial cable

   D. All of the above

   E. None of the above

   Answer: D.

5. *What is the most popular LAN wiring?*

   A. Fiber

   B. Twisted pair

   C. Coaxial cable

   D. UTP CAT-3

   E. CAT-5

   Answer: E.

6. *What features make servers robust and reliable?*

   A. Hot-swappable power supplies

   B. Multiple CPUs

   C. Error detecting and correcting RAM

   D. Hot-swappable fans

   Answer: B, C, and D, because hot-swap power supply makes them easy to repair.

7. *What is the IEEE designation for Ethernet?*

   A. IEEE 802.5

   B. IEEE 802.11

   C. IEEE 802.2

   D. IEEE 802.3

   E. IEEE 802.4

   Answer: D.

8. *The Universal Naming Convention (UNC) designates servers how?*

   A. \

   B. \\

   C. First

   D. Last

   Answer: B, but C is okay.

9. *How fast is Ethernet?*
   A. 10 Mbps
   B. 100 Mbps
   C. 1 Gbps
   D. 10 Gbps
   E. A, B, and C
   F. All of the above
   Answer: E today—10 GBps is coming, but not yet implemented.

10. *What internetworking components work in OSI Layers 1 and 2?*
    A. Repeaters
    B. Switches
    C. Gateways
    D. Routers
    Answer: B.

11. *What internetworking components work on the same layers?*
    A. Switches and bridges
    B. Repeaters and bridges
    C. Routers and gateways
    D. Clients and servers
    Answer: A, but D is also okay, because they sometimes work on the same layers.

12. *What is an Internet gateway?*
    A. A switch
    B. A bridge
    C. A gateway
    D. A router
    Answer: D.

13. *What are the hottest LAN applications?*
    A. VoIP and disk serving
    B. Groupware and printer serving
    C. VoIP and Web-based client/server applications
    D. Disk and printer sharing
    Answer: C, because of their potential cast savings and business development opportunities.

14. *What RAID level is the most expensive to implement?*

    A. 0

    B. 1

    C. 0+1

    D. 5

    Answer: C.

15. *What RAID level requires only one disk to back up three other disks?*

    A. 0

    B. 1

    C. 0+1

    D. 5

    Answer: D.

16. *Ethernet uses what MAC protocol?*

    A. Token passing

    B. DLC

    C. Bus collision

    D. CSMA/CD

    Answer: D.

17. *TCP/IP runs on?*

    A. Ethernet

    B. Token Ring

    C. ArcNet

    D. ATM

    E. All of the above

    F. A, B, and D

    Answer: E.

18. *What software is most likely to be Microsoft's biggest competitor?*

    A. NetWare

    B. UNIX

    C. DOS

    D. POSIX

    Answer: B, because it is cheap and used widely in the Internet.

19. *What wiring specification covers premises wiring?*
    A. IEEE 802.3
    B. EIA RS-232 D
    C. TIA/EIA-568
    D. CAT-5
    Answer: C.

20. *Single-mode fiber is described by* _____
    A. 125/62.5
    B. T-568a
    C. 125/8.3
    D. CAT-5
    Answer: C.

Chapter 7: Saving Telecommunications Costs

1. *What ISDN service is similar to a T-1 channel?*
    A. Basic Rate Interface (BRI)
    B. Primary Channel Interface (PCI)
    C. Primary Rate Interface (PRI)
    Answer: C.

2. *What high-speed digital service is seldom sold directly to end-user organizations?*
    A. ISDN
    B. SONET
    C. T-1
    D. SMDS
    Answer: B.

3. *What digital transmission service operates at the highest speeds?*
    A. T-1
    B. Frame relay
    C. ATM
    D. X.25 packet networks
    Answer: C.

4. *What T-carrier circuit is twice the speed of a T-1 channel?*

   A. T-1c

   B. T-3

   C. T-2

   D. T-4

   Answer: A.

5. *What does a DACS do?*

   A. Switches T-1 channels

   B. Multiplexes T-3 channels

   C. Cross-connects DS-0 channels

   D. Cross-connects DS-4 channels

   Answer: C.

6. *What does CIR stand for?*

   A. Committed Interface Rate

   B. Committed Information Reduction

   C. Continual Inter-hop Rate

   D. Committed Information Rate

   Answer: D.

7. *What technology uses CIR?*

   A. X.25 packet-switched networks

   B. Fast packet networks

   C. ATM

   D. SMDS

   Answer: B.

8. *What should not exceed CIR?*

   A. LAN-to-LAN data traffic

   B. FRAD traffic

   C. Voice and video traffic

   D. Terminal to host traffic

   Answer: C.

9. *What technology uses cells?*

   A. SONET

   B. Fast packet networks

   C. ATM

   D. SMDS

   Answer: C.

10. *How large are cells?*

    A. 53 characters

    B. 47 characters

    C. 128 characters

    D. 4,096 characters

    Answer: A.

11. *Do cells have error checking?*

    A. No

    B. Header only

    C. Yes – all cells have it

    D. Payload only

    Answer: C—SMDS cells have data error checking. ATM cells have header error checking.

12. *What transmission technology uses payloads?*

    A. Frame relay

    B. SMDS

    C. ATM

    D. SONET

    Answer: D.

13. *What technology functions in OSI Layer 1?*

    A. Frame relay

    B. SMDS

    C. ATM

    D. SONET

    Answer: D.

14. *What is the top SONET speed?*

    A. 51.84 Mbps

    B. 39.813 Gbps

    C. 622.08 Mbps

    D. 9.9 Gbps

    Answer: B.

15. *What is the base SONET speed?*

    A. 51.84 Mbps

    B. 25 Mbps

    C. 1.544 Mbps

    D. 6.312 Mbps

    Answer: A.

16. *What is a frame relay frame size?*

    A. 128 characters

    B. 106 characters

    C. 4096 characters

    D. 810 characters

    Answer: C.

17. *LANE is important with _____?*

    A. Frame relay

    B. X.25 packet networks

    C. The Internet

    D. ATM

    Answer: D.

18. *Can ATM be run over copper wire?*

    A. No

    B. Yes - always

    C. At speeds of 25 Mbps and 155 Mbps

    D. At speeds up to 9.9 Gbps

    Answer: C.

19. *How many fibers in a SONET ring?*

    A. 2

    B. 4

    C. 8

    D. 6

    Answer: A and B.

20. *A T-1 span runs between two facilities. The average data load is 256 Kbps. To replace it with frame relay service and get the best performance, what access speed should be used?*

    A. 256 Kbps

    B. 1.544 Mbps

    C. T-1C access

    D. 512 Kbps

    Answer: C—Higher speed is better. The highest speed would give the best performance.

Chapter 8: RF, Satellite, and Cellular Communications

1. *What is CDMA?*

    A. Code Divided Multiplexing Access

    B. Code Division Multiplexing Access

    C. Code Division Multiple Access

    D. Code Divided Multiple Access

    Answer: C.

2. *What frequencies communicate with satellites?*

    A. 800/900MHz

    B. 12/14GHz

    C. 200/300GHz

    D. 1400/1600KHz

    Answer: B.

3. *What is a characteristic of microwave networks?*

   A. Frequencies are in the KHz range.

   B. Rain and weather do not affect transmission.

   C. They have limited transmission capacity.

   D. They use Line of Sight (LOS) transmission.

   Answer: D.

4. *What is a bad characteristic of satellite transmission?*

   A. Satellite antennas must shoot up in the sky.

   B. Satellite uses microwave frequencies.

   C. All satellite antennas are big.

   D. Some satellite links have significant propagation delays.

   Answer: D.

5. *Why would one use private microwave or satellite networks?*

   A. They do not pay telephone companies for point-to-point channels.

   B. It is fun.

   C. They put cool dish antennas on your roof.

   D. They have the highest security.

   Answer: A.

6. *What general type of multiplexing is similar to the operation of standard analog cellular phones?*

   A. FDM

   B. CDM

   C. TDM

   D. TDMA

   Answer: A.

7. *What helps wireless phones communicate with the Internet?*

   A. FDM

   B. CDMA

   C. GSM

   D. WAP

   Answer: D.

8. *What will follow GSM?*

    A. 3G

    B. WAP

    C. AMPS

    D. N-AMPS

    Answer: A.

9. *Which frequency sharing technique is most effective, TDMA or CDMA?*

    Answer: CDMA.

10. *Which is more widely used, CDMA or TDMA?*

     Answer: If CDMA is not more widely use today, it will become the most widely used.

11. *About how far apart are PCS cell sites?*

     A. 24 miles

     B. 300 Km

     C. 12 miles

     D. 25,000 feet

     Answer: C.

12. *What frequency range does Nextel use?*

     A. 900MHz

     B. 1,600MHz

     C. 24GHz

     D. 800MHz

     Answer: D.

13. *Weather satellites use what orbit?*

     A. LEO

     B. MEO

     C. GEO

     D. Stationary EO

     Answer: C.

14. *The Global Positioning System (GPS) uses what orbit?*

    A. LEO

    B. MEO

    C. GEO

    D. Non-stationary EO

    Answer: B.

15. *What do most North American cell phones use?*

    A. AMPS

    B. TDMA

    C. FDM

    D. PCS

    Answer: A.

16. *Do cellular plans where all calls are local calls really save money?*

    A. Absolutely

    B. Maybe

    C. Only if you use exactly all the minutes of the plan each month

    D. No

    Answer: C.

Chapter 9: Telecommunications Technologies Providing New Business Opportunities

1. *What technology is at the core of the Internet?*

    A. HTML

    B. WWW

    C. TCP/IP

    D. DSL

    Answer: C—The TCP/IP protocol suite was developed with the earliest implementation of the Internet.

2. *What technology is used by the World Wide Web?*

   A. DSL

   B. Cable modems

   C. HTML

   D. TCP/IP

   Answer: C—Hyper-Text Markup Language.

3. *What is closely related to HTML?*

   A. HTTP

   B. FTP

   C. RADSL

   D. Gnutella

   Answer: A—Hyper-Text Transfer Protocol.

4. *What is a key Internet architectural feature?*

   A. HTML

   B. DSL

   C. Cable modems

   D. NAPS

   Answer: D—Network Access Points (NAPS).

5. *How many major NAPs are in the Internet today?*

   A. 5

   B. 15

   C. 50

   D. 100

   Answer: B—There are probably around 15 major NAPs.

6. *Domain name suffixes are?*

   A. .ac, .uk, and .nz

   B. .com, .org, and .mil

   C. .rec, .web, and .net

   D. All of the above

   E. None of the above

   Answer: D—The A suffixes are for countries, the B suffixes are in common use, and the C suffixes are planned for future use.

7. *What type of service is the Internet at OSI Layer 3?*

   A. TCP

   B. Connection-less

   C. Connection-oriented

   D. Circuit-switched

   Answer: B.

8. *What type of service is the Internet at OSI Layer 4?*

   A. IP

   B. Connection-less

   C. Connection-oriented

   D. Circuit-switched

   Answer: C.

9. *What is the top cable modem speed?*

   A. 56 Mbps

   B. 10 Mbps

   C. 27 Mbps

   D. 1.544 Mbps

   Answer: A.

10. *What are different types of DSL?*

    A. ADSL, RADSL, VDSL

    B. xDSL, nDSL, uDSL

    C. SDLS, ODSL, KDSL

    D. DSL Lite, MDSL, HDSL

    Answer: A.

11. *What component is used in a VoIP network?*

    A. Gateways

    B. Ethernet Cards

    C. Switches and routers

    D. PCs

    E. All of the above

    F. None of the above

    Answer: E.

12. *Which technology has the best long-term capacity growth potential?*

    A. DSL

    B. Cable modems

    C. Dial-up lines

    D. None of the above

    Answer: B.

13. *What technology uses existing telephone lines?*

    A. DSL

    B. T-1

    C. E-1

    D. TCP/IP

    Answer: A—TCP cable can run over phones lines as well.

14. *A major cable modem market player is?*

    A. MCI

    B. Verizon

    C. Sprint

    D. AT&T

    Answer: D.

15. *What range of frequencies are carried on cable modem CATV systems most typically?*

    A. 340MHz

    B. 50KHz

    C. 10GHz

    D. 1GHz

    Answer: D.

16. *What is the typical maximum distance of a DSL link?*

    A. 12,000 feet

    B. 5,000 feet

    C. 20 miles

    D. 18,000 feet

    Answer: D.

INDEX

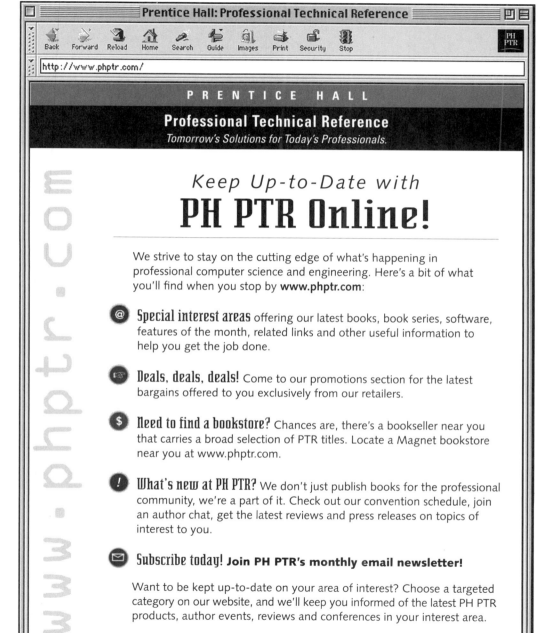